TO WITHDRAWN
Kings Hwy

Technologies for Inclusive Education:

Beyond Traditional Integration Approaches

David Griol Barres
Carlos III University of Madrid, Spain

Zoraida Callejas Carrión
University of Granada, Spain

Ramón López–Cózar Delgado
University of Granada, Spain

TOURO COLLEGE LIBRARY
WITHDRAWN

Information Science
REFERENCE

KH

Managing Director:	Lindsay Johnston
Editorial Director:	Joel Gamon
Book Production Manager:	Jennifer Romanchak
Publishing Systems Analyst:	Adrienne Freeland
Development Editor:	Myla Merkel
Assistant Acquisitions Editor:	Kayla Wolfe
Typesetter:	Deanna Jo Zombro
Cover Design:	Nick Newcomer

Published in the United States of America by
Information Science Reference (an imprint of IGI Global)
701 E. Chocolate Avenue
Hershey PA 17033
Tel: 717-533-8845
Fax: 717-533-8661
E-mail: cust@igi-global.com
Web site: http://www.igi-global.com

Copyright © 2013 by IGI Global. All rights reserved. No part of this publication may be reproduced, stored or distributed in any form or by any means, electronic or mechanical, including photocopying, without written permission from the publisher. Product or company names used in this set are for identification purposes only. Inclusion of the names of the products or companies does not indicate a claim of ownership by IGI Global of the trademark or registered trademark.

Library of Congress Cataloging-in-Publication Data

Technologies for inclusive education : beyond traditional integration approaches / David Griol Barres, Zoraida Callejas Carrion and Ramon Lopez-Cozar Delgado, Editors
      p. cm.
  Includes bibliographical references and index.
  Summary: "This book introduces the basic concepts, current research guidelines and future perspectives on the current state of inclusive education by highlighting technological advances in applied e-learning, cognitive learning and education multimedia"--Provided by publisher.
  ISBN 978-1-4666-2530-3 (hardcover) -- ISBN 978-1-4666-2531-0 (ebook) -- ISBN 978-1-4666-2532-7 (print & perpetual access) 1. Inclusive education. 2. Special education. 3. Educational technology. I. Griol Barres, David, 1976- II. Callejas Carrion, Zoraida, 1982- III. Lopez-Cozar Delgado, Ramon.
  LC1201.T46 2013
  371.33--dc23
                            2012026061

British Cataloguing in Publication Data
A Cataloguing in Publication record for this book is available from the British Library.

All work contributed to this book is new, previously-unpublished material. The views expressed in this book are those of the authors, but not necessarily of the publisher.

11/12/13

Editorial Advisory Board

Gloria Inés Álvarez Vargas, *Pontificia Universidad Javeriana, Colombia*
Juan Carlos Augusto, *University of Ulster, North Ireland*
Hynek Boril, *University of Texas, USA*
Javier Carbó Rubiera, *Carlos III University of Madrid, Spain*
Juan Gómez Romero, *Carlos III University of Madrid, Spain*
Lluís F. Hurtado Oliver, *Technical University of Valencia, Spain*
Ana María Iglesias Maqueda, *Carlos III University of Madrid, Spain*
Kristiina Jokinen, *University of Helsinki, Finland*
Eduardo Lleida Solano, *University of Zaragoza, Spain*
Jan Nouza, *Technical University of Liberec, Czech Republic*
Alejandra Martínez Monés, *University of Valladolid, Spain*
Paul McKevitt, *University of Ulster, North Ireland*
Michael McTear, *University of Ulster, North Ireland*
José Manuel Molina López, *Carlos III University of Madrid, Spain*
Diana Pérez Marín, *Juan Carlos I University, Spain*
María José Rodríguez Fórtiz, *University of Granada, Spain*
Araceli Sanchis de Miguel, *Carlos III University of Madrid, Spain*
David del Valle Agudo, *PyxelArts, Spain*

Table of Contents

Section 1
Multimodal Interfaces

Chapter 1
David Griol Barres, Carlos III University of Madrid, Spain
Zoraida Callejas Carrión, University of Granada, Spain
José M. Molina López, Carlos III University of Madrid, Spain
Araceli Sanchis de Miguel, Carlos III University of Madrid, Spain

Chapter 2
William R. Rodríguez, Antonio Nariño University, Colombia & University of Zaragoza, Spain
Oscar Saz, Carnegie Mellon University, USA & University of Zaragoza, Spain
Eduardo Lleida, University of Zaragoza, Spain

Chapter 3
Kristiina Jokinen, University of Helsinki, Finland & University of Tampere, Finland
Päivi Majaranta, University of Tampere, Finland

Chapter 4
Beatriz López Mencía, Universidad Politécnica de Madrid, Spain
David Díaz Pardo, Universidad Politécnica de Madrid, Spain
Alvaro Hernández Trapote, Universidad Politécnica de Madrid, Spain
Luis A. Hernández Gómez, Universidad Politécnica de Madrid, Spain

Section 2
Virtual Environments

Section 3
User Modelling

Section 4
Adapted Contents

Section 5
Devices and Simulators

Detailed Table of Contents

Section 1
Multimodal Interfaces

David Griol Barres, Carlos III University of Madrid, Spain
Zoraida Callejas Carrión, University of Granada, Spain
José M. Molina López, Carlos III University of Madrid, Spain
Araceli Sanchis de Miguel, Carlos III University of Madrid, Spain

Continuous advances in the development of information technologies have currently led to the possibility of accessing learning contents from anywhere, at anytime, and almost instantaneously. However, accessibility is not always the main objective in the design of educative applications, specifically to facilitate their adoption by disabled people. Different technologies have recently emerged to foster the accessibility of computers and new mobile devices, favoring a more natural communication between the student and the developed educative systems. This chapter describes innovative uses of multimodal dialog systems in education, with special emphasis in the advantages that they provide for creating inclusive applications and learning activities.

William R. Rodríguez, Antonio Nariño University, Colombia & University of Zaragoza, Spain
Oscar Saz, Carnegie Mellon University, USA & University of Zaragoza, Spain
Eduardo Lleida, University of Zaragoza, Spain

This chapter reports the results after two years of deployment of PreLingua, a free computer-based tool for voice therapy, in different educational institutions. PreLingua gathers a set of activities that use speech processing techniques and an adapted interface to train patients who present speech development delays or special voice needs in the environment of special education. Its visual interface is especially designed for children with cognitive disabilities and maps relevant voice parameters like intensity, vocal onset, durations of sounds, fundamental frequency, and formant frequencies to visually attractive graphics. Reports of successful results of the use of PreLingua have been gathered in several countries by audiologists, speech therapists, and other professionals in the fields of voice therapy, and also, in other fields such as early stimulation, mutism, and attention-deficit disorders. This chapter brings together the experiences of these professionals on the use of the tool and how the use of an interface paradigm that maps acoustic features directly to visual elements in a screen can provide improvements in voice disorders in patients with cognitive and speech delays.

#### Chapter 3

In this chapter, the authors explore possibilities to use novel face and gaze tracking technology in educational applications, especially in interactive teaching agents for second language learning. They focus on non-verbal feedback that provides information about how well the speaker has understood the presented information, and how well the interaction is progressing. Such feedback is important in interactive applications in general, and in educational systems, it is effectively used to construct a shared context in which learning can take place: the teacher can use feedback signals to tailor the presentation appropriate for the student. This chapter surveys previous work, relevant technology, and future prospects for such multimodal interactive systems. It also sketches future educational systems which encourage the students to learn foreign languages in a natural and inclusive manner, via participating in interaction using natural communication strategies.

This chapter describes a collection of experiences and recommendations related with the design and evaluation of interactive applications integrating Embodied Conversational Agents (ECA) technology in real environments of use with children in Special Education. Benefits and challenges of using ECAs in this context are presented. These benefits and challenges have guided the creation of Special Education reinforcement applications incorporating ECAs, which have been used for extended periods of time at Infanta Elena Special Education School in Madrid. Co-design principles were applied in the development of two of the applications discussed here, with the participation of the school's teaching staff and children with severe motor and mental disabilities (mainly with cerebral palsy). From the design experience a set of recommendations and observations were extracted, which the authors hope may serve as guidance for the scientific and educational communities when undertaking further research. For example, in an application to reinforce the learning of emotions it believe it beneficial to include ECAs that display a number of exaggerated facial expressions together with a combination of auditory and gestural reinforcements. The ECA should show its eyes and mouth clearly, in order to help the children focus their attention. These and other ECA strategies have been analysed to provide reinforcement in learning and also to attract the children's attention when interacting with the application.

Section 2
Virtual Environments

Chapter 5

Kiran Pala, International Institute of Information Technology, India
Suryakanth V Gangashetty, International Institute of Information Technology, India

In human beings, learning is a life-long and continuous process; it can encompass both active and passive activities in accordance with social changes and the development of society. In this era, the development and use of technologies have changed the face of information accessibility. Similarly, such technologies facilitate learners with new and different options to engage in learning through interactive tasks and content delivered through CD-ROMs, websites, communication software on the internet, and virtual games, which have had a significant impact on human learning and education. The significant question arises on which type of content and what way of representation of the content are required in this connection. Researchers need to reconsider any approach to teaching or providing platform to learners which is concerned with an explanation of how learning ability and development are prompted by an exposure to the target in view of the dramatic differences in experiences of learners. This chapter defines the concept of Virtual Environment (VE) based learning discussing how a VE differs from the traditional classrooms approaches. Thus, this chapter presents a unique framework and a formalism for interactive linearity or non-linearity in controlling the structure of learning activity or interaction. These activities aim at addressing the relationship between the main constructs targeted toward developing a VE. This chapter takes stock of various distributed models and projects a framework on how the learners can be engaged continuously in learning activities according to their previous linguistic and educational experiences. It also focuses on how a learner can be reported to the admin or tutor and self assessments.

Chapter 6

Juan Mateu, Universidad Autónoma de Madrid, Spain
María José Lasala, IES Ernest Lluch, Spain
Xavier Alamán, Universidad Autónoma de Madrid, Spain

In this chapter, the authors present an introduction to the use of virtual worlds in education, an analysis of the stronger and weaker points that such environments offer for high school education, and an experience on applying such technologies for the inclusion at a concrete high school in Cunit (Spain). In this high school, there is a need for teaching immigrant children the Catalan language when they arrive, in order to allow them to continue their studies integrated with the rest of the students. The chapter describes an experience on using virtual worlds for achieving such goal, based on the open software platform called "OpenSim."

Section 3
User Modelling

Chapter 7

Diana Pérez-Marín, Universidad Rey Juan Carlos, Spain
Ismael Pascual-Nieto, Universidad Rey Juan Carlos, Spain

According to User-Centered Design, computer interactive systems should be implemented taking into account the users' preferences. However, in some cases, it is not easy to apply conventional Human-Computer interaction evaluation techniques to identify the users' needs and improve the user-system interaction. Therefore, this chapter proposes a procedure to model the interaction behaviour from the analysis of conversational agent dialog logs. A case study in which the procedure has been applied to model the behaviour of 20 children when interacting with multiple personality Pedagogic Conversational Agents is described as an illustrative sample of the goodness and practical application of the procedure.

Chapter 8

Ana Pérez Pérez, University of Granada, Spain
Zoraida Callejas Carrión, University of Granada, Spain
Ramón López-Cózar Delgado, University of Granada, Spain
David Griol Barres, Carlos III University of Madrid, Spain

New technologies have demonstrated a great potential to improve the social, labour, and educational integration of people with special needs. That is why there is a special interest of academia and industry to develop tools to assist this people, improving their autonomy and quality of life. Usually, intellectual disabilities are linked with speech and language disorders. In this chapter, the authors present a review on the efforts directed towards designing and developing speech technologies adapted to people with intellectual disabilities. Also, they describe the work they have conducted to study how to gather speech resources, which can be used to build speech-based systems that help them to communicate more effectively.

Chapter 9

Karla Muñoz, University of Ulster, UK
Paul Mc Kevitt, University of Ulster, UK
Tom Lunney, University of Ulster, UK
Julieta Noguez, Tecnológico de Monterrey, México
Luis Neri, Tecnológico de Monterrey, México

Students' performance and motivation are influenced by their emotions. Game-based learning (GBL) environments comprise elements that facilitate learning and the creation of an emotional connection with students. GBL environments include Intelligent Tutoring Systems (ITSs) to ensure personalized learning. ITSs reason about students' needs and characteristics (student modeling) to provide suitable instruction (tutor modeling). The authors' research is focused on the design and implementation of an emotional student model for GBL environments based on the Control-Value Theory of achievement emotions by Pekrun et al. (2007). The model reasons about answers to questions in game dialogues and contextual variables related to student behavior acquired through students' interaction with PlayPhysics. The authors' model is implemented using Dynamic Bayesian Networks (DBNs), which are derived using Probabilistic Relational Models (PRMs), machine learning techniques, and statistical methods. This work compares an earlier approach that uses Multinomial Logistic Regression (MLR) and cross-tabulation for learning the structure and conditional probability tables with an approach that employs Necessary Path Condition and Expectation Maximization algorithms. Results showed that the latter approach is more effective at classifying the control of outcome-prospective emotions. Future work will focus on applying this approach to classification of activity and outcome-retrospective emotions.

The Basque Government has published two calls to create digital educational objects for the programme called Eskola 2.0. After having provided schools with technological equipment, these calls aim to increase the use of learning technology in the classroom. More than 300 didactic sequences have been developed, which vary greatly in visual design, content structure, organization, and pedagogical aspects. Even though accessibility is one of the quality criteria, the reality is that they are hardly accessible and inclusive. DeustoTech Learning research group has carried out a survey of the educational objects approved in these calls up to November 2011. The authors evaluated pedagogical and technological aspects to find out how inclusive they are. In this chapter, they provide the results of the survey and propose a set of guidelines for designing more accessible and inclusive objects in the future.

#### Chapter 11

Practitioners have been using three communication aids in conducting many school activities at both special needs and regular schools. In the simplest system, voices and sounds are transformed into dot codes, edited with pictures and text, and printed out with an ordinary color printer; the printed dot codes are traced to be decoded into the originals by using a handy tool, Sound Reader. In the most complex system, in addition to audio files, multiple media files such as movies, web pages, html files, and PowerPoint files can be linked to each dot code; just touching the printed dot code with sound or scanner pens reproduces their audio or multimedia, respectively. The present chapter reports the software and hardware used in developing originally handmade teaching materials with dot codes and various school activities performed at both special needs and regular schools.

#### Chapter 12

Computational linguistics can offer tools for automatic grading of written texts. "Evaluator" is such a tool. It uses FreeLing as a morpho-syntactic analyzer, providing words, lemmas, and part of speech tags for each word in a text. Multi-words can also be identified and their grammar identified. "Evaluator" also manages leveled glossaries, like the one developed by the Instituto Cervantes, as well as other electronically available dictionaries. All these glossaries enable the tool to identify most words in texts, grading them into the six levels scale of the Common European Framework of Reference for Languages. To assign a lexical level to the text under analysis, a statistical distribution of leveled qualified lemmas is used. Other ways to assign a lexical level to a text by using corpora of a preset level are also suggested. The syntactic analysis is based on a collection of grammar structures leveled by following the descriptors given by the Instituto Cervantes. These grammar structures are identified within the text using quantitative indices which level a text by comparing it with a given corpus. Finally, semantic identification is done using semantic fields as defined by the Instituto Cervantes. Latent Semantic Analysis is also used to group texts dealing with the same topic together. All these methods have been tested and applied to real texts written in Spanish by native speakers and learners.

Section 5
Devices and Simulators

Chapter 13

Ana Iglesias, Universidad Carlos III de Madrid, Spain
Belén Ruiz-Mezcua, Universidad Carlos III de Madrid, Spain
Juan Francisco López, Spanish Centre of Captioning and Audio Description, Spain
Diego Carrero Figueroa, Spanish Centre of Captioning and Audio Description, Spain

This chapter explores new communication technologies and methods for avoiding accessibility and communication barriers in the educational environment. It is focused on providing real-time captions so students with hearing disabilities and foreign students, among others, could participate in an inclusive way in and outside the classroom. The inclusive proposals are based on the APEINTA educational project, which aims for accessible education for all. The research work proposes the use of mobile devices for teacher and students in order to provide more flexibility using the APEINTA real-time captioning service. This allows using this service from anywhere and at anytime, not only in the classroom.

Chapter 14

Francisco J. Liébana-Cabanillas, University of Granada, Spain
Myriam Martínez-Fiestas, University of Granada, Spain
Francisco Rejón-Guardia, University of Granada, Spain

The purpose of this chapter is to contextualize the situation of the use of remote response devices or clickers in education and identify the benefits that tools such as Q-Click software can bring to university teaching and to different groups of students. To fulfil this objective, the authors conducted research in classes with students who rated 149 different aspects related to the use of such software, including its use in class, benefits, and implications for follow-up assessment of the subject, attention, and class quality. This information was then compared to other groups of students studying the same subject who did not use clickers in class. The findings confirm the original proposal verifying the usefulness of these tools in university teaching for the important consequences for students and teachers.

Chapter 15

    Francisco J. Liébana-Cabanillas, University of Granada, Spain
    Myriam Martínez-Fiestas, University of Granada, Spain
    María Isabel Viedma-del-Jesús, University of Granada, Spain

The purpose of this chapter is to discuss the use of business management simulators in university teaching, specifically the use of marketing simulators, identifying the main advantages and disadvantages for students. The marketing simulator Simbrand was used and evaluated by 104 students in a general marketing class at the University of Granada. Their responses to a survey about the implications that simulator use has on student attention, motivation, the ability to follow course material and the quality of the classes that use this tool are outlined below. The findings provide solid theoretical evidence of the usefulness and advantages of these tools in university teaching for both students and faculty.

Preface

The concept of inclusive education implies providing all students with the same opportunities to learn and receive a high quality education regardless of their personal, social, or cultural background. It is a new area which goes beyond traditional integration approaches in order to endow the educative system with the capability to adapt to the diversity of the students without the use of special classrooms to separate students with different abilities and facilitating the full participation of everyone.

In order to make inclusive education a reality in the near future, technological advances in applied e-learning, cognitive learning, virtual learning environments, educational multimedia, web-based teaching, and learning and tutoring systems, become fundamental. In addition, novel approaches to human-computer interaction are essential to make these contents available for every student regardless of their disabilities and learning styles.

The objective of this edited volume is discussing the current state of the arts in these topics, bringing together the perspectives from different knowledge areas such as human-computer interaction, virtual environments, educative multimedia, and adaptation to educational special needs. This way, it will help researchers to broaden their research spheres and improve their understanding of how Technology and Education can enrich mutually. It will also help postgraduate and doctoral students in identifying new and challenging research problems in all the areas involved.

The 15 chapters of this book have been organized in the following 5 sections: 1) Multimodal Interfaces, 2) Virtual Environments, 3) User Modeling, 4) Adapted Contents, and 5) Devices and Simulators.

The first section describes the potential of multimodal interfaces to facilitate universal access to learning contents. Chapter 1 presents a state of the art of the advances in the development of multimodal conversational interfaces to guarantee accessibility to educational technology. Chapter 2 describes the case of the PreLingua tool for voice therapy, which merges speech processing techniques and an adapted visual interface to train patients who present speech development delays or special voice needs in the environment of special education. Chapter 3 explores additional possibilities for interactive teaching agents that process non-verbal input modalities such as eye-gaze and facial expressions. Embodied conversational agents combine the modalities described in the previous chapters, as discussed in Chapter 4, which closes the section with a study of the use of embodied conversational agents in interactive applications for children with special needs.

The second section is comprised of two chapters that describe the pedagogical possibilities of virtual worlds. Chapter 5 presents a study about using virtual environments for long-life learning and their differences with respect to traditional teaching approaches; while Chapter 6 describes practical experiences of the pros and cons of applying such technologies for inclusive middle education.

In the third section, several approaches to user modeling are discussed. In Chapter 7, conversational behaviors are modeled in order to provide adapted human-computer interaction. In Chapter 8, this adaptation is tackled from the perspective of adjusting speech-based interfaces to the language disorders that are associated with certain intellectual disabilities. In Chapter 9, the user model is compiled using emotional parameters in game-based learning, as they are closely related to the student's performance and motivation.

The fourth section examines contents adapted to users with special needs. The section starts with Chapter 10, which analyzes a vast amount of digital educational objects with respect to their accessibility. Chapter 11 presents three communication aids in which the multimedia learning contents are transformed into dot codes for special needs and regular schools. Chapter 12 presents the Evaluator tool, which can be used for automatic grading adapted to the language skills of the students.

The fifth section focuses on devices and simulators. Chapter 13 explores the possibilities of mobile devices including a captioning service for disabled and non-native users. Chapter 14 and 15 center in university teaching, the former discusses the applications of remote response devices, and the latter the use of simulators to explain abstract concepts.

David Griol Barres
Carlos III University of Madrid, Spain

Zoraida Callejas Carrión
University of Granada, Spain

Ramón López-Cózar Delgado
University of Granada, Spain

Acknowledgment

This book is the result of the efforts of many people. We would like to thank all the authors for their very interesting contributions, as well as the members of the Editorial Advisory Board for their support and valuable comments. Also special thanks go to Myla Merkel from IGI Global for her feedback and help; it is greatly appreciated.

Section 1
Multimodal Interfaces

Chapter 1
Towards the Use of Dialog Systems to Facilitate Inclusive Education

David Griol Barres
Carlos III University of Madrid, Spain

José M. Molina López
Carlos III University of Madrid, Spain

Zoraida Callejas Carrión
University of Granada, Spain

Araceli Sanchis de Miguel
Carlos III University of Madrid, Spain

ABSTRACT

Continuous advances in the development of information technologies have currently led to the possibility of accessing learning contents from anywhere, at anytime, and almost instantaneously. However, accessibility is not always the main objective in the design of educative applications, specifically to facilitate their adoption by disabled people. Different technologies have recently emerged to foster the accessibility of computers and new mobile devices, favoring a more natural communication between the student and the developed educative systems. This chapter describes innovative uses of multimodal dialog systems in education, with special emphasis in the advantages that they provide for creating inclusive applications and learning activities.

1. INTRODUCTION

Technological advances currently reached by computers and mobile devices allow their use to access information and a number of services. In addition, users want to access these services anywhere and anytime in a natural, intuitive and efficient way. Speech-based interfaces have become one of the main options to facilitate this kind of communication as it is a good solution to the shrinking size of mobile devices, eases the communication in environments where this access is not possible using traditional input interfaces (e.g., keyboard and mouse), and facilitates information access for people with visual or motor disabilities.

With the advances of speech, image and video technology, human-computer interaction (HCI) has reached a new phase, in which multimodal

DOI: 10.4018/978-1-4666-2530-3.ch001

Copyright © 2013, IGI Global. Copying or distributing in print or electronic forms without written permission of IGI Global is prohibited.

information is a key point to enhance the communication between humans and machines. Unlike traditional keyboard- and mouse-based interfaces, multimodal interfaces enable greater flexibility in the input and output, as they permit users to employ different input modalities as well as to obtain responses through different means, for example, speech, gestures, and facial expressions. This is especially important for users with special needs, for whom the traditional interfaces might not be suitable (McTear, 2004; López-Cózar and Araki, 2005; Wahlster, 2006).

In addition, the widespread use of mobile technology implementing wireless communications enables a new type of advanced applications to access information. As a result, users can effectively access huge amounts of information and services from almost everywhere and through different communication modalities.

There is a large variety of applications in which spoken dialog systems can be used. One of the most wide-spread is providing information on a specific topic, such as flight/railway and booking information, tourist and travel information, weather forecast, banking systems, or conference help (Glass et al., 1995; Zue et al., 2000; Bohus and Rudnicky, 2005; Andeani et al., 2006; Callejas and López-Cózar, 2008). In some cases, spoken interaction can be the only way to access information, as, for example when the screen is too small to display information (e.g. hand-held devices) or when the eyes of the user are busy in other tasks (e.g. driving) (Mattasoni et al., 2002; Jokinen et al., 2004; Weng et al., 2006). Spoken interaction is also useful for remote control devices and robots, especially in smart environments (Lemon et al., 2001; Montoro et al., 2006; Ábalos et al., 2006; Menezes et al., 2007; Augusto, 2009). Finally, one of the most demanding applications for fully natural and understandable dialogs are virtual agents and companions (Hubal et al., 2000; Catizone et al., 2003; Corradini et al., 2005).

With the growing maturity of speech technologies, the possibilities for integrating conversation and discourse in e-learning are receiving greater attention, including tutoring, question-answering, conversation practice for language learners, pedagogical agents and learning companions, and dialogs to promote reflection and metacognitive skills. This chapter focuses on some of the most important challenges that researchers have recently envisioned for future multimodal interfaces applied to educative purposes. It describes current efforts to develop intelligent, adaptive, proactive, portable and affective multimodal interfaces. All these concepts are not mutually exclusive, for example, the system's intelligence can be concerned with the system's adaptation enabling better portability to different environments.

To deal with all these important topics required for the design of educative multimodal interfaces, this chapter is organized as follows. Section 2 provides an overview of the main modules and functionalities required for the development of spoken dialog systems. Section 3 describes the main principles involved in the development of educative multimodal interfaces. This section also provides important examples showing the benefits of the integration of this kind of systems in educative applications. Section 4 describes our work related to the development of educative multimodal interfaces describing two systems developed to respectively facilitate the access to Internet and learn foreign languages. Finally, Section 5 presents the conclusions and outlines possibilities for future research directions.

2. DIALOG SYSTEMS: MODULAR ARCHITECTURE AND PROCESSES

The complexity of the interaction between the user and the dialog system can vary and some of the previously described components might not be used. For example, for a simple menu, semantic analysis is not necessary. However, for a conversational companion all the modules must be used in order to interpret the user input, take justified decisions on what the system will respond, and finally tailor the answer to user needs and expectations. This way, the implementation of multimodal dialog systems is a complex task in which a number of technologies are involved, including signal processing, phonetics, linguistics, natural language processing, affective computing, graphics and interface design, animation techniques, telecommunications, sociology and psychology. The complexity is usually addressed by dividing the implementation into simpler problems, each associated with a system's module that carries out specific functions. Usually, this division is based on the traditional architecture of spoken dialog systems: automatic speech recognition (ASR), spoken language understanding (SLU), dialog management (DM), natural language generation (NLG) and text-to-speech synthesis (TTS).

Speech recognition is the process of obtaining a sentence (text string) from a voice signal (Rabiner et al., 1996). It is a very complex task given the diversity of factors that can affect the input, basically concerned with the speaker, the interaction context and the transmission channel. Different applications demand different complexity on the speech recognizer. Cole et al. (1997) identified eight parameters that allow an optimal tailoring of the recognizer: speech mode, speech style, dependency, vocabulary, language model, perplexity, signal-to-noise ratio (SNR) and transduction. Nowadays, general-purpose ASR systems are usually based on Hidden Markov Models (HMMs) (Rabiner and Juang, 1993).

Spoken Language Understanding is the process of extracting the semantics from a text string (Minker, 1998). It generally involves employing morphological, lexical, syntactical, semantic, discourse and pragmatic knowledge. In a first stage, lexical and morphological knowledge allow dividing the words in their constituents distinguishing lexemes and morphemes. Syntactic analysis yields a hierarchical structure of the sentences, whereas the semantic analysis extracts the meaning of a complex syntactic structure from the meaning of its constituents. There are currently two major approaches to carry out SLU: rule-based (Mairesse et al., 2009) and statistical (Meza et al., 2008), including some hybrid methods (Liu et al., 2006).

Dialog Management is concerned with deciding the next action to be carried out by the dialog system. The simplest dialog model is implemented as a finite-state machine, in which machine states represent dialog states and the transitions between states are determined by the user's actions. Frame-based approaches have been developed to overcome the lack of flexibility of the state-based dialog models, and are used in most current commercial systems. For complex application domains, plan-based dialog models can be used. They rely on the fact that humans communicate to achieve goals, and during the interaction, the humans' mental state might change (Chu et al., 2005). Currently, the application of machine-learning approaches to model dialog strategies is a very active research area (Griol et al., 2008; Williams and Young, 2007; Cuayáhuitl et al., 2006; Lemon et al., 2006).

Natural language generation is the process of obtaining texts in natural language from a non-linguistic representation of information. It is usually carried out in five steps: content organization, content distribution in sentences, lexicalization, generation of referential expressions and linguistic realization. The simplest approach uses predefined text messages (e.g. error messages and warnings). Although intuitive, this approach is very inflexible (Reiter, 1995). The next level of sophistication is template-based generation, in which the same message structure can be produced with slight differences. This approach is used mainly for multi-sentence generation, particularly in applications where texts are fairly regular in structure, such as business reports (Reiter, 1995). Phrase-based systems employ what can be considered generalized templates at the sentence level (in which case the phrases resemble phrase structure grammar rules), or at the discourse level (in which case they are often called text plans) (Elhadad and

Robin, 1996). Finally, in feature-based systems, each possible minimal alternative of expression is represented by a single feature to obtain the maximum level of generalization and flexibility (Oh and Rudnicky, 2000).

Text-to-speech synthesizers transform text strings into acoustic signals. A TTS system is composed of two parts: front-end and back-end. The front-end carries out two major tasks. Firstly, it converts text strings containing symbols such as numbers and abbreviations into their equivalent words. This process is often called text normalization, pre-processing or tokenization. Secondly, it assigns a phonetic transcription to each word, which requires dividing and marking the text into prosodic units, i.e. phrases, clauses, and sentences. The back-end (often referred to as the synthesizer) converts the words in text format into sound. Concatenative synthesis employs pre-recorded units of human voice that are put together to obtain words. It generally produces the most natural synthesized speech; however, differences between variations in speech and in the nature of the automated techniques for segmenting the waveforms sometimes result in audible glitches.

3. SPOKEN DIALOG SYSTEMS AND EDUCATION

With the growing maturity of conversational technologies, the possibilities for integrating conversation and discourse in educative applications are receiving greater attention, including tutoring (Pon-Barry et al., 2006), question-answering (Wang et al., 2007), conversation practice for language learners (Fryer et al., 2006), pedagogical agents and learning companions (Cavazza et al., 2010), and dialogs to promote reflection and metacognitive skills (Kerly et al., 2008).

The design, implementation and strategies of dialog systems employed in e-learning applications vary widely, reflecting the diverse nature of the evolving speech technologies. The conversa-

tions are generally mediated through simple text based forms (Heffernan, 2002), with users typing responses and questions at a keyboard. Some systems use embodied dialog systems (Graesser et al., 2001) capable of displaying emotion and gesture, whereas others employ a simpler avatar (Kerly et al., 2008b). Speech output, using text to speech synthesis is used in some systems (Graesser et al., 2001), and speech input systems are increasingly viable (Litman and Silliman, 2004) (Bos et al., 2002).

According to Roda et al. (Roda et al., 2001), enhanced e-learning systems are expected to i) accelerate the learning process, ii) facilitate access, iii) personalize the learning process, and iv) supply a richer learning environment. In addition, three main emerging approaches are described to integrate dialog systems in learning environments at the individual as well as at the group level:

1. Advanced help and learning process facilitation tools;
2. Personal coaches equipped with specific domain knowledge;
3. Role-playing actors in simulated experiential learning environments.

Dialog systems as advanced help and learning process facilitation tools are designed to provide an advanced helping service. To do this, they integrate structured knowledge models about the application domain and the environment. Although this kind of systems can be very useful, they are usually considered to be annoying and not intelligent. Their main limitations are due the inability to contextualize the users' actions within the set of possible uses sequences of the computer application. This way, the dialog system does not have any knowledge related to the user and cannot be adapted according to their preferences and motivations. In addition, they do not usually include dialog functionalities and can only be used to solve isolated questions, providing information already present in the corresponding manual of the application. This way, these systems do not incorporate any learning model. Examples of this kind of systems are the Microsoft Conversational Agents integrated in the Office desktop applications, as well as similar agents that are available in database applications.

Dialog systems as personal coaches integrate information about the domain of the application. Systems of this kind are characterized by the possibility to represent and continuously update information that represents the cognitive and social users' state. The main objective is to guide and manage users in the learning process, providing suggestions and other interaction functionalities not only with the developed application but also with the rest of students. To do this, these applications usually integrate realistic and interactive interfaces.

K-Inca is an artificial conversational agent designed to help people to adopt knowledge management practices (Angehrn et. al 2001) (Roda et al., 2001). Users' profiles have been included to represent their similarity with a set of predefined hierarchic behavior profiles, providing a personalized helping service that takes into account tutoring (e.g., providing specific exercises), suggestions and stimuli that modify the way in which the system interacts with their users.

Dialog systems as role-playing actors in simulated experiential learning environments are systems which are able to carry out a specific function in a very realistic way inside a simulated environment that emulates the real learning environment. These systems integrate knowledge about this environment or domain application (tasks, behaviors, objects, relationships, etc.) and are able to maintain a dialog updating and adapting this knowledge by considering users' social and cognitive state.

The Change VIBE (C-VIBE) system (Angehrn, 2001) has been developed to interact within the EIS simulated environment (Manzoni and Angehrn, 1997), currently used in leading schools and universities to train managers in the theory and practice of managing change and organizational transformation facing the natural resistance to innovation and change latent in organizations. Students interact in this platform by means of avatars and with the main objective of managing (individually or in group) a specific mission that is proposed in a Virtual Board Room.

3.1 Tutoring Applications

Tutoring is one of the most substantially research areas for the use of natural language dialog in e-learning. In educational domains, Kumar et. al. (20011) have shown that agents playing the role of a tutor in a collaborative learning environment can lead to over one grade improvement. Additional works (Liu and Chee, 2004) have explored a variety of interaction patterns and tactics that could be used in multi-party educational situations.

Most of the existing research on interaction strategies for dialog systems used in various interactive settings has focused on task-related strategies. In the case of conversational tutors, the task (or work) related interaction include aspects like instructing students about the task, delivering appropriate interventions in suitable form (e.g. socratic dialog, hints), providing feedback and other such tactics (Graesser et. al., 2005). Some studies (Rosé et. al., 2001b; Wang and Johnson, 2008) have evaluated the effect of these task related conversational behavior in tutorial dialog scenarios. Work in the area of affective computing and its application to tutorial dialog has focused on identification of student's emotional states (D'Mello et. al., 2008) and using those to improve choice of task related behavior by tutors.

The AutoTutor project (Graesser et al., 1999) provides tutorial dialogs on subjects including university level computer literacy and physics. The tutoring tactics employed by this system assist students in actively constructing knowledge, and are based on extensive analysis of naturalistic tutoring sessions by human tutors. AutoTutor includes the use of a dialog manager, curriculum scripts and latent semantic analysis. This system was demonstrated to give an important improvement when compared to control conditions for gains in learning and memory.

Another tutoring system employing dialog is Ms Lindquist (Heffernan, 2003), which offers "coached practice" to high school students in algebra by scaffolding "learning by doing" rather than offering explicit instruction. Early work with the system found that students using Ms Lindquist did fewer problems, but that they learned equally well or better than students who were simply told the answer. The results also suggested that the dialog was beneficial in maintaining student motivation. The authors concluded that Ms Lindquist was a "Less is More" approach, where learners tackled fewer problems, but learnt more per problem when they were engaged in an intelligent dialog (Heffernan, 2003).

CycleTalk (Forbus et. al., 1999) is an intelligent tutoring system that helps students to learn principles of thermodynamic cycles in the context of a power plant design task. Teams of two students work on designing a Rankine cycle using a Thermodynamics simulation software package. As a part of the design lab during which this learning task is performed, students participated in a collaborative design interaction for 30-45 minutes using ConcertChat, a text based collaboration environment (Mühlpfordt and Wessner, 2005). ITSPOKE is a tutoring spoken dialog system which engages the students in a spoken dialog to provide feedback and correct misconceptions (Litman and Silliman, 2004). It is speech-based dialog system that uses a text-based system for tutoring conceptual physics. A list with additional projects developed at the University of Pittsburgh can be found at http://www.cs.pitt.edu/~litman/itspoke.html.

Another example of natural language tutoring is the Geometry Explanation Tutor (Aleven et al., 2004), where students explain their answers to geometry problems in their own words. The system uses a knowledge-based approach to recognize explanations as correct or partially correct, and a statistical text classifier when the knowledge-based method fails. Studies with this system found that students who explain in a dialog learn better to provide general explanations for problem-solving steps (in terms of geometry theorems and definitions) than those who explain by means of a menu

The Oscar conversational intelligent tutoring system (CITS) (Latham et al. 2012) aims to mimic a human tutor by implicitly modeling the learning style during tutoring, personalizing the tutorial to boost confidence and improving the effectiveness of the learning experience. The system uses natural language to provide communication about specific topics with the users and dynamically predicts and adapts to a student's learning style. It is implemented using the Index of Learning Styles (ILS) model (Felder and Silverman, 1988) to deliver an SQL tutorial. The results of an evaluation carried out with real students that all learning styles in the ILS model were successfully predicted from a natural language tutoring conversation, with an accuracy of 61–100%.

An educational dialog system to support e-learning in the subject of geometry is described in (Kim, 2007). Knowledge in the system was created and represented by XML-based AIML (Artificial Intelligence Markup language). The system can answer the student's questions by referring and saving the previous knowledge while having a conversation with a student. To do this, context information related to the student is considered using an overlay student model. An educational dialog system was evaluated to test the efficiency of the designed and implemented system with geometry learning.

An educational environment developed for a modular spoken dialog system is described in (Gustafson et al., 1998). The aim of the environment is to provide students, with different backgrounds, means to understand the behavior of spoken dialog systems. Dialog is recorded in a dialog tree whose nodes are dialog objects, which model the constituents of the dialog and consist of parameters for modeling dialog structure, focus structure and a process description describing the actions of the dialog system. The educational system has been used in a number of courses at various universities in Sweden.

Other question-answering systems have included a student discussion board (Feng et al., 2006) where the dialog system mines a corpus to retrieve an answer based on cosine similarities between the query post and the corpus passages, and the Intelligent Verilog Compiler Project (Taylor and Moore, 2006), which allows learners to ask questions in English that query the same ontology as is used to provide the system's 'help' texts. This style of use most closely mirrors the most common use in commercial environments where dialog systems are used for information retrieval.

3.2 Learning Companions and Embodied Dialog Systems

Developing more human-like systems seems to improve interaction by establishing a more engaging relation with this kind of systems (Dehn and van Mulken, 2000). Learning companions are simulated characters that act as a mate of the student, and take a non-authoritative role in a social learning environment (Chou et al., 2003). This way, a number of Embodied Dialog systems (ECA) have been developed to assist students during the learning process. According to research and evaluation studies in the field of intelligent interfaces, ECAs (Gratch et al., 2002) have shown to be a good interaction metaphor when acting in the role of counselors (Marsella et al., 2003), personal trainers (Bickmore, 2003), or healthy living advisors (de Rosis et al., 2003). Indeed, ECAs have the potential to involve users in a human-like conversation using verbal and non-verbal signals for providing feedback, showing empathy and emotions in their behavior (Cassell, 2001). Due to these features, ECAs can be successfully employed as interaction metaphor

in the pedagogical domain (Johnson et al., 2004) and in other domains where it is important to settle long-term relations with the users (Bickmore and Picard, 2005).

These agents, which may employ gesture, synthesized speech and emotional facial displays, have been investigated in domains ranging from helping children to learn plant biology (Lester et al., 1999) to continuing medical education (Shaw et al., 1999) and naval training (Rickel and Johnson, 1999). Research into the roles which may be played by a pedagogical agent or learning companion has investigated agents as mentors, peers, experts or instructors (Baylor, and Kim, 2005). In some systems the student must teach the agent (Chan and Baskin, 1998), or interact with peer agents or co-learners (Dillenbourg and Self, 1992), who may even include trouble makers intended to provoke cognitive dissonance to prompt learning (Aimeur et al., 1997). Researchers have also investigated user preferences for the agent expertise. Findings suggest that in general, similarities in competency between an agent and learner have positive impacts on the learners' affective attainments, for example, academically strong students showed higher self-efficacy beliefs in a task after working with a high-competency agent, while academically weak students showed higher self-efficacy after working with a low-competency agent (Kim, 2007).

Moreover, even if ECAs have shown to have a good impact on settling an emphatic relation with the user (de Rosis et al., 2005; Cassell et al. 2000) (Ai et al., 2006) (Bailly et al., 2010) (Edlund et al., 2008), involving them in a deeper and intimate interaction, it is difficult to communicate with these agents whenever needed (i.e. when the user is not in front of a computer but he/she has the need to get suggestions and advices). For example, DESIA (Johnson et al., 2004) is a step in this direction. This agent, presented in Carmen's Bright IDEAS, has been adapted for running successfully on a handheld device in order to assist in a psychosocial intervention for acquiring problem solving skills (Marsella et al., 2003).

Another example is the VU-MAS architecture, a Virtual University Multi-Agent System (MAS), is described in (De Carolis et al., 2006). Each student can interact with VU-MAS using a personal agent, called MyCoach, represented as an ECA. The main goal of this agent is to monitor the student activities, following his/her learning improvements, but also to select useful material according to the recognized student's goals and needs. The agent is also capable to proactively provide the student with useful suggestions whenever it is needed. As it is designed to run on a smart phone or a PDA, this agent combines e-learning capabilities with mobile computing, thus realizing an m-learning experience where the student can feel always in touch with his advisor.

3.3 Other Applications

There may be possibilities to integrate dialog systems in Learning 2.0 communities, as assistants, moderators, guides or as virtual peers within the community. Dialog and anthropomorphic characteristics of pedagogical and dialog systems may help support the social dimension of e-learning activities, and the social context has been argued to catalyze the cultivation and motivation for knowledge (Chou et al., 2003).

For example, dialog systems have been proposed to offer conversation practice for language learners. Jia (Jia, 2002) found that users were dissatisfied with the responses provided by a basic ALICEbot (www.alicebot.org) implementation, and the pattern-matching mechanism was deemed insufficient for use as a foreign language practice environment. In contrast, Jabberwacky (Fryer and Carpenter, 2006) (www.jabberwacky.com) uses a very different technology to ALICEbots, learning from all its previous conversations. It has been suggested for providing language practice; Fryer and Carpenter note that agents are willing to repeat the same material as often as students require.

They also argue that chatbots give students the opportunity to use varying language structures and vocabulary (for example slang and taboo words), which they may otherwise get little chance to experience (Fryer and Carpenter, 2006).

Spoken dialog systems have also been proposed to improve phonetic and linguistic skills. Vocaliza is a dialog application for computer-aided speech therapy in the Spanish language, which helps in the daily work of speech therapists who teach linguistic skills to Spanish speakers with different language pathologies (Vaquero et al., 2006). The Listem system (Literacy Innovation that Speech Technology Enables) is an automated Reading Tutor that displays stories on a computer screen, and listens to children read aloud (Mostow, 2012).

Finally, dialog is also used as a prompt for reflection. Grigoriadou et al. describe a system where the learner reads a text about a historical event before stating their position about the significance of an issue and their justification of this opinion (Grigoriadou et al., 2003). Answers are classified as scientific, towards-scientific or non-scientific, and a dialog generator produces "appropriate reflective diagnostic and learning dialog for the learner". CALMsystem (Kerly et al., 2008) promotes reflection of a different kind. Users answer questions on the domain, and state their confidence in their ability to answer correctly. The system infers a knowledge level for the student based on their answers, and encourages the learner to engage in a dialog to reflect on their self-assessment and any differences between their belief and that of the system about their knowledge levels. Studies have shown this dialog improved self-assessment accuracy significantly more than reflection based only on visual inspection of the system and learner beliefs (Kerly and Bull, 2008). Motivation and user engagement enhancements have also been frequently noted (Baylor and Kim, 2005), (Heffernan, 2003), (Fryer and Carpenter, 2006). In some cases motivation may be actively supported through deliberate motivational tutoring techniques; in others it may be a useful by-product of exposure to a novel technique.

If motivational benefits are to be retained, then this novelty cannot be relied upon, and further research into deliberate scaffolding of affect may be required. A key feature of dialog systems in educative applications is the use of a natural communication method. The user of natural language allows users' cognitive resources to be spent on the learning task, rather than stretched by the interface (Beun et al., 2003). Computer literacy, and familiarity with online chatting media, is becoming ubiquitous and a greater number of users are expected to find conversing with their learning tools a feasible option.

This section has demonstrated the wide variety in conversational systems in e-learning. Implementations may employ full embodied dialog systems with emotion or gesture display, synthetic voice output, simple text-based output, dialog with an accompanying avatar, and many variants or combinations of these. Developers have integrated conversational capabilities into systems for a range of reasons.

4. EXAMPLES OF EDUCATIVE DIALOG SYSTEMS

In this section we describe two interactive multimodal interfaces that we have developed covering some of the issues described in the previous sections.

4.1 The *VoiceApp* Multimodal Dialog System

The *VoiceApp* system (Griol et al, 2011) has been developed as a framework for the study of the XHTML+Voice technology to develop multimodal dialog systems that improve the accessibility to information on the Internet (http://www.w3.org/TR/xhtml+voice/). The XML, XHTML and VoiceXML (http://www.w3.org/

TR/voicexml20/) programming languages respectively deal with the visual design of the application and allow spoken dialog with the user. This way, multimodal interaction capabilities have been integrated for both the input and output of the system. The use of additional programming languages, as PHP and JavaScript, as well as relational database management systems such as MySQL, facilitates the incorporation of adaptive features and the dynamic generation of contents for the application.

Accessibility has been defined as one of the most important design requisites of the system. This way, detailed instructions, help messages, and menus have been also incorporated to facilitate the interaction with the different applications in the system. Previous interactions of the users are also taken into account to adapt the system, considering users' most used application, recent topics searched using the application, or errors detected after each interaction with the system.

In order to interact with the XHTML+Voice documents that make up the system, a web search engine supporting speech interaction and the specifications of this language is required. There are different models for implementing this multimodal interaction on mobile devices. The fat client model employs embedded speech recognition on the specific device and allows conducting speech processing locally. The thin client model involves speech processing on a portal server and is suitable for mobile phones. The implementation of the *VoiceApp* multimodal application for both computers and mobile devices is based on the fat client model, including a multimodal browser and embedded speech recognition on the corresponding device, and a web application server in which the system is stored.

The development of oral interfaces with XHTML+Voice implies the definition of grammars, which delimit the speech communication with the system. The *<grammar>* element is used to provide a speech or DTMF grammar that specifies a set of utterances that a user may speak to perform an action or supply information, and for a matching utterance, returns a corresponding semantic interpretation. We have defined a specific strategy to cover the widest range of search criteria in *VoiceApp* by means of the definition of speech recognition grammars in the different applications. This strategy is based on different aspects such as the dynamic generation of the grammars built from the results generated by the interaction with a specific application, the definition of grammars that includes complete sentences to support the naturalness of the interaction with the system (e.g., to facilitate a more natural communication and cover more functionalities in *Voice Pronunciation*), and the use of the ICAO phonetic alphabet (http://www.icao.int/icao/en/trivia/alphabet.htm) in the cases in which spelling of the words is required in order not to restrict the contents of the search or in situations in which repetitive recognition errors are detected (e.g., in order not to delimit the topics to search using Voice Browser).

The system consists of several modules to access web information. Firstly, the *Voice Dictionary* application offers a single environment where users can search contents in the Wikipedia encyclopedia with the main feature that the access to the application and the results provided by the search are entirely facilitated to the user either through visual modalities or by means of speech. Once the result of an initial search is displayed on the screen and communicated to the user by means of speech, they can easily access any of the links included in the result of the search or visit the rest of applications in the system with the possibility of interrupting the system's speech in any case. This functionality is achieved by means of the dynamic generation of the corresponding grammars, in which the different links that are present in the result of a specific search are included in the dynamic XHTML+Voice page automatically generated by means of a PHP script that captures the different information sources to inform the user about them (headings, text, contents, formulas,

links, etc.). Figure 1 shows the initial page of this application.

Secondly, Google is currently one of the most important companies for the management of information on the Internet due to its web search engine and a number of applications and services developed to access information on the net. This way, the *Voice Browser* application has been developed with the main objective of allowing the speech access to facilitate both the search and presentation of the results in the interaction with the Google search engine. The application interface receives the contents provided by the user and displays the results both visually and using synthesized speech. The application also allows the multimodal selection of any of the links included in the result of the search by numbering them and allowing using their titles as voice commands (Figure 1).

Thirdly, the *Voice Pronunciation* application has been developed with the main objective of implementing a web environment that facilitates second-language learning with two games that help to acquire new vocabulary and train the words pronunciation. The game *Words* shows on the screen and synthesizes orally the definition of one of the over one hundred thousand words stored in a database of the application and the user must guess the word. The game *Pictures* uses images stored in a database and annotated with different difficulties, whose exact name must be correctly uttered by the user to continue in the game and increase the score (Figure 2). The specific problems and errors detected during the previous interactions of the users with this application are taken into account for the selection of the different words and images and to consequently adapt both games to the specific evolution of each user during the learning process.

A number of tests and verifications have been carried out to maximize the functionalities and accessibility of the different applications included in the *VoiceApp* system. These tests have been very important to detect and correct programming errors and accessibility problems. One of

Figure 1. Main page of the Voice Dictionary application and screen showing the result of a search using the Voice Browser application

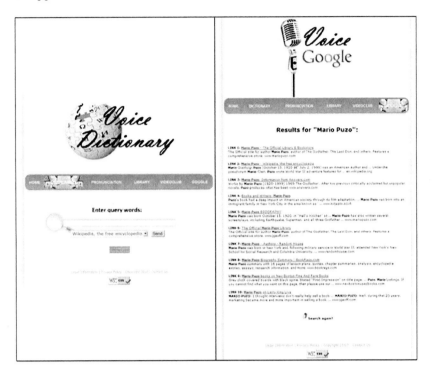

the main identified problems was related to the generation of inconsistencies when words with similar pronunciation were reserved to both interact with by the Opera search engine and the different applications in the system. These inconsistencies have been limited to the maximum so that the possible matches between selected words have been eliminated in the different applications.

Figure 2. Main page of the Voice Pronunciation application and the Words functionality

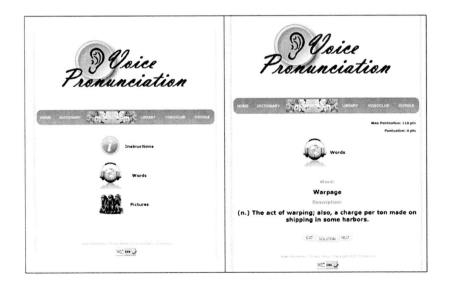

Current research lines include the adaptation of the system for its interaction using additional languages, a more detailed assessment of each specific application, and the incorporation of new features in each one of them. Another important research line consists of the adaptation of the different applications taking into account specific user profiles considering more detailed information about their preferences and evolution.

4.2 The LEGA System

The LEGA system (*Learning English? Go Ahead!*) (Griol et al., 2012) has been developed to facilitate self-learning English for foreign students. The design of the system considered the required capacities defined by the Association of Language Testers of Europe (ALTE), the Common European Framework of Reference for Languages (CEFR, http://www.coe.int/t/dg4/linguistic/CADRE_EN.asp), and the corresponding equivalence with Cambridge ESOL examinations

(Figure 3). This way, the system is focused on the skills and kind of exercises included in two of the most representative ESOL exams: First Certificate in English (FCE) and Certificate in Advanced English (CAE).

Through the access to the main page of the web-based application, users find a friendly system to visualize and complete different exercises and tests. The application provides access to these exercises by means of traditional input interfaces (i.e., mouse and keyboard), using tactile devices such as tablet-PCs or mobile phones, by means of speech, or even alternating both visual and speech modalities.

The architecture of the system includes three main elements. Dynamic web pages are used to display the different exercises and interact with users dynamically. They have been developed using the VoiceXML and PHP programming languages. As can be observed in Figures 4 and 5, the application shows the type of examination and selected block, the randomly selected exercise by

Figure 3. Relationship between the Common European Framework of Reference for Languages and the exams of Cambridge EOSL

CEFR level		Skills	Equivalence Cambridge EOSL
Basic User	A1	Can understand and elaborate basic spoken and written structures.	
	A2	Can understand and communicate sentences and frequently used expressions related to areas of most immediate relevance.	Key English Test (KET)
Independent User	B1	Can understand the main standard inputs, deal with most situations in an area where the language is spoken, and produce simple connected text on topics which are familiar or of personal interest.	English Self Study Platform (PET)
	B2	Can understand the main ideas of complex topics, interact with a degree of fluency and spontaneity with native speakers, and produce clear, detailed text on a wide range of subjects.	First Certificate in English (FCE)
Proficient User	C1	Can understand and produce a wide range of well-structured texts, express him/herself fluently and spontaneously, and use language flexibly and effectively for social, academic and professional purposes.	Certificate in Advanced English (CAE)
	C2	Can understand with ease virtually everything heard or read, and express him/herself spontaneously, very fluently and precisely in the most complex situations.	Certificate of Proficiency in English (CPE)
	Listening	Reading	Speaking	Writing

the application within the block and corresponding subsection, instructions, accumulated mark until the current and time remaining to complete the exercise. Each time students provide an erroneous answer in any of the questions, they receive a feedback explaining the reasons why it is not the right answer for the described situation. The different controls embedded in the page code allow the selection of the response by touching the screen, using the keyboard and mouse, playback audio files in the listening exercises, and interaction through speech for the assessment of oral expression.

The Application Database stores the different exercises, organized according to the kind of examination and corresponding block and sections. To incorporate a new exercise in the application it is required to introduce the statement, set of possible answers, valid answer, route of possible external files and feedback to the student for each of the options. This structure allows easy incorporation of new content in the application and modification of existing without advanced

knowledge of databases using the phpMyAdmin tool (http://www.phpmyadmin.net). Each exercise is numbered with a unique code.

Finally, the Users Database stores the specific information related to each one of the users registered in the application. This feature allows including in this database information on the previous interactions of each user (exercises that have been tried and mistakes made). This information is taken into account by the application for the selection among the possible exercises of each block and the generation of recommendations that take into account students specific skills and relevant exercises that they should emphasize.

In summary, the LEGA system has been developed after a detailed study of Common European Framework of Reference for Languages and the ESOL program of the University of Cambridge. The main objective of the system is the integration of different technologies that make possible to emulate the different exercises so that the interaction with the system is similar to the real conditions that students are going to find during

Figure 4. Visual exercise included in a FCE exam

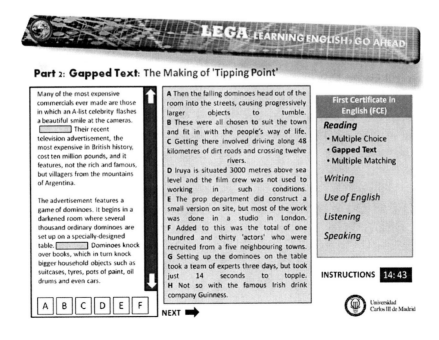

Figure 5. Oral exercise included in a CAE exam

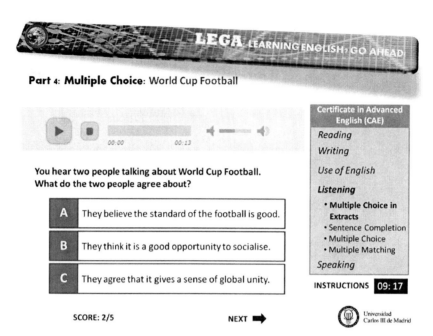

the examination. Among these technologies, the VoiceXML language makes possible the spoken interaction with the system. In addition, it is possible to access the application by means of conventional computers or by means of mobile devices with the possibility of speech and/or tactile interaction. Finally, the system also considers the specific evolution of each student and the analysis of the errors to adapt the system by taking into account these important features. As future work we want to incorporate new contents and complete a detailed evaluation of each one of the modules of the system, as well as the extension of the number of functionalities related to the adaptation of the system.

5. CONCLUSION AND FUTURE RESEARCH DIRECTIONS

This chapter has explored the variety of conversational agent applications and techniques in the e-learning literature, identifying a variety of purposes and strategies including tutoring, language practice, learning companions, pedagogical agents, question answering and encouraging learner reflection. Reported benefits to learners include improvements in grades, motivation, engagement and metacognitive skills. Professors may also benefit from the ability of conversational systems to provide assessment, reporting and additional classroom tools. Through detailed examples we have described innovative uses for conversational agents in e-learning, and demonstrated their use as tools in a larger e-learning system and for the provision of support to parallel classroom activities. We have also explored a range of issues relating to the development of multimodal dialog systems, including questions regarding the design of conversational process and issues relating to technical implementation. We conclude that dialog systems have a valuable role to play in future e-learning and blended learning systems and we expect their use to become increasingly common and progressively more capable as this technology continues to develop. Finally, we have also described two systems developed using some of the innovative applications of multimodal dialogue systems described in the chapter.

REFERENCES

Ábalos, N., Espejo, G., López-Cózar, R., Callejas, Z., & Griol, D. (2010). A multimodal dialog system for an ambient intelligent application in home environments. *Lecture Notes in Computer Science, 6231*, 491–498. doi:10.1007/978-3-642-15760-8_62

Ai, H., Litman, D., Forbes-Riley, K., Rotaru, M., Tetreault, J., & Purandare, A. (2006). Using systems and user performance features to improve emotion detection in spoken tutoring dialogs. *Proceedings of Interspeech'06-ICSLP*, (pp. 797–800).

Aimeur, E., Dufort, H., Leibu, D., & Frasson, C. (1997). Some Justifications for the Learning by Disturbing Strategy. *Proceedings of International Conference on Artificial Intelligence in Education*, (pp. 119-126).

Aleven, V., Ogan, A., Popescu, O., Torrey, C., & Koedinger, K. (2004). Evaluating the effectiveness of a tutorial dialog system for self-explanation. *Proceedings of International Conference on Intelligent Tutoring Systems*, (pp. 443-454).

Andeani, G., Fabbrizio, D. D., Gilbert, M., Gillick, D., Hakkani-Tur, D., & Lemon, O. (2006). Let's DISCOH: Collecting an annotated open corpus with dialogue acts and reward signals for natural language helpdesks. *Proceedings of IEEE Workshop on Spoken Language Technology (SLT'06)*, (pp. 218–221).

Angehrn, A. (2001). C-VIBE: A virtual interactive business environment addressing change management learning. *Proceedings of IEEE International Conference on Advanced Learning Technologies (ICALT'01)*, (pp. 174-177).

Angehrn, A., Nabeth, T., Razmerita, L., & Roda, C. (2001). K-InCA: Using artificial agents for helping people to learn new behaviours. *Proceedings of IEEE International Conference on Advanced Learning Technologies (ICALT'01)*, (pp. 225-226).

Augusto, J. (2009). Ambient intelligence: Opportunities and consequences of its use in smart classrooms. *Italics, 8*(2), 53–63.

Bailly, G., Raidt, S., & Elisei, F. (2010). Gaze, dialog systems and face-to-face communication. *Speech Communication, 52*(6), 598–612. doi:10.1016/j.specom.2010.02.015

Baylor, A. L., & Kim, Y. (2005). Simulating instructional roles through pedagogical agents. *International Journal of Artificial Intelligence in Education, 15*(2), 95–115.

Beun, R.-J., de Vos, E., & Witteman, C. (2003). Embodied dialog systems: Effects on memory performance and anthropomorphisation. *Proceedings of International Conference on Intelligent Virtual Agents*, (pp. 315-319).

Bickmore, T. (2003). *Relational agents: Effecting change through human-computer relationships.* PhD Thesis, Media Arts & Sciences, Massachusetts Institute of Technology.

Bickmore, T. W., & Picard, R. W. (2005). Establishing and maintaining long-term human-computer relationships. *ACM Transactions on Computer-Human Interaction, 12*(2), 293–327. doi:10.1145/1067860.1067867

Bohus, D., & Rudnicky, A. (2005). LARRI: A language-based maintenance and repair assistant. *Spoken Multimodal Human-Computer Dialogue in Mobile Environments, 28*, 203–218. doi:10.1007/1-4020-3075-4_12

Bos, J., Klein, E., Lemon, O., & Oka, T. (1999). The verbmobil prototype system - A software engineering perspective. *Journal of Natural Language Engineering, 5*(1), 95–112. doi:10.1017/S1351324999002132

Callejas, Z., & López-Cózar, R. (2008). Influence of contextual information in emotion annotation for spoken dialogue systems. *Speech Communication, 50*(5), 416–433. doi:10.1016/j.specom.2008.01.001

Cassell, J., Sullivan, J., Prevost, S., & Churchill, E. F. (2001). *Embodied dialog systems.* The MIT Press.

Catizone, R., Setzer, A., & Wilks, Y. (2003). Multimodal dialog management in the COMIC Project. *Proceedings of EACL'03 Workshop on Dialog Systems: Interaction, Adaptation, and Styles of Management,* (pp. 25–34).

Cavazza, M., de la Camara, R. S., & Turunen, M. (2010). How was your day? A companion ECA. *Proceedings of AAMAS'10 Conference,* (pp. 1629-1630).

Chan, T.-W., & Baskin, A. B. (1988). Studying with the prince: The computer as a learning companion. *Proceedings of International Conference on Intelligent Tutoring Systems,* (pp. 194-200).

Chou, C.-Y., Chan, T.-W., & Lin, C.-J. (2003). Redefining the learning companion: The past, present and future of educational agents. *Computers & Education, 40,* 255–269. doi:10.1016/S0360-1315(02)00130-6

Chu, S.-W., O'Neill, I., Hanna, P., & McTear, M. (2005). An approach to multistrategy dialog management. *Proceedings of Interspeech'05-Eurospeech,* Lisbon, Portugal, (pp. 865–868).

Cole, R., Mariani, J., Uszkoreit, H., Varile, G. B., Zaenen, A., Zampolli, A., & Zue, V. (Eds.). (1997). *Survey of the state of the art in human language technology.* Cambridge University Press.

Corradini, A., Mehta, M., Bernsen, N. O., & Charfuelán, M. (2005). Animating an interactive conversational character for an educational game system. *Proceedings of the International Conference on Intelligent User Interfaces,* (pp. 183–190).

Cuayáhuitl, H., Renals, S., Lemon, O., & Shimodaira, H. (2006). Reinforcement learning of dialog strategies with hierarchical abstract machines. *Proceedings of IEEE/ACL SLT'06 Workshop,* (pp. 182–186).

D'Mello, S. K., Craig, S. D., Gholson, B., Frankin, S., Picard, R., & Graesser, A. C. (2005). Integrating affect sensors in an intelligent tutoring system. *Proceedings of Workshop on Affective Interactions: The Computer in the Affective Loop at IUI,* (pp. 7-13).

De Carolis, B., Pelachaud, C., Poggi, I., & Steedman, M. (2003). APML, a markup language for believable behavior generation. In Prendinger, H., & Ishizuka, M. (Eds.), *Life-like characters: Tools, affective functions and applications.* Berlin, Germany: Springer.

de Rosis, F., Cavalluzzi, A., Mazzotta, I., & Novielli, N. (2005). Can embodied dialog systems induce empathy in users? *Proceedings of AISB'05 Virtual Social Characters Symposium,* (pp. 1-8).

Dehn, D. M., & van Mulken, S. (2000). The impact of animated interface agents: A review of empirical research. *International Journal of Human-Computer Studies, 52*(1), 1–22. doi:10.1006/ijhc.1999.0325

Dillenbourg, P., & Self, J. (1992). *People power: A human-computer collaborative learning system in intelligent tutoring systems* (pp. 651–660). Berlin, Germany: Springer-Verlag.

Edlund, J., Gustafson, J., Heldner, M., & Hjalmarsson, A. (2008). Towards human-like spoken dialog systems. *Speech Communication, 50*(8-9), 630–645. doi:10.1016/j.specom.2008.04.002

Elhadad, M., & Robin, J. (1996). An overview of SURGE: A reusable comprehensive syntactic realization component. *Proceedings of the Eighth International Natural Language Generation Workshop*, (pp. 1–4).

Felder, R. M., & Silverman, L. K. (1988). Learning and teaching styles in engineering education. *English Education*, *78*(7), 674–681.

Feng, D., Shaw, E., Kim, J., & Hovy, E. (2006). An intelligent discussion-bot for answering student queries in threaded discussions. *Proceedings of International Conference on Intelligent User Interfaces*, (pp. 171-177).

Forbus, K. D., Whalley, P. B., Evrett, J. O., Ureel, L., Brokowski, M., Baher, J., & Kuehne, S. E. (1999). CyclePad: An articulate virtual laboratory for engineering thermodynamics. *Artificial Intelligence*, *114*(1-2), 297–347. doi:10.1016/S0004-3702(99)00080-6

Fryer, L., & Carpenter, R. (2006). Bots as language learning tools. Language learning and technology. *Language Learning & Technology*, *10*(3), 8–14.

Glass, J., Flammia, G., Goodine, D., Phillips, M., Polifroni, J., & Sakai, S. (1995). Multilingual spoken-language understanding in the MIT Voyager system. *Speech Communication*, *17*, 1–18. doi:10.1016/0167-6393(95)00008-C

Graesser, A. C., Chipman, P., Haynes, B. C., & Olney, A. (2005). AutoTutor: An intelligent tutoring system with mixed-initiative dialog. *IEEE Transactions on Education*, *48*, 612–618. doi:10.1109/TE.2005.856149

Graesser, A. C., Person, N. K., & Harter, D. (2001). Teaching tactics and dialog in AutoTutor. *International Journal of Artificial Intelligence in Education*, *12*, 23–39.

Graesser, A. C., Wiemer-Hastings, K., Wiemer-Hastings, P., & Kreuz, R. TRG. (1999). AutoTutor: A simulation of a human tutor. *Journal of Cognitive Systems Research*, *1*, 35–51. doi:10.1016/S1389-0417(99)00005-4

Gratch, J., Rickel, J., Andre, J., Badler, N., Cassell, J., & Petajan, E. (2002). Creating interactive virtual humans: Some assembly required. *IEEE Intelligent Systems*, *17*(4), 54–63. doi:10.1109/MIS.2002.1024753

Grigoriadou, M., Tsaganou, G., & Cavoura, T. (2003). Dialog-based reflective system for historical text comprehension. *Proceedings of Workshop on Learner Modelling for Reflection at Artificial Intelligence in Education*.

Griol, D., Hurtado, L. F., Segarra, E., & Sanchis, E. (2008). A statistical approach to spoken dialog systems design and evaluation. *Speech Communication*, *50*(8-9), 666–682. doi:10.1016/j.specom.2008.04.001

Griol, D., Molina, J. M., Callejas, Z., & López-Cózar, R. (2012). (in press). Desarrollo de actividades de evaluación para un sistema on-line de aprendizaje de idiomas. *Revista Relada*, *6*.

Griol, D., Molina, J. M., & Corrales, V. (2011). Lecture Notes in Computer Science: *Vol. 7023*. *The VoiceApp System: Speech technologies to access the Semantic Web* (pp. 393–402). CAEPIA. doi:10.1007/978-3-642-25274-7_40

Gustafson, J., Elmberg, P., Carlson, R., & Jönsson, A. (1998). An educational dialogue system with a user controllable dialogue manager. *Proceedings of ICSLP*, *98*, 33–37.

Heffernan, N. T. (2003). Web-based evaluations showing both cognitive and motivational benefits of the Ms. Lindquist tutor. In Hoppe, U., Verdejo, F., & Kay, J. (Eds.), *Artificial intelligence in education* (pp. 115–122). Amsterdam, The Netherlands: IOS Press.

Hubal, R. C., Frank, G. A., & Guinn, C. I. (2000). AVATALK virtual humans for training with computer generated forces. *Proceedings of 9th Conference on Computer Generated Forces and Behavioral Representation*, Orlando, (pp. 617–623).

Jia, J. (2002). *The study of the application of a keywords-based chatbot system on the teaching of foreign languages*. University of Augsburg.

Johnson, W. L., LaBore, L., & Chiu, Y. C. (2004). A pedagogical agent for psychosocial intervention on a handheld computer. *Proceedings of AAAI Fall Symposium on Dialogue Systems for Health Communication*, (pp. 22-24).

Jokinen, K., Kanto, K., & Rissanen, J. (2004). Adaptative user modelling in AthosMail. *Lecture Notes in Computer Science*, *3196*, 149–158. doi:10.1007/978-3-540-30111-0_12

Kerly, A., Ellis, R., & Bull, S. (2008). Dialog systems in e-learning. *Proceedings of, AI-08*, 169–182.

Kerly, A., Ellis, R., & Bull, S. (2008). Children's interactions with inspectable and negotiated learner models. *Proceedings of International Conference on Intelligent Tutoring Systems*, (pp. 132-141).

Kerly, A., Ellis, R., & Bull, S. (2008). CALM-system: A dialog system for learner modelling. *Knowledge-Based Systems*, *21*(3), 238–246. doi:10.1016/j.knosys.2007.11.015

Kim, Y. (2007). Desirable characteristics of learning companions. *International Journal of Artificial Intelligence in Education*, *17*(4), 371–388.

Kumar, R., & Rose, C. P. (2011). Architecture for building dialog systems that support collaborative learning. *IEEE Transactions in Learning Technology*, *4*(1), 21–34. doi:10.1109/TLT.2010.41

Latham, A., Crockett, K. A., McLean, D., & Edmonds, B. A. (2012). Conversational intelligent tutoring system to automatically predict learning styles. *Computers & Education*, *59*(1), 95–109. doi:10.1016/j.compedu.2011.11.001

Lemon, O., Georgila, K., & Henderson, J. (2006). Evaluating Effectiveness and portability of reinforcement learned dialog strategies with real users: The TALK TownInfo evaluation. *Proceedings of IEEE-ACL SLT'06*, Palm Beach, Aruba, (pp. 178–181).

Lester, J. C., Stone, B. A., & Stelling, G. D. (1999). Lifelike pedagogical agents for mixed-initiative problem solving in constructivist learning environments. *User Modeling and User-Adapted Interaction*, *9*, 1–44. doi:10.1023/A:1008374607830

Litman, D. J., & Silliman, S. (2004). ITSPOKE: An intelligent tutoring spoken dialog system. *Proceedings of Human Language Technology Conference: North American Chapter of the Association for Computational Linguistics*, (pp. 5-8).

Liu, Y., & Chee, Y. S. (2004). Designing interaction models in a multiparty 3D learning environment. *Proceedings of 12th International Conference on Computers in Education (ICCE 2004)*, (pp. 293–302).

López-Cózar, R., & Araki, M. (2005). *Spoken, multilingual and multimodal dialog systems: Development and assessment*. John Wiley and Sons.

Mairesse, F., Gasic, M., Jurcícek, F., Keizer, S., Thomson, B., Yu, K., & Young, S. (2009). Spoken language understanding from unaligned data using discriminative classification models. *Proceedings of ICASSP*, *09*, 4749–4752.

Manzoni, J. F., & Angehrn, A. (1997). Understanding organizational dynamics of IT-enabled change: A multimedia simulation approach. *Journal of Management Information Systems*, *14*(3), 109–140.

Marsella, S. C., Johnson, W. L., & LaBore, C. M. (2003). Interactive pedagogical drama for health interventions. In Hoppe, I. U. (Eds.), *Artificial intelligence in education: Shaping the future of learning through intelligent technologies* (pp. 341–348). Amsterdam, The Netherlands: IOS Press.

Mattasoni, M., Omologo, M., Santarelli, A., & Svaizer, P. (2002). On the joint use of noise reduction and MLLR adaptation for in-car hands-free speech recognition. *Proceedings of International Conference on Acoustics, Speech, and Signal Processing (ICASSP'02)*, (pp. 289–292).

McTear, M. F. (2004). *Spoken dialog technology.* Springer. doi:10.1007/978-0-85729-414-2

Menezes, P., Lerasle, F., Dias, J., & Germa, T. (2007). Towards an interactive humanoid companion with visual tracking modalities. *International Journal of Advanced Robotic Systems*, 48–78.

Meza, I., Riedel, S., & Lemon, O. (2008). Accurate statistical spoken language understanding from limited development resources. *Proceedings of ICASSP, 08*, 5021–5024.

Minker, W. (1998). Stochastic versus rule-based speech understanding for information retrieval. *Speech Communication, 25*(4), 223–247. doi:10.1016/S0167-6393(98)00038-7

Montoro, G., Haya, P. A., Alamán, X., López-Cózar, R., & Callejas, Z. (2006). A proposal for an XML definition of a dynamic spoken interface for ambient intelligence. *Proceedings of International Conference on Intelligent Computing (ICIC'06)*, (pp. 711–716).

Mostow, J. (2012). Why and how our automated reading tutor listens. *Proceedings of International Symposium on Automatic Detection of Errors in Pronunciation Training (ISADEPT)*, (pp. 43-52).

Mühlpfordt, M., & Wessner, M. (2005). Explicit Referencing in chat supports collaborative learning. *Proceedings of 6th International Conference on Computer-Supported Collaborative Learning (CSCL'05)*, (pp. 662-671).

Oh, A., & Rudnicky, A. (2000). Stochastic language generation for spoken dialog systems. *Proceedings of ANLP/NAACL Workshop on Conversational Systems*, (pp. 27–32).

Pon-Barry, H., Schultz, K., Bratt, E. O., Clark, B., & Peters, S. (2006). Responding to student uncertainty in spoken tutorial dialog systems. *International Journal of Artificial Intelligence in Education, 16*, 171–194.

Rabiner, L. R., & Juang, B. H. (1993). *Fundamentals of speech recognition.* Prentice-Hall.

Rabiner, L. R., Juang, B. H., & Lee, C. H. (1996). An overview of automatic speech recognition. In Lee, C. H., Soong, F. K., & Paliwal, K. K. (Eds.), *Automatic speech and speaker recognition: Advanced topics* (pp. 1–30). Kluwer Academic Publishers. doi:10.1007/978-1-4613-1367-0_1

Reiter, E. (1995). NLG vs. templates. *Proceedings of the Fifth European Workshop in Natural Language Generation*, (pp. 95–105).

Rickel, J., & Johnson, W. L. (1999). Animated agents for procedural training in virtual reality: Perception, cognition, and motor control. *Applied Artificial Intelligence, 13*, 343–382. doi:10.1080/088395199117315

Roda, C., Angehrn, A., & Nabeth, T. (2001). Dialog systems for advanced learning: Applications and research. *Proceedings of BotShow'01 Conference*, (pp. 1-7).

Roda, C., Angehrn, A., & Nabeth, T. (2001). Matching competencies to enhance organizational knowledge sharing: An intelligent agents approach. *Proceedings of 7th International Netties Conference*, (pp. 931-937).

Rosé, C. P., Moore, J. D., VanLehn, K., & Allbritton, D. (2001). A comparative evaluation of Socratic versus didactic tutoring. *Proceedings of Cognitive Sciences Society.*

Shaw, E., Johnson, W. L., & Ganeshan, R. (1999). Pedagogical agents on the Web. *Proceedings of International Conference on Autonomous Agents,* (pp. 283-290). ACM Press.

Taylor, K., & Moore, S. (2006). Adding question answering to an e-tutor for programming languages. *Proceedings of 26th SGAI International Conference on Innovative Techniques and Applications of Artificial Intelligence,* (pp. 193-206). Cambridge, UK: Springer.

Vaquero, C., Saz, O., Lleida, E., Marcos, J., & Canalís, C. (2006). VOCALIZA: An application for computer-aided speech therapy in Spanish language. *Proceedings of IV Jornadas en Tecnología del Habla,* (pp. 321–326).

Wahlster, W. (Ed.). (2006). *SmartKom: Foundations of multimodal dialog systems.* Springer. doi:10.1007/3-540-36678-4

Wang, N., & Johnson, L. W. (2008). The politeness effect in an intelligent foreign language tutoring system. *Proceedings of 9th International Conference Intelligent Tutoring Systems,* (pp. 70-280).

Wang, Y., Wang, W., & Huang, C. (2007). Enhanced semantic question answering system for e-learning environment. *Proceedings of AINAW'07 Conference,* (pp. 1023-1028).

Weng, F., Varges, S., Raghunathan, B., Ratiu, F., Pon-Barry, H., & Lathrop, B. ... Shriberg, L. (2006). CHAT: A conversational helper for automotive tasks. *Proceedings of the 9th International Conference on Spoken Language Processing (Interspeech-ICSLP),* (pp. 1061–1064).

Williams, J., & Young, S. (2007). Partially observable Markov decision processes for spoken dialog systems. *Computer Speech & Language, 21*(2), 393–422. doi:10.1016/j.csl.2006.06.008

Zue, V. W., & Glass, J. R. (2000). Conversational interfaces: Advances and challenges. *Proceedings of the IEEE, 88,* 1166–1180. doi:10.1109/5.880078

ADDITIONAL READING

Bezold, M., & Minker, W. (2011). *Adaptive multimodal interactive systems.* Springer. doi:10.1007/978-1-4419-9710-4

Clark, B., Lemon, O., Gruenstein, A., Bratt, E., Fry, J., & Peters, S. ... Treeratpituk, P. (2005), A general purpose architecture for intelligent tutoring systems. *Advances in Natural Multimodal Dialogue Systems,* (pp. 287–305).

Graesser, A. C., VanLehn, K., Rosé, C., Jordan, P. W., & Harter, D. (2001). Intelligent tutoring systems with conversational dialogue. *AI Magazine, 22*(4), 39–51.

Grifoni, P. (Ed.). (2009). *Multimodal human-computer interaction and pervasive services.* Hershey, PA: IGI Global. doi:10.4018/978-1-60566-386-9

Jokinen, K. (2009). *Constructive dialog modelling: Speech interaction and rational agents.* Wiley.

Kurkovsky, S. (Ed.). (2009). *Multimodality in mobile computing and mobile devices: Methods for adaptable usability.* Hershey, PA: IGI Global. doi:10.4018/978-1-60566-978-6

Macías, J. A., Granollers, A., & Latorre, P. M. (Eds.). (2009). *New trends on human-computer interaction.* Springer. doi:10.1007/978-1-84882-352-5

Maragos, P., Potamianos, A., & Graos, P. (Eds.). (2010). *Multimodal processing and interaction: Audio, video, text.* Springer.

Tzovaras, D. (Ed.). (2010). *Multimodal user interfaces: From signals to interaction.* Springer.

Veletsianos, G., Heller, R., Overmyer, S., & Procter, M. (2010). Conversational agents in virtual worlds: Bridging disciplines. *British Journal of Educational Technology*, *41*(1), 123–140. doi:10.1111/j.1467-8535.2009.01027.x

KEY TERMS AND DEFINITIONS

Automatic Speech Recognition (ASR): Technique to determine the word sequence in a speech signal. To do this, this technology first detects basic units in the signal, e.g. phonemes, which are then combined to determine words.

Dialog Management (DM): Implementation of the "intelligent" behaviour of the conversational system. It receives some sort of internal representation obtained from the user input and decides the next action the system must carry out.

Multimodal Dialog System: Computer program that emulates a dialog between two human beings and process two or more combined user input modes such as speech, pen, touch, manual gestures, gaze, and head and body movement in a coordinated manner with multimedia system output.

Natural Language Generation (NLG): Creation of messages in text mode, grammatical and semantically correct, which will be either displayed on screen or converted into speech by means of text-to-speech synthesis.

Spoken Language Understanding (SLU): Technique to obtain the semantic content of the sequence of words provided by the ASR module. It must face a variety of phenomena, for example, ellipsis, anaphora and ungrammatical structures typical of spontaneous speech.

Speech Synthesis: Artificial generation of human-like speech. A particular kind of speech synthesis technique is called Text-To-Speech synthesis (TTS), the goal of which is to transform into speech of any input sentence in text format.

VoiceXML: Standard XML-based language to access web applications by means of speech.

XHTML+Voice (X+V): XML-based language that combines traditional web access using XHTML and speech-based access to web pages using VoiceXML.

Chapter 2
Experiences Using a Free Tool for Voice Therapy Based on Speech Technologies

William R. Rodríguez
Antonio Nariño University, Colombia & University of Zaragoza, Spain

Oscar Saz
Carnegie Mellon University, USA & University of Zaragoza, Spain

Eduardo Lleida
University of Zaragoza, Spain

ABSTRACT

This chapter reports the results after two years of deployment of PreLingua, a free computer-based tool for voice therapy, in different educational institutions. PreLingua gathers a set of activities that use speech processing techniques and an adapted interface to train patients who present speech development delays or special voice needs in the environment of special education. Its visual interface is especially designed for children with cognitive disabilities and maps relevant voice parameters like intensity, vocal onset, durations of sounds, fundamental frequency, and formant frequencies to visually attractive graphics. Reports of successful results of the use of PreLingua have been gathered in several countries by audiologists, speech therapists, and other professionals in the fields of voice therapy, and also, in other fields such as early stimulation, mutism, and attention-deficit disorders. This chapter brings together the experiences of these professionals on the use of the tool and how the use of an interface paradigm that maps acoustic features directly to visual elements in a screen can provide improvements in voice disorders in patients with cognitive and speech delays.

DOI: 10.4018/978-1-4666-2530-3.ch002

Copyright © 2013, IGI Global. Copying or distributing in print or electronic forms without written permission of IGI Global is prohibited.

INTRODUCTION

Different disorders or pathologies can reduce the ability of an individual to control the production of voice. These disorders may be caused by structural anomalies, such as weakness of laryngeal structures or muscles; by pathological conditions including vocal nodules, polyps or vocal fold thickening, by vocal abuse or vocal misuse, and by certain cases of disabilities (Kenneth, 1966; Kornilov, 2004). The main consequence of these disorders is the reduction in the communication skills of those who suffer them, which eventually excludes them from normal social relationships and lowers their standard of living. In many cases, voice therapy is the solution to train or to educate the patient's altered voice via extensive interaction with a skilled therapist. In general, alterations of the voice are any acoustical disturbance which affects the quality of parameters of the voice such as intensity, fundamental frequency, durations of sounds, formants, or various combinations of them (Arias and Estape, 2005; Aronso, 1993).

As the first step of the treatment, the patient must be examined by a speech therapist, where the consultation between them may result in the recommendation of voice therapy as the appropriate solution to the disorder or pathology. Therapists have developed through the years a handful of techniques aimed to train the different voice skills; for instance, to work vocalic articulation, patient and therapist sit in front of a mirror to work the tongue movements through imitation, or they blow up balloons to work blowing abilities. In general, the time required to provide this therapy for a single patient can make it impractical when working with a large population, and access to voice therapy becomes costly and time consuming.

Computer-based tools can be helpful for this purpose. This kind of tools are based on robust techniques of signal processing and speech technologies like voice activity detection, energy estimation, tracking of fundamental frequency, and formant estimation. By combining these techniques, the tools allow to work different parameters in voice therapy like voiced/unvoiced sounds, voice intensity, tone modulation, rhythm, vocal onset and sound duration. Therapists can, in some cases, use them to provide enhanced treatment to some of their patients. However, the resources are not always sufficient to provide the acquisition of voice skills in individuals with handicaps due to the price of computer-aided tools for voice therapy, the limitations for the training of vocalic articulation and the lack of available tools for the different languages, including Spanish.

The work presented here describes the set of interactive tools that were developed to reduce the time and the level of computer expertise required from the therapist for providing the interactive component of the therapy. This tool, called PreLingua, uses speech processing to train patients with speech development delays, or special voice needs of handicapped individuals in a special education environment. The tool covers the first stage of language acquisition (phonatory skills) and includes voice activity detection, the control of voice intensity, blow, vocal onset, phonation time, tone, and, vocalic articulation activity in Spanish language. Its visual interface does not require any previous configuration and is especially designed for children and people with cognitive disabilities by using attractive graphics representing important voice parameters in real time, and in the vocalic articulation, an special avatar was designed in order to make the children understand how to locate their articulatory structures in the generation of the Spanish vowels (Rodriguez et al., 2010).

To test the effectiveness of PreLingua, a study was conducted in two schools for special education in Spain and Latin America, the results show that PreLingua can actually help patients with speech disorders to improve their voice capabilities, and its interface is really easy to use, very motivating and understandable to young users. As PreLingua is a free tool available on line, it is possible to benefit a large number of Hispanic-speaking countries from this work. A large amount of feedback has been collected over time; some of this feedback has led to further improvements in the tool, while other has provided examples of individual cases where PreLingua has provided a fruitful help to therapists and patients.

This chapter gives initially a short background to voice therapy tools and outlines the design of PreLingua, focusing on the graphical interface and the feedback loop that converts acoustic parameters to visual elements in the computer. The results of the use of PreLingua in patients with voice disorders are provided, along with several experiences of use by the professionals and some cases of success in patients with disabilities. This will lead to state the directions of future research as well as the conclusions of this work.

BACKGROUND

Traditional voice therapy techniques may include, for instance, sitting down with the patient in front of a mirror to work tongue movements through imitation, or imitate musical instruments to work tonality, or blowing up balloons to work blowing abilities, etc.; situations where the time required providing this therapy for a single patient can make it impractical when working with a large population. Other option is the use of Computer-Aided tools for voice therapy which bridge this gap with more time efficient and more robust voice therapy, but they present limitations as the difficulty of training vocalic articulation, the lack of available tools for many languages, including Spanish, or the high costs of their development (Cucchiarini et al., 2008).

This kind of tools for voice therapy based on speech technologies has been a major issue since the 1990's. Some of the most remarkable efforts in this area comprehend the following: Speech Viewer III developed in 1997 by IBM (Speech Viewer III, 2005), was the most popular commercial software for speech therapy although currently is not having any more support from

its company. This application used a very simple speech interface which allows training voice activity detection, varying intensity, pitch and vocal onset. Vox Games developed by CTS Informatica in Brazil (VoxGames, 2009), is a pack of games developed to clinical therapy with the aim of stimulating the voice and speech modification in children and young adults. Voice Games M5176, by KAY Elemetrics Corp. (Voice Games, 2010), provides an environment for speech therapy which focuses on the control of intensity and pitch amplitude. Dr. Speech developed by Tiger DRS (Dr. Speech, 1999), is a comprehensive speech/voice assessment and training software system which is intended for use by professionals in voice and speech fields. In this last tool, the vowel tracking is possible but the feedback to the user is a plot representation of the formants or resonant frequencies which is hardly understandable by non-professional users.

In the area of academic research, several works have addressed this field and have studied issues like the use of different speech processing techniques, different types of feedback and different levels of interaction. Works like Orto-Logo-Paedia (Öster et al., 2002); the ISAEUS consortium (García-Gómez et al., 1999), SPECO (Vicsi et al., 1999), the ISLE project (Atwell et al., 2003) or LISTEN (Rasmussen et al., 2011) are some of the most well-known examples. Orto-Logo-Paedia (Öster et al., 2002, Hatzis et al., 2003), and its predecessor Optical-Logo-Therapy (Hatzis et al., 1997; Hatzis, 1999) aimed for the training of different phonetic features by the use of phonetic maps. SPECO (Vicsi et al., 1999) and ISAEUS (García-Gómez et al., 1999) were oriented in a similar way to the training of designated phonemes like vowels or fricatives. Their novel interest was their ability to produce the tools in several languages like Spanish, German and French in ISAEUS or Hungarian, Slovenian, Swedish and English in SPECO. These tools, and other studies like (Öster, 1996) were mainly aimed to the hearing impaired community. LISTEN has focused on reading tutors, providing feedback on intonation abilities for children with speech difficulties in American English. Most of the research works, and all of the previously mentioned, obtained the voice parameters directly from the user's acoustical information, but other techniques using Automatic Speech Recognition (ASR) and pattern recognition have been used in (Kirschning and Cole, 2007), to provide language therapy in children with hearing disabilities, or for preliterate children in the Tball project (Tepperman et al., 2006; Black et al., 2008).

Following all these efforts, the Communication Technologies Group of the Aragon Institute for Engineering Research in the University of Zaragoza (Spain) started developing tools in the framework of COMUNICA (Saz et al., 2009; Rodríguez et al., 2008) as an initiative for providing free tools to the speech and language therapy community in the Hispanic world. One of the tools created was PreLingua which began as a tool for pre-linguistic communication and was expanded into a tool for voice therapy. The paradigms for the development of PreLingua are focused on two issues: First, the use of speech processing techniques like the digital model of voice production, linear prediction analysis, estimation of the fundamental frequency and formants and homomorphic analysis (Rodríguez et al., 2011; Rabiner et al., 1978) to detect voice parameters from a patient speech. Second, the presentation of these parameters to the patient with an especially designed interface where the patients can see in a graphical way their speech production; this visual feedback loop is designed to make the patients correct the impediments in their speech through repeated practice, and, through the imitation of an avatar for the vocalic articulation all in real time. The tool has improved continuously in the last three years according to the suggestions made by teachers and therapists, for instance, the last version integrates new features for the assessment and measurement of acoustic parameters for the monitoring of the patients. Nowadays PreLingua has thousands of users and it is becoming a reference tool for voice therapy among therapists in Spanish speaking countries.

DESIGNING AND INTERFACE OF PRELINGUA

PreLingua has a special design in order to facilitate the therapist's work and to motivate young users and users with disabilities. The tool is designed in Spanish and can be downloaded from the website www.vocaliza.es, once installed, a simply microphone set up on a computer is required to access and work on the different activities. PreLingua is powered by the Allegro graphic engine (Allegro, 1998) and runs as a standalone application for Windows machines.

As shown in Figure 1, the activities in PreLingua form a pyramid with five levels according to five increasing degrees of difficulty in the activities. The lower level corresponds to Voice Activity games, level 2 to the control of Intensity, level 3 to Blow, Vocal Onset and Phonation Time, level 4 corresponds to the Tone activities and, finally, level 5 to vocalic articulation activities. The tool considers these parameters/levels because they are measurable by means of different speech processing algorithms (Rodríguez et al., 2012). All the activities and the speech processing within are performed in real time. The graphic user interface is designed according to children's level of cognition, for instance, simple objects or animals that appear or move on the screen in presence of voice in the basic level, or interfaces more complex where the voice's tone or intensity is used to modify the position of a certain object or character on the screen. The feedback given by the game is the completion of a goal; for instance, reaching the end of a labyrinth in which a cartoon is controlled up and down accordingly to the voice parameters. In order to train the basis of

Figure 1. PreLingua main interface

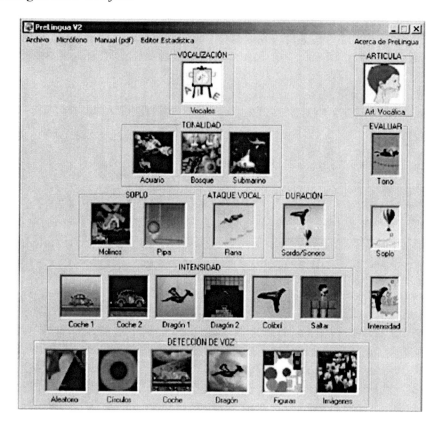

vocalization features, the special activity called ARTICULA was developed (Rodriguez et al., 2010) creating a more natural and understandable interface for users. This tool aims to show the patient how to place the most basic elements of the vocal tract (tongue, mouth aperture and lips) in the articulation of the different vowels through a moving avatar. The interfaces for some of these activities can be seen in Figure 2.

In order to provide an objective assessment on the phonatory faculties of a given patient, PreLingua offers a section to evaluate three different features like intensity, blow and tone in individual sessions. In the Articula activity the system also evaluates each vowel for each session if the therapist decides so. This evaluation section is located at the right hand side of the PreLingua main window (Figure 1). The therapist can use the reports and images as attachments to the clinical information.

Voice Detection: Level 1

The level provides activities with animated graphics to represent voiced sounds in real time. This feature is especially oriented to children in the very early stages of development who still do not associate their production of sounds to changes in their environment. When the voice segment is analyzed and the energy exceeds an established threshold, the sonority of the segment is studied to ensure that it is a voiced segment when the minimum sonority threshold is reached. When the segment is classified as voiced segment, the system produces a reaction on the screen in which a set of simple shapes and colors will interact around the screen like in Figure 2(a). In similar activities, a simple character like a car is moved on the screen only when the voice is detected.

Figure 2. Some activities in PreLingua

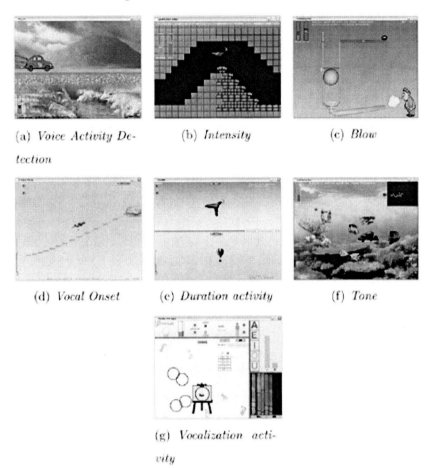

(a) *Voice Activity Detection*

(b) *Intensity*

(c) *Blow*

(d) *Vocal Onset*

(e) *Duration activity*

(f) *Tone*

(g) *Vocalization activity*

Intensity: Level 2

Patients with the ability to distinguish their own speech production might find necessary to learn the control of the volume of this vocal production. In this case, the intensity of the voice is used to modify the position of a certain object or character on the screen. The feedback given by the game is the completion of a goal; for instance, reaching the end of a labyrinth in which a given character is controlled up and down in the vertical axis accordingly to the intensity of the voice production as in Figure 2(b).

Blow, Vocal Onset, and Phonation Time: Level 3

This level covers three important aspects related to the importance of breathing in the production of voice: Blow, Vocal Onset and Phonation Time. The Blow activities make use of the intensity value estimated in unvoiced segments, then, there is an animation on the screen associated to these segments like a blowpipe in Figure 2(c). In this game the therapist can change the threshold in order to modify the degree of difficulty. Vocal Onset helps the patient to control the attack of the vocal folds, which is very useful in stuttering cases. In this activity, a character (frog) is controlled by the patient's vocal onset, with the frog jumping in each vocal attack of the user as in Figure 2(d); in this case, the therapist can set up the space between the bases where the frog jumps.

The Phonation Time activity is aimed to help the therapist assess the voiced and unvoiced phonation time of the patient. Maximum Phonation Time (MPT) and Maximum Exhaling Time (MET) imply abilities in voice production and provide information about the efficiency of the glottal closure (Arias and Estape, 2005). In this activity (shown in Figure 2(e)) the patient is instructed to sustain a voiced sound as long as possible following deep inspiration; this voiced segment produces the flight of a character (bird) and the system calculates the MPT value. After that, the child is instructed to sustain an unvoiced sound as long as possible following deep inspiration, which makes the flight of a second object/character (balloon) and the system shows the MET value. When the activity is completed the system provides the ratio MET/MPT which can be used to evaluate the glottal closure by the therapist.

Tone: Level 4

Tone activities are designed to help patients who need to improve pitch control and develop the smooth modulation of tone contour. Control of tone is required in a correct speech production and it is extremely needed in some speech features like prosody. Once the system obtains an estimation of the pitch frequency by the autocorrelation method, the system moves a graphic element like a fish according to the pitch contour and the goal is to follow the other animals on the main stage (Figure 2 (f)).

Vocalization: Level 5

This stage is important because the transition between the production of voice and the production of speech and language occurs with vowels. The set of vowels for every language is different, so the strategy in the activities to motivate vocalization in

PreLingua has been designed purely for the vowels in Spanish. This language contains five vowels (/a/, /e/, /i/, /o/ and /u/ in their SAMPA notation) whose representation in the space of the formant frequencies F1 and F2 is a triangle. The canonical values of F1 and F2 for the five Spanish vowels are given by several authors (Martínez-Celdrán, 1989) but these values are purely theoretical and vary largely among different speakers, especially in the case of high pitched voices of women and children. Hence, in PreLingua a formant normalization was applied with the vocal tract length in order to obtain a better estimation for each user.

Within the vocalization activity, the therapist selects the gender and height of the user and the system re-adjust the expected formant values for a person of similar physical characteristics. As showed in Figure 2(g), the activity allows training each vowel (vowel /a/ in this case) showing a dartboard, and the position for the darts is the normalized F1 against the normalized F2 obtained from the user's voice after the normalization process. The goal is to aim and hit inside the desired target region for each vowel. This activity also shows the voice spectrum with the evolution of the unnormalized formants in real time.

Articula

A more natural approach to the training of vowels was proposed as a separated activity using a more robust technique for formant estimation called ARTICULA. This activity reinforces the patient how to position the most basic elements of the vocal tract (tongue, mouth aperture and lips) in the articulation of the different vowels. It is well known that the vocalic sounds are determined primarily by tongue position, the degree of constriction and the lip shape. These characteristics can be correlated to the acoustic features of the vowels which can be identified by the first and seconds formants (Rodriguez & Lleida, 2009) in order to animate a boy or girl avatar and whose interface can be seen in Figure 3. Here, the ava-

Figure 3. ARTICULA activity

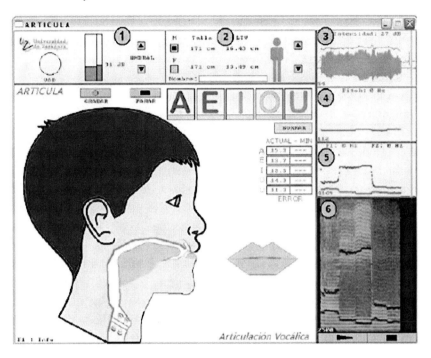

tar has been developed with a static part (skull), and three dynamics components (tongue, jaw and lips). The normalized formant frequencies modify the horizontal and vertical positions of these components, based on the premises that first formant F1 is correlated with the elevation of the tongue and second formant F2 is correlated with tongue frontness (Watt et al., 2002) achieving a better natural representation of the avatar. Articula also provides useful additional information to the therapist about user's voice parameters such as intensity, pitch, formants (not normalized) and spectrum in real time, as shows Figure 3 in items 3, 4, 5, and 6.

RESULTS AND EXPERIENCES OF THE USE OF PRELINGUA

PreLingua is currently being used in more than 15 Spanish speaking countries and by December 2011 has reached over 8,440 registered users. Some of the therapists who are using the tool in countries

such as Spain, Colombia, Costa Rica and Uruguay have participated in an experimental study using PreLingua or have shared their experiences and results with this tool. The results of the study and their reports provide several cases of success with the application of the tool in patients with disabilities that help understand how PreLingua can help individuals with disabilities to improve their communication abilities (Rodriguez, 2011).

Experimental Study with PreLingua

PreLingua was tested for three months in the Center of Special Education "CEDESNID" in Bogota (Colombia) and the Public School for Special Education (CPEE) "Alborada" in Zaragoza (Spain). The test was applied in users with different disabilities (cognitive and/or motor) that affected their voice skills in many different ways. Due to the difficulty of comparing users with different affections to the voice no control group was defined; instead, a longitudinal study was made where patients from the two educative institutions worked with PreLingua and a comparison was made of their voice skills at the beginning of the study and their voice skills after 12 weeks of therapy with PreLingua. 27 subjects were found as potential users of the system and the user selection was made by the therapists based on their capability of understanding the proposed therapy.

At the initial stage of the study, each user was evaluated by the therapist through a speech therapy evaluation form in order to assess their voice skills (subjective assessment); afterward, the therapists used PreLingua for 12 weeks with each user; and, finally, the therapists repeated the same speech therapy evaluation with each user to assess changes in the voice skills of the subjects. The therapists were free to decide how to use PreLingua with each subject, focusing on those skills which might be more helpful or necessary for the patient.

An objective assessment of the subjects was made with data from the first 3 weeks of therapy with PreLingua and from the last 3 weeks of therapy with PreLingua. Subjects performed the evaluation activities mentioned in the previous Section and the results in intensity, blow, tone and Articula were stored for a posterior statistical analysis. Only the Mean Square Error (MSE) between the proposed pattern and the user's performance was considered; and the mean value and standard deviation of this value was calculated for the initial and final sessions separately. The final aim was to detect significant differences between the results of the activities at the beginning and the end of the therapy to detect improvements in the capabilities of the subjects.

Results

The results described here are divided in objective measurements from the statistical analysis of the results stored by PreLingua and subjective measurements from the pre and post speech therapy evaluation forms for each user.

The objective measures provided the following results. By considering a significance level of 99% (p <.01) the study showed improvements in 14.8% of the subjects in the control of intensity, 18.5% of the subjects improved in blow production, only 3.7% improved in tone control and 8.3% improved in vocalic production (at least one of the vowels). A more relaxed threshold, but still determining high significance of 95% (p <.05) provided improvements in 29.6% of the subjects in intensity, 25.9% improved in blow production, 22.2% of the subjects improved in the control of tone and 20.8% improved in the production of vowels. Finally, a level of significance of 80% (p <.2) marked improvements in 55.6% of the subjects in intensity, 55.6% of the subjects improved in the production of blow, 29.6% improved in the control of tone and 33.3% of the subjects improved vocalization.

In general, control of intensity and blow were the activities where more subjects achieved significant improvements at all the significance levels. These results were especially encouraging for blowing activities, as they require a higher level of concentration compared to the intensity activities which usually require less skill from the subjects. Fewer subjects achieved significant improvements in the control of tone, possibly influenced by the short duration of the therapy study, as subjects require a high level of awareness to improve in this feature and more time would be required to achieve a better control of the vocal folds by the patient. Regarding the vocalic articulation activity, it is well known that the articulation process is affected by geometrical features of the patient's vocal cavity. Some of the subjects presented malformations in the hard and soft palates, crooked teeth and/or hypotonia or hypertonia, and achieving real significant improvements in these cases would require larger amounts of work.

The subjective assessment included traditional aspects in speech therapy as: Intensity, Blow Duration, Tone, Tongue Praxis and Rhythm. All of them were evaluated in subjective scales according to each topic for evaluation; for instance, rhythm was evaluated as normal, tachylalia, gasped or bradylalia; or tone was evaluated as normal, monotonous or robotic. Blow duration was the skill where a larger number of subjects had an improvement according to the therapists, followed by intensity and rhythm. In the intensity feature, 12 subjects had a positive change after therapy, for instance changing from strained voice to normal voice (although with some difficulties) or increasing skill in asthenic voices. 18 subjects improved in blow duration, where some of them changed from normal blow to normal with increased skill, or another who changed from altered blow to normal with difficulties. Regarding tone, only 7 subjects experienced a positive evolution of their skills, most of them getting closer to a normal intonation compared to their previous monotonous intonation. Tongue praxias was the skills where Articula acted during therapy, with 8 cases improving their performance for the therapists; in all cases increasing their skills in the tongue movements. The rhythm aspect was treated by activities in PreLingua like Vocal Onset and Phonation Time, 12 subjects showed an improvement in this skill, most of them achieving a normal rhythm. Finally, additional skills were observed by the therapist at the end of the study. Out of the 27 cases of study, 21 of them achieved skills which were not the primary outcomes of the study; these skills included increases in attention time, higher ability to follow instructions, better control of blow direction and socialization skills.

At the end of the experience, the therapists were asked to evaluate the work with PreLingua. They considered it to be very easy to use and very attractive for all the patients (disabled children and some adults). They observed improvements during the 12 weeks of work with PreLingua, highlighting the ability of sustained blowing instead of disrupted blowing and better continuous patterns (tableland and rising–falling) in voiced utterances. Other observations mentioned cognitive issues, as some subjects showed improvements

in paying attention, better levels of concentration and memorization and a high motivation of the user. Regarding sensor-perceptual issues, some subjects showed better spatial location (on the screen) and coordination, as well as improvements in visual and auditory perception. In communication skills some subjects showed an increase in voiced utterances and the recognition of the different characters inside PreLingua. An issue often mentioned by the therapists was related to socialization skills, as they mentioned positive attitudes like team playing, taking turns to play, helping each other, healthy competition and self-demand in some cases.

User's Experiences

All the computer-aided tools at the COMUNICA project (Rodríguez et al., 2008) are available in its web site www.vocaliza.es since 2008, and only a valid e-mail address is required to download any tool from that web page. Users come from Spain and Spanish speaking Latin American countries, where the need for speech therapy tools targeting Spanish has always been high. Figure 4 shows the geographic distribution of the first 500 registered users with mayor density in Spain and a growing tendency in Latin-America countries. This impact and outreach to the community has been possible due to extensive diffusion work in oral and poster presentations in national and international conferences, seminars in special education schools or by direct recommendations among therapists. Furthermore, to provide more support about how to use the tools in COMUNICA, including PreLingua, in February of 2009 a YouTube channel was opened with video-tutorials which have been, been played more than 4250 times in the case of the PreLingua video. These reproductions include not only Spanish speaking countries but other countries where the use of PreLingua arises from the ease of the tool to work basic aspects of the voice like intensity, duration of sound, vocal onset and tone, which are independent of the language.

Figure 4. First 500 registered users

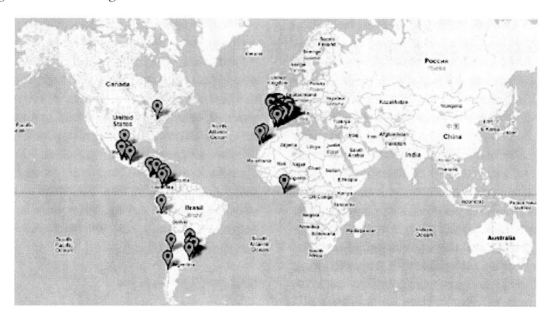

Also, PreLingua is present in different blogs related to speech therapy and special education where the therapists consider the tool very useful and easy to use and share their opinions and experiences using the tool. In some cases, therapists have created their own materials and tutorials to work with PreLingua which they have shared freely with other, creating a community which has helped expand the capabilities of PreLingua as a tool. All these elements, altogether with other media notes like TV and radio interviews and press articles, show the high impact of PreLingua in the speech therapy community.

Regarding the use of the tool, the therapists agree that it is easy to use and very intuitive, since it does not require previous configurations and the activities work with one click and in real time, and, the most relevant aspect highlighted by the therapists is that PreLingua is free software and it can be downloaded easily. They also mention that it is possible to get from patients a quick motivation, pleasure for playing with the tool and more willingness to attend therapy. Regarding the training of vocalic articulation through an avatar, the therapists mention a large change in

the methodology of work by reducing the time of therapy with the patient, and highlight the appropriate and apprehensive interface to train vocalic articulation in real time, since the naturalness of the interface makes it easier for the patients to imitate the vocalic pattern shown by the system. On the other hand, the therapists expressed the need that the tool continues improving its development in order to consider adult patients with altered voices, also, that the tool works in other platforms like Linux and Apple, and the possibility to work with consonant-vowel sounds.

Cases of Success

Singular cases of success reported include the de-muting of a child in Valencia Spain, and the elimination of a problem with the phoneme /s/ in A Coruña Spain. In Colombia, a patient with cerebral palsy improved his manner of breath, the blowing directionality, and thanks to the vocalic articulation activity through the avatar, the patient improved the mobility of the his phono-articulators structures and gained clarity in the sounds generated. In Uruguay, the therapists reported four cases with diagnoses of cerebral palsy, hearing loss, stuttering and autism respectively, where the patients improved the maintenance of sound, the blowing force, better modulation of tone, attention to visual stimuli and motivation in the use of the tool. In other case reported in Uruguay, a stuttering boy improved his ability to maintain sounds and his speech fluency. Finally, in a case reported outside of the mentioned study, a child with deep cognitive delay without oral communication achieved voiced utterances after continuous therapy with levels 1 and 2 of the pyramid of PreLingua (voice detection and intensity), and according to the therapist's comment the child enjoyed the therapy activity games inside PreLingua.

FUTURE RESEARCH DIRECTIONS

Several aspects are open for the improvement of PreLingua and related tools in the future. A very relevant issue is the increase in robustness of the speech processing algorithms embedded in the application. The acoustic conditions in which it has to operate can significantly vary due to the features of different users and the changes in the room and microphone where the therapy takes place. Robust processing which can work successfully independent of any of these factors is necessary to keep providing effective therapy in all cases.

Another improvement for the future is the possibility of developing a new multi-platform tool based in PreLingua which works the different aspects of voice therapy thought any web browser in a client-server architecture. This would ensure access to the features and functionalities of Pre-Lingua independently of the machine which the therapist or user is running. In this architecture, all the speech processing and analysis is performed in the remote server, while the client just presents the graphic interface and captures the speech to be transmitted to the server, receiving the results of the analysis to update the visualization. This

feature can be useful in special education institutions with low resources where the therapists can have access to PreLingua remotely without requiring any special software.

Many issues for the future of PreLingua arise from the feedback provided by therapists and users in general of the tool. One demand refers to the need of developing an alternative user interface which is more suitable for adults without disabilities, so the functionalities of PreLingua could be used by individuals with voice disorders not related to acquisition delays or handicaps. Furthermore, the experiences of the therapists presented in this Chapter suggest that new uses of the technologies included in PreLingua could be used for other areas such as early stimulation, hearing impairments, muteness, cases of stroke, autism, apraxia and attention-deficit disorders in special therapy sessions or in multi-sensorial rooms, where it is possible to work with patients with deep cognitive disorders.

CONCLUSION

The experiences collected from the users and the cases of success reported up to now show that the free tool for voice therapy PreLingua has impacted positively in the therapeutic community that uses it. Its potential for application is not only limited to voice therapy activities, since it has been extended to several scenarios of special education with successful results. The use of speech technologies in this kind of applications can definitely support the work of therapists and improve the quality of life of people with disabilities.

Especially significant are the results of the study run in the schools in Colombia and Spain which have shown analytically how the use of PreLingua can help patients with very different voice disorders improve their voice production in a short space such as 12 sessions. Further studies with larger populations and longer periods should expand these results and provide further evidence.

These results support the design of intuitive interfaces where acoustic features are directly mapped into graphical elements in the computer screen for speech training. The direct visualization of these elements allows for individuals with cognitive and development disorders to understand easily how changes in their voice features affect their environment, thus providing a simple and useful way to correct disorders in the voice production. Other visualization methods like periodograms, spectrograms or 3-D modeled talking heads difficult this feedback due to their higher levels of abstraction. Further advantages of these types of interfaces are the improvement on other characteristics like attention or motivation.

Communication is one of the most important features that define our quality of living. Those individuals who, for different reasons, have difficulties in it see themselves excluded from normal social interactions. All the efforts, like the one presented in this Chapter, that can successfully improve the communicative skills of this population are necessary to insure their inclusion. Cases of success in this area have to serve as further encouragement to new work which can help achieve the goal of providing sufficient communication to everybody in society.

ACKNOWLEDGMENT

This work was supported under TIN-2008-06856-C05-04 from MEC of the Spanish government and Santander Bank scholarships.

The authors want to acknowledge to Center of Special Education "CEDESNID" in Bogota (Colombia), and the School for Especial Education "Alborada" in Zaragoza (Spain), for their collaboration applying and testing the tool.

REFERENCES

Allegro, Free software. (1998). *A game programming library.* Retrieved on January 14, 2012, from http://www.liballeg.org

Arias, C., & Estape, M. (2005). *Disfonía infantil.* Barcelona, Spain: Ars Medical.

Aronso, A. (1993). *Clinical voice disorders* (3rd ed.). New York, NY: Thieme.

Atwell, E., Howarth, P., & Souter, C. (2003). The ISLE corpus: Italian and German spoken learners' English. *ICAME JOURNAL - Computers in English Linguistics, 27,* 5-18.

Black, M., Tepperman, J., Kazemzadeh, A., Lee, S., & Narayanan, S. (2008). *Pronunciation verification of English letter-sounds in preliterate children.* Paper presented at the 10th International Conference on Spoken Language Processing (ICSLP - Interspeech), Brisbane, Australia.

Cucchiarini, C., Lembrechts, D., & Strik, H. (2008, April). *HLT and communicative disabilities: The need for co-operation between government, industry and academia.* Paper presented at LangTech 2008, Rome, Italy.

Dr. Speech. Tiger DRS INC. (1999). *Tool for a comprehensive speech/voice assessment.* Retrieved January 14, 2012, from http://www.drspeech.com

García-Gómez, R., López-Barquilla, R., Puertas-Tera, J.-I., Parera-Bermúdez, J., Haton, M.-C., & Haton, J.-P. … Hohmann, S. (1999). *Speech training for deaf and hearing impaired people: ISAEUS Consortium.* Paper presented at the 6th European Conference on Speech Communication and Technology (Eurospeech-Interspeech), Budapest, Hungary.

Hatzis, A. (1999). *Optical logo-therapy: Computer-based audio-visual feedback using interactive visual displays for speech training.* Unpublished doctoral dissertation, University of Sheffield, U.K.

Hatzis, A., Green, P., Carmichael, J., Cunningham, S., Palmer, R., Parker, M., & O'Neill, P. (2003). *An integrated toolkit deploying speech technology for computer based speech training with application to dysarthric speakers*. Paper presented at the 8th European Conference on Speech Communication and Technology (Eurospeech-Interspeech), Geneva, Switzerland.

Hatzis, A., Green, P.-D., & Howard, S.-J. (1997). *Optical logo-therapy (OLT): A computer-based real time visual feedback application for speech training*. Paper presented at the 5th European Conference on Speech Communication and Technology (Eurospeech-Interspeech), Rhodes, Greece.

Kenneth, D. (1966). *Voice therapy for children with laryngeal dysfunction*. Paper presented at the Annual Convention of the American Speech and Hearing Association. Washington, USA

Kornilov, A.-U. (2004). *The biofeedback program for speech rehabilitation of oncological patients after full larynx removal surgical treatment*. Paper presented at the 9th International Conference Speech and Computer (SPECOM), St. Petersburg, Russia.

Martínez-Celdrán, E. (1989). *Fonología general y Española: Fonología funcional*. Barcelona, Spain: Teide.

Oester, A. M., House, D., Protopapas, A., & Hatzis, A. (2002, May). *Presentation of a new EU project for speech therapy: OLP (Ortho-Logo-Paedia)*. Paper presented at the XV Swedish Phonetics Conference (Fonetik 2002), Stockholm, Sweden.

Öster, A.-M. (1996). *Clinical applications of computer-based speech training for children with hearing impairment*. Paper presented at the 4th International Conference on Spoken Language Processing (ICSLP-Interspeech), Philadelphia (PA), USA.

Rabiner, L., & Schafer, R. (1978). *Digital processing of speech signals*. Upper Saddle River, NJ: Prentice-Hall.

Rasmussen, M. H., Mostow, J., Tan, Z. H., Lindberg, B., & Li, Y. (2011, August). *Evaluating tracking accuracy of an automatic reading tutor*. Paper presented at the 2011 Workshop on Speech and Language Technologies in Education (SLaTE), Venice, Italy.

Rodríguez, W. R. (2011). *Tecnologías del habla en la educación de la voz infantil alterada*. Zaragoza, Spain: Editorial Académica Española.

Rodríguez, W. R., & Lleida, E. (2009, September). *Formant estimation in children's speech and its application for a Spanish speech therapy tool*. Paper presented at the 2009 Workshop on Speech and Language Technologies in Education (SLaTE), Wroxall Abbey Estates, United Kingdom.

Rodríguez, W. R., Saz, O., & Lleida, E. (2010, September). *ARTICULA - A tool for Spanish vowel training in real time*. Paper presented at the 2010 Workshop on Second Language Studies Acquisition, Learning, Education and Technology, Tokio, Japan.

Rodríguez, W. R., Saz, O., & Lleida, E. (2012). A prelingual tool for education of altered voices. *Speech Communication, 54*(5), 583–600. doi:10.1016/j.specom.2011.05.006

Rodríguez, W. R., Saz, O., Lleida, E., Vaquero, C., & Escartín, A. (2008, October). *COMUNICA - Tools for speech and language therapy*. Paper presented at the First Workshop on Children, Computer and Interaction (WOCCI), Chania, Grece.

Saz, O., Yin, E., Lleida, E., Rose, R., Vaquero, C., & Rodríguez, W. R. (2009). Tools and technologies for computer-aided speech and language therapy. *Speech Communication, 51*(10), 948–967. doi:10.1016/j.specom.2009.04.006

Speech Viewer, I. B. M., III. (2005), *Software for speech therapy*. This product has been discontinued. Retrieved January 14, 2012, from http://www.synapseadaptive.com/edmark/prod/sv3/

Tepperman, J., Silva, J., Kazemzadeh, A., You, H., Lee, S., Alwan, A., & Narayanan, S. (2006). *Pronunciation verification of children's speech for automatic literacy assessment*. Paper presented at the 9th International Conference on Spoken Language Processing (ICSLP - Interspeech), Pittsburgh (PA), USA.

Vicsi, K., Roach, P., Oester, A., Kacic, Z., Barczikay, P., & Sinka, I. (1999, August). *SPECO: A multimedia multilingual teaching and training system for speech handicapped children*. Paper presented at the 6th European Conference on Speech Communication, Budapest, Hungary.

Voice Games Model 5167B. Key Elemetrics. (2010). *Tool for voice therapy*. Retrieved January 14, 2012, from http://www.kayelemetrics.com/index.php?option=com_product&view=product&Itemid=3&controller=product&cid%5B%5D=53&task=pro_details

VoxGames. (2009). *Software for speech and voice therapy*. CTS Informatica, Brasil. Retrieved January 14, 2012, from http://www.ctsinformatica.com.br/#voxGames.html{paginaProduto!7&1

Watt, D., & Fabricius, A. (2002). Evaluation of a technique for improving the mapping of multiple speakers' vowel space in the f1–f2 plane. *Leeds Working Papers in Linguistics and Phonetics, 9*, 159–173.

ADDITIONAL READING

Bonet, N. (2009). Rehabilitación de la voz infantil. *Audiología Práctica, 1*, 10–13.

Bosch, L. (2004). *Evaluación fonológica del habla infantil*. Barcelona, Spain: Masson.

Cabero, J., Córdoba, M., & Fernández, J. (2008). *Ordenador y discapacidad*. Sevilla, Spain: CEPE.

Gurlekian, J., Elisei, N., & Eleta, M. (2000). *Caracterización articulatoria de los sonidos vocálicos del español de Buenos Aires mediante técnicas de resonancia magnética*. Tech. rep., Laboratorio de Investigaciones Sensoriales. Retrieved January 14, 2012, from http://www.lis.secyt.gov.ar/index.php?l=en

Hirano, M. (1981). *Clinical examination of voice*. New York, NY: Springer.

Hurtado, D., & Soto, F. (2005). *Tecnologías de ayuda en contextos escolares*. Murcia, Spain: Consejería de Educación y Cultura.

Makhoul, J. (1975). Linear prediction: A tutorial review. *Proceedings of the IEEE, 63*, 561–580. doi:10.1109/PROC.1975.9792

Puyuelo, M., Rondal, J., & Wiig, E. (2004). *Evaluación del lenguaje*. Barcelona, Spain: Masson.

Sánchez, R. (2002). *Ordenador y discapacidad*. Madrid, Spain: CEPE.

Stevens, K. (1998). *Acoustic phonetics*. Cambridge, MA: The MIT Press.

KEY TERMS AND DEFINITIONS

Fundamental Frequency (Pitch): The immediate result of vocal cord vibration is the fundamental frequency of the voice, which determines its pitch. In physical terms, the frequency of vibration as the foremost vocal attribute corresponds to the number of air puffs per second, counted as cycles per second (Hz).

Language Acquisition: The natural process in which a student learns all the processes of language, starting in babbling as an infant and finishing in the functional language as a child.

Resonant Frequency (Formant): The resonant frequencies which arise from the vocal tract column are known as the formants and corresponds a groups of emphasized energy-harmonics of the voice.

Speech Technologies: Engineering techniques for the simulation of different parts of the oral communication like speech recognition, speech synthesis or voice analysis.

Speech/Voice Therapy: The corrective treatment, carried by a specialist in speech/voice pathology, for the improvement in oral communication of patients with different language or voice disorders.

Talking Head: An avatar whose lips, tongue and jaw movements are synchronized to the articulatory properties of the output speech.

Voice Intensity: Vocal attribute referred to voice volume which depends primarily on the amplitude of vocal cord vibrations and thus on the pressure of the subglottic airstream.

Chapter 3

Eye–Gaze and Facial Expressions as Feedback Signals in Educational Interactions

Kristiina Jokinen
University of Helsinki, Finland & University of Tampere, Finland

Päivi Majaranta
University of Tampere, Finland

ABSTRACT

In this chapter, the authors explore possibilities to use novel face and gaze tracking technology in educational applications, especially in interactive teaching agents for second language learning. They focus on non-verbal feedback that provides information about how well the speaker has understood the presented information, and how well the interaction is progressing. Such feedback is important in interactive applications in general, and in educational systems, it is effectively used to construct a shared context in which learning can take place: the teacher can use feedback signals to tailor the presentation appropriate for the student. This chapter surveys previous work, relevant technology, and future prospects for such multimodal interactive systems. It also sketches future educational systems which encourage the students to learn foreign languages in a natural and inclusive manner, via participating in interaction using natural communication strategies.

INTRODUCTION

With the development of personal computer technology in the 1980's, also educational applications started to get developed. Personal computers allowed educators to design and develop their own software, and various applications emerged for both instructional and support purposes; see an overview of the history and design of the educational systems in Reiser (2001a, b). Since the early applications, however, technology has taken big leaps, and especially interface technology has advanced much beyond text and mouse

DOI: 10.4018/978-1-4666-2530-3.ch003

Copyright © 2013, IGI Global. Copying or distributing in print or electronic forms without written permission of IGI Global is prohibited.

input. For instance, the techniques regarding the perception of the user, such as eye-gaze and face tracking, have become robust and easier to use in ordinary applications. They have been used in game applications (Isokoski et al., 2009), although their use in educational applications is not so common (however, some related research is conducted with respect to translation, see e.g. Hyrskykari et al., 2000).

In this chapter, we explore possibilities to use novel face and gaze tracking technology in educational applications. Our goal is to contribute to education technology by integrating novel interface technology and dialogue modelling techniques into a practical interactive learning tool that assists students in second language learning (L2-learning). Language learning differs from math and physics learning in that the main goal is to learn to *communicate* with other people using the new language, i.e. to learn to use the new language as a tool in everyday social situations. From this perspective, the support device for a language learner must be highly interactive, something that allows learning and training in interactive settings, and also learning of the interaction itself. Here we approach Jonassen (2000) who, in his review article, searchers for a new transformative view of educational technology. Jonassen advocates the constructivist view of learning, according to which teaching is not just transmitting knowledge from the teacher to the student, but a two-way dynamic situation where the knowledge is constructed through interaction and communication. Jonassen mainly focuses on collaborative learning, but it is clear that in L2-learning, dynamic interaction with the teacher is crucial, since it essentially sets out the practices and strategies which the student should adopt as part of the communicative repertoire for the language to be learnt.

Communication is social activity, bound by social and cultural norms and obligations, and learning, in particular L2-learning, is also governed by communicative practices. Because of this,

it is important to support L2 learners' pragmatic and interactional competence, and to develop their awareness of the differences between native and target languages both on lexical-syntactic and pragmatic levels. The learning of various patterns and practices of language use, including structure and organization of interactions, requires pedagogy that Hall (1999) has described as "prosaics of interaction": the learners' attention is directed to the pertinent features in the interaction context and linguistic resources, and through the systematic study of the interactive practices, the learners are thus helped to detect relevant patterns. Hall proposes that appropriate pedagogical activities in this respect should include analysis of videotapes, following the methodology of linguistic anthropology and discourse analysis. Furthermore, the analysis should concern recurring and goal-directed interactions like mealtime talk, faculty meetings, advice sessions, service encounters, etc., since the students, at least in the beginning of their studies, may not be able to detect the necessary features in less ritualized language uses. According to Hall (1999), the situations function as "cultural maps" of the social environment, and introduce the language learner, a newcomer, to relevant socio-cultural information.

While it is vital for students to develop a critical awareness of the language use, it is also important that they can take part in different communicative situations themselves, and become familiar with the appropriate use of linguistic resources in real interactions. Often suitable human partners may not be available for this kind of practise purposes, especially for beginners, who mostly need drill exercises to master simple interactions rather than complicated exchanges of information. For such repetitive learning situations, automated agents can prove useful assistants, as they can provide practise anytime without getting tired or frustrated.

In our work, the main learning context is assumed to be for individual language learners who want to get exercise on their interaction skills with a computer agent. When learning a second language, not only verbal information (words, grammar) needs to be learnt, but also paralinguistic information. These skills can also be learnt interactively: if the learner is repeatedly exposed to a certain kind of communicative situation and if the communicative action taken in that situation by the learner results in a successful goal achievement, the same action is likely to be used again in similar situations. We thus set our goal in what Jonassen (2000) considers the most challenging alternative in educational technology, namely to learn together with the computer. This means that the student does not only get assistance and learn from the computer, but enters into a real interaction with the teacher agent which acts like a partner in a communicative situation.

We can also imagine a peer context in which two or more students talk to each other, with a purpose of practising their language and communication skills among themselves. The computer agent would then function as a monitoring agent that may be able to jump into the conversation in order to correct the learners' grammatical or lexical problems, provide further information, or suggest a new conversation topic. In fact, the peer group may engage participants in interaction more than student-teacher encounters, since the conversations can also be more relaxed, and thus alleviate the student's fear of needing to produce "correct" sentences. The peer group may thus encourage the language learners to talk more and consequently, get more practise. It should be pointed out that the peer group resembles collaborative learning situation, in which the students work together on a task or a problem, and share information to solve problems and create solutions; in L2-learning, the task is to learn spoken interaction. However, in collaborative learning contexts the role of the computer has mainly been a tool or a shared working space through which the group communicates and shares information (see Resta & Laferrière, 2007, for a discussion on various collaborative learning technologies), whereas in our case, quite contrary, the computer has a more

active and agent-like role (cf. Jokinen, 2009, for a discussion concerning the change of the computer metaphor from a tool to an agent).

The article is structured as follows. Previous work on educational applications and issues related to interaction management will be surveyed in the next section, while the current technological context will be introduced in the section following this. We then continue with a discussion on facial expressions and their communicative functions, and also present a draft of the system and some experimental results. Finally, we draw some conclusions and the present prospects and research topics for the future.

PREVIOUS RESEARCH

Educational Interactive Applications

During the early years, educational software industry boomed especially with applications related to game-based technology. It became common to talk about *edutainment* or *edugames* where game playing is one of the important means to learn skills and concepts. The game provides a fun way of learning and requires the player to make immediate and meaningful decisions. Thus educational content can be learnt in the context of a game as part of the game activity; in other words, the application is simultaneously entertaining and educational. Although games have been used in teaching through the history, the game as an educational product which is designed and developed especially for the learning purpose was new. However, educational experts had reservations concerning the edutainment technology and applications were judged as poor learning tools and of no value (Randel et al., 1992). It was argued that it is not clear what kind of learning takes place (skills transfer, memorizing), or if learning indeed increases with game playing at all. Much of the discussion in game development also concerned the question if the game was just a means to convey a message, or if it is a message itself, a cultural artefact. Discussion took mostly place in the game development community, but it also provides background for the present-day edutainment applications and education technology.

Modern edutainment community is not debating so much about whether the game is a means or an expression as such, but focuses on the design and development of Serious Games, i.e. games whose primary purpose is not only to amuse or entertain, but to train and investigate. Educational games, for instance, aim at teaching or providing educational content, and research has shown that technology indeed has a positive effect on the student's learning scores, motivation, and inventive thinking. However, there are also obstacles in integrating technology into learning and teaching. These can be traced back to the attitudes and beliefs about the technology, as well as to expectations and practices around the subject, knowledge and skills, besides the infrastructure resources and assessment methodology (see on a general level e.g. Hew & Brush, 2007).

Many current educational applications and tutoring systems have been developed especially for domains such as mathematics, physics, and computer programming. For instance, Intelligent Tutoring Systems (ITS) guide students in problem-solving activities, and use a cognitive model of the domain in order to adapt instructions to the needs and skills of the individual learners (Corbett & Anderson, 2001; Koedinger & Corbett, 2006). Another example is the AutoTutor system (Graesser et al., 2005) which simulates a human tutor and can converse with the student in natural language. In AutoTutor, an animated conversational agent and 3D simulations are used to engage the student in the learning situation, which is modelled on the basis of constructivist learning theories (Driscoll, 2000), where learning is seen as an active construction of knowledge, and the teacher is a mediator whose aim is to create suitable learning environments where the construction of knowledge can take place.

Interactive tutoring has also been a productive application domain for spoken dialogue systems. It requires fairly rich interaction capabilities and thus provides a good testing ground for various models concerning presentation strategies, error handling, emotions, adaptation, etc. For instance, the ITSPOKE system (http://www.cs.pitt.edu/~litman/itspoke.html) is an Intelligent Tutoring Spoken Dialogue System, which focuses on dialogue-based interactions and aims at combining spoken language technology with instructional technology. The text-based tutoring system teaches simple physics problems to students. It has been used to collect a large corpus of the students' interactions with the system, and the corpus has been used for studying tutor responses and various aspects of communication such as emotions and user uncertainty, as well as simulation and evaluation of dialogue systems. Another example of dialogue-based tutoring systems is described by Griol et al. (2011) who present a multiagent framework for teaching support and the student's self-learning. The system facilitates more natural interaction between the system and the students, and it is developed within the area of Ambient Intelligence. The framework emphasizes intuitive interfaces that are embedded in everyday objects, and respond to the users and their presence in an intuitive and natural manner.

In the domain of second language learning (L2-learning), traditional Computer-Aided Language Learning (CALL) systems have been one of the key technologies in assisting learners to master a new language. The main functions of automated language training systems deal with corrections of the learners' pronunciation or accent. However, a major problem in the conventional CALL systems has been that the students are assigned a passive role: they need to repeat or read aloud sentences learnt from written choices, and there is no active practice or training for the problematic points, or for the interaction as a whole. In this regard, the progress of Automatic Speech Recognition (ASR) has pushed forward the research on CALL systems, since the more robust recognition allows experimentation with systems that can recognize spontaneous speech of the learners (cf. Yamazaki et al., 2008). Also chatbots have been used as language learning devices and in particular, used to allow students to participate in conversations in the target language, see Fryer and Carpenter (2006) for an overview. However, Fryer and Carpenter (2006) also point out that albeit the popularity of chatbot technology and possibilities for creating one's own chatbots, there is not yet ones which have been designed specifically for language learning.

One of the main concerns in learning environments is the form and amount of support that the system provides. In a series of articles, Aleven has discussed interactive learning environments (Aleven et al., 2003; 2004; 2005; 2006), and focused especially on the support that the educational system provides. Ideally, the learner can concentrate on the tasks and get help for learning the skills and concepts necessary for the successful completion of the task. Support for the task can comprise various hints, feedback, discussion or more information about the task, and the computational framework is implemented within the framework of the Intelligent Tutor System (ITS). An important research question is the optimal use of the support device, and in particular, its effect on the student's learning outcome: what are the optimal choices in the learning environments, so that the interaction would be beneficial for learning. However, it has also been noticed that the problematic areas in ITS concern the students' help-seeking skills and especially their meta-knowledge, i.e. the student's knowledge of their own knowledge (Aleven et al., 2003). In order to be able to seek for assistance, the students do not only need to know how to obtain additional information, but also, and more importantly, they have to know whether their current knowledge is enough to succeed on their own or whether more guidance is needed. This is a concern for self-guided education applications in general: the

students' self-awareness and knowledge of their own knowledge are necessary for the student to be able to take full use of the tutoring system and its facilities.

Below we will take this point further and discuss it with respect to spoken dialogue management. Feedback giving behaviour is usually related to the concept of grounding, which refers to the agents construction of shared understanding of each other's underlying goals and intentions (see Traum, 1994; Jokinen, 1994). It has been modelled e.g. via presentation-acceptance cycle (Clark & Wilkes-Gibbs, 1986), whereby the agents present new information on their goals to the partner, and consequently evaluate the value of the presented information with respect to the current context and their own intentions. In interaction modelling, grounding is a sign of the agents' cooperation (Allwood et al., 2000) which drives the interaction forward.

We claim that the optimal support in interactive tutorial systems is related to the optimal feedback behaviour of the tutor, learnt through interactions with the student. Central in the learning is to become aware of the student's level of understanding, and the tutor can learn this by observing signals that are generally used to express acknowledgement, agreement, and understanding. By observing the student's verbal and non-verbal behaviour, the teacher can benefit from perceiving the student's face and gaze which function as signals of the student's focus of attention and state of understanding.

Multimodal Interaction

In human-human communication, non-verbal signals such as pauses, intonation, nods, smiles, frowns, eye-gaze, gesturing etc. are effectively used to signal the speaker's understanding and emotions (Feldman & Rim, 1991). The relation between verbal and non-verbal communication is actively researched. Topics deal with such various issues as emotional speech (Douglas et al., 2003), alignment (Pickering & Garrod, 2004), synchrony and copying (Heldner et al., 2010, Manzini et al., 2010, Jokinen & Pärkson, 2011), audiovisual speech (Swerts & Krahmer, 2005), communicative functions of gestures and face expressions (Allwood et al., 2007; Jokinen et al., 2007), and the use and function of non-propositional vocalisations such as laughs and sighs (Campbell, 2007). Face and gesture communication has been widely studied (Kendon, 2004), and models implemented in the context of embodied conversational agents (André & Pelachaud, 2010; Nakano & Nishida, 2007) and robotics (e.g. Staudte & Crocker, 2009).

Also the embodiment of linguistic knowledge via action and interaction has been much discussed in experimental psychology and neuroscience. Although we will not go into details of this type of research due to complex nature of the relation between signal level data and cognitive representations, it is good to point out that interesting research is being conducted on the relation between sensorimotor activity and linguistic representations (concepts), and cognitive language skills and their motor representations in certain brain regions (see e.g. Tomasello, 1992; Arbib, 2003). This will, hopefully, result in better understanding of the principles guiding the ways in which the environment affects the individual's behaviour, and how the individual's knowledge is based on active experience.

When studying multimodal aspects of communication, such as gestures and facial expressions, cultural differences become more obvious. E.g. gesturing conveys tacit information about the partner's understanding, emotions, and attitudes that is important for the purpose and smooth operation of communication. Often certain gestures are typical for the speakers of a particular language and cultural context; see e.g. Kendon (2005) for Neapolitan gesturing where the gestures are important meaning conveying devices. Also Rehm et al. (2009) found differences in the German and Japanese speakers and their gesturing, while Navarretta et al. (2012) found that there are differ-

ences in the feedback providing nodding practices among the speakers in the closely related Nordic cultures. For instance, Finns tend to nod with single nods, while Swedish and Danish speakers use more repeated nods.

Very few educational computer systems have taken the culture into account. One exception is Johnson et al. (2004) who describe a language tutoring system that also considers cultural differences in gesture usage. Our goal is to study multimodal behaviour in intercultural context, and in particular to explore differences between Japanese and Finnish in a more detailed manner. In fact, we want to put forward a claim that the fluency of language speaking is not only related to verbal production, but can also be measured by the use of the "correct" type of gesturing besides the spoken ability. Moreover, there are cultural differences in the use of eye-gaze, facial expressions, and body posture, in a similar manner as there are cultural differences in the use of gestures.

Our focus is on non-verbal feedback that is used to construct a shared context in which learning can take place. In this context, face and gaze tracking technology becomes highly relevant as facial expressions and gaze are common feedback signals that tacitly indicate the learner's attitudes, engagement, and level of understanding. These signals are important in everyday interactions, but they also function as important primary means for interaction for users with special needs. Thus our work also supports the goal to build multimodal interactive systems which encourage the students to learn language in a natural and inclusive manner, via participating in interactions that support rich communication possibilities and allow different interaction strategies to be used.

In the following section, we will give an overview of the development and advances in face and eye-tracking technology that provides an excellent starting point for developing constructive learning environments in general, and tools for communication training for L2-learning in particular.

NOVEL TECHNOLOGIES FOR INTERACTION

Eye tracking makes it possible to record eye movements and gaze direction in real time. An eye tracking device records the eye movements and a computer program maps the gaze points into screen coordinates or objects in the environment. Before gaze direction can be interpreted reliably, the tracker must be calibrated. This is done by asking the user to look at a set of predefined points on the screen while the computer analyses the eye movements and calculates the gaze vector. Since gaze tracking is based on eye movements, eye glass frames, reflections on lenses, drooping eyelids, squeezing of the eyes while laughing or large head movements may disturb the tracker's ability to clearly track the eyes (especially the pupils) and thus cause errors in the tracking. However, the overall quality, stability and usability of the systems have increased substantially from the early days of eye tracking (Hansen & Majaranta, 2012). For example, modern trackers can recover from tracking errors quickly as soon as the eye(s) returns to the view of the camera, and they support fairly robust, long-lasting calibrations. Traditionally, eye tracking has mostly been utilized as a research tool for medical and psychological, marketing or usability research or by people with severe disabilities as a communication aids (Majaranta & Räihä, 2007). The improvement in the quality of systems and the increase in user population give great motivation for research on gaze-enhanced applications. Today, eye tracking is no longer a niche technology used exclusively by research laboratories; advances in the technology have extended the potential user group remarkably (Donegan et al., 2009; Majaranta et al.- 2009).

Eye gaze is a natural indication of people's focus of visual attention. Gaze is also proactive in nature, thus anticipating actions: we often gather visual information from our surroundings before performing motor actions (Land & Furneaux, 1997). Humans are accustomed to using eye gaze

to facilitate interaction with other humans, e.g. interlocutors monitor their partners' gaze direction of to establish joint attention that facilitates mutual understanding, either in real life, or in computer based applications (Qvarfordt et al., 2005). Gaze has been used to create attentive (proactive) applications that adjust their operation based on where the user is looking at (Hyrskykari et al., 2003). Eye tracking can also be used in education at various levels. Sibert et al. (2000) used eye tracking to support students who had trouble in learning to read; the eye tracker followed the user's gaze and provided auditory support if the student got stuck. Related to learning foreign language, there have been several attempts to develop gaze-based support for systems that help in the task of translating foreign text, either as a separate translation task or during natural reading (Takagi, 1998; Khiat et al. 2004; Hyrskykari et al., 2000). Gaze interaction can also play a big role in enabling communication for people with disabilities as their main interaction method at home as well as at school (Millar, 2010).

Eye tracking has been used as a (passive) research tool to study interaction between a software agent and a human and find out the effectiveness of the agent in attracting or directing the user's attention, or the naturalness of the interaction in general (Witkowski et al., 2001; Prendinger et al., 2005). We wish to use gaze tracking to improve natural interactions between humans and artificial tutors. In fact, previous research has already found eye tracking useful in the context of tutoring agents and conversational interfaces. For example Wang et al. (2006) exploited both head and eye movements in interaction with software agents. Their system could recognize simple gaze and head gestures for simple "yes" or "no" responses. In addition, they used information from the user's gaze direction to track where the student's attention was targeted at. The agent could provide additional information about the topic under focus, or attract the learner's attention to other related material. Preliminary results indicated that eye tracking may improve interaction and lead to stronger motivation in learning.

Eye tracking can also improve human-robot interaction by providing natural means for tele-operation of a robot (see e.g. Decker & Piep-meier, 2008; Atienza, R. & Zelinsky, A. 2003). Instead of a simple control method, we are more interested in using gaze as a natural means for communications between human and the robot. For example, Yonezawa et al. (2007) used gaze tracking in interactions with a toy robot. The toy robot could move its head towards a target in the environment, which caused the human participants to also (subconsciously) direct their gaze towards the target. "Eye-contact" with the robot, on the other hand, seemed to be interpreted as a positive signal that resulted in favorable feelings toward the robot. Head movements and gaze behaviour have also a crucial role in coordinating turn-taking in human-human conversations. With the help of eye tracking, this information can be exploited in multimodal human-human (Jokinen et al., 2010a, b) or in human-robot interaction (Staudte & Crocker, 2009).

The ability to recognize, not only gaze direc-tion, but also facial expressions and even emotions, may significantly improve human-technology interaction (Surakka & Vanhala, 2011). We cannot measure emotions directly as such, but we can detect external changes that with high confidence reflect certain emotions. Facial expressions are caused by activation of muscles on the face. Those can be either reactions to our internal feelings or they can be voluntarily produced (e.g. social smile). Facial expressions can also be commu-nicative, e.g. a voluntary raise of the eye brow during conversation, or voluntary frowning as a selection method in assistive computer control (Surakka et al., 2004).

It has been suggested (Ekman, 1999) that there are six basic, discrete emotions (anger, discust, fear, joy, sadness, and surprise) with universally recognizable facial expressions. The six basic emo-tions are fairly easy to detect either by a human or

by a computer, as they are constructed by certain characteristic changes, i.e. visible expressions, on the face. Those facial expressions can be coded using the Facial Action Coding System (FACS) developed by Ekman and Friesen (1978). For the purposes of affective computing, it is not necessary to track the full set of facial actions (Partala, 2005; Dimberg, 1990), since the most typical positive or negative emotions can usually be detected by simply measuring zygomaticus major (muscle required for smiling) and corrucator supercilii (muscle required for frowning).

There are various optional technologies that can be used for measuring the facial muscle activations (Pantic & Rothkrantz, 2000; Fasel & Luettin, 2003). One of the most used techniques is facial electromyography (EMG) that can measure muscle activations on the face and thus detect activity in e.g. the above mentioned zygomaticus major and corrucator supercilii. For example, Branco et al. (2005) used EMG to measure facial expressions during a word processing task and found that an increase in task difficulty is related to an increase in specific muscle activity. There are also computer vision and video-based systems that detect facial expressions from video image (Gizatdinova & Surakka, 2010). For example, El Kaliouby and Robinson (2005) demonstrated how complex mental states such as agreeing, concentrating, disagreeing, interested, thinking and unsure, could be inferred from head and facial expressions in real time from a video.

Other possible methods to detect emotions include, for example, electrodermal activity, skin conductance, cardiac measures (for heart rate, see e.g. Anttonen & Surakka, 2005), blood pressure, brain activity, bodily activation and posture. The measures can be related either on the affective valence (positive, negative) or the arousal (calm, excited) or both. For an overview of these mea-sures, see Partala (2005). In spoken dialogue management, emotion recognition and affective interfaces have been a popular topic in order to increase robustness of the interactive system. For instance, Andre et al. (2004) discuss how this is important, while Callejas & Lopez-Cozar (2008) have used different techniques to improve the emotion recognition from the speech signal. A review of the emotion recognition problems and possible solutions can be found in Pittermann et al. (2010).

The Face Interface prototype, developed at Tampere University of Technology in collaboration with University of Tampere, Finland (Rantanen et al., 2010), provides a contactless alternative to the facial electromyography. The Face Interface combines head-mounted, video-based gaze tracking with capacitive facial movement detection. Facial activity (e.g. smiling, frowning, mouth corners down, eyebrows up) is measured with a contact-free capacitive sensors located on top the frames of the glasses. Eye movements are measured using video based methods. The system has two video cameras, one of which is directed towards the eye and the other towards the surroundings of the person. This allows both eye movements and head movements to be tracked in real time. The Face Interface exemplifies an easy-to-wear wireless system for measuring behavioural and emotion-related signals from the head area. It can measure also spontaneous eye movements and facial activations. At University of Tampere, we have used Face Interface for studying voluntary facial activations as a method for regulating more spontaneous physiological changes during virtual social stimulation (Vanhala et al., in press), and we have also developed several alternative technologies that allow wireless signal and information measurement less obtrusively than the traditional electrode technology in the context of human-technology interaction (e.g. Surakka et al., 2004).

FACE AND GAZE AS SOCIAL SIGNALS

Interaction technology is currently going towards the processing of spontaneous speech and multi-

modal recognition techniques, and in doing so it incorporates information about the gestures and body movements. We look at the communication from the holistic point of view, and nonverbal communication is regarded as part of the natural means to exchange information in conversations, indicating especially the engagement of the interlocutors in their communicative behaviour. We also assume that this is an indication of the participants' collaboration with each other (Jokinen, 2009). In this section, we will more closely look at the different research in studying the use non-verbal signals, especially face and gaze, to build mutual rapport and manage the conversation and social interaction.

As argued earlier, language mastering includes multimodal interaction and social communication skills. When learning a foreign language, it is necessary to learn, besides words and syntactic structures, the whole paralinguistic context that includes non-verbal signals such as eye-gaze and facial expressions.

Direct and averted gaze can signal the sender's motivational tendencies to approach or to avoid the object of attention, and this can be reflected in both the direction (approach or avoid) and intensity of the reaction (Hietanen et al., 2008). Similarly, such aspects as looking at the conversational partner or looking away provide indirect cues of the partner's willingness to continue interaction, while gazing at particular elements in the vision field tell us what the partner's focus of attention is, and thus give guidance for appropriate presentation of information as well as suitable analysis and response to the partner's contribution. Eye contact is not only important in human-human communications. The amount of eye contact between an artificial agent and the human significantly affects the human's experience of the agent's friendliness and dominance (Fukayama et al., 2002).

Also turn-taking is usually accompanied by the speaker looking down, whereas acceptance as the next speaker is accompanied by mutual gazing with the previous speaker. When the speakers end their turn, they rapidly gaze the other participants as if looking for feedback or turn-acceptance from them (Kendon, 1967; Argyle & Cook, 1976: Jokinen et al., 2009, 2010).

Facial emotional expressions can change the way the conversation partner interprets non-emotional information (Surakka et al., 1999). Technological systems that exploit biofeedback to detect and react to emotions can seem more natural (Picard, 1997; 1999) and improve performance (Partala & Surakka, 2004). For example, therapeutic applications can be effective in teaching people to overcome their fears (Vanhala & Surakka, 2008) or emotionally adaptive gaming may be able to provide optional emotional experience by customizing certain elements of the game such as difficulty (Saari et al., 2009). Affect-aware tutors can also significantly improve learning results (Woolf et al., 2009). If the affective tutor can recognize emotions such as frustration, it could react accordingly and provide additional help on the subject that seems to be (overly) challenging for the student. According to Woolf et al. (2009), affective interventions encourage learning, lessen student humiliation and provide support and motivation. In our study, we use facial expressions as an additional information channel in the estimation of where the student may hesitate or experience difficulties in understanding the topic under discussion.

As pointed out by Woolf et al. (2009), there have been concerns that one cannot exploit emotion recognition in human-technology interaction until a clear theory of emotion is articulated. However, as Woolf et al. discuss, it has been shown in several studies related to affective computing (e.g., Picard et al., 2004) that, even with limited ability to detect emotions, computers can react more naturally – which results in more positive learning experience. Furthermore, the efforts to improve affective computing have improved our knowledge of the phenomenon itself, and thus it is worth the effort to develop the practice and theory simultaneously.

The use of a combination of head and hand gestures enables speakers to simultaneously be engaged in the conversation and show feedback to the partner. In multiparty dialogue, gaze/head orientation is important for advertising to whom the speaker's utterance is addressed, and is therefore part of a complex system of collaborative and communicative behaviour. Also in two-party dialogue systems, speakers use gestures, head and gaze to create a space within which interaction takes place. Indeed, speech and gesturing are interactionally significant events that allow speakers to better manage the complexities that arise in the dialogue, and especially in multiparty conversations. These events and the recipients' responses contribute to the incremental construction of utterances.

It is also hypothesized that speakers' head and hand movements will be different from those of the listeners, and experiments in Battersby (2011) show that this indeed the case. Moreover, findings indicate that in tutoring type dialogues, the primary recipient is more likely to be looking at the speaker than at the secondary recipient, and the preference of the primary recipient to look at the speaker is stronger than that of the secondary recipient. Hence, in an interactive situation, the partner whom the speaker is addressing is more likely to reciprocate the interest and attention than the partner who is overlooking the interaction. Moreover, it was found that the speakers are more likely to gesture and move their hands than non-speakers, with the interpretation that the movement is an important signal in the interaction, and fit into a feedback cycle showing collaboration between the speaker and the partners. Battersby (2011) further shows that the partners respond faster and more frequently to simultaneous engagement events than to baseline events, i.e. they are faster in their actions when the speaker is in synchrony with them. In other words, in fluent conversational interactions, the participants tend to show cooperation with each other in behaving in a synchronous manner and thus the interaction is faster and seems to proceed in a smooth manner (cf. also Jokinen & Pärkson, (2011) for the synchrony from the point of view of dialogue cooperation).

It is shown that participants follow the partner's gaze and fix their eyes on the participant's head and eyes also when the partner is virtually present or a virtual agent (Gullberg, 2009), thus supporting the view that gaze and head are related to socially important signalling. Walsh (2011) discusses the relationship between language, interaction and learning from the point of view of classroom interactions, and focuses on the use of interaction as a central means to effective teaching. Corbett and Anderson (2001) showed that immediate feedback contributes to learning, while instructional design aims at arranging planned and designed environments so that they most adequately support learning processes.

In addition to gestures, eye contact and facial expressions – which are on focus in this chapter – there are also a number of other parameters that should be taken into account while considering socio-emotional communication between human and agents or robots such as bodily actions and proximity (see e.g. Partala et al., 2004) that are out of the scope of this chapter. Below, we exemplify our idea of exploiting the non-verbal signals in language education by presenting a model for interaction that takes into account all these interaction modalities.

TUTORING SYSTEMS AND MODELS

As an example of a tutoring system, the architecture of the Cognitive Tutor (Koedinger et al., 1997) is presented in Figure 1. This has later been combined with the Help Tutor which supports the student's help-seeking behaviour by tracing their actions relative to a (meta)cognitive model (Aleven et al., 2006). Although our model is based on different technology, it is still useful to compare this with the Cognitive Tutor architecture. We will

focus on the models for multimodal (face, gaze) feedback to indicate understanding, misunderstanding, and non-understanding in conversational interactions. This is combined with a model of joint attention and engagement in language learning situations. Eye-gaze can tell us when the learner concentrates on a difficult task, or is looking for a help from the partner. We will test if and how non-verbal feedback helps the teacher to adjust their verbal presentation.

The various aspects of Cognitive Tutor type tutoring systems are designed to support and enhance learning. One way to do this is especially through interaction, or *instructional interventions*. These interventions concern guidance, strategies or tools, and the tools can be distinguished depending on the type of learning supported. It is common to talk about information tools which provide information to be learned, scaffolding tools which support learning efforts, and cognitive tools which allow interaction with the information (Hannafin, Land & Oliver, 1999). Besides tools, also several instructional principles are available for metacognitive process of tutoring systems. These include representation of student competence and the learning goals and metacognitive skills, promotion of abstract understanding of the problem-solving knowledge, providing immediate feedback on errors, supporting metacognition before, during, and after the problem-solving process, minimizing working memory load, and communicating the goal structure underlying the problem solving and the metacognitive learning goals (see details in Anderson et al., 1995; Aleven et al., 2006).

Our goal is to develop a tool that allows independent practice on drill exercises, and our vision is to assist in learning language by providing fun, intuitive, and interactive learning environment. Our model consists of a dialogue manager engine which is based on simple finite state technology (Jokinen & McTear, 2009) and provides straightforward Question-Answer -type interaction. The interaction can take place in two different modes:

Figure 1. Cognitive tutor architecture (Adapted from Aleven et al 2004)

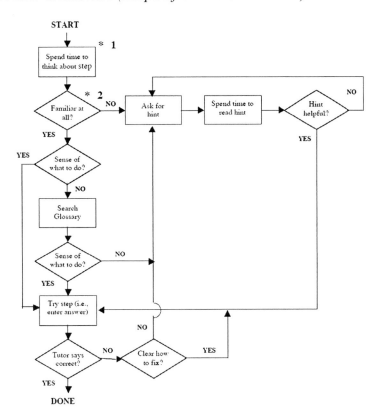

the Teacher mode and the Student mode. The Teacher mode is used when the teacher needs to explain grammar rules or correct pronunciation. It is a teacher initiated mode where the teacher has the right to speak and lead the conversation but at the same time is obliged to pay attention to the student and the student's feedback signals so as to be able to tailor the presentation according to the partner's level of understanding. The input to the Teacher mode are the observations of the student's face and gaze through the eye-tracker and a component that can recognize facial expressions like the Face Interface Technology. It can make competent inferences about the student's state of attention, willingness to interact and the level of understanding. Accordingly, the teacher can ask clarification questions and confirmations (e.g., is this clear?) and provide further information as necessary. The second mode is that of the Learner, and it is student initiated mode where the student,

by evoking a clarification question can lead the conversation and ask for further information from the Teacher.

The mode shift occurs always when the teacher recognizes that the student utterance is a question or a request, while the teaching mode is a default mode and occurs when the teacher starts providing information or explanation. In the first version, the student utterances are selected from a small set of predefined alternatives such as: *ok, I'm fine, I don't understand, this is too difficult* (repeat explanation), *I want to sleep, bye bye*. Later, we hope to extend the set by more complex expressions. Further ideas for the future development of the system are discussed below.

We envisage that the automated tutor will be intelligent agent, e.g. a robot companion that can speak and move to play the role of a conversational partner. For instance, Wilcock & Jokinen (2011) demonstrate how speech can be added to a robot simulator to talk about issues related to web information. In an analogous manner, an intelligent Tutor can talk about the topics the students find interesting, and thus provide a practice companion on conversational chitchats in the foreign language. It is also possible to focus on a certain type of vocabulary, so as to provide drills on a particular set of words or certain grammatical points. Furthermore, we can deal with questions that concern how gaze is used in interaction situations. The participants' eye-gaze can be monitored and used to predict turn taking points and also to model the student's hesitation or puzzlement. For an interactive setup, possible levels are, e.g.

1. The robot tutor is "eye aware", i.e. it knows if it is looked at or not. Although the robot may not understand gaze direction and who is looking at it, this information helps the robot to know if the other members are listening to it, or if it is expected to say something.
2. The robot tutor is fully "gaze aware", i.e. it gets information from gaze trackers that follow the other participants' gaze direction, and thus it knows where the students' visual attention is targeted at.
3. The robot is "both gaze and context aware", i.e. it uses knowledge both from eye tracking as well as e.g. a "scene camera" to get information of objects as well as gestures / body posture etc. of other participants. This enables the robot tutor to have "joint attention" with the student.

FUTURE RESEARCH

Future research is related to the further sophistication of the technology. For instance, some cognitive and emotional signals can also be detected via the eye tracker, by observing the changes in the pupil size. Changes in the pupil size reflect changes in the affective state (Partala & Surakka,

2002) but dilated pupil may also indicate increased cognitive load (Hyönä et al., 1995). Pupil size is also present in natural conversations; people react to the changes in other people's pupils and it affects their feelings of the opposite person even if they are not aware of the changes in the pupil size (Hess & Petrovitch, 1987).

Interaction management can also be more sophisticated. While we have focused on the student's multimodal feedback giving behaviour, it is possible to take other type of *conversational* signals into account as well. The employment of a speech recognizer need not be used only for comparing the student's pronunciation with the native speaker's pronunciation, but also to affect interaction at the conversational level. Here techniques commonly deployed to increase robustness of spoken dialogue systems can be adopted. For instance, knowledge of previous system misunderstandings is an efficient means to help the system to select the correct dialogue management frame, and helps the system to make the correction transparent to the student who may not even be aware of some mistakes made by the speech recognizer (Lopez-Cozar et al., 2010). Interaction with the system can thus proceed more naturally. Moreover, emotion detection can prove to be very useful in dialogue management: the student's frustration or enjoyment is another signal that can be effectively used to guide the interaction by lowering or increasing the difficulty level of the task (see some techniques in recognizing the affective state of the user by including the history of the interaction e.g. in Callejas and Lopez-Cozar 2008).

Other research questions are related to the usability of educational systems and their educational suitability for improved learning outcomes. Instead of just evaluating the use of the system and the user's views and attitudes, we might also want to inquire if the educational interactions can be designed so that they provide optimal learning opportunities and positive learning outcomes.

CONCLUSION

Previous work in educational applications and L2 learning technology has built various models to enable interactive learning, but has not fully taken advantage of novel technology that can bring forward subtle coordination and feedback possibilities with respect to the learner's paralinguistic behaviour. In this article we have explored these possibilities and focussed on the eye-tracking and face-tracking technology to enhance interaction and to assist the automated language teacher in assessing the student's interest level and intake of the learnt substance. We have provided a comprehensive survey of the current state of eye-tracking technology and discussed challenges for its use in educational applications to make the interaction more natural and reliable. We conclude that the models that take into account the learner's facial expressions and eye-gaze are necessary for the system to recognize the student's nonverbal feedback, and to fully understand how the student is progressing in the learning. The student's gaze patterns and facial expressions can correlate with the student's understanding of the presented information (understood/not understood) as well as with the student's experience of their own production in the new language (difficult, easy). The teacher agent can then provide learning opportunities for continuous and self-initiated learning events, and thus encourage the students to express themselves in a foreign language. Besides improving the student's interaction skills, this can also empower the students to make choices concerning interaction and linguistic resources available.

REFERENCES

Aleven, V., McLaren, B., Roll, I., & Koedinger, K. (2004). Toward tutoring help seeking: Applying cognitive modeling to meta-cognitive skills. In J. C. Lester, R. M. Vicario, & F. Paraguaçu (Eds.), *Proceedings of Seventh International Conference on Intelligent Tutoring Systems, ITS 2004* (pp. 227-239). Berlin, Germany: Springer Verlag.

Aleven, V., McLaren, B. M., Roll, I., & Koedinger, K. R. (2006). Toward meta-cognitive tutoring: A model of help seeking with a cognitive tutor. *International Journal of Artificial Intelligence in Education, 16*, 101–128.

Aleven, V., Roll, I., McLaren, B. M., Ryu, E. J., & Koedinger, K. R. (2005). An architecture to combine meta-cognitive and cognitive tutoring: Pilot testing the help tutor. *Proceedings of 12th International Conference on Artificial Intelligence in Education* (pp. 17–24). Amsterdam, The Netherlands: IOS.

Aleven, V., Stahl, E., Schworm, S., Fischer, F., & Wallace, R. M. (2003). Help seeking and help design in interactive learning environments. *Review of Educational Research, 73*(2), 277–320. doi:10.3102/00346543073003277

Allwood, J., Traum, D., & Jokinen, K. (2000). Cooperation, dialogue and ethics. *International Journal of Human-Computer Studies, Special Issue on Collaboration. Cooperation and Conflict in Dialogue Systems, 53*(6), 871–914.

Anderson, J. R., Corbett, A. T., Koedinger, K. R., & Pelletier, R. (1995). Cognitive tutors: Lessons learned. *Journal of the Learning Sciences, 4*(2), 167–207. doi:10.1207/s15327809jls0402_2

André, E., & Pelachaud, C. (2010). Interacting with embodied conversational agents. In Jokinen, K., & Cheng, F. (Eds.), *New trends in speech-based interactive systems*. Springer Publishers.

Andre, E., Rehm, M. L., Minker, W., & Bifihler, D. (2004). *Endowing spoken language dialogue systems with emotional intelligence* (pp. 178–187). Irsee, Germany: Tutorial and Research Workshop Affective Dialogue Systems. doi:10.1007/978-3-540-24842-2_17

Anttonen, J., & Surakka, V. (2005). Emotions and heart rate while sitting on a chair. *Proceedings of CHI 2005* (pp. 491-499). ACM Press.

Arbib, M. (2003). The evolving mirror system: A neural basis for language readiness. In Christiansen, M., & Kirby, S. (Eds.), *Language evolution* (pp. 182–200). Oxford, UK: Oxford University Press. doi:10.1093/acprof:o so/9780199244843.003.0010

Argyle, M., & Cook, M. (1976). *Gaze and mutual gaze*. Cambridge, UK Cambridge: University Press.

Atienza, R., & Zelinsky, A. (2002). Active gaze tracking for human-robot interaction. *Proceedings of 4th IEEE International Conference on Multimodal Interfaces* (pp. 261-266).

Branco, P., Firth, P., Encarnao, L. M., & Bonato, P. (2005). Faces of emotion in human-computer interaction. *Proceedings of CHI 2005* (1236-1239). New York, NY: ACM.

Callejas, Z., & López-Cózar, R. (2008). Influence of contextual information in emotion annotation for spoken dialogue systems. *Speech Communication*, *50*(5), 416–433. doi:10.1016/j. specom.2008.01.001

Campbell, N. (2007). On the use of nonverbal speech sounds in human communication. In Campbell, N. (Ed.), *Verbal and Nonverbal Communication Behaviors* (*Vol. 4775*, pp. 117–128). LNAI. doi:10.1007/978-3-540-76442-7_11

Clark, H., & Wilkes-Gibbs, D. (1986). Referring as a collaborative process. *Cognition*, *22*, 1–39. doi:10.1016/0010-0277(86)90010-7

Decker, D., & Piepmeier, J. A. (2008). Gaze tracking interface for robotic control. *40th Southeastern Symposium on System Theory* (pp. 274-278).

Dimberg, U. (1990). Facial electromyography and emotional reactions. *Psychophysiology*, *19*, 643–647. doi:10.1111/j.1469-8986.1982. tb02516.x

Donegan, M., Morris, J. D., Corno, F., Signorile, I., Chio, A., & Pasian, V. (2009). Understanding users and their needs. *Universal Access in the Information Society*, *8*(4), 259–275. doi:10.1007/ s10209-009-0148-1

Douglas, C. E., Campbell, N., Cowie, R., & Roach, P. (2003). Emotional speech: Towards a new generation of databases. *Speech Communication*, *40*, 33–60. doi:10.1016/S0167-6393(02)00070-5

Driscoll, M. (2000). *Psychology of learning for instruction*. Boston, MA: Allyn & Bacon.

Duchowski, A. (2007). *Eye tracking methodology: Theory and practice*. Springer.

Ekman, P. (1999). Basic emotions. In Dalgleish, T., & Power, T. (Eds.), *The handbook of cognition and emotion* (pp. 45–60). Sussex, UK: John Wiley & Sons.

Ekman, P., & Friesen, W. V. (1978). *Facial action coding system (FACS): A technique for the measurement of facial action*. Palo Alto, CA: Consulting Psychologists Press.

El Kaliouby, R., & Robinson, P. (2005). Generalization of a vision-based computational model of mind-reading. *First International Conference on Affective Computing and Intelligent Interaction*. Beijing, China.

Fasel, B., & Luettin, J. (2003). Automatic facial expression analysis: A survey. *Pattern Recognition*, *36*, 259–275. doi:10.1016/S0031-3203(02)00052-3

Feldman, R. S., & Rim, B. (1991). *Fundamentals of nonverbal behavior*. Cambridge University Press.

Fryer, L., & Carpenter, R. (2006). Emerging technologies: Bots as language learning tools. *Language Learning & Technology*, *10*(3), 8–14.

Gizatdinova, Y., & Surakka, V. (2010). Automatic edge-based localization of facial features from images with complex facial expressions. *Pattern Recognition Letters, 31*(15), 2436–2446. doi:10.1016/j.patrec.2010.07.020

Graesser, A. C., Chipman, P., Haynes, B. C., & Olney, A. (2005). AutoTutor: An intelligent tutoring system with mixed-initiative dialogue. *IEEE Transactions on Education, 48*(4), 612–618. doi:10.1109/TE.2005.856149

Griol, D., Gracia-Herrero, J., & Molina, J. M. (2011). TheEducAgent platform: Intelligent conversational agents for e-learning applications. In Novais, P., Preuveneers, D., & Corchado, J. M. (Eds.), *Ambient intelligence – Software and applications. Advances in Intelligent and Soft Computing Series (Vol. 92,* pp. 117–124). Springer.

Hall, J. K. (1999). A prosaics of interaction. The development of interactional competence in another language. In Hinkel, E. (Ed.), *Culture in second language teaching and learning. Cambridge applied linguistics series* (pp. 137–151). Cambridge, UK: Cambridge University Press.

Hansen, D. W., & Majaranta, P. (2012). Basics of camera-based gaze tracking. In Majaranta, P. (Eds.), *Gaze interaction and applications of eye tracking: Advances in assistive technologies* (pp. 21–26). Hershey, PA: IGI Global.

Harnard, S. (1990). The symbol grounding problem. *Physica D. Nonlinear Phenomena, 42,* 335–346. doi:10.1016/0167-2789(90)90087-6

Hazlett, R. (2003). Measurement of user frustration: A biologic approach. *Extended Abstracts CHI 2003* (pp. 734-735). New York, NY: ACM.

Heldner, M., Edlund, J., & Hirschberg, J. (2010). Pitch similarity in the vicinity of backchannels. *Proceedings of Interspeech, 2010,* 3054–3057.

Hew, K. F., & Brush, T. (2007). Integrating technology into K-12 teaching and learning: Current knowledge gaps and recommendations for future research. *Educational Technology Research and Development, 55*(3), 223–252. doi:10.1007/s11423-006-9022-5

Hietanen, J. K., Leppänen, J. M., Peltola, M. J., Linna-aho, K., & Ruuhiala, H. J. (2008). Seeing direct and averted gaze activates the approach–avoidance motivational brain systems. *Neuropsychologia, 46*(9), 2423–2430. doi:10.1016/j.neuropsychologia.2008.02.029

Hyönä, J., Tommola, J., & Alaja, A.-M. (1995). Pupil dilation as a measure of processing load in simultaneous interpretation and other language tasks. *The Quarterly Journal of Experimental Psychology, 48A,* 598–612.

Hyrskykari, A., Majaranta, P., Aaltonen, A., & Räihä, K.-J. (2000). Design issues of iDict: A gaze-assisted translation aid. *Proceedings of Eye Tracking Research and Applications, Symposium (ETRA 2000)* (pp. 9-14). New York, NY: ACM.

Hyrskykari, A., Majaranta, P., & Räihä, K.-J. (2005). From gaze control to attentive interfaces. *Proceedings of HCII 2005,* Las Vegas, NV.

Isokoski, P., Joos, M., Martin, B., & Spakov, O. (2009). Gaze controlled games. *Universal Access in the Information Society, 8*(4), 323–337. doi:10.1007/s10209-009-0146-3

Jokinen, K. (2009). *Constructive dialogue management – Speech interaction and rational agents.* John Wiley & Sons.

Jokinen, K., Harada, K., Nishida, M., & Yamamoto, S. (2010a). Turn alignment using eye-gaze and speech in spoken interaction. *Proceedings of Interspeech 2010,* Makuhari Messe, Japan.

Jokinen, K., Nishida, M., & Yamamoto, S. (2010b). On eye-gaze and turn-taking. *Proceedings of the Workshop on Eye Gaze in Intelligent Human Machine Interaction* (EGIHMI '10) (pp. 118-123). New York, NY: ACM.

Jokinen, K., Nishida, M., & Yamamoto, S. (2010c). Collecting and annotating conversational eye-gaze data. *Proceedings of Multimodal Corpora: Advances in Capturing, Coding and Analyzing Multimodality* (MMC 2010), LREC-2010. Valetta, Malta.

Jokinen, K., & Pärkson, S. (2011). Synchrony and copying in conversational interactions. *Proceedings of the 3rd Nordic Symposium on Multimodal Communication* (pp. 18-24). NEALT Proceedings Series 15.

Jonassen, D. H. (2000). Transforming learning with technology: Beyond modernism and postmodernism or whoever controls the technology creates the reality. *Educational Technology, 40*(2), 21–25.

Kendon, A. (1967). Some functions of gaze direction in social interaction. *Acta Psychologica, 26*, 22–63. doi:10.1016/0001-6918(67)90005-4

Kendon, A. (2005). *Gesture: Visible action as utterance*. Cambridge University Press.

Khiat, A., Matsumoto, Y., & Ogasawara, T. (2004b). Task specific eye movements understanding for a gaze-sensitive dictionary. *Proceedings of the 9th International Conference on Intelligent User Interface* (IUI 04) (pp. 265-267). New York, NY: ACM.

Land, M. F., & Furneaux, S. (1997). The knowledge base of the oculomotor system. *Philosophical Transactions of the Royal Society of London. Series B, Biological Sciences, 352*(1358), 1231–1239. doi:10.1098/rstb.1997.0105

López-Cózar, R., Callejas, Z., & Griol, D. (2010). Using knowledge of misunderstandings to increase the robustness of spoken dialogue systems. *Knowledge-Based Systems, 23*(5), 471–485. doi:10.1016/j.knosys.2010.03.004

Majaranta, P., Bates, R., & Donegan, M. (2009). Eye-tracking. In Stephanidis, C. (Ed.), *The universal access handbook* (pp. 587–606). Lawrence Erlbaum Associates, Inc. doi:10.1201/9781420064995-c36

Majaranta, P., & Räihä, K.-J. (2007). Text entry by gaze: Utilizing eye-tracking. In MacKenzie, I. S., & Tanaka-Ishii, K. (Eds.), *Text entry systems: Mobility, accessibility, universality* (pp. 175–187). Morgan Kaufmann.

Mancini, M., Castellano, G., Bevacqua, E., & Peters, C. (2007). Lecture Notes in Computer Science: *Vol. 4418. Copying behaviour of expressive motion* (pp. 180–191). Berlin, Germany: Springer.

Millar, S. (2010). Using eye gaze in school. In Wilson, A., & Gow, R. (Eds.), *The eyes have it! The use of eye gaze to support communication* (pp. 28–34). Edinburgh, UK: CALL Scotland, The University of Edinburgh.

Nakano, Y., & Nishida, T. (2007). Attentional behaviours as nonverbal communicative signals in situated interactions with conversational agents. In Nishida, T. (Ed.), *Engineering approaches to conversational informatics* (pp. 85–102). John Wiley & Sons, Ltd. doi:10.1002/9780470512470.ch5

Pantic, M., & Rothkrantz, L. J. (2000). Automatic analysis of facial expressions: The state of the art. [PAMI]. *IEEE Transactions on Pattern Analysis and Machine Intelligence, 22*, 1424–1445. doi:10.1109/34.895976

Partala, T., & Surakka, V. (2002). Pupil size variation as an indication of affective processing. *International Journal of Human-Computer Studies, 59*, 185–198. doi:10.1016/S1071-5819(03)00017-X

Partala, T., & Surakka, V. (2004). The effects of affective interventions in human–computer interaction. *Interacting with Computers, 16*, 295–309. doi:10.1016/j.intcom.2003.12.001

Partala, T., Surakka, V., & Lahti, J. (2004). Affective effects of agent proximity in conversational systems. *Proceedings of NordiCHI, 2004*, 353–356. New York, NY: ACM. doi:10.1145/1028014.1028070

Picard, R. (1997). *Affective computing.* MIT Press.

Picard, R. (1999). Affective computing for HCI. In H.-J. Bullinger & J. Ziegler (Eds.), *Proceedings of HCI International (the 8th International Conference on Human-Computer Interaction) on Human-Computer Interaction: Ergonomics and User Interfaces,* Vol. I. (pp. 829-833). Hillsdale, NJ: L. Erlbaum Associates Inc.

Pickering, M., & Garrod, S. (2004). Towards a mechanistic psychology of dialogue. *The Behavioral and Brain Sciences, 27*, 169–226. doi:10.1017/S0140525X04000056

Pittermann, J., Pittermann, A., & Minker, W. (2010). *Handling emotions in human-computer dialogues.* Springer. doi:10.1007/978-90-481-3129-7

Prendinger, H., Ma, C., Yingzi, J., Nakasone, A., & Ishizuka, M. (2005). Understanding the effect of life-like interface agents through users' eye movements. *Proceedings of the 7th International Conference on Multimodal Interfaces* (ICMI '05) (pp. 108-115). New York, NY: ACM.

Qvarfordt, P., Beymer, D., & Zhai, S. (2005). RealTourist – A study of augmenting human-human and human-computer dialogue with eye-gaze overlay. *INTERACT 2005, LNCS 3585/2005,* (pp. 767-780).

Randel, J. M., Morris, B. A., Wetzel, C. D., & Whitehill, B. V. (1992). The effectiveness of games for educational purposes: A review of recent research. *Simulation & Gaming, 23*(3), 261–276. doi:10.1177/1046878192233001

Rantanen, V., Niemenlehto, P.-H., Verho, J., & Lekkala, J. (2010). Capacitive facial movement detection for human-computer interaction to click by frowning and lifting eyebrows. *Medical & Biological Engineering & Computing, 48*(1), 39–47. doi:10.1007/s11517-009-0565-6

Rehm, M., Nakano, Y., Andre, E., & Nishida, T. (2009). From observation to simulation: Generating culture-specific behavior for interactive systems. *AI & Society, 24*(3), 267–280. doi:10.1007/s00146-009-0216-3

Reiser, R. (2001a). A history of instructional design and technology: Part I: A history of instructional media. *Educational Technology Research and Development, 49*(1), 53–64. doi:10.1007/BF02504506

Reiser, R. (2001b). A history of instructional design and technology: Part II: A history of instructional design. *Educational Technology Research and Development, 49*(2), 57–67. doi:10.1007/BF02504928

Resta, P., & Laferrière, T. (2007). Technology in support of collaborative learning. *Educational Psychology Review, 19*(1), 65–83. doi:10.1007/s10648-007-9042-7

Saari, T., Turpeinen, M., Kuikkaniemi, K., Kosunen, I., & Ravaja, N. (2009). Emotionally adapted games – An example of a first person shooter. In Jacko, J. A. (Ed.), *Human-Computer Interaction, Part IV, HCII 2009, LNCS 5613* (pp. 406–415). Berlin, Germany: Springer-Verlag. doi:10.1007/978-3-642-02583-9_45

Sibert, J. L., Gokturk, M., & Lavine, R. A. (2000). The reading assistant: Eye gaze triggered auditory prompting for reading remediation. *Proceedings of the Symposium on User Interface Software and Technology (UIST '00)* (pp. 101-107). New York, NY: ACM.

Staudte, M., & Crocker, M. W. (2009). Visual attention in spoken human-robot interaction. *Proceedings of the 4th ACM/ IEEE International Conference on Human Robot Interaction (HRI '09)* (pp. 77-84). New York, NY: ACM.

Surakka, V., Illi, M., & Isokoski, P. (2004). Gazing and frowning as a new human-computer interaction technique. *ACM Transactions on Applied Perception*, *1*(1), 40–56. doi:10.1145/1008722.1008726

Surakka, V., Sams, M., & Hietanen, J. K. (1999). Modulation of neutral face evaluation by laterally presented emotional expressions. *Perceptual and Motor Skills*, *88*, 595–606. doi:10.2466/pms.1999.88.2.595

Surakka, V., & Vanhala, T. (2011). Emotions in human-computer interaction. In Kappas, A., & Krämer, N. (Eds.), *Face-to-face communication over the Internet: Emotions in a Web of culture, language, and technology* (pp. 213–236). Cambridge University Press. doi:10.1017/CBO9780511977589.011

Swerts, M., & Krahmer, E. (2005). Audiovisual prosody and feeling of knowing. *Journal of Memory and Language*, *53*, 81–94. doi:10.1016/j.jml.2005.02.003

Takagi, H. (1998). Development of an eye-movement enhanced translation support system. *Proceedings of the Third Asian Pacific Computer and Human Interaction* (pp. 114-119). IEEE Computer Society.

Vanhala, T., & Surakka, V. (2008). Computer-assisted regulation of emotional and social processes. In Or, J. (Ed.), *Affective computing: Focus on emotion expression, synthesis, and recognition* (pp. 405–420). Vienna, Austria: I-Tech Education and Publishing. doi:10.5772/6168

Vanhala, T., Surakka, V., Courgeon, M., Martin, J.-C., & Jacquemin, C. (in press). Voluntary facial activations regulate physiological arousal and subjective experiences during virtual social stimulation. [in press]. *ACM Transactions on Applied Perception*.

Walsh, S. (2011). *Exploring classroom discourse. Language in Action Routledge Introductions to Applied Linguistics*. Routledge.

Wang, H., Chignell, M., & Ishizuka, M. (2006). Empathic tutoring software agents using real-time eye tracking. *Proceedings of the 2006 Symposium on Eye Tracking Research & Applications* (ETRA '06) (pp. 73-78). New York, NY: ACM.

Wilcock, G., & Jokinen, K. (2011). Emergent verbal behaviour in human-robot interaction. In L.-C. Delgado, et al. (Eds.), *Proceedings of the Third International Conference on Spoken Dialogue Systems: Ambient Intelligence (IWSDS)*, (pp. 375–380). Granada, Spain, September 2011.

Witkowski, M., Arafa, Y., & deBruijn, O. (2001). Evaluating user reaction to character agent mediated displays using eye-tracking equipment. *Proceedings of the Symposium on Information Agents for Electronic Commerce* (AISB'01) (pp. 79-87).

Woolf, B., Burleson, W., Arroyo, I., Dragon, T., Cooper, D., & Picard, R. (2009). Affect-aware tutors: recognising and responding to student affect. *International Journal of Learning Technology*, *4*(3/4), 129–164. doi:10.1504/IJLT.2009.028804

Yamazaki, H., Kitamura, K., Harada, K., & Yamamoto, S. (2008). *Creation of learner corpus and its application to speech recognition.* International Conference on Language Resources and Evaluation, LREC2008, Marrakech, Morocco.

Yonezawa, T., Yamazoe, H., Utsumi, A., & Abe, S. (2007). Gaze-communicative behavior of stuffed-toy robot with joint attention and eye contact based on ambient gaze-tracking. *Proceedings of the 9th International Conference on Multimodal Interfaces* (ICMI '07) (pp. 140-145). New York, NY: ACM.

ADDITIONAL READING

Hadelich, K., & Crocker, M. W. (2006). Gaze alignment of interlocutors in conversational dialogues. *Proceedings of the 2006 Symposium on Eye-Tracking Research & Applications* (ETRA '10) (Austin, Texas, March 22-24, 2010) (pp. 38-38). New York, NY: ACM. doi: 10.1145/1117309.1117322

Hayhoe, M., & Ballard, D. (2005). Eye movements in natural behavior. *Trends in Cognitive Sciences*, *9*, 188–194. doi:10.1016/j.tics.2005.02.009

Jacob, R. J. K. (1993). What you look at is what you get. *Computer*, *26*(7), 65–66. doi:10.1109/MC.1993.274943

Kirriemuir, J., & McFarlane, A. (2004). *Literature review in games and learning.* Report 8. Bristol. Nesta Futurelab. Retrieved from http://telearn.archives-ouvertes.fr/hal-00190453/

Kuriyama, N., Terai, A., Yasuhara, M., Tokunaga, T., Yamagishi, K., & Kusumi, T. (2011) Gaze matching of referring expressions in collaborative problem solving. *Proceedings of International Workshop on Dual Eye Tracking, in CSCW* (DUET 2011) (Aarhus, Demark, September 25, 2011).

Maglio, P. P., & Campbell, C. S. (2003). Attentive agents. *Communications of the ACM*, *46*(3), 47–51. doi:10.1145/636772.636797

Porta, M. (2008). Implementing eye-based user-aware e-learning. *Extended Abstracts on Human Factors in Computing Systems* (CHI '08) (pp. 3087-3092). New York, NY: ACM. doi:10.1145/1358628.1358812

Qvarfordt, P., & Zhai, S. (2005). Conversing with the user based on eye-gaze patterns. *Proceedings of the SIGCHI Conference on Human Factors in Computing Systems* (CHI'05) (pp. 221-230). New York, NY: ACM. doi:10.1145/1054972.1055004

Richardson, D., & Dale, R. (2005). Looking to understand: The coupling between speakers' and listeners' eye movements and its relationship to discourse comprehension. *Cognitive Science*, *29*(6), 1045–1060. doi:10.1207/s15516709cog0000_29

Roy, D., Ghitza, Y., Bartelma, J., & Kehoe, C. (2004). Visual memory augmentation: Using eye gaze as an attention filter. *Proceedings of the Eighth International Symposium on Wearable Computers* (31 October - 3 November 2004) (pp. 128-131). Washington, DC: IEEE Computer Society. doi:10.1109/ISWC.2004.47

KEY TERMS AND DEFINITIONS

Conversational Feedback: Refers to a verbal or non-verbal act whereby the interlocutor provides evaluative and regulating information to the speaker. Feedback can concern the partner's willingness to continue interaction, their agreeing with the presented information, or their level of understanding in a given situation. Verbal feedback consists of particular feedback words or short vocalisations (often referred to as *backchannelling*), while non-verbal feedback can be expressed by hand gestures, nodding, facial expressions, and body posture.

Conversational Interface: Is a type of interactive interface which uses dialogue technology to engage the user in a conversation with the system. Compared with simple dialogue systems, it aims at allowing the user to talk freely on any topic, take initiative to clarify topics, and follow natural communication patterns in dialogue management. The interface is usually speech-based, although written language can also be used. Nowadays it is common to integrate various multimodal technologies which allow rich communication possibilities.

Educational Technology: Refers to technological applications and tools that primarily aim at assisting in teaching and facilitating learning. It uses general computational techniques, methods, and models, and applies them to learning theories in order to design software and build automatic systems. Nowadays many online learning opportunities and collaborative learning applications are increasing.

Eye Tracking: Is a technique used to record and measure eye movements. Eye tracking is often used as a synonym with *gaze tracking* where the viewer's gaze direction or "point of regard" is analyzed based on the gaze vector. By mapping the gaze coordinates to objects in the environment, we can estimate what the user is looking at e.g. on the computer screen.

Face Tracking: Refers to the technique used to detect a human face and to measure changes in the face. Face recognition is exploited especially in security related applications. Face tracking is also used to detect facial features and changes in the expression, enabling emotion recognition for affective computing.

Multimodal Interaction: Provides the user with multiple modes of interfacing with the system. Both the input and the output method may include several combined modes, such as speech, gaze, head or body movements, tactile feedback etc.

Natural Communication: Refers to communication that is typical of humans when communicating with each other. In a narrow sense it refers to the use of natural language, while in a wider sense, it also includes paralinguistic aspects, social signaling, and cultural context.

Second Language Learning: Refers to the process through which people learn a second language. It includes knowledge and skills in language and culture. It is often interchangeably used with *foreign language learning*. Although difference can be drawn in the situation in which the learning takes place: the former concerns learning a language in the context of the language to be learnt, while the latter refers to language learning in one's native environment. As an academic study, it is often called *Second Language Acquisition*.

Chapter 4
Embodied Conversational Agents in Interactive Applications for Children with Special Educational Needs

Beatriz López Mencía
Universidad Politécnica de Madrid, Spain

Alvaro Hernández Trapote
Universidad Politécnica de Madrid, Spain

David Díaz Pardo
Universidad Politécnica de Madrid, Spain

Luis A. Hernández Gómez
Universidad Politécnica de Madrid, Spain

ABSTRACT

This chapter describes a collection of experiences and recommendations related with the design and evaluation of interactive applications integrating Embodied Conversational Agents (ECA) technology in real environments of use with children in Special Education. Benefits and challenges of using ECAs in this context are presented. These benefits and challenges have guided the creation of Special Education reinforcement applications incorporating ECAs, which have been used for extended periods of time at Infanta Elena Special Education School in Madrid. Co-design principles were applied in the development of two of the applications discussed here, with the participation of the school's teaching staff and children with severe motor and mental disabilities (mainly with cerebral palsy). From the design experience a set of recommendations and observations were extracted, which the authors hope may serve as guidance for the scientific and educational communities when undertaking further research. For example, in an application to reinforce the learning of emotions it believe it beneficial to include ECAs that display a number of exaggerated facial expressions together with a combination of auditory and gestural reinforcements. The ECA should show its eyes and mouth clearly, in order to help the children focus their attention. These and other ECA strategies have been analysed to provide reinforcement in learning and also to attract the children's attention when interacting with the application.

DOI: 10.4018/978-1-4666-2530-3.ch004

Copyright © 2013, IGI Global. Copying or distributing in print or electronic forms without written permission of IGI Global is prohibited.

INTRODUCTION

Special Education addresses the specific needs of children with disabilities so that they may achieve the maximum possible degree of personal development. Computer-based interactive multimedia technologies can be used to reinforce learning in children with special educational needs (Vazquez & Rota, 2002) and to improve their social integration (Kiung et al., 2008), their affective communication skills and their ability to express emotions (Baron-Cohen et al., 2009), (Picard, 2009).

One interaction tool that is particularly promising is the Embodied Conversational Agent, or ECA. An ECA is an animated human-like avatar capable, to some degree, of engaging in conversation with real human users. This involves the ability to understand and generate speech, hand movements and facial expressions (Cassell, 2000). It is possible to give ECAs expressiveness and social capabilities that make them helpful in educational contexts (see, e.g., (Wik & Hjalmarsson, 2009)).

Noteworthy educational benefits of ECAs have been identified in the literature. For instance, a virtual agent can be designed to play different roles *vis-à-vis* the user. This is useful for mimicking peer tutoring, with an ECA in the role of peer, which takes advantage of on the observation that children pay more attention when another child explains something to them than when the teacher does so (Bolich, 2001). It has also been shown that the rapport between children and ECAs contributes to improving communication efficiency, increasing motivation and interest and obtaining improved learning results compared to systems featuring only text or voice outputs (Atkinson, 2002), (Gratch et al. 2007). ECAs can be designed to perform a great variety of gestures and facial expressions with different levels of intensity. Expressions can be exaggerated, and the evidence suggests that this can be used to improve learning by imitation. For example, Massaro (Massaro et al., 2000) gave the ECA Baldi lip, tongue and tooth movements to help deaf children learn to speak.

These are but a few examples to illustrate the fact that the analysis of the potential of ECAs in educational contexts, to support specific aspects of learning, is emerging as an important field of research embracing the scientific and educational communities. The relative novelty of this line of research requires that the very place and the possibilities of ECAs need to be explored. Moreover, incorporating this technology in interactive systems entails general interaction design challenges, and specific ones concerning evaluation in real user contexts, to which special considerations must be added for the particular context of learning reinforcement for children with special educational needs (Sánchez and García, 2003). Typical usability tests cannot be applied directly since metrics for effectiveness, efficiency and satisfaction cannot easily be obtained from the children. Furthermore, there are large differences in ability between children.

We propose to approach the specific complications in designing interactive special education support applications incorporating ECAs, through the adoption of design methods that allow, and take into account, collaboration between the child and the educator, as well as the research team itself. With this collaborative approach we have sought to explore the capabilities of ECAs in the classroom, in especially designed educational applications that are easy to use and that may be adapted dynamically to the needs of the children and the educators. In this chapter we illustrate the process through the description of our design experiences with two software applications for Special Education support featuring ECA technology. We took inspiration from the co-design methodology proposed by Sanders (Sanders and Stappers, 2008), which provided researchers and engineers, as well as children and teachers – for whom the applications were designed –, the opportunity to bring their creativity together.

We describe the research we have been undertaking with the Public School for Special Education (CPEE) Infanta Elena in Madrid. This collaboration has involved a multidisciplinary team: researchers and students from ETSIT-UPM, and teachers, therapists and children with severe mental and physical disabilities from the School, particularly children with Cerebral Palsy. We have been working together using collaborative design and long iteration cycles, in a real environment of use, to develop educational tools with ECA technology for disabled children in the School (two will be described in this chapter). The result is enriching for all parties. On the development side, the approach provides insights regarding the usefulness and the potential of ECA technology in applications for Special Education, both in purely technological terms, and also from the point of view of the experience of use, from the observation of the children's daily interaction with the technology. On the educational side, Special Education teachers are able to use helpful technology easily in their classrooms.

The chapter is structured as follows. First we provide an introduction to Embodied Conversational Agent technology, focusing on the possibilities that it may offer in the scope of Special Education, and on the main challenges for the integration of ECAs in real applications. Then we describe the central application design experiences carried out in collaboration with the CPEE Infanta Elena in Madrid. To illustrate these experiences we present a new support tool called "Emo," designed to reinforce the learning of emotions and facial expressions in children between 4 and 7 years of age with Cerebral Palsy; and then "Animaddin," a tool that helps teachers to create interactive stories with ECAs using a digital blackboard. Finally, we discuss the main conclusions that may be extracted from these design experiences, and point to important avenues to further develop this field.

BACKGROUND: ECAs IN SPECIAL EDUCATION

ECAs are very versatile interactive objects for the education environment, by virtue of a variety of communicational possibilities they possess, including a potentially wide palette of gestural (and verbal) expressiveness and social skills (e.g., (Wik and Hjalmarsson, 2009)). As with all objects of promise, potential benefits are accompanied by difficulties. In this section we review the benefits and challenges identified in the literature with regard to the use of ECAs in the education environment.

Benefits

Different Roles

One is free to create an animated agent with the appearance one wishes. One can create a child or adult, a male or a female, etc. Likewise, ECAs can be created to have specific personalities and social roles. These can be exploited or educational purposes. This is the idea behind the Pedagogical Conversational Agents proposed by Marín, which take the role either of a teacher of a student (Marín, 2010). This sort of ECAs is usually associated with task-oriented scenarios (Johnson et al., 2000).

Different educational benefits can be obtained depending on the role of the avatar in the application (Marín, 2010). For instance, the "Protégé effect" can be exploited, which is the observation that children are more engaged in the learning activity when they have to explain it to a peer, to a companion in the learning process. The ECA can be designed to play such a role. Another effect that has been observed is called the Proteo effect, which is that children see the avatar as a model to follow, thus increasing their motivation. The Persona effect (Lester et al., 1997) is also worth mentioning. It is the observation that the sole presence of the ECA in an interactive application can have a positive effect on how the student perceives the learning experience.

We now present a couple of examples of research experiences in which ECAs are designed to play different roles to produce beneficial effects.

ECA as a Teacher

Virtual teachers have been developed with complex pedagogical functions, like language acquisition (or autistic or hearing impaired children). Encouraging results have been obtained, both with regard to the effectiveness of the learning and the popularity among the children (Massaro, 2006).

ECA as a Student/Classmate

Learning with a peer, a technique that is being increasingly employed, is based on observations that children pay more attention when another child is explaining something to them, rather than the teacher. This is known as "peer tutoring" (Bolich, 2001). Various strategies can be used with this technique. For instance, the ECA can be made to be on the same level as the real pupil, and then they can both do exercises or solve the problem at hand either in collaboration or in competition. Rasseneur provides an example with the AMICO system which allows flexibility in the use of these strategies in the context of a mathematics application (Rasseneur et al, 2002). A noteworthy piece of work was carried out by Tartaro and Cassel, who designed a virtual companion that proved more engaging for autistic children than did real companions (Tartaro & Cassell, 2008).

Confidence

Motivation and confidence are two very important factors to improve the social skills of children and reduce their stress when interacting with other people. It has been shown that using ECAs in learning tools can help increase the children's motivation and interest, improving over results obtained with systems with only text or speech outputs ((Atkinson, 2002)(Gratch et al.,2007) (Moreno et al., 2001)). New challenges and the fun factor have also been shown to elevate children's level of commitment to pursue learning objectives (Corradini et al., 2005).

Verbal and Non-Verbal Communication

The capabilities of ECAs to display different types of movement, gestures and facial expressions make them very well suited to reinforce the learning of these non-verbal communication skills. For instance, an ECA can be made to display expressions in a wide range of intensities, from the very subtle and muted to the wildly exaggerated. When gestures are made very clearly the child can see more easily the gesture he is trying to learn by imitation. He can even see anatomical areas that it would be hard to notice otherwise.

The educational benefits of the expressive potential of ECAs have been explored in many of research approaches in the field. Eskenazi has given an overview of research efforts that have introduced speech technologies in educational applications, and observed that many of them use also visual information to improve learning. Worth mentioning here is the work carried out by Ron Cole's group at the Centre for Spoken Language Research (University of Colorado Boulder), relying on a wide variety of tools with which they have developed applications for deaf children and children with language impairments. In Engwall's study on pronunciation and articulation learning in Swedish, children obtain better results with an ECA tutor than with a real teacher (Engwall, 2008). Massaro uses details in the lip, tongue and teeth movements (which would not normally be picked up in interactions with a human) of ECA "Baldi" to help children to learn to speak (Massaro et al., 2000). Other work, especially that focused on the generation and teaching of sign language, has used not only but also Movements of the body have also been exploited, in addition to facial and articulatory movement, especially in work oriented toward the generation and teaching of sign language (an example for Spanish sign language can be found in (San-Segundo et al., 2010)). Yet another possibility with the expressive range of ECAs is to work with the emotional dimension of communication. In (Mohamad et al., 2005) emotions are incorporated to ECA outputs as a learning motivation support for children with disabilities.

Challenges

Notwithstanding the above benefits of ECAs in special education, there are still major aspects to improve concerning the design and evaluation of special education applications with ECAs in real context of use (Sanchez and García, 2003). We now describe some of the main challenges to the development and adoption of applications for children with special educational needs.

Social Factors

The first obstacle for the introduction of ECA technology in special education is that it is not mature enough. The technology is not widely known. It might be met with indifference or even rejection on the part of teaching staff in charge of integrating the educational applications in the programme of activities for the children. In fact, we got some such reactions when proposing applications with ECAs to some teachers in some schools we approached, although we cannot be sure of the reasons, whether the use of ECAs itself, the nature of the applications or simply habit and unwillingness to introduce new elements in their education programmes. In any case, it is important to develop the technology with stability, flexibility and ease of use and integration (into applications) in mind.

The abundance of computer-based resources can also be a problem. Gone are the times when computer use was not very intensive and specialized options for users were limited. Now there is a wealth of computer-based tools and educators

may feel saturated when considering the amount of options open to them. Hence, there is a need to underline the potential benefits of using ECAs and to make them more widely known. However, it is important to introduce the technology appropriately, in such a way as not to generate false expectations or narrow views of the possibilities through undue generalisations from particular implementations (every particular instance of use of the technology necessarily has limitations).

Finally, Sanchez and García (2003) point out that it is also important to consider other kinds of interaction difficulties: those that people with intellectual disabilities may have with technology. Cognitive overload (from having to handle too much information and having too many options to choose from) and loss of attention (due to waiting times or the presence of sources of distraction) are factors that have to be taken into account with care, in any case, but especially for the intellectually challenged.

Designing Applications with ECAs

When designing applications for people with disabilities methodologies and guidelines that are adapted to the respective target groups should be followed to guarantee accessible and standardized designs. Introducing animated agents that give new capabilities to applications can make existing guidelines and methodologies obsolete, or at least missing new relevant aspects of the interaction that should be considered.

There are guidelines for Web environments (e.g., WAI (http://www.w3.org/WAI/), User Agent Accessibility Guidelines (http://www.w3.org/TR/UAAG10/) and the SIDAR foundation (http://www.sidar.org/)), as well as user-centred design guidelines (ISO, 1999) that propose involving end-users actively in the design process, making sure they clearly understand the tasks they are required to perform, in order to ensure the best possible fit between the technology and the users. We have taken a user-centred approach inspired in the work of Sanders, from which we have taken the idea of co-design *"to refer to the creativity of designers and people not trained in design working together in the design development process"* (Sanders and Stappers,2008). Today there is a trend among researchers to lean toward this collaborative design approach (Hornof, 2009) based on first-hand requests from potential users, ensuring the best possible adaptation of technology to its users (Hemmert et al., 2010). The trend is also observable in child education, with an increasing number of creative techniques that seek to extract information directly from the child, with the participation also of parents or teachers (Mazzone et al., 2010).

The problem with many of these techniques is that it is difficult to apply them to children with special needs. These children often have great difficulty to express what they want, which makes it important to take special care to involve them in the design process in a way that adequately elicits the required information from them. As Muñoz points out, for certain disabilities such as cerebral palsy treatment has to be individualized, since each child has his own peculiarities and a different set of difficulties (Muñoz, 2007). When designing applications for these children, the information flow and the actions that are made available to them when using the educational application have to be appropriately adapted to the specific needs of each child.

With these requirements in mind it is not only difficult to apply existing standard design methodologies, but also to create all-encompassing design guidelines for children with special needs. Rather than closely adhering to standard procedures to create prototypes, the way forward might be to gradually introduce technology in multidisciplinary environments including parents, children, researchers, teachers etc., and to perform regular evaluations, with flexibility governing the design process.

Evaluation

How can we know that the application we design succeeds in meeting its educational purposes to the satisfaction of its users, the children and the teachers? What evaluation method best captures the benefits and limitations of the interaction experience in this context? Today it is still very much a challenge to adapt evaluation methodologies proposed for interactive systems to the context of educational support. As with the general problem with the design process, it is difficult to apply traditional evaluation methods based on measures of effectiveness, efficiency and user satisfaction.

To begin with, it is not easy to obtain measures directly from the children. It is often necessary for teachers or carers to actively help during the experiment (for instance, holding the child's head or body), which inevitably causes interference in the production of experimental data. Another important peculiarity concerns the collection of data reflecting the childrens' subjective views on the interaction. Traditional methods rely on questionnaires or interviews. Due to the limitations of expression of the children, which will vary for each particular child depending on his or her type and degree of disability, it may be challenging to obtain meaningful responses from them regarding their experience using the system. Some studies use adapted scales, for instance showing pictograms and smileys (Maguire et al., 2006), but if the child has a severe disability it will be difficult to employ even these adapted scales. The wide disparities in the disabilities of children even in the same class only add to the difficulty. An alternative to obtain this sort of subjective information is though the teacher, carer or other people who know the child well, acting as interpreters of the reactions and opinions expressed by the child. This approach lends itself to qualitative methods of evaluation that take into account the collaboration between the evaluator, the child, the educator and/or other carers (Guha et al., 2010). Along these lines

Garzotto and Bordogna propose an interesting evaluation experience in which children without disabilities collaborate with the disabled children and the experts (Garzotto and Bordogna, 2010). Their design and evaluation procedure is to present an initial prototype, evaluate the needs of the children and define design criteria in meetings and semi-structured interviews with the experts –teachers, educators and therapists–, and to carry out a preliminary evaluation with a few children before using the application at school. This suggests a multidisciplinary approach is a sound one for carrying out evaluations in this environment.

Another peculiarity of interactive educational support applications is that they usually requires a long evaluation process. In one case, for instance, use of a toy robot in a number of families selected for the study was monitored for six to ten months (Fernaeus et al., 2010). In this long-term evaluation process the families themselves recorded the use of the toy with cameras, and later the experimenter analysed the video footage and extracted observations regarding play, interaction, life-cycle and maintenance. In recent years Living Labs have been proposed as central elements in methodologies for long term evaluation of usage in real or realistic settings (see, e.g., the European Network of Living Labs (www.openlivinglabs.eu)). The increasing prominence of Living Labs may be signaling a trend toward long-term, collaborative evaluation in meaningful (more realistic) settings. These characteristics are desirable, precisely, as we have seen, in the evaluation of interactive systems for special education, due to the nature and limitations present in this context.

The preceding discussion of the state of the art underlines the potential of using ECAs in education, and in special education in particular, as supporting tools to treat specific aspects of learning. It is a line of research with a lot of potential, but it is also, by the same token, relatively young, and the place and possibilities of animated agents in educational applications have yet to be adequately explored. This is especially true in the case of special education.

Seeking to answer the aforementioned challenges, in the following pages we present our experiences introducing embodied conversational agents in applications used in support programmes for special education using collaborative design methods involving the children and teaching staff. Particular attention was given to the requirement that the applications be easy to use, flexible enough so that they may be continually adapted to the needs of the children and their educators, and, connected with this, as useful as possible within the educational programmes designed in the school, that is, subordinating research goals purely centred on the features and behavior of the ECAs to the need to provide useful tools that would serve specific educational purposes within the programme in which the study was framed. In any case, we have been able to derive both design-and evaluation-related insights centred on the possibilities of enrichment of learning support for children with special educational needs, using ECAs and including long term effects.

A COLLECTION OF EXPERIENCES TO DESIGN APPLICATIONS WITH ECAs IN THE C.P.E.E. INFANTA ELENA OF MADRID

With the aim to study the role of an ECA in Special Education, in this section we explore both the possibilities that this technology may offer in this area and also its integration in the development of new educative applications for children with Special Needs. Considering the "Aprendiendo" application as a starting point, we develop a continuous process using co-design techniques to create two innovative applications, "Emo" and "Animaddin," which help to integrate ECAs into an educational environment. In Figure 1 we illustrate this continuous process scheme to create applications.

Figure 1. Continuous process for generate new applications

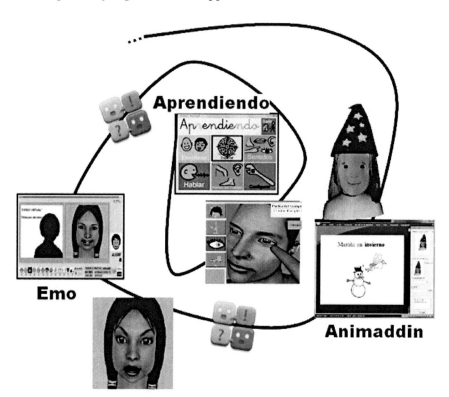

Aprendiendo is an educational tool for children between 6 and 12 years old. This tool tries to fully exploit the ECA capabilities by exploring five learning areas. After a lengthy period of use of this application in the Infanta Elena School, and due to the intricacy of the ECA functionality in each area, it was decided to create a new application centred in one ECA ability which was pointed out as the most interesting one by the teachers: ECA facial expression and exaggerated gestures to reinforce the learning for communicating and understanding the emotional behaviour. Thus, using several co-design techniques (such us brainstorming, interviews with teaching staff, prototype tests with children in the classroom environment, etc), we developed "Emo" application. This tool uses the ECA expressivity to teach small children (between 4 and 7 years of age) how to perform several gestures with their face in order to express different emotions.

Later, taking into consideration the knowledge and experience acquired developing "Emo," we created "Animaddin." This is an application which adds interactivity and emotions to traditional story telling at School. The initial purpose of this development was to explore the interaction possibilities that new devices such as interactive digital blackboards could offer in the context of Special Education. Thus, "Animaddin" takes advantage of both touch interaction and ECA life-size to help teachers to integrate ECA technology in the class easily, using technology they are familiar with (PowerPoint, from the Microsoft Office package).

In order to describe how these educational applications were developed using a number of ECA functionalities to cover several specific needs in the school, in the next subsection we describe "Aprendiendo" as a starting point of the work that followed. After this we relate the process to create "Emo," describing the co-design techniques that we have used. Later we describe the "Animaddin" application and the creative process behind it. Finally, we draw general conclusions from this collection of experiences.

Starting Point: Aprendiendo

We started our ECA research work within the Special Education area, in 2007, with the "Aprendiendo" application. This research was directed by Prof. Dr. Luis A. Hernández Gómez, working in collaboration with researcher Dr. Álvaro Hernández-Trapote, who supervised several Master's theses which collect various results extracted throughout the development and testing of "Aprendiendo" (theses: (Cortarelo, 2007), (Blázquez, 2007), (Bersano, 2007); see also (Hernández-Trapote et al., 2007)). "Aprendiendo" has been designed following the educational criteria from teachers from Infanta Elena School in Madrid. We now present an overview of the possibilities of ECA technology that were exploited in "Aprendiendo."

A Short Description of ECA Capabilities in "Aprendiendo"

Facial Expression

The gestures of an ECA are used to develop a module in which the Embodied Conversational Agent uses her facial gestures to express emotions. Using this module the children are supposed imitate the emotion performed by the ECA. The goal is that the children learn several emotions: happy, sad, angry, tired, "I like it," "I don't like it," smiling, surprised, being in love and scared. We used some predetermined emotions of the Haptek software in order to implement the emotional states.

Mouth Articulation Control

The ECA ability to control the articulation of their mouths, and, specifically, their capability to synchronise lips and speech lead us to implement a module for speech learning. This module helps the children learn how to pronounce and vocalize certain words. It offers two possibilities for integrating the speech and the visual feedback of an ECA. The first is a text-to-speech converter; the second is using pre-recorded words, which could be selected from a list (categorized as bilabial, dental, plosive, etc) and they can be pronounced using several modes (stressing the first phoneme, stressing syllables or saying the whole word).

Head Movements

"Aprendiendo" has a module for learning spatial orientation using the ECA capability to perform head movements. The main objective of this module is to reinforce the learning of the basic concepts of spatial orientation: up, down, right and left.

Body Movements

Including an ECA with a 3D body enabled us to build a module in "Aprendiendo" for learning the parts of the body. This module uses the ECA ability of moving different parts of her body and emphasizes them by using deictic gestures which point at different parts of the ECA's body.

Physical Appearance

The image processing (i.e., changing the ECA's skin texture in order to get an exaggerated blush) allowed us to shape the appearance of the Embodied Conversational Agents. Therefore ECA physical appearance can be modified and different characters could be developed in order to emphasize some specific physical features. This ECA ability is used in a module in "Aprendiendo" for learning the senses. In this module children can see an ECA with her different parts of the body related with the senses emphasized in red (eyesight, hearing, sense of smelling, taste and sense of touch).

In addition, "Aprendiendo" offers several configuration options, which makes it possible to use different ECA characters. In addition, ECA technology could be integrated with other multimedia elements such as images or videos. The main configuration options are:

- Selecting the virtual character and its background. Four different characters have been implemented: a woman, a man, a boy and a girl. For each of these characters it is possible to select a colour from a palette for the background.
- Selecting the learning mode. The application has four modalities for learning, which were designed following to the teaching staff's advice. The different modalities (usage options) are: *Basic,* which has the buttons and the virtual agent as its only elements; *Picture,* which shows pictures with each concept for reinforcing the learning; *Photo,* which is similar, but using photos instead of pictures; and *Webcam,* which allows the student to practice the concepts comparing his/her own actions (displayed in a webcam window) with those of the ECA.

Using the Application in the School

Javier Poza Blázquez (Blázquez, 2007) and Luca Bersano (Bersano, 2007) carried out an evaluation of the "Aprendiendo" software with teachers and children at the School. They obtained very good results in terms of user acceptance and motivation with the application. During the 2008 school year "Aprendiendo" was being used at the CPEE Infanta Elena School. At the beginning of the 2009 school year we decided to monitor how they were using the software at the school. After the first meeting we realised that they were no longer using the software at the school. According to the teachers, they didn't use it because children had lost their motivation in their interaction with the application, and they no longer found it fun. The teachers explained that the reason might be that

the software covered too many learning areas and the ECA could turn out to be too repetitive for children. We would also like to observe that today schools are provided with new didactic equipment and they have also access to a large amount of resources on the internet. In sum, we believe that the novelty effect of the ECA technology had diminished. Today teachers and children seem to be more demanding with new applications. This makes it more important that new applications meet teachers and users' expectations regarding functionality and design.

With this in mind we proposed the creation of new applications with ECAs involving both children and teachers actively. We now present our experience in the development process of two innovative tools, "Emo" and "Animaddin," for children with severe physical and psychic disabilities from the Infanta Elena Special Education School in Madrid.

"Emo"

In this subsection we describe the process undergone to create the application "Emo," building on the experience we acquired during the development and evaluation of "Aprendiendo." Throughout this process we employed several co-design techniques and focused on two recurrent interactive issues: the ECA and the multimedia components. These two issues were previously identified as key elements by the teacher staff while they were working with "Aprendiendo," and, therefore, we regarded them as two important elements to take into account during the whole development process of the new interactive applications.

In Figure 2 we present the overall development scheme of "Emo" application, showing the co-design techniques which were used. In our approach we have combined traditional user-centred design methodologies (such as brainstorming or prototype testing) with other techniques which carefully involve all the relevant parties (children,

Figure 2. The "Emo" development process

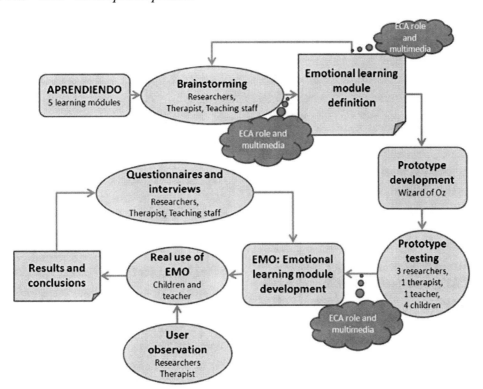

teaching staff, researchers) during the development process. We next describe how all these techniques were applied.

Brainstorming

The process began with a meeting in which, apart from the three researchers from Universidad Politécnica de Madrid, there were three teachers and a therapist from Infanta Elena School. In this meeting we carried out a brainstorming session. This is a traditional method to generate creativity within groups of people. In these sessions people express their ideas regarding a specific problem or a proposal. We took "Aprendiendo" as a starting point in our meeting, and we generated ideas for the development of a new educational application. The main outcomes of this session were the following:

- Unlike with the "Aprendiendo" tool, it was decided that the new application would be focused only on one learning module.

- Considering the multimedia issues, the teaching staff pointed out the importance of the WebCam device. They explained that the children's interest in the application was increased when they saw themselves "in the PC" with the Webcam. Consequently we decided to upgrade the use of this technology in the new application as a "virtual mirror" for the children. We decided that the functionality of the new application should be to reinforce the children's learning of facial expressions and emotions. Thus, the "virtual mirror" would mimic the traditional teaching method of learning emotions using a real mirror in the classroom. We decided also to use pictograms together with the ECA's emotions as learning reinforcement.

• We decided to set the role of the Embodied Conversational Agent as a virtual peer for learning, and we chose a girl character for the ECA. The teaching staff proposed to add interactivity to the ECA behaviour. Therefore we decided the ECA would ask the children to perform the emotions and we also decided to extend the list of the emotion-related states the ECA could perform (adding "I am hungry," "I love you," "I don't want to be alone," "I want to be alone," "I love you"). At the same time we planned to add a new ability for the ECA: giving feedback to the children corresponding to the emotion that the children perform (e.g., "great!," "well done!"). For designing the interaction we considered two possibilities. The first was to use an automatic emotion recognition system, but it was immediately rejected. The main reason was that the automatic emotion recognition system we had required an exaggerated gestural input in order to produce a good result with the classification of the user's emotional states. The children that were going to use the application have severe physical disabilities; therefore they would be unable to use this system. The second option was to use the Wizard of Oz method, where the teacher would be the Wizard during the interaction with the application. This method was considered more appropriate. We also considered which would be the most suitable voice for the ECA. The first option was to use a text-to-speech system, but we rejected this option because at this moment we were unable to obtain an automatic text-to-speech with a highly expressive girl's voice. Thus, we decided to use pre-recorded speech.

We put together all of these requirements, we designed a paper prototype and then we moved on to the implementation phase.

Designing the ECA Behaviour

During the brainstorming session, the teacher staff defined the gestures and actions that the ECA should perform. It was decided to keep on using the emotional states from "Aprendiendo," the design of which is presented in (Cortarelo, 2007). With the aim to enhance the ECA's interactive behaviour, it was decided to add a phrase for each emotional state, so the ECA names aloud the emotion that she is performing. Besides this, as we have mentioned before, new emotions and actions were added. When creating the avatar's behaviour we copied as accurately as possible the gestural behaviour displayed in class by the teachers themselves. A broader explanation of the new emotions design can be found in (López-Mencía, 2011).

Preliminary Validation of ECA Behaviour

In an early stage of the development process we had a second meeting with the teaching staff and the therapist. The object of this meeting was to check whether the prototype we were developing matched their mental model of the application functionality.

The design of the application was accepted and their overall opinion was positive. The ECA's facial expressions and emotional states were validated and accepted by the teaching staff. Regarding the synchronization between the ECA's speech and gesture they decided that first the ECA should perform the gesture, then say the phrase, and finally the ECA should perform the gesture again, until the teacher (controlling the system as a Wizard) switches the gesture off. Thus, children would be able to see the ECA's facial expression for as long as they need.

Finally, the teaching staff was not completely happy with the visual design of the multimedia elements. After a new brainstorming session we made several aesthetic and layout changes in the interface. Thus a complete list of specifications for developing the new application was defined. Later we developed a functional prototype of the application. Implementation details can be seen in (Portela, 2010).

Prototype Testing

The therapist and two teachers selected four children to test the prototype. They are children with Cerebral Palsy, and have severe motor and speech disabilities. They were between 4 and 14 years old. We aimed to see how children of different ages interact with the application, seeking to define the optimal age range to use the tool. The testing performance was controlled by a Wizard of Oz. The teacher acted as a wizard and controlled the system's response. During the testing session a therapist, the researchers and the teacher (wizard) were present. The therapist helped the younger children with severe motor disabilities. She stood behind their wheelchair and held their head when necessary. The wizard was located at a moderate distance from the children, so they could notice his presence, but didn't realise that he was controlling the interface. The wizard could see the child's webcam signal in his monitor, and trigger the appropriate ECA behaviour using a control panel. The average duration of the interaction was 10 minutes. Figure 3 shows the testing environment.

At the end of the session, we exchanged impressions with the teacher and the therapist and we reached the following conclusions regarding the prototype testing:

- With regarding to the multimedia elements, we realised that several children (between 4 and 5 years of age) were too young to pictogram reinforcement, because they didn't know the pictogram code. Therefore, we decided that pictogram reinforcement would be optional. In addition, due to the scarcity of computers at the school and in order to make it easier to use the application in class, the teaching staff proposed to add the possibility of using the application with only one PC. This led to adding the option to include both the ECA control panel and the user interface on the same screen.

- The teaching staff proposed to add welcome and farewell messages from the ECA. This way the children would be able to understand better when the interaction starts and ends. We observed that children responded with enthusiasm to the application reinforcement's phrases, so it was proposed to add more of these phrases and sounds (such as clapping). We further observed that sometimes the children didn't look at the ECA while she was showing the emotion and instead they looked at themselves in the "virtual mirror." For this reason it was decided to add a visual and audio reinforcement as a call of attention. The ECA would say "look at me!," and optionally a blinking frame around the ECA could be also added as a visual stimulus to attract the child's attention.

Figure 3. Testing environment using a Wizard of Oz

- We were also able to validate the ECA's face expressions and behaviour with the children. First of all, the wizard tested all the emotions with the children, and after this first round of familiarisation, he would focus only those emotions which seemed to appeal more to the children (such as "I love you," "Scared," "Happy," "Sad"…). Thus, the Wizard played these emotions repeatedly and tended to ignore the less exaggerated ones (e.g., "I want to be alone," "I want more"). In addition, in order to evaluate this first interaction with the application, at the end of the session we asked the children if they had liked the experience. They responded with positive enthusiasm.

EMO: ECAs for Learning Emotions

Based on the conclusions and recommendations extracted from the prototype testing, a final version of Emo, the application for learning emotions, was developed. Figure 4 shows what the interface looks like. It has two main frames, one of them contains the Embodied Conversational Agent and the other shows the webcam signal as a "virtual mirror." Optionally, a pictogram showing the emotion that the ECA is performing can appear to the right of the ECA frame, as additional learning reinforcement. The Wizard's ECA control panel was placed at the bottom of the interface.

We describe next the role of the ECA in this new learning application:

- Generation of expression patterns to be imitated. As we have mentioned before, the available emotions and facial expressions were defined by the teaching staff at Infanta Elena. These are "Hungry," "Surprised,""Like,""Dislike," "Angry," "Smiling," "Tired," "Sad," "Happy," "I want more," "I love you," "I want to be alone," "I don't want to be alone." The teacher (Wizard) can choose an emotional state by pressing the button that represents it. The ECA then acts out the emotion; afterwards the ECA says aloud the name of the emotion / action that is being performed, and again the ECA acts out the emotion until the Wizard switches the emotion off.
- Encouraging children to interact with the system. Besides expressing emotions, the virtual agent can also ask the children to

Figure 4. Emo interface

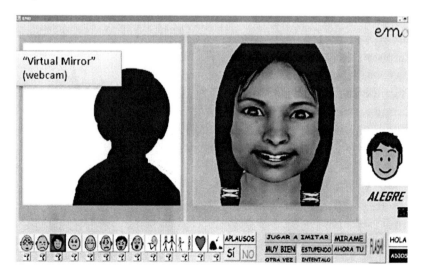

perform the same emotion she is acting out. There is a row of pictures that represent emotional states or actions. Underneath each picture there is a question mark (?) button. If pressed, the virtual agent asks a question in relation to the corresponding picture. For example, "How do you get angry?"

- Learning reinforcement. Reinforcements were included at the request of the teachers and therapists, who highlighted their importance in the learning process. In addition to "yes" and "no" responses from the ECA (visual and auditory stimuli), we included applause and encouragement phrases such as "Well done!," "Fantastic!," "Great!" or "Try again!"

- Capturing the children's attention though direct requests by the ECA. The teachers hope that this function will help the children increase their levels of concentration with the tasks. There are also reinforcement phrases to try to draw the child's attention to the avatar's face: "Play with me! Imitate my face!," "Look!," "It's your turn." Optionally, the Wizard can activate a blinking frame around the ECA as a visual stimulus to attract the child's attention.

A more detailed description of the architecture of this application can be found in (López-Mencía, 2011).

Testing "Emo" in a Real Environment

Once we had developed a stable version of "Emo" we decided to perform a final test with the children. We chose the same four children who had participated in the previous test. The reason is that they were considered to be a representative group by the teaching staff. Also, although they all suffer from Cerebral Palsy, each child has his own peculiarities within the disability. Moreover, had we chosen different children for the final test we wouldn't have been able to tell whether

any observed differences in the course of the interactions might correspond to the fact that the changes done in the prototype worked properly in the final application.

We tested the application in the computer room. During the testing session researchers, the therapist and the teacher (wizard) were present. We recorded the sessions using two camera angles: a frontal medium close up shot of the child's face and a lateral wide shot capturing both the child and teacher. We did not consider it necessary to record the avatar's actions in video as they could be completely logged from the audio files and the button events from the wizard interface. The average duration of the interaction with the application was 8 minutes. A more detailed description of the data extracted and analysed can be found in (López-Mencía et al., 2010)

After the testing session, we exchanged opinions and impressions with the teaching staff. The following observations were made:

- The control panel was easy to use for the teacher (wizard).
- The learning reinforcements were working properly.
- Children did focus their attention on the ECA and they tried to mimic the ECA's facial expressions.
- Children showed enthusiasm and they didn't show boredom cues during the interaction with the application.

Consequently, we concluded that the ECA was functioning as desired: an expression model for imitation, an attention attractor and an audio-visual motivational learning reinforcement.

Monitoring the Application

After the final version of "Emo" was tested at the school, we installed the application there so that the teaching staff would be able to integrate the application in their daily teaching activities.

In order to monitor the use of the application, first we provided a questionnaire to be filled-in by the teaching staff periodically. We included the following dimensions in the questionnaire: Usefulness of the application, Children's motivation, Enjoyment, Children's lack of attention, Children's assimilation audio-visual reinforcement, Ease of use of the application, and interaction strategy employed by the teacher (whether as a hidden Wizard of Oz or using the system within one screen).

After using the application during approximately 3 months in the school, we returned to monitor how the application was being used and what was the teaching staff's opinion of it. We had a meeting with the school therapist and she answered the questionnaire giving a positive overall opinion of the application. On a five-point likert response format, she awarded 5 points for the items application usefulness and children's motivation and attention during the interaction. She also gave a high positive mark (4) for the items children's assimilation of reinforcements and ease to use for the teaching staff. On the other hand, she gave a low mark (2) for enjoyment of the application. She pointed out that the application wasn't fun by itself, but, rather, the enjoyment came from the teacher's feedback or from other children around the one who was using the application. Regarding the interaction strategy, she told us that the most common one was to use the application on one screen only. After the therapist finished the questionnaire, we were invited to attend a class to see the application in use. From this experience we highlight the following observations:

- A kind of "near-wizard of Oz" strategy was employed, where teachers use only one screen for interacting with the application. The child was in front of the screen and the teacher was behind the child. The teacher controlled the ECA by using the control panel located in the bottom part of the interface, with the mouse of the PC. Thus,

the children didn't realise that the teacher was the "wizard" who controlled the ECA.
- The application is suitable for being used with children between 4 and 7 years of age.
- The application was used with children with different levels of disability. During the session in which we were present, a girl without motor disability used the application. She was able to control the ECA by using the control panel buttons. She preferred to use the application by herself, and she even showed embarrassment when the teacher controlled the ECA. She displayed an interesting behaviour, trying to communicate with another girl in the classroom using the ECA's facial expressions. It could be worthwhile to study this behaviour in future research.
- The teacher suggested we enrich the interaction. Specifically, they wanted to use the ECA to tell stories to the children. As we will see next, we decided to implement this functionality in a new application called "Animaddin."

"Animaddin"

At the beginning of the 2010/2011 school year, we had another meeting at Infanta Elena School, to monitor progress with "Emo." Researchers from Universidad Politécnica de Madrid, the therapist and the teaching staff who had participated in the development of "Emo" were at the meeting. The interactive multimedia elements and the role of ECA were discussed, and new directions explored, taking into consideration both the teaching staff's experience with "Emo" and the new computer material that the Infanta Elena School had been provided with. It was decided that a new application would be created to make the integration of the ECA technology in the educational programme easier for the teaching staff. The main conclusions from the meeting were the following:

- The teaching staff suggested that the children were tired of using always the same Animated Agent in "Emo." They suggested we add new ECA characters. At this point it is reasonable to ponder whether the children were tired of the ECA character itself or tired of its behaviour, as "Emo" is a tool in which the ECA always uses the same phrases and emotions and it has no configuration options. Whatever the case may have been, we listened to the teaching staff's requests and we decided to implement new ECA characters. We discussed the possibility of creating new characters using photorealistic technology, which could make it possible for children could see "themselves" made into ECA characters. We thought this might increase their motivation to express the gestures.
- The teaching staff also wished to put their new interactive devices to use, particularly a digital touch-whiteboard. This technology, despite the fact that neither the children nor the teachers were familiar with it at the time, offered the opportunity to develop new applications around it. The ECA technology could be shown in life-like size and new interaction schemes between the teacher, the ECA appearing in the whiteboard and the children could be explored. With these possibilities in mind, we decided to focus the development of the new application around the ECA and the digital whiteboard.

We began to define a completely new application for the digital whiteboard which would embed ECA technology in the context of "Fairy Martita" stories. The idea was to get the ECA identified with Martita by the children. Martita the fairy is the main character in a collection of stories called "Fairy Martita," by Mª Candelaria Imbernon, included in her Thesis (López, 2009). She developed an educational program with the children from Infanta Elena School. In this program she used a collection of "Fairy Martita" stories to boost the children's learning abilities and their active participation in the classroom during a storytelling session. The idea now was to combine this new interactive technology to encourage participation in the classroom and help children with special needs to develop their communication skills and literacy.

It was further argued that ECA technology would be helpful for both the children and the teaching staff as follows:

- An ECA might be a motivation enhancer for children in this context, more so than in the previous efforts related above. The ECA could help the children increase their participation in the story telling. Adding an ECA equipped with gestural and emotional behaviour (which was previously designed for "Emo") to the new application would also help the children increase their comprehension and awareness of the story.
- An ECA would be important for the teaching staff, as it would help them apply different interaction strategies with the aim to involve the children in the story and increase their participation in the telling of the story.

In Figure 5 we show the "Animaddin" development scheme. The figure summarises the steps and techniques of the co-design process.

As shown in the figure 5, from the beginning we worked on two main tasks in parallel: the development of new ECA characters and the development of a new tool including an ECA as an interactive character in the context of storytelling. Nevertheless, both tasks ended up being connected, as we will see in the following subsection. We would like to underline that the experience we acquired during the development process for "Emo" contributed positively to the development of "Animaddin." In fact, we followed the same

Figure 5. "Animaddin" development scheme

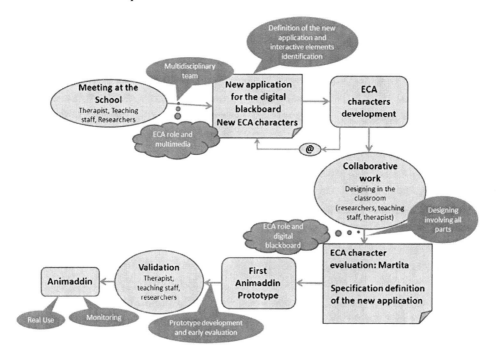

development guidelines used in the creation of "Emo": we built a multidisciplinary team, identified the interactive elements around which we had to work, and applied a set of co-design principles and techniques. In the following subsections we describe all the steps of the development process of "Animaddin" in detail.

Developing Different ECA Characters

We created several animated agents with different appearances using the People Putty tool by Haptek. To create photorealistic characters we used pictures of the faces of two children at Infanta Elena school (with due permission from their parents). The teaching staff also sent us several fairy Martita pictures so that we could develop an avatar with Martita's appearance. In total we built the following ECA characters: Martita, two "children" from the school, a teacher, a boy and a cat. The development details of the new ECA characters can be found in (Arias, 2011). Figure 6 shows pictures of these characters.

Collaborative Work in the Classroom

Once we had developed the ECA characters, we carried out a collaborative work session at the school. The same multidisciplinary team was there (researchers, teaching staff and the therapist). These were the main outcomes from this session:

- First we introduced the new ECA characters. The teaching staff discarded non-human-like ECAs, such as the cat. They also discarded the teacher and the boy because they had accessory features around their eyes and mouth (e.g., glasses) which made parts of their faces less visible, which is not ideal for the purpose of attracting the child's attention to their interlocutor. The photorealistic ECAs were also set aside, anticipating that the children might be unable to recognise themselves in them. Fairy Martita was well received, so further development efforts would revolve around her.

Figure 6. The new ECA characters

- We then defined the specifications for the new application in the context of the interactive storytelling, for which we moved to a classroom and worked in front of the digital whiteboard itself (a SmartBoard 600i). The research team and two teachers participated in this session. We decided to create a new application that would be configurable by the teaching staff and which could be integrated easily with the format of the educational tools they were using already at the school (that is, compatible with PowerPoint presentations, which are the main format for the Fairy Martita tales). It was proposed to add a gestural and emotional ECA with the appearance of Martita. This ECA should be able to speak and it would also be desirable to have the possibility of adding new accessories (e.g., a hat). At this point we suggested adding an automatic text-to-speech engine to provide the flexibility of building new stories. We also analysed the interaction on the digital whiteboard. It was decided

that the level of touch interaction would be limited to allowing the child to press "Yes" or "No" question buttons located in the upper part of the whiteboard, as a way to increase their interaction with the story. We also considered the possibility of using a Wizard of Oz approach to control certain ECA actions during the interaction. However, we did not find a specific design to everyone's satisfaction.

Initial Working Prototype

The specifications that were defined in that meeting guided work on the initial prototype. It should be noted that the specifications were not very precise, and some aspects were left to the judgment of the research team. Regarding the functionality of the application, it was decided to give the tool enough flexibility to make it possible to adapt an unlimited number of stories for it. Seeking total integration with tools that were readily available and which the teachers were already familiar with, the implementation of the application was planned as a PowerPoint add-in. This would also allow the reuse of stories that were already available in PowerPoint format, as well as the dissemination of ECA technology in new application contexts.

Some paper prototypes were drawn, taking into account the agreed requirements, which included the following:

- It should be possible to select different ECA characters and accessories (i.e. hats)
- There should be an area to introduce the text which is going to be spoken by the ECA, or a selector feature for gestures associated with utterances. Regarding the synchronization of speech and gestures, some possibilities were discussed that would allow the teacher to have some way to control the behavior of the ECA. A fine-grained approach could add more complexity but also more control over the scene. On the other hand, simpler mechanisms would limit the possibilities of configuration, but have other advantages. An overall balance between development complexity, flexibility of the tool and ease of use was sought, always keeping in mind not to over-complicate things for the task the application was intended for.
- The interface should feature an area to preview the final result of the setup before inserting the element in the presentation.

VSTO (Visual Studio Tools for Office) was chosen as the development environment for the prototype. VSTO is a collection of development tools which are installed in Visual Studio and grant access to Microsoft Office capabilities and the creation of new controls and add-ins for this office suite. Luis González, in his master thesis (Arias, 2011), provides a solid justification of this choice of development tool, mainly based on its speed, power and flexibility compared to another available options.

Early Validation of the Prototype

When the idea of the initial prototype was mature, we programmed a further meeting with the teaching staff (teachers and therapists) and the research team. The goal was to find out whether the "paradigm" of embedding an ECA in the PowerPoint stories was aligned with the learning methodology and the mental model of the teaching staff. It was considered relevant to assess this validation in an early stage of development because using the new application requires a more intense participation of the teaching staff (e.g., for the configuration of the different ECAs).

Overall, the prototype was well received and only some minor changes regarding the appearance of the interface and the flow of the interaction were suggested. These were the highlights of the meeting:

- Providing the possibility of changing the appearance of the ECAs was considered to be a good idea, but 'Martita' was to remain the main character. Some changes were requested for the background color of the Animated Agent.
- The capabilities developed for the ECA were validated. Among them was the use of gestures/emotions and locutions to reinforce the children's motivation and help them understand the story as it unfolds. For example, when the story asks *"What does Martita wears in winter? A scarf?,"* reinforcement could be achieved by nodding and the sentence *"Yes!, so she isn't cold!."*
- Different possibilities to synchronise gestures and speech were explained. It was decided to make the process simpler, allowing only to select whether the ECA speaks first and then makes the gesture or vice versa. The ECA element would be loaded with the corresponding slide and the actions (i.e. speech and gestures) would be acted out immediately.

- Regarding the position in which the ECA element is inserted in the slide, it was agreed to locate it in a default position and then to let the teacher move it manually (dragging it with the mouse) to a different position.
- 'Martita' the fairy was to wear only one accessory: a hat.
- The teaching staff suggested the inclusion of a button to repeat the configured action in the preview area.

Animaddin

Finally, following the aforementioned guidelines, the 'Animaddin' PowerPoint add-in was developed. As was pointed out in the section discussing the initial working prototype, the add-in was implemented using VSTO tools for Visual Studio. In this programming environment the animated agent is integrated through an ActiveX object, provided by Haptek, which offers an API to set up and to control the avatar. For further techni-cal details of the implementation the reader may refer to (Arias, 2011) or (López-Mencía, 2011).

The 'Animaddin' add-in is a PowerPoint COM object which can be incorporated into presentations through the "Add-ins" menu option. The add-in appears (by default) on the right side of the presentation, and it offers a set of controls for the set-up of the agent (see Figure 7).

The controls which the 'Animaddin' add-in offers are:

- Selection of the ECA character. Although the 'Martita' avatar will be used mostly at the Infanta Elena School, the add-in offers a range of characters to choose from in case the children get bored with the main one. These animated agents have been described above in the section on "Emo."
- Selection of the ECA's accessories. This is a feature of the application even though, as mentioned above, currently only Martita's hat is available.

Figure 7. Animaddin add-in

- Selection of the ECA's emotion. The facial expressions and emotions from 'Emo' application are used.
- A box to insert text to be uttered by the ECA. At present a Spanish free text-to-speech is used provisionally (Isabel by Nuance - the former Scansoft). We plan to work on the improvement of this feature in order to be able to include a synthesizer that is better adapted to the learning context.
- Coarse-grained synchronization of speech and gestures. Two possibilities are allowed: speech first, then gesture or gesture first, then speech.
- Play the configured actions. This plays a preview of the ECA's behaviour before it is inserted in the slide.

Effective Use and Monitoring

Now that 'Animaddin' has been developed we plan to deploy the teaching tool at the school and then monitor its use and the beneficial effects (as well as the problems) that may be associated with it. The children have started to get involved in this key task. Their reactions will provide invaluable information for the research team. Unfortunately, the children's communication limitations and the novelty of the electronic whiteboard technology (which hadn't yet been installed and used with the children at the beginning of the development process) have delayed their participation, as final users, in the co-design process.

CONCLUSION

In this chapter we have described two experiences of incorporation of Embodied conversational Agents in two learning reinforcement applications for special education: "Emo" and "Animaddin." We have underlined the most important elements of the co-design approach followed. From these experiences we have identified and validated a

set of features that ECAs bring to educational applications. The following are some of the more important observations to take into account when designing and evaluating these systems:

- Exaggerated facial expressions performed by the ECA can serve as a model to support the learning of emotion recognition and expression through imitation.
- ECAs claim the attention of children.
- Combining auditory and gesture (visual) reinforcement of gestures through the use of an ECA can help children learn gestures and understand stories.
- ECAs in an active role when interacting with a child can encourage him or her to participate in activities.
- Using an ECA with repetitive interaction patterns for long periods of time can induce boredom and tiredness in children.
- Regarding the physical appearance of the ECA, it is important that the eyes and the mouth be completely visible; animated agents created from pictures of children should be avoided, while we have observed that an ECA inspired in a character in a story was particularly well received.

We have also described the role of the people involved in the creation process of these tools. Partial results were presented and conclusions discussed for each of the two co-design experiences described.

In Emo facial expressions performed by ECAs were exploited to help children with cerebral palsy improve their learning of emotions. Use of the application in class and the qualitative feedback from the teaching staff confirm that it increases the children's motivation and it provides benefits to their educational experience. In addition, its continual use in the school opens the opportunity to add further functionalities for future use –such as an emotion communicator–, for children with different disabilities.

Animaddin makes use of a relatively new interface: the interactive whiteboard. This application allows animating stories with ECAs, interactively, through the whiteboard. This is achieved by configuring an ECA as a PowerPoint add-in (in the Microsoft Office package). Teachers are then able to configure and manipulate the ECAs easily using tools they are familiar with. The tool can be used with pre-recorded audio files, but it also features text-to-speech conversion to produce new utterances the teacher or the child may wish to create. We should ponder at this point whether it is desirable to include synthetic speech rather than natural (recorded) utterances for applications targeted at disabled children. Maguire consider that although natural speech is more intelligible and pleasant, synthetic speech may be acceptable if it sounds natural (Maguire et al., 2006). In any case, developing a text-to-speech converter that is adapted to the needs of children, sounds like a child and can produce clear and intelligible, yet exaggerated, expression is a challenge, an area of research in its own right, to be undertaken in future work.

Animaddin has some similarities with videogames. In it the ECA does not change and there is no direct dialogue, but, rather, exchanges in the changing context of a story. Educational videogames, also known as "serious games" (these are videogames in which the pedagogical component is more important than entertainment (Susi and Backlund, 2007)), constitute an interesting and active line of research, both in the industry and in the academic sphere. Regardless of whether we think of Animaddin as a videogame or not, what is important is that it allows educators to design the interaction control of the ECA themselves, adapting it (pre-programming it) to suit the needs at each particular moment in time, and to the capabilities of each particular child, which may vary greatly with respect to those of other children with different types and degrees of disability.

Our research approach with Animaddin has more similarities with opensource, configurable and sharable design (not unlike the Scratch language, a developed at MIT; http://scratch.mit.edu). It provides teachers with new flexible educational tools that they can adapt to complement other, more traditional materials that they use in the classroom, following the current trend in education of generating shared environments. Teachers are becoming increasingly accustomed to integrating technology, social networks and online tools into the activities of the educational community, for which a variety of resources are being developed, such as Moodle and Google Apps for Education. As corresponds to this approach we have sought to give as much visibility as possible to the project (through online news media, social networks and discussion fora), making the material freely available, so that Animaddin may be used by all those who may find it helpful.

Recommendations

Both of the applications described in this chapter were developed following user-centred co-design and evaluation principles with due consideration to the presence of ECAs and the context of use. The experienced has enabled us to put together a set of recommendations or guidelines for future developments in similar contexts López-Mencía et al., 2010b). For the design and evaluation process we believe the following notes are helpful:

- The process should be undertaken with a multidisciplinary team including developers, researchers, teachers, therapists and the children themselves.
- The aspect or module that is to be developed should be clearly defined, as should the interactive elements of the application.
- It is beneficial to combine and adapt available design and evaluation methods that engage all of the actors involved in the process.

- Prototypes should be tested with the teachers and children already in the early stages of development.
- The function of the interactive elements under development should be evaluated at all stages of the co-design process.
- Real usage of the application should be a part of the design and evaluation process.
- It is important to monitor the use of the system for long periods of time to extract observations that will allow redesigning or extracting insights that may lead to new directions of research.

Regarding the observed effects, benefits and limitations of ECAs in Special education, their use is recommended:

- As a tool to reinforce learning
- To attract the attention of the child
- As an alternative means of interation that encourages the child to respond or participate.

A final note of gratitude is due, first of all, to the teaching staff and the children at CPEE Infanta Elena, Madrid, without whose invaluable collaboration throughout the entire design, evaluation and monitoring process the work presented in his chapter would not have been possible. Regarding the technical implementation, recognition is due to the students at Universidad Politécnica de Madrid who worked in some phases of development as part of their Master's project and were an integral part of the research team.

FUTURE RESEARCH DIRECTIONS

The first and most obvious line of work, in following the co-design approach, is to continue collaborating with the staff at the school, monitoring the use of the Animaddin application, continuing its adaptation to the evolving educational needs,

seeking to increase the users' satisfaction with it. Long-term monitoring and impact evaluation based on real usage is in itself increasingly relevant to the scientific community. Furthermore, this may lead to further ideas for new applications.

Since the beginning of our research on reinforcement tools for special education we have sought to provide a text-to-speech converter that is suitable for the children. By suitable we mean that the voice be that of a child and that it be adaptable to the expressive and pronunciation needs of the children with disabilities using the tools. Synthetic speech has improved during the course of these years in terms of the quality and expressiveness of the voices, but it is still hard to find free software that meets these requirements. Consequently, we are pondering the possibility of developing a text-to-speech converter for children and make it available to the research community.

Sharing experiences and the technology itself has been a major element of our work, through which we have received feedback from the users which has helped direct and refine our designs. We consider it would be highly beneficial to all to broaden the visibility of our ongoing projects. We have already begun to publish them on online journals and a forum created for this purpose. Future efforts are to include intensifying our presence on the Internet, with the development of a portal for resource-sharing and increasing our visibility through social networks and other fora and online publications.

Finally, preliminary testing in the school led to the idea of developing an automatic data-collection system that provides access to information set in shared formats so that it may be easily shared and analysed by other researchers, developers and educators. A more innovative possibility would be to collect usage data in real-time, as is done with website monitoring tools such as Google Analytics. This would make interaction with the school's teaching staff more effective. The researchers could access and analyse the flow of monitoring data and plan meetings and visits to the school when the observations should call for it (the most basic case for the use of such a system would be to detect when usage rates drop –through lack of data coming in–, which might be taken as an indication that the needs at the school should be re-evaluated).

ACKNOWLEDGMENT

The activities described in this chapter were funded by the Spanish Ministry of Science and Technology as part of the TEC2009-14719-C02-02 project. We thank the teaching staff at CPEE Infanta Elena for their invaluable help and recommendations. Our gratitude goes also to Virginia León, Luca Bersano, Javier Poza, Jorge López, Jose Luis Naranjo and Luis González Arias for their work in developing the applications.

REFERENCES

Arias, J. L. G. (2011). *Diseño y desarrollo de una herramienta informática para apoyo en educación especial con soporte de pizarra digital interactiva*. Master Thesis, Escuela Superior de Ingeniería Informática. Universidad de Vigo.

Atkinson, R. (2002). Optimizing learning from examples using animated pedagogical agents. *Journal of Educational Psychology, 94*(2), 416–427. doi:10.1037/0022-0663.94.2.416

Baron-Cohen, S., Golan, O., & Ashwin, E. (2009). Can emotion recognition be taught to children with autism spectrum conditions? *Philosophical Transactions of the Royal Society B. Biological Sciences, 364*, 3567–3574. doi:10.1098/rstb.2009.0191

Bersano, L. (2007). *Aprendiendo, desarrollo y evaluación de una herramienta informática para niños y niñas con necesidades educativas especiales*. Master's thesis, Politécnico di Torino.

Blázquez, J. P. (2008). *Aprendiendo: desarrollo y evaluación de una herramienta informática para niños y niñas con necesidades educativas especiales*. Master's thesis, Universidad Politécnica de Madrid.

Bolich, B. J. (2001). Peer tutoring and social behaviors: A review. *International Journal of Special Education, 16*(2).

Cassell, J. (2000). Embodied conversational interface agents. *Communications of the ACM, 43*(4), 70–78. doi:10.1145/332051.332075

Corradini, A., Mehta, M., Bernsen, N., & Charfuelan, M. (2005). Animating an interactive conversational character for an educational game system. In *Proceedings of the 10th International Conference on Intelligent User Interfaces* (pp. 183-190). ACM.

Cortarelo, V. L. (2007). *Desarrollo de herramientas de apoyo docente basadas en agentes animados para educación especial*. Master's thesis, Universidad Politécnica de Madrid.

Engwall, O. (2008). *Can audio-visual instructions help learners improve their articulation?- an ultrasound study of short term changes* (pp. 2631–2634). INTERSPEECH.

Eskenazi, M. (2009). An overview of spoken language technology for education. *Speech Communication, 51*(10), 832–844. doi:10.1016/j.specom.2009.04.005

Fernaeus, Y., Hakansson, M., Jacobsson, M., & Ljungblad, S. (2010). How do you play with a robotic toy animal? A long-term study of pleo. In *Proceedings of the 9th International Conference on Interaction Design and Children* (pp. 39-48). ACM.

Garzotto, F., & Bordogna, M. (2010). Paper-based multimedia interaction as learning tool for disabled children. In *Proceedings of the 9th International Conference on Interaction Design and Children* (pp. 79-88). ACM.

Gratch, J., Wang, N., Okhmatovskaia, A., Lamothe, F., Morales, M., van der Werf, R. J., & Morency, L. (2007). Can virtual humans be more engaging than real ones? In J. A. Jacko (Ed.), *Proceedings of the 12th International Conference on Human-Computer Interaction (HCI'07): Intelligent Multimodal Interaction Environments* (pp. 286-297).

Guha, M., Druin, A., & Fails, J. (2010). Investigating the impact of design processes on children. In *Proceedings of the 9th International Conference on Interaction Design and Children* (pp. 198-201). ACM.

Hemmert, F., Hamann, S., Lowe, M., Zeipelt, J., & Joost, G. (2010). Co-designing with children: A comparison of embodied and disembodied sketching techniques in the design of child age communication devices. In *Proceedings of the 9th International Conference on Interaction Design and Children* (pp. 202-205).ACM.

Hernández-Trapote, A., López-Mencía, B., Bersano, L., & Hernández-Gómez, L. (2007). *Aprendiendo: Uso de la tecnología de agentes conversacionales personificados en el ámbito de la educación especial*. Paper presented at the Simposio Nacional de Tecnologías de la Información y las Comunicaciones en la Educación. Congreso Español de Informática. Zaragoza, Spain.

Hornof, A. (2009). Designing with children with severe motor impairments. In *Proceedings of the 27th International Conference on Human Factors in Computing Systems* (pp. 2177-2180). ACM.

ISO/IEC. (1999). *ISO/IEC 13407: Human-centred design processes for interactive systems*.

Johnson, W., Rickel, J., & Lester, J. (2000). Animated pedagogical agents: Face-to-face interaction in interactive learning environments. *International Journal of Artificial Intelligence in Education, 11*, 47–78.

Karna, E., Nuutinen, J., Pihlainen-Bednarik, K., & Vellonen, V. (2010). Designing technologies with children with special needs: Children in the centre (CIC) framework. In *Proceedings of the 9th International Conference on Interaction Design and Children* (pp. 218-221). ACM.

Kiung, N. G., Liew, Y. T., Saripan, M. I., Abas, A. F., & Noordin, N. K. (2008). Flexi e-learning system: Disabled friendly education system. *European Journal of Soil Science, 7*(2).

Lester, J. C., Converse, S. A., Kahler, S. E., Barlow, S. T., Stone, B. A., & Bhogal, R. S. (1997). The persona effect: Affective impact of animated pedagogical agents. In *Proceedings of the SIGCHI Conference on Human Factors in Computing Systems*, (pp. 359-366).

Lopez, M. C. I. (2009). *El desarrollo de las habilidades de alfabetización emergente en el contexto de la lectura de cuentos*. PhD Thesis, Departamento de Didáctica y Organización Escolar. Universidad de Murcia.

López-Mencía, B. (2011). *Agentes conversacionales personificados en sistemas interactivos: Diseño y evaluación*. PhD Thesis, Universidad Politécnica de Madrid.

Lopez-Mencia, B., Pardo, D., Hernandez-Trapote, A., Hernandez, L., & Relaño, J. (2010). A collaborative approach to the design and evaluation of an interactive learning tool for children with special educational needs. In *Proceedings of the 9th International Conference on Interaction Design and Children* (pp. 226-229). ACM.

Lopez-Mencía, B., Pardo, D., Roa-Seiler, N., Hernandez-Trapote, A., Hernandez, L., & Rodriguez, M. (2010). *Look at me: An emotion learning reinforcement tool for children with severe motor disability*. Paper presented at Multimodal Corpora: Advances in Capturing, Coding and Analyzing Multimodality -LREC 2010.

Maguire, M., Elton, E., Osman, Z., & Nicolle, C. (2006). Design of a virtual learning environment: For students with special needs. *An Interdisciplinary Journal on Humans in ICT Environments, 2*(1), 119–153.

Marín, D. P. (2010). *Uso de agentes conversacionales pedagógicos en sistemas de aprendizaje híbrido (b-learning)*. Paper presented at IV Seminario de Investigación en Tecnologías de la Información Aplicadas a la Educación, Madrid, Spain.

Massaro, D. (2006). Embodied agents in language learning for children with language challenges. In K. Miesenberger, J. Klaus, W. Zagler, & A. Karshmer (Eds.), *Proceedings of the 10th International Conference on Computers Helping People with Special Needs, ICCHP 2006* (pp. 809-816). University of Linz, Austria. Berlin, Germany: Springer.

Massaro, D., Cohen, M., Beskow, J., & Cole, R. (2000). Developing and evaluating conversational agents. In Cassell, J., Sullivan, J., Prevost, S., & Churchill, E. (Eds.), *Embodied conversational agents* (pp. 287–318). Cambridge, MA: MIT Press.

Mazzone, E., Iivari, N., Tikkanen, R., Read, J., & Beale, R. (2010). Considering context, content, management, and engagement in design activities with children. In *Proceedings of the 9th International Conference on Interaction Design and Children* (pp. 108-117). ACM.

Mohamad, Y., Velasco, C., & Tebarth, H. (2005). Development and evaluation of emotional interface agents in training of learning disabled children. In *Proceedings of the First Workshop on Emotion in HCI*.

Moreno, R., Mayer, R., Spires, H., & Lester, J. (2001). The case for social agency in computer-based teaching: Do students learn more deeply when they interact with animated pedagogical agents? *Cognition and Instruction, 19*(2), 177–213. doi:10.1207/S1532690XCI1902_02

Muñoz, A. M. (2007). *La parálisis cerebral. Technical report, Observatorio de la Discapacidad Institutos de Mayores y Servicios Sociales.* IMSERSO.

Picard, R. W. (2009). Future affective technology for autism and emotion communication. *Philosophical Transactions of the Royal Society B. Biological Sciences, 364*, 3575–3584. doi:10.1098/rstb.2009.0143

Portela, J. R. L. (2010). *Diseño y usabilidad de interfaces hombre-máquina con agentes animados para apoyo a la enseñanza en educación especial*. Master's thesis, Universidad Politécnica de Madrid.

Rasseneur, D., Delozanne, E., Jacoboni, P., & Grugeon, B. (2002). Learning with virtual agents: Competition and cooperation in AMICO. *Intelligent Tutoring Systems: 6th International Conference* (pp. 129-142).

San-Segundo, R., Pardo, J., Ferreiros, J., Sama, V., Barra-Chicote, R., & Lucas, J. (2010). Spoken Spanish generation from sign language. *Interacting with Computers, 22*(2), 123–139. doi:10.1016/j.intcom.2009.11.011

Sánchez Benavente, R., & García Cuenca, A. (2003). *Diseño de contenidos accesibles para personas con discapacidad intelectual*. Paper presented at I Jornadas Científico-Técnicas IAE / AFANIAS: La accesibilidad a Internet de personas con discapacidad intelectual, Madrid, Spain.

Sanders, E., & Stappers, P. (2008). Co-creation and the new landscapes of design. *CoDesign, 4*(1), 5–18. doi:10.1080/15710880701875068

Susi, T., Johannesson, M., & Backlund, P. (2007). *Serious games: An overview*. Technical report, University of Skovde (HS-IKI-TR-07-001).

Tartaro, A., & Cassell, J. (2008). Playing with virtual peers: Bootstrapping contingent discourse in children with autism. *Proceedings of the 8th International Conference for the Learning Sciences-Volume 2* (pp. 382-389).

Vázquez Reyes, C. M., & Fernández Rota, M. E. (2002). *El proyecto de la Agencia Europea sobre la aplicación de las Tecnologías de la Comunicación e Información a la educación del alumnado con necesidades educativas especiales.* Tecnoneet.

Wik, P., & Hjalmarsson, A. (2009). Embodied conversational agents in computer assisted language learning. *Speech Communication, 51*(10), 1024–1037. doi:10.1016/j.specom.2009.05.006

ADDITIONAL READING

Abascal, J., Arrue, M., Garay, N., & Tomás, J. (2003). USERfit tool: A tool to facilitate design for all. In *Proceedings of the User Interfaces for All 7th International Conference on Universal Access: Theoretical Perspectives, Practice, and Experience* (pp. 141-152).

Adamo-Villani, N. (2006). A virtual learning environment for deaf children: Design and evaluation. *IJASET International Journal of Applied Science, Engineering, and Technology, 16,* 18–23.

Bickmore, T. W. (2003). *Relational agents: Effecting change through human-computer relationships.* PhD Thesis, Massachusetts Institute of Technology.

Brave, S., Nass, C., & Hutchinson, K. (2005). Computers that care: Investigating the effects of orientation of emotion exhibited by an embodied computer agent. *International Journal of Human-Computer Studies, 62*(2), 161–178. doi:10.1016/j.ijhcs.2004.11.002

Cole, R., Massaro, D., De Villiers, J., Rundle, B., Shobaki, K., & Wouters, J. … Solcher, D. (1999). New tools for interactive speech and language training: Using animated conversational agents in the classrooms of profoundly deaf children. In *Proceedings of ESCA/SOCRATES Workshop on Method and Tool Innovations for Speech Science Education* (pp. 45-52).

Correia, S., Pedrosa, S., Costa, J., & Estanqueiro, M. (2009). Little Mozart: Establishing long term relationships with (virtual) companions. In *Proceedings of the 9th International Conference on Intelligent Virtual Agents Intelligent Virtual Agents* (pp. 492-493). Berlin, Germany: Springer-Verlag.

Cosi, P., Delmonte, R., Biscetti, S., Cole, R. A., Pellom, B., & van Vuren, S. (2004). Italian literacy tutor: Tools and technologies for individuals with cognitive disabilities. In *Proceedings of the InSTIL/ICALL Symposium on Computer Assisted Learning.*

Dautenhahn, K., & Werry, I. (2004). Towards interactive robots in autism therapy: Background, motivation and challenges. *Pragmatics & Cognition, 12*(1), 1–35. doi:10.1075/pc.12.1.03dau

Di Blas, N., Paolini, P., & Sabiescu, A. (2010). Collective digital storytelling at school as a whole-class interaction. In *Proceedings of the 9th International Conference on Interaction Design and Children* (pp. 11-19). ACM.

Farr, W., Yuill, N., Harris, E., & Hinske, S. (2010). In my own words: configuration of tangibles, object interaction and children with autism. In *Proceedings of the 9th International Conference on Interaction Design and Children* (pp. 30-38). ACM.

Fransen, S., & Markopoulos, P. (2010). Let robots do the talking. In *Proceedings of the 9th International Conference on Interaction Design and Children* (pp. 59-68). ACM.

Garay, N., Cearreta, I., Lopez, J., & Fajardo, I. (2006). Human technology. *Assistive Technology and Affective Mediation. Special Issue on Human Technologies for Special Needs, 2*(1), 55–83.

Hanna, L., Risden, K., & Alexander, K. (1997). Guidelines for usability testing with children. *Interaction, 4*(5), 9–14. doi:10.1145/264044.264045

Koda, T., & Maes, P. (1996). Agents with faces: The effects of personification of agents. In *Proceedings of HCI'96* (pp. 98-103).

Lanyi, C., Geiszt, Z., Karolyi, P., Tilinger, A., & Magyar, V. (2006). Virtual reality in special needs early education. *The International Journal of Virtual Reality, 5*(4), 55–68.

Marco, J., Cerezo, E., & Baldassarri, S. (2007). *Desarrollo de interfaces naturales para aplicaciones educativas dirigidas a niños*. Paper presented at the VIII Congreso Internacional de Interacción Persona-Ordenador, Zaragoza, Spain.

Markopoulos, P., Read, J., & MacFarlane, S. (Eds.). (2008). *Evaluating children's interactive products: Principles and practices for interaction designers*. Morgan Kaufmann Pub.

Moridis, C., Klados, M., Terzis, V., Economides, A., Karabatakis, V., Karlovasitou, A., & Bamidis, P. (2010). Affective learning: Empathetic embodied conversational agents to modulate brain oscillations. In *Proceedings of the XII Mediterranean Conference on Medical and Biological Engineering and Computing* (pp. 675-678). Springer.

Paniagua Martín, F., Colomo Palacios, R., & García-Crespo, A. (2009). Mas: learning support software platform for people with disabilities. In *Proceedings of the 1st ACM SIGMM International Workshop on Media Studies and Implementations that Help Improving Access to Disabled Users* (pp. 47-52). ACM.

Picard, R. (2000). *Affective computing*. The MIT Press.

Raya, R., Ceres, R., Roa, J., & Rocon, E. (2010). Assessment of the involuntary motion of children with motor impairments to improve the accessibility of an inertial interface. In *Proceedings of the 9th International Conference on Interaction Design and Children* (pp. 128-137). ACM.

Rickel, J. (2001). Intelligent virtual agents for education and training: Opportunities and challenges. In *Proceedings of the Intelligent Virtual Agents* (pp.15-22). Springer.

San-Segundo, R., Cordoba, R., Ferreiros, J., Macias-Guarasa, J., Montero, J., Fernandez, F., & D'haro, L. (2009). Speech technology at home: Enhanced interfaces for people with disabilities. *Intelligent Automation and Soft Computing, 15*, 645–664.

Sanchez, J. (2008). User-centered technologies for blind children. *Human Technology Journal of Advertising Research, 45*(2), 96–122.

Sanders, L. (2008). An evolving map of design practice and design research. *Interaction, 15*(6), 13–17. doi:10.1145/1409040.1409043

Saz, O., Yin, S., Lleida, E., Rose, R., Vaquero, C., & Rodriguez, W. (2009). Tools and technologies for computer-aided speech and language therapy. *Speech Communication, 51*(10), 948–967. doi:10.1016/j.specom.2009.04.006

Tartaro, A. (2007). *Autorable virtual peers for children with autism. Doctoral Consortium Presentation at Human Factors in Computer Systems (CHI2007)*. Extended Abstracts.

Zaman, B., & Abeele, V. (2010). Laddering with young children in user experience evaluations: Theoretical groundings and a practical case. In *Proceedings of the 9th International Conference on Interaction Design and Children* (pp. 156-165). ACM.

Zhang, Z., Shrubsole, P., & Janse, M. (2010). Learning environmental factors through playful interaction. In *Proceedings of the 9th International Conference on Interaction Design and Children* (pp. 166-173). ACM.

KEY TERMS AND DEFINITIONS

Co-Design: We use co-design in a broader sense to refer to the creativity of designers and people not trained in design working together in the design development process.

Embodied Conversational Agent (ECA): A representation of a virtual human capable of engaging in conversation with humans by both understanding and producing speech, hand gestures and facial expressions.

Special Education: Special Education addresses the specific needs of children with disabilities so that they may achieve the maximum possible degree of personal development.

Section 2
Virtual Environments

Chapter 5
Virtual Environments Can Mediate Continuous Learning

Kiran Pala
International Institute of Information Technology, India

Suryakanth V Gangashetty
International Institute of Information Technology, India

ABSTRACT

In human beings, learning is a life-long and continuous process; it can encompass both active and passive activities in accordance with social changes and the development of society. In this era, the development and use of technologies have changed the face of information accessibility. Similarly, such technologies facilitate learners with new and different options to engage in learning through interactive tasks and content delivered through CD-ROMs, websites, communication software on the internet, and virtual games, which have had a significant impact on human learning and education. The significant question arises on which type of content and what way of representation of the content are required in this connection. Researchers need to reconsider any approach to teaching or providing platform to learners which is concerned with an explanation of how learning ability and development are prompted by an exposure to the target in view of the dramatic differences in experiences of learners. This chapter defines the concept of Virtual Environment (VE) based learning discussing how a VE differs from the traditional classrooms approaches. Thus, this chapter presents a unique framework and a formalism for interactive linearity or non-linearity in controlling the structure of learning activity or interaction. These activities aim at addressing the relationship between the main constructs targeted toward developing a VE. This chapter takes stock of various distributed models and projects a framework on how the learners can be engaged continuously in learning activities according to their previous linguistic and educational experiences. It also focuses on how a learner can be reported to the admin or tutor and self assessments.

DOI: 10.4018/978-1-4666-2530-3.ch005

Copyright © 2013, IGI Global. Copying or distributing in print or electronic forms without written permission of IGI Global is prohibited.

INTRODUCTION

"The illiterate of the 21st century," according to futurist Alvin Toffler, "will not be those who cannot read and write, but those who cannot learn, unlearn, and relearn." (Pond 2003, p.13)

In a world of globalization and reduced distances, technology has become a part of an individual's life and has created a new global economy. In the current circumstances, the nature and purpose of the educational system has changed due to the developmental implications of this new global economy, commerce and technology. The US Department of Labor (1999) has recognized and clarified that there is a need for a change to the nature of educational system to meet the demands of personal education and development with new avenues of technology. And the information availability has to be "powered by technology, fueled by information and driven by knowledge" (US Department of Labor, 1999). Especially, the application of information technology in education may be attributed to numerous factors such as linguistic heterogeneity of a country or region, specific social attitudes, or the desire to promote national identity etc.

To develop any country, it is necessary to develop the education system of that country. And to build a proper and effective education system, any country requires huge human resources and infrastructure which constitute basic needs. Producing effective human resources according to a nation's requirements and developmental strategies is a huge time taking process and in addition, a costlier matter. Concerns over the relevance of the quality and imperative of expanding learning opportunities like new skills or languages etc. to the development of an educational system should be squared up to the demands driven by the global changes.

Generally, VEs consist in not just real world simulations; internet or online based content or multimedia material which includes radio and television also fall under the gamut of VEs. More specifically, introducing VE is more important on grounds of justification derived from calibration of a multitude of learning requirements and personal demands. On the other hand, national educational policies can be formulated, in broader terms, on the basis of new techniques and strategies in the growth of learning channeled by the introduction of VEs. To be briefer, what can be said about VEs in precise terms is that VEs are high potential and powerful tools for enabling educational changes and reforms in the nature of learning and teaching methods which will thereby change the access and selection of content (Pala, In press).

This expansion of accessibility and availability of informational base with the help of various VEs strengthens the relevance of selection and informational access to the increasingly digital workplace, and beefs up learning quality by, among others, making teaching and learning an intertwined engaging and active process connected to real life. Getting information to learn is a linear activity, but learning, that is, interpreting and perceiving that information, is a non-linear activity. Also the perception of information depends, among other things, on the intensity of interest, that is, motivation toward the particular objective. If the objective is not of significance or need, the learner will take the input and interpret it narrowing down the space of interpretations. If, on the other hand, the learners' interest is more intensified, they can operate on the same information forming a plethora of connections to other sources. From another angle, if their needs are not of immediate requirement, the perceptual information will undergo a blocking and the cascaded information will be carried forward to later stages of learning.

A huge development of information and communication technologies (ICT) and their applications has penetrated into various domains of education, agriculture and other fields too. This has come as a new revolution especially in education and academics in which the implementation of ICT is maximized by using the relevant tools and equipments in teaching and learning process in the form of communication media.

Two types ICT can be distinguished on the basis of their application level:

- ICT as a subject i.e., studying computations and building ICTs
- ICT as a supportive tool in studies or learning (i.e., computer-based learning, education management information systems, presentation, research)

In contemporary conditions ICTs are able to support and facilitate a strong platform for satisfying the learning requirements available in world class settings for competency and performance-based curricula (Oliver, 2000). From many years academicians practiced and adopted these curricula with very limited technological resources and tools; now due to the widespread availability of ICTs, restrictions and impediments have been removed. In addition, new possibilities of implementing novel pedagogical methods now drive forms of further learning. With the growing concerns of learners about access to higher bandwidths, more direct forms of communication and access to rich sharable resources in different modes of content, the capability to support these quality learning settings by means of personalization of methods and content has had a drastic impact on the trajectories of learning in the real world. With the development of computer networks, the standalone computer has transformed into a technology that sustains the social networks of work and community.

Interaction with computers can enable people with shared interests to form and continue relationships within communities. As it has been observed that virtually based and mediated community members are more heterogeneous in social characteristics but often more homogeneous in interactive attitudes (Oliver, 2000; Oliver, 2002), these communities and individuals largely tend to occupy conforming space and time and they are

knit together in interaction and sharing their tasks, thoughts. Online communities have removed earlier fears of dehumanizing effects by providing emotional support and sociability as well as information and instrumental aid (Shurville & Browne, 2007). The number of relationships can expand at least tenfold when the virtual environment is introduced to mediate human communication processes for activities like organizing, filtering, summarizing, categorizing, directing, sequencing, and regulating. (Oliver, 2002) This underscores, to a large extent, the impact of online VEs on people, communities, organizations, and society, as well as the ability to "network" among larger groupings of individuals and to make any link available when needed (Oliver, 2002; Duffy & Cunningham, 1996). New software tools, applications and systems like social media, social networking websites for coordinating and interaction have alleviated some of the problems of interaction in (online) communication, say, information overload and propagated normless behavior. Aspects of social cognition become reconfigured with the changing scenario of social media that mediate forms of social relationships, interpersonal emotional bonds and negotiations which are redefined in a dynamic process of layering of social interests, understanding of socially engaged emotions, thoughts on issues that relate to trans-individual concerns about issues in jobs, education, recreation, sports and life in general.

In this 21st era, we have an availability of highly developed technologies like touch screen gadgets, and new generation spectrums pave the way for a curtailment of social presence and face-to-face meetings for engendering and nurturing primary group relationships thereby turning them into a myth. Nowadays, interaction through internet is possible for close relationships among general friends, personal friends as it also depends on the intention of the users and relatively on the act of spending time online to build relations or actualize communication of information. As has been suggested above, there is an emotional support factor that involves, though in a virtual world, smiles, hugs and kisses children receive from their parents and companionship:-), xxx, ◇,:-(etc. when real execution is not possible and the VE communication has reduced the distances between people. For example, using email to communicate when one or both are travelling, parents exchange, share their views and problems and offer solutions to children through monitoring, and thus make them understand new skills by supporting one another during parent-child crises. These new kinds of online ties are real and not virtually second-rate. One can easily observe through witness cases in marriages and court cases among former electronic pen pals, virtual classmates who hug each other on their graduation day that VEs are changing the shape of human life in remarkably visible ways never seen hitherto fore. The online VEs are being used in the same way as face-to-face meetings for interaction, and conveying a matrix of meanings socially constructed is thus used to sustain traditional community relationships (Oliver, 2002). The communication through VE provides information and social support in both specialized and broad senses to virtual space.

The interaction through VE can be classified as two types based on the response time in a broader sense: 1) Active interaction – mobile, video conferencing, online chatting etc. 2) Passive interaction –using emails, responding to forums questions, content reading on screen and replying, blogging etc. *"John Perry Barlow, has proclaimed, "With the development of the Internet and with the increasing pervasiveness of communication between networked computers, we are in the middle of the most transforming technological event since the capture of fire"* (Barlow, Birkets, Kelly, and Slouka,, 1995, p.40). On the other side, an ad for Mark Slouka's 1995 book War of the Worlds warned, "Face-to-face communication is Starr Roxanne Hiltz and Barry Wellman Despite the lack of physical space." (Hiltz, & Wellman, 1997). However, some of the debates about the nature of the internet have continued the

longstanding exchange between computerphiles and computerphobes (Hiltz & Wellman, 1997). In some of the domains, instead of face-to-face interaction, understanding by viewing the functionality is more important. For example, in forms of chemical reactions, formation of mathematical equations in mathematics and physics etc, -especially where the abstraction and imagination are involved-- the synchronization of audio and videos is distinctively required. VE facilitates learners to exchange emotional support, information, a sense of belonging and understanding of the meaning of the abstraction by using the synchronization of the content and context with different modes and actions of the relevant situation. For example, a chemical process of NACL (salt) displaying the exchange of chemical bonds and formation of salt with an animation of video and audio will be more understandable. An online VE combines the characteristics of online communities, interaction between individuals and computer-supported workgroups (Hiltz & Wellman, 1997). This should take care of "medium affect" in interactions between groups and individuals by virtue of the types of social structures emerging in postindustrial societies (Hiltz & Wellman, 1997).

In fact, VE is a solution to the huge demands of the knowledge society in terms of a fulfillment of educational needs and requirements and simultaneous personalization of education or learning. Here an attempt would be made to limit the present discussion to the design of a VE, as seen through the pedagogical telescope in a knowledge society. VEs have enabled learning through forms of multiple intelligences and different pedagogical methods like learning through games (simulation and web based); this enables active learning, that is, the reception of information processes through all senses. VE provides education policy makers, planners and practitioners with a systematic process to formulate, plan and evaluate education development programs enhanced by information and communication technologies (ICTs) (Hiltz & Wellman, 1997; Paquette, 2002; Girard, Paquette,

Miara & Lundgren, 1999). The following factors need to be probed and factored in for the purpose of building VEs using ICT for learning or teaching. The major roles and responsibilities are: (Dev/World Bank, 2007).

- Mapping the national, technological and educational situations
- Formulation and assessment of ICT-enhanced programs
- Plans for physical and human requirements
- Plans for ICT-enhanced content
- Generation of program costs
- Creation of a master plan
- Monitoring, implementation, effectiveness and impact.

Merits of Using Virtual Environments in Education

Virtual environments (VE) reduce the training costs in many ways, including that of enabling the cost-savings of e-learning (e.g. less travel, accommodation, more work time available, lower teaching costs, etc) as well as streamlining the administration of training programs across different organizations. Notable merits of using VEs in learning are (Adv/Micro, 2011; LMS/time, 2011; LMS/Simply, 2011).

Consolidation of all Training Information into one System: There are significant benefits to having all the training information in a single, consolidated system. At a glance, we can review and report on the status of company-wide training programs, identifying the staff who have completed certain qualifications, and much more. Instead of searching through several disparate systems and paper files to find what one needs, VE puts all training information at the fingertips.

Centralized Learning and Environment to Ensure Consistency: The information or content in VE is available to all individuals 24X7 from any location with web access. Multiple users can access the VE at any given point in time. VE ensures consistency in delivery and evaluation since each user sees the exact same material in the exact same manner and can be evaluated through common pre-testing and/or post-testing methods.

Tracking and Reporting for Enhanced Performance: VE allows highly secured and reliable tracking of the learners' learning path and progress against the learning path, review or assessment records. Based on their performance and necessity, the tutor of the VE can offer different levels in that course by adjusting itself to the individually customized requirements of the learners in a more adaptive manner.

Immediate Capabilities Evaluation: VE allows a tutor or evaluator to review, by periodically scheduled assessments, the retention level of the learner in actual time. Learners have to be also evaluated prior to their choosing the content components. As in educational institutes, learners review their performance based on the tests and quizzes.

Simplifying Learning Processes: The highly user experienced VE is easy to use and is instructed very well, a new user is able to use it easily. VE accommodates various features- documentation and administration, recording and tracking events and programs, classroom learning, to name a few. VE is an alternative for many learners because of its pragmatic and persuasive approach.

Easy to Use: VE is easy to use for the new user. VE provides user friendly interfaces to access the content and interact with tutors or other participants. A novice user is also comfortable with using this.

Direct to the "Point": Only relevant information is included in the modules that the users have access to. They can be assured of the fact that it will be direct to the point and they will only be learning what they really need so they will not be wasting any time.

Control on System: Learning strategies can be managed easily according to one's unique learning needs. Users can spend more time on areas in which they have difficulties. Modules are available at any time at their home or other best suitable places. VE gives them the power to manipulate their learning pace.

Minimizes Photocopying: Learners are able to get their homework resources and assignments at their workplace or at home online thanks to VEs. Giving learners texts online is not only helpful with regards to minimizing photocopying, but also reserves classroom time for other productive learning activities.

Learner can Easily Access Missed Classes: The advantage of having accessible resources is that when learners miss their classes, they can immediately find out exactly what they missed. They also communicate with their tutors and classmates online if they have questions.

Security and Privacy: Password security gives authorized users to access the information and courses. Administrators may, in such a case, grant partial or full access rights based on individual roles. It is easy to maintain a high privacy of learners' accounts and their credentials by not giving access to any other individuals even for viewing purpose.

Organization: Organization is particularly valuable with large class sizes or for large companies. A VE will take over and coordinate all of the administrative work. A good system will allow every step of the organizational process to be done online from enrolling students and employees to setting reminders for projects and deadlines as well as taking exams and accepting homework assignments. A VE will even grade the work.

Multifunctional: A VE has evolved to do just anything we could imagine. Not only do VEs work well for distance learning in colleges and universities, but they can be used for corporate training, pre-employment testing and also in cutting down the heavy amount of administrative work.

Access to Multiuser: VEs provide training for more people at the same time in a quick manner with the same consistency and 24X7.

Ease of Upgradation of Content: VEs are highly flexible for social interaction. VEs tend to

be course centered rather than student centered. At this time, VE does not accommodate a complete range of teaching styles, though a lot of promising opportunities and possibilities lie ahead.

Bi-directional Interaction: VEs facilitates bi-directional interaction; this in can be active and passive according to the response time. Active interaction will be facilitated by using online collaboration tools, including chat rooms, video-conferencing, direct calling and sms sent to tutors or participants. Passive interaction will take place with online collaboration tools which include posts to forums, blogs, feedback messages, and emails etc. To make this interaction VE brings individuals and groups together irrespective of culture and geographical space.

Limitations

VEs have the following limitations (LMS/blog, 2011; Per/minu, 2011; Dis/e-lms, 2011):

- There are fewer possibilities of face-to-face instructions with the instructor especially by means of a personalization of environment whenever the learner requires it.
- Reducing fraud tolerances in VEs requires tasks like logging into others' accounts and more security barricades. Security of data and personal information adds up to the paraphernalia of stringent security measures. While some applications include privacy settings, these are generally not subject to the institution's authentication protocols.
- Using a VE is difficult for computer illiterates.
- Regular review of content is required to reduce redundancy and out-of-datedness.
- In VEs we have all types of content; but filtering according to domain is very important and for this, rich computational resources are required. Building domain specific resources for different modes of

content will be expensive and a time consuming task.

- Initial development of VE is not cost effective for small audiences and offline VEs.
- Compatibility issues like localization of the content, technology differences of end-users' computers, representation of content on interfaces and operating system compatibilities etc. can also hamper the working of VEs.
- Slow or unreliable internet connections, power-offs, poor maintenance of third party applications, poor design of interface navigations can be frustrating.
- Some courses such as traditional hands-on courses like engineering, drawing etc. can be difficult to simulate in VEs.

However, the experience of introducing different ICTs in the classroom and other educational settings all over the world over the past several decades suggests that the full realization of the potential educational benefits of ICTs is not automatic. Rather, they come as an operationally constrained outcome of more adapted techniques and processes of optimization that come with reduced costs with increasing robustness. In addition, innovative online based educational programs are often implemented so that they come within the reach of the larger masses, and it is also targeted to promote proficiency in various fields and wider communication.

Nowadays, learning inside or outside classrooms cannot be any more linear and indicative of information transmission activity. It has changed the face and pace towards educational entertainment field, for example: Khan Academy or Edututor etc. Educational and academic organizations have recognized that learning is continuous process and it requires continuous interaction with the environment within which learners are growing and living. In such situations, the importance of the environment has increased significantly in all kinds of learning. Especially, personalization

of learning has serious needs as it has made a significant mark. On other hand, there is a serious problem in the management of human resources in most developing countries. Therefore, virtual environments play a significant role in fulfilling the needs of a country's educational growth and development.

However, even if technologies have developed to a large extent to make up what modern life is today, there are some questions that need to be addressed in the process of designing and development of an alternative learning platform that can constitute a virtual environment. How are this interaction and virtual environments related? What are the factors that affect the learner in continuous interactions with virtual environment? How are those factors interrelated with the growth of learning? What are the detailed forms of such interactions? Examples from social media and networking websites data can certainly be given in this regard. What is also interesting is that linguistic structures that constitute the cognitive structures of mind are formatted and re-formatted in response to such interaction with the environment as is clearly visible in cases of visuo-spatially mediated lexical learning. VEs are not only 3D simulations; they are also web-based or online applications. This is where courses or learning events are designed, constructed and delivered using VE and many of its communication possibilities are available in this fashion. Many models and methods such as delivery models like high-tech classrooms, distributed classrooms, multimedia individual instruction, on-line teaching, personalization platforms, and communities of practice and performance support systems are available for these learning events (Pala, Singh and Ganagashetty, 2011).

We would like to compare the main features of the existing models and present an architecture that can support interaction with environment. The choice of a combination of delivery models is determined by decisions based on instructional engineering and cognitively oriented learning strategies. Such strategies have major consequences on the selection of resources for information processing, collaboration, assistance and management of the learning activities through a virtual environment for human learning processes through interaction. This interaction process can be integrated in different courses in a flexible manner to open means of facilitating learners' needs and understanding.

BACKGROUND

According EnGauge the 21st century skills are digital age literacy, inventive thinking, higher-order thinking and sound reasoning, effective communication, and high productivity. Here functional literacy, visual literacy, scientific literacy, technological literacy, information literacy, cultural literacy, and global awareness as a part of the digital age literacy itself and all other functional properties have been shown in Table 1 (Blurton, 1999; Tinio, 2003). These days, using of technologies related to ICTs in educational institutes are more ubiquitous.

Institutes have been better prepared to make the current generations of learners more efficient, and thus effective use of these mechanisms is seen as representing a competitive edge in an increasingly globalizing job market and social needs in

Table 1. Technological literacy in the digital age (Tinio, 2003)

Digital Age Literacy	
Functional Literacy	Ability to decipher meaning and express ideas in a range of media; this includes the use of images, graphics, video, charts and graphs or visual literacy
Scientific Literacy	Understanding of both the theoretical and applied aspects of science and mathematics
Technological Literacy	Competence in the use of information and communication technologies
Information Literacy	Ability to find, evaluate and make appropriate use of information, including via the use if ICTs
Cultural Literacy	Appreciation of the diversity of cultures
Global Awareness	Understanding of how nations, corporations, and communities all over the world are inter-related
Inventive Thinking	
Adaptability	Ability to adapt and manage in a complex, interdependent world
Curiosity	Desire to know
Creativity	Ability to use imagination to create new things
Risk-taking	Ability to take risks
Higher-Order Thinking Creative Problem-Solving and Logical Thinking that Result in Sound Judgments	
Effective Communication	
Teaming	Ability to work in a team
Collaboration and Interpersonal Skills	Ability to interact smoothly and work effectively with others
Personal and Social Responsibility	Be accountable for the way they use ICTs and to learn to use ICTs for the public good
Interactive Communication	Competence in conveying, transmitting, accessing and understanding information
High Productivity	Ability to prioritize, plan, and manage programs and projects to achieve the desired results. Ability to apply what they learn in the classroom to real-life contexts to create relevant, high-quality products

the market. For that the promotion of potential ICTs in education is tied to its use as a tool for raising acquisition quality, including encouraging the shift of a learner-centered environment from a simply teacher-centered pedagogy (Tinto, 2003)—which, in its worst form, is characterized by memorization and rote learning.

Recent research has developed various emerging pedagogies which we can combine with ICTs and enable in VE. We have listed here the emerging pedagogy advantages and functionalities with ICTs.

Active Learning: It is more relevant to learner's real-life problems so that abstraction will be lower and learners will engage in solving problems practically. This makes sure that the learner will be far from memorization and rote learning. Here the VEs can be used to test the learners' capability of calculations and analysis of information. This facilitates learners' understanding of the construction of meanings of new information. Availability and accessibility through VEs is "just-in-time" learning i.e. learners can choose what to learn when they need to learn it (Johnson, and Johnson, and Smith, 1991; Tinio, 2003).

Collaborative Learning: Here the VEs facilitate interaction and cooperation among learners and mentors regardless of where they are (Pala, Singh and Gangashetty, 2011). In this case VEs provide support to learners to access different cultures and people. Hence learners can enhance their communicative skills as well global awareness. What appears to be an obstacle is that modeling (simulations) the real-world interactions is not possible in this method. But one advantage is that in this method learners' learning space is so vast it includes peers, mentors and experts from various fields (Bruffee, 1999, Tinio 2003).

Creative Learning: By enabling VEs to adapt to this pedagogy, we can see that problem solving abilities will be more effective. This is because of the fact that in this method the learner will manipulate the received information and tries to provide own solutions which are relevant to the

real-world products. On top of this, here learners apply their critical thinking abilities on the received information rather than doing just regurgitation of the information (Torrance, and Myers, 1970).

Integrative Learning: It promotes a thematic, integrative approach to learning (Klein, 2005; Tinio, 2003). In this approach understanding issues and positions contextually is more independent. It eliminates the artificial separation between different disciplines, and between theory and practice that characterizes the traditional classroom approach (Bannan-Ritland, 2003).

Evaluative learning: It is a learner oriented approach and diagnostic. It is different from static, text or print-based educational technologies; VE enables learner to encourage learning through many different learning pathways and many different articulations of knowledge (Pelgrum and Anderson, 1999). VEs also enable learners to explore and discover, rather than merely listen and remember, the content (Tinio, 2003).

Various researches have shown that the appropriate use of technologies can catalyze the paradigmatic shift in both content and pedagogy methods (Paquette, 2002). If designed and implemented properly, technology-supported reforms in education can promote the interaction for acquisition of the knowledge and skills that will empower learners for lifelong learning. Continuous learning per se requires, among other things, an enriched process of socialization and transmission of cultural structures into minds through elaborate forms of education, rules, mores and a whole matrix of experiential induction in the cognitive niche. From the beginning of the human life interaction with environment is an important part of this process. Interaction between learner groups and individuals brings together such processes of culturalization and socialization into a greater cohesion. Interaction requires that an environment be real or virtual which includes email, bulletin boards and newsgroups, synchronous chat systems, computer conference systems, group decision support systems, and most re-

Table 2. A comparison of a traditional pedagogy and an emerging pedagogy enabled by ICTs as VE (Tinio, 2003)

Aspect	Less ('traditional pedagogy')	More ('emerging pedagogy')
Active	Activities prescribed by teacher Whole class instruction Little variation in activities Pace determined by the programme	Activities determined by learners Small groups Many different activities Pace determined by learners
Collaborative	Individual Homogenous groups Everyone for him/herself	Working in teams Heterogeneous groups Supporting each other
Creative	Reproductive learning Apply known solutions to problems	Productive learning Find new solutions to problems
Integrative	No link between theory and practice Separate subjects Discipline-based Individual teachers	Integrating theory and practice Relations between subjects Thematic Teams of teachers
Evaluative	Teacher-directed Summative	Student-directed Diagnostic

cently, homepages on the World-Wide Web etc. (Hiltz, and Wellman, 1997; Blurton, 1999; Paquette, 2002; Pala, Singh and Gangashetty, 2011). Some of the systems are specifically structured to maintain that kind of permanent discussions between communities. These days this kind of communities has increased actively sustaining what is necessary for them to continue (Hiltz, and Wellman, 1997).

Such communities are majorly using, sharing and exchanging the information. In this process a huge interaction takes place that leads one to learn some new information about the particular domain which they are dealing with through interaction. Also, there is a need to understand the construction of meaning of the particular domain or topic embedded in the specific domain.

Such community-based meanings and their forms vary in constrained ways, if not wildly. They need to be understood and harnessed if their richness adds to much of what one brings to bear on the task and process of learning things by means of a robust scaffolding accumulated from various sources. After the entry of the technology into human's personal and professional life, the definition of community has expanded to the virtual too. The virtual communities have grown up through:

- Conferencing, groupware, and email systems in many corporations (Rheingold, 1993).
- Email and bulletin boards in such diverse non-corporate groups for communica-

Figure 1. Interaction is a bridge between learner and environment in learning process. Interaction is an activity which can be an act of observing.

TOURO COLLEGE LIBRARY

tion between meetings and for connecting to dispersed local groups. (Wellman, and Salaff, et al, 1996).

- Interactive Web pages by organizations as diverse as the IEEE, ACM for exchange of information among members or customers. (Hiltz, and Wellman, 1997).
- Exchanging daily email digests filled with hundreds of messages.
- Virtual environments such as multi-user domains (MUDs), in which participants enter and which broadly encompass highly involving social worlds, like gaming social media, networking, professional communities (Rheingold, 1993; Hiltz, and Wellman, 1997).
- Temporary project teams formed around specific tasks, meeting primarily online, and then dissolving when the project is over (Hiltz, and Wellman, 1997).
- Courses and degree programs through the Virtual Classrooms serving for the past decade as a detailed example of the nature of communities on the net. (Hiltz, and Wellman, 1997).

Given that community and individuals are intertwined in a complex network of exchange, transfer, manipulation and mutual shaping of information and meanings, the role of VEs becomes very significant in that a VE facilitates a community and individuals to extend educational opportunities in both formal and informal ways. These ways can be summarized below:

- Access to a variety of information sources irrespective of time and space;
- Access to a variety of information forms and types to unlimited number;
- Learner-centered learning settings based on information access and inquiry;
- Environments centered on problem-centered and inquiry-based activities;

- Authentic settings of content and learners accounts;
- Tutors as coaches and mentors rather than content experts;
- Privacy and reliability of the content and learners activities,
- Adaptable nature of learners' activities;
- Ease of activation of learners' ability based assessments;
- Possibility of implementing different types of curricula like competency and performance based and pedagogy methods (Stephenson, 2001)

Lexical Learning and Multilingualism

Lexicon is an important part of language and lexical competence is at the cross-section of language, cognition and environment. This means that lexical learning is both biologically and culturally constrained. Hence, here we would like to concentrate on vocabulary learning of a language, i.e., construction of meanings of lexical items in non-native languages as a subject in the context of multilingualism. In a world of globalization that reduces distances and removes cultural barricades, multilingualism has become a very important skill/trait. However, natural multilingualism is still not so common. In other words to become a multilingual, most people have to learn new languages as non-native speakers (Pala and Ganagashetty, In Press).

Going beyond more than two languages is very common for many people all over the world. This is quite visible in multilingual and multicultural countries; for example, India has almost 13 scheduled languages which have evolved with different cultures (Emeneau, 1956, 1980). These days most of the countries demand that their people need to know more than two languages. This demand arrives from commerce and trade between countries and states. Due to historical, political, socio-economic and cultural reasons two or more languages are used in different spheres of life, but it is also common in the case of individuals who need to communicate in several languages and in schools where two or more languages are taught.

Learning is a humans' basic attitude and it relates to aptitude as well; it largely depends on the socio-cultural term "purpose". It is well-known that adults' learning another language other than their first language has been considered to be a second language (L2). Importantly, the process of gaining L2 competence is affected by many variables like psychological, linguistic, socio-economical, anthropological and neurobiological factors and constraints (status, identity, previous education, culture etc) which are, of course, dynamic (Saville-Troike, M., 2006). Related to this are cases of learning style and learning strategies. Language learning styles and strategies appear to be among the most important variables influencing performance in a second language (Oxford & Rebecca 1989). Every human being has his/her own styles and strategies of learning (Felder, R.M. and Soloman, B.A., 1993). The learning style encompasses aspects of the learner's cognitive, affective, and behavioral elements (Oxford & Ehrman, 1988). Learning styles mediate between two major modules in brain and behavior of a human being: comprehension (input) and production (output) of language.

Learning a language especially the lexical items i.e. vocabulary is not like adding another digit to the existing set of digits as in computer or in a digital machine (for example 1+1=2). It is a different process i.e. understanding of the meaning is a very important constraint in the learning process. In the process of understanding or construction of meaning for a specific situation or for an object or a lexical item, personal experience, exposure to the relevant labeled or coined word, or use of the particular lexical item are necessary in human learning. Once the exposure to the lexical item happens through an experience or use of the label, conceptualization of the word starts taking place at that time. Here the perceptual process of the word will also guide lexical learning in initiating an interaction with the environment in all conditions

wherever this word or the lexical item is needed or such situation occurs. The other vital information that is claimed to be facilitatory in helping adult learners learn the vocabulary of the target language is the unique background of individual learners. The word 'background' is used here to mean the sum total of psycho-social, behavioral, educational and cultural experiences that the learners bring to bear upon non-native language learning in general. Any learning tool or something that purports to teach vocabulary learning can do better if such information is optimized for the individual needs of adult language learners. Learning vocabulary of a language essentially involves understanding and construction of a meaning of the particular lexical item. This construction of meaning is directly related to the perception of the learners in the terms specified here.

In a very general sense, languages shape and are also shaped by the perceptual organization in human beings. It is more so, when this perceptual organization is molded, formatted and changed by the surrounding linguistic and cultural settings. Thus, perception and language are related in many ways. Research on how language connects to the world has been from the perspective of how lexicon mediates spatial, temporal and causal relations (Miller and Johnson-Laird, 1976; Langacker, 1999), how the structure of language has a parallel reflection in socio-cultural practices (Jackendoff, 2007), and also how language relates to aspects of cognitive processing including memory, vision etc (Talmy, 2000; Pinker, 2007). Relevant though these issues are, however here we will be concerned primarily about how perception of the world affects communication about it. This issue has different nuances associated with it.

Neurobiological Aspects of Language Development

Language development follows a specific trajectory. It is neither random, nor very systematic. Language development from a cognitive point of

Figure 2. Human language learning effects with various factors, in a broad sense deriving from various fields; the above diagram shows how each field is interrelated and interaction with the other in terms of human language learning

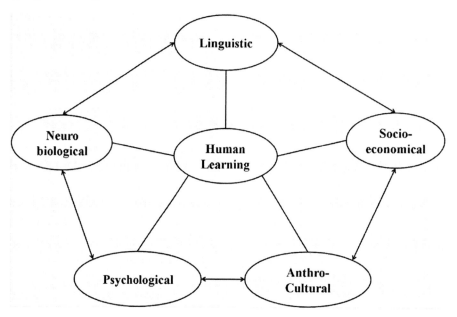

view can be looked at just like other ontogenetic developments of other cognitive modules such as vision, memory, motor system. But the patterns of language development closely correlate with those of other cognitive modules in the context of maturational constraints that organize brain development (Stemmer and Whitaker, 2008).

Children's babbling stages start relatively early in life around 1-3 months of life. At this stage children are all uniform in discriminating phonemes of any language, which suggests that there may be some innate neural structures for auditory-acoustic-phonetic tasks in human temporal lobe. So phonological development starts pretty early in the ontological trajectory of a child's linguistic profile. As children start producing single words, both phonological development at the suprasegmental level (prosody, rhythm etc.) and lexicon building get a head start along with the ongoing conceptual development. It has been found that the lexico-semantic event related potential (ERP) N400 component emerges around 12–14 months of children's life, thus indicating that lexical se-

mantics is closely followed by early phonological development. LAN and P600 responses which are an index of syntactic maturity emerge a little around 24-30 months of life in children (Stemmer and Whitaker, 2008). All this suggests that there is a certain well-defined sequence in which language development occurs and this mirrors development in neural structures; neural structures underlying language processing also follow such a pattern. Neurofunctional brain lateralization of language areas shows how a symmetrically organized functional brain gradually becomes reorganized into an asymmetrically organized brain with the left hemisphere taking the lead in language processing. Brain structures known for language processing like Broca's area, Wernicke's area, auditory cortex all emerge in close synchrony as language develops through its own patterned sequence of development of components of language; and growth in perisylvian areas in both hemispheres goes on till puberty (Locke, 1997; Paradis, 2004). Along with the development in motor skills, child's language development is coupled to these areas which become more and more specialized (though not exclusively) for language. During language acquisition, human brain not only continually reorganizes itself around localized structures, but also becomes more neurofunctionally robust, efficient and patterned.

Innateness, Language Development, and Brain

The fact that after brain lesions, language gets relocated and reorganized in the contralateral hemisphere shows that language module whatever it grows to become is not fully genetically hardwired. Neuroplasticty in language development suggests that even if there might be some genetic guidance in neural growth, language localization in brain is not fully innate as far as one considers innate structures underlying language module in brain. Innate principles guiding language acquisition have also been advanced as an argument for nativism, but closer examination of this issue also points to the same direction. Even if there might be some circumscribed period within which genes map out but do not determine the contours of language development, there is no fixed or stable critical period for language learning/acquisition (Herschensohn, 2007). Similarly, Newport, Bavelier and Neville (2001) have also argued for differential patterns of critical period for different components of language: vocabulary learning seems to be far less resistant to critical period, but morphology and syntax are less resilient with respect to their learning by late learners and adults. All this indicates that neurofunctional system for language module is more flexible and plastic and less innate. And this is the reason why children's acquisition of language is driven by such neuroplastic system which is sensitive to the grammatical patterns of the language children are exposed to. In some sense, language is neither innate nor learned. There happens a wiring of neural structures underlying language development and it is neurofunctionally grown in humans (Torey, 2009).

Memory-Language Associations

Language is organized as a relation between form and meaning (Cruse, DA, 1986, Lantolf, J.P., 2009); it comprises a lexicon that contains words along with conceptual information, and a grammar for forming/constructing the rule-governed forms. Language is instantiated in the brain structures which subserve other functions as well. There is a division of labor in human memory in terms of declarative vs. procedural (DP) distinction (Ullman, M.T., 2001a, 2001b). Declarative memory is for facts and events that are memorized; while the use of knowledge for implementation in real world involves procedural memory and it depends largely on the temporal-parietal/medial-lobe substrates of declarative memory system marked as the mental lexicon (Ullman, M.T., 2001a, 2001b; Cruse, DA, 1986). The learning and execution of motor and cognitive skills, especially those involving sequences of grammatical rules are processed by frontal basal-ganglia as it is known as the procedural memory system. The knowledge of these rules may be defined as the mental grammar. This mental grammar, which subserves the combination of lexical items into complex representations, depends on a distinct neural system.

In later stages i.e. after puberty the activity of memory will be more procedural than declarative. The procedural memory is directly linked to motor-sensory activity; the remembrance of activity is more of precision than of recalling. For example, bike riding is an activity which is related to motor sensory unit; the rider after knowing i.e. experiencing the bike riding on a particular road initially keeps focused more on the road than at later stages of driving. Because the experienced information has been molded as an information structure within the procedural memory, the experience of the word meaning will similarly give off higher precision than the memorized word in the construction of a sentence when the experience is proceduralized, so to say.

Rehearsal, Narration, and Meaning Construction

Rehearsal activity is required for an understanding of the meaning and construction of a sentence. Whenever a person listens to or perceives a sound as a linguistic input, he/she will implement a rehearsal of the activity in his/her thoughts, and thereby this rehearsal will help him/her in use of this new sound in different nuances and situations. Reading the text a number of times can be of help in memorization but construction of the sentence will be possible when the learner understands the meaning of the word. Any rehearsal activity has to be cast in the inner thought processes which manipulate the symbolic items and constructions through an iterative procedure of linguistic processing. Learning and interaction with the environment have an intricate role in such processes as they modulate the learners in orienting themselves to the relevant items of linguistic exposure. Thus, content informationally received through senses depends on domain knowledge. Activation of senses, in turn, depends on visual, tactile, auditory modes etc.

Interpretation happens with the text narration of the stimuli. The learner's interpretation is to take place against their previous background i.e. experience and it will change only after the learner comes to know the use of the particular text. For example, a doctor, a lawyer and a house-wife etc. will vary in their interpretation of text as a function of how they assign specific meanings to the texts that they come to bring under their interpretations.

Outline of Current Learning Methods and Models

In humans, learning is non-linear activity and every human being receives information from various resources through their senses. These senses become activated on different occasions. Senses and memory are related and directly depend on each other. This becomes evident through a description of the learning activities of the following kind.

Formal Learning: Class room learning activities like face-to-face teaching or interaction inside the classroom and exams etc. are a linear learning activity. Here a clear purpose has been described before the learner enters the activity, for example, getting a certificate or degree or diploma. It was defined in a particular period.

Informal Learning: In outside classroom activities like distance-mode studies, self-learning etc. sometimes the goal has been defined but not in a complete manner. It is not defined within the limits of a definite time bound. It is a non-linear form of learning and not necessarily aimed at a certificate or diploma or a degree. In this approach one can be a tutor or mentor himself/herself.

Instructionalism: A traditional way of learning is instructionalism which is the most common approach in the educational sector. The idea of instructionalism is "to instruct", to build the knowledge of facts, relations, rules or principle of one kind or another per se; so it is complementary to training (Instru/cypr, 2011). The perspective is to focus on teaching but not learning and it is completely teacher-centered. It is a process in which being situated in a physical classroom with an instructor or teacher and informing the learners or students of the stuff in a particular domain are commonplace (Harel, and Papert, 1990). During the instruction, it is not necessary to interact with the learners, and there is a pervasive feeling that the instructor has the appropriate knowledge and others have not. In this method "instructor" thinks that the teacher 'pours' the knowledge into the student (Instru/cypr, 2011).

As we discussed above, education has taken a paradigm shift towards learner-centered personalization, virtual classrooms etc. using ICTs and their supplementary components. In such a context, in contrast to instructionalism various pedagogical methods have been proposed and implemented.

Project-based Learning: Project Based Learning is a teaching and learning model that emphasizes student-centered instruction by assigning projects. It is a dynamic approach to teaching in which students explore real-world problems and challenges (Hmelo-Silver, 2004), simultaneously developing cross-curriculum skills while working in small collaborative groups. Projects put students in an active role—problem solver, decision maker, investigator, documentarian (Poikela, and Nummenmaa, 2006). Project based learning has some challenges, nonetheless: (Blumenfeld, and et al 1991; Poikela, and Nummenmaa, 2006)

- Recognizing situations that make a way for good projects
- Structuring problems as learning opportunities
- Collaborating with colleagues to develop interdisciplinary projects
- Managing the learning process
- Integrating technologies wherever appropriate
- Developing authentic assessments

Procedural Learning: Procedural Based Learning Approach necessarily involves being able to solve a certain task by applying a procedure. Learners must *demonstrate* their ability to select/apply a procedure. As procedural learning is a knowledge of how to do something, such learning enables a student to apply a rule. It is the method of learning in which problems are solved by set of rules, algorithms, and procedures (Yates, and Kenneth, 2007).

Distance Learning: In the educational sphere, it is a method which involves interaction at a distance between instructors and learners, and enables a timely reaction of the instructor to learners (Honeyman and Miller, 1993); posting or broadcasting learning materials to learners is not distance learning. Instructors must be involved in receiving feedback from learners. In terms of VEs, distance learning includes internet-based live instructor broadcasts, video-conferencing,

chat and scheduled online conference discussions, and even e-mail courses or discussions.

Learning through Multimedia: Multimedia is a presentation of content that relies on both text and graphics. It is a combination of various digital media types, such as text, images, sound, and video, into an integrated multisensory inter-active application or presentation for conveying a message or information to an audience (Mayer and Moreno, 1998; Shank, 2005).

In multimedia learning environments, the learner engages in three important cognitive processes. 1) *Selecting* is applied to incoming verbal information to yield a text base and is applied to incoming visual information to yield an image base. 2) *Organizing* is applied to the word base to create a verbally-based model of the to-be-explained system and is applied to the image base to create a visually-based model of the to-be-explained system. Finally, the third process, *integrating*, occurs when the learner builds connections between corresponding events (or states or parts) in the verbally-based model and the visually-based model. It is better to present an explanation in words and pictures than solely in words (Mayer and Moreno, 1998; Dillenbourg, and et al, 2002; Shank, 2005; Pala, Singh and Gangashetty, 2011)

Multimodal Learning: Multimodal learning involves relating information from multiple sources. For example, images and 3D depth scans are correlated at the first-order level as depth discontinuities often manifest as strong edges in images (Ngiam, and Khosla, et al., 2011).

Learning through Games: Conventional classroom based learning has some limitations that make it unsuitable, especially in case of vocabulary learning for academic domains. In this process virtual games have largely paved the way for the shift of the learning paradigm. 1) In Image Identification game, a sequence of images will be displayed and the user has to identify the names of the images and has to choose from the available options for each image. 2) Word Matching game is about matching words. 3) Image-Name Matching games are a matching kind of game except that in one set all the images will be given and in the other set the names of the images will be given in a jumbled order. 4) In Deep Meaning game, the user has to find the correct meaning of the given word among the options. An image is presented and the user has to select the correct explanation out of the ones given (Pala, Singh and Gangashetty, 2011).

LEARNING IS AN ENTERTAINMENT ACTIVITY

VEs will open up new horizons for teaching, entertainment, and learning (bi-directional) in a continuous process. Typical VEs are very complex and a VE may consist of several components including speech recognition, gesture recognition, language understanding, dialogue management, emotion, reasoning, planning, inference, verbal and nonverbal output, (Gratch et al 2007a, 2007b). VEs can serve as colleagues or advisors in training, helping a student to study language and culture (Johnson, et al 2005; Johnsen et al, 2005) or negotiation skills (Traum et al 2005). A VE can also help physicians in treating psychological disorders (Kenny et al, 2009). It can work as virtual guides and helps in designing (Jan et al 2009; Bartle, 2004), museum documents (Swartout et al, 2010).Thus, VEs pave the way for more sophisticated handling and compatibility in getting information from various sources and different formats. Every human being is unique in terms of what he/she understands and how he/she interprets things. But with respect to receiving information from the environment, humans use the commonly denominated sensory input mechanisms. VEs capitalize on this fact and are designed with this in mind. In a way, here different formats of the same information mediated by VEs enable a better and more comfortable interaction between humans and machines. As discussed above, in humans learnt information is linked with memories and formed as cognitive structures with respect to how such structures enact their roles in perception, mapping, information processing etc. Additionally, human beings have a very strong tendency toward adaptation. This tendency helps them in better understanding and learning. However, to inculcate such processes upon machines, we have to build machines that can learn in such a niche. This process will take place fast if VEs are better optimized and adapted for such tasks as demanding a high degree of sophistication in the interaction scenarios.

But undoubtedly, taking VEs to such an interactive and adaptation level will require a huge access to knowledge processing that can have broader implications for how humans interact, enact and evolve in their ecological niche where we live to grow, learn and act. In order to achieve this, most of the time from engineering perspectives we have had to depend on ways to compile and process the behavioral and linguistic data (structured and unstructured). Language processing techniques also are just one of the approaches toward such a goal. This interaction can make it possible for one to approach the imagined goal of VEs perhaps in a more efficient way. In a more practical sense, the interaction can be both formal and informal i.e. in class room or outside of the classroom in educational settings. To reach the imagined VE goal, an interaction between human and machine is required and in fact changes in pedagogical settings will bring such a platform to make this kind of condition viable.

These days World Wide Web (WWW) is so common that an increasing number of users are building ways in using this web technology for both developing and using web applications. That is why it is quite clear that *"Virtual Environments (VE)"* can be a good environment for creating interactive conditions between machines and human beings; for this purpose VEs require a lot of effort in terms of time and human data for simulation. The effective construction of a VE for an educational system is so complex that we require a multifaceted process in accordance with the interaction method that involves not just technology—indeed, given enough initial capital, and proper human resources for developing and verifying content at initial state, developing application, getting the technology is the easiest part—but also curriculum and pedagogy, institutional readiness, tutor competencies, and long-term financing, among others (Dillenbourg, 2002).

We should be aware of the broad issues in the use of ICTs (effectiveness, cost, equity, and sustainability) and the challenges those policy-makers have to take in decision making –educational policy and planning, infrastructure, capacity building, language and content, and financing; and learning factors (resources and constraints) are all involved in education and construction of a VE. Apart from these, some of the principles involved in the optimization of VEs are also of paramount importance.

Principles for the Design of Virtual Environments

Education development succeeds or fails on the basis of the nature and quality of educational policies and strategies and sound practices (Paquette, 2002; Dillenbourg, 2002). Technology is only a tool; no technology can fix a bad educational philosophy or compensate for bad practice. But technology can facilitate people to help accelerate learners' learning process, and in fact, there is a huge scope for understanding the meaning of learning in a broader space. ICTs are not one monolithic entity; they differ in their properties, scope, and potential. For example, an audio technology deals with sound only and a video technology depicts sound and motion. Similarly, a CD provides multimedia digital content and a web version adds interactivity. But a VE can bring them together on a single platform. To bring out such a platform, we propose that ten major principles should be taken into account

while designing and developing a VE (Hiltz, and Wellman, 1997; Girard, Paquette, Miara and Lundgren 1999; Paquette, 2002; Dillenbourg, 2002; Johnson, and Wang, and Wu, 2007; Pala, Singh and Ganagashetty, 2011).

1. An environment should be centered on the learner. The roles of other actors, tutors, administrators, agents and developers should also be defined according to the learners' activities.

2. An environment should fully facilitate lifelong and continuous learning by making possible the use of distance as an asset. Environment must be available anytime and anyplace to the learner.

3. An environment should propagate relative pedagogy by bringing together the learner's self and a group interaction activity in constructing individual/collective knowledge by taking into consideration learners' characteristics to integrate available information from the environment within a context of use. In other words, transformation of information into knowledge is exceedingly important.

4. An environment should be flexible enough to integrate different pedagogy methods which are domain and learners specific. For example, if an environment is process-oriented, then the learner can build knowledge by solving problems.

5. An environment should offer just-in-time information by making information available at the moment when information is necessary for an activity i.e. availability of resources like tutor help or suggestions or hints in problem-solving etc.

6. An environment should aim to develop social skills and positive attitudes towards learning.

7. An environment should facilitate bi-directional interaction between actors in various ways for accessing and processing information, such as software applications available for search of information and

communication, for process-related advice, for collaboration among learners as well as between individuals or group learners and tutors in the learning process.

8. Data representation is very important and heavily loaded as well in the environment designing process. The environment should support the learning process through various seamlessly integrated resources, tools and documents within a coherent set of objectives, tools and methods and different presentation methods for the purpose of estimating learners' aptitude and attitude towards the content and domain.

9. An environment should be adaptive to learners' individual capabilities and styles of learning process. Also it should make estimates to categorize learners from different surroundings or cultures as teams or groups based on similar needs of learners; it is modular in order to facilitate its adaptation, updating or its re-engineering.

10. An environment should also be accountable for learners' privacy and security of content delivery and for personal records within the specified time.

Outline of Virtual Environment Design, Architecture, and Process

Research shows that the discussion on virtual classrooms and virtual learning started since 80's. Initially people compared traditional approaches in a large number of courses in various disciplines which include sociology, mathematics, English composition, management, and computer science (Paquette, et al, 1993; (Hiltz, 1990). At later stages of development of virtual classrooms, an initiation was taken to design and develop, offer, and assess the effectiveness of virtual classrooms plus videotaped lectures via computer science as a subject with different modes of delivery. Students' or learners' objective performance was tested using various evaluation techniques including pre- and

post-course questionnaires, direct observation of online activities, interviews with selected students, quasi experimental comparison of test or course grades (Paquette, 2002).

Here we have proposed a design of an architecture with consideration of previous applications, various pedagogies and a persons' learning process. The kind of learning whose parameters are specified here is majorly towards an understanding of the situational meaning and construction of meaning (especially lexical meaning). This has been designed with the incorporation of relevant linguistic phenomena that constitute processes of meaning construction and language understanding. This is required given the fact that linguistic constraints shape and modulate the syntactic and semantic factors that operate on the organizational principles of learning processes.

User Interface Module: User-friendly and less complicated user interface will be designed to elicit appropriate information, like individual linguistic knowledge, learning styles, previous academic knowledge, etc. on the basis of user responses paired with a set of questions that will be presented to the learners in the form of a questionnaire. The functionality of such an interface will be like that of some of the existing social websites such as Facebook, Bibo, Youtube, Orkut etc.

Learner Gradation Module: Learner gradation module receives information through the user-interface from learners. On the basis of the received information from the learners through the system, measuring and grading the learning activity of the learners can be attempted at (Johns, J., Mahadevan, S. and Woolf, B., 2006). In the process of interaction this module will adapt to the learners' abilities that involve experience of the domain i.e. previous knowledge about the domain; this method is required to proceed to provide content etc. For example, if the content is theory-oriented and the learner does not show any interest in reading or faces a difficulty in reading, the learner can have a flexibility to choose the same content in audio format from the domain

Figure 3. Block diagram of the envisaged architecture of a virtual environment

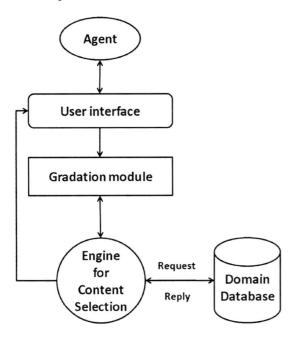

database. This information will be adopted by this module so that while logging into the system next time the user can revert to the previous state of the content representation mode.

Domain Database: The content to be provided to the learners needs be to be selected and organized as a database that can be accessed by the core engine. Content preparation for learning tasks requires manual efforts and is therefore, a time consuming and expensive task. The collection of the content and its organization as a database will be done in parallel. In order to simplify this task, I will explore various possible techniques for automatic selection of the content. Since in this study we have proposed approach toward "meaning construction" of lexical items, it requires relations also. Ontology is a formal representation of knowledge as a set of concepts within a domain, and the relationships between those concepts. Building domain-specific ontologies is,

Figure 4. This diagram shows the flow of system functionality process

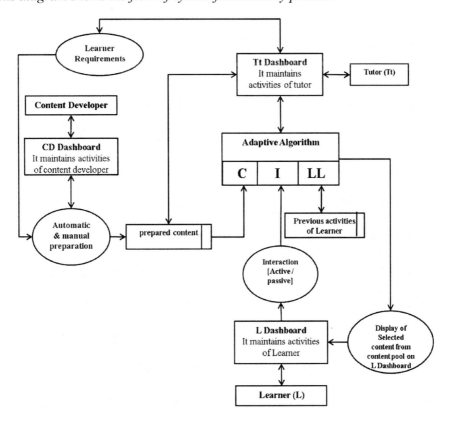

in itself, a challenging task. To reduce the cost of the building such ontologies interactive games are more effective with minimal efforts (Pala, Singh and Ganashetty, 2011).

Content Selection Module (Engine): The content selection module is an engine that draws the content from the domain database selectively on the basis of the output of the above mentioned learner gradation module and displays the output to the learner through user-interface. The engine has a crucial role in this entire process; the engine has the capability of adaptation. It receives the information from the gradation module for selection of content according to the type of interaction, level of learner and mode of the content. These parameters defined in the previous module will provide one with the state of the behavior of learners for him/her to understand the meaning of the situation. This state will be adjusted by the engine which runs an adaptive algorithm. Hence, whenever the same learner logs into the system next time, the engine will suggest to the learner what he/she should/can do in view of the previous behavior since the entire interaction has already been going through this engine. The engine also operates on the basis of the following mechanisms/ constraints for selection of the content along with the gradation module's data.

Representational Parameters (RP): These parameters are majorly related to the user interface; these parameters are a part of interaction, navigation, color of content and webpage, accessibility of content and the weight of application. This ensures that as few distractions as possible are built into the interface so as not to cause the learner to deviate from the focus.

Learner Level (LE): The level of the learner is very important. Based on the learner's level the content developer will prepare the content.

Type of Interaction (TI): It completely depends on learners' nature of action as to whether they want to interact with the tutor or group etc. Depending on this, they will choose active interaction, else passive.

Mode of Content: It also depends on learners' nature of action, domain information and content availability in the requested mode.

Domain Information: This is defined by the learners' interest and the type of knowledge they would like to perceive.

Time (t): Time is related to how much time the learner spends on each activity.

Practical Constraints (PC): The practical constraints refer to all those technical and non-technical constraints that may occur in the process such as technological illiteracy, technical maintenance issues (insufficient internet bandwidth or slow internet speed, server configuration, power supply), unavailability of human resources (tutor or group and content developer), financial crunches and privacy threats to learner accounts, content and databases from hackers.

All these data will be handled by an adaptive algorithm which develops with the self-organizing maps. Self-organizing maps (SOM) are one kind of feedforward neural network. It is a biologically inspired network, i.e. motivated by the functionality of cerebral cortex in human brain (Haykin, 1999). The goal of this network is to respond to preserve and organize the properties and features of a neighborhood function in a certain input space. It adapts the unsupervised learning method for training data, since the space is low-dimensional (Ultsch, 2007).

Functional Process

All the components in the VE interact with one other while they are engaged in the learners' learning process. The roles and responsibilities of each component are defined and have their own limitations and activities. The key motive behind developing a VE is to facilitate continuous learning through enriched and varied interaction and to improve the learner's learning capabilities in construction of meaning of a lexical item. The cognitive levels of the learner should enhance accordingly. The software application for this VE

Figure 5. An equation for selection and display of content to learners. This equation will function according to learner's options.

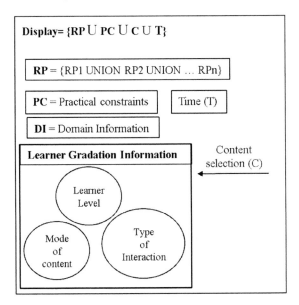

has followed 3 layered architecture designs. Here we have discussed the envisaged architecture of the VE in terms of software engineering processes.

The software application for this VE has followed a 3 layered architecture design. Here we have discussed the envisaged architecture of VE in terms of software engineering process.

We have followed a 3 layered architecture with a consideration of the following factors:

- The client side where the learner can take course and gives exams.
- The tutor interacts with the learner(s) to evaluate the submissions and provide suggestions.
- The server side also consists of a content developer who interacts with the tutor and administrator to upload content.
- The data side where the data are processed with an existing application server.

Figure 6. Block diagram of agent interaction process with virtual environment

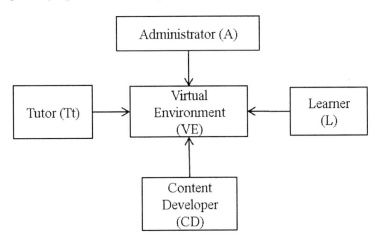

Figure 7. Three layered architecture virtual environment application

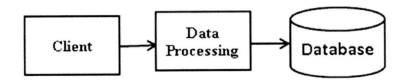

• Learner entered data (exams or tasks) will be stored in respective databases.
• The database also consists of details of all the learners, tutors and content developers, evaluators and the reports of the learners.

Learner: After registration, the learners will have their own account. They may edit or update the account settings. The learner has to login first and now after logging into the system, they can register for the courses as they choose. Learners can upload/download the content, give the exams and their performance is thereby evaluated. Learners get performance records following this procedure. They can use and view chats, discussion forum, FAQ's etc. as defined in the table above.

Content Developer: The content developer has to register to get authorization. The content developer registers the courses and users for the course content. Content developers will prepare the content and upload the materials to the content pool. Content developers interact with the tutor to get the updates about the content and course details.

Tutor: In tutors' account all the information regarding lectures, contact information etc. is available. Tutors have to evaluate the tests given by the learners, if applicable. Tutors have responsibilities for interacting, if needed, with the learners and the content developer. They provide feedback to the users and system administrator. Tutors can also view the forums, discussion and give the response as shown in Table 3.

Administrator: The administrator is the controller of the process functionality. The administrator has all the rights to provide permission to others to access databases, add or remove the users and to define the courses according to relevant requirements.

Figure 8. Accessibility to agents according to their functional responsibilities

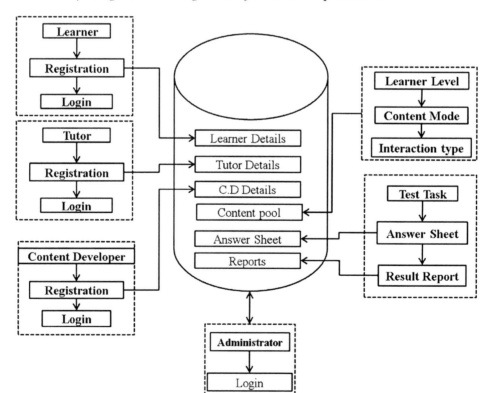

Table 3. Functional requirements of agents have been described

Agent	Interaction (classification based on response time)			Roles & Responsibility
	Active	**Passive**	**With Whom**	
Learner	Online chatting, discussions, video-conferencing, mobile chatting, multi-user games webinars, twit postings, etc.	Downloading materials, emailing, taking exam, FAQ's, writing feedbacks, single-user games, watching animations, forums, reading content on screens, writing blogs	Other learners, Tutors, Administrator	Social actor, Navigator, Explorer, Problem solver, Interactor and Producer in the learning scenario, Interacting with groups or individuals
Tutor	Chat, forums, discussions, feedback, online chatting, online discussions, video-conferencing, mobile chatting, multi-user games webinars, twittering	e-mailing, uploading materials, writing feedbacks, suggestions, clarifying doubts though forums, single-user games, watching animations, FAQ'[s	Learners, Content developer, Administrator	Advising to learners, Evaluator of learners productions, Help in using environment
Administrator	Replying through live chats, video-conferencing, phoning	Replying to feedbacks	Tutor, Content developer, Learner	Decision maker, Controller, Network Manager
Content Developer	Replying through live chats, video-conferencing, phoning	Modifying and updating content modes, uploading	Tutor, Administrator	Knowledge base builder, Designer of learning materials, Designer of the content development, Media Producer, Pedagogical scene builder

Engineering Process

Modularity: While the implementation of the architecture processes has to be divided into various modules or components. Each module or component plays a different role in the system as discussed below.

Home Page and Login: This page contains information about the application and general instructions, login window, forgot password link and other such options.

Registration Pages: All the users have to register before accessing the dashboard in this application. In this page the users have to give few details to maintain their credentials and the score.

Content Developer Dashboard: All the registered content developers can access their personal account page. All the course related details will be displayed here with very brief information about their activities.

Tutor Dashboard: All the registered tutors can access their personal account page. All the details related to course, tests, evaluations will be displayed here with very brief information about their activities.

Test Page: Once the user is chosen or selected for writing the test, s/he will be moved to the test page. Here the questions will be displayed with the options that one needs to choose.

Admin Page: This is a control panel to upload items into the database and some more facilities to change the application according to the user needs.

Course Page: The learner should go through this page to carry out checking of the availability of his/her courses. During the period when the learner takes a course, he/she also interacts with the tutor according to their nature of interest. Learners also have the facility to provide feedback to each task he/she completed for the respective authorities.

Information Hiding: Security and privacy are major functional aspects in this system. In this process the learners cannot access any database, and they cannot access other learners' score reports. This ensures persistent privacy. Any tutor cannot also access everything fully to control and make any changes to the submissions, and their role has been defined to be limited to certain boundaries. Similarly, content developers also cannot access or change the learners' reports and the tutor's page unless permitted by the administrator. Content developers have been permitted strictly to manage the course content editing and upload. Evaluators cannot access any database except to enter marks of the test-task.

Control Hierarchy: The control hierarchy is very crucial in any system; in view of the VE that has been developed in the current context, four main categories of users of VE are administrator, tutor, content developer and learner who together build the hierarchy of the system.

Quality Attributes: Below are some of the quality attributes which are taken into consideration while designing and implementing the system.

Scalability: It is the measure of an increase of the number of learners, content developers and tutors. Depending on the course and test requirements, the system database should be strong enough to handle such conditions.

Extensibility: VEs should have the capacity to deal with new changes at the architecture level. In fact, it has a facility to collect feedback and

Figure 9. The hierarchy in the VE application

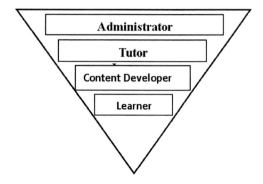

based on the feedback the system may see further modifications in the future.

Reusability: The system should always have flexibility for one to add new features to it.

Robustness: The technologies used to build the VE make it robust, and it can function quite well in difficult conditions, such as at low bandwidths.

Security: The security of the system has been given high priority; the databases cannot be accessed without the permissions by the administrator.

Fault tolerance: The VE is stable and can recover from any major failure which can occur at any level of the system (for example at Learner level, Admin level or Tutor level or Content Developer level) (Pressman, 1992; Sommerville 2004).

FUTURE RESEARCH DIRECTIONS

It now behooves us to look into the implications as they come out of the system architecture of VEs and their efficiency in tasks, performance and goals. This becomes more crucial given the vast gap that exists between learning and success. Success does not come equipped with learning. Learning is always fraught with difficulties and problems which need to be addressed, if not outright eliminated. And VEs appear to mediate such processes that make an attempt to reduce the gap. When VEs link people to machines, they become social networks, or the basic building blocks of societies. Building social groups which are, for example, relatively densely knit and tightly bound networks of people is a formidable task. Most studies on virtual social networks have looked at collaborative and cooperative work, or how people work together online despite being separated in space (usually) and in time (often). VEs are different from these social networks in that VEs are not fully homogenizing in the goals and functions specified. It is not always optimal and conceptually motivated to bring forth a tendency toward homogeneity and this is truer of language learning. On the other hand, VEs constitute or become social networks when VEs tie in people and machines in an intricate plexus which emerges out of small minuscule seemingly automated components, processes and individuals maintaining a delicate balance between some form of autonomy and flexibly controlled randomness.

CONCLUSION

The features and aspects of VEs have been discussed within the context of language learning, especially lexical learning. Potential ramifications derived from the implications of using VEs and its limitations have also been dealt with in the current paper. The envisaged architecture of a VE has also been delineated here with a specification of its functional organization and computational optimization.

The basic objectives about effects on learners were all supported by the results of both studies, including the following:

- Reaching "excellence" in the course using virtual environment is equal or superior to that in the traditional classroom.
- Learners will report higher subjective satisfaction with the VE than with the traditional classroom on a number of dimensions, including access to their professors and the overall quality of the educational experience.
- Learners perceive the meaning with the accumulating experience and interaction with groups or individuals can be personal or interpersonal. The more they perceive meaning from the narration, more critical thinking will take place.

Overall, this ICT approach toward the issue of helping learning build lexical competence with digital scaffolding has much to do with the nature of lexical learning and lexical competence. They are much less constrained and malleable by developmental and environmental constraints. VEs just home in on this aspect of lexical learning to integrate the learner in a seamless network of educational setting, instructors, learning content, digital forms of interaction and the learners themselves. The construction of meaning in the entire integrated matrix emerges out of the whole with an entrenched causal loop where language learning is boosted and roofed over with a cognitive niche construction that characterizes the whole seamless network of educational setting, instructors, learning content, digital forms of interaction and the learners.

REFERENCES

Bannan-Ritland, B. (2003). The role of design in research: The integrative learning design framework. *Educational Researcher*, *32*(1), 21–24. doi:10.3102/0013189X032001021

Barlow, J. P., Birkets, S., Kelly, K., & Slouka, M. (1995). What are we doing online? *Harper's*, *291*(1), 35–46.

Bartle, R. A. (2004). *Designing virtual worlds*. New Riders Pub.

Blumenfeld, P. C., Soloway, E., Marx, R. W., Krajcik, J. S., Guzdial, M., & Palincsar, A. (1991). Motivating project-based learning: Sustaining the doing, supporting the learning. *Educational Psychologist*, *26*(3), 369–398. doi:10.1207/s15326985ep2603&4_8

Blurton, C. (1999) New Directions of ICT-Use in Education, *World Communication and Information Report*, Retrieved December 11, 2011 from http://www.unesco.org/education/educprog/lwf/dl/edict.pdf.

Bruffee, K. A. (1999). *Collaborative learning: Higher education, interdependence, and the authority of knowledge.* Johns Hopkins University Press. doi:10.2307/358879

Cruse, D. A. (1986). *Lexical semantics.* Cambridge University Press.

Dev/World Bank. (2007). *ICT-in-education toolkit for decision makers, planners & practitioners,* version 2.0. Retrieved 1 December, 2011, from www.ictinedtoolkit.org

Dillenbourg, P., Schneider, D., Synteta, P., et al. (2002). Virtual learning environments. In A. Dimitracopoulou (Ed.), *Proceedings of the 3rd Hellenic Conference "Information & Communication Technologies in Education"* (pp. 3-18). Kastaniotis Editions, Greece.

Dis/e-lms. (2011). *What are e-learning pros and cons?* Retrieved 1 December, 2011, from http://e-lms.org/product-overview/elearning-faq/127-elearning-advantages-and-disadvantages

Duffy, T., & Cunningham, D. (1996). Constructivism: Implications for the design and delivery of instruction. In Jonassen, D. H. (Ed.), *Handbook of research for educational telecommunications and technology* (pp. 170–198). New York, NY: MacMillan.

Emeneau, M. B. (1956). India as a linguistic area. *Linguistics* (pp. 32:3-16).

Emeneau, M. B. (1980). *Language and linguistic area. Essays by Murray B. Emeneau (Selected and introduced by Anwar S. Dil).* Stanford, CA: Stanford University Press.

Felder, R. M., & Soloman, B. A. (1993). *Learning styles and strategies* (*Vol. 2*).

Girard, J., Paquette, G., Miara, A., & Lundgren, K. (1999). Intelligent assistance for web-based telelearning. In Lajoie, S., & Vivet, M. (Eds.), *AI in education – Open learning environments.* IOS Press.

Gratch, J., Wang, N., Gerten, J., Fast, E., & Duffy, R. (2007). *Creating rapport with virtual agents. Intelligent Virtual Agents* (pp. 125–138). Springer.

Gratch, J., Wang, N., Okhmatovskaia, A., Lamothe, F., Morales, M., van der Werf, R., & Morency, L. P. (2007). *Can virtual humans be more engaging than real ones? HCI Intelligent Multimodal Interaction Environments* (pp. 286–297). Springer. doi:10.1007/978-3-540-73110-8_30

Harel, I., & Papert, S. (1990). *Instructionalist products vs. constructionist tools: The role of technology-based multimedia in children's learning.* Cambridge, MA: MIT Media Laboratory.

Haykin, S. (1999). Self-organizing maps. In *Neural networks - A comprehensive foundation* (2nd ed.). Prentice-Hall.

Herschensohn, J. (2007). *Language development and age.* New York, NY: Cambridge University Press. doi:10.1017/CBO9780511486487

Hiltz, R. (1990). Evaluating the virtual classroom. In Harasim, L. (Ed.), *Online education: Perspectives on a new environments* (pp. 133–184). New York, NY: Praeger Publishers.

Hiltz, S. R., & Wellman, B. (1997). Asynchronous learning networks as a virtual classroom. *Communications of the ACM, 40*(9), 44–49. doi:10.1145/260750.260764

Hmelo-Silver, C. E. (2004). Problem-based learning: What and how do students learn? *Educational Psychology Review, 16*(3), 235–266. doi:10.1023/B:EDPR.0000034022.16470.f3

Honeyman, M., & Miller, G. (1993). *Agriculture distance education: A valid alternative for higher education? Proceedings of the 20th Annual National Agricultural Education Research Meeting* (pp. 67–73).

Instru/cypr. (2011). *Process of education.* Retrieved 1 December, 2011, from http://cyprain.blogspot.com/2010/02/process-of-education.html

Jackendoff, R. (2007). *Language, consciousness and culture*. Cambridge, MA: MIT Press.

Jan, D., Roque, A., Leuski, A., Morie, J., & Traum, D. (2009). *A virtual tour guide for virtual worlds. Intelligent Virtual Agents* (pp. 372–378). Springer.

Johns, J., Mahadevan, S., & Woolf, B. (2006). *Estimating student proficiency using an item response theory model. Intelligent Tutoring Systems* (pp. 473–480). Springer.

Johnsen, K., Dickerson, R., Raij, A., Lok, B., Jackson, J., & Shin, M. … Lind, D. S. (2005). Experiences in using immersive virtual characters to educate medical communication skills. *Proceedings VR 2005* (pp. 179-186). IEEE.

Johnson, D. W., Johnson, R. T., & Smith, K. A. (1991). *Active learning*. Interaction Book Co.

Johnson, W. L., Wang, N., & Wu, S. (2007). Experience with serious games for learning foreign languages and cultures. *Proceedings of the SimTecT Conference.*

Kenny, P., Parsons, T., & Rizzo, A. (2009). *Human computer interaction in virtual standardized patient systems. Human-Computer Interaction: Interacting in Various Application Domains* (pp. 514–523). Springer. doi:10.1007/978-3-642-02583-9_56

Klein, J. T. (2005). Integrative learning and interdisciplinary studies. *Peer Review, 7*(4), 8–10.

Langacker, R. W. (1999). *Grammar and conceptualization*. New York, NY: Mouton de Gruyter. doi:10.1515/9783110800524

Lantolf, J. P. (2009). Second language learning as a mediated process. *Language Teaching, 33*(2), 79–96. doi:10.1017/S0261444800015329

(2001). Learner-managed learning- an emerging pedagogy for online learning. InStephenson, J. (Ed.), *Teaching and learning online: Pedagogies for new technologies*. London, UK: Kogan Page.

LMS-Adv/Micro. (2011). *Five advantages of using a learning management system.* Retrieved 5 December, 2011, from http://www.microburst-learning.com/knowledgecenter.php

LMS/blog. (2011). *What LMS is best for pupils, teachers and program developers? Advantages vs disadvantages.* Retrieved 1 December, 2011, from http://njw789.blogspot.com/

LMS/Simply. (2011). *Advantages of using a learning management system.* Retrieved 5 December, 2011, from http://www.simplydigi.com/blog/2011/05/24/advantages-of-using-a-learning-management-system

LMS/time. (2011). *The LMS- Learning systems made easy!* Retrieved 5 December, 2011, from http://www.timelesslearntech.com/blog/5-advantages-of-using-the-learning-management-system-lms/

Locke, J. L. (1997). A theory of neurolinguistic development. *Brain and Language, 58*, 265–326. doi:10.1006/brln.1997.1791

Mayer, R. E., & Moreno, R. (1998). A cognitive theory of multimedia learning: Implications for design principles. *Electronic Proceedings of the CHI'98.*

Miller, G., & Johnson, L. P. (1976). *Language and perception*. Cambridge, UK: Cambridge University Press.

Newport, E. L., Bavelier, D., & Neville, H. J. (2001). Critical thinking about critical periods: Perspectives on a critical period for language acquisition. In Dupoux, E. (Ed.), *Language, brain, and cognitive development*. Cambridge, MA: MIT Press.

Ngiam, J., Khosla, A., Kim, M., Nam, J., Lee, H., & Ng, A. Y. (2011) *Multimodal deep learning.* NIPS Workshop on Deep Learning and Unsupervised Feature Learning. 2010.

Oliver, R. (2000). Creating meaningful contexts for learning in web-based settings. In *Proceedings of Open Learning* (pp. 53–62). Brisbane, Australia: Learning Network, Queensland.

Oliver, R. (2002) *The role of ICT in higher education for the 21st century: ICT as a change agent for education.* Retrieved 14 November, 2011, from http://www. edna.edu.au

Oxford, R. (1989). *The role of styles and strategies in second language learning. ERIC Digest-ED317087.* Washington, DC: ERIC Clearinghouse on Languages and Linguistics.

Oxford, R., Ehrman, M., & Lavine, R. (1991). *Style wars: Teacher-student style conflicts in the language classroom, Challenges in the 1990s for college foreign language programs* (pp. 1–25). Heinle & Heinle Pub.

Pala, K., & Ganagashetty, S. V. (in press). Experience of speech perception mediates lexical learning. In *Proceedings of International Conference on Speech and Prosodic Interfaces.*

Pala, K., Singh, A. K., & Gangashetty, S. V. (2011). Games for academic vocabulary learning through a virtual environment. In *Proceedings of International Conference on Asian Language Processing (IALP),* (pp. 295-298). IEEE

Paquette, G. (2002). *Designing virtual learning centers.* Retrieved December 22, 2011, from http://hal.archives-ouvertes.fr/docs/00/19/06/67/PDF/Paquette-Gilbert-Chap16-2001.pdf

Paquette, G., Bergeron, G., & Bourdeau, J. (1993). The virtual classroom revisited. *TeleTeaching '93 Proceedings,* Trondheim, Norway.

Paradis, M. (2004). *A neurolinguistic theory of bilingualism.* Amsterdam, The Netherlands: John Benjamins.

Pelgrum, W. J., & Anderson, R. E. (1999). *ICT and the emerging paradigm for life long learning: A worldwide educational assessment of infrastructure, goals and practices.* International Association for the Evaluation of Educational Achievement.

Per/minu. (2011). *Perceived advantages and disadvantages.* Retrieved 1 December, 2011, from http://minutebio.com/blog/2009/03/24/perceived-advantages-and-disadvantages/

Pinker, S. (2007). *The stuff of thought.* New York, NY: Viking.

Poikela, E., & Nummenmaa, A. R. (2006). *Understanding problem-based learning.* University of Tampere.

Pond, W. K. (2003). *Lifelong learning–The changing face of higher education. eLearning Summit, 2003.* California: La Quinta Resort.

Pressman, R. S. (1992). *Software engineering-A practitioner's approach-required.* McGraw Hill.

Rheingold, H. (1993). *The virtual community: Homesteading on the electronic frontier.* Reading, MA: Addison-Wesley.

Shank, P. (2005). *The value of multimedia in learning.* Adobe Motion Design Center.

Shurville, S., & Browne, T. (2007). Introduction: ICT-driven change in higher education: Learning from e-learning. *Journal of Organisation Transformation & Social Change, 3*(3), 245–250. doi:10.1386/jots.3.3.245_2

Sommerville, I. (2004). *Software engineering* (7th ed.). Addison-Wesley.

Stemmer, B., & Whitaker, H. A. (2008). *Handbook of the neuroscience of language.* San Diego, CA: Academic Press.

Swartout, W., Traum, D., Artstein, R., Noren, D., Debevec, P., & Bronnenkant, K. … Piepol, D. (2010). Ada and Grace: Toward realistic and engaging virtual museum guides. *Intelligent Virtual Agents* (pp. 286-300). Springer.

Talmy, L. (2000). *Toward a cognitive semantics.* Cambridge, MA: MIT Press.

Tinio, V. L., & UNDP, Asia-Pacific Development Information Programme and e-ASEAN Task Force. (2003). *ICT in education.* e-ASEAN Task Force.

Torey, Z. (2009). *The crucible of consciousness.* Cambridge, MA: MIT Press.

Torrance, E. P., & Myers, R. E. (1970). *Creative learning and teaching.* HarperCollins Publishers.

Traum, D., Roque, A., Leuski, A., Georgiou, P., Gerten, J., & Martinovski, B. … Vaswani, A. (2007). Hassan: A virtual human for tactical questioning. *Proceedings of the 8th SIGdial Workshop on Discourse and Dialogue* (pp. 71-74).

Ullman, M. T. (2001a). A neurocognitive perspective on language: The declarative/procedural model. *Nature Reviews. Neuroscience, 2*(1), 717–726. doi:10.1038/35094573

Ullman, M. T. (2001b). The declarative/procedural model of lexicon and grammar. *Journal of Psycholinguistic Research, 30*(1). doi:10.1023/A:1005204207369

Ultsch, A. (2007). Emergence in self-organizing feature maps. In *Proceedings Workshop on Self-Organizing Maps* (WSOM '07), Bielefeld, Germany.

US Department of Labor. (1999). *Futurework—Trends and challenges for work in the 21st century.* Quoted in EnGauge, "21st Century Skills," North Central Regional Educational Laboratory. Retrieved 31 May, 2002, from http://www.ncrel.org/engauge/skills/21skills.htm

Wellman, B., Salaff, J., Dimitrova, L. G., Garton, L., Gulia, M., & Haythornthwaite, C. (1996). Computer networks as social networks: Collaborative work, telework, and virtual community. *Annual Review of Sociology, 22*, 213–238. doi:10.1146/annurev.soc.22.1.213

Yates, K. A. (2007). *Towards a taxonomy of cognitive task analysis methods: A search for cognition and task analysis interactions.* Unpublished Doctoral Dissertation, University of Southern California, Los Angeles.

ADDITIONAL READING

Aroyo, L., & Dicheva, D. (2004). The new challenges for e-learning: The educational Semantic Web. *Journal of Educational Technology & Society, 74*, 59–69.

Becker, K. (2005). *Games and learning styles.* Special Session on Computer Games for Learning and Teaching, at the The IASTED International Conference on Education and Technology.

Biemiller, A. (2009). Teaching vocabulary: Early, direct, and sequential. *American Educator, 25*(1), 24–28.

Camp, G. (1996). Problem-based learning: A paradigm shift or a passing fad? *Medical Education Online, 1.*

Castro, F., Vellido, A., Nebot, A., & Mugica, F. (2007). Applying data mining techniques to e-learning problems. In Tedman, R. A., & Tedman, D. K. (Eds.), *Evolution of teaching and learning paradigms in intelligent environment* (pp. 183–221). Springer. doi:10.1007/978-3-540-71974-8_8

Collis, B., & Wende, M. (2002). *Models of technology and change in higher education: An international comparative survey on the current and future use of ICT in higher education.* Cheps.

Garris, R., Ahlers, R., & Driskell, J. E. (2002). Games, motivation, and learning: A research and practice model. *Simulation & Gaming, 33*(4), 441–467. doi:10.1177/1046878102238607

Guichon, N., & McLornan, S. (2008). The effects of multimodality on L2 learners: Implications for CALL resource design. *System, 36*(1), 85–93. doi:10.1016/j.system.2007.11.005

Hampel, R., & Hauck, M. (2006). Computer-mediated language learning: Making meaning in multimodal virtual learning spaces. *The JALT CALL, 2*(2), 3–18.

Hill, J., Ray, C. K., Blair, J. R. S., & Carver, C. A., Jr. (2003). Puzzles and games: addressing different learning styles in teaching operating systems concepts. *Proceedings of the 34th SIGCSE technical symposium on Computer science education* (pp. 182-186). ACM.

Jenkins, J. R., Matlock, B., & Slocum, T. A. (1989). Two approaches to vocabulary instruction: The teaching of individual word meanings and practice in deriving word meaning from context. *Reading Research Quarterly, 24*(2), 215–235. doi:10.2307/747865

Kroll, J. F., Michael, E., Tokowicz, N., & Dufour, R. (2002). The development of lexical fluency in a second language. *Second Language Research, 18*(2). doi:10.1191/0267658302sr201oa

Lonigan, C. J., Burgess, S. R., & Anthony, J. L. (2000). Development of emergent literacy and early reading skills in preschool children: Evidence from a latent-variable longitudinal study. *Developmental Psychology, 36*(5), 596–613. doi:10.1037/0012-1649.36.5.596

Lu, F., Li, X., Liu, Q., Yang, Z., Tan, G., & He, T. (2007). Research on personalized e-learning system using fuzzy set based clustering algorithm. *Computational Science-ICCS, 2007*, 587–590. Springer.

Mendes, M. E. S., & Sacks, L. (2004). Dynamic knowledge representation for e-learning applications. *Studies in Fuzziness and Soft Computing, 139*, 259–282. Physica-Verlag. doi:10.1007/978-3-540-45218-8_12

Merrill, M. D. (2002). First principles of instruction. *Educational Technology Research and Development, 50*(3), 43–59. doi:10.1007/BF02505024

No Child Left Behind Act. (2002). Pub. L. No. 107-110, 115 Stat. 1425.

Pala, K., et al. (2009). The relevance of variations in auditory perception for second language teaching and learning. In *Proceedings of the 4th, LTC-HLT09*, Poland.

Paquette, G. (1997). Virtual learning centres for 21st century organisations. In Verdejo, F., & Davies, G. (Eds.), *The virtual campus* (pp. 18–34). London, UK: Chapman & Hall.

Pearson, P. D., & Hiebert, E. H. (2007). Vocabulary assessment: What we know and what we need to learn. *Reading Research Quarterly, 42*(2), 282–296. doi:10.1598/RRQ.42.2.4

Prensky, M. (2001). *The digital game-based learning revolution.* Digital Game-Based Learning, 2001.

Prensky, M. (2005). Computer games and learning: Digital game-based learning. In Raessens, J., & Goldstein, J. H. (Eds.), *Handbook of computer game studies* (pp. 97–122).

Roblyer, M. D. (2006). *Integrating educational technology into teaching (Vol. 2)*. Pearson/Merrill Prentice Hall.

Romero, C., & Ventura, S. (2007). Educational data mining: A survey from 1995 to 2005. *Expert Systems with Applications, 33*(1), 135–146. doi:10.1016/j.eswa.2006.04.005

Sampson, D., Karagiannidis, C., & Cardinali, F. (2002). An architecture for web-based e-learning promoting re-usable adaptive educational e-content. *Journal of Educational Technology & Society*, *5*(4), 27–37. Retrieved from http://ifets. ieee. org/periodical/issues.html

Savery, J. R., & Duffy, T. M. (1996). Problem based learning: An instructional model and its constructivist framework. In Wilson, B. G. (Ed.), *Constructivist learning environments: Case studies in instructional design* (pp. 135–148).

Schwienhorst, K. (2002). Why virtual, why environments? Implementing virtual reality concepts in computer-assisted language learning. *Simulation & Gaming*, *33*(2), 196.

Sjolander, K., Beskow, J., Gustafson, J., Lewin, E., Carlson, R., & Granstrom, B. (1998). *Web-based educational tools for speech technology*. Fifth International Conference on Spoken Language Processing.

Sycara, K. P. (1998). The many faces of agents. *AI Magazine*, (Summer): 1998.

Tam, M. (2000). Constructivism, instructional design, and technology: Implications for transforming distance learning. *Journal of Educational Technology & Society*, *3*(2), 50–60.

Warschauer, M. (1996). Comparing face to face and electronic discussion in the second language classroom. *CALICO Journal*, *13*, 7–25.

Wen, D., Graf, S., Lan, C. H., Anderson, T., Dickson, K., et al. (2007). Adaptive Assessment in Web-based learning. *2007 IEEE International Conference on Multimedia and Expo,* (pp. 1846-1849). IEEE.

Wilson, B. G. (1996). *Constructivist learning environments: Case studies in instructional design*. Educational Technology Pubns.

KEY TERMS AND DEFINITIONS

Assessment Techniques: These are combination of methods to estimate learner's learning process ability which includes attitude and aptitude.

Degree of Adaptiveness: It is estimation; it shows range of assimilation capacity of a learner who involves in a particular process or a procedure.

Formal Learning: It is a linear activity in learning to reach certain state in a particular time period.

Informal Learning: In learning, it is a non-linear activity without proper defined goal and unlimited time, flexibility to explore, highly-efficient learning.

Interaction: Is an activity to transform information from source to destination to interpret and construct the meaning of activity. The source and destinations can be different or within.

Learning: It is a process of "meaning construction" of an activity with help of different kinds of inputs.

Technology in Education: Using technological developments in field of education to enhance richness in localizing and strengthen standards.

Virtual Environment: It is an environment which can facilitates interaction between users or participants or own to transfer information source to destination in a meaningful way as similar to physical environment.

Chapter 6
Education for Inclusion Using Virtual Worlds:
An Experience Using OpenSim

Juan Mateu
Universidad Autónoma de Madrid, Spain

María José Lasala
IES Ernest Lluch, Spain

Xavier Alamán
Universidad Autónoma de Madrid, Spain

ABSTRACT

In this chapter, the authors present an introduction to the use of virtual worlds in education, an analysis of the stronger and weaker points that such environments offer for high school education, and an experience on applying such technologies for the inclusion at a concrete high school in Cunit (Spain). In this high school, there is a need for teaching immigrant children the Catalan language when they arrive, in order to allow them to continue their studies integrated with the rest of the students. The chapter describes an experience on using virtual worlds for achieving such goal, based on the open software platform called "OpenSim."

INTRODUCTION

Over the years, education has suffered a series of changes regarding the educational models with the aim of improving the educational quality. In fact, the emergence of new technologies has been a key factor for developing new ways of teaching.

In this chapter we will discuss the main educational models that have appeared and those that are being used in the classroom. These educational models have many common features, thus opening the possibility of using them simultaneously. In traditional education the teaching-learning process is based on formal classroom-based education, where students and teachers are both present in the learning environment. The e-learning model

DOI: 10.4018/978-1-4666-2530-3.ch006

Copyright © 2013, IGI Global. Copying or distributing in print or electronic forms without written permission of IGI Global is prohibited.

was developed to offer new educational models that do not have this location constraint.

In first place, we will analyze educational models that are emerging through the use of Information and Communication Technologies (ICT). In second place, we will discuss how current learning theories support the application of virtual worlds in education. In third place we will analyze the advantages and disadvantages of the application of virtual worlds in the classroom. We will also briefly discuss the most widely used virtual world platforms in education and some examples of projects where virtual worlds are applied to the educational context. In fourth place, we will describe what inclusive education is and we will propose the use of virtual worlds to promote the integration of cultural diversity and to improve the communication and social skills of the students. Finally, we will present a case study of such application of virtual worlds.

ICT AND EDUCATION: E-LEARNING AND BEYOND

E-learning is a distance education model that uses Information and Communication Technologies (ICT) in the teaching-learning process. E-learning provides new tools for communication such as chat, forums, email and other forms of teacher-student interaction and student-student interaction. The interactions between students and teachers can be synchronous, for example when participating in a chat room, or asynchronous, for example when sending a question by email.

Learning management systems (LMS) are one of the main tools used in e-learning. Moodle probably is the most used LMS, being very easy to install and use. It includes tools such as chat, forums and efficient management of students and their grades; teachers can even give specific feedback on student activities. There are also other platforms such as the Sakai project or Dokeos that are used in various areas of education. The major-

ity of schools base the decision of what learning platform to use on the availability of software licenses. Open software plays an important role in this area.

The emergence of Web 2.0 has allowed the use of other tools and platforms for online learning in collaborative spaces. The emergence of social networks, forums, wikis, blogs and other tools can complement online learning. Web 2.0 encourages more active participation in the network, through the contribution of knowledge and experience from the active users, thus developing the so called "collective intelligence." Users are generating content that is filtered through the "collective" to ensure a good level of accuracy. Web 2.0 users are producers and consumers of information while users of the traditional web (Web 1.0) are only consumers of information. E-learning can be complemented with some of these Web 2.0 applications such as Youtube, Wikipedia, Slideshare, Flickr and others, thus enriching the teaching-learning process.

Following the evolution of the educational methods, there is a variant of e-learning called b-learning (blended learning) which aims to combine classroom teaching (face-to-face) with virtual learning. Blended learning can help to address some issues within e-learning, such as the lack of physical student-teacher interaction, the student's low capability for independent learning, and the lack of student's competence in the use of ICT.

Both e-learning and blended learning are educational models which aim to develop some important skills: knowing how to find relevant information on the web; team-working; and decision making based on diverse information.

Another variant of e-learning is m-learning (mobile learning) in which learning takes place using mobile devices such as smartphones, tablets, i-pods or any device that has wireless connectivity. M-learning is growing quickly because most students have mobile devices and use them frequently. An example of m-learning is a student traveling on the train on the way to college while she is connected to the virtual campus of the university, reading notes or sending an e-mail to a professor.

Some universities are adapting their virtual presence and their on-line materials to be displayed correctly on mobile devices. An example is the Open University of Catalunya (UOC), which has adapted its virtual campus to smartphones and tablets. For example, the amount of virtual campus tours using mobile devices has reached up to 90.000 per month. However, despite the great potential of mobile learning, adaptation of the virtual campuses to mobile devices is still very limited.

An educational model very similar to m-learning is u-learning (ubiquitous learning) in which learning takes place anywhere, anytime and on any subject. This teaching method uses the technologies present in Web 2.0 on a variety of devices such as mobile devices, interactive television, etc. For example, within u-learning, the student can have video-conference and interactive sessions using digital TV.

An emerging educational model is c-learning (cloud learning), based on the paradigm of cloud computing. Students belong to virtual communities such as Ning, Youtube, WordPress and Twitter, interacting and sharing information through computers, PDA, tablets, smartphones, etc. Students can engage in collaborative work using cloud-computing applications, such as Zoho, Google Docs or Dropbox. C-learning uses a wide variety of tools such as virtual worlds (Second Life, OpenSim...), social networks (Facebook, Twitter...), blogs, forums, wikis, etc.

Another type of learning is situated learning. Situated learning was defined first by Jean Lave and Etienne Wenger (Lave and Wenger, 1991) as a model of learning in a community of practice. This type of learning allows students to explore real life situations trying to solve problems through socialization, by observing other's behavior and imitating it.

For example, The River City project (Ketelhut, 2007) is an example of application of situated learning using virtual worlds (see below). The River City allows students to focus in a particular scenario in which they must investigate and explore the reason why people are getting sick. Students collect data to form hypotheses and perform experimental design to discover the causes of the epidemic in the virtual world.

Situated learning can include a wide range of activities related to places such as workshops, kitchens, greenhouses or gardens, which are used as classrooms. With the help of virtual worlds we can simulate these scenarios and allow the students to explore and interact with other avatars that may be experts in the field.

Finally, we'd like to present a teaching method called v-learning (virtual learning) where you use virtual worlds as a tool in the teaching-learning process. V-learning breaks the spatial barriers in the learning environment, while still allowing a learning experience that is close to the traditional class. Furthermore, the big advantage of using this new method is the ability to engage in realistic simulations in a 3D environment, providing the student with meaningful experiences. Virtual worlds can also be integrated with learning management systems like Moodle: an example of such integration is SLOODLE.

For example, Transurb Technirail is a company that provides e-learning training for their urban rail and subway train drivers by an immersive 3D environment that is integrated with a learning management system (Dockeos). Reports on the performance of the drivers during the simulations are stored in Dockeos. Currently, engineers are simulating the Transurb 25km railway to help metro drivers getting familiar with the new metro system in Kuala Lumpur.

A new approach to learning tries to integrate all the teaching methods described above through what is called a Personal Learning Environment (PLE). A PLE is a way of learning where students set their own goals, choose the most appropriate tools and contents for their learning and interact with other people to form their personal learning network (PLN) in order to actively share information and experiences. The younger generations are becoming more autonomous and self-taught in the use of ICT, thus they will not only use learning management systems (LMS), but also many other tools, services and people. With PLE we can integrate formal learning with informal learning, the latter related with virtual educational communities. The student will actively participate in social networks, create and participate in blogs and wikis, etc. Of course, Web 2.0 is key factor for the development of learning through PLEs.

VIRTUAL WORLDS AND EDUCATION

In this section we will focus on the use of virtual worlds in education, and we will analyze the opportunities this method provides, as well as the problems that are preventing its wider use.

A virtual world can be defined as "a synchronous, persistent network of people, represented as avatars, facilitated by networked computers" (Bell, 2008).

Virtual worlds like Second Life or OpenSim are classified as massive multi-user virtual environments (MUVE) because many people can interact with each other in real time at the same virtual space. In virtual worlds we can create 3D objects and interact with other avatars through text chat or voice chat and we can even buy or sell objects using its own currency (i.e., the Linden Dollar used in Second Life).

Virtual worlds began to be used in education in the 70's, but it has not been until the emergence of some key technologies (high speed networks, computer graphics, etc.) that their use and deployment has generalized. One of the potentials of virtual worlds in education is the easy application of constructivist learning. This methodology, originally proposed by Vigotsky (Vygotsky, 1978), proposes that students construct their learning based on their own experiences, observations and collaborations with the rest of the group.

Constructivist learning is considered a dynamic, participatory and interactive methodology, where students construct their own knowledge to solve any problem posed.

Thus, the use of virtual worlds in the classroom will be based on the features present in constructivist theories: teachers present a series of teaching-learning activities and the students have to solve them by immersion in virtual worlds through their avatar. The constructivist approach to virtual worlds considers the role of the teacher as the facilitator of learning. This approach fits perfectly with other teaching methods that are based on "learning by doing," "learning by playing" and "learning by watching." With all these approaches the flow of communication is changed, avoiding the traditional one-way communication channel from teacher to students. Thus, the students engage in a more active role and feel more involved in the learning process.

Bloom's taxonomy (Bloom, 1956) proposes that there are three learning domains: the cognitive domain, the affective domain and the psychomotor domain. By using virtual worlds in education we can address the higher levels in this taxonomy, which usually are the more difficult to deal with. For example, students are encouraged to analyze, evaluate and create (cognitive domain) and then receive positive feedback (affective domain), thus inducing a positive attitude, higher motivation, an improved interest in learning, and a more attentive attitude.

A very important concept today is that of emotional intelligence. Emotional intelligence is the ability to recognize feelings in oneself and others and the ability to handle them properly. Researchers, such as Daniel Goleman, have produced many studies and theories on emotional intelligence (Goleman, 1998), and on how emotions can play a role in many areas, including education. One way to work the emotions is through educational games that help students to express their feelings based on experiences obtained in these educational games. We can work emotional intelligence through the use of virtual worlds, where students will be immersed in a virtual environment where they will experience sensations and feelings that are very difficult to reproduce using traditional methods.

According to Roger Schank (Schank, 2002), appropriate teaching methods should be based on simulations that are as close as possible to reality. This would allow the student to "learn by doing" through real life situations, using role-playing scenarios. Virtual worlds precisely help us to do that, allowing us to take decisions, set goals and priorities, make predictions, learn from mistakes, etc. in an almost-real environment.

Within virtual worlds social learning is favored: students may learn new behaviors through observation of social factors in the environment. They watch desirable behaviors (and positive consequences) and learn them by imitation. It also promotes cooperative learning where students help each other; this may be a very useful tool to eliminate conflicts among students with different cultural backgrounds. Cooperative learning helps to build self-confidence and to encourage social interactions in heterogeneous groups. Both collaborative learning and cooperative learning are based on the constructivist paradigm.

Several types of communication are available in virtual worlds for this kind of collaborative learning. Synchronous communication occurs when all the persons that are communicating are present at the same time -such as during a chat session-, while asynchronous communication occurs when not all the people are present at the same time, for example when using off-line messages. In virtual worlds we can also find verbal communication -textual or oral-, as well as nonverbal communication, the latter being related with the appearance, position and gestures of the avatar, for example.

We can also highlight two types of learning: formal learning, which is the most traditional and is used in educational institutions; and informal learning, that takes place at everyday situations, and can be accomplished through virtual worlds.

Students can use virtual worlds from their homes as a form of entertainment, but unconsciously learning from the feedback received during their activities. Students need to acquire a broad range of knowledge and skills to integrate in society, and approximately 80% of these skills are acquired through informal learning. Virtual worlds may support and enhance this process.

Virtual worlds applied to education try to enrich and improve the student's learning experience. Virtual worlds encourage students to experience 3D environments that would be difficult to experience in traditional education. However, it is a big challenge for teachers using immersive learning environments because they require a great effort to learn their use, to adapt the syllabus, and to develop the educational activities. The rewards are high, however.

Currently, virtual worlds are mainly used by universities. Some universities use virtual worlds as a marketing tool to attract new students to their campuses, while others use them as an educational tool, especially for performing simulations of real situations. However, the use of virtual environments in secondary schools is just beginning: there is still much to be done to establish 3D e-learning in secondary education.

Secondary education imposes some particular requirements. For example, it is broadly recognized the need to work a series of basic skills, such as learning to learn, digital literacy, mathematical competence, social and civic competence, etc. In some countries, such as in Spain, these requirements are enforced by Law. These skills are acquired gradually throughout the period of secondary studies. While teaching any specific subject, you can work these core competencies and link them to other skills found in other areas. For example, when using a computer program for calculations during the math class, both mathematical competences and -to a lesser extent- digital competences, are being achieved.

Most of these basic skills may be developed using virtual worlds. Virtual worlds fit neatly into existing educational models, both from the point of view of methodology and from the point of view of acquisition of basic skills, which are different for the various educational levels of the students. The orientation of the teaching-learning process should be directed towards the development of learning skills and knowledge, not only to teaching.

The immersion in 3D virtual environments offers the students the possibility of developing some basic skills through exploration and interaction that are difficult to achieve with other tools. The creation of 3D objects -for example creating a virtual building- may develop student's creativity. Virtual worlds can be used to simulate case studies based on a specific context in which students learn to investigate, formulate their own hypotheses and make decisions to solve the realistic problems, thus developing a critical and reflective attitude.

Virtual worlds have many advantages, but also have a number of problems that have prevented or delayed its implementation and use in secondary education.

The first problem is that virtual worlds need powerful computers and high-speed network connections to work properly. Unfortunately, many secondary schools still have a very limited computer infrastructure and a low bandwidth connection. Furthermore, many times these connections are protected with a firewall that is administered by external authorities, and thus it is administratively difficult to set up connections and ports to access the virtual worlds, both within and outside the schools.

The second problem is the high number of students per classroom, which in some cases can reach up to 25 or 30. This problem is mainly due to economical reasons, and is further aggravated with the presence of students with special educational needs that, also for economical reasons, do not have the special care they would need. Implementing new learning methodologies with such number and diversity of students is always difficult.

The third problem is the need for faculty training on new technologies. Teachers lack the knowledge and practice on the use of 3D environments applied to the teaching-learning process. Furthermore, a certain sector of teachers, especially the older ones, is reluctant to innovate and adapt their teaching methodologies to the current times. Nowadays students are digital natives and need new learning methods to keep their interest in learning. Traditional methodological approaches may cause in the student boredom and loss of interest in the study; students need to feel that they are part of new and meaningful experiences. The fact that some teachers may be reluctant to use new technologies is mainly caused by the fear of not properly controlling the various devices in a multimedia classroom, such as computers, interactive whiteboards, etc.

Nevertheless, there is another sector of the faculty that is interested in using new technologies in order to provide a more appropriate teaching for the XXI century. However, when these motivated teachers face problems such as these mentioned above (low bandwidth, poor infrastructure, firewall restrictions, lack of training, etc.) they may get frustrated and give up.

To overcome this possible frustration a good solution is to foster the collaboration among the teachers interested in new learning methods. Fostering collaboration among teachers to create interesting educational projects would facilitate the efficient implementation of virtual worlds in the classroom. Creating educational projects related to 3D virtual environments helps to establish dialogue and consensus among the faculty. Having more dialogue among teachers helps to establish relations between different departments and this in turn will allow finding cross-cutting themes that are part of the curricula.

An example of an initiative involving several schools is the *Comenius Programme*. The Comenius Programme aims to strengthen the European dimension in the field of nursery, primary and secondary education, promoting mobility and cooperation among schools. The *NIFLAR Project* is an example of a Comenius Project between a Spanish secondary education institute and a center of Dutch secondary education that proposes using virtual worlds for language learning.

One important issue is that teachers have to learn how to use virtual worlds to teach: it is not enough just to know how to use virtual worlds. Teachers should study the educational use of virtual worlds, defining the goals and seeing how to adapt the various educational areas to 3D virtual environments. This whole process is quite complex and time-consuming and should be studied in detail before applying the technology to the classroom. Furthermore, once this is achieved there is still a lot of work ahead in order to prepare the materials and teaching-learning activities adapted to 3D environments.

The students may also present some adaptation problems to this technology. The students may see virtual worlds as a game, without realizing the educational objectives to be achieved. Therefore, the use of virtual worlds in the classroom may cause distraction, the students not paying attention to the teaching-learning activities proposed and getting lost in unimportant aspects. In addition, some students who have fewer resources and have scarce experience in the use of new technologies may have a steep learning curve when dealing with virtual worlds.

Finally, the last agent involved is the family of the students, which should be aware of the objectives pursued in the use of virtual worlds. It is important that the student's family is involved and help students in making appropriate use of virtual worlds at their own homes. Although virtual worlds that are used at school will be monitored and closed to external access, students can always be curious about other virtual worlds, so the family must be aware of the potential dangers that may arise in this direction. The students should be monitored by family members not to venture into other virtual worlds that may have inappropriate contents.

Table 1 summarizes the major problems inherent to the use and implementation of virtual worlds in the classroom, separated by the main agents involved in the teaching process.

Finally let's briefly discuss a concept related with virtual worlds: the so called "serious games." These are computer based games that use entertainment as a way of training in a particular topic, and have recently gained strength in education. "Serious games" is a useful learning method

Table 1. Weak points in the use of virtual worlds in secondary education

Problem	Agent involved
Lack of acceptance by students	Students
Virtual worlds provide distraction or display inappropriate content	
Steep learning curve (especially for low-income students)	
Lack of knowledge and training in virtual worlds	Teachers
Lack of dialogue and consensus among teachers	
Poor infrastructure and low bandwidth	School and educational institutions
Difficulties to control connections and opening of new ports	
High ratio of students in classrooms	
Failure to create more educational projects on virtual worlds	
Lack of information about virtual worlds	Family
Lack of involvement in the child's learning process	
Poor control and monitoring of the use of virtual worlds outside school.	

that allows the use of your own experiences in making decisions and encourages teamwork. Virtual worlds, of course, are quite appropriate for implementing serious games. An example of a fairly widespread platform for serious games is Unity 3D.

Virtual World Platforms

After analyzing the main positive and negative aspects of the application of virtual worlds in the classroom, we will focus now on the different platforms available for their deployment.

Probably the most popular virtual world platform is Second Life. Although Second Life is an excellent 3D virtual environment, there are a number of aspects that spoil its suitability for secondary education. In first place, Second Life is a closed environment and you have to pay for using it. The limited budget of schools makes this a significant problem. A second problem is age limitations for entering Second Life. Second Life is aimed to adults, so it cannot be used by minors: you have to be over 18 years old to be admitted in SL. Linden Labs (the company that created Second Life) developed a version for teens named Teen Second Life, but it was not as successful as expected and finally was abandoned. On the other hand, and independently of age restrictions, Second Life is an environment that gives access to content that can be considered inappropriate for high school students.

An example of educational use of Second Life, focused in the process of language learning, is EduNation. EduNation islands are maintained by a community of educators that constitute a virtual non-profit organization that provide educational simulations, virtual classrooms, and virtual world telecollaboration and class exchanges.

Active Worlds is the second most used virtual world platform for education and has a high demand from educators. Active Worlds launched an educational community called The Active Worlds Educational Universe (AWEDU) that engages educational institutions, teachers and students into exploring new educational theories and discovering new paradigms of social learning, among other things.

An example of educational project within Active Worlds is the River City Project, which will be discussed latter. Active Worlds provides web browser integration, support for VoIP and is more geared to education than the other virtual world platforms. However, it is a pay platform, and this makes its implementation in Spanish public schools problematic.

There is a widely used open source platform for virtual worlds: OpenSim. It is delivered under a BSD license so it can be used with no software cost. In addition, there is a community of programmers who are continuously creating new versions to further improve the software. OpenSim offers a free and scalable platform where you can create islands on your own servers. With OpenSim you can create a fully controlled land, thus preventing your students from accessing inappropriate content or contacting inappropriate people. With OpenSim only authorized students and teachers can interact within the designated areas, preventing access to unauthorized people. OpenSim has a discussion list associated in which educators discuss about educational projects, techniques for creating 3D objects and programming their behavior, resources for the classroom, problems while using the platform, and scheduled events on OpenSim.

Alice is an innovative 3D programming environment that allows learning object-oriented programming. Using Alice you can create an animation for telling a story, play an interactive game, or create a video to be shared on the web. Alice is a teaching tool for introductory computing, using an easy 3D graphics-based interface that provides an attractive first experience in programming.

Finally, Edusim is a multi-user 3D virtual world platform and authoring toolkit for classroom interactive whiteboards. It is a means of allowing students to practice with 3D virtual environments by manipulating objects using the interactive whiteboard surface.

SOME EXAMPLES OF VIRTUAL WORLDS FOR EDUCATION

In this section we will discuss some projects that have experimented with virtual worlds for secondary education.

The *AVATAR Project* (Added Value of teAching in a virtuAl woRld) is a two-year project completed in November 2011 and co-financed by the European Commission under the Lifelong Learning Programme Sub-Comenius. AVATAR (Feliz. and Santoveña, 2009) investigated the use of virtual worlds for education and sought to provide a methodology for that type of applications. The main objective of the project was to improve the quality of teaching and education in secondary schools through an innovative learning environment using a virtual world. This project enabled the development of ICT skills to both students and teachers through the v-learning educational model, increasing the level of student participation

The *NIFLAR Project* (Jauregi *et al.*, 2010) aimed to enrich, innovate and improve the learning process by using video conferencing and virtual worlds for interaction among students from Spain and Holland. There was a special focus on socio-cultural interaction. They performed tutoring sessions, familiarization with the environment sessions, specification of the pedagogical approach tasks, institutional contacts, and interaction sessions.

V-LeaF (Virtual LEArning platForm) is an educational platform developed by the Universidad Autonoma de Madrid, which promoted cooperative and collaborative learning versus traditional learning. V-LeaF (Rico *et al.*, 2009) provides specific documentation for high school students and a number of resources for learning in virtual worlds, such as manuals for creating and

manipulating 3D objects or manuals for learning how to give behavior to objects using the LSL language. V-LeaF offers an attractive way of learning to program computers. The platform was based in the OpenSim software and the project involved several high schools in Spain. One of them developed the case study on inclusive education that will be described below.

3D Learning Experiences Services (3DLES, 2011) includes several educational projects developed with OpenSim for secondary education in the Netherlands. An interesting project under 3DLES consists in two virtual towns, one of them speaking English (Chatterdale) and the other speaking French (Parolay). Students tour the two villages while practicing speaking with the inhabitants thereof, which are pretending to be traders, doctors, pharmacists, etc. Residents of both towns are teachers and university students that are learning languages, using headphones to interact while immersed in simulations of real life situations.

The *River City Project* (Ketelhut, 2007) was funded by the National Science Foundation and consist in an interactive simulation for science students in order to learn how to do scientific research and acquire other related skills. The River City project is developed under the Active Worlds platform, with a licensing agreement with Harvard University. The River City Project simulates a city besieged by health problems. Students are organized in small research groups trying to find why residents are getting sick, using technology to track clues and figure out the causes of the disease, developing and testing hypotheses through experiments and extracting conclusions from the collected data.

The *Vertex Project* (Bailey and Moar, 2002) was held at elementary schools in the United Kingdom and included students from 9 to 11 and their teachers. Elementary schools were in different geographical areas and diverse cultural spaces. In the context of the classroom, about 32 children with limited access to computers participated. Students combined traditional activities such as writing a story, draw a scene or make a collage with the use of software tools like Adobe Photoshop or 3D Studio Max. Students worked in small groups while trying to imagine, plan and design their virtual worlds, with the educational goal of developing their creativity and imagination. The project worked with different areas of the curriculum (literacy, art, ICT…) by performing different tasks. They observed that within a multi-user world, students improve their communication skills, learn to cooperate and improve their self-esteem and confidence.

The *AVALON Project* (Access to Virtual and Action Learning live Online) was a two-year project funded by the European Commission as a part of the Education and Culture DG Lifelong Learning Programme. The AVALON project (Deutschmann *et al.*, 2010) was aimed to language teachers, language learners, teacher trainers, learning technologists and other professionals interested in the field of education. The AVALON project created activities to promote language learning among students using materials in both 2D and 3D. This project sought to develop best practices in teaching and learning of languages in multi-user environments (MUVEs) like Second Life or OpenSim.

WiloStar3D (WiloStar3D, 2011) is a virtual school that offers distance education using virtual worlds. WiloStar3D has a curriculum approved by the USA educational authorities (SACS). The methodology used by WiloStar3D is based on constructivism in which students learn to experience and interact in the virtual world. Students can take different roles, according to the activity, participating in media projects with other students. WiloStar3D improves reading comprehension, improves problem-solving ability, and promotes creativity using active learning in a safe and reliable virtual world.

ARC: The impending Gale is a project developed by Game Environment Applying Real Skills (GEARS) using a 3D virtual learning environment.

GEARS (Barkand and Kush, 2009) is a division of the National Network of Digital Schools (NNDS) that integrates the Lincoln Interactive curriculum in order to reinforce the concepts taught in traditional classes and provides innovative and effective educational experiences. The Lincoln Interactive curriculum is designed for K-12 online students and consists of over 250 asynchronous online courses. They created an online community called the Social and Educational Virtual World (VSEW). This community allowed access to the Lincoln online curriculum to more than 15.000 students. The VSEW 3D social spaces contain avatars, chat, Voice Over Internet Protocol (VoIP) communication, areas for tutoring with teachers and various social objects that can interact with avatars.

Euroland (Ligorio *et al.*, 2000) is a project based on collaborative activities carried out among several classrooms in the Netherlands and Italy, which was developed under Active Worlds. Euroland implied the creation of a 3D virtual world that was initially empty and was progressively populated with "culture houses" (Ligorio, 2001). This project involved seven schools that built seven cultural houses. For example, students in Rome built "The Dutch House of Art"; students of Bari built a house for a travel agency; and students of Milan built "The Dutch House of Food."

VIRTUAL WORLDS AND EDUCATION FOR INCLUSION

Schools always aim to provide quality education, and that has to embrace inclusive education. Inclusive education seeks to address the diversity of students in the classroom and to find cohesion among all the members of the educational environment (teachers, parents, students, educational administration…)

Inclusive education is guided primarily by the following principles:

- The students should be taught respect for human rights.
- The education community should encourage personal and professional development of the students as well as cohesion among equals.
- The diversity of any member of the school community should be considered as a richness of the educational environment that promotes the values of social cohesion and interdependence.
- The students should share a common educational environment in which each member is valued equally, with the aim of encouraging both excellence and equality among students.

Inclusion involves identifying and minimizing the difficulties of learning and participation as well as maximizing the educational resources. Inclusive education seeks to provide equal opportunities to any student that has a perceived social stigma, which can be related to gender, race, physical or mental disability, or even culture.

Before using virtual worlds in inclusive education we have to define clearly the teaching methods that will be used, in order to ensure that the teaching-learning process is successful in reaching the desired objectives. The use of virtual worlds can help to avoid the risk of marginalization and social exclusion by breaking some barriers for the inclusion that exist in the real world. For example, avatar interactions can facilitate verbal and nonverbal communication skills (Babu *et al.*, 2007). Virtual worlds are spaces that allow testing social alternatives through actions and reflections on the feelings and thoughts (Sheehy and Fergunson, 2008).

An interesting example of using virtual worlds for inclusion is the treatment of Autism or Asperger Syndrome by Brigadoon. Brigadoon is a private island in Second Life which aims to promote social skills among people who have trouble interacting face to face with other people. At the island of Brigadoon, students can learn socialization skills through a 3D environment similar to the "real world," but that it is less stressful for them. Building objects in the virtual world, sitting and chatting with other people in a garden, sailing a boat, or organizing bonfires on the beach with other persons, are some of the scenarios that show the potential of virtual worlds. Such scenarios allow experiencing new sensations, forming emotional bonds with others, learning to work in groups and improving the social skills.

CASE STUDY: EDUCATION FOR INCLUSION USING VIRTUAL WORLDS

The IES Ernest Lluch is a public high school located in Cunit, at the north-east of Spain, in the region of Catalonia, where they speak their own language: Catalan. In the area of Cunit there is a high rate of immigration and usually the children of these newcomers attend to the public school. One consequence of this fact is the need for teaching these children the Catalan language when they arrive, to allow them to pursuit their studies integrated with the rest of the children at the school. In addition, many of these children come from developing countries (Morocco, Ecuador, Bolivia, Brazil, etc.) and have a low income and educational profile. In order to integrate these children in the mainstream Catalonian educational system the "Welcome Course" was created, where the recently arrived children spend several hours a day learning Catalan language and culture as well as other necessary basic skills.

From 2008-09 several didactic applications with digital contents have been used to help in this "Welcome Course." Moreover, from 2009-10 several projects that involved virtual worlds were initiated, being used as a resource for newcomers to learn the Catalan language, customs and traditions in a fun and practical way. Students learned without effort, effectively engaging and playing with this "serious game." This system had the appeal of combining traditional teaching methodologies with innovative technology.

To understand how these new applications are used, in first place we are going to explain the context, the institutional framework and the educational problems we faced.

The "Ernest Lluch" high school is located at Cunit, a town of in the province of Tarragona (Catalonia-Spain). It is a secondary school that has recently grown in line with the needs of the population of the town. This center has traditionally been keen to address diversity in the classroom. The Open Classroom (dedicated to teens with social or behavioral problems), the Unit for External Schooling (in charge of non-academic teaching) and the Welcome Course are good examples of this.

The Welcome Course is the first contact point and subsequent meeting place for students that have recently arrived to Catalonia. These students may come from other Spanish regions, from other Spanish-speaking countries, or elsewhere. The common characteristic is that they do not speak Catalan, which is the working language at the school. The school has to provide an appropriate educational response to this type of students. Each student should follow a curriculum as individualized as possible that takes into account his educational background and specific needs. Delivering this kind of individualized learning is a difficult task.

A good way to work with this diversity is the "working on projects" approach. Each student (or pair of students) works during the class in her particular project, which may be different to the rest of the students. Each project is tailored to their particular level of knowledge and progress. The use of ICT (Information and Communication Technologies) and CLT (Collaborative Learning Technologies) greatly facilitates this complex task.

To reach the desired goals, the classroom environment is designed to be as welcoming and open as possible. As it was said above, it is essential

that the student is competent in Catalan to join the regular classroom as quickly as possible. This process may take from one quarter to a couple of academic years. It would be impossible for students to continue their studies without this prior knowledge. The vocabulary, writing, reading, spelling and oral communication are, therefore, the center of the activities.

The Welcome Course covers ages from 12 to 16, although some older students may be also attending. Each student has an Intensive Individualized Plan with the adequate curricular adaptations and modifications as dictated by the Spanish Law. The focus is in the acquisition of language proficiency, but not forgetting other interdisciplinary skills.

Thus, the Welcome Course focuses in oral language, simulating everyday situations through playing and using resources that can create a climate conducive to communication and participation. The goal is not only to prepare the student for the studies at the school, but also to help the teenager to join the new society in which she lives. The Catalan language will become the nexus of union and cohesion of this disparate group class.

In our search for new methodologies and resources that could help in this task we ended using ICT resources of all kinds: Web 2.0 applications, class blogs, wikis, webquest, social networks such as Twitter and Messenger, and finally -with the help of projects Espurna, VLeaf, and Spiral-, 3D virtual worlds.

Espurna Project (Espurna, 2011) has been one of the drives for using ICT resources at our school. This project, managed by the Department of Education of the Generalitat of Catalonia and the Institute of Educational Sciences at the Autonomous University of Barcelona, consolidated definitely with its current format in 2008. It consists on an online learning space, which began in 2006 as a support for innovation in the "Welcome Courses" and in the "Open Classrooms." During the current academic year it has begun to be also used in regular classrooms of primary and secondary schools in Catalonia.

This project provides teachers and students with hundreds of activities and resources of all kinds accessible on the web and, at the same time, it allows these two collectives to share their own experiences and resources. (Alart *et al.*, 2010).

One of the initiatives under the Espurna project was the use of a virtual world as a meeting place for teachers interested in the use of ICT in the classroom. We collectively promoted the use, for example, of Twitter and Google, and finally we created a 3D Virtual School. After a series of tests with students using Lively (a 3D virtual world environment provided by Google that now has been closed), we choose Second Life (SL), provided by Linden Labs, to continue experimenting with virtual worlds.

Since 2007 the headquarters and meeting place for Espurna were located in the Second Life "island" named Edunation II. In October 2009 the Espurna 3D School opened. Every two weeks the team members met there to coordinate the project. As a result, every two weeks new activities were launched: practical sessions on the educational possibilities of virtual worlds. The goal was to investigate the possibilities of the environment in order to use it with our students.

We used SL to prepare, for example, conference presentations, seminars, introductory courses, teacher training courses, a summer school, etc. It was not only a meeting place but basically a learning and teaching space for teachers.

Some of the workshops we organized in the virtual world covered basic use of SL (avatar tailoring, group management, chat and voice-chat use, building objects, developing scripts, creating animations, etc.), but others were focused in more general issues, such as short courses on Google Wave, Latex, SL as a tool for language practice, demonstrations of interactive whiteboards, the use of Twitter, etc. The video created for the 2009-10 closing meeting of the Espurna 3D School illustrates quite well all these activities (Espurna, 2010).

The use of SL has become essential for us, as we work in geographically separated parts of Catalonia. For writing articles, creating schedules, etc. we use collaborative tools such as Google docs or type.me. Nevertheless, the real-time interaction that can be achieved with SL is a great advantage, besides being fun, dynamic and highly creative. The monitoring of all activities is done through the portal Ning (Espurna-Ning, 2011).

The first experiences involving students where done under the umbrella of the V-Leaf project (Virtual Learning Platform), developed at the School of Engineering of the Universidad Autonoma de Madrid (Rico *et al.* 2009). The main goal of this project was to use the new capabilities of interaction and the intrinsic appeal of virtual worlds to engage students in a greater participation in their learning process.

The main objectives and pedagogical needs that had to be addressed were:

- To learn the language, customs and traditions of Catalonia.
- To improve listening and reading capabilities.
- To improve writing capabilities (guided and free) and oral expression.
- To attend the diversity in the classroom, following the rhythm of work and learning of each student, taking into account her motivations, needs and background knowledge.
- To practice Catalan language by playing (virtual gymkhanas), establishing relationships, describing landscapes, sorting objects, answering tests or learning the vocabulary appropriate for each task.
- To facilitate teacher-learner as well as learner-learner interaction, using simulations of everyday life.
- To encourage students' attention by diversifying the resources and stimulating their work.

- To design an educational methodology for virtual worlds.
- To promote the work in the classroom using different types of aggregations: individual work, work in pairs, work in small groups and work in large groups. The goal is to enrich social relations, respect for peers, respect for teachers, as well as to facilitate class cohesion.
- To develop a multidisciplinary project in which other knowledge areas (besides Catalan language) have accommodation, such as mathematics, social sciences, arts, technology, etc.
- To practice how to use games as an effective learning method.
- To strengthen and broaden students' knowledge from complementary activities within virtual worlds, while consolidating previously learned concepts.

Now we will describe the experiences we made using virtual worlds as a tool for inclusive education.

First Experience Using Virtual Worlds

The first contact with virtual worlds in the context of the Welcome Course began during the 2009-2010 academic year. During the second quarter of this year the students of the course spent a couple of hours each week working in this experience. Students used a couple of Second Life avatars in turns, under the teacher supervision. They were not given any specific goal or mission, the idea was to allow them exploring the environment and to see what reactions they had to the fact that their teacher allowed them to "play" during the class. We wanted to see whether there was a possibility for educational uses of this new technology.

Once in the virtual world, they went to the Espurna headquarters, they went to an educational sandbox (where they edited their appearance and

learned how to create objects), and they visited other locations of interest (science museums, art museums, zoos, etc.) The objective, as stated above, was to motivate students to learn the language, customs and culture of Catalonia using an innovative learning methodology. The methodology was very different to that we were using routinely in the classroom. Although we had already used Web 2.0 resources from the Espurna portals and we had already created our own class blog, using virtual worlds was a further step in innovation.

How was this experience put into practice?

1. Using the text chat between the students and the teacher or just among students. As the way of interacting inside the virtual world is "chatting," this encourages practicing language. The teacher was physically at their side while they were chatting in the virtual world, so they were continuously asking questions to the teacher on how to write well, practicing both oral and written communication.
2. Learning how to create objects in the virtual world. This is a fun but complicated task, and therefore they had to understand in detail the explanations given in the classroom (in Catalan) and then they had to work together (again, encouraging communication) to solve the problems they found.
3. Manipulating objects within the virtual world. We used the vocabulary learnt in the current didactical unit and built objects with these forms or names. For example they worked on numbers, colors, shapes, seasons, food, etc.
4. Visiting different locations in Second Life. These virtual "tours" served to review the names of the objects they encountered along the way: furniture, animals, plants or places, and so on.

Figure 1. Welcome course students working with the virtual world

Cultural Week Workshops

Seeing that the initial experience with the Welcome Course students had been positive, we decided to make a second experience during the "Cultural Week." This is an activity that is held once a year: during a whole week regular classes in the high school are substituted by thematic workshops on cultural issues. We proposed and delivered a workshop on "virtual worlds."

In this experience the goal was more playful than during the Welcome Course. The workshop consisted mainly in an introduction to virtual worlds, being also the first attempt to work with the V-Leaf platform provided to us by the Universidad Autonoma de Madrid. It was a 5 hour workshop spread over two days; this was time enough for the kids to get an idea about what a virtual world is, to learn how to move and edit their own avatar; and to start doing some basic building.

The experience was highly positive and a decision was made on continuing experimenting with this technology. We asked the V-Leaf project to provide us our own virtual space (a virtual island) so that we could use it routinely. During the following courses, 2010-2011 and 2011-2012, we repeated the workshop on virtual worlds during the cultural week with a big success in demand and satisfaction.

"Let's Have a Beach" Project

The third experience was the "Let's have a beach" project, involving the Welcome Course students and the V-Leaf platform. Since May 2010 we worked with Welcome Course students with the goal of reaching a little beyond in our educational experience with virtual worlds. This time the results obtained by the students were evaluated and had a 30% impact in their grade for the third quarter. They had to choose between "Let's make a football field," or "Let's have a beach" activities (Lasala, 2011).

They were explained that we had an "island" just for us and that each of them was going to have her own avatar and could customize it. They were allowed to build all kinds of objects with the only condition that all the communication during the task should be in Catalan. The teacher would help, but this time they should make a greater effort.

Firstly, they prepared a dossier. They took notes in a logbook, looked for objects and vocabulary for the specific topic (beach or football), worked on spelling, sought the web for the typical measurements and colors of the objects, and translated all of it to Catalan. Once this preliminary work was done, each student described and drawn to scale the object he had chosen to build in the virtual world (a lighthouse, a ball, football goal, the referee's clothing, a boat, a beach scooter, an umbrella, etc.).

Secondly, they practiced building skills, looking for textures, learning to handle simple scripts (small computer programs that give behavior to objects) and managing avatars animations.

Finally, the project was implemented. Due to time constraints only the "Let's have a beach" project was finally developed in the virtual world.

The project mixed traditional learning procedures (dossiers, books, searching on the dictionary) with innovative technologies (web, 3D virtual worlds). The effort made by the students was huge, because they had to work in a virtual world unknown to them, but there was also a reward:

Figure 2. Beach built by the welcome course students

the fast, efficient and fun learning of the Catalan language. The kids were quite involved and excited about the project; they realized they were attempting something that very few high school students have the opportunity to do, something completely new. They worked quite hard and motivated; in particular some students who often have a lack of working habits and motivation.

Two factors that also helped were that their teacher was one more player in the world and that there was an atmosphere of sharing all the knowledge they obtained. The students researched by themselves, interacted with the objects, sought answers, and practiced and discovered things that sometimes the teacher had not yet explained. They were experimenting and simulating everyday situations that helped them to adapt to the environment in which they lived (school, friends, town, etc.)

We have verified that this way of working makes students learn how to collaborate with each other: they share knowledge and support mutually as they get tangible results from the start. They are not only building in the virtual world but they are also building their own knowledge.

The fact that they conceive the platform as a game also helps. They realize that they are working, but in a pleasant way. For them the virtual world is like a chat, a social network, similar to which they are accustomed to use in their spare

time. They find very motivating being able to speak with each other freely through chat. Affective relationships are established between them and between them and the teacher. They practice the language freely, without shame to write a bad sentence or without the teacher making them to shut up because they might disturb his companions, as might occur during an ordinary class.

Another strong point of the experience is that you can also work on the basic skills, on the development of Multiple Intelligences and on the interdisciplinary aspects of the curriculum. In these initial trials some interdisciplinary aspects have emerged, such as working with measurements and scales (mathematics) and with colors and appearances (arts). However in this experience the mathematics and the art departments were not involved. To make a more complete project and to get deeper into each subject, other departments will be involved in the project during the next academic years (Technology, Art & design, Social sciences, Spanish language, Foreign language, Music).

"Pine, Pinecone, Pinion" Project

During 2011 we began to develop a more complex and elaborated project that involves professionals from different fields. It is the "Pine, pinecone, pinion" project, that involves nursery children, teenagers from residential homes for adolescents at risk (CRAE: juvenile shelters managed by SAGESSA) and the Welcome Course at the Cunit high school. The Department of Environmental Issues of the Generalitat of Catalonia and the Rural Agents Agency are also participating.

The topic is environmental education. The project aims to establish itself as a tool for education of children and adolescents in environmental issues. During the summer 2011 the children from the CRAE made several treks into the forest accompanied by Rural Agents. They gathered information and materials to be used latter by the nursery teachers at the classroom. The project name has its meaning: its base is the "pine," which is composed of boxes ("pinecones") organized by topics. The "pinions" are the natural materials obtained during the excursions (leaves, pine cones, branches, stones, etc.), which are included in the boxes, accompanied with worksheets for the classroom activities at the nursery.

Once all the materials were picked up by the CRAE teenagers, the forest and the routes were represented in the 3D virtual world by the high school students at Cunit. This virtual forest would be used by the nursery children, or by other high school students, to experiment a recreation of the original treks.

The objectives for nursery children and CRAES teenagers were to develop a closer relationship with natural environments by learning what a forest is; knowing the forest plants and animals and their needs; observing the natural, physical and social elements; learning how to be in the forest; participating in environmental activities; raising awareness on the appropriate behaviors in a natural environment; and improving social skills.

The objectives for the students in the Welcome Course were practicing Catalan language and learning about the forest through the building of virtual spaces for the other project participants (children and CRAE adolescents).

Figure 3. Working session on knowing and caring the forest

ESPURNIK Project

After using the V-Leaf platform, which is based on OpenSim (OS, an open software version of Second Life), the Espurna project decided to launch its own virtual world platform (also based in OS): Espurnik. A large number of educational projects are now arising, stimulated by training courses offered to teachers (Barlam, Lasala *et al.*, 2011).

During the third quarter of 2011 an introductory course on Espurnik was delivered. It was a 30-hour course whose target was the collective of primary teachers, secondary teachers and Espurna Project participants. About 30 people attended, and several interesting initiatives emerged from the course. Running rules were established (necessary for the proper administration of our OS) and, more importantly, we designed together the worksheets for the projects the participants would later deploy in their classrooms (for an example, see Lasala, M.J., 2011b). Virtual islands were allocated to educational centers and an open and shared timetable was established inside the virtual world. The teachers continued throughout the summer the practices and projects they had already started. The course ended with a face to face meeting in order to know each other in "real life" (till that moment we had only met virtually in OS); to solve possible doubts; and to develop plans for the continuation of the work done so far (Lasala, 2011c).

After the success of this first training course for teachers, it was decided to repeat the experience. This time it started in October 2011 and covered a total of 40 hours of training by May 2012. This course is coordinated by several trainers and technicians, and the basic idea is using three Working Groups (one of them completely virtual) for learning how to employ virtual worlds for education. More than 65 people are attending, all of them teachers and other professionals related with education.

Collaborative activities, sharing resources and innovation are guidelines that continuously appear on the projects that are arising; this also shows at the moment of application in the classroom. Once the teacher has completed the initial training she may be granted a virtual space (an island) and become part of Espurnik with her students. A follow-up of the training activities and of other Espurnik activities is available online (Espurnik, 2011).

An example of the type of projects that are being implemented is the Welcome Course at Cunit high school, where parts of the educational units are delivered within the 3D virtual world. Some of the activities that we have put into practice are:

- Work performed to know the Catalan alphabet (activities especially aimed at students with no knowledge of the Latin alphabet).
- Activities about the basic vocabulary of body parts, clothing, colors, numbers, shapes, seasons, animals, food, transportation, etc.
- Simulations of everyday conversations, personal introductions, greetings, shopping, localization in space, job applications, etc.
- Building 3D objects to create thematic environments.
- Writing poems of a famous Catalan poet and teacher, which were posted in panels within the virtual world. This activity was part of the Saint Jordi 2010 festival at the high school. Once the poems were posted, the students read them aloud and recorded the reading, working on vocabulary and reading comprehension with an emphasis on correct pronunciation and intonation.

The area in which we work is helping the recently arrived immigrant students to integrate in the Catalan society, by helping them to learn the language and traditions of Catalonia. In the Welcome Course we have a mixture of ages (12 to16 years old), with different levels of language and learning skills. Some of them hardly can write or read in their own language, while others just lack knowledge of the Catalan language. Each student has his own individualized Learning Plan, so once one concrete activity in the virtual world is prepared, any student can take advantage of it depending on the units in which she is working at that time, her date of arrival at the Centre or her background knowledge.

Besides the acquisition of Catalan language, other basic skills are also obtained with the use of Espurnik at the classroom: communication skills; information processing and digital competence; learning to learn; and socialization and citizenship.

There are a lot of practical activities that have been carried out in the virtual world: simulated conversations (voice and text) with classmates and with the teacher, tests, vocabulary acquisition, morphosyntax, synonyms, antonyms, plurals, verb forms, etc.

These activities are generally done in the classroom, but also some children engage in them out of school hours. At the beginning of the course we have focused more on the activity of tailoring their avatars, in order to have them identified with their virtual "alter ego" so that during the rest of the course they were more motivated when working in the different tasks.

Virtual world sessions were not strictly scheduled. We spent about two to four hours a week working inside Espurnik, trying that the moments of connection were the last hours of the morning or the afternoon in order to take advantage of their motivation in working in the virtual world.

The experience was totally adapted to diversity and cohesion, which was one of the main goals (Barlam, Marín *et al.*, 2011). Students had a very different starting point on their knowledge and skills, and needed to adapt as quickly as possible to the Catalan educational system. Activities varied in difficulty level taking into account the country of origin, language, date of arrival, and knowledge and skill levels in the different topics (language, mathematics, history, etc.)

LESSONS LEARNED AND CONCLUSION

Nowadays, students are digital natives: it is necessary to adapt the curriculum to include new tools and methodologies that will motivate them. A virtual world is a 3D environment that is ideally suited to the curriculum of the XXI century, allowing us to work a set of skills that are very difficult to develop using traditional education. Virtual worlds allow making simulations of specific scenarios where students can research and draw their own conclusions.

Many of the students play in virtual worlds (SIMS, Haboo), chat on Messenger or belong to social networks such as Facebook or Twitter. They are hoping to be allowed to use the computer during class hours, but most teachers do not give such permission, assuming this may be a waste of time and cause a delay in the timing of their classroom programming. Instead, in our Welcome Course we took advantage of this interest in new technologies and in online gaming for improving motivation and engagement.

After working with our students we have found the following advantages in using virtual worlds:

- Student supervision and monitoring of the process is simpler to perform.
- Attention to diversity is guaranteed: each student is working at the level she needs.
- Students are more involved in their own learning.
- The high motivation of the students had an impact in their evaluation. Being motivated, the attitude and interest improved (30% of the grade), this in turn had a positive impact in tasks and procedures (30% of the grade), and finally this helped to improve their knowledge of the concepts (40% of the grade).
- Students can work individually, in pairs, in small groups or in large groups, which is sometimes difficult to achieve in a traditional class.

- Evaluation can be made in a variety of forms: initial, continuous, formative and final.
- Concrete educational goals are really achieved and can be easily modified or adapted in case of need.
- Other benefits are obtained, which are complementary to these obtained using the traditional methodology or even using methodologies that are based on use of blogs, Moodle, wikis, online webquests, etc.
- Using closed virtual worlds (as opposed to Second Life) students find only what the teacher wants them to find, not being distracted with other things.
- Blended learning is possible, where face to face teaching and virtual activities are happening simultaneously.
- Students who have not integrated well into the educational system are incorporated more easily using these methodologies.
- There is an increase in the inclusion in education: virtual worlds soften the inclusion barriers (race, social or economic status, disabilities, etc.)

But we have also encountered some difficulties, the two main ones being:

- The need for advanced technical infrastructures at the school (good computers and good internet connection).
- The high amount of teacher's work required for preparing the virtual world activities, as well as the need of previous training of the teacher in virtual worlds.

ACKNOWLEDGMENT

This work was partially funded by ASIES (Adapting Social & Intelligent Environments to Support people with special needs), Ministerio de

Economía y Competividad (TIN2010-17344), and e-Madrid (Investigaciónn y desarrollo de tecnologías para el e-learning en la Comunidad de Madrid) S2009/TIC-1650.

REFERENCES

Alart, N., Barlam, R., Girona, M., & Lasala, M. J. (2010). Espurn@, metodología i cooperació per al canvi. *Perspectiva escolar*, Vol. 344, (pp. 32-42). Barcelona.

Alvarez, M. (2006). *Second Life and school: The use of virtual worlds in high school education. Undergraduate term paper for the course "Game for Web."*. San Antonio, TX, USA: Trinity University.

Babu, S., Suma, E., Barnes, T., & Hodges, L. F. (2007). *Can immersive virtual humans teach social conversational protocols?* IEEE Virtual Reality Conference March 10–14, NC.

Bailey, F., & Moar, M. (2002).*The vertex project: Exploring the creative use of shared 3D virtual worlds in the primary (K-12) classroom.* SIGGRAPH'02.

Barkand, J., & Kush, J. (2009). GEARS a 3D virtual learning environment and virtual social and educational world used in online secondary schools. *Electronic Journal of e-Learning, 7*(3), 215-224.

Barlam, R., Lasala, M. J., Marín, J., Masalles, J., & Pinya, C. (2010). Espurnik, proposta educativa en tres dimensions. *AULA de Innovación Educativa, 205*(19), 77-78. Retrieved April 13, 2012, from http://aula.grao.com/revistas/aula/205-lenguas-integradas-y-competencias-basicas/espurnik-propuesta-educativa-en-tres-dimensiones

Barlam, R., Marín, J., & Oliveres, C. (2011). Enseñar en la sociedad del conocimiento. Reflexiones desde el pupitre. *Cuadernos de Educación, 63.*

Basogain, X., Olabe, M., Espinosa, K., & dos Reis, A. (2009). *Supporting the education with 3D environments and MUVEs.* X Congreso Internacional de Interacción Persona – Computador, INTERACCION'2009.

Bell, M. W. (2008). Toward a definition of virtual worlds. *Journal of Virtual Worlds Research, 1*(1), 1–5.

Bloom, B. S. (1956). *The taxonomy of educational objectives: Classification of educational goals. Handbook 1: The cognitive domain.* New York, NY: McKay Press.

Deutschmann, M., Outakoski, H., Panichi, L., & Schneider, C. (2010). Virtual learning, real heritage benefits and challenges of virtual worlds for the learning of indigenous minority languages. *Conference Proceedings International Conference ICT for Language Learning,* 3rd Conference ed.

3DLES. (2011). Retrieved from http://3dles.com/

Espurna. (2010). Retrieved from http://www.youtube.com/watch?v=Fe1k8gwKGM8&feature=related

Espurna. (2011). Retrieved from http://www.espurna.cat/

Espurna-Ning. (2011). Retrieved from http://espurna.ning.com/

Espurnik. (2011). Retrieved from http://www.youtube.com/watch?v=x4fy3_t5K0Y&feature=youtu.be&hd=1

Feliz, T., & Santoveña, S. M. (2009). *El proyecto Added Value of Teaching in a Virtual World (AVATAR) (Valor añadido de la enseñanza en un mundo virtual).* Programa Comenius, Lifelong Learning Programme.

Goleman, D. (1998). *Working with emotional intelligence.* New York, NY: Bantam Books.

Hernández, J., Pennesi, M., Sobrino, D., & Vázquez, A. (2011). Experiencias educativas en las aulas del siglo XXI. *Fundación Telefónica,* Madrid 2011 (pp. 404-409). Retrieved April 13, 2012 from http://es.scribd.com/doc/58800585/Experiencias-educativas-en-las-aulas-del-siglo-XXI

Hew, K. F., & Cheung, W. S. (2010). Use of three-dimensional (3-D) immersive virtual worlds in K-12 and higher education settings: A review of the research. *British Journal of Educational Technology, 41,* 33–55. doi:10.1111/j.1467-8535.2008.00900.x

Inman, C., Wright, V. H., & Hartman, J. A. (2010). Use of Second Life in K-12 and higher education: A review of research. *Journal of Interactive Online Learning, 9*(1).

Jauregi, M. K., Canto, S., de Graaff, R., & Koenraad, T. (2010). Social interaction through video-webcommunication and virtual worlds: An added value for education. In *Short paper in CD Proceedings Online Education,* Berlin, (pp. 1-6). Berlin, Germany: ICWE.

Jerónimo, J. A. (2011). *Promover el aprendizaje en los mundos virtuales con una docencia innovadora.* Universidad Nacional Autónoma de México, Virtual Educa México 2011.

Ketelhut, D. J. (2007). The impact of student self-efficacy on scientific inquiry skills: An exploratory investigation in River City, a multi-user virtual environment. *Journal of Science Education and Technology, 16*(1), 99–111. doi:10.1007/s10956-006-9038-y

Kluge, S., & Riley, L. (2008). Teaching in virtual worlds: Opportunities and challenges. *Issues in Informing Science and Information Technology, 5.*

Lasala, M. J. (2011). *Proyectos educativos en aula d'acollida basados en mundos virtuales 3D: Fem una platja (hagamos una playa).* En: Experiencias educativas en las aulas del siglo XXI. Innovación con TIC.

Lasala, M. J. (2011b). *Espurnik'11.* Retrieved from http://www.slideshare.net/aulaacollidacunit/ficha-prctica-espurnik11

Lasala, M. J. (2011c). *Experiencias didacticas mundos virtuales y redes sociales en la enseanza secundaria obligatoria.* Retrieved from http://www.slideshare.net/aulaacollidacunit/experiencias-didcticas-mundos-virtuales-y-redes-sociales-en-la-enseanza-secundaria-obligatoria

Lave, J., & Wenger, E. (1991). *Situated learning: Legitimate peripheral participation.* Cambridge, UK: University of Cambridge Press. doi:10.1017/CBO9780511815355

Ligori, M. B., & Van Veen, K. (2006). Constructing a successful cross-national virtual learning environment in primary and secondary education. *AACE Journal, 14*(2), 103–128.

Ligorio, M. B. (2001, March). *Euroland: A virtual community.* Paper presented at the Conference Computer Supported Collaborative Learning. Maastricht, Amsterdam.

Ligorio, M. B., Talamo, A., & Simons, R. S. (2000, March). *Euroland: A virtual world fostering collaborative learning at a distance.* Paper presented at the First Research Workshop of EDEN Research and Innovation in Open and Distance Learning, Prague.

Ligorio, M. B., & Trimpe, J. D. (2000). *Euroland: Active knowledge building through different formats of mediated communication.* Unpublished, Katholieke University of Nijmegen, Netherlands.

Molka-Danielsen, J., & Deutschman, M. (2009). *Learning and teaching in the virtual world of Second Life.* Trondheim, Norway: Tapir Academic Press.

Revuelta, F. I. (2011). Competencia digital: Desarrollo de aprendizajes con mundos virtuales en la escuela 2.0. *Edutec-e. Revista Electrónica de Tecnología Educativa, 37.*

Rico, M., Camacho, D., Alaman, X., & Pulido, E. (2009). A high school educational platform based on virtual worlds. *2nd Workshop on Methods and Cases in Computing Education (MCCE 2009)*, Barcelona, Spain, (pp. 46-51).

Rico, M., Martínez-Muñoz, G., Alamán, X., Camacho, D., & Pulido, E. (2010). A programming experience of high school students in a virtual world platform. *International Journal of Engineering Education, 2010*.

Rodger, S. H., Bashford, M., Dyck, L., Hayes, J., Liang, L., Nelson, D., & Qin, H. (2010). Enhancing K-12 education with Alice programming adventures. *Proceedings of ITiCSE, 2010*, 234–238.

Schank, R. (2002). *Designing world-class e-learning: How IBM, GE, Harvard Business School, and Columbia University are succeeding at e-learning*. McGraw-Hill Professional.

Sheehy, K. (2010). Virtual environments: Issues and opportunities for researching inclusive educational practices. In Peachey, A., Gillen, J., Livingstone, D., & Smith-Robbins, S. (Eds.), *Researching learning in virtual worlds*. Human-Computer Interaction Series. doi:10.1007/978-1-84996-047-2_1

Sheehy, K., & Ferguson, R. (2008). Educational inclusion, new technologies. In Scott, T. B., & Livingston, J. L. (Eds.), *Leading edge educational technology*. New York, NY: Nova Science.

The New Media Consortium & the EDUCAUSE Learning Initiative. (2007). *The 2007 horizon report* (pp. 18).

Vygotsky, L. S. (1978). *Mind in society*. Harvard University Press.

WiloStar3D. (2011). Retrieved from http://www.wilostar3d.com/

ADDITIONAL READING

Antonacci, D. M., & Modaress, N. (2005). *Second Life: The educational possibilities of a massively multiplayer virtual world*. EDUCAUSE Western Regional Conference.

Antonacci, D. M., & Modress, N. (2008). Envisioning the Educational possibilities of user-created virtual worlds. *AACE Journal, 16*(2), 115–126.

Ares, N. (2007). Appropriating roles and relations of power in collaborative learning. *International Journal of Qualitative Studies in Education, 21*(2), 99–121. doi:10.1080/09518390701256472

Bronack, S. C., Riedl, R. E., & Tashner, J. H. (2004). *Teaching in a virtual world*. League of Worlds Annual Meeting, Helsinki, Finland.

Bronack, S. C., Riedl, R. E., & Tashner, J. H. (2005). Teaching in 3D: Developing learning communities in a multi-user virtual environment. *Society for Information Technology and Teacher Education International Conference*, 2005, Vol. 1, (pp. 2166-2170).

Bronack, S. C., Rieldl, R. E., & Tashner, J. H. (2006). Learning in the zone: A social constructivist framework for distance education in a 3-dimensional virtual world. *Interactive Learning Environments, 14*(3), 219–232. doi:10.1080/10494820600909157

Campbell, M. (2009). Using virtual world technologies to improve the professional decision-making capacities of pre-graduate teachers. In Mendez-Vilas, A., Solano Martin, A., Mesa Gonzalez, J. A., & Mesa Gonzalez, J. (Eds.), *Research, reflections and innovations in integrating ICT in education*.

Ching-Song, W., Yan, C., & Jiann-Gwo, D. (2009). *A 3D virtual world teaching and learning platform for computer science courses in Second Life*. International Conference on Computational Intelligence and Software Engineering CiSE 2009.

Dalgarno, B., Lee, M. J. W., Carlson, L., Gregory, S., & Tynan, B. (2010). 3D immersive virtual worlds in higher education: An Australian and New Zealand scoping study. *Proceedings ASCI-LITE* Sydney 2010.

De Freitas, S. (2008). *Serious virtual worlds: A scoping study*. JISC e-Learning Programme.

Dickey, M. D. (2005). Three-dimensional virtual worlds and distance learning: Two case studies of active worlds as a medium for distance education. *British Journal of Educational Technology, 36*(3), 439–451. doi:10.1111/j.1467-8535.2005.00477.x

Dickey, M. D. (2011). World of Warcraft and the impact of game culture and play in an undergraduate game design course. *Journal Computer & Education, 56*(1), 200–209. doi:10.1016/j.compedu.2010.08.005

Elund, J., Clayden, J., & Green, L. (2010). Getting to know your avatar in Second Life. *Australian Journal of Communication, 37*(2), 73–86.

Esteves, M., Fonseca, B., Morgado, L., & Martins, P. (2009). Using Second Life for problem based learning in computer science programming: Pedagogy, education and innovation in 3-D virtual worlds. *Journal of Virtual Worlds Research, 2*(1).

Esteves, M., Fonseca, B., Morgado, L., & Martins, P. (2011). Improving teaching and learning of computer programming through the use of the Second Life virtual world. *British Journal of Educational Technology, 42*(4). doi:10.1111/j.1467-8535.2010.01056.x

Fewster, R., Chafer, J., & Wood, D. (2010). Staging Second Life in real and virtual spaces. In Vincenti, G., & Bramam, J. (Eds.), *Teaching through multiuser virtual environments: Applying dynamic elements to the modern classroom* (pp. 217–235). Hershey, PA: IGI Global. doi:10.4018/978-1-61692-822-3.ch013

Fominykh, M., Prasolova-Førland, E., Morozov, M., & Gerasimov, A. (2009). Virtual campus in the context of an educational virtual city: A case study. In G. Siemens & C. Fulford (Eds.), *Proceedings of World Conference on Educational Multimedia, Hypermedia and Telecommunications 2009* (pp. 559-568). Chesapeake, VA: AACE.

Gilman, R., Tashner, J., Bronack, S., Riedl, R., & Cheney, A. (2007). Crossing continents: Bringing teachers and learners together through a 3D immersive world. *Educators' eZine*, April 2007. Retrieved April 13, 2012, from http://www.techlearning.com/story/showArticle.php?articleID=196604336

Graaff, R., & Koenraad, A. L. M. (2011). *Research based guidelines on designing tasks for intercultural communicative competence using video web communication and 3D virtual worlds*. Manual on 3D in Secondary Education, NIFLAR Project.

Jauregi, K., Canto, S., de Graaff, R., Koenraad, T., & Moonen, M. (2011). Verbal interaction in Second Life: Towards a pedagogic framework for task design. *Computer Assisted Language Learning Journal, 24*(1), 77–101. doi:10.1080/09588221.2010.538699

Kelton, A. J. (2007). Second Life: Reaching into the virtual world for real-world learning. *EDUCAUSE Research Bulletin, 17*, 1–13.

Kemp, J., & Livingstone, D. (2006). Putting a Second Life "metaverse" skin on learning management systems. *Proceedings of the Second Life Education Workshop at SLCC* (pp. 13-18).

Koenraad, A. L. M. (2009, March). *Learning blends and 3D Virtual Worlds to promote oral skills development in modern language education*. Paper presented at CALICO 2009 Conference, Phoenix, Arizona.

Lim, J. K. S., & Edirisinghe, E. M. (2007). *Teaching computer science using second life as a learning environment.* In *Proceedings ASCILITE ICT: Providing Choices for Learners and Learning.* Singapore, 2007.

Molka-Danielsen, J. (2011). Exploring the role of virtual worlds in the evolution of a co-creation design culture. *SCIS, Vol. 86 of Lecture Notes in Business Information Processing,* (pp. 3-15). Springer.

Molka-Danielsen, J., & Chabada, M. (2010). Application of the 3D multi user virtual environment of Second Life to emergency evacuation simulation. *HICSS, 2010,* 1–9.

Nie, M., Roush, P., & Wheeler, M. (2010). Second Life for digital photography: An exploratory study. *Contemporary Educational Technology, 1*(3), 267–280.

Ryan, M. (2008). *16 ways to use Second Life in your classroom: Pedagogical approaches and virtual assignments.* Research Learning in Virtual Environments.

Schank, R. C. (1997). *Virtual learning. A revolutionary approach to building a highly skilled workforce.* New York, NY: McGrawHill. doi:10.1002/pfi.4140400511

Schank, R. C. (2005). *Lessons in learning, e-learning, and training: Reflections and perspectives for the enlightened trainer: Reflections and perspectives for the bewildered trainer.* Pfeiffer & Company.

Sheehy, K., Fergunson, R., & Clough, G. (2010). *Virtual worlds: Controversies at the frontier of education.* Nova Science Publishers Inc.

Sim, J., James, J., McDonald, M., Scutter, S., & Wood, D. (2011). *The use of 3D simulation learning in healthcare disciplines: A pilot study.* In 8th ASMMIRT 2011 'The Perfect Blend', Adelaide, South Australia.

Tashner, J. H., Riedl, R. E., & Bronack, S. C. (2005). Virtual worlds: Further development of web-based teaching. *Hawaii International Conference on Education* (2005), Vol. 1, (pp. 4579-4588).

Tashner, J. H., Riedl, R. E., Bronack, S. C., Cheney, A. L., Gilman, R. M., Sanders, R. L., & Angel, R. B. (2007). *Learning communities in 3D immersive worlds: Evolving online instruction.* Hawaii International Conference on Education, Oahu, Hawaii.

Wallace, P., & Maryott, J. (2009). The impact of avatar self-representation on collaboration in virtual worlds. *Innovate: Journal of Online Education, 5*(5).

Wood, D. (2010). The benefits and unanticipated challenges in the use of 3D virtual learning environments in the undergraduate media arts curriculum. In Vincenti, G., & Bramam, J. (Eds.), *Teaching through multi-user virtual environments: Applying dynamic elements to the modern classroom* (pp. 236–257). Hershey, PA: IGI Global. doi:10.4018/978-1-61692-822-3.ch014

Wood, D. (2010). Communicating in virtual worlds through a Web 2.0 application. *Telecommunications Journal of Australia, 60*(2), 19.1-19.16.

Wood, D., Ussery, J., & Morris, C. (2010, March). *Health care, virtual worlds and education.* Lead panel presented at the Virtual Worlds Best Practice 2010 Third Annual Conference.

KEY TERMS AND DEFINITIONS

B-Learning: Blended learning, a education model that combines classroom teaching (face-to-face) with e-Learning.

E-Learning: A distance education model that uses Information and Communication Technologies (ICT) in the teaching-learning process.

Information and Communication Technologies (ICT): All the technologies developed around the computer and the computer networks. They include software components (programs) as well as hardware components (for example, tangible interfaces, interactive blackboards, etc.).

M-Learning: Mobile learning, a distance educational model in which learning takes place using mobile devices such as smartphones, tablets, i-pods or any other device that has wireless connectivity.

U-Learning: Ubiquitous learning, a distance educational model in which learning takes place anywhere, anytime and on any subject.

Virtual World: A synchronous, persistent network of people, represented as avatars, facilitated by networked computers.

V-Learning: Virtual learning, a distance educational model that uses virtual worlds as a tool in the teaching-learning process.

Section 3
User Modelling

Chapter 7
A Proposal to Model Interaction from the Analysis of Student – Pedagogic Conversational Agent Logs

Diana Pérez-Marín
Universidad Rey Juan Carlos, Spain

Ismael Pascual-Nieto
Universidad Rey Juan Carlos, Spain

ABSTRACT

According to User-Centered Design, computer interactive systems should be implemented taking into account the users' preferences. However, in some cases, it is not easy to apply conventional Human-Computer interaction evaluation techniques to identify the users' needs and improve the user-system interaction. Therefore, this chapter proposes a procedure to model the interaction behaviour from the analysis of conversational agent dialog logs. A case study in which the procedure has been applied to model the behaviour of 20 children when interacting with multiple personality Pedagogic Conversational Agents is described as an illustrative sample of the goodness and practical application of the procedure.

INTRODUCTION

In the last years, there has been a great evolution in the design and application of computer systems. Moreover, the users of these computer systems are not longer restricted to people with computer skills. Therefore, computer applications should provide an intuitive and friendly interface to make their use easier.

Human-Computer Interaction (Dix et al. 2004) studies how to design, evaluate and implement interactive computer systems to be used by human beings. It could be considered complementary to classic Software Engineering models and techniques (Pressman, 2009) to develop applications.

DOI: 10.4018/978-1-4666-2530-3.ch007

Copyright © 2013, IGI Global. Copying or distributing in print or electronic forms without written permission of IGI Global is prohibited.

For instance, User Centered Design (UCD) could be applied in iterative software life cycles to take into account the opinion and needs of the users during the all the process (Abascal, Moriyón 2002).

That way, it is reduced the risk that when the users get the final application, they claimed that it is different from what they indicated. On the other hand, users feel that their opinion is being taken into account and participate in the design of the interface that evolves according to their comments. However, sometimes it is not easy to directly ask the users for their opinion because they cannot attend regular meetings, they have some kind of impairment or they are simply too young to clearly express what they think. In those cases, the benefits of UCD could be lost.

In this chapter, a procedure to model the interaction of those users with the system from their logs is proposed. The users can interact with any prototype of the system on their own, at any computer connected to Internet, and a log system registers the information needed to extract the indicators. The design questions can then be answered from that information, without directly asking the user, but taking into account all the variables to be modelled.

In particular, User Centered Design extended with this procedure could be useful for the design and evaluation of Pedagogic Conversational Agents (PCA). PCAs can be defined as lifelike autonomous character that cohabite the learning environment creating a rich face-to-face interface with the student (Johnson et al. 2000).

However, it is still not clear which features should have those characters to improve the learning or the level of engagement of the students (Pérez-Marín, Pascual-Nieto 2011). Therefore, depending on the features of the students the agents could be designed accordingly. Moreover, in the case of children, and as an illustrative sample of how to apply the proposed procedure to model the children-agent interaction, we present a case study in which the logs of 20 conversations were analyzed to answer some design questions and provide some answers, without having to directly ask the children.

The chapter is organized as follows: section "Related Work" presents a review of the existing methods and techniques to model and evaluate Human-Computer Interaction; Section "Proposal" describes the proposed procedure to model the interaction from the logs; Section "Case Study" focuses on the how the procedure has been applied; and, Section "Conclusion" ends the paper with the main conclusions and lines of future work.

RELATED WORK

Evaluation is key in User Centered Designs because from the comments and opinions of the users the prototypes of the computer interactive system evolve to new versions. In order to evaluate the system, several procedures and techniques have been proposed that can be applied in different phases of the software life cycle.

Several main evaluation methods can be distinguished (see Figure 1 for a general overview based on Dix et al. 2004):

- Evaluation through expert analysis: heuristics, standards or cognitive walkthroughs are used to identify potential difficulties from the point of view of the expert.
- Evaluation through user participation: users interact with the system as they would normally do when the computer application is released, and/or they complete some tasks as indicated by the researchers or to fill in some questionnaires.

Evaluation through Expert Analysis

Several experts are usually needed to perform the evaluation. The reason is because it is more likely that several experts find out the usability problems instead of just one expert. They can use

Figure 1. Summary of the existing evaluation methods

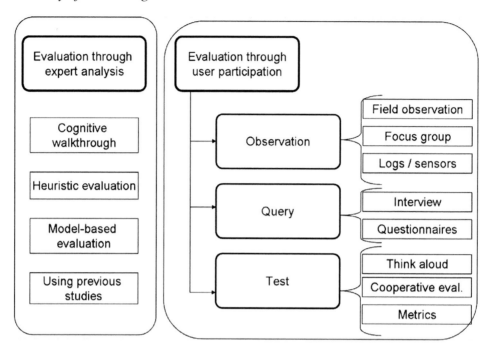

their previous knowledge, standards or heuristics to tackle the evaluation.

In particular, using the cognitive walkthrough technique, the evaluators have to go through each step of the interaction with the system in order to accomplish some task. They have to think about who the users are, and what kind of experience and knowledge can assume about them to decide whether they would be able to perform the tasks. For instance, in the evaluation of an educational system for children with Special Needs they should take into account which specific features the system should have.

A heuristic can be defined as a guideline or general principle or rule of thumb that can guide a design decision. Nielsen (1993) proposed a list of usability heuristics that can be used, among others, by the experts using the heuristic evaluation to check whether the system follows them, or which violations can be detected and solved. For instance, according to Nielsen, the experts could focus on checking the visibility of the system status, the matching between the system and

real world, the consistency of the interface, how errors are prevented and shown, the aesthetics of the design, and the help and documentation.

On the other hand, experts could rely their evaluation on some already existing models, using the model-based evaluation. For instance, if the experts have to evaluate a new Word Processor, they could rely on standards di facto such as Microsoft Word as it is used by many users all over the world so it constitutes a reference.

Finally, the experts could also use previous studies. If a similar system was evaluated previously, the findings could be reused and that way, it would not be necessary to repeat the whole evaluation again.

Evaluation through User Participation

The evaluation is not based on the opinion of the experts, but on the collaboration with users. They could answer some questions in an interview or questionnaire, complete some tasks with the system or just interact with it as they would do once it is released, for instance to evaluate its usability.

For the sake of grouping these possibilities, we have identified three main categories of evaluation techniques through user participation: observation, query and test. Under the observation category, we have grouped all the techniques in which the users just interact with the system but without completing predefined tasks, they could have some sensors on them and some logs could be registered, and it is recommended that although it is possible that the researcher is in the same room, they do not interfere with the users. Under the query category, we have grouped all the techniques in which the users are directly asked for their opinion. Finally, under the test category, we have grouped all the techniques in which the users have to complete predefined tasks and talk about them.

According to that classification, the techniques identified for observation can be: field observation, focus group, physiological sensors and logs. During the field observation, the researchers should just observe and write on their books the way in which the users interact with the system on their own. No predefined tasks are asked to complete, and no dialogue between the evaluator and the users should be established (although it is possible to combine this technique with query techniques too). For instance, the field observation could be useful to identify which tasks the users are able to easily perform to be kept in future versions and which options of the menus are less used or how they are accessed by the users.

For the focus group, from 6 to 9 users and evaluators talk about aspects related to the system. Among them, one (an expert evaluator) is designated as the moderator of the group. It is very important to have a moderator as s/he is in charge of preparing the list of topics to discuss and gather the information during the talk. On the other hand, the moderator should not strongly control the talk of the group. S/he should let people speak freely to capture their spontaneous reactions and evolution of ideas during the talk.

Logs are traditionally used to automatically gather statistics about the use of the system. One of their main benefits is that they can provide much objective information. Even, by using sensors they could provide physiological information such as heart rate, orientation of the gaze, facial gestures, etc. On the other hand, they can be difficult to process without a systematic approach to model and without having a clear idea of which indicators are being found. Furthermore, they have been traditionally used for the launch of the system when it was already in production.

Regarding the techniques identified for query, it can be distinguished the interview and the use of questionnaires. One of the main advantages of this method is that you have information directly provided from the user. However, users may find difficult to answer some design questions or they could not be able to clearly express their opinions because they are too young or they have some kind of impairment.

In any case, both interviews and questionnaires have to be prepared before the evaluation. Interviews can follow a closed structure with a predefined sequence of questions, or a more open structure allowing the users more freedom in their answers and the evaluator can ask new questions depending on the answers of the users to detect something new or find out more details about an interesting aspect. In both cases, it is usually advisable to start with more general questions to more focused questions. Moreover, given that the amount of time spent with each participant could be high, the number of users to which this technique can be applied is limited.

On the other hand, questionnaires have a close list of items and they can be filled in by many users at the same time. One of the main advantages is that it is possible to get more information, although it may be subjective. It is also advisable that the questionnaire is anonymous so that it is not possible to identify which user has written something and that way, users may feel more freedom to give their opinion. The limitation is that even in open items in which more general questions can be asked, there is no the possibility of directly asking the user for more information about some detail.

Finally, three techniques can be classified in the test category: think aloud, cooperative evaluation and metrics. Think aloud consists in asking the users to talk aloud what they are thinking about their feeling and opinions about any aspect of the system while they are interacting with it. This is an efficient way to get information from a small number of users from a cognitive point of view to understand their mental model. However, some users find it difficult to talk alone. Hence, the cooperative evaluation is an alternative in which instead of just one user, two users are interacting with the system, and they are asked to talk aloud about their thoughts and feelings. Regarding the metrics technique, it consists in getting objective and subjective measures. For instance, some objective measures could be how many errors the users make, how long they take in completing each task in average, etc. Subjective measures could be comments, perceptions, preferences, etc.

PROPOSAL: PROCEDURE TO MODEL THE INTERACTION FROM THE LOGS

The proposed procedure combines the ideas of the metrics and logs evaluation through user participation techniques. It is intended to extend the User Centered Design (UCD) taking into account information directly from users (not evaluation through expert analysis) but without the need of asking them to talk aloud, in groups, fill in questionnaires or to answer interviews. This is because we believe that those techniques are adequate for adults, but in some cases as children or people with some kind of impairment they could not be applied and the benefits of UCD could be lost.

Hence, it is our insight that taking metrics is a good option to capture much information of any

user interacting with the computer. However, it should be done systematically to produce a valid behaviour model. Moreover, and opposite to the traditional use of logs in the final production phase, we believe that logs can be effectively used in previous phases of the software life cycle too, and that could keep the benefits of this type of evaluation while reducing its limitations.

The main steps of the procedure to model the interaction are as follows:

1. **Identification of variables**. The evaluators have to ask themselves which variables they want to model. This could be done by preparing some design questions. Each variable could be related to one or more questions.
2. **Logs registration**. To register the interaction of the users with the system in logs. It is advisable to apply some templates or markup language to make the processing of the logs easier, and in some cases even automatic.
3. **Identification of levels**. To identify several levels of log analysis depending on the depth of the behaviour model to be created.
4. **Extraction of indicators and relationships.** For each level, to extract indicators for each variable of the model and possible relationships among the variables.
5. **Creation of the behaviour model.** To answer the design questions and provide the behaviour model.

Figure 2 shows an overview of the proposed procedure. As can be seen the procedure can be represented as a triangle that relates the variables of the model, the indicators of the logs and the interaction between the users and the system.

CASE STUDY: PRACTICAL APPLICATION OF THE PROCEDURE

The proposed procedure has been applied for the first time to model the interaction behaviour of a

Figure 2. Overview of the procedure to generate the model from the logs

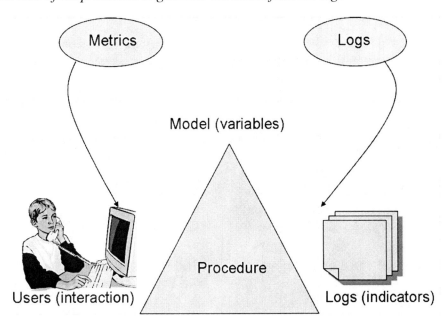

group of children with a Pedagogic Conversational Agent. The full description of the agent is out of the scope of this chapter, given that the goal here is to study how to model the interaction. However, to give an idea of the interface of the system, it should be said that it is like the Messenger with the face of the agent on the left, and the text conversation on the right. Moreover, the face of the agent changes according to its mood: informative, tester, cheerful or grumpy.

Step 1: Identification of Variables

To identify the variables to model, the following design questions were raised:

Question 1: Do children prefer that the agent has a good or bad temper? Could it be that by designing cheerful agents, the children are more encouraged to study, or on the contrary, could it be that by designing bad-tempered agents that tell the students not to rest on their laurels, students start devoting more effort and time to their study? (*Variable: agent personality*)

Question 2: Do children prefer that the agent provides them with new information or with formative assessment? (*Variable: agent informativeness*)

Question 3: Would children like to change the personality of the agent? (*Variable: agent personality*)

Question 4: Could it be identified a new 'Police Effect' according to which an agent with a tester personality that only asks questions is rejected by the students because they feel they are constantly under questioning? (*Variables: agent personality and informativeness*)

Question 5: Are children less aggressive in their interactions with the agent than adults interacting with agents? (*Variable: user aggresiveness*)

Question 6: Do children keep a coherent conversation with the agent? How long in average do they think their answer? (*Variable: coherence of the conversation*)

Question 7: Are children kind with the agent? Are they more kind with certain type of agent personalities? (*Variable: user amiability*)

Question 8: Are there gender differences? (*Variable: user gender*)

Question 9: Are there differences between children who are more familiarized with the use of computers than children who are less familiarized? (*Variable: use of computer competence*)

Question 10: Would children tolerate a new interaction with the same agents and conversation? What would be the changes between the first round of conversations and the following rounds? Would they start complaining? (*Variable: user tolerance*)

Table 1 sums up the variables of the model and their related design questions.

Step 2: Logs Registration

The second step is to gather the user logs. We asked permission to the teachers and parents of 20 children of a Spanish school to register their natural language conversation with the agent during one class (1 hour). The children were not provided instructions on how to use the system or asked any doubt during the interaction. The students were motivated by telling them that the agent would teach them study techniques, and that they could use the computer during the whole hour and even to choose the temper of the agent (informative, tester, cheerful or grumpy).

Table 1. Variables of the model and their related design questions

Variable	Questions
Agent personality	1,3,4
Agent informativeness	2,4
User aggresiveness	5
Coherence of the conversation	6
User amiability	7
User gender	8
Use of computer competence	9
User tolerance	10

Step 3: Identification of Levels

Once the logs were gathered, three level of log analysis were identified from the most general to the most specific: in level 1, the interaction of each child with a different temper of the agent is studied (the agent was provided a different name according to the temper to make the analysis easier, in particular Tim was informative, Mario was tester, Nim was cheerful and Ñom was grumpy); in level 2, it is studied how each child freely chooses each agent; and, in level 3, the natural language conversation is analyzed.

Step 4: Extraction of Indicators and Relationships for Each Level

Level 1 of Analysis: At the Level of Each Temper of the Agent

18 students referred to Tim (informative) as a boy. Only 2 students stated they think that 'it was a robot that knows a lot of things' or 'it is an intelligent object'. In any case, the adjective that was most used to describe Tim was intelligent. In fact, to the question why they like it, students usually answered because the agent told them important things, and he was right.

In the case of Mario, all the students referred to it as a boy, and to the question about what they think of the agent, the most common answers were a simple 'I like it'. Two students highlighted that they like the way in which the agent formulated questions to make them think. In any case, the sentences most used to refer to this agent was 'he is intelligent to make you questions to find out if you know how to study and he knows very well how to do it'. In fact, to the question why they like the agent, students usually answered because he was able to make them questions to find out what you know. The most common adjective to describe Mario was curious.

In the case of Nim, all the students referred to the agent as a boy, and to the question about what they think about him, students were enthusiast in their answers. Sentences referring to Nim were usually in the form: 'Nim is superb!!!', 'I like soooo much Nim' or, 'Nim is so good'. In fact, the adjective most used to describe Nim was good, and students said that they like Nim because he motivates them.

In the case of Ñom, all the students also referred to the agent as a boy, and to the question about what they think about him, they mostly answered that they dislike him because he was angry and grumpy. On the other hand, 9 out of the 20 children said that they liked Ñom because he told them that they could do better and not to rest on their laurels. Some sentences used by the children to refer to Ñom was 'he is a bit grumpy but he tries you to do better', or 'I dislike Ñom', being 'bad' the adjective most used for Ñom.

Table 2 sums up the results of the analysis of the logs at the level of each agent according to three criteria: how many students have regarded the agent as a human being, the most usual sentence to refer to the agent, and the most used adjective to describe it.

Level 2 of Analysis: At the Level of the Student Personal Choice of Agent

Table 3 shows the percentages of times in which each agent was asked in the first place to keep the conversation after the four moods have been introduced, both in the case of the conversations of the first round, the second and the third round of interaction.

As can be seen, when the children were given the option of choosing the temper they wanted, in the first round they mostly chose Mario (the tester agent), and in the second round they mostly chose Tim (the happy and informative agent).

It has also been observed that children usually kept talking to an agent of the same temper during at least three dialogue turns before asking for a different agent. Ñom was usually the last

Table 2. Summary table of the analysis of the logs at the level of each temper

Agent	Tim	Mario	Nim	Ñom
Personality	Happy and informative	Tester and thinker	Happy and encouraging	Bad-temper and grumpy
# of students who have regarded the agent as a human being	18/20	ALL	ALL	ALL
Most used sentence to refer to the agent	'Tim told me important things and he is right'	'Mario is intelligent to make you questions to find out if you know how to study'.	'Nim is superb!!!'	'I dislike Ñom'
Most used adjective to refer to the agent	intelligent	curious	good	bad

Table 3. Analysis of the logs at the level of the student personal choice of agent

Percentage/Agent	Tim	Mario	Nim	Ñom	None
First round	17.39	**39.13**	21.74	13.04	8.70
Second round	**41.67**	8.33	0.00	0.00	50.00
Third round	0	**100.0**	0.00	0.00	0.00
Total	25.00	**30.56**	13.89	8.33	22.22

option, and children asked for him when they did not have other option (i.e. the other agents had run out of sentences). On the other hand, when children started to get tired after many dialogue turns, they asked for Nim, and they would thank him for his jokes, and in some cases, even they directly asked him for more jokes.

Level 3 of Analysis: At the Level of the Conversation

Table 4 presents the results for the following indicators at the level of the whole agent-student conversation: average duration, aggressiveness level, coherence of the conversation, amiability of the student with the agent, number of students who asked for a certain temper first, number of changes requested by the students for the agent and the number of students who ended the conversation after talking to the agent in all the available moods.

The *average duration* of the conversations was around 10 minutes, decreasing from an average of 13 minutes in the first round conversations down to nearly 4 minutes in the second round conversations (only one student used the agent for a third round conversation). Similarly as the changes of the duration of the conversations, the duration of each interaction is around 10 seconds

Table 4. Analysis of the logs at the level of the conversation

Criterion	Average	Deviation
Duration of the conversation	9' 43"	5' 57"
Aggressiveness	0.11	0.32
Coherence	8.86	1.36
Amiability	9.81	0.58
# of changes requested for Tim	1	--
# of changes requested for for Mario	0	--
# of changes requested for Nim	1	--
# of changes requested for Ñom	14	--
# of students who finished the conversation	24	--

in average, decreasing from 10.85 in the first round conversations to 7.08 in the second round conversations.

The *aggressiveness level* of the conversation was measured from 0 (lack of aggressiveness) to 10 (complete aggressiveness) depending on the number of insults written by the students. Its value is insignificant, both in the case of first, second and third round of conversations. This result is quite interesting because according to Angeli and Brahnam (2008), many adults may have insulted the agents when the answer was the same, or different from what they would expect for a second dialogue (i.e. a human being would not repeat again the same sentences).

On the contrary, children did not seem to care about the agent repeating again the same sentences, they did not complain, and they just devoted a little less time to the interaction, but in most cases even completed the dialogue in the second round (and in one case even during a third round). The only little aggressiveness observed against the agents in a second round was in the log of one child who started typing letters without forming correct words, and other child who answered that he was 123 years old.

The *coherence of the conversation* was measured from 0 (lack of coherence) to 10 (complete coherence) as the naturalness of the answers of the student to the questions of the agent, and if the sentences of the students were as expected in the flow of the conversation. For instance, if the agent asks what the student thinks about him, the answer of the student is coherent if it deals with the opinion of the student about the agent. The average value for coherence is around 9 in both the first and second round conversations. This is quite high and it could be an indicative that not only the children did not insult the agents, but they correctly answered to their requests and followed the normal flow of the conversation, even in the second round.

The only little coherence breaks registered in the logs was due to children asking for a temper that was not longer available. It was particularly relevant in the case of Nim. Some children would ask for Nim many consecutive times. Thus, Nim would run out of sentences, and the system would say to the child that s/he must choose between Tim, Mario or Ñom, but the child wanted to speak to Nim, so s/he would ask several times for Nim, until s/he finally accepted that Nim was not longer available.

A different aspect between the coherence in first and second round conversations is that students uttered longer and more justified sentences in the first round, while in the second round, the sentences were shorter and some of them even monosyllabic (i.e. just answering 'Yes' to all the questions asked by Mario). This could be explained by the novelty effect of the first round.

The *amiability* of the student with the agent was measured from 0 (lack of amiability) to 10 (complete amiability) as the kindness of the students' sentences. For instance, if the student provides sentences such as: 'how intelligent of you to tell me that!' is more amiable than if the student provides sentences such as: 'I am getting bored of your nonsenses'.

The average value for amiability is around 10 (the maximum value). This is because children were really kind to the agents, and highly tolerant to any possible mistake. The only little problem with amiability was that even without being aggressive and insulting the agent, two children were quite brusque with Ñom. They would not accept Ñom's comments, so even without being asked, they told Ñom that he was not right, and that they did not like his attitude.

Only one student would change Tim but she did not say how, while the rest of the children would keep Tim the same, in words of one student 'because he has to be like he is'. The same child also said that she would like to change Nim, although again she did not explain how. No child would change Mario. On the other hand, 14 out of the 20 children would like to change Ñom so that he becomes happier.

There were a total of 24 conversations (because some children completed more than one conversation). Only one child did not complete the first round conversations, while 5 children completed the second round conversations, and no child completed a third round conversation.

Table 5 shows the average results for boys and for girls to make the comparison easier. The results are only given for the first round conversations, because no boy completed a second-third round conversation (it could be due because there were less boys in the class).

The average duration of the girls-agents conversations (around 13 minutes) is higher than the average duration of the boys-agents conversations (around 12 minutes), as well as the duration of each interaction (around 12 seconds for girls, and 10 seconds for boys). All the same, it should also be taken into account the typing speed factor.

Although as commented before, in general, aggressiveness is insignificant, in the case of the girls is completely 0. Similarly, although in general, amiability is high, in the case of the girls is maximum: 10, and the coherence is a little high (9.38) than in the case of the boys (8.29).

The girls asked for more changes of the agents. This is particularly relevant for the case of Ñom, 8 girls asked for its change in contrast to only 2

Table 5. Analysis of possible gender differences for the first round conversations

Criterion	Girls	Boys
Duration of the conversation	12' 06"	9' 79"
Aggressiveness	0	0.14
Coherence	9.38	8.29
Amiability	1	0
# of changes requested for Tim	0	0
# of changes requested for for Mario	0	0
# of changes requested for Nim	1	0
# of changes requested for Ñom	8	2
# of students who finished the conversation	13	6

Table 6. Analysis of possible differences because of the degree of familiarity with the use of computers

Criterion	Value
Duration of the Conversation	**Min Sec**
Average-deviation duration for 0-hour/day computer users	16' 35"
Average-deviation duration for 1-hour/day computer users	14' 17"
Average-deviation duration for 2-hour/day computer users	18' 32"
Average-deviation duration for >2-hours/day computer users	11' 23"
Duration of the Agent-Student Interaction	**Seconds**
Average-deviation duration for 0-hour/day computer users	8.33
Average-deviation duration for 1-hour/day computer users	12.21
Average-deviation duration for 2-hour/day computer users	20.00
Average-deviation duration for >2-hours/day computer users	7.20
Aggressiveness	**[0-10]**
Average-deviation for 0-hour/day computer users	0
Average-deviation for 1-hour/day computer users	0
Average-deviation for 2-hour/day computer users	0.5
Average-deviation for >2-hours/day computer users	0
Coherence	**[0-10]**
Average-deviation for 0-hour/day computer users	8.83
Average-deviation for 1-hour/day computer users	8.86
Average-deviation for 2-hour/day computer users	8.50
Average-deviation for >2-hours/day computer users	9.00
Amiability	**[0-10]**
Average-deviation for 0-hour/day computer users	10
Average-deviation for 1-hour/day computer users	10
Average-deviation for 2-hour/day computer users	9-1
Average-deviation for >2-hours/day computer users	10
# of Changes Requested	**Number**
For Tim (0-hour/day,1-hour/day,2-hours/day,>2-hours/day)	1,0,0,0
For Mario (0-hour/day,1-hour/day,2-hours/day,>2-hours/day)	0,0,0,0
For Nim (0-hour/day,1-hour/day,2-hours/day,>2-hours/day)	1,0,0,0

continued in following column

Table 6. Continued

Criterion	Value
For Ñom (0-hour/day,1-hour/day,2-hours/day,>2-hours/day)	4,4,1,2
# of Students who Finished the Conversation	**Number**
0-hour/day computer users	7
1-hour/day computer users	5
2-hour/day computer users	2
>2-hours/day computer users	5

boys. Only one boy did not complete the first turn conversation with all the agents, and this could be caused because he had to share the computer, and the other child took longer than the average to finish his conversation. Finally, Table 6 shows the average results for children according to the number of hours that they use the computer at home per day.

There are not significant differences, and while it could be thought that students who are less familiarized with the computer would have devoted more time to the conversation, it was the students who spent 2 hours per day with the computers the ones who spent more time in the conversations with an average duration of 18 minutes, and spent 20 seconds in average per interaction.

Irrespectively of the number of hours to use the computer at home, Mario is the first agent asked. There was only one case of little aggressiveness, and he was a boy who used the computer 2 hours per day at home. All coherence values are above 8 and all amiability values are above 9 without significant differences either. It is interesting to observe that even children who never used the computer at home behaved just the same than the rest of their colleagues.

Step 5: Creation of the Behaviour Model

Finally, the following behaviour model was produced to answer all the questions initially raised.

Question 1: Do children prefer that the agent has a good or bad temper? Could it be that by designing cheerful agents, the children are more encouraged to study, or on the contrary, could it be that by designing bad-tempered agents that tell the students not to rest on their laurels, students start devoting more effort and time to their study?

According to the exploratory study, children might prefer happy talkative agents from the tested personalities. This is because when the children had the possibility of freely choosing the temper of the agent, they chose happy and informative or tester personalities.

Question 2: Do children prefer that the agent provides them with new information or with formative assessment?

There is not a unanimous answer to that question. Nevertheless, in general, children chose the tester personality and Mario was the only agent that no children attempted to change.

Question 3: Would children like to change the personality of the agent?

Children do not tend to like changing the personality of the agent. On the contrary, they usually consider the agent as a human child with a personality on his own. Thus, they believe that the agent should be as he is. Moreover, when they are given the possibility of choosing different agents, they do not usually keep changing the personality of the agent, but they try to keep the same agent for at least three turns of the conversation. Some children are even annoyed to be asked again if they want to change the personality.

Question 4: Could it be identified a new 'Police Effect' according to which an agent with a tester personality that only asks questions is rejected by the students because they feel they are constantly under questioning?

A Police Effect cannot be identified. Children seemed unaware of being under questioning, and they enjoyed answering to the computer provided that they were told that the goal of the agent was just to help them by finding out what they knew. It is also important to observe that the domain was study techniques, and all the children knew that there was not a course on study techniques. The results achieved could have been different for other domains in which children may have thought that they were taking an exam.

Question 5: Are children less aggressive in their interactions with the agent than adults interacting with agents?

Yes, they are. According to Angeli and Brahnam (2008) the language used by adults can be quite aggressive when interacting with the agents, particularly when the agents make some mistake in the conversation. However, in the case of the children, only one child started typing letters without forming words, but it was the only kind of little aggressiveness registered. No child insulted the agents, even after having completed two conversations and interacted with all the different agents; and, they were tolerant with the agent even when they asked for a mood that was not longer available. The reaction of the children was to keep asking for the agent, until they accepted that they had to ask for a different mood.

Question 6: Do children keep a coherent conversation with the agent? How long in average do they think their answer?

Yes, they follow the normal flow of the conversation with an average value of 8.86 in a scale from 0 (lack of coherence) to 10 (complete coherence) according to the analysis of the logs. It is important to register it because it could indicate that the children are engaged by the conversation and they are not just randomly answering, even when the interactions are quite fast. In particular, there is an average of 9.43 seconds, and a total length for the conversations of around 10 minutes.

Question 7: Are children kind with the agent? Are they more kind with certain type of agent personalities?

Yes, they are. The amiability factor was measured by a human judge who analyzed all the logs in a scale from 0 (lack of amiability) to 10 (complete amiability) as 9.81. Children are kind to all agents, and only two boys were unkind to Ñom, but it was just because they wanted to express their disagreement with his grumpy attitude.

Question 8: Are there gender differences?

There are not significant gender differences. Boys and girls behaved similarly when interacting with the pedagogic agent. It could just be observed that boys did not complete second and third conversations, and the only little aggressive unkind behavior registered was found in the logs of two boys-agents conversations.

Question 9: Are there differences between children who are more familiarized with the use of computers than children who are less familiarized?

There are not significant differences between students who are not familiarized with computers. All children were able to interact with the agents without any difficulty, and in general, even when they were not allowed to use the computer at home more than 1 hour per day, the results were very similar to those of the students who used the computer more than 2 hours per day. It is also important to take into account that these students

were used to go to the computer lab for their lessons at school, and they were all familiarized with the Messenger interface of the application.

Question 10: Would children tolerate a new interaction with the same agents and conversation? What would be the changes between the first round of conversations and the following rounds? Would they start complaining?

Children could tolerate even third round of conversations with the same agents and dialogue. They do not seem to care that the conversation is just the same, showing only a decrease of the time per interaction and the total length of the conversation. Again, the aggressiveness levels registered are practically zero, and the amiability and coherence levels are around 8-9.

CONCLUSION

A procedure to model the interaction behavior has been proposed extending the metrics and logs evaluation techniques for the User Centered Design. We consider that this procedure should be used whenever the users are not directly available to ask because they are too young or they have some kind of impairment. That way, the interaction model can still be created according to their preferences and needs from the indicators of the logs to some variables of the model.

The procedure has been applied to the particular case of modelling the children-Pedagogic Conversational Agents interaction as an illustrative sample. We have chosen this domain because, in the last years, it has attracted a great deal of interest. However, it is not clear which guidelines should be followed to design effective pedagogic agents for children. The application of the procedure has allowed us to create an initial behaviour model for the children-agent interaction.

REFERENCES

Abascal, J., & Moriyón, R. (2002). Tendencias en interacción persona computador. *Revista Iberoamericana de Inteligencia Artificia, 16*, 9–24.

Angeli, A. D., & Brahnam, S. (2008). I hate you! Disinhibition with virtual partners. *Interacting with Computers, 20*(3), 302–310. doi:10.1016/j.intcom.2008.02.004

Dix, A., Finlay, J., Abowd, G., & Beale, R. (2004). *Human-computer interaction*. Prentice Hall.

Johnson, W., Rickel, J., & Lester, J. (2000). Animated pedagogical agents: Face-to-face interaction in interactive learning environments. *Journal of Artificial Intelligence in Education, 11*, 47–78.

Nielsen, J. (1993). *Usability engineering*. Cambridge.

Pérez-Marín, D., & Pascual-Nieto, I. (2011). *Conversational agents and natural language interaction: Techniques and effective practices*. Hershey, PA: IGI Global. doi:10.4018/978-1-60960-617-6

Pressman, R. (2009). *Software engineering: A practitioner's approach*. McGraw Hill.

ADDITIONAL READING

Allen, J., Byron, D., Dzikovska, M., Ferguson, G., Galescu, L., & Stent, A. (2001). Towards conversational human-computer interaction. *AI Magazine, 22*(4), 27–37.

Bernsen, N. O. (1997). Towards a tool for predicting speech functionality. *Speech Communication, 23*(3), 181–210. doi:10.1016/S0167-6393(97)00046-0

Bernsen, N. O. (2001). Natural human-human-system interaction. In Earnshaw, R., Guedj, R., Van Dam, A., & Vince, J. (Eds.), *Frontiers of human-centred computing, on-line communities and virtual environments* (pp. 347–363). Berlin, Germany: Springer. doi:10.1007/978-1-4471-0259-5_25

Chapanis, A. (1975). Interactive human communication. *Scientific American, 232*, 36–42. doi:10.1038/scientificamerican0375-36

Chen, F. (2006). *Designing human interface in speech technology*. Dordrecht, The Netherlands: Springer.

Doran, C., Aberdeen, J., Damianos, L., & Hirschman, L. (2001). Comparing several aspects of human-computer and human-human dialogues. In *Proceedings of the Second SIGDIAL Workshop on Discourse and Dialog*, (pp. 1-10).

Hauptmann, A. G., & Rudnicky, A. I. (1990). A comparison of speech and typed input. In *Proceedings of the Speech and Natural Language Workshop*, (pp. 219-224).

Jensen, C., Farnham, S. D., Drucker, S. M., & Kollock, P. (2000). The effect of communication modality in cooperation in online environments. In *Proceedings of CHI 2000*.

Lai, J., & Yankelovich, N. (2006). Speech interface design. In Brown, K. (Ed.), *Encyclopedia of language & linguistics* (pp. 764–770). Amsterdam, The Netherlands: Elsevier.

Lazar, J., Heidi, J., & Hochheiser, H. (2010). *Research methods in human-computer interaction*. Wiley.

Maes, S. H. (2000). Elements of conversational computing - A paradigm shift. In *ICSLP-2000, Proceedings of the Sixth International Conference on Spoken Language Processings*, Vol. 1, (pp. 130-133).

Maybury, M., & Wahlster, W. (Eds.). (1998). *Readings on intelligent user interfaces* (pp. 620–630). San Francisco, CA: Morgan-Kaufmann.

Minker, W., Pittermann, J., Pittermann, A., Strauß, P. M., & Bühler, D. (2007). Challenges in speech-based human-computer interfaces. *International Journal of Speech Technology*, *10*(2-3), 109–119. doi:10.1007/s10772-009-9023-y

Ochsman, R. B., & Chapanis, A. (1974). The effects of 10 communication modes on the behavior of teams during communicative problem-solving. *International Journal of Man-Machine Studies*, *6*(5), 579–620. doi:10.1016/S0020-7373(74)80019-2

Oviatt, S. L. (1996). User-centered modeling for spoken language and multimodal interfaces. *IEEE MultiMedia*, *3*(4), 26–35. doi:10.1109/93.556458

Oviatt, S. L. (1997). Usability and interface design. In Cole, R. A., Mariani, J., Uszkoreit, H., Zaenen, A., & Zue, V. (Eds.), *Survey of the state of the art in human language technology*. Cambridge, UK: Cambridge University Press.

Oviatt, S. L., & Cohen, P. R. (1991). The contributing influence of speech and interaction on human discourse patterns. In J. W. S. Sullivan & S. W. Tyler (Eds.), *Intelligent user interfaces*, (pp. 69-83). New York, NY: Addison-Wesley Publishing Co. (ACM Press Frontier Series).

Oviatt, S. L., Cohen, R. C., & Wang, M. (1994). Toward interface design for human language technology: Modality and structure as determinants of linguistic complexity. *Speech Communication*, *15*(3-4), 283–300. doi:10.1016/0167-6393(94)90079-5

Rogers, Y., Sharp, H., & Preece, J. (2011). *Interaction design: Beyond human-computer interaction* (3rd ed.). John Wiley & Sons, Inc.

KEY TERMS AND DEFINITIONS

Cognitive Walkthrough Technique: Evaluators go through each step of the interaction with the system in order to accomplish some task and evaluate whether the users would be able to accomplish it.

Field Observation: Researchers observe and write on their books the way in which the users interact with the system on their own.

Focus Group: 6 to 9 users and evaluators talk about aspects related to the system.

Heuristic: Guideline or general principle or rule of thumb that can guide a design decision.

Human-Computer Interaction: A research field that studies how to design, evaluate and implement interactive computer systems to be used by human beings.

Log: A written register of the user interactions with a certain system.

Model-Based Evaluation: Experts rely their evaluation on some already existing models.

Pedagogic Conversational Agents (PCA): Lifelike autonomous character that cohabite the learning environment creating a rich face-to-face interface with the student.

Think Aloud: Consists in asking the users to talk aloud what they are thinking about their feeling and opinions about any aspect of the system while they are interacting with it. However, some users find it difficult to talk alone. Hence, the cooperative evaluation is an alternative in which instead of just one user, two users are interacting with the system, and they are asked to talk aloud about their thoughts and feelings.

User Centered Design (UCD): An iterative software methodology that takes into account the opinion and needs of the users during the all the process.

Chapter 8
On the Use of Speech Technologies to Achieve Inclusive Education for People with Intellectual Disabilities

Ana Pérez Pérez
University of Granada, Spain

Ramón López-Cózar Delgado
University of Granada, Spain

Zoraida Callejas Carrión
University of Granada, Spain

David Griol Barres
Carlos III University of Madrid, Spain

ABSTRACT

New technologies have demonstrated a great potential to improve the social, labour, and educational integration of people with special needs. That is why there is a special interest of academia and industry to develop tools to assist this people, improving their autonomy and quality of life. Usually, intellectual disabilities are linked with speech and language disorders. In this chapter, the authors present a review on the efforts directed towards designing and developing speech technologies adapted to people with intellectual disabilities. Also, they describe the work they have conducted to study how to gather speech resources, which can be used to build speech-based systems that help them to communicate more effectively.

INTRODUCTION

According to the World Health Organization, the 15% of the world population is affected by some physical, mental or sensorial disability, which hinders their personal development and social integration, education or employment (WHO-

DOI: 10.4018/978-1-4666-2530-3.ch008

11). The research area of inclusive education was introduced to avoid such situation by aiming at the maximum development of every student. In order to do so, it is necessary to identify and define guidelines for the students with special educational needs.

These students require during all their schooling period a certain support and specific education attention. Brennan (1984) stated that it is possible

Copyright © 2013, IGI Global. Copying or distributing in print or electronic forms without written permission of IGI Global is prohibited.

to identify a special education need when a deficiency (physical, sensorial, intellectual, emotional, social or any combination of these) affects learning up to the point that partial or full access to special curriculums is necessary.

The Warnock Report (Aguilar, 1991; Warnock, 1979) establishes that this must be done paying particular attention to the social structure and emotional climate in which education takes place, favouring the cohesion of all members of the community.

Such social implications in special needs education and inclusive education in general, make it necessary to emphasize communication and dialogue. However, many intellectually impaired people have difficulties communicating because of speech problems derived from their disability.

Speech technologies specially oriented to people with disabilities aims at improving their quality of life, increasing their autonomy and facilitating their capacity to communicate with other people. In this chapter we make a review on how speech technologies can help students with special educational needs interact with other people, reducing the impact of their disability. We will pay special attention to the recent work carried out in our research team in the study of speech resources for intellectually impaired users.

The rest of the chapter is organized as follows. Section 1 presents an introduction to the most frequent communication, language and speech impairments. Section 2 describes the state of the art technologies developed to mitigate the impact of such impairments. Concretely speech technologies that help intellectually impaired people are discussed in section 3. Section 4 describes the study carried out by our team about collecting corpora to automatically recognize speech of people with intellectual disability. Finally, section 5 presents the conclusions and outlines future work guidelines.

1. COMMUNICATION, LANGUAGE, AND SPEECH IMPAIRMENTS

The primary means of human communication is the oral language, as it allows individuals to express and understand ideas, thoughts, feelings, knowledge and activities. As highlighted by (Vila, 2008), language is a very powerful tool, "a specifically human communicative behaviour that plays important functions in a cognitive level, social and communication, allowing humans to make explicit their intentions, stabilize them, change them in regulations very complex of human action and enter to a positive plain of cognitive and behavioural auto regulation, which cannot be reached without language" (Puyuelo, 1997).

Language is acquired by learning through the interaction of biological, cognitive, psychosocial and environmental agents (Puyuelo, 2003) and it is started at birth (Montoya, 2009). (Miretti, 2003) defines three learning stages:

- **Pre-linguistic level:** from birth up to twelve months. Babies transfer information through the tone, intensity and rhythm of crying.
- **Linguistic level:** between twelve months and five years. It is a period when vocabulary acquisition grows quickly learning more phonemes, although phonologic development is not complete until the next level (Puyuelo, 2000).
- **Pure verbal level:** between five and twelve years. The meaning of words is symbolized and abstractions are built as required in the learning process of mathematics.

With children, language assessment must be executed according to evolutionary principles. Any deviation of the expected conduct is an indicative of pathology (Lezak, 1983; National, 2011). The pathologies of human communication are usually classified into four areas (Gutierrez-, 2003). Firstly, phonopathies which are voice alterations such as rhinophonia, rhinolalia, dysphonia, aphonia or dysodia (Perello, 1973). The second class are speech disorders: dyslalias, dysarthria and diglossia. (Perello, 1990). Thirdly, there are the modifications of the emission rhythm of spoken language: arrhythmias, dysrhythmias, bradyphasia, bradyarthia, physiological dysphemia, and persistent dysphemia (Serra, 1982). The fourth group is comprised of logopathies. This field is the largest since it deals with all aspects of human communication. It includes simple or severe language delay, oral language delay (aphasia, dysphasia, perturbation of psychic origin, autism, mental trauma...), written language delay (agraphia, dysgraphia, dysorthography, agrammatism), read language delay (alexia, dyslexia), mathematical language delay (acalculia, dyscalculia), musical language delay (amusia), dactilologic language delay (akinesia, dyskinesia), symbolic language delay (asymbolia) and mimic language delay (amimia, hyponymy, paramimia) (Perello, 1989).

The previous classification attends to a symptomatic criterion. Some authors have proposed alternative classification criteria. For example (Peña, 1988) proposes topographic and functional classification, attending to the organs that are affected: hearing, speech or alterations of nervous systems. Also the pathologies can be classified according to the initial reasons for their appearance: genetic lesions (vascular, tumour traumatic, toxic, infectious, degenerative or metabolic), environmental or emotional reasons. Finally, they can also be classified according to temporal criteria as whether the onset of the disease occurs in development stages or in adulthood.

2. DISABILITY AND TECHNOLOGIES

As discussed above, the 15% of the world population is affected of some physical, mental or sensorial disability. Moreover, the majority of people will be affected of some type of transitory or permanent disability in some moment of their life. This number is increasing due to the ageing of the population and the global increase of the chronic health troubles, such as diabetes, cardiovascular illnesses and mental impairments. Thus, there is a growing conscience of the importance of the integration of people with disabilities in society and the technology sector is playing a key role trying to improve their autonomy and quality of life.

However, technologies may also be a barrier for this people if their needs and peculiarities are not taken into account in the technology development process (European, 1999). Thus, it is important to admit that the Information Society can provide more opportunities and independence for some people with disability, but also can generate an opposite effect, preventing them from accessing information and participating in the society. In this sense the adoption of legislation, the disposition of adapted installations and the Universal Design build the three pillars that sustain the equality of opportunities and the promotion of the rights of people with disabilities (Valle, 2011). The term "Universal Design" refers to all the techniques whose objective is to ease the life for people by means of products and services more usable by people of all ages, characteristics and abilities (Stockholm, 2004). An example is assistive technology, which consists of a set of devices and other solutions to support people with physic, mental or sensorial deficiencies (Laplante, 1992).

Among these technologies, Automatic Speech Recognition (ASR) can be used to interpret the acoustic signal proceeding from a human speaker and obtain a textual representation that can be analysed by a Natural Language Processing (NLP) system (Casacuberta, 1987; Lee, 1996). Thus this technology can eliminate multiple barriers helping people with visual and motor impairments to access information through natural language, allowing them to access services that are traditionally visual, such as webs or software with graphical user interfaces. These systems are usually receive oral commands and present information using a speech synthesizer, such as the MyVoice dialogue system (Cerva, 2007), which allows people with motor disability to work using a computer through oral commands, and the Italian Literacy Tutor (ILT) that is a tutor created for Italian students with cognitive disabilities (Cosi, 2004).

Although as pointed out above the most widespread use of speech-based systems as assistive technology is to help visually and motor impaired people, they have also demonstrated a great potential for the treatment of language disorders, as discussed in the next section.

3. SPEECH TECHNOLOGIES TO HELP INTELLECTUALLY IMPAIRED PEOPLE

In this section we describe briefly some of the most representative tools developed for the therapy of language.

SpeechViewer III is a tool developed by IBM which supports therapists and educators in the treatment of communication disorders of different aged people. It can be used to manage the control of the tone, the intensity, the sonority, the duration of the voice, analysis of spectres and pronunciation of phonemes (Speechviewer). The tool is comprised of several modules which allow analyzing the treatment and clinical management of each disorder. Speech Viewer also follows the progress and performance of the patient and incorporates graphics, speech patterns, notes and voice files for the therapeutic exercises.

Video Voice, by Micro Video Corporation, provides games that help to control pitch, amplitude and duration of voice and other speech problems associated with autism, apraxia, brain damage and other disabilities.

Dr. Speech, developed by Tiger DRS is a system that has several interactive games where children receive feedback from the change of tone, phonation and intensity.

VoxGames, developed by CTS Computer Company, is a package of 25 games developed for clinical phoniatric therapy, allowing to control the intensity, tone, or time of phonation.

COMUNICA is a set of tools to support therapists, providing training from pre-linguistic to pragmatic levels of language to facilitate learning the Spanish language in a fast, effective and even unsupervised manner, using speech technology. The project consists of: *PreLingua* for children with problems in the development of the pre-language stage, *VOCALIZA* for *students* with problems in the articulatory level, *VocalizaL2* to work on pronunciation accuracy and *CUENTAME* which trains the functional level of language. As the tools described above, *COMUNICA* is a professional support *program* (Vaquero, 2006; Rodriguez, 2011).

MUSA is an instrument for the rehabilitation of people with auditory and language problems. The goal is to train the intensity and duration of vocal production as well as the intonation, rhythmic structures, voiced sounds, deaf and fricatives. It contains files corresponding to two semantic fields (family and animals) (Ruiz, 1994). As the COMUNICA project, its drawback is that it is destined to help in the therapy sessions.

Orto-Logo-Paedia is a system that provides a visual feedback to the user about the correct positioning of the articulatory elements (tongue, palate, teeth) to correctly produce the different sounds (Oester, 2002).

PEAKS is a system for the automatic evaluation of speech and voice disorders for patients who had their larynx removed due to cancer, and children with cleft lip and palate. The users have to read a text or names of pictures and then their speech is analyzed by automatic speech recognition and prosodic analysis (Maier, 2009).

The previously described tools have been developed to help professionals during rehabilitation sessions and speech therapy, in order to assist them and make sessions more effective, but they are not aimed at directly helping the disabled users in a daily basis, for example when they need to be understood when they are trying to communicate.

Most speech-based tools currently available to help people with disabilities communicate are based on displaying images or synthesizing voice from a textual input. Those which accept spoken input have to address the challenge of developing a speech recognizer that obtains acceptable recognition rates with users who suffer from speech disorders. Usually, this has been done by specializing in a certain pathology, which allows optimizing the acoustic features employed by the recognizer (Kain, 2007). Three systems developed with this approach are the following.

STARDUST (Speech Training And Recognition for Dysarthric Users of Assistive Technology) is a system that uses speech recognition errors to recognize people with mild and even severe dysarthria (Hawley, 2003). The objective of this system is the control of assistive technologies in a home through the voices of people with dysarthria.

VIVOCA (Voice-Input Voice-Output Communication Aid). Is a system with speech input and output, designed to help people with speech disorders, focusing on the users with moderate or severe dysarthria, mainly in situations where the speed and intelligibility is crucial (Hawley, 2006).

Dragon Dictate is a speech recognition software initially developed for Microsoft Windows, which has been used in studies of automatic recognition of dysarthric speech (Ferrier, 1995).

One of the main problems with the adaptation of speech-based systems to specific pathologies is that people with other disorders may not be able to use such systems efficiently, specially people who suffer from several language disorders, which is usually the case of intellectually disabled people. Thus, more effort must be done in order to collect resources to build general-purpose systems.

4. APPROACH TO GENERATE SPEECH RESOURCES FOR PEOPLE WITH INTELLECTUAL DISABILITY

In our research team we have been interested in gathering, studying and comparing corpora that can be used to train speech recognizers for intellectually disabled people, covering a varied range of the pathologies and communication levels. In order to do this, we have used two corpora of average Spanish speakers, and collected a new corpus with intellectually impaired people.

The first corpus we used was Albayzín (Casacuberta, 1991) the Spanish reference corpus that consists of a total of 6800 balanced elocutions, which were recorded by 304 speakers. We have used in our research 699 sentences recorded by 11 female speakers.

Secondly, we have been used a corpus previously obtained from a Call-Center, that consists of 200 sentences and a reduced grammar on the routing of calls within our Department. It has been used for comparison purposes as it was recorded with lower quality than Albayzín.

Thirdly, we collected a corpus of recordings with people with intellectual disability in collaboration with the APAFA association (Association of parents, relatives and friends of intellectually disabled people in the North of the province of Almeria, Spain), which we have named APAFA corpus. The participants were 15 persons (4 women and 11 men) who were arranged in three groups attending to their verbal communication level (low, medium or high). This classification was made by specialists belonging to the APAFA association.

4.1 Collection of the APAFA Corpus

The APAFA corpus is comprised of 1965 recordings. We have finalized a first collection stage in which we were interested in recording words that could be used as commands for a simple speech-based system.

The participants recorded a list of 131 words related to their daily activities in the residence where they live, related to food (*water, apple, dish...*) bedrooms (*pillow, bed, duvet, bedside table...*) personal hygiene (*shampoo, gel, shower, toilet...*) clothes (*shirt, pullover, trousers...*) and frequently used adjectives (*cold, happy, angry, hot...*).

The recording phase took place in the residence of the APAFA association, It was carried out in several sessions not to tire the participants out, and in the moments were the residence was not very busy in order to avoid external noises in the recordings.

In order to carry out the recordings, we could not employ the usual tools based on reading a text that appears in the screen as only three participants could actually read. Thus, we had to come up with alternative methods to carry out the recordings. The method chosen was that the monitor who is responsible for the care and supervision of the participant read aloud the word that had to be recorded and the participant repeated it afterwards.

This method also had some drawbacks, for example, many recordings had unnecessary noises because they were started before the monitor finished saying the word to the participant. Moreover, some participants began to repeat the word while the monitor was still pronouncing it. Thus, it was necessary to listen to all the recordings in order to detect and correct these issues, discarding those that were considered useless.

Although significant differences were detected among the three groups of participants, they had a lot of common difficulties. For example, the participants found it hard to pronounce words containing more than three syllables words that contain certain phonemes, such as the Spanish "r" and "ñ". Also, some participants had characteristic pronunciations such as prolonging the end of the some words (e.g. the Spanish word "cama" (bed) was pronounced as "camaaaaaaaaa").

4.2 Experiments

In order to carry out a preliminary study about the possibilities of each corpus for developing speech-based systems to enhance user quality of life, we implemented several speech recognizers using the HTK toolkit (Young, 2006). We trained and tested them using different combinations of the corpora, which are summarized in Table 1.

The best results for all the tests were obtained using monophonemes instead of triphonemes. Hence, for clarity we for clarity we only report the results obtained with monophonemes.

The tests carried out were as follows:

- **100%ALB1 / ALB2:** We made two sets from the Albayzin corpus corresponding to the recordings of the same 699 sentences by 2 different speakers (ALB1, ALB2), and used one of them for training and the other for testing.

Table 1. Corpora used for the initial evaluation of the speech recognizers

Test Code	Training	Test
100%ALB1/ALB2	Full Albayzín Corpus with monophonemes	Albayzín Corpus
60%ALB1/40%ALB1	60% Corpus Albayzín with monophonemes	40% Albayzín Corpus
100%ALB1/CCT	Full Albayzín Corpus with monophonemes	Call-Center Corpus
CCTR/CCT	Call-Center Corpus	Call-Center Corpus
CCTR/ALB2	Call-Center Corpus	Albayzín Corpus
100%ALB1/100%APAFA	Full Albayzín Corpus with monophonemes	Full APAFA Corpus
60%APAFA/40%APAFA	60%APAFA Corpus	40% APAFA Corpus

- **60%ALB1 / 40%ALB1:** 60% of the utterances in ALB1 were used for training and the rest for testing.
- **100%ALB1 / CCT:** ALB1 was used for training and the Call-Center Test (CCT) set for testing.
- **CCTR / CCT:** Call-Center Training set for training (CCTR) and Call-Center Testing set (CCT) for testing.
- **CCTR / ALB2:** Call-Center Training set for training (CCTR) and Albayzín set for testing (ALB2) consists of 200 phrases.
- **100%ALB1 / 100%APAFA:** Albayzín set for training (ALB1) and APAFA corpus for testing.
- **60%APAFA/40%APAFA:** APAFA was separated into two sets: 60% for training and 40% for testing.

The results of the tests are shown in Figure 1. As can be observed, the recordings made by speakers without language disorders (Albayzín corpus) are not suitable to recognize the speech of intellectually disabled people. The low recognition rates highlight the importance of collecting speech resources specifically for disabled people or to adapt the already existing ones.

Also, the recognition rate was low when the Call-Center corpus was used for training and the Albayzín corpus was used for testing, given that the Call-Center corpus was not phonetically balanced. Moreover, the recognition rates corresponding to the APAFA corpus were very low compared with others, because of the difficulty of recognizing speech of people with disabilities. A second experiment was carried out to study the results of the different communication groups of the APAFA corpus, evaluating the results by participant. The experimental conditions are summarized in Table 2.

The results are shown in Figure 2. The level of verbal communication of each participant is:

- High verbal communication: subjects 1, 2, 3, 4 and 5.
- Medium verbal communication: subjects 6, 7, 8, 9 and 10.
- Low verbal communication: subjects 11, 12, 13, 14 and 15.

It is important to keep in mind that the criteria for grouping the subjects were provided by the experts of the APAFA association. Hence, it is possible that not all subjects in the low verbal group

Figure 1. Results from evaluation of the speech recognizers

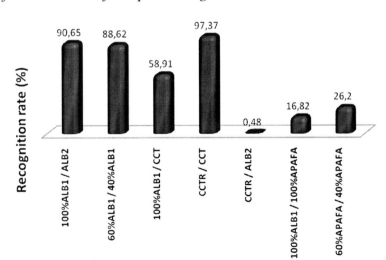

Table 2. Tests with APAFA corpus

100%ALB1/ APAAIND	60%APAFAGROUP/ 40%APAFAGROUP	100%APAFA/ APAFAIND	60%APAFA/ 40%APAFAIND
Full Corpus Albayzín with monophonemes/ individual tests with APAFA corpus	60% APAFA corpus divided by groups of communication/ 40% APAFA corpus divided by groups of communication	Full APAFA corpus/individual tests realize with APAFA corpus	60% APAFA corpus/ individual tests realize with 40% APAFA corpus

Figure 2. Experimental results with the APAFA corpus

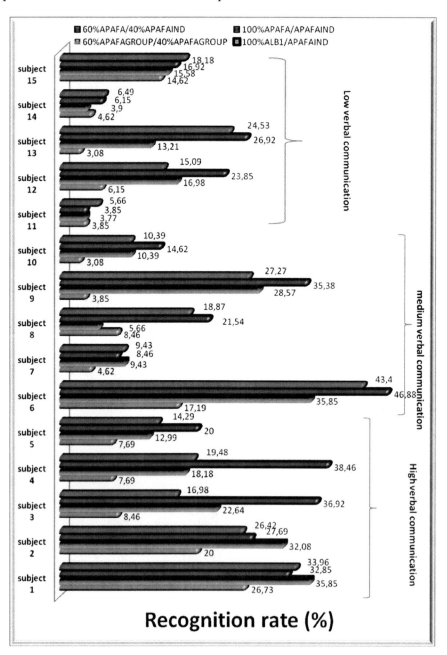

Table 3. Median improvement introduced

Communication Level	Median
High Communication	-1.89%
Medium Communication	0%
Low Communication	2.59%

obtain the worst speech recognition results. Figure 2 shows that the recognition rates obtained are not good if the recognizer is trained with the Albayzín corpus and tests are made with the recordings of the APAFA corpus.

It can be observed that in general, for the high communication group better results are obtained when the recognizer is trained only with recordings made by this group, obtaining worse results when we added recordings from the other groups. For the medium communication group, the results obtained for the recognizer trained with the full APAFA corpus were similar to those obtained training it just with the speech samples from this group. Finally, for the low verbal group, better recognition rates are obtained with the full corpus than building a recognizer specifically for this group.

These results are corroborated by calculating the median improvement introduced by considering 60%APAFA/40%APAFAIND compared to using 60%APAFAGROUP/40%APAFAGROUP, as reflected in the Table 3.

5. CONCLUSION AND FUTURE WORK

Speech technologies can play a very important role in enhancing the quality of life of people with special educational needs related to intellectual impairments and the associated language disorders. These technologies can give them the possibility to be better understood by others, decreasing the degree of frustration for not being understood and increasing their autonomy. In this chapter we have presented a review of some tools currently

available to assist this people. Most of them are used for creating software to help specialists and speech therapists, whereas others are designed to be, directly used by the disabled people and are usually focused on a specific pathology.

We have collected resources that can be employed in the development of assistive, speech-based such systems, to be used by intellectually disabled people.

Our experimental results show that speech recognition of people with a low communication level might benefit from resources collected from speakers with different levels of communication. Thus, we believe that there is a relevant opportunity for academia and industry to build on the previous efforts in order to developed speech-based tools for more diverse target users.

As a future work, we plan to study the adaptation of the already available resources gathered non-disabled speakers to the recognition of intellectually disabled users. Also, we plan to extend the APAFA corpus to cover a wider range of pathologies and making it more phonetically balanced.

REFERENCES

Aguilar, L. A. (1991). El informe Warnock. *Cuadernos de Pedagogía, 197*, 62–64.

Barry, S. (1994). Speech viewer 2. *Child Language Teaching and Therapy, 10*, 206–213. doi:10.1177/026565909401000207

Brennan, W. K. (1984). *Curriculum for special needs (children with special needs series)*. Philadelphia, PA: Open University Press.

Casacuberta, F., García, R., Llisterri, J., Nadeu, C., Pardo, J. M., & Rubio, A. (1991). Development of Spanish corpora for speech research (Albayzin). In *Proceedings of the Workshop International Cooperation Standardization Speech Databases Speech I/O Assessment Methods*, (pp. 26-28). Chiavari, Italy.

Casacuberta, F., & Vidal, E. (1987). *Reconocimiento automático del habla*. Barcelona, Spain: Marcombo-Boixareo Editores.

Cerva, P., & Nouza, J. (2007). Design and development of voice controlled aids for motor-handicapped persons. In *Proceedings of the 11th International Conference on Spoken Language Processing (Interspeech'07-Eurospeech)*, Antwerp, Belgium, (pp. 2521-2524).

Cosi, P., Delmonte, R., Biscette, S., Cole, R. A., Pellom, B., & van Vuren, S. (2004). Italian literacy tutor: Tools and technologies for individuals with cognitive disabilities. In *Proceedings of the ESCA ETRW NLP Speech Technology Advanced Language Learning Systems Symposium*, Venice, Italy, (pp. 207–214).

European Disability Forum. (1999). *European manifesto on the information society and disabled people*. Brussels, Belgium: European Disability Forum.

European Institute for Design and Disability. (2004). *The EIDD Stockholm declaration*. Stockholm, Sweden: Author.

Ferrier, L., Shane, H., Ballard, H., Carpenter, T., & Benoit, A. (1995). Dysarthric speakers' intelligibility and speech characteristics in relation to computer speech recognition. *Augmentative and Alternative Communication, 11*(3), 165–175. doi:10.1080/07434619512331277289

Gutiérrez, R. (2003). *Patología de la comunicación humana: Una taxonomía integradora*. Conferencia de clausura del XVI Congreso Nacional de Fepal, (pp. 467-486). Sevilla, Spain: Universidad de Sevilla.

Hawley, M., Enderby, P., Green, P., Brownsell, S., Hatzis, A., & Parker, M. … Carmichael, J. (2003). STARDUST: Speech training and recognition for dysarthric users of assistive technology. In *Proceedings of the 7th Conference of the Association for the Advancement of Assistive Technology in Europe* (AAATE). Dublin, Ireland.

Hawley, M., Enderby, P., Green, P., Cunningham, S., & Palmer, R. (2006). Development of a voice-input voice-output communication aid (VIVOCA) for people with severe dysarthria. *Computer Science, 4061*, 882–885.

Kain, A. B., Hosom, J. P., Niu, X., Van Santen, J. P. H., Fried-Oken, M., & Staehely, J. (2007). Improving the intelligibility of dysarthric speech. *Speech Communication, 49*(9), 743–759. doi:10.1016/j.specom.2007.05.001

LaPlante, M. P., Hendershot, G. E., & Moss, A. J. (1992). Assistive technology devices and home accessibility features: Prevalence, payment, need, and trends. *Advance Data from Vital and Health Statistics, 217*, 2–13.

Lee, C., Soong, F. K., & Paliwal, K. K. (1996). *Automatic speech and speaker recognition: Advanced topics*. Boston, MA: Kluwer Academic Publishers. doi:10.1007/978-1-4613-1367-0

Lezak, M. (1983). *Neuropsychological assessment*. New York, NY: Oxford University Press.

Maier, A., Haderlein, T., Eysholdt, U., Rosanowski, F., Batliner, A., Schuster, M., & Nöth, E. (2009). PEAKS-A system for the automatic evaluation of voice and speech disorders. *Speech Communication, 51*, 425–437. doi:10.1016/j.specom.2009.01.004

Miretti, M. (2003). *La lengua oral en la educación inicial*. Rosario, Argentina: Homo Sapiens.

Montoya, Z. (2009). *El desarrollo del lenguaje. Carta de la Salud, 155*. Santiago de Cali, Colombia: Fundación Valle del Lili.

National Dissemination Center for Children with Disabilities. (2011). *Speech and language impairments*. Washington, DC: Author.

Oester, A.-M., House, D., Protopapas, A., & Hatzis, A. (2002). Presentation of a new EU project for speech therapy: OLP (Ortho-Logo-Paedia). In *Proceedings of the XV Swedish Phonetics Conference*, Stockholm, Sweden, (pp. 45–48).

Peña, J. (1988). *Manual de logopedia*. Barcelona, Spain: Masson.

Perelló, J. (1990). *Trastornos del habla*. Barcelona, Spain: Masson.

Perelló, J., Miquel, J. A. S., & Llorach, A. (1973). *Alteraciones de la voz*. Barcelona, Spain: Científico-Médica.

Perelló, J., & Tortosa, F. (1989). *Fundamentos audiofoniátricos*. Barcelona, Spain: Científico-Médica.

Puyuelo, M. (1997). *Casos clínicos en logopedia*. Barcelona, Spain: Masson.

Puyuelo, M. (2003). *Manual de desarrollo y alteraciones del lenguaje: aspectos evolutivos y patología en el niño y adulto*. Barcelona, Spain: Masson.

Puyuelo, M., Rondal, A., & Wiig, E. (2000). *Evaluación del lenguaje*. Barcelona, Spain: MASSON.

Rodríguez, W.-R., Saz, O., & Lleida, E. (2011). A prelingual tool for the education of altered voices. *Speech Communication, 40*(4).

Ruiz, C. (1994). El proyecto MUSA. *Apanda, 2*, 14–19.

Serra, M., Vallejo, J., Goday, P. S., & Cabrero, F. J. (1982). Trastornos de la fluidez del habla: Disfemia y taquifemia. *Rev. Logop. Fonoaud, 2*(2), 69–78.

Valle, R. E. (2011). TIC y accesibilidad: Programa Red XXI Educacyl Digital. *Educación Especial y Mundo Digital, 2*, 202–215. Almería, Spain: Universidad de Almería.

Vaquero, C., Saz, O., Lleida, E., Marcos, J. M., & Canalís, C. (2006). *VOCALIZA: An application for computer-aided speech therapy in Spanish language* (pp. 321–326). Zaragoza: IV Jornadas en Tecnologías del Habla.

Vila, J. M. (2008). Alteraciones del habla. *Pediatría Integral, 11. XXII Congress of the Society of Pediatric Outpatient and Primary Care*, (pp. 56-59).

Warnock, M. (1979). Children with special needs: The Warnock Report. *British Medical Journal, 1*, 667–668. doi:10.1136/bmj.1.6164.667

World Health Organization. (2011). *World report on disability*. Geneva, Switzerland: World Health Organization.

Young, S., Evermann, G., Gales, M., Hain, H., Kershaw, D., & Liu, X. (2006). *The HTK book*. Cambridge, UK: Cambridge University.

ADDITIONAL READING

Cole, R., Mariani, J., Uszkoreit, H., Varile, G., Zaenen, A., Zue, V., & Zampolli, A. (Eds.). (1997). *Survey of the state of the art in human language technology*. Cambridge, UK: Cambridge University Press.

Gold, B., & Morgan, H. (1999). *Speech and audio signal processing: Processing and perception of speech and music*. New York, NY: John Willey & Sons.

Gonzalez, A.-P., Gisbert, M., Guillen, A., Jiménez, B., Lladó, F., & Rallo, R. (1996). Las nuevas tecnologías en la educación. In Salinas, A. (Eds.), *Redes de Comunicación, Redes de Aprendizaje, EDUTEC'95* (pp. 409–422). Palma de Mallorca, Spain: Universitat de les Illes Balears.

Jiménez, A. (2003). Nuevas tecnologías y discapacidad. *Documentación Social, 130*, 91–107.

Koon, R.-A., & de la Vega, M.-E. (2000). *El impacto tecnológico en personas con discapacidad. CIIEE 2000, Córdoba. España, Ministerio de Educación y Ciencia. (1994). Proyecto LAO: Logopedia asistida por ordenador*. España, Spain: Ministerio de Educación y Ciencia.

López-Cózar, R., & Ariaki, M. (2005). *Spoken, multilingual and multimodal dialogue systems: Development and assessment*. UK: John Wiley & Sons.

Martínez, M.-J., García, F. A., Pérez, F. M., & Soto, F. J. (2003). *Proyecto para la estimulación sensoriomotriz de niños plurideficientes con grave afectación a través del ordenador. Conclusiones de un estudio piloto*. Comunicación oral presentada al IV Congreso Iberoamericano de Informática en la Educación Especial. (CIIE). Madrid.

Massie, T., & Salisbury, J. K. (1994). *The phantom haptic interface: A device for probing virtual objects*. Chicago, IL: ASME International Mechanical Engineering Exposition and Congress.

McTear, M. F., Conn, N., & Phillips, N. (2000). *Speech recognition software: a tool for people with dyslexia* (pp. 81–84). INTERSPEECH.

Rabiner, L., & Juang, B. H. (1993). *Fundamentals of speech recognition*. New Jersey: Prentice Hall.

Rabiner, L. R., Juang, B. H., & Lee, C. H. (1996). An overview of automatic speech recognition. In Lee, C.-H., Soong, F. K., & Paliwal, K. K. (Eds.), *Automatic speech and speaker recognition: Advanced topics* (pp. 1–30). Kluwer Academic Publisher. doi:10.1007/978-1-4613-1367-0_1

Torres, J. (2003). *Trastornos del lenguaje en niños con necesidades educativas especiales*. Barcelona, Spain: CEAC.

KEY TERMS AND DEFINITIONS

Automatic Speech Recognizer: System capable of analysing the acoustic signal corresponding to a human utterance in order to identify the words that were pronounced.

Disability: Restriction or absence (due to a deficiency) of the capacity to carry out an activity of the way, or inside a margin, which is considered normal for the human.

Intellectual Disability: Type of disability that involves a deficit in intelligence and incapacity to achieve certain levels of autonomy and social responsibility.

Special Educational Needs: Necessity of a student for additional educational support derived from a special condition.

Speech Impairment: Alteration and perturbation in the production and reception of speech.

Speech Technologies: set of technologies used to process the human language and use it as the primary means for human-machine communication.

Chapter 9
An Emotional Student Model for Game-Based Learning

Karla Muñoz
University of Ulster, UK

Tom Lunney
University of Ulster, UK

Paul Mc Kevitt
University of Ulster, UK

Julieta Noguez
Tecnológico de Monterrey, México

Luis Neri
Tecnológico de Monterrey, México

ABSTRACT

Students' performance and motivation are influenced by their emotions. Game-based learning (GBL) environments comprise elements that facilitate learning and the creation of an emotional connection with students. GBL environments include Intelligent Tutoring Systems (ITSs) to ensure personalized learning. ITSs reason about students' needs and characteristics (student modeling) to provide suitable instruction (tutor modeling). The authors' research is focused on the design and implementation of an emotional student model for GBL environments based on the Control-Value Theory of achievement emotions by Pekrun et al. (2007). The model reasons about answers to questions in game dialogues and contextual variables related to student behavior acquired through students' interaction with PlayPhysics. The authors' model is implemented using Dynamic Bayesian Networks (DBNs), which are derived using Probabilistic Relational Models (PRMs), machine learning techniques, and statistical methods. This work compares an earlier approach that uses Multinomial Logistic Regression (MLR) and cross-tabulation for learning the structure and conditional probability tables with an approach that employs Necessary Path Condition and Expectation Maximization algorithms. Results showed that the latter approach is more effective at classifying the control of outcome-prospective emotions. Future work will focus on applying this approach to classification of activity and outcome-retrospective emotions.

DOI: 10.4018/978-1-4666-2530-3.ch009

Copyright © 2013, IGI Global. Copying or distributing in print or electronic forms without written permission of IGI Global is prohibited.

INTRODUCTION

Information technologies for supporting education have evolved into increasingly sophisticated environments. Virtual environments, tele-presence, video games, intelligent tutoring, haptic devices and social environments are only some of the technologies that have been applied successfully. However, challenges are still present in the area of personalized emotional learning. Emotion is considered an essential component of human experience and from a Human-Computer Interaction (HCI) viewpoint, Graphical-User Interfaces (GUIs) that do not address emotion appropriately are perceived as socially-impaired and can limit users' performance (Brave & Nass, 2008). As a result, two research areas, Edutainment and Computer Tutoring, i.e. Intelligent Tutoring Systems (ITSs), have concentrated efforts on recognizing or showing emotion (Picard et al., 2004). Incorporation of affective modeling promises enhanced student motivation, learning and understanding. The topic of "emotion in education" is also gaining popularity in the field of Cognitive Psychology. Theories that aim to provide an enhanced explanation of the origin of emotion in an educational context are important (Schutz & Pekrun, 2007).

Whilst attempting to reason about or understand emotion, common questions appear, such as how emotion arises and the emotions most relevant for the teaching-learning experience. As part of the endeavor in finding the most suitable answers to these questions, this chapter reviews related work in the areas of ITSs and Edutainment, which aims to identify emotion. In addition, approaches, such as recognizing the physical effects of emotion (D'Mello et al., 2008), which have been derived and used to recognize and reason about emotion are examined and discussed by outlining their advantages and disadvantages. This chapter also focuses on examining cognitive psychology theories, such as the Ortony, Clore and Collins (OCC) model (Ortony, Clore & Collins, 1990), which have previously been used as

a basis to implement emotional student models and other theories that have not been previously employed, such as the Control-Value theory of achievement emotions by Pekrun, Frenzel, Goetz and Perry (2007).

We have developed PlayPhysics, an emotional game-based learning environment for teaching Physics at undergraduate level. It was designed to derive and evaluate our emotional student model and facilitate students' in self-reporting their emotions. PlayPhysics is a space adventure, where the student, an astronaut, has to overcome challenges using his/her Physics knowledge of vectors, circular and linear kinematics and Newton's laws for particles and rigid bodies. The first challenge involves piloting the Alpha Centauri spaceship in order to arrive at the Athena space station before the ship's fuel is exhausted. PlayPhysics is implemented with the Unity Game Engine, Hugin Lite, MySQL and Java. The design and implementation of PlayPhysics are also discussed in this chapter.

This chapter focuses mainly on the analysis, design and implementation of an emotional student model using contextual and feasible variables related to students' observable behavior for game-based learning. The approach employed is Cognitive-Based Affective User Modeling (CB-AUM), which involves employing the Control-Value Theory (Pekrun et al., 2007) as a basis. Control-Value Theory has not been employed previously for implementing an emotional and computational student model. As part of our research methodology, we employ Probabilistic Relational Models (PRMs) to facilitate the derivation of Dynamic Bayesian Networks (DBNs) (Sucar & Noguez, 2008).

DBNs enable us to handle uncertainty and incorporate previous domain knowledge (Jensen & Nielsen, 2007). Multinomial Logistic Regression (MLR) was employed to select the most significant regressors (Kinnear & Gray, 2010) and cross-tabulation was employed for setting the probabilities in the Conditional Probability Tables (CPTs) in previous work, where we obtained promising results for classifying *outcome prospective emotions* into positive and negative-neutral categories (Muñoz, Mc Kevitt, Lunney, Noguez & Neri, 2011). MLR is a method used to predict category membership using categorical variables as factors and it has the advantage of knowing the contribution of each regressor to the prediction. However, here we compare the previous approach with one using the Necessary Path Condition (NPC) algorithm for structural learning and the Expectation Maximization (EM) algorithm for learning the probabilities in the CPTs (Bashar, Parr, McClean, Scotney & Nauck, 2010; Hugin Lite, 2012). Results from our tests with high school and undergraduate students at Tecnológico de Monterrey (ITESM-CCM) are presented comparing the effectiveness of both approaches. We also compare our results to related work and discuss future research directions.

BACKGROUND AND RELATED WORK

Emotion is a component of human experience that has been shown to influence cognition, perception, learning and performance (Brave & Nass, 2008; Westerinck, Ouwerkerk, Overbeek, Pasveer, & De Ruyter, 2008). As a result, computer tutoring aims to react suitably to emotion, which requires highly responsive systems, capable of adapting to the rich behavior patterns exhibited by interacting humans. However, to know if the desired effects will be achieved, it is necessary to enable these systems to identify and model the learner's affective or motivational states.

Affective Computing is a research area focused on enabling computers to recognise and show emotion (Picard, 1995). It is an interdisciplinary field comprising Computer Science, Psychology, and Cognitive Science (Tao & Tan, 2005). When a computer tutor recognizes the student's affective state, it can respond accordingly to it, e.g. motivating students and improving the learning

process. As a result, computers are able to provide suitable support to improve users' experiences, facilitate performance and encourage the creation of meaningful relationships with users by promoting their trust and give a sensation of competence (Brave & Nass, 2008). Intelligent Tutoring Systems (ITS) and serious games have been influenced by Affective Computing, and have adopted the goals of understanding and expressing emotions. Simultaneously, educational games or GBL environments incorporate ITSs to ensure personalised instruction, i.e. be aware of students' characteristics and needs, and the achievement of learning goals.

Edutainment

Edutainment is a concept that combines aspects of teaching and learning with the characteristics of video games in order to provide attractive learning environments for students. These systems combine specific teaching methods and characteristics of video games to engage students in familiar ways and make it easy to support their learning (Qianping, Wei & Bo, 2007; Rapeepisarn, Wong, Fung, & Depickere, 2006). Their main goal is to enhance the educational value of games though the addition of pedagogical techniques in order to convey educational content in a less stressful way. As a result, students can enjoy this process and increase their interest in the content that is taught. This may enhance the quality and efficiency of the teaching-learning process between professors and students.

Game Based Learning (GBL) enables learning through experiencing the effects of the students' own actions in situated contexts and facilitates the connection between learning and real-world experiences (Van Eck, 2006). GBL environments are comprised of specific elements, e.g. narrative, characters, sounds, actions, challenges and goals, which interact creating a unique experience, known as "game play" (Rollings & Adams, 2003). GBL is effective, since playing has been considered and employed as a primary instructional strategy and a form of socialization. Therefore, Edutainment environments are effective at focusing students' attention and enabling students to play in order to learn and enjoy the experience of learning (Qianping et al., 2007). According to Lazzaro (2004), it is for this emotional experience that people play games. In addition, GBL environments comprise elements that have an emotional character, e.g. narrative, sounds or music and graphics or animations. As a result, they are capable of establishing an emotional bond with the learner (Sykes, 2006).

Educative computer games are also being adapted to be affective learning tools. These provide immediate feedback and reward learning and mastering through different modalities, e.g. heroic music, new characters, power-ups, progression of story and high scores (Sykes, 2006). Malone (1981) signalled that the characteristics of video games, e.g. challenge, fantasy and curiosity, can also encourage learning in these environments. Learners need clear goals that must be uncertain and relevant not only from an educational perspective, but also from the game fantasy viewpoint. It is important to remember that not all fantasies appeal to all users, as personal preferences and gender influence users' choices. However, fantasy or storytelling is important because users have contact with other contexts that assist them in achieving an enhanced understanding of the specific problem that they want to solve.

Overcoming Design Problems in Edutainment

Developing Edutainment systems is not a simple endeavor as these kinds of systems require balancing of entertainment and educational strategies. Some common problems encountered in GBL environment design are balancing game and learning content, supporting the curriculum and ensuring that learning actually happened (Carpenter & Windsor, 2006; Conati, 2002; Sykes, 2006; Van Eck, 2006).

In addition, research in the Edutainment field is also pursuing personalization (Paireekreng, Rapeepisarn & Wong, 2009), Therefore, ITSs are also used in combination with GBL environments in order to achieve personalized instruction and ensure the achievement of the learning goals (Conati, 2002; McQuiggan, Mott & Lester, 2008). Since emotional and cognitive capabilities have been demonstrated to be deeply intertwined (Norman, Ortony & Russell, 2003), the field of Affective Computing merged with the field of ITSs. Researchers began to focus on the creation of a new generation of ITSs, which are capable of recognizing or predicting the learner's emotional state and showing affect (Picard et al., 2004).

Towards a New Generation of ITSs

The rise of ITSs is due to several facts such as the transformation of educational and teaching methods that evolved in order to achieve an enhanced awareness of cognitive processes, learning styles and interaction methods. Another important event is the information technology (IT) revolution that has encouraged novel ideas for processing and saving information, software development and the creation of networks. The advance in AI techniques has also been meaningful in achieving adaptable instruction, managing suitably resources, evaluating students' learning or encouraging collaboration. Additionally, student data is easily accumulable and can be employed to achieve enhanced understanding about students' behaviour, i.e. Educational Data Mining (EDM). Furthermore, novel interaction techniques have arisen in order to follow and record students' progress.

ITSs keep track of the student's performance over time, provide targeted feedback when necessary, select the most suitable pedagogical action and adapt to each student's preferences and pace of learning. ITSs take a student centred approach, where AI techniques are used to model or reason about students' characteristics, skills, behaviour or needs over time and respond accordingly to them (Woolf, 2009). These models attempt to infer what students should know and understand together with their misconceptions and learning preferences. Sometimes this entails using psychological and cognitive theories that explain how students acquire knowledge and how lecturers diagnose learning as a basis.

The new generation of ITSs attempts to address the integration of the emotional dimension in addition to addressing students' knowledge, learning and understanding successfully. The ultimate goal is to manage and hold students' motivation whilst learning (Du Boulay & Luckin, 2001), since emotional, motivational and cognitive processes have proved to be deeply interrelated and play different but equally important roles (Norman et al., 2003; Pekrun et al., 2007). Cognitive processes manage the semantic meaning, analysis, memorisation and understanding of the world. Additionally, affective processes focus on performing judgements and evaluations.

From the student modelling viewpoint, handling students motivation has comprised efforts in (1) identifying students' preferred learning styles (Kelly & Tangney, 2002), (2) diagnosing students' motivation (De Vicente & Pain, 2002; Del Soldato & Du Boulay, 1995), (3) recognising students' attitudes (Arroyo & Woolf, 2005), inferring students' level of self-efficacy (McQuiggan et al., 2008) and more recently inferring students' affective or emotional state (Conati & Maclaren, 2009; D'Mello et al., 2008; Porayska-Pomsta, Mavrikis & Pain, 2008). The latter has received increased attention due to recent research that has shown that emotional or affective states influence students' motivation, decisions and performance (Picard, 1995; Picard et al., 2004). Two approaches are employed to provide this new generation of tutors with the capabilities of understanding and reasoning about affect: (1) observing how human tutors reason about the learners' affective states as in Sarrafzadeh, Alexander, Dadgostar, Fan and

Bigdeli (2008) and observing how learners experience emotion as in Conati and Maclaren (2009).

Student Modeling

A student model is an important element of an ITS, as it is useful for reasoning about how people learn, specifically how new knowledge is filtered and integrated into a person's existing cognitive structure. Several representations have been deployed in implementing student models. Student models based on Bayesian networks (BN) have been deployed in diagnosis, the task being to infer the cognitive state of the student from observable data. A proposed classification of Bayesian student models is given in Mayo and Mitrovic (2001): (1) expert-centric student models is the product of domain analysis, in which an expert specifies either directly or indirectly the complete structure and conditional probabilities of the Bayesian student model; (2) efficiency-centric models that involves partial specification or restriction of the model and fitting domain knowledge to it, and (3) data-centric models, in which the structure and conditional probabilities of the network are learned from data. However, the effort required to define the network structure, the difficulty to obtain the parameters and the computational complexity of the inference algorithms, have to be considered when implementing these types of models. The main problem is the cost and time spent on building and refining a model for each domain. Therefore, a representation that simplifies this process is very important.

The student model is a representation of knowledge with the purpose of classification or prediction (Han & Kamber, 2006). ITSs perform continuous observations of student behavior linked to student performance in order to adapt feedback to encourage student interest and learning (Woolf, 2009). Cognitive student models are derived from domain models or expert knowledge models, since these are composed of the concepts that students have to grasp and comprehend or techniques that students may use for solving a specific problem or case study. Therefore, domain models represent these facts and methods, which are signaled by expert lecturers as those required to solve successfully domain problems or issues related to the instructional technique employed by these experts to provide feedback. The level of difficulty and time involved in the process of representing the domain is influenced by the domain complexity or structure.

Emotion in Computing and Education

Predicting emotion from its origin or CB-AUM is a computational approach for affective student modeling that uses cognitive psychology theory as a basis for reasoning about emotion. The most commonly employed is the OCC (Ortony, Clore and Collins) model (Ortony et al., 1990), which defines different types of emotions according to the sources that originate them. This theory suggests that events, agents and objects can elicit an emotion. To ensure that an individual is experiencing an emotion, it is necessary to have knowledge of their goals, social standards, attitudes, cultural context and personality traits, since this theory states that a threshold level has to be reached to experience an emotion. This approach has advantages such as it can be employed for online learning and uses feasible and low-bandwidth contextual variables, but has not yet demonstrated reasonable success (Jaques, Vicari, Pesty & Martin, 2011; Sabourin, Mott & Lester, 2011).

Identifying the physical and physiological effects of emotion is an approach that requires hardware. As a result, these kinds of ITSs are only available with full capabilities for reasonably recognizing emotion only in laboratory settings (D'Mello et al., 2008), are prone to failure (Burleson & Picard, 2007) and are considerably expensive to bring to classroom settings (Arroyo et al., 2009). This approach involves using self-reports or the opinions of expert judges to map patterns

of behavior to affective states and has shown the most successful to date. The 'hybrid approach' to reasoning about and indentifying emotion, which combines both approaches, inherits the strengths and weaknesses of both approaches and is expected to be the most successful way forward. However, it has still not shown significantly accurate results (Conati & Maclaren, 2009).

Once the computer tutor is able to predict or recognise the learner's affective, emotional or motivational state with certain accuracy, the new generation of interactive tutors focus on changing the learner's state to one optimal to attaining knowledge and understanding, i.e. encouraging the learner's motivation. Until now, there is no consensus about what is the learner's optimal state. D'Mello et al. (2008) focus on promoting flow during interaction, which was related to affective state engagement. Therefore the research was focused on changing negative affective states, e.g. boredom, frustration and confusion. Also, Conati & Maclaren (2009) focus on changing negative emotional states, distress and reproach, for joy and admiration respectively. Pekrun (2006) suggests that positive and negative achievement emotions, i.e. highly related to achievement activities and outcomes, do not necessarily produce a corresponding positive or negative effect on learning. This phenomenon is due to a complex pattern, which is the result of the interplay of task demands and different mechanisms, e.g. learning strategies, interest and motivation to learn, cognitive resources, social and cultural antecedents, personality antecedents and achievement goals.

In order to reason about emotion, it is meaningful to understand the origin of emotions and their characteristics. Two challenges are how to predict or recognize the learner's motivational and emotional states and how to suitably respond to them. Emotion is dynamic, short lasting and intentional. Self-reports are considered evidence of emotions, since they are subjective and only the person has access to them. Emotion influences students' motivation, learning and performance and plays a main role in the students' physiology process and behavior, the employed learning strategies and the use of the available cognitive resources.

Finally, to create an emotional student model it is important to relate the relevant emotions to the educational experiences. Achievement emotions are emotions that occur in educational settings when students want to achieve relevant activities and outcomes, e.g. boredom and frustration. The Control-Value Theory of achievement emotions by Pekrun et al. (2007) defines that control and value appraisals are the most relevant when determining these emotions. This theory has not been employed previously in work to create a computational and emotional student model. Therefore, our research focuses on this goal. In addition, this section discussed that reasoning about and addressing emotion in computer tutoring is meaningful to enable students' to focus and enjoy the experience of learning. Also, GBL environments facilitate the creation of this emotional bond and include ITSs to enhance their understanding of students' needs and capability to adapt instruction. The following section describes the adaptation of the Control-Value theory to a GBL environment setting.

FORMALISATION OF THE EMOTIONAL STUDENT MODEL

The work here focuses on using the Control-Value Theory of Achievement emotions by Pekrun et al. (2007) to create an emotional student model which can reason about students' emotions from answers to questions in game dialogues and observable and contextual variables, which are of low-bandwidth and feasible. Therefore, our hypothesis is that Control-Value Theory can be adapted to online Game-based learning environments settings and can reason about emotion accurately, i.e. approximately the precision of humans recognizing emotion (Keltner & Lerner, 2010). Hence, this is done by following a Cognitive-Based Affective-User Modeling (CB-AUM) approach, which reasons

about emotion from its origin using a psychological and cognitive theory of emotion. We decided to employ Dynamic Bayesian Networks (DBNs) to characterize our emotional student model, since they are proven to handle domain uncertainty effectively, enable us to include previous information from the domain and to represent the evolution of students' behavior over time. The latter is key, since as mentioned earlier emotion is dynamic, short lasting and intentional (Brave & Nass, 2008). Therefore, we require a knowledge representation that can fulfill these characteristics and DBNs are currently shown to be suitable in recognizing or reasoning about emotion (Conati & Maclaren, 2009; Sabourin et al., 2011).

In order to facilitate the derivation of DBNs, i.e. identifying the relevant observable variables to derive its structure and Conditional Probability Tables (CPTs), we have employed a combination of Probabilistic Relational Models (PRMs) and Multinomial Logistic Regression (MLR) (Muñoz et al., 2011). MLR is one of the preferred methods in Psychology for classifying category membership, since it requires fewer assumptions than discriminant analysis, such as multivariate normality or homogeneity of variance-covariance matrices. Also, it can handle categorical regressors effectively. As mentioned earlier, we employed this technique previously and it proved to be effective in predicting negative-neutral emotions, achieving an accuracy of 75%. In that research *control* was predicted by the student's attitude towards Physics and *value* was predicted successfully by the student's confidence in achieving a successful outcome. However, it was observed that this approach comprising analysis of correlation, MLR and cross-tabulation, conducted mainly manually, is highly time consuming. Therefore, in addition to the PRMs approach, here we use specific machine learning techniques, which involve less effort and require investing less time.

PRMs have been employed previously in research to facilitate the derivation of Bayesian Belief Networks (BBNs) and create student models that comprise the domain knowledge and concepts that students have to understand and learn (Sucar & Noguez, 2008). The PRMs approach assumes that a domain can be characterized as a series of objects with properties and relationships between them (Koller, 1999). In our research, this technique is employed to derive three PRMs, one corresponding to each type of *achievement emotion*, i.e. emotions originated from the achievement of relevant activities or outcomes, defined by Pekrun et al. (2007): (1) *prospective outcome*, (2) *activity* and (3) *retrospective outcome emotions*. These three types of emotions arise depending on the time frame and the object focus, e.g. outcome or activity. It is important to underline that achievement emotions are domain dependent. People that experiences specific emotions studying Physics do not experience the same emotions learning English. Here, we focus specifically on the creation and evaluation of the DBN corresponding to the *prospective outcome* emotions.

Adapting the Control-Value Theory to a GBL Environment Setting

As mentioned earlier, the Control-Value Theory assumes that control and value appraisals are the most relevant determining emotion. The subjective *control* over an activity and its outcomes is assumed to be related to causal expectancies and attributions, e.g. that the activity can be initiated and successfully performed or performing the activity will enable students to achieve their objectives. As a result, we inferred that control is related to students' self-efficacy, i.e. beliefs of performing in specific ways and attaining specific goals. *Value* is related to the relevant outcome or activity per se, or for its utility to contribute to later outcomes. Table 1 shows categorization of control and value and its relationship to the *prospective outcome* emotions.

It is observed that Pekrun et al. (2007) relate value and control to different factors according to the time frame, focus and educational setting

in their Achievement Emotions Questionnaire (AEQ) (Pekrun, Goetz & Perry, 2005). The AEQ is a self-report tool with statements and a scale from 1 to 5, where 1 corresponds to "strongly disagree" and 5 to "strongly agree", designed through Structural Equation Modeling (SEM) in order to determine if a student experience an emotion in classroom, tests and learning settings. The AEQ is comprised of affective, cognitive, physiological and motivational factors. We employed the factors in the AEQ to identify the employed constructs and derive our own questions in order to introduce and adapt them in game dialogues. For example: "I feel confident that I will be able to master the material". From this statement, it is observed that the student confidence is related to control or value.

Prospective outcome achievement emotions are emotions experienced by students before performing an activity and attempting to achieve its outcome. The value in this time frame is related to the students' expectancy of being able to perform an activity effectively with a successful outcome or the possibility of failing to take into account the control that they have over the outcome, i.e. if they believe that they have or can acquire the knowledge, skills and capabilities in order to achieve a successful or failed outcome or if they feel that the outcome will be achieved anyway due to the characteristics of the situation. We identified some factors from the AEQ, such as "perceived level of difficulty", "confidence towards achieving a successful outcome" or "source of motivation", but

Table 1. Prospective outcome emotions

Prospective outcome emotion	Value	Control
Anticipatory joy	Positive (achieving a successful outcome)	High
Hope		Medium
Hopelessness	Positive/Negative	Low
Anxiety	Negative (possibility of failing)	Medium
Hopelessness		High

Figure 1. Prospective outcome emotions PRM

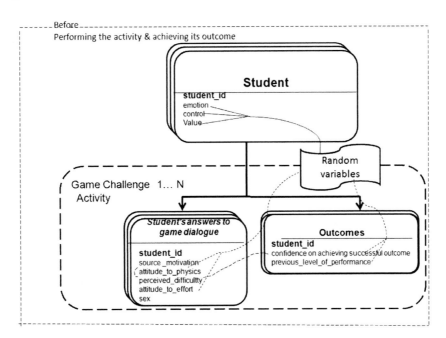

we do not know how these variables are related, if at all, to control and value. Furthermore, we do not know if these variables are related to each other. Figure 1 shows the PRM derived for the *prospective outcome emotions*. The dashed lines between properties indicate relationships, which are not certain and are necessary to verify. To select the contextual variables relevant to the online learning experience in the GBL environment, we considered a subset of the contextual variables employed by McQuiggan, Mott and Lester (2008) and Del Soldato and Du Boulay (1995), which were previously employed to diagnose students' level of self-efficacy and motivation respectively. These works were selected, since motivation and self-efficacy are deeply interrelated to emotion and are mentioned in the Control-Value Theory and the AEQ.

To know how these variables are related, it was observed that we need data from students' interaction in game dialogues and game challenges; since the ultimate goal is that our emotional student model can reason about emotion in online game-based learning (GBL) environment

settings. Also, this GBL environment should enable and encourage students to self-report their emotional state, since as Ortony et al. (1990) mentioned that self-reports are taken as evidence of emotions, as the experience of emotion is subjective and students are the only ones that have access to it. For example we cannot be sure that a person sees a green car as green with 100% certainty. However, if the person says that the car is green, we believe that the person is seen it in a green color. Also, we decided that the GBL environment setting would not have full capabilities of intelligent tutoring, since we want to study the emotions that arise when tutoring is not fully adaptable and intelligent in order to have a base to compare with when adaptable instructional strategies are implemented. Additionally, as mentioned earlier, deciding which affective and cognitive strategies are suitable to apply and how these should be conveyed are considered other challenges of the personalized and adaptable computer tutoring field.

Research Methodology

From the ideas discussed in the "Background and Related work" section, we decided that our methodology will comprise creating a GBL environment that allow students to learn and self-reporting their emotions, and then ask students to interact with the GBL environment in order to acquire data. We selected a GBL environment instead of a VLE, since GBL environments facilitate the establishment of an emotional link for inherent affective characteristics, e.g. narrative, sounds, color. Data mining and machine learning techniques are applied, specifically Necessary Path Condition (NPC) algorithm for structural learning and Expectation Maximization (EM) algorithm (Bashar et al., 2010; Hugin Lite, 2012) for parametric learning. The latter entails computing the log-likelihood in respect of the parameter values. The NPC algorithm enables us to incorporate domain knowledge about the relationships or conditional dependencies between variables when relationships are uncertain owing to scarce data. In addition NPC learning has an enhanced performance on small data sets when compared with the Peter-Clarkson (PC) algorithm. The PRMs originated from the Control-Value Theory are employed to clarify the relations according to the theory. Instead of using cross-tabulation and the observations to obtain the Conditional Probability Tables (CPTs) as in our previous work (Muñoz et al., 2011) we employed the EM algorithm, which makes the process of derivation faster and easier. The accuracy of classification of this model is compared with the accuracy of classification achieved by the model derived in previous work (Muñoz et al., 2011).

PLAYPHYSICS DESIGN AND IMPLEMENTATION

This section discusses our case study, the design and implementation of PlayPhysics, an affec-tive GBL environment for teaching Physics at undergraduate and high school levels. Our case study focuses on collecting data from students' self-reporting of emotion and answers to questions in game dialogue and interaction.

Analysis

We decided to focus on creating a GBL environment for teaching Physics, since students have been shown to find it difficult to comprehend underlying theories of Physics and hence find it difficult to stay engaged (Er & Dag, 2009). To create an application that addresses lecturers' and students' needs, an online survey was conducted. Fifty three students and four lecturers of an introductory Physics course from Tecnológico de Monterrey (ITESM-CCM) and Trinity College Dublin participated in the survey. From this survey, students' background as game players, personality traits and preferred feedback were examined. Also, it was noted that some topics were considered the most difficult, specifically the application of Newton's laws for particles and rigid bodies and principles of linear and circular kinematics. Therefore, PlayPhysics focused on these topics.

Design

PlayPhysics is a GBL environment that enables students to perform a pre-test on these topics to make them aware of their current level of understanding and knowledge. Then it enables them to play a Role Playing Game (RPG) implemented with Java, MySQL, 3D Studio Max, Poser, Hugin Lite, Jakarta Tomcat and the Unity Game Engine. The Unity Game Engine was selected to implement PlayPhysics, since it supports online gaming through the installation of the Unity Web Player in the web-browser (Unity Technologies, 2011). In the RPG, the student is an astronaut contacted by NASA with the purpose of performing a rescue mission by travelling to the Athena space station. The super computer, which was affected by a virus,

Figure 2. PlayPhysics game dialogue

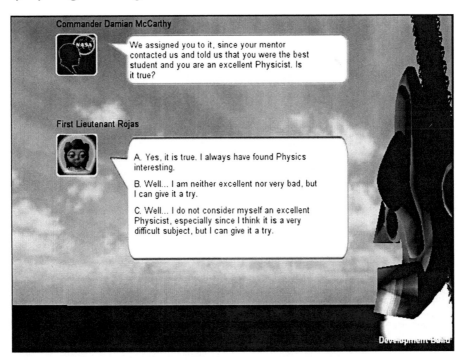

attacked the crew and the captain, Captain Foster is trapped. The first challenge comprises docking the Alpha Centauri spaceship with Athena. When the student is first contacted by NASA they are asked questions about their attitude to Physics, the level of difficulty of the mission according to the students' perspective, the source of motivation to take the mission, the effort that they are willing to spend and how confident they are in achieving a successful outcome. Figure 2 shows a screenshot depicting the PlayPhysics game dialogue. In this specific case, it illustrates the question enquiring about students' attitude towards Physics.

In addition, PlayPhysics includes a learning companion, the M8 robot, which provides hints to students if required. It was designed in this manner, since we did not want to interfere with students' independence. The M8 robot is not a highly effective instructor and companion, since we wanted to know what emotions happen in GBL environments that do not have highly adaptable instructional capabilities. Figure 3 presents the GUI corresponding to the first challenge. A con-

trol panel is displayed if the student chooses the cockpit view or internal spaceship view. The student can then interact in first person and employ the arrows and buttons in the control panel to set the required parameters to operate the spaceship and achieve the main goal corresponding to the first challenge, which involves arriving at the Athena station. The student also can switch to the outside view and watch how the spaceship is moving towards the space station from a third person perspective. The M8 robot appears in the screen on the right if it needs to convey a message, or ask the student to self-report his or her emotional state. The affective feedback provided by the M8 robot is limited to mimicking the emotions that the student self-reports, since knowing how to address and respond to students' emotions is still an ongoing question. For example, if the student reports that he or she is enjoying the learning experience M8 smiles, does a small dance with the upper part of its body and says "I am also having fun". Students can self-report their emotional state anytime using the *EmoReport* wheel.

Figure 3. PlayPhysics first challenge GUI

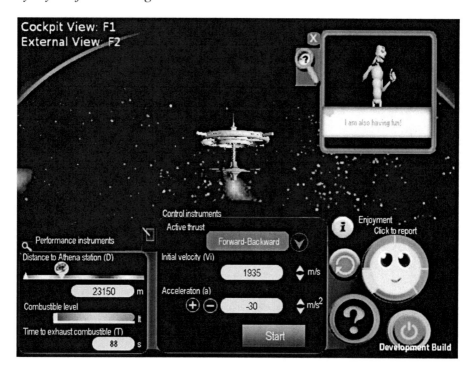

Game Challenge Design and Domain Knowledge Representation

PlayPhysics scenarios were designed with the assistance of an expert in Astrophysics. In the first challenge or Physics scenario of PlayPhysics, the Alpha Centauri spaceship, is heading at a constant speed towards the space station Athena. The purpose of this challenge is that the student selects appropriate values for Physics variables in order to stop Alpha Centauri precisely at Athena's rotational axis, in order to facilitate docking and entering it before the remaining fuel is exhausted (see Figure 3). The theme addressed in this phase is one-dimensional rectilinear motion with constant deceleration, one of the core topics of an introductory Physics course at undergraduate level. The complete scenario is introduced by M8 as follows:

"The objective of this challenge is to position the Alpha Centauri spaceship just below Athena station. You will have to move the spaceship in a linear path by setting the initial velocity and ac-

celeration (use the mouse to click arrows). Pay attention to the distance to the space station, the time and the available fuel. You need to arrive close to Athena station, so you can dock before the fuel runs out."

The condition variables, assigned randomly by PlayPhysics, are the initial distance from Alpha Centauri to Athena, D, and the remaining time to exhaust Alpha Centauri's fuel, T. The value ranges corresponding to these variables were defined as $D \in [15, 70]$ km and $T \in [80, 120]$ s. On the other hand, the exploration variables, variables for which the student has to select appropriate values, are: i) the direction of Alpha Centauri's acceleration (towards Athena Station '←', or away from it '→'), ii) the magnitude of this acceleration "a", which must be in the range $a = [0, 100]$ m/s^2, and iii) the initial speed "v_i" of Alpha Centauri, which must be in the range $v_i = [1000, 2000]$ m/s.

The first parameter that the student has to choose is the direction of the acceleration (towards the station '←', or away from it '→'). This is very important, since the chosen direction has to be '→'; otherwise, the spaceship will never stop at Athena's position, but will continue increasing its speed until the fuel is exhausted and then will continue moving at constant speed in interplanetary space forever. As a result, the astronaut will die. In this case PlayPhysics displays the player character with a sad and worried face saying that "he or she is lost in infinity". The student has to try the challenge again. However, M8 asks for the emotion of the student before restarting the game challenge. If the student decides to require a hint from M8, M8 will try to clarify the student misconception by saying: "Oops…Alpha Centauri didn't stop at Athena's axis. Its speed continued increasing".

Once Alpha Centauri's acceleration direction is correctly set, the student can focus on selecting the values corresponding to Alpha Centauri's deceleration magnitude "a" and initial speed "v_i" in order to precisely stop at Athena's rotation axis. The corresponding values ranges ($a \in \left[0, 100\right]$ m/s² and $v_i \in \left[1000, 2000\right]$ m/s²) were defined in order to make the solution non-trivial. For example, the student may be tempted to select a very large value for the deceleration magnitude ($a >$ 40 m/s²), which causes Alpha Centauri to stop very quickly, as a result not using all the remaining fuel.

However, humans cannot stand accelerations that are greater than 4g, where g represents the gravitational acceleration on Earth (g = 9.8 m/s²). Therefore, in this case, PlayPhysics displays the player character in a purple color, i.e. blood entered the brain showing that he or she passed out, with an accompanying thinking bubble saying "Too much acceleration". The student may restart the game challenge in order to try again and asks for a hint from the M8 in order to clarify what happened. M8 says: "It seems that the magnitude of

the acceleration is too large (more than 4g)…the astronaut blacked out". Therefore, the student will have to select a smaller value for the deceleration $\left(a \geq 40m / s^2\right)$ in order to continue and try to overcome the challenge. On the other hand, if the student selects a very small value for a, there is a risk of exceeding the time limit, T, which is required to complete the challenge.

In order to evaluate how effective the student selections for a and v_i, PlayPhysics calculates the breaking distance, d_s, and the time used to stop, t_s, for Alpha Centauri. These quantities are calculated using Equations 1 and 2.

$$d_s = \frac{v_i^2}{2a} \tag{1}$$

$$t_s = \frac{v_i}{a} \tag{2}$$

PlayPhysics compares t_s with T. If $t_s > T$ PlayPhysics assigns a low grade to the student, because the fuel ran out before Alpha Centauri arrived at Athena and as a result the astronaut is not saved.

If $t_s <= T$, PlayPhysics calculates the relative error, e_d, of the distance, defined by Equation 3.

$$e_d = \frac{d_s - D}{D} \tag{3}$$

This relative error will be small, if the calculations accordingly by the student are accurate. For small values of e_d, the grade or score assigned to the student is higher. A very high grade is obtained when the absolute value of e_d is smaller than 0.02 (a relative error of 2%), and a low grade is obtained when the relative error is larger than 0.10. PlayPhysics also evaluates the student selection according to the resulting breaking time t_s. For each set of randomly assigned condition values, D and T, PlayPhysics calculates the corresponding time interval, Δt, for all possible values of t_s that are consistent with valid values of a and v_i. Higher grades or scores are assigned for smaller values of t_s, because less fuel was consumed.

As can be seen, the student's selection of values for a and v_i is not trivial because they have to satisfy all the conditions imposed by the scenario, achieving the least value for the breaking time, not surpassing the maximum acceleration limit (40 m/s²), not exceeding the fuel exhaustion time and achieving the smallest relative error in the breaking distance. The solution to the scenario is relatively simple when D and T are large, since the combinations of a and v_i that fulfill all the requirements are greater. On the contrary, if T and/or D are too small, the valid combinations become scarce.

EVALUATION

In the winter of 2011, eighty-four high school and undergraduate students undertaking a Physics course at Tecnológico de Monterrey, Mexico City campus (ITESM-CCM), interacted with

PlayPhysics. Students solved a pre-test, afterwards they interacted with the first challenge of PlayPhysics and finally solved a post-test and qualitative questionnaire. Students self-reported their emotional state before, during and after performing the game activity.

This work centres on the emotions reported before interacting with the game challenge. As a result, the data collected and recorded in the database was employed to validate and compare the performance of the emotional student model derived and presented for the *prospective outcome emotions* in Muñoz et al. (2011) with the one derived using NPC structural learning and EM learning algorithms in this work. The former DBN model was created using cross-tabulation and MLR using the data collected from a sample of sixty-six undergraduate students of Physics in September 2010 (Muñoz et al., 2011). This same data was reused in this work to derive the DBN model applying NPC structural learning and EM learning, which are implemented in Hugin Lite (Hugin Expert A/S, 2011), which also has a Java API, e.g. HAPI. The motivation for this investigation arose from observing that the derivation of

Figure 4. Prospective outcome emotions DBN derived using cross-tabulation and MLR

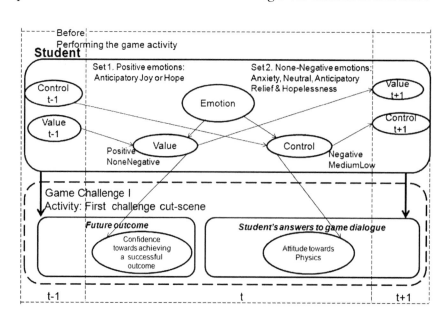

Figure 5. Prospective outcome emotions DBN derived using NPC and EM algorithms

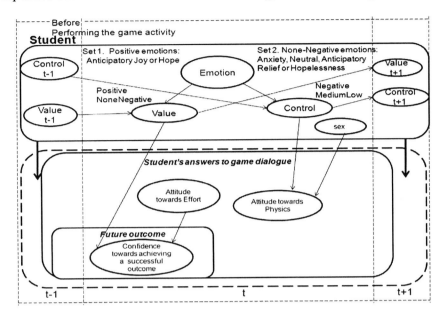

the previous DBN was time consuming and the classification accuracy needed to be improved. Figures 4 and 5 show the comparable DBNs:

The data corresponding to sixty-six students on September 2010 was employed for deriving the network structure in Figure 5 using the NPC algorithm. Hugin Lite required us to address the links that were identified as uncertain. Confidence was linked to the node Value only and Control was linked to Emotion. The data corresponding to the eighty-four students was employed to evaluate this model and the model in Figure 4, derived in previous research (Muñoz et al., 2011). We decide to employ the same sets of data to perform a fair comparison of their performance. As can be seen the DBN structure in Figure 5 includes two additional nodes, *gender* and *attitude towards effort*, in contrast to the DBN in Figure 4. What this indicates is that in this specific population, students' sex, male or female, is associated to their attitude towards Physics. There were 40 males and 26 females in this sample, 27 males corresponding to 57.5% from the male sample reported to have a neutral or negative attitude towards Physics, while 22 females corre-

sponding to 84.6% from the female sample reported to have a neutral or negative attitude towards Physics. When analyzing the Pearson correlation between the *attitude towards physics* and *students' sex*, this resulted to be negative and equal to 0.284 and significant at 0.05 level where there are 66 pairs of values, i.e. $r(66) = -0.284$. The square of the correlation (r^2) or coefficient of determination is usually employed to analyze the effect size. In this case r^2 is equal to 0.0806, since it is less than 0.09 and larger than 0.01 the effect is small and 1% or 8% of the variance between these variables is shared. Whilst analyzing the Pearson correlation between the students' attitude towards effort and the students' confidence, this was found to be significant at 0.05 level, positive and equals to 0.281, which is related to observing that 71.9% of the students on this specific sample have a positive attitude towards effort and reported to have a high level of confidence and 55.9% of students that do not have or have a negative attitude towards effort reported to have a low or medium level of confidence, i.e. $r(66) = 0.281$ and $r^2=0.079$. This correlation has a small effect over student confidence.

Results of the performance of both models classifying emotions, control and value are summarized and presented in Tables 2, 3 and 4 respectively. As can be observed, both models classify emotion significantly with approximately 70% accuracy. This is due to being capable of classifying the categorical variable value with the same accuracy (also 70%). In this case the valence of the defined set of emotions agrees with their value. This can be understood as students that evaluate as positive (positive emotion) the probable outcome of the task expect to succeed (positive value), whilst students that evaluate as negative (negative emotion) the probable outcome of the task expect to fail (negative value). Also, it is not clear if positive emotions are classified with 58.1% accuracy, or they are classified with this percentage only by chance, since the p-value is not significant. However, it is clear that negative and neutral emotions are classified with 80.5% accuracy by both models. In addition, control is classified with an accuracy of 63% by both models. However, in the model attained using NPC and EM algorithms, it can be affirmed that high control is classified with 6.3% accuracy, while low and medium control are classified with 98.1% accuracy. It is clear that to achieve an enhanced discrimination and reasoning of emotion, other variables that classify control more accurately should be identified. In comparison to Control-Value Theory, we are including the neutral or no-emotion, since Pekrun et al. (2007) state that if there is no control or value, there is no emotion, which we interpret as the student not having any interest in the outcome or the task, i.e. the outcome or the task is irrelevant, the student does not focus on failure or success and does not feel the motivation to compel himself or herself to manage and accomplish the task. As a result, we decided to locate the neutral emotion in the set of negative emotions, since they are emotions that we would like to address using adaptive instructions.

Focusing on the 33 cases (80.5%) that were classified accurately and correspond to the negative-none emotion set, it was observed that 13 cases corresponded to a neutral emotion, 11 cases to anticipatory relief, 6 cases to anxiety and 3 cases to hopelessness.

The emotional student model derived for reasoning about *prospective outcome emotions* using MLR revealed that the value of emotion is influenced by students' confidence and con-

Table 2. Comparison of performance classifying emotion

Prospective outcome emotions DBN model	Emotion set	Cases correctly classified	Cases incorrectly classified	Binomial test result (Bernoulli trials)
MLR & cross-tabulation derived (Muñoz et al., 2011) Accuracy ≈ 70% p =0.001, g =0.38 Large size effect	Positive emotions (anticipatory joy and hope) 43 out of 84 students	25 (58.1%)	18 (41.9%)	p = 0.360 is not significant Medium size effect g = 0.16
	None-negative emotions (neutral, anxiety, anticipatory relief and hopelessness) 41 out of 84 students	33 (80.5%)	8 (19.5%)	p = 1.1222 x 10⁻⁴, p<0.05 is significant Large size effect g = 0.61
NPC structural learning & EM learning derived Accuracy ≈ 70% p =0.001, g =0.38 Large size effect	Positive emotions (anticipatory joy and hope) 43 out of 84 students	25 (58.1%)	18 (41.9%)	p = 0.360 is not significant. Medium size effect g = 0.16
	None-negative emotions (neutral, anxiety, anticipatory relief and hopelessness) 41 out of 84 students	33 (80.5%)	8 (19.5%)	p = 1.1222 x 10⁻⁴, p<0.05 is significant Large size effect g = 0.61

Table 3. Comparison of performance classifying control

Prospective outcome emotions DBN model	Control	Cases correctly classified	Cases incorrectly classified	Binomial test result (Bernoulli trials)
MLR & cross-tabulation derived (Muñoz et al., 2011) Accuracy = 63% p=0.021, g = 0.26 Large size effect	High 32 out of 84 cases corresponded to high control	14 (43.8%)	18 (56.3%)	p = 0.597 is not significant Small size effect g = 0.12
	Medium-low 52 out of 84 cases corresponded to medium-low control	39 (75%)	13 (25%)	p = 4.0954 x 10^{-4} is significant Large size effect g = 0.5
NPC structural learning & EM learning derived Accuracy = 63% p=0.021, g = 0.26 Large size effect	High 32 out of 84 cases corresponded to high control	2 (6.3%)	30 (93.8%)	p = 2.4633 x10^{-7} is significant Large size effect g = 0.875
	Medium-low 52 out of 84 cases corresponded to medium-low control	51 (98.1%)	1 (1.9%)	p = 2.3537 x10^{-14} is significant Large size effect g =0.962

trol is influenced by students' attitude towards Physics. However, when we derived this model using the NPC algorithm, this was confirmed, but also revealed that for this specific population, students' gender has a small influence over the attitude towards Physics and frequently females have a more negative attitude towards Physics than males. Additionally, it was also revealed that students' attitudes towards effort has a small influence over students' confidence, which is directly proportional, i.e. students' confidence decreases if the student has a negative attitude towards effort.

RELATION TO OTHER WORK

Students' attitudes towards the subject, confidence and effort are three constructs evaluated by Pekrun et al. (2007) using the AEQ questionnaire (Pekrun et al., 2005). It is also observed that approximately 70% of achievements emotions value is accurately

Table 4. Comparison of performance classifying value

Prospective outcome emotions DBN model	Value	Cases correctly classified	Cases incorrectly classified	Binomial test result (Bernoulli trials)
MLR & cross-tabulation derived (Muñoz et al., 2011) Accuracy ≈ 70% p =0.001, g =0.38 Large size effect	Positive 43 out of 84 cases corresponded to positive value	25 (58.1%)	18 (41.9%)	p = 0.360 is not significant Medium size effect g = 0.26
	None-negative 41 out of 84 cases corresponded to none-negative value	33 (80.5%)	8 (19.5%)	p = 1.1222 x 10^{-4} is significant Large size effect g = 0.6
NPC structural learning & EM learning derived Accuracy ≈ 70% p=0.001, g =0.38 Large size effect	Positive 43 out of 84 cases corresponded to positive value	25 (58.1%)	18 (41.9%)	p = 0.360 is not significant Medium size effect g = 0.26
	None-negative 41 out of 84 cases corresponded to none-negative value	33 (80.5%)	8 (19.5%)	p = 1.1222 x 10^{-4} is significant Large size effect g = 0.6

classified by students' confidence and this is owing to more accurately classifying the category none-negative. In Control-Value Theory, value is related to the focus of the student on succeeding or avoiding failure, and hence, it makes sense that the value is related to students' confidence. Also, it is observed that the value agrees with students' valence, which is linked with attractiveness or evasiveness of an event, in this case achieving a successful outcome or failing. A difference of our work compared with the work by Pekrun et al. (2007) is that we are including the neutral or no-emotion category, since in our case, we do not know if the activity is relevant from the student's viewpoint, therefore, we do not know if value or control exists.

Del Soldato and Du Boulay (1995) following the theory of Keller (1983) also noted that effort, confidence and student interest are involved in students' motivation, which, unsurprisingly correlated to student's motivation in our work, since motivation is also influenced by students' emotion. In addition, students' beliefs of confidence are also related to students' self-efficacy. Therefore, McQuiggan et al. (2008) in an effort to identify students' affective aspects focus on classifying students' level of self-efficacy. In addition, our results show that the emotional student model achieved by applying the NPC and EM algorithms is more effective of classifying control, since this model proved to classify correctly 6.3% of the cases related to High control. The model obtained through MLR cannot ensure that 43.8% of the cases classified correctly in this category were not categorized by chance. However, it is noted that 98.1% of the cases classified as medium-low control were correctly classified. As a result, the control perceived is influenced by students' attitude towards Physics, agreeing with what Pekrun et al. (2007) stated about achievement emotions, which depend on the subject domain. Therefore, we can observe that the Control-Value Theory shows promise while employed as a basis for deriving an emotional student model for GBL.

FUTURE RESEARCH DIRECTIONS

This research evaluated the DBN that we derived to classify *prospective-outcome* achievement emotions. As NPC and EM algorithms proved more effective than MLR and cross-tabulation and are less time consuming, we will use them to derive the DBNs corresponding to *activity achievement emotions* and *retrospective-outcome achievement emotions*. We acquired from the interaction of these 84 students at ITESM-CCM approximately 1073 registries, which will be employed to reason about emotion using contextual variables related to the game activity, such as time invested and mouse location. In addition, we will acquire interaction and Galvanic Skin Response (GSR) data corresponding to 10 students to evaluate if data corresponding to the student internal context enhances the prediction accuracy. We selected GSR, since research has shown that it is more effective than Heart Rate (HR) signals (Rajae-Joordens, 2008). However, Pekrun et al. (2005) employ questions about the students' heart rate on the AEQ as evidence to determine if the student is feeling a specific emotional state. In addition, more challenges will be designed for PlayPhysics and research can be focused on identifying how to suitably respond to students' emotion in order to enhance learning and engagement.

CONCLUSION

This chapter reviews the state of the art of Edutainment, ITSs, Student Modeling and Emotion in Computing and Education. Three approaches to recognizing emotion were identified. The Cognitive-based User Modeling (CB-AUM) approach was employed in this work using Control-value Theory of achievement emotions (Pekrun et al., 2007) as a basis. We are the first employing this theory to derive a computational student model of this nature. The model uses answers to questions in game dialogues and contextual variables for reasoning about emotion acquired through the student interaction with PlayPhysics, an emotional game-based learning environment for teaching Physics that comprises self-reporting capabilities. Results showed promise on classifying negative-neutral emotions, emotion overall is classified with 70% accuracy. Therefore, using Control-Value Theory to derive our emotional model showed potential and can be employed in online GBL environments, since it uses contextual and feasible variables. Two approaches to derive DBNs were compared: (1) using MLR and cross-tabulation and (2) using NPC and EM algorithms. The latter results in being more effective at classifying control and at finding other relevant relationships between variables involved in the classification. In addition, the process is less time consuming. As a result, this approach will be employed to derive the DBNs corresponding to the *activity* and *retrospective-outcome achievement emotions*. PRMs were employed in combination with both approaches to facilitate the derivation of DBNs and the identification of potential observable variables. Data corresponding to the interaction and the student GSR will also be collected in order to determine if evidence related to the internal student context when employed in combination with contextual variables enhances the accuracy of the model.

ACKNOWLEDGMENT

We would like to convey our gratitude to the members of the e-learning research team at ITESM-CCM, Victor Robledo, Dr. Moises Alancastre, Dr. Lourdes Muñoz, Dr. Gilberto Huesca, Gerardo Aguilar and Benjamín Hernández, for their support during the testing of PlayPhysics. In addition, we would like to acknowledge the support and assistance provided by the lecturers of Physics at ITESM-CCM, Lamberto Álvarez, Carlos Salinas, Flor Ortínez, Ahylim Zamayoa and Enrique Muñoz. Also, we thank the participants

of this research, high school and undergraduate students of engineering undertaking a Physics course, who gave constructive feedback and helped with data gathering related to their GBL experience. In addition, thanks to Prof. Mark Shevlin from the Psychology Research Institute, Lee Cadieux from the Art and Design Research Institute, Prof. Sally McClean and Dr. Girijesh Prasad and Dr. Abdul Satti from the Computer Science Research Institute and the Intelligent Systems Research Centre (ISRC) at the University of Ulster for the advice provided during this research. We also like to acknowledge advice on statistical methods by Dr. Deaglan Page and Dr. Donncha Hanna from the School of Psychology at Queen's University Belfast. In respect of the implementation of PlayPhysics, we would like to thank the technical support offered by Dennis Heaney from BeepBlip Games and Gabriel Deak at the ISRC. Additionally, thanks to Richard Walsh from ZooCreative for his assistance in modeling PlayPhysics' player characters and Peter Starostin for creating LowMax, the free rig that was adapted to create the learning companion robot, M8.

REFERENCES

Arroyo, I., Cooper, D. G., Burleson, W., Woolf, B. P., Muldner, C., & Christopherson, R. (2009). *Emotion sensors go to school*. Paper presented at the 14th International Conference on Artificial Intelligence in Education (AIED 2009): Building Learning Systems that Care: From Knowledge Representation to Affective Modelling.

Arroyo, I., & Woolf, B. P. (2005). Inferring learning and attitudes from a Bayesian network of log file data. In C. K. Looi, G. Mc Calla, B. Bredeweg, & J. Breuker (Eds.), *Proceedings of the 12th International Conference on Artificial Intelligence in Education, Frontiers in Artificial Intelligence and Applications* (Vol. 125, pp. 33-40). Amsterdam, The Netherlands: IOS Press.

Bashar, A., Parr, G., McClean, S., Scotney, B., & Nauck, D. (2010, 7-9 July 2010). *Learning-based call admission control framework for QoS management in heterogeneous networks*. Paper presented at the Proc. of Networked Digital Technologies (NDT 2010), Part II, Prague, Czech Republic.

Brave, S., & Nass, C. (2008). Emotion in human-computer interaction. In Sears, A., & Jacko, J. A. (Eds.), *The human computer interaction handbook: Fundamentals, evolving technologies and emerging applications* (2nd ed.). New York, NY: Lawrence Earlbaum Associates, Taylor & Francis Group.

Burleson, W., & Picard, R. W. (2007). Evidence for gender specific approaches to the development of emotionally intelligent learning companions. *IEEE Intelligent Systems*, *22*(4), 62–69. doi:10.1109/MIS.2007.69

Carpenter, A., & Windsor, H. (2006, 24 January 2010). A head of the game? - Games in education. *Serious Games Source*. Retrieved from http://seriousgamessource.com/features/feature_061306_ahead_of_the_game.php

Conati, C. (2002). Probabilistic assessment of user's emotions in educational games. *Applied Artificial Intelligence*, *16*, 555–575. doi:10.1080/08839510290030390

Conati, C., & Maclaren, H. (2009). Empirically building and evaluating a probabilistic model of user affect. *User Modeling and User-Adapted Interaction*, *19*(3), 267–303. doi:10.1007/s11257-009-9062-8

D'Mello, S., Jackson, T., Craig, S., Morgan, B., Chipman, P., White, H., et al. (2008). *AutoTutor detects and responds to learners affective and cognitive states*. Paper presented at the International Conference of Intelligent Tutoring Systems, Workshop on Emotional and Cognitive Issues.

De Vicente, A., & Pain, H. (2002). *Informing the detection of the student's motivational state: An empirical study*. Paper presented at the 6th International Conference on Intelligent Tutoring Systems (ITS 2002).

Del Soldato, T., & Du Boulay, B. (1995). Implementation of motivational tactics in tutoring systems. *Journal of Artificial Intelligence in Education*, *6*(4), 337–378.

Du Boulay, B., & Luckin, R. (2001). Modelling human teaching tactics and strategies for tutoring systems. *International Journal of Artificial Intelligence in Education*, *12*, 235–256.

Er, N. F., & Dag, H. (2009). *Comparison of cost-free computational tools for teaching physics*. Paper presented at the Fifth International Conference on Soft Computing, Computing with Words and Perceptions on Systems Analysis, Decision and Control (ICSCCW 2009).

Han, J., & Kamber, M. (2006). *Data mining: Concepts and techniques* (2nd ed.). San Francisco, CA: Elsevier.

Hugin Expert A/S. (2011, 19 August 2011). Hugin Lite - Evaluation. *Hugin expert: The leading support tool*. Retrieved from http://www.hugin.com/productsservices/demo/hugin-lite

Hugin Lite. (2012, 18 January 2012). Hugin help pages. *Hugin Lite*. Retrieved from http://download.hugin.com/webdocs/manuals/7.4/Htmlhelp/descr_NPC_algorithm_pane.html

Jaques, P. A., Vicari, R. M., Pesty, S., & Martin, J.-C. (2011). *Evaluating a cognitive-based affective student model*. Paper presented at the 4th International Conference of Affective Computing and Intelligent Interaction (ACII 2011) Part I.

Jensen, F. V., & Nielsen, T. D. (2007). *Bayesian networks and decision graphs* (2nd ed.). Berlin, Germany: Springer. doi:10.1007/978-0-387-68282-2

Keller, J. M. (1983). Motivational design of instruction. In Reigeluth, C. M. (Ed.), *Instructional-design theories and models: An overview of their current status* (*Vol. 1*, pp. 386–434). Hillsdale, NJ: Lawrence Erlbaum Associates.

Kelly, D., & Tangney, B. (2002). *Incorporating learning characteristics into an intelligent tutor*. Paper presented at the 6th International Conference Intelligent Tutoring Systems (ITS 2002).

Keltner, D., & Lerner, J. S. (2010). Emotion. In Fiske, S. T., Gilbert, D. T., Lindzey, G., & Jongsma, A. E. (Eds.), *Handbook of social psychology* (5th ed., *Vol. 1*, pp. 317–352). Hoboken, NJ: Wiley.

Kinnear, P. R., & Gray, C. D. (2010). *PASW statistics 17 made simple*. East Sussex, UK: Psychology Press.

Koller, D. (1999). Probabilistic relational models. In S. Džeroski & P. Flach (Eds.), *Proceedings of the 9th International Workshop of Inductive Logic Programming (ILP-99)* (Vol. 1634, pp. 3-13). Pittsburgh, PA: Springer.

Lazzaro, N. (25 October, 2011). Why we play games: Four keys to more emotion without story. *XEO Design*. Retrieved from http://www.xeodesign.com/xeodesign_whyweplaygames.pdf

Malone, T. W. (1981). Toward a theory of intrinsically motivating instruction. *Cognitive Science*, *6*(4), 333–369. doi:10.1207/s15516709cog0504_2

Mayo, M., & Mitrovic, A. (2001). Optimizing ITS behaviour with Bayesian networks and decision theory. *International Journal of Artificial Intelligence in Education*, *12*(2), 124–153.

McQuiggan, S. W., Mott, B. W., & Lester, J. C. (2008). Modeling self-efficacy in intelligent tutoring systems: An inductive approach. *User Modeling and User-Adapted Interaction*, *18*(1 - 2), 81-123.

Muñoz, K., Mc Kevitt, P., Lunney, T., Noguez, J., & Neri, L. (2011). An emotional student model for game-play adaptation. *Entertainment Computing*, *2*(2), 133–141. doi:10.1016/j.entcom.2010.12.006

Norman, D. A., Ortony, A., & Russell, D. M. (2003). Affect and machine design: Lessons for the development of autonomous machines. *IBM Systems Journal*, *42*(1), 38–44. doi:10.1147/sj.421.0038

Ortony, A., Clore, G. L., & Collins, A. (1990). *The cognitive structure of emotions*. New York, NY: University Press.

Paireekreng, W., Rapeepisarn, K., & Wong, K. W. (2009). Time-based personalised mobile game downloading. In Pan, Z., Cheok, D. A., & Müller, W. (Eds.), *Transactions on Edutainment II, LNCS 5660* (*Vol. 2*, pp. 59–69). Berlin, Germany: Springer-Verlag. doi:10.1007/978-3-642-03270-7_5

Pekrun, R. (2006). The control-value theory of achievement emotions: Assumptions, corollaries, and implications for educational research and practice. *Educational Psychology Review*, *18*(4), 315–341. doi:10.1007/s10648-006-9029-9

Pekrun, R., Frenzel, A. C., Goetz, T., & Perry, R. P. (2007). The control value theory of achievement emotions. An integrative approach to emotions in education. In Schutz, P. A., & Pekrun, R. (Eds.), *Emotion in education* (pp. 13–36). London, UK: Elsevier. doi:10.1016/B978-012372545-5/50003-4

Pekrun, R., Goetz, T., & Perry, R. P. (2005). *Achievement emotions questionnaire (AEQ). User's manual*. University of Munich.

Picard, R. W. (1995). *Affective computing*. Unpublished Technical report. Massachusetts Institute of Technology (MIT).

Picard, R. W., Papert, S., Bender, W., Blumberg, B., Breazeal, C., & Cavallo, D. (2004). Affective learning –A manifesto. *BT Technology Journal*, *22*(4), 253–269. doi:10.1023/B:BTTJ.0000047603.37042.33

Porayska-Pomsta, K., Mavrikis, M., & Pain, H. (2008). Diagnosing and acting on student affect: The tutor's perspective. *User Modeling and User-Adapted Interaction*, *18*, 125–173. doi:10.1007/s11257-007-9041-x

Qianping, W., Wei, T., & Bo, S. (2007). *Research and design of edutainment*. Paper presented at the First IEEE International Symposium on Information Technologies and Applications in Education (ISITAE '07).

Rajae-Joordens, R. J. E. (2008). Measuring experiences in gaming and TV applications: Investigating the added value of a multi-view auto-stereoscopic 3D display. In Westerinck, J. H. D. M., Ouwerkerk, M., & Overbeek, T. J. M. (Eds.), *Probing experience: From assessment of user emotions and behaviour to development of products* (*Vol. 8*, pp. 77–90). Netherlands: Springer.

Rapeepisarn, K., Wong, K. W., Fung, C. C., & Depickere, A. (2006, 4-6 December). *Similarities and differences between "learn through play" and "edutainment"*. Paper presented at the 3rd Austrasalian Conference on Interactive Entertainment (IE 2006), Perth, Australia.

Rollings, A., & Adams, E. (2003). *On game design*. Old Tappan, NJ: Pearson.

Sabourin, J., Mott, B. W., & Lester, J. C. (2011). *Modelling learner affect with theoretical grounded dynamic Bayesian networks*. Paper presented at the 4th International Conference of Affective Computing and Intelligent Interaction (ACII 2011) Part I.

Sarrafzadeh, A., Alexander, S., Dadgostar, F., Fan, C., & Bigdeli, A. (2008). How do you know that I don't understand? A look at the future of intelligent tutoring systems. *Computers in Human Behavior*, *24*(4), 1342–1363. doi:10.1016/j.chb.2007.07.008

Schutz, P. A., & Pekrun, R. (Eds.). (2007). *Emotion in education*. San Diego, CA: Elsevier.

Sucar, L. E., & Noguez, J. (2008). Student modeling. In Pourret, O., Naïm, P., & Marcot, B. (Eds.), *Bayesian networks: A practical guide to applications* (pp. 173–185). West Sussex, UK: J. Wiley & Sons.

Sykes, J. (2006). Affective gaming: Advancing the argument for game-based learning. In Pivec, M. (Ed.), *Affective and emotional aspects of human-computer interaction* (pp. 3–7). Amsterdam, The Netherlands: IOS Press.

Tao, J., & Tan, T. (2005, 22-24 October 2005). *Affective computing: A review*. Paper presented at the Affective Computing and Intelligent Interaction (ACII 2005), Beijing, China.

Unity Technologies. (2011, 19 August 2011). *Unity 3*. Retrieved from http://unity3d.com/unity/

Van Eck, R. (2006). Digital game-based learning: It's not just the digital natives who are restless. *EDUCAUSE Review*, *41*(2), 16–30. Retrieved from http://www.educause.edu/EDUCAUSE+Review/EDUCAUSEReviewMagazineVolume41/DigitalGameBasedLearningItsNot/158041

Westerinck, J. H. D. M., Ouwerkerk, M., Overbeek, T. J. M., Pasveer, W. F., & De Ruyter, B. (2008). *Probing experience: From assessment of user emotions and behaviour to development of products*. Dordrecht, The Netherlands: Springer.

Woolf, B. P. (2009). *Building intelligent interactive tutors: Student-centered strategies for revolutionizing e-learning*. Burlington, MA: Elsevier, Inc.

ADDITIONAL READING

Dalgleish, T., & Power, T. (Eds.). (1999). *The handbook of cognition and emotion*. Sussex, UK: John Wiley and Sons, Ltd. doi:10.1002/0470013494

Darwin, C. R. (1872). *The expression of the emotions in man and animals* (1st ed.). London, UK: John Murray. doi:10.1037/10001-000

Sears, A., & Jacko, J. A. (Eds.). (2007). *The human computer interaction handbook: Fundamentals, evolving technologies and emerging applications* (2nd ed.). New York, NY: Lawrence Earlbaum Associates, Taylor & Francis Group. doi:10.1201/9781410615862

KEY TERMS AND DEFINITIONS

Achievement Emotions: Are emotions that arise in learning and educational settings where the achievement of activities and their outcomes is pursued.

Control-Value Theory: Is a cognitive theory by Pekrun et al. (2007) in which control and value appraisal are assumed the most relevant to determine emotion.

Dynamic Bayesian Networks: Are a type of machine learning technique used for achieving knowledge representation that are highly effective handling the uncertainty of domains that evolve over time and incorporate previous knowledge of the domain.

Educational Data Mining: Is a discipline focused on developing methods for analyzing data from educational settings in order to achieve an enhanced understanding and awareness of the student and the environment in which he/she learns.

Game-based Learning Environments: Are a type of *Edutainment* environment, i.e. games used with the serious purpose of teaching in parallel to keep students' engagement.

Intelligent Tutoring Systems (ITSs): Are a type of computer tutoring that have the capability of adapting teaching and feedback to students' needs and skills and, in addition, to the capability of reasoning about students' characteristics.

Probabilistic Relational Models: Are an object representation of the domain, i.e. parameters, classes and the relations between them, which facilitate the derivation of Bayesian Belief Networks (BBNs).

Student Modeling: Is the process involved on deriving a knowledge representation of the student comprising needs, skills, knowledge, learning preferences or other characteristics in order to achieve personalization through an enhanced understanding of student behavior.

Section 4
Adapted Contents

Chapter 10
Analyzing the Level of Inclusion of Digital Educational Objects in Eskola 2.0

Mª Luz Guenaga
DeustoTech Learning – Deusto Foundation, Spain & University of Deusto, Spain

Iratxe Mentxaka
DeustoTech Learning – Deusto Foundation, Spain & University of Deusto, Spain

Susana Romero
DeustoTech Learning – Deusto Foundation, Spain & University of Deusto, Spain

Andoni Eguíluz
DeustoTech Learning – Deusto Foundation, Spain & University of Deusto, Spain

ABSTRACT

The Basque Government has published two calls to create digital educational objects for the programme called Eskola 2.0. After having provided schools with technological equipment, these calls aim to increase the use of learning technology in the classroom. More than 300 didactic sequences have been developed, which vary greatly in visual design, content structure, organization, and pedagogical aspects. Even though accessibility is one of the quality criteria, the reality is that they are hardly accessible and inclusive. DeustoTech Learning research group has carried out a survey of the educational objects approved in these calls up to November 2011. The authors evaluated pedagogical and technological aspects to find out how inclusive they are. In this chapter, they provide the results of the survey and propose a set of guidelines for designing more accessible and inclusive objects in the future.

INTRODUCTION

In July 2009, the Council of Ministers of the Spanish Government promoted a programme entitled Escuela 2.0 (Moncloa, 2009) which invested over 100 million Euros in equipping 400,000 students and 20,000 teachers with laptops, digitalizing 14,400 classrooms with Wi-Fi connection, digital whiteboards and other technology aimed at enhancing learning. This programme was established in the 2009-2010 academic year, starting with 5th –year primary school students, and each year it covers one new academic level.

DOI: 10.4018/978-1-4666-2530-3.ch010

Copyright © 2013, IGI Global. Copying or distributing in print or electronic forms without written permission of IGI Global is prohibited.

In the Basque Country competences on education are transferred from the central Ministry of Education to the Basque Government Department of Education, who endorsed this programme and called it Eskola 2.0

Many changes have taken place in a very short period of time: computers in the classroom, Internet connection, multimedia and audiovisual content at hand, changes in pedagogical models, competence-based learning, training teachers in Information and Communication Technologies (ICTs), etc. The present academic year, 2011-2012, is the third in which the Eskola 2.0 programme is being carried out. There are already three years of students with their own notebook to work with in class, but there are still many challenges for all participants in the educational process (teachers, institutions, schools, parents, students…)

Schools have been provided with technological infrastructure, but a key aspect is having quality educational content to enhance learning with the use of technology. This is the aim of these calls and the result has been more than 300 educational

sequences in core subjects of the Basque curriculum. Content producers received a few guidelines, so each has applied their own pedagogical and technological design criteria and the results have been quite varied.

In this chapter we present an evaluation of Digital Educational Objects uploaded to Agrega (AgregaGV 2012), the website where the Basque government shares all the content under its/a Creative Common license when it approves pedagogical and technical evaluation.

We analyze the accessibility and adaptability of this content for students and we assess the relation between the previously mentioned variables and the level of accessibility. This analysis will conclude with a set of guidelines for the design of inclusive educational content. Furthermore, we will provide content creators with a proposal on how to improve their material without the need of a total redesign. It is not the same to create educational content from scratch, with the proper guidelines to make it inclusive, as improving existing material and making it more adaptable.

Figure 1. Information of the DEO provided by Agrega search engine

One of the main interests of our work is to facilitate the Basque Government with a design style guide so that it can serve as a reference for other educational content designers. In fact, the call itself talked about a set of guidelines for producing content but this is not available yet. This guide will explain how to design the interface, -whose technology improves inclusive education-, the recommended extension and instructional design of educational objects, different levels and intensity of interaction and what the target audience of the content may be.

This guide will ease the creation of inclusive educational content and will improve the accessibility and adaptability to students according to their personal and functional characteristics. Ultimately, it will improve the overall quality of the content and will benefit all users.

ICT IN THE CLASSROOM, NEW CHALLENGES

Learning and teaching tools have changed a great deal/significantly in the last few years and the unstoppable advance of technology means this is an ongoing condition. We have passed from chalk and board, pen and paper to laptop, digital board, digital educational content, web 2.0 applications and many other possibilities. Changes need time, but the problem is that technology advances so fast and in so many directions that there is no time to keep up to date. This, added to the fact that today's students were born in the digital era and they are familiar with technology, generates a lack of self-confidence among teachers. They fear that students have better skills than them using ICTs, but they have to realize that a change has taken place in the role of teachers: they are no longer the guardians of knowledge.

In recent years teachers have invested many hours attending *ICT training courses*. From word processors, spreadsheets and operative systems to Internet, search engines, web 2.0 applications (forum, wiki, blog…), digital boards and Learning Management Systems used in each educational institution. Moreover, from time to time they are faced with the change of technology and/or version in their educational institution due to emerging technologies, the updating of existing ones or policy changes. Despite the number of hours needed for training, many teachers do not feel self-confident using ICTs and demand even more training. They ask for training specifically related to their areas of knowledge. They are not so interested in how a forum works but how to use it pedagogically in their science, history or language class. Teachers demand educational content in order to make the best of the technological infrastructure they have. They ask for orientation and courses on how to use and integrate these educational digital objects into the curriculum.

The term Digital Educational Object (DEO) refers to digital and interactive educational content structured in didactic sequences, which has been designed with a pedagogical objective and can be used in different educational contexts. In this definition we highlight two main characteristics: *reusability*, digital objects designed to be used freely in different contexts; and *granularity*, that is to say, an object consists of several educational elements that have, by themselves, an educational purpose and can also be used in different contexts (Cuadrillero, Serna and Corrochano, 2007; Polsani, P. R. 2003).

One of the most urgent problems is the *lack of digital educational content* available to make the best of technological infrastructure, even more so if we try to find material in the Basque language. Teachers who are more concerned have been creating or adapting their material to new technological tools. Others do not have sufficient ICT skills or time to do this. There are many technologies available and it is a real challenge for teachers to keep up to date on didactic aspects of their subjects and on ICT at the same time. But professional producers will slowly satisfy their needs for educational content. That is why the

Basque government has published a public call in the last two years to stimulate an increase in production.

The *pedagogical approach* has also changed from content-based to competence-based education. Many experienced teachers have not found this an easy change to understand and apply. They had their subjects structured in traditional chapters, content and concepts, and they have to change to teach competences like teamwork, social and civic competence, autonomy and personal initiative or learning to learn. They find it difficult to find the way to do it, to apply the competences in their particular areas of knowledge and to evaluate them.

All these changes make it more evident that *the centre of the learning process is the student*. The teacher becomes the guide, tutor or moderator of learning. We need more interactive models, with self-evaluation, with clear orientations for teachers and students, with no closed agendas and models where teachers do not know everything. Students have to discover the knowledge and construct their learning. This is why inclusive design is now even more relevant than ever.

The Call of the Basque Government to Create Digital Educational Objects

In 2009 and 2010 the Basque Government published two separate calls (BOPV 2009; BOPV 2010) to create Digital Educational Objects (DEOs) that «*will have an open character, will enable the development and exchange of didactic material among teachers, and will enhance collaborative, personalized and meaningful learning processes*» (BOPV 2010).

Below we describe the main characteristics of the last of the two calls. To understand the result and conclusions of our survey we have to take into account that the educational objects were developed under these conditions and with a considerably tight time limit.

- Content focus on core areas of knowledge of the 5th and 6th years of primary school and 1st and 2nd courses of secondary school.
- Content has to be bilingual (Basque and Spanish) or trilingual in some areas (Basque, Spanish and English).
- Each project has to include eight teaching sequences with an average duration of three working sessions. A didactic sequence is a planned organization of activities aimed at progression and is designed to achieve a specific learning, that is to say, co-related activities with a specific didactic goal.
- The whole content and resources included have to be copyright-free and original.
- It is recommended to include a variety of formats like text, image, audio, video, animations, hypertext, simulations and specific material for Digital Interactive Boards.
- Content has to run online and offline, which sometimes means creating equivalent material or providing alternative content and activities which can be carried out without Internet connection.
- All content and resources have to be developed with free and open software.
- Content has to adapt to different ICT skills of teachers. As far as possible content should serve several stages and teachers should be able to use it for different purposes, depending on their ICT competence and experience.
- The resulting educational content will be distributed under the Creative Commons license on the Agrega web site of the Basque and Spanish governments (Agrega 2012). Copying, modifying and distributing it for non-commercial use will be allowed.
- Teaching strategy is focused on the student more than in the content itself. The methodology focuses in the development of competences.

Educational content has to be packaged and has to meet the LOM.ES and SCORM international educational standards. This makes it possible to interoperate with other content and tools that meet the same standards, to provide metadata that describes the educational content in a pedagogical and technological way, and it also enables description of the educational object's level of inclusion. It also makes it possible to develop search engines, classification and advanced tools that manage this metadata. Moreover, with this information, teachers are able to determine whether the material is useful or not. According to the Spanish Centre on Educational Information and Communication (CNICE), educational metadata has to describe, store, organize and manage educational objects so they can be retrieved, searched and reused as educational resources. If a digital resource does not have metadata, it cannot be considered an educational object (Bueno de la Fuente, G. 2006).

Projects funded in this call must have a pedagogical consultant with a minimum of two year's experience in approved centres teaching the area covered by the project. This professional will be responsible for the pedagogical adequacy of the project, which will then be evaluated by a counsellor assigned by the Basque Government. This evaluator will supervise the whole process and content, making sure it fits the curricula, level of difficulty, activities, simulations, teacher's guide and all pedagogical aspects of the project.

How Inclusion is Assessed

In this changing scenario teachers find the need to deal with diversity, students with different functional characteristics, disabilities and learning styles that could personalize and adapt their learning process with the use of technology. Accessible and adaptable educational content is extremely valuable for an inclusive education.

One of the Basque Government's recommendations in the last call (but not in the first one) is to design accessible content for students with disabilities: «*accessibility: design controls and presentation format appropriate to the needs of students with disabilities*». This was one of the evaluation criteria scoring five points over the total 150.

From DeustoTech Learning group we understand inclusive design as not only making content accessible for students with disabilities but including the possibility to adapt educational content to all students according to several variables like learning pace, personal aptitudes, technological skills, attention to diversity, etc. This has to be integrated into the design of educational objects and was included in the following evaluation criteria in the call of the Basque Government. Each of the following criteria was also weighted with five points over 150:

Criteria related to pedagogical quality that affects the inclusive design of the educational content:
- Relevance to students
- Development of personal initiative, decision-making, and the development of meta-cognitive skills and learning strategies that allow students to plan, regulate and evaluate their own intellectual activity.

Other technical criteria that improve inclusion (accessibility and usability):
- Interface design, referring to it as «*visual quality of text, graphics, animations, video, sound, etc…*»
- Navigation design, mentioned as «*organization of information and the possibilities to access it*»
- Personalization, educational content should «*allow customized itineraries and include evaluation and correction tutoring systems*»

With reference to linguistic quality, the call focuses on:
- Presentation clarity and precision.

○ Non-discriminatory use of language *«for social, linguistic, cultural, ethnic, gender or any other reasons»*

A total of 40 points over 150 are in some way related to the inclusive character of the educational content supported by the Basque Government. This includes not only direct accessibility issues for students with disabilities but also features related to adaptation to students, interface design and non-discrimination. Meeting this criteria not only benefits students with disabilities but everyone, because every student has their own characteristics and learning should take them into account and be adaptable.

Difficulties in Making Inclusion a Reality

DeustoTech Learning research group has a background in technological accessibility and usability, educational content design and learning technologies. We participated in the 2010 call by creating educational content for the subject of Technology in the 1st year of secondary school. As content producers, we have detected several problems in making educational content accessible and inclusive in the context of this call. We have directly faced some of these difficulties and we have also shared experience with other producers.

In many cases content producers do not know many of the problems that students with disabilities have when accessing digital learning content and tools. They ignore guidelines, standards and legislation on accessibility and they do not have sufficient skills in human-computer interaction to afford pedagogical and technical design taking inclusion as a priority. Time is tight and evaluation is focused on pedagogical aspects, so producers have these as the main goal of the product.

There is confusion about some features of the content to be created. Neither producers nor the Basque Government have a unique criterion concerning key features of content; e.g. the kind of activities to be included: they may vary from simple digitalized documents with no interaction to complex simulations that explain abstract concepts. There is no guideline to the minimum number of simulations or interactive activities to be included or the best or worst practices in this sense.

In DeustoTech Learning we are researching on innovative technologies in education applied to different areas of knowledge. In this sense we try to promote the use of Web 2.0 tools in a pedagogical way in the area of Technology. The point is that these activities were classified as too difficult for teachers' average ICT literacy, and flash-based animations were preferred instead.

The average duration of each of the eight educational sequences was established in the call as three hours, though after several reviews with experts in the area, the final product included many activities, multimedia resources, theoretical explanations, simulations and evaluation, which take much longer than three hours to be completed. This is related to the initial aim of the proposal, which was to create educational content to complement the traditional learning process. In some cases it has changed to the point that the project covers almost a whole course subject.

One aspect that led to misunderstanding was the target users of digital objects. Initially we understood it was oriented to teachers who will use it in their class or ask their students to use it at home. We oriented the presentation, navigation schema, language, guides and everything to teachers, but in the middle of the project we realized that the Basque Government required material to be self-explanatory for the student. They wanted students to be as autonomous as possible, so issues such as self-evaluation, simulations or explanation of the theoretical concepts were key aspects that we had not taken into account. This implied a total re-design of the project, which delayed our progress considerably.

All the difficulties described make producers focus on educational content, attractive interface design, organization and structure of the information, development of multimedia resources that complement theoretical explanations, interactive activities, simulations and self-assessment that help the students aware of their progress in the area…but the high demand and tight time schedules do not allow us to give the necessary importance to key aspects like accessibility for students with disabilities, usability to make content user friendly and other issues that promote the user's inclusion and adaptation.

REVIEW OF PEDAGOGICAL AND TECHNOLOGICAL PRINCIPLES

Inclusive learning can be understood from different points of view. We have focused on pedagogical and technical features of the Digital Educational Objects that affect accessibility and adaptation to the student. For that purpose we have analyzed existing pedagogical models and how they are implemented in DEOs. On the other hand, we have conducted a review of accessibility and usability guidelines that promote the capability of educational content to adapt to diversity of students and facilitate the full participation of everyone.

Pedagogical Variables

When drawing up the pedagogical design of a digital educational object (DEO), we have to take some decisions about graphical design, structure and logical sequence, style of interaction, help system, etc. When we design a DEO, we have to realize that we are designing a product that will cause a change in the user providing him/her with a specific learning. It is not only a matter of how to organize content but also to decide the best didactic strategy. In this sense learning theories or pedagogical models have an important influence on the design of any DEO, even more so if we want to create this content within the framework of an inclusive education. That is why we have

paid special attention to the analysis of pedagogical models, underlying each DEO we have studied (Gros, B. 2000).

Analyzing the theoretical framework of the pedagogical approach throughout history we can distinguish six instructional models (Gros, B. 2000, Sarramona, J. 2000; Martínez Otero, V. 2003). At the first stage in history the valid educational model was the *traditional model* focused more on the development of character and human faculties through discipline. The basis of the study was mainly classical authors and the methodology was authoritarian, rote and repetitive. This phase evolved into the romantic model, highlighting as a matter of study the natural, spontaneous and free development of the individual. It meant a change towards freedom of expression.

The educational landscape changed in a radical way through Skinner's *behaviorist pedagogical model,* which promoted a model of education where the teacher was responsible for guiding students towards the acquisition of observable skills and competences. From this pedagogical model we can already identify synergies with the pedagogical design of DEOs since they use principles based on this theory, such as: decomposition of information into units, design of activities that require a user response, reinforcement planning, observable objectives, analysis and grading of tasks...

Another pedagogical model close to the preceding one is the *cognitive model*. Instructional models of this trend focus on motivational factors, providing students with alternatives to explore according to their own interests. It pays special attention to the study of perception, comprehension, recall, information management and memory. This model could be identified with educational multimedia programs, hypertext or simulations.

In the *constructivist model* there is no a single knowledge, as there are sufficient degrees of freedom in the environment to allow people to build their own theories. The educational objective is to encourage students to develop socially acceptable systems to explore their ideas, opinions and arguments. Educational programmes that respond to this pedagogic model focus on learning by discovery, in which the students learn to value their own skills, to learn for themselves and build their own meanings.

Finally, the latest educational trend would be the *social model*. Educational programmes that address these social theories emphasize the value of learning contexts and cooperation. The theory of situated learning, for example, argues that you can only learn something when the learner is able to attribute a meaning to their activity. The construction of knowledge becomes something shared: collaborative learning. Some examples of programmes based on this theory would be communication programs or learning in social networks.

After reviewing the theoretical framework of instructional theories, we find that EDOs might fit three models of education, the cognitive, the constructivist and the social models. Thus when designing our assessment tool for cataloguing EDOs, we decided to focus on these three theories establishing a series of indicators that help us identify each item with one of these pedagogical models. Indicators refer to instructional goals or objectives of the programmes, the methodology and evaluation.

Interactivity is another dimension of educational programmes to be taken into account when designing an EDO and is closely related to accessibility. In fact, authors like Gonzalez define educational objects as «interactive content units» (Gonzalez, M. 2007). We understand interactivity as the possibility of establishing a two-way communication in the instructional process, that is, allowing users to search for information, make decisions and respond to the proposals offered by the system (Sanchez, J. and Romance, A. R. 2000). In relation to interactivity we can identify several levels, from programmes that only allow the user to access, follow links or go forward or backward, semiinteractive programmes in which

the user accesses the content and can select the sequence or timing of execution, to structured programmes with many branches in which the user can select content from different points of view (Regil, L. 2003).

The design of interaction in an educational programme refers to a variety of aspects such as the type of application that allows a program, the existence of multimedia resources and the specific role of these resources, attention to diversity, the possibility of guided navigation, exploratory or participatory, the design of an intuitive interface, the ability to generate knowledge, etc. Basing ourselves on these aspects, we have established a series of indicators that we believe will allow us to define the level of interactivity of EDOs. We have also defined indicators oriented to the technical-instructive adequacy and to didactic adequacy of educational objects. For this purpose we have taken as a basis the educational quality assessment scale of multimedia software by Reparaz, developed in the PEMGU project (Reparaz, Sobrino and Mir, 1999).

When we defined Digital Educational Objects, we mentioned reusability and granularity (Sicilia M, A. and García, E. 2003). In some studies these characteristics have been related to the level of complexity, type of elements and structure or architecture of digital objects (Cuadrillero, Serna and Corrochano, 2007). We decided to include these two factors in our evaluation tool, adding questions like the existence of levels of difficulty, analysis of complexity of multimedia resources, consistency of structure and number of elements, content blocks and links on the screen at the same time (Wiley, D. A. 2000).

Through this research we wish to detect a correlation between the theories of learning and the interactivity level of a DEO; in parallel we aim to analyze the level of accessibility of this content. We are also looking for a possible relationship between the complexity of a DEO and its capability of being accessible. It is important to know whether the more complex and interactive a DEO is, the more accessible it will be too, or in that case we restrict the possibility of it being accessible.

Technological Variables

In order to create technological accessibility indicators, we relied on the UNE 139803:2004 rule (AENOR 2003), the Spanish guide to Web accessibility, ISO 24751 «Individualized adaptability and accessibility in e-learning, education and training» and in Web Content Accessibility Guidelines 2.0 (WCAG 2.0), the recognized standard on Web accessibility at a European level. These guidelines were specifically developed for Web content but they can be applied to all kinds of multimedia and audiovisual resources, even those accessed without an Internet connection.

WCAG 2.0 being the most recent and widely used guidelines in Europe, we based our survey on these sets of rules in order to evaluate the technical accessibility of the Digital Educational Objects. They are based on four key principles (WCAG 2.0 2012):

1. **Perceivable:** Information and user interface components must be presentable to users in ways they can perceive.
2. **Operable:** User interface components and navigation must be operable.
3. **Understandable:** Information and the operation of user interface must be understandable.
4. **Robust:** Content must be robust enough so that it can be interpreted reliably by a wide variety of user agents, including assistive technologies.

WCAG 2.0 has three conformance levels called A, double-A (AA) and triple-A (AAA). If a web page conforms level A, it means that it satisfies all success criteria of level A; if it conforms level AA it means that the web page meets all A and AA success criteria, and so on.

For the purpose of this survey we have taken into account the less restrictive criteria related to audiovisual content, those of level A. We have also included usability aspects of the interface that affect the structure, organization, navigation and ease of use of the educational content.

More specific studies on the standards for developing educational objects have focused on accessibility and usability (CNICE, 2006). Regarding accessibility, they also recommend WCAG guidelines and Guidelines for the Development of Educational Applications. For usability, they refer to ISO 9126, but it has now been replaced by ISO/IEC 25000:2005.

ANALYZING THE INCLUSIVE DESIGN OF DIGITAL EDUCATIONAL OBJECTS

In previous sections we introduced the conditions under which Digital Educational Objects have been developed for the Basque government. They are the result of a call that fixes specific characteristics on the content and educational and technological design. Taking them as the basis of our survey, we analyzed how inclusive they are, to what degree they take accessibility for students with disabilities into account or how they may adapt to students' learning styles or preferences.

It is important to point out that these are the first experiences in creating digital educational objects addressing the Basque curriculum. Everyone involved in the development has seen, explored and used many educational objects, material, multimedia and interactive content… but in general there was a lack of expertise and clear, common objectives of what we want as a result of the project.

The Survey Evaluation Tool

Based on our review of pedagogical models and accessibility and usability literature, we have created a form to evaluate digital educational objects approved and uploaded to Agrega. It collects data

Figure 2. Part of the evaluation form used for the survey

FICHA DE EVALUACIÓN DE LAS ODES DE ESKOLA 2.O

Título:

Autor/editorial/guía de estilo:

Área:

Nivel educativo:

1. ANÁLISIS DEL MODELO PEDAGÓGICO:

1.1. METAS / OBJETIVOS: ¿Cuál es el objetivo último del material?

* **(conductista)** Moldeamiento de la conducta, adquisición de competencias y destrezas observables. ☐

* **(cognitivista)** Desarrollo cognitivo y emocional, es decir, adquisición de conocimientos, comprensión y manejo de la información. ☐

* **(constructivista)** Formar personas activas, capaces de tomar decisiones, de reflexionar y de argumentar. ☐

* **(social)** Desarrollar la personalidad y las capacidades cognitivas del alumno para la mejora de la calidad de la sociedad. ☐

1.2. METODOLOGÍA: ¿Qué tipo de metodologías predominan en el programa?

* **(conductista)** Técnicas de modificación de la conducta y fragmentación del material de aprendizaje. ☐

* **(cognitivista)** Aprendizaje por descubrimiento proponiendo actividades para que el alumno explore, busque, reflexione e innove. ☐

* **(constructivista)** Metodologías progresivas y secuenciales según el grado de logro de estados mentales. ☐

* **(social)** Metodologías progresivas, secuenciales y colaborativas enfocadas a la producción social. ☐

on pedagogical and technological aspects for accessibility and inclusion (Nesbit, J., Belfer, K. and Vargo, J. (2003). This form is divided into three sections: 1- pedagogical model, 2-interaction level and 3-accessibility.

Each *pedagogical model* or paradigm has different objectives, methodology, teacher-student interaction, learning objective and evaluation. In the case of these educational objects, there is no interaction between teacher and student, because the technology does not support it, so this item has been left out of the evaluation.

Regarding the objectives, our interest is the aim of each learning object, which may be different. Some objects are centred on competences, others

on the acquisition of concepts, on social learning, etc. That is why the first question of the form was the ultimate objective of the content.

The type and variety of activities gives an idea of how complete the content is. It may include individual, group or collaborative activities, and students may have to apply concepts, discover or construct the knowledge, not just click on the correct answer.

It is recommended to have some kind of evaluation, which can be self-evaluation, co-evaluation, initial, formative or summative. We have analyzed the evaluation included in each educational object and its type.

The *interaction level* determines the learning model allowed the student. We focused on the following issues:

- Student initiative, if the content is totally guided, explorative or participative.
- The interface, its structure, complexity, type and number of elements.
- If the content has to be applied individually, in small or larger groups.
- Attention to diversity, characteristics that improve inclusion, like learning pace, language used, etc.
- Type, variety and function of the resources included.
- Type of activities.
- Feedback and evaluation.

Finally, we checked a number of elements directly related to *technological accessibility*, like whether the text of links is meaningful and the existence of subtitles, audio description, textual alternatives or playback controls.

Difficulties Addressed during the Survey

We analyzed 54 digital objects with the previously described form and we found some difficulties due to the variety of designs. The style, structure, extension, level of interaction and overall design of the DEOs are very different. Some of them are simple activities, with or without theoretical explanations; others include a very small set of exercises with some multimedia or audiovisual content; and the most complex ones include a great variety of resources, media, simulations and interactive activities and cover a great part of the subject. This variety makes it very difficult to evaluate the same criteria in different educational objects, so different educational objects with the same evaluation tool and compare their characteristics. For example, when we try to determine the accessibility of a DEO, it may prove to be very accessible but just because it is a web page with a simple non-interactive activity. Can we compare

Figure 3. Playback controls should be included in video, animations and audio

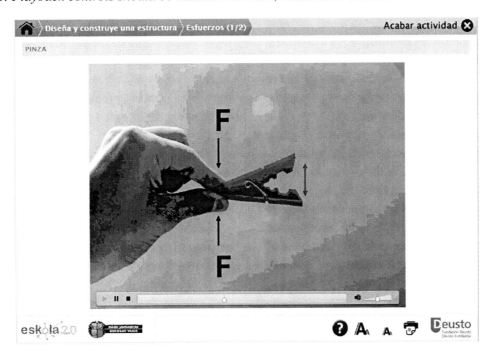

its accessibility with an interactive simulation about mechanical structures?

We have mentioned that each DEO has to have an online and offline version, or at least it should have alternative versions, content or activities that can be played without an Internet connection. In some cases the offline version is not properly uploaded or the content is not complete, so we cannot evaluate the full version. In other cases they just do not work, so they were discarded from the survey.

It is difficult to determine which unique theoretical model follows each educational object. Models are very close to each other so, in many cases, we can say that the project includes more than one: in some aspects it is close to one model and in other aspects it is closer to another.

It is possible to include links to external Web pages like Youtube, Wikipedia, etc. and to create activities with external tools like Geogebra, JClic, ThatQuiz or Smart Notebook. This enriches the material but makes the content creator lose the control over the accessibility and usability of the result. The interface and type of interaction with these tools is often closed and does not allow the author to modify it. Some DEOs have made wide use of this kind of external resource; in these cases it is difficult to determine what to evaluate because we find three levels of authoring: 1-their own original material, 2- content created by the producers with other authoring tools, 3- totally external material created by another.

As a conclusion, we lack a general design guide that clarifies not only aspects related to accessibility and inclusion, but also those that determine the scope and expected result of the project. This lack of guidance has led to misunderstanding. In future calls we recommend the inclusion of a guide that would improve the accessibility and level of inclusion of the generated educational content, and therefore, the overall quality of the project.

The Results

From 23rd to 25th of November 2011 we downloaded a sample of 57 digital educational objects from 356 objects existing in Agrega at that moment. We selected one or two objects from each author-project trying to analyze digital objects of all styles and areas of knowledge. From the 284 educational objects oriented to primary school we selected 30, and from the 72 for secondary school we analyzed 24.

Most educational objects follow the cognitive/constructivist (52%) or constructivist/social (30%) pedagogical model. 57% of them has a guided schema where the student has no scope for initiative and must follow a concrete learning path. This is not the best option for inclusive learning and more exploratory and participative models are recommended because they promote inclusion. Participative and exploratory models allow students to personalize their pace, the content, the sequencing... In addition, they make students become a more active agent in the construction of their knowledge.

Individual (37%) and small group activities (43%) are the most used, a result which goes against the current trend towards cooperative, collaborative and social learning. On the other hand, most objects follow conditional sequence, which means that students cannot go on if they do not fulfil a condition. This reduces the possibility of adapting their learning path and goes against inclusive learning.

62% of the educational objects analyzed do not include any kind of evaluation. The evaluation approach can be carried out in many different ways but it has to exist somehow. Authors can choose an auto-evaluation system, co-evaluation or formative evaluation, but it is important for students to know what they are going to learn and what the evaluation criteria and methodology is.

From the accessibility and inclusion point of view, educational content should promote the development of competences, attention to diversity and motivation. In this sense we must say that evaluated objects have a good level of activities covering these areas. 87% of them include activities that develop critical thinking, 85% have activities to consolidate knowledge and 37% offer recreational activities.

As expected, more complete objects include a wider variety of multimedia and audiovisual resources, which may have more than one function. 77% have demonstrative functions, 50% have a motivating function and 88% instructive functions. We have classified educational objects in terms of their complexity relating to the number, type and variety of the resources they have. 33% have a high level of complexity with 3 or more type of multimedia resources, 19% have a medium level and 48% are simple educational objects (one type of resource).

In general there is a lack of equivalent alternatives to audiovisual content in text format, subtitles or audio description (see Table 1). When analyzing technical accessibility, we realized that educational objects which include a wider variety and higher number of audiovisual resources pay less attention to alternatives. There is only one educational object (see Figure 4) that includes subtitles and we have to remark that it is an educational object oriented to language learning. They aim of the subtitle is to help understand the content of the video and to relate pronunciation to written language. Therefore, we cannot say that subtitles are oriented towards improving the accessibility of people with disabilities, but it is more closely related to the didactic objective of the content.

Another aspect to be taken into account regarding accessibility is the existence of text alternatives to non-text resources. Only 21% of the analyzed objects include text alternatives and 12% of them include equivalent alternatives to resources that are only audio or only video. Regarding audio description, there is not a single educational object that includes it for video or image.

Producers were concerned about making links understandable with proper text (70%); an example can be seen in the following figure. Although they have not been as careful in terms of playback controls, only 26% of educational objects include more than a simple play button in their audiovisual resources.

Figure 4. Educational object with video that includes subtitles

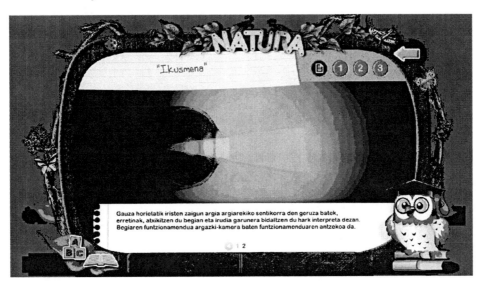

Table 1. Relation between the level of complexity and the accessibility of resources

Level of complexity	Educational Digital Objects		DEOs that include subtitles		DEOs with no-textual resources that have alternative text		DEOs including audiodescription		DEOs with only-audio or only-video having equivalent alternative	
High	18	33%	1	1%	2	4%	0	0%	3	6%
Medium	10	19%	0	0%	6	11%	0	0%	3	6%
Low	26	48%	0	0%	3	6%	0	0%	0	0%
TOTAL	54		1		11		0		6	

Figure 5. Example of links with meaningful text

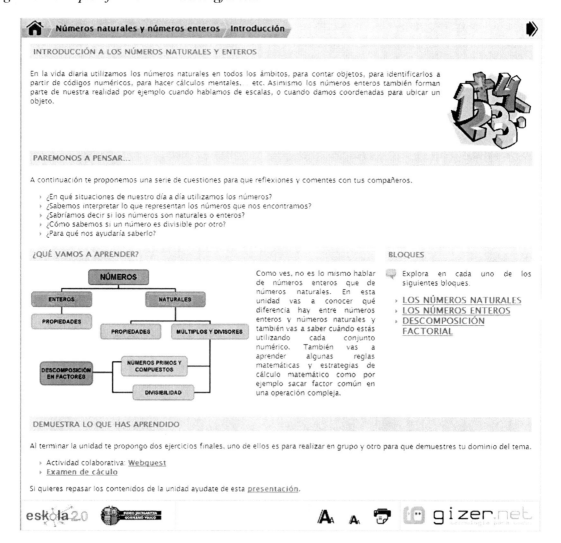

DESIGN GUIDELINES FOR CREATING INCLUSIVE DIGITAL EDUCATIONAL OBJECTS

Based on our personal experience as content producers, the evaluation of digital educational objects and the results obtained from the survey, we propose a set of guidelines on improving accessibility and inclusion of educational objects. This is a guide that should be shared with authors so that they may take it into account from the beginning of the project.

From the pedagogical point of view, an educational object should be designed following a concrete instructional model. It cannot be said that one pedagogical model is better than another, but there are some models that suit the latest educational trends and existing educational technology better.

Current technology trends are social networks, blogs, wikis, interactive simulations or augmented reality, so advances in technology align social learning. If we are to have more inclusive learning, we have to promote collaborative and student-centred learning. We have to use pedagogical models that treat students as the main character and are adaptable to their needs, learning pace… a collaborative learning that benefits from technology and is going in the same direction as society.

With reference to the interactive design of a digital object, authors should use all capacities offered by educational technology. We would like to highlight multimedia resources because they are rich and multifunctional. We can use them to: explain and demonstrate concepts and processes, as a positive and negative reinforcement, as a motivating element or as an accessible alternative for people with disabilities. There are other elements that will ease interaction between students and learning content, like a logical navigation schema, an intuitive interface or the possibility to register the progress of students and give them immediate feedback on completion of activities. We can offer an open pedagogical model to students and they can select and construct their learning according to their interests.

In this sense we recommend following a methodology focused on shared work in small and large groups, an exploratory and mainly participative learning. We are in favour of didactics that promote the search for knowledge, the exchange of ideas, arguing and ultimately, the shared construction of knowledge. With collaborative work the members of a team can compensate their different levels of knowledge and experience so that all learn from each other. Thanks to technology like wiki, blog or social networks, we can work these didactics in an integrated, innovative and motivating way.

As we have mentioned, technology offers a wide variety of didactic possibilities. We would like to highlight the rise of simulations, virtual reality and game-based learning. Both simulations and virtual reality scenarios provide students with a complete and visual way to know and understand concepts and processes and the possibility of interacting with them (Brito, Nava and Mejía, 2007). Thanks to subtitling, audio description and text alternatives, these technologies are also available for students with disabilities. On the other hand, game-based learning is highly motivating; it promotes the acquisition of meaningful learning and enables sharing with multidisciplinary teams (Sánchez Gómez, M. 2007).

We have to take into account interaction due to the simple fact that interrelating knowledge stimulates better memory, in addition to increased motivation. We also recommend considering factors that enable motivation, freedom of knowledge and that attend the educational needs and interests of students.

Inclusive education, understood as an open and accessible-for-all learning system, does not mean discarding any educational quality standards. A digital object may include a wide and varied educational offer that responds to user needs in different ways. This can be done with simulations, video tutorials, research practices, information analysis, collaborative work, etc. We recommend an educational offer that allows different learning in an integrated, open and social way.

When an educational content producer aims to create accessible digital content, there are many issues to be taken into account. The World Wide Web Consortium (W3C) classifies disabilities into: hearing, cognitive and neurological, physical, speaking and visual contexts. If we want to design content adequate for these groups, it is necessary to know the problems they face when accessing technology and, most of all, the capabilities they have. Besides W3C guidelines, there are more specific standards to be applied such as UNE 153010 for subtitling. It is not enough to add a subtitle to a video or audio, it has to meet existing standards and guidelines.

Detailed below are the design guidelines related to different functional characteristics. Some guidelines should be included in more than one category, because they benefit several user groups, but they have been assigned to the most meaningful one:

Users with hearing impairment

- Audio content from video or audio should include captions, subtitles and/or sign language.
- Media players should provide volume controls, as well as options to adjust text size and colours of captions.

Users with cognitive and neuronal problems

- Complexity in all aspects should be avoided. Navigation schema, content structure and organization, the language used and the extension of text should be as simple and clear as possible.
- Information should be provided with complementary media to make it more understandable. E.g. a text could be illustrated with an image, or a complex image could be explained with an audio or text description.

- The playback of audiovisual and multimedia resources should be controlled by the user. Avoid moving, blinking or flickering content that do not have an educational function.
- Time-limited content and activities should be long enough or adaptable so that all users have enough time to complete them.
- Content organization, structure and general layout has to be predictable, consistent and coherent. Besides there should be visual and non-visual cues that help to locate oneself in the overall structure of the content.

Users with physical difficulties

- Interaction should be totally available through the keyboard. Other alternative input devices are usually compatible with keyboard input (e.g. Braille display, alternative keyboards, pointers).

Users with speech impairment

- Interaction should not rely on voice only.
- Contact information should not be simply a telephone number, email, fax or an online form; there should be other types of contact possibilities.

Visually impaired users

- The interface should be as adaptable as possible to the user. It should allow changing the style sheet, text font, colour and size, layout of the interface content blocks, image and video size.
- All visual content should be of high quality; there should be sufficient contrast between foreground and background colour combinations.
- Visual information like images, controls and video should have equivalent text or audio alternatives, e.g. the following image shows a map partially described through text.

Figure 6. ESCALAS

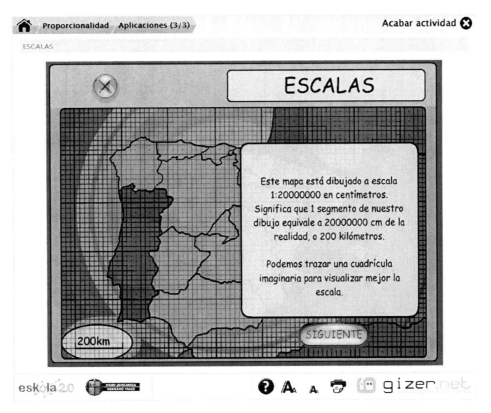

As for the base technology for the project, Adobe Flash seems to be a good option. Besides being a *de facto* standard for the development and visualization of multimedia content, it also includes a set of tools oriented to designing accessible content. However, when possible, we recommend providing different formats in case there are problems with the plug-ins needed to play it.

HTML is also a recommendable option for the overall layout of the content. Applying WCAG guidelines and other usability and pedagogical criteria ensures high quality and inclusive educational content.

FUTURE RESEARCH

There are many ways in which we are working to complete the research described in this chapter.

These are some of the areas we are dealing with to continue our work:

Many analyzed educational objects are extremely good and have great educational potential. They include interactive activities, rich audiovisual content, simulations and diverse evaluation schemas. We believe an in-depth analysis of accessibility and how it could be implemented at minimum cost is important. It is relevant for producers to know what kind of resources should be added or modified and how. So we are developing a series of recommendations to help make the most complete and complex digital objects more accessible.

Mobile devices are becoming increasingly important in people's daily lives and particularly for students of primary and secondary school. We are working on completing access tests from different devices, giving importance to a multi-device design approach. We are analyzing the latest ICT access devices such as tablets, digital boards and mobile phones, observing how they affect accessibility, and trying to propose new ways of using and dealing with them.

DeustoTech Learning group is working on the construction of a usability and accessibility laboratory to carry out user testing. It would be of great value to conduct an analysis of real users in a simulated classroom and see how they interact with the educational content. Proposed recommendations could be contrasted with user testing.

As for specific tools to obtain digital accessibility, we should analyze specific hardware and software tools for accessibility and inclusion, and the possibilities and recommendations for making common multimedia resources accessible.

Apart from analyzing already made digital objects, we think it is important to participate again in the development of specific objects, because there are many aspects that are closely associated with the creation of educational material. We are working on developing new educational objects and adapting existing ones, taking into account given recommendations, measuring times, effort and costs (which are essential for educational content producers). In that sense, we believe it is important to collaborate with more digital educational content development teams in order to share evaluation and feedback.

Finally, we are trying to provide the Basque Government this assessment with the goal of designing a follow-up study in two directions: developers (parameters, technologies, difficulties...) and students (degree of use, access difficulties, satisfaction before and after changes...).

CONCLUSION

We assume that 100% accessibility is impossible and that the total inclusion of all types of students is unaffordable. However, there is much that people involved in the creation of educational content can do to improve current concern, awareness and knowledge about these issues. Pedagogical and technical design are both key factors that determine the level of inclusion of educational content.

The first thing is knowledge. Content designers should know their users, their characteristics, when and how they access technology, what their expectations are ... They should talk to them at every stage of the development and final users should be part of the team.

Next, producers should be made aware of inclusion. They should think about the wide variety of students that use their products: students with disabilities, with limited Internet connection, with obsolete equipment, those who do not follow the traditional educational path, with different pedagogical and ICT skills, etc. They see these students as potential customers and also be aware of the fact that students need to be integrated and not discriminated.

Finally, awareness. If content producers know their users and are concerned about the problems or difficulties they face when using educational objects, their awareness for creating inclusive content will increase.

It is also important to have clear design guidelines oriented to inclusion. We have tried to contribute with our recommendations, derived from the analysis of existing educational objects in Agrega and the review of pedagogical and technological literature in the area. Taking into account these design criteria not only benefits students with disabilities but also improves the overall quality of the content and all users will make the most of their learning experience.

REFERENCES

W3C. (2012). *Web accessibility initiative*. Retrieved December, 2012, from http://www.w3.org/WAI/

AENOR. (2004). *UNE 139802:2003 Aplicaciones informáticas para personas con discapacidad. Requisitos de accesibilidad al ordenador. Software.* In *Software. Requisitos de calidad y ergonomía.* Asociación Española de Normalización y Certificación, AENOR.

Agrega. (2012). *Agrega: Repository of digital educational objects.* Retrieved November 2012 from http://agrega.hezkuntza.net

BOPV. (2009). *ORDEN de 17 de noviembre de 2009, de la Consejera de Educación, Universidades e Investigación, por la que se convocan ayudas para la elaboración de Objetos Digitales Educativos (ODEs) en la Comunidad Autónoma Vasca.* Boletín Oficial del País Vasco n° 253, lunes 7-dic-2009.

BOPV. (2010). *ORDEN de 15 de junio de 2010, de la Consejera de Educación, Universidades e Investigación, por la que se convocan ayudas para la elaboración de Objetos Digitales Educativos (ODEs) en la Comunidad Autónoma Vasca.* Boletín Oficial del País Vasco n° 128, martes 6-jul-2010.

Brito, L., Nava, O., & Mejía, J. A. (2007). *Desarrollo de objetos reutilizables aplicados en el aprendizaje virtual.* In *Proceedings of IV Simposio Pluridisciplinar sobre Diseño, Evaluación y Desarrollo de Contenidos Educativos Reutilizables, SPDECE 07,* September 2007, Bilbao.

Bueno de la Fuente, G. (2006). *Organización, gestión de la información e interoperabilidad: Metadatos.* Curso de Tecnologías Aplicadas al Desarrollo de Contenidos Educativos Multimedia Interactivos CNICE. Retrieved November 2012 from http://www.tecnotic.com

CNICE. (2006). Accesibilidad, TIC y educación. *Serie Informes, 17.* Retrieved December 20, 2012, from http://ares.cnice.mec.es/informes/17

Cuadrillero Menéndez, J. A., Serna Nocedal, A., & Corrochano, J. H. (2007). Estudio sobre la granularidad de objetos de aprendizaje almacenados en repositorios de libre acceso. In *Proceedings of IV Simposio Pluridisciplinar sobre Diseño, Evaluación y Desarrollo de Contenidos Educativos Reutilizables,* SPDECE 07, September 2007, Bilbao.

González, M. (2005). Cómo desarrollar contenidos para la formación online basados en objetos de aprendizaje. *Revista de Educación a Distancia, 3.* Retrieved December 20, 2012, from http://www.um.es/ead/red/M3/

Gros, B. (2000). *El ordenador invisible: Hacia la apropiación del ordenador en la enseñanza.* Barcelona, Spain: Gedisa.

Martínez González, R. A., Miláns del Bosch, M., Pérez Herrero, H., & Sampedro Nuño, A. (2007). Psychopedagogical components and processes in e-learning. Lessons from an unsuccessful on-line course. *Computers in Human Behavior, 23*(1). Retrieved December 20, 2012, from http://www.sciencedirect.com/

Martinez-Otero Perez. V. (2003). *Teoría y práctica de la educación.* Madrid, Spain: CCS.

Moncloa. (2009). *Council of Ministers 2009-07-31.* La Moncloa. Retrieved November 2012 from http://www.lamoncloa.gob.es

Nesbit, J., Belfer, K., & Vargo, J. (2003). A convergent participation model for evaluation of learning objects. *Canadian Journal of Learning and Technology, 28*(3).

Polsani, P. R. (2003). Use and abuse of reusable learning objects. *Journal of Digital Information, 3*(4).

Priego, L., & López, F. (2006). *Metodología para el uso de estándares internacionales en la creación de objetos de aprendizaje.* Retrieved from http://www.cs.buap.mx/~cuartocongreso/webs/apdf/A14.pdf

Regil, L. (2003). *Interactividad y construcción de la mirada*. Barcelona, Spain: Infonomía.

Sánchez, J., & Romance, A. R. (2000). Multimedia. In Rios, J. M., & Cebrián de la Serna, M. (Eds.), *Nuevas tecnologías de la información y de la comunicación aplicadas a la educación*. Málaga, Spain: Aljibe.

Sánchez Gómez, M. (2007). *Buenas prácticas en la creación de Serious Games (Objetos de aprendizaje Reutilizables)*. In *Proceedings of IV Simposio Pluridisciplinar sobre Diseño, Evaluación y Desarrollo de Contenidos Educativos Reutilizables*, SPDECE 07, September 2007, Bilbao.

Sarramona López, J. (2000). *Teoría de la educación: Reflexión y normativa pedagógica*. Barcelona, Spain: Ariel.

Sicilia, M, A., & García, E. (2003). On the concepts of usability and reusability of learning objects. *International Review of Research in Open and Distance Learning, 4*(2).

Sobrino, A. (2000). Evaluación del software educativo. In Reparaz, C., Sobrino, S., & Mir, J. I. (Eds.), *Integración curricular de las nuevas tecnologías*. Barcelona, Spain: Ariel.

Usability.gov. (2011). *Usability.gov is the primary government source for information on usability and user-centered design*. HHS Web Communications and New Media Division, U.S. Department of Health and Human Services. Retrieved December, 2012, from http://www.usability.gov/about/index.html

WCAG 2.0 (2008) *Web content accessibility guidelines 2.0*. Retrieved December 20, 2012, from http://www.w3.org/TR/WCAG20/

Wiley, D. A. (2000). Connecting learning objects to instructional design theory: A definition, a metaphor, and a taxonomy. *Learning Technology, 2830*(435), 1–35.

ADDITIONAL READING

Churchill, D. (2007). Towards a useful classification of learning objects. *Educational Technology Research and Development, 55*(5). doi:10.1007/s11423-006-9000-y

Fernandez-Manjon, B., & Sancho, P. (2002). Creating cost-effective adaptive educational hypermedia based on markup technologies and e-learning standards. *Interactive Educational Multimedia, 4*, 1–11.

Kay, R. H., & Knaack, L. (2007). Evaluating the learning in learning objects. *Open Learning, 22*(1), 5–28. doi:10.1080/02680510601100135

Koohang, A., Floyd, K., Santiago, J., Greene, S., & Harman, K. (2008). Design, development, and implementation of an open source learning object repository. *Issues in Informing Science & Information Technology, 5*(1), 487–498.

Koohang, A., Floyd, K., & Stewart, C. (2011). Design of an open source learning objects authoring tool: The LO creator. *Interdisciplinary Journal of E-Learning & Learning Objects, 7*, 111–123.

Leacock, T. L., & Nesbit, J. C. (2007). A framework for evaluating the quality of multimedia learning resources. *Journal of Educational Technology & Society, 10*(2), 44–59.

Northrup, P. (2007). *Learning objects for instruction: Design and evaluation*. Information Science Publishing. doi:10.4018/978-1-59904-334-0

KEY TERMS AND DEFINITIONS

Design Guideline: Best practices and not written rules that improve the quality of something, in our case educational content. Design guidelines include in our survey pedagogical and technological aspects, and in the last case accessibility and usability guidelines that aim to create inclusive educational content.

Digital Educational Object: It refers to digital and interactive educational content, structured in didactic sequences that have been design with a pedagogical objective to be used in different educational contexts.

Functional Diversity: It refers to the functional characteristics that determine how users access and read (play or reproduce) technological tools or content. Nowadays we do not talk about disabilities (e.g. blindness) but the characteristic of not being able to use the sight function to access technology. It can be due to a problem with the eyes or because there is a condition, temporary or permanent, that does not allow the use of sight (e.g. a tool to be used while driving a car). So we talk about functional diversity when accessing technology rather than disability.

Metadata: It is data about data. Educational content is the core of the survey (the core data), and above it we define a set of data that define the educational content itself (metadata). This data describes generic characteristics that allow users or technology to do advanced searches, cataloguing or create applications based on them. E.g. course, subject, language, author, type of content, etc.

Pedagogical Model: It is the educational line that underlies any educational object. It refers to the aims and educational objectives, to contents, to the methodology chosen to achieve those objectives, to student-teacher interaction and to the evaluation approach.

Shareable Content Object Reference Model (SCORM): It is a set of international standards to create educational objects. The aim is to create objects that are accessible, adaptable to user needs, durable (capable to resist the rapid evolution of technology), interoperable with different systems and reusable. It describes the content aggregation model, run-time environment, sequencing and navigation.

Technological Accessibility: It describes how possible or easy is a technological tool or content to be accessed by users with disabilities. Technology is accessible if it can be accessed and processed (read, played, and understood) by people with functional diversity; this includes people with visual, hearing, cognitive and physical impairment.

Usability: It is the degree in which something is easy to use, user-friendly. It includes terms like efficacy (you get what you expected), efficiency (you get it in a reasonable time) and satisfaction (you have a good and nice experience).

Chapter 11
School Activities Using Handmade Teaching Materials with Dot Codes

Shigeru Ikuta
Otsuma Women's University, Japan

Emi Endo
*School for the Mentally Challenged at Otsuka,
University of Tsukuba, Japan*

Fumio Nemoto
*School for the Mentally Challenged at Otsuka,
University of Tsukuba, Japan*

Satomi Kaiami
*School for the Mentally Challenged at Otsuka,
University of Tsukuba, Japan*

Takahide Ezoe
Shinjuku Japanese Language Institute, Japan

ABSTRACT

Practitioners have been using three communication aids in conducting many school activities at both special needs and regular schools. In the simplest system, voices and sounds are transformed into dot codes, edited with pictures and text, and printed out with an ordinary color printer; the printed dot codes are traced to be decoded into the originals by using a handy tool, Sound Reader. In the most complex system, in addition to audio files, multiple media files such as movies, web pages, html files, and PowerPoint files can be linked to each dot code; just touching the printed dot code with sound or scanner pens reproduces their audio or multimedia, respectively. The present chapter reports the software and hardware used in developing originally handmade teaching materials with dot codes and various school activities performed at both special needs and regular schools.

INTRODUCTION

It is very important for students with severe verbal and mental challenges to express their thoughts and needs to others by using various means such as signs, gestures, and tools; these communicative means enhance their lives and help them get along with others and function in society. To provide essential support for such students is an important task of special needs schools (Johnston, Beard, & Carpenter, 2007).

Developers and researchers have created many teaching aids based on an assistive technology (AT). Among these, voice output communica-

DOI: 10.4018/978-1-4666-2530-3.ch011

Copyright © 2013, IGI Global. Copying or distributing in print or electronic forms without written permission of IGI Global is prohibited.

tion aids (VOCAs) are widely known and used for students with severe verbal and mental challenges; the school activities with such VOCAs sometimes work very effectively on such students (Ace Center, 2000; Axistive, 2011; Disabled Living Foundation, 2011; Gateway, 2011; Inclusive Design Research Center, 2011; Sussex community, 2011). In most VOCAs, however, output numbers and length are restricted. Therefore, we have been using three communication aids that can decode the dot codes printed on paper (Anderson et al., 2008; Ikuta, 2008a; Ikuta, 2008b; Ikuta et al., 2011; Kaneko et al., 2011; Ikuta, 2011). By using these systems, schoolteachers can create original handmade teaching materials suitable for the independent needs and desires of each student in their class.

In this chapter, we report several school activities including two long-term ones, undertaken at both regular and special needs schools, using the Sound Pronunciation System (SPS) developed by Olympus (1999). In this system, voices and sounds are imported into a personal computer (PC) through a microphone or voice recorder, then transformed into two-dimensional dot codes, edited to include text and pictures, and finally output with an ordinary color printer. Then, the dot codes on the printed sheet can be traced with a handy tool, *Sound Reader*, which decodes them into the original voices and sounds (Okawara et al., 2008; Ohshima et al., 2007; Ohshima et al., 2008).

The *first* long-term activity is a sensible, three-year approach to "Student A." The SPS is used to facilitate communication with his family and classmates, and his transformations are described carefully. As a result of these efforts, he learns how to *communicate* with others and experiences the pleasures and satisfactions of everyday life. Furthermore, he gains competence and confidence and is now living peacefully. He also masters changing his clothes by himself, increasing his ability to perform tasks necessary for daily life, and is living confidently (Nemoto & Ikuta, 2010).

The *second* long-term school activity was conducted for students with intellectual and expressive language disabilities, where many handmade sheets with the voices of their homeroom teacher and volunteers, in addition to pictures, words, and phrases, enable them to acquire vocabulary, grasp word meanings, as well as achieve meaningful relationships (Ishitobi, Ezoe, & Ikuta, 2010).

From the abovementioned school activities, we demonstrate that it is essential for schoolteachers to develop *original* handmade teaching materials for supporting the independent needs and desires of each student. However, students with hand/finger or severe mental challenges at special needs schools and those in the lower grades at regular schools cannot trace the dot codes correctly to join in the same activities with their classmates. We, therefore, have started collaborative research with two venture business companies, Gridmark (2004) and Apollo Japan (2005), to develop *new* handmade teaching materials with a newly developed dot code and test them in school activities (Kaneko et al., 2011; Ikuta, 2011). These new dot codes are called Grid Onput (Gridmark, 2004) and Screen Code (Apollo Japan, 2005), and their "sound pens" are called SPEAKING PEN and Speakun, respectively. Just *touching* the printed dot codes with these pens reproduces original voices and sounds clearly, instead of *tracing* longer dot codes. The Grid Onput system has several interesting characteristics such as linking more than one audio file to *one* dot code and more than one multimedia file such as movies, web pages, html files, and PowerPoint files to *the same* dot code. These valuable new features enable the students with challenges to enhance their learning activities.

The SPS system cannot exceed an audio length of 40 s because the audio is directly printed on a sheet as two-dimensional dot codes. The software for the new sound pens, SPEAKING PEN and Speakun, however, can edit and compress the original voices and sounds effectively and save them onto a micro SD card in the pens (For example, a total of 30 min of voice recordings can be compressed into a 31 MB file.). Therefore, content developers need no longer worry about limiting the length of each voice and sound.

In this study, we also introduce new software and hardware recently developed for the sound pens, in addition to the SPS; a wealth of know-how in developing original handmade teaching materials; and various school activities performed at both special needs and regular schools.

BACKGROUND

The Congress of the United States of America originally passed the Education of All Handicapped Children Act in 1975 (Kendall, 1978). This law, now called the Individuals with Disabilities Education Act (IDEA), outlines rules and regulations that define categories of disabilities and special education programming. Several revisions have been made to the original law, but the revision of 1997 included, for the first time, a definition for AT and a requirement for AT consideration and services for students with disabilities (Office of Special Education and Rehabilitative Services, 1997, 2004; Anderson, Fukushima, & Ikuta, 2009). This was called "a defining moment" for AT (Edyburn, 2000) because schools for the first time were required to consider AT for all students with disabilities. The Japan's Ministry of Education, Culture, Sports, Science and Technology likewise passed "the State of Special Needs Education Act in 21st century in Japan" (2001), covering similar ground.

IDEA defines 13 categories of students with disabilities:

- Autism
- Deaf-blindness
- Emotional disturbance
- Hearing impairment
- Mental retardation
- Multiple disabilities

- Orthopedic impairment
- Other health impairment
- Specific learning disability
- Speech or language impairment
- Traumatic brain injury
- Visual impairment.

Augmentative and Alternative Communication (AAC) Technology has been widely used to give students with severe speech, language, and communication difficulties the opportunity to achieve successful communication and relationships with others (Belson, 2003). AAC systems use symbols that represent the message the student is communicating. These symbols range from one word to a full sentence or to several sentences. The evaluation process for the selection of the right communication systems for a student with a severe speech-language deficit consists of an evaluation by many professionals who must help the student and individuals involved daily with the student to learn to use an AT device in order to facilitate better communication skills (Johnston, Beard, & Carpenter, 2007). AT devices range from no tech to light tech to high tech, allowing for greater selection of the type of communication device that a student needs (Vanderheiden, 1984). The practical use of AT devices in a classroom was described by Dell, Newton, and Petroff (2008).

VOCAs are widely used as AT devices; a VOCA is an electronic device that assists students who are unable to use natural speech to express their needs and thoughts and exchange information with other students during everyday conversations. Among the high tech AAC devices, various types of voice output devices such as single-level and multi-level outputs are used. There are various VOCAs available that are appropriate for students with various abilities and needs (Ace Center, 2000; Axistive, 2011; Disabled Living Foundation, 2011; Gateway, 2011; Inclusive Design Research Center, 2011; Johnston, Beard, & Carpenter, 2007; Sussex Community, 2011). In most VOCAs, however, their output numbers and length are restricted.

Therefore, we have been developing original handmade teaching materials with dot codes—which pronounce original voices and sounds by using handy teaching aids decoding them printed on paper and conducting school activities both at special needs and regular schools by using these materials for students with severe mental and hand or finger challenges (Ohshima et al., 2007; Anderson, Fukushima, & Ikuta, 2009; Ikuta, 2008a; Ikuta, 2008b; Ikuta & Ezoe, 2008; Ohshima et al., 2008; Okawara et al., 2008; Ikuta & Ezoe, 2009a; Ikuta & Ezoe, 2009b; Ikuta & Ezoe, 2009c; Ikuta, 2011; Ikuta et al., 2011). The Scan Talk (ST) code developed by Olympus (1999), which can be printed on ordinary paper, was first used; tracing the dot codes with a handy tool, Sound Reader, reproduced the original voices and sounds clearly.

We have recently started using new dot codes, Screen Code (Apollo Japan, 2005) and Grid Onput (Gridmark, 2004); by just touching such printed dot codes, which are nearly invisible to the naked eye, with specially designed sound pens, original voices and sounds can be reproduced. The Grid Onput system has an attractive characteristic: in addition to the audio files, more than one multimedia file such as movies, web pages, html files, and PowerPoint files can be linked to the dot code (Kaneko et al., 2011; Ikuta, 2011). School activities with this new dot code may enable students with disabilities to enhance their experiences and learn more widely and successfully.

DOT CODES: SCHOOL ACTIVITIES USING HANDMADE TEACHING MATERIALS AND AIDES

Scan Talk Code: Hardware and Software

The ST code was invented by Olympus (1999) more than 10 years ago. SPS with ST codes uses two key technologies. One is software called Sound Card Print Lite (SCPL), which enables the transformation of voices and sounds into ST codes. In addition, it can edit these voices and sounds to include text and pictures, and output the edited format with an ordinary color printer. The other technology is hardware, called Sound Reader, which traces the dot codes on the printed sheet and decodes them into the original voices and sounds.

Figure 1 shows a screenshot of SCPL. You can see four icons on the left, which can open a blank sheet, import pictures, import audio files, and prepare text input boxes on the sheet, respectively. Imported voices are encoded as two-dimensional dot codes, along with text and pictures, in the figure. This edited format is a part of handmade sheets developed by the student school library assistants at Kashiwagi Elementary School in Hachioji, Tokyo. We can listen to the original voices by right clicking the dot codes during editing. SCPL is a simple program that most teachers can use easily without referring to manuals.

Figure 2 shows an SR with a handmade carrier and sheet, which can decode the printed dot codes into the original voices and sounds; the students must trace them while pressing the yellow button.

Scan Talk Code: School Activities

Let's Read More Books!

The teachers at Kashiwagi Elementary School in Hachioji, Tokyo, made a brochure, encouraging students to read more than 300 books over their six years. In addition, the teachers drew posters and put them on the wall, and students' mothers often helped with storytelling before the day's lessons began.

Every elementary schools in Japan have student school library assistants from higher grades, who put the books on the bookshelves and recommend more books for students to read. The library assistants at Kashiwagi Elementary School worked on an exciting activity to introduce the plots of

Figure 1. Screenshot of sound card print lite

Figure 2. Sound reader with handmade carrier and sheet

books to lower grades using the SPS. First, they recorded the plots of the books with their voices through a microphone connected to a PC. Then, they transformed these recordings into dot codes and edited them with the title and picture of the book cover by using SCPL. Finally, they printed the edited format using an ordinary color printer and laminated it. They made more than 50 sheets with dot codes, introducing the books to the lower grades. The location of the books on the bookshelves of the school library was also given by the dot codes at the bottom of each sheet.

Figure 3. Students in the school library

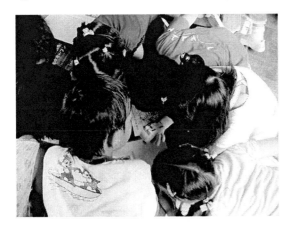

Then, in the gymnasium, the library assistants showed all students how to use the SR. When the students first saw the demonstration of the SR, they were amazed. The lower grade students also learned how to use the SR in their "reading hours" and could listen to the plots of the books by tracing the dot codes on the sheets (Figure 3).

The higher grade students felt a sense of pride from introducing the plots of books to the lower grade students. The teachers now consider the SR a necessary tool for activities such as "Introduction of books recommended by higher grades," "Introduction of books recommended by their mothers," "Introduction of books recommended by teachers," and "Introduction of books recommended by authors themselves." These activities successfully encourage the students to read more books (Ohshima et al., 2007; Ohshima et al., 2008).

The library assistants' current activity, in co-operation with their teachers, enabled even the lower grade students to participate, although some of them had trouble tracing the dot codes with the SR. To overcome this difficulty, we began using new dot codes that can pronounce voice and sound just by touching them with new "sound pens," as illustrated in a later section.

In a "Period for Integrated Study"

A "Period for Integrated Study" is required in elementary (beginning in third grade) and through lower and upper secondary schools in Japan. Most schools address one of the following subjects in this period: international understanding, information study, environment study, health and welfare, or regional problems.

At Moto-Hachioji-Higashi Elementary School in Hachioji, Tokyo, a native speaker teaches international understanding through English lessons every year. However, because of the shoestring budget, each class received only several hours' lessons, and the teachers faced other problems such as lack of communication with the native speaker and lack of suitable textbooks.

The teachers, therefore, discussed the curriculum with the native speaker and developed teaching materials using her voice. They worked out a four-hour-long lesson and attractive teaching materials that could be used enjoyably during and between lessons. They made more than 200 cards using dot codes with the native speaker's voice (Figure 4). On the front side of each card, a simple word was depicted as dot codes with text and a picture. On the reverse side, the conversations using the word were listed as dot codes. All students considerably enjoyed using these cards with dot codes and learning "international understanding" from a cheerful assistant language teacher. Several cards were collected on each page, edited, and published as "Hello Book 1" and "Hello Book 2" (Ikuta & Ezoe, 2008; Ikuta & Ezoe, 2009a). These published books are now used at more than 10 elementary schools in Hachioji and Hino cities in Tokyo and at Kirigaoka School for the Physically Challenged, affiliated with the University of Tsukuba. Two more side readers, "Emi and Alex with Sound Reader I" and "Emi and Alex with Sound Reader II" were published and used in their classes (Ikuta & Ezoe, 2009b; Ikuta & Ezoe, 2009c).

Figure 4. Cards with dot codes in English learning

"Student A" and His Transformation

Student A is an individual with Sotos syndrome, and his IQ corresponds to that of a 1.9-year-old child. He has no expressive language except one Japanese hiragana character. In the past, he always needed help and support with communicating. He was usually gentle and did not actively fight with anyone. He expressed his thoughts through gestures. However, sometimes teachers and classmates could not understand him, and when he grew frustrated, he would regularly kick walls and beat on desks. Therefore, we first struggled to help him understand a sequence of diary programs at his school and to enhance his communication ability with his classmates and teachers. We hoped that he could successfully and repeatedly experience communication (Nemoto & Ikuta, 2010).

We first made a support book with many pictures for him: a method frequently used at schools for special needs education. However, he only pointed out his favorite pictures and could not actually express himself to teachers and classmates by using such a support book. Moreover, he could not learn sign language because of poor hand movement. He sometimes used VOCAs to

introduce himself, but soon lost interest in the VOCA system. After these efforts, we finally turned to the SPS. We began by creating sheets with voices and sounds by using the SPS and attempted to extend his ability to communicate with the teachers and classmates at his school.

At the beginning of the present activity, he could not trace the dot codes on the printed sheets correctly, so he began to move his hand smoothly along the horizontal code. A handmade teaching aid was developed to allow him to correctly slide a small button on a rail. We also developed another aid to help him understand the correlation between "tracing" and "sound," where voice and melody were emitted following his correct sliding of the small button. A rail guide was also made to slide the SR along the printed dot codes, with red spots pasted at both ends of the dot codes, as shown in Figure 5, so that he could easily understand where to begin and end tracing.

After two months of struggling with dot codes, a breakthrough occurred when he was studying with a female classmate in their "Language of Amounts and Quantities" class. After waiting for him to successfully trace the dot codes that spoke her name, she responded to him with a smile and

Figure 5. Teaching materials with a rail guide

touched his hand (Figure 6). He finally realized that tracing dot codes reproduced voices and sounds, and resulted in successful communication with his classmates. He began trying his best to trace even longer dot codes and then succeeded in tracing a 27-cm-long code the very same day.

Half a year after he began using the SPS, the teacher had him act as the master of the morning meeting held daily in Japanese schools. By tracing the dot codes, he played a voice saying "Now let's begin the morning meeting!" Every student stood up and greeted each other, saying "Good morning, everyone!" He then called each student's name for attendance one after another by tracing the dot codes printed on the sheets. Each classmate,

when called by him, answered by raising his or her hand and saying, "Present." All students were moved by his earnest efforts and said, "A tool that can reproduce voices to help him communicate is really a wonderful device." Thus we were convinced that the present challenge was a success.

When nearly one year had passed after he began using the SPS, by using the sheets bound into a book for his self-introduction, he learned to introduce himself to student teachers and university students who came to experience nursing care.

At the school cultural festival, he also described his experience of successfully growing squash to the audience by using the SR (Figure 7). While raising pumpkins for Life Environment Studies, he took pictures with a digital camera and then asked his homeroom teacher to make a sheet with dot codes. He then traced the dot codes, saying with his gestures, "I raised pumpkins as best as I could and harvested four pumpkins," as shown in Figure 8.

Student A's mother made a summer vacation diary with voices and sounds for her son by using the SPS. He presented his happy memories of summer vacation by tracing the dot codes of the sheet to his class (Figure 9). Tracing the printed dot codes reproduced "I went to the fireworks festival with Student B," and then Student B replied to Student A, "Yes, we went together." The

Figure 6. Smiling and touching

Figure 7. At the school festival

Figure 8. Gesturing "four fruits"

voice saying, "I was scared when fragments of fireworks sometimes came down around us," was reproduced, and all his classmates responded with a nod. Student A also nodded with a smile.

He brought a bound file, containing many cards with the dot codes of his mother's voice as well as sounds from a sing-along machine and computer games, to a supporting organization after school and on holidays, and proudly showed it off to the staff and volunteers. They said they had never seen him so happy. Nowadays, he takes several bound files and sheets home and "*talks*" to his family by tracing them: "Today I did an interesting activity at school," "Student C was absent," and so on.

Figure 9. Showing his memories

Using Support Books with Sound

Other long-term school activities with support books consisting of many cards with voices and sounds were undertaken for two students with intellectual and expressive language disabilities. Their teachers wanted them to gain communication experience, taste the joy of being able to express themselves to teachers and classmates, and cultivate relationships with others (Ishitobi, Ezoe, & Ikuta, 2010).

At the beginning of these activities, the students took us to places they wanted to share, expressed their desires with gestures, and took the items they wanted. They did not speak in words, but enjoyed exchanging their ideas with others.

The first activity was performed at the "Language of Amounts and Quantities" class held once a week; the two students in question had experienced tracing dot codes with the SR before the present activities. We created various cards with dot codes for them, in which words necessary not only at school but also outside and at home were selected in cooperation with their mothers. On each card, two words with opposite meanings (for example, "large" and "small") or several related words (for example, "good morning," "hello," and "good-bye") used in similar situations were displayed (Figure 10). These cards were laminated and bound as a support book, and can be replaced with new cards at any time.

Student C could trace the dot codes with an SR, but Student D, who could not trace them himself, attempted the activities with the modified SR on small casters, as shown in Figure 2. Through the classes, they learned to match the voices produced by the dot codes with real words, real places at school, and the real man or woman printed on the sheets, and behave suitably for real occasions. In a class, they considerably enjoyed tracing the dot codes.

We guided them to not only reproduce voices and sounds with the SR but also learn the relationships between the reproduced sound and

Figure 10. Handmade card with opposite words

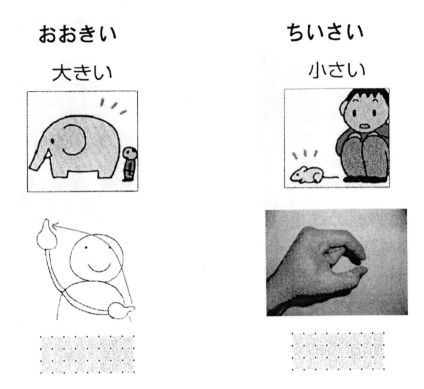

real meanings and situations by describing the real situations with their fingers and enacting the scenes from an illustration.

They learned how to select a suitable word from a card in order to express their feelings; they could select and trace the dot codes properly, producing a suitable word such as "delicious" or "tasteless" and touching their cheek to express their feelings correctly.

During these activities, when Student C selected the dot codes, reproducing "Please give me one more glass of orange juice," Student D made a breakthrough. He suddenly picked up the SR just used by Student C and reproduced the voice saying, "Please give me one more glass of orange juice" again by pushing the replay button on the SR. That was the moment when he realized that the voice reproduced by the SR could ask the teacher his own requests. This realization was prompted by the convenient replay function on the SR, which consists of a button that will issue the voice or sound previously emitted. Such accidental discoveries sometimes help students enhance their understanding of vocabulary.

Screen Code: Hardware and Software

A new sound pen called "Speakun," shown in Figure 11, pronounces voice and sound just by lightly *touching* the dot codes, instead of *tracing* them. The software for developing handmade teaching materials suitable for this sound pen is called "Garyu-Tensei" (Apollo Japan, 2008). The dot codes placed over the text and pictures on the sheet are called "Screen code," developed by Apollo Japan (2005), which can be printed with any model of OKIdata color printer as almost invisible to the naked eye. (In the previous SPS system, the dot code, placed over text and picitures, hides them.)

Figure 11. Speakun and handmade sheet

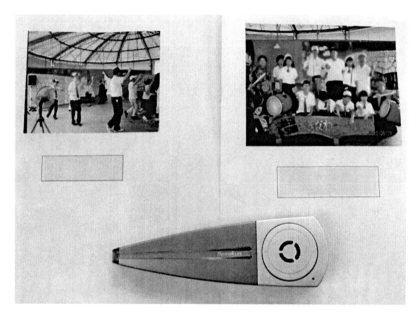

To embed dot codes suitable for Speakun, bitmap image (bmp) files to be marked with squares or circles must be prepared beforehand. As shown in Figure 12, "Garyu-Tensei" has three panels. First, one of the bitmap image files is selected, and then the positions linked with voices and sounds are marked with a square or circle object. Each marked position is serially linked with the corresponding voice or sound file by selecting a suitable audio file. Both these procedures are repeated for all marked positions in all bmp files. The selected bmp files and the linked audio files are listed in the upper- and lower-right panels, respectively.

After linking all necessary audio files to the marked positions of all bmp files, selecting "Output Voices" in the "Data Output" pull-down menu produces an executable file that can be installed into the Micro SD card of a Speakun pen. This executable file can be renamed as desired and then multiple executable files can be saved onto one Micro SD card. Pushing the "Next Content Button" of the Speakun pen easily selects the file suitable for the corresponding content.

Each printed dot code is read by infrared rays emitted by the Speakun pen. The linkage between the dot codes and the corresponding original audio on the Micro SD card is interpreted, thus reproducing the original voice or sound.

For the contents of "Hello Book 1" and "Hello Book 2," the new dot codes were placed over the older ones used for the SPS, so that the students who had used the SR could easily see where the voices are embedded.

Screen Code: School Activities

Foreign Language Learning

At Kirigaoka School for the Physically Challenged, affiliated with the University of Tsukuba, all grades have foreign language activities (English lessons) at least once a week. They have been using the handmade supplementary readers for "Hello Book 1" and "Hello Book 2" (Ikuta & Ezoe, 2008; Ikuta & Ezoe, 2009a) developed for the previous SPS for more than two years, and have experienced many enjoyable learning opportunities and greatly improved their communication skills in

Figure 12. Screenshot of "Garyu-Tensei"

English. However, students with hand or finger challenges could not trace such long dot codes and could not join in the same activities as their classmates, and felt lonely.

To provide such disabled students with the same learning opportunity, the supplementary readers for "Hello Book 1" and "Hello Book 2" developed for the previous SPS were transformed to use the present Speakun pen. The new dot codes were positioned over the older ones so that each student could easily understand the points to be touched.

These new handmade supplementary readers were first used in the fifth and sixth grade joint English class consisting of 14 students. Even students with hand or finger challenges could touch the new dot codes and reproduce the voices successfully using the Speakun pen. They shouted for joy, and the feeling of exultation and smiles filled the class (Figure 13). These new handmade supplementary readers and sound pens were also welcomed in the junior and senior high school English classes.

Storytelling with "Jizo (Stone Statue) with a School Bag"

A storytelling activity using the new handmade content for "Jizo (Stone Statue) with a School Bag" was performed in the English class at Kirigaoka School for the Physically Challenged; the story and its illustrations were created by Koseko and Kitashima (1980), respectively, on the basis of a true incident that happened in Hachioji, Tokyo, during World War II. This book is widely used

Figure 13. English lesson using Speakun

Figure 14. Storytelling activity with sharing earphones

Figure 15. SPEAKING PEN and handmade sheets

for peace education at many elementary schools in Hachioji. All students listened to the story by touching the dot codes with the new sound pens. Some of them listened to the story by sharing earphones (Figure 14) and were eager to know the true story of "Jizo with a School Bag." Their teacher advised them to read its original book.

Grid Onput: Hardware and Software

New dot codes that can handle more than one multimedia file such as movies, html files, web pages, and PowerPoint files, in addition to audio files, are called Grid Onput (Gridmark, 2004). The sound pen for Grid Onput is called SPEAKING PEN, which is shown in Figure 15 along with handmade sheets.

The software for developing contents with the latest dot codes is called GridLayouter (OKIdata, 2009), as shown in Figure 16. It presents the user three frames, a thumbnail frame on the left, a main frame in the center, and a property frame on the right. One page of a pdf file published in the previous procedure is selected and displayed in the center, i.e., the main view panel, where the positions linked to voice and sound should be marked with a square or circle object. The marked postions are numbered sequentially in the right property panel.

For the handmade contents for "Hello Books 1 & 2" and "Jizo (Stone statue) with a School Bag," new dot codes were placed over the older ones for the SPS, so that the students who have experienced previous activities with the SR and Speakun can easily find the positions to be touched.

However, for the content of "Let's Read More Books," the dot codes are distributed across the entire sheet so that even blind students can use it; thus, touching any position on the sheet with the new SEAKING PEN can reporduce the original voices and sounds. The superimposed dot codes printed with a specially designed OKIdata c380dn color printer are also nearly invisible to the naked eye.

Content developers prepare an assembly source program linking each dot code with the correspong MP3 audio file and a batch file to compile such a program and make it excutable. The generated executable file is installed into the Micro SD card of a SPEAKING PEN.

By performing the extensive coding of an assembly source program, more than one audio file can be linked to one dot code, and thus, advanced content such as a bilingual (trilingual, and so on) supplementary reader can be developed. The handmade billingual content of "Jizo (stone statue) with a School Bag" shown in Figure 16 enables storytelling in both Japanese and English by touching specially designed icons placed in the

Figure 16. Screenshot of GridLayouter for a bilingual side reader

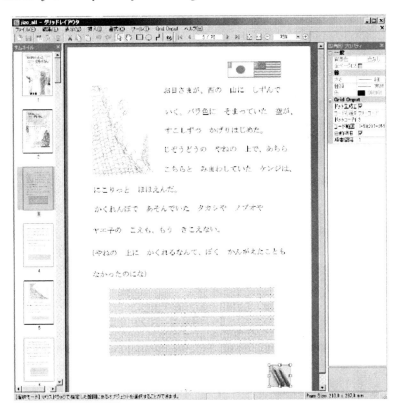

upper-right corner of the first page of the content. This supplementary reader is also available for the previously used SR (SPS) in only one edition because the new dot codes for a SPEAKING PEN are placed at the lower-right corner of each sheet, instead of covering the SR codes with them.

The present Grid Onput system has another enhanced feature: in addition to audio files, each dot code can be linked with more than one multimedia file such as movies, pictures, web pages, html files, and PowerPoint files. The linked multimedia is displayed on the screen of a PC connected to the new G1-Scanner pen (OKIdata, 2009) shown in Figure 17. For example, each picture in Figure 18 is first marked with a square or circle by using the GridLayouter and then linked to the corresponding voice or sound by editing and compiling an assembly source program, as noted above. A second content file, such as a movie, can be further linked to each dot code by using another program, "Grid Content Studio" (OKIdata, 2009).

The Grid Content Studio shown in Figure 19 also consists of three panels: a content list panel on the left, a preview panel in the upper right, and a link list panel in the lower right. All multimedia files linked to the dot codes are first drag-and-dropped into the content list panel. These added files are linked with the corresponding dot codes serially by using the link list panel. Finally, selecting the "Save" button saves the linking as an

Figure 17. G1-Scanner

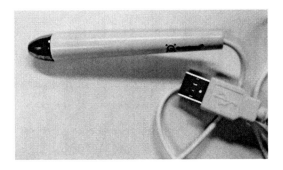

Figure 18. GridLaouter for audio linking

executable file. The movies linked to each picture in Figure 18 are video recordings of each school activity performed at both the School for the Mentally Challenged at Otsuka and Kirigaoka School for the Physically Challenged. Each movie linked to the picture in Figure 18 is reproduced on the PC screen or tablet by both activiting its excutable file and touching the dot codes with a G1-Scanner; for example, the embedded html file with a movie is executed.

Figure 19. Grid Content Studio for multimedia linking

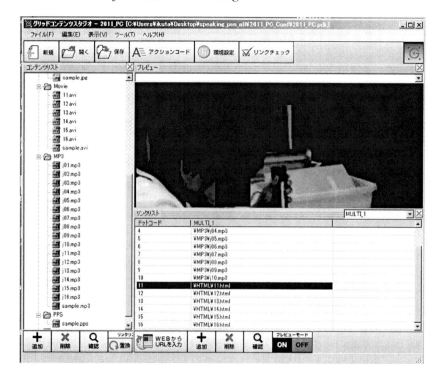

However, the biggest limitation of the new Grid Onput system might be that printing such dot codes is currently restricted to a costly model of OKIdata, c380dn. To overcome this limitation, a specially designed sheet shown in Figure 20 can be prepared, where the order of each dot code, which can be linked with any audios and movies by editing its assembly source program and using Grid Content Studio, is imprinted on each square beforehand. Each square on the sheet should first be pasted on the target object and can then be touched with a SPEAKING PEN or G1-Scanner.

Grid Onput: School Activities

"Let's Read More Books"

The teachers at Kashiwagi Elementary School in Hachioji encourage the students to read more than 300 books during the six years, as noted in the SPS section. Their mothers often help with storytelling before the start of the day's lessons, and the students at Otsuma Women's University also recommend many books to their students by using handmade pop-up advertisements with voices by using the SPS.

Figure 20. Specially designed "magical" sheet

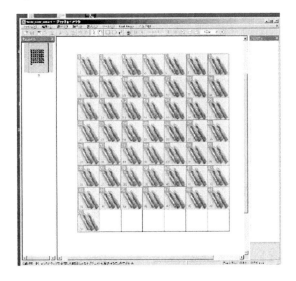

In the present activity, the library assistants, in cooperation with their teachers, from the upper grades made two handmade advertisements for "Let's Read More Book 1" and "Let's Read More Book 2" with the new SPEAKING PEN to promote reading. Touching the dot codes overlying the picture of the book cover replayed the library assistants' introductory speeches on the recommended books. The dot codes for these advertisements were superimposed on the entire picture of each book cover, and therefore, even lower grade students could easily replay and listen to such speeches just by touching any position on the sheet with a SPEAKING PEN.

The delegate for the library assistants first introduced the "Let's Read More Books" activity to all students at an assembly in the school gymnasium, demonstrating how the new SPEAKING PEN can reproduce voices and sounds. The students were surprised and impressed that by just lightly touching the dot codes, almost invisible to the naked eye, reproduced the library assistants' voices. The two handmade advertisements and several SPEAKING PENs are always available in their school library.

The library assistants' present activity, in cooperation with their teachers, enabled even the lower grade students to participate, because they did not need to trace the longer dot codes, unlike with the previous SPS.

Self-Help Supports

To improve *listening and telling activities*, activities such as "Looking back," "Matching Words with Pictures," "Cultivating Listening," and "Writing Composition and Its Presentation" have been performed using the new SPEAKING PEN at the School for the Mentally Challenged at Otsuka, affiliated with the University of Tsukuba.

In the "Looking back" activity, students who were weak at writing superimposed their spoken feelings and thoughts as dot codes on the memorial pictures and photos, and presented their memories to classmates by touching them on the sheet with a SPEAKING PEN.

In the "Matching Words with Pictures" activity, many handmade sheets on which dot codes were superimposed on words and pictures/photos were prepared to cultivate their vocabulary acquisition. The students ticked the dot codes off on their fingers, pointed their fingers at the real item, and brought it to the teacher after the production of linked voice and sound with the new SPEAKING PEN.

In the "Cultivating Listening" activity, various handmade sheets were made where the dot codes for the SPEAKING PEN were superimposed across the entire picture, so that the students could easily use it. The sounds of various vehicles, animals, telephones, slurping noodles, fireworks, thunder, etc., were prepared for the sheets (Figure 21). The listening abilities of the students were greatly improved through these efforts with the new handmade materials and sound pens; some students learned now to reply to questions like "What sound is this?" and exchange several words with their classmates. The lower grade students were first surprised and then impressed that just touching the picture/photos reproduced voices and sounds clearly, and they scrambled for both the sheets and SPEAKING PENs during breaks in class. A severely mentally challenged student first floundered, but he learned to put the SPEAKING PEN near his ear to indicate listening to the voice produced from the sound pen.

In the "Writing Composition and Its Presentation" activity, the students who were poor at writing became able to present and confirm their feelings and thoughts experienced at various school events by touching the memorial picture/photos on the sheet by using a SPEAKING PEN; the voices were superimposed beforehand by the students themselves or their homeroom teacher. The students who could write their feelings and thoughts in only short sentences learned to tick their writing texts off on their fingers while their voice was reproduced. The pieces produced during the "Writing Composition and Its Presentation" activity were displayed on the walls of the hallway, where anyone could listen to the students' feelings and thoughts, at any time. These efforts became very enjoyable and allowed the students to share their memories with each other.

At the recent "Field Day Festival," a junior high school student with intellectual and language expressive disabilities was able to act as the master of the festival, in cooperation with her homeroom teacher, by using the sheets with dot codes available for the new SPEAKING PEN (Figure 22).

At Seibi Special Needs Education School, Suginami, Tokyo, the teachers created a specially designed handmade teaching aid with the SPEAKING PEN for the students with Down syndrome and autism, as even they can handle it easily. This aid consists of a SPEAKING PEN

Figure 22. Procession of the field day festival

Figure 21. Activity for improving listening

stored in a handmade wooden box, as shown in Figure 23. The students can move handmade wooden blocks with dot codes, instead of touching the dot codes with the pen, in learning the relationships between pictures and words and their pronunciations. A student could repeat the pronunciations himself after reproducing them by the SPEAKING PEN. They are now attempting to serve as masters of morning meetings using such a handmade wooden box with a SPEAKING PEN and handmade blocks embedded with a stream of morning meeting sentences. The teachers at both the School for Special Needs Education, Faculty of Education, Hirosaki University, Hirosaki, Aomori, and ABIKO Special Needs Educational School for the Mentally Challenged, Abiko, Chiba, have now begun developing handmade teaching materials for their classes and performing school activities using them, in cooperation with us.

Extracurricular Activities

One of the present authors (S. I.) with his university students created handmade content for "Let's Play Tama Zoo" by using the Grid Onput system; he expects students to learn in advance before visiting the Tama zoo as an extracurricular activity. Nearly 200 audios and 23 movies are included in the content.

The students can answer more than 70 animal quizzes on the basis of two hints for each animal and then verify their correct answers by using a SPEAKING PEN; three audios, two hints and its answer, are linked to each dot code, and movies are linked to some dot codes in addition to the audio files.

The first and second grade students at Kirigaoka School for the Physically Challenged enjoyed the content very much during their lunch break. By touching the dot codes superimposed over the animals' silhouettes on the sheet, they could hear two hints for each animal and enjoy thinking and answering the quizzes. The students also enjoyed seeing the movies placed over some of the animals' silhouettes on the zoo map. They shouted for joy, and the feeling of exultation and smiles filled the class. Some of the students were hand- or finger-challenged, but they could use the present content perfectly. They could not part from the table holding the contents even at the end of lunch break.

The new handmade content and SPEAKING PEN were also welcomed in the fifth and sixth grade joint-class (Figure 24) as well as the seventh grade class. The present Tama zoo content was also welcomed very much at the School for the Mentally Challenged at Otsuka and several regular elementary schools in Hachioji and Hino, Tokyo.

FUTURE RESEARCH DIRECTIONS

In "Foreign Language Learning" activities, the dot codes for the new sound pens (the SPEAKING PEN and Speakun) were superimposed on the older ones for the previous SPS, so that the students who had previously used such handmade

Figure 23. Handmade apparatus for SPEAKING PEN

Figure 24. Extracurricular activity with handmade multimedia content

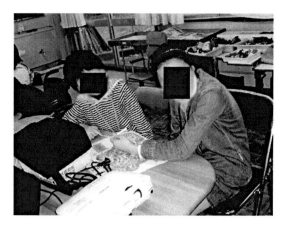

content could easily understand the position to be touched. Even the students with hand and finger challenges could use these new materials and participate in the same school activities as did other students, and then gain competence and confidence in themselves.

In the "Let's Read More Books" activity performed by the upper grades library assistants, new dot codes were placed over all pictures of the book covers, enabling even the lower grade students to reproduce the introductory speeches by just touching the picture embedded with new dot codes for the new sound pen, instead of tracing the longer ones for the SPS.

In the "Self-Help Support" activities, the students with intellectual and expressive language disabilities and autism could join in using the new sound pens, and could share their feelings and thoughts with their classmates. Even the students with severe mental challenges could participate in these activities.

In the Screen Code and Grid Onput systems, the dot codes are distributed across the entire sheet so that even blind students can use it; touching any position on the sheet can reporoduce the original voices and sounds.

By editing an assembly source program for the Grid Onput system, more than one voice and sound may be embedded in one dot code. The bi-lingual supplementary reader for foreign language classes, as shown in Figure 16, was developed in just one edition. This functionality might be very useful in developing handmade teaching materials for students with various challenges; the relationship between two items (the name of a bird and its call, for example) might be placed over one dot code. The supplementary reader, which can be used with both previous SPS and new sound pens, is also available in only one edition. Some of the students at the regular and special needs schools are still fond of *tracing* dot codes rather than *touching* them; *tracing* dot codes might be still important for such students to motivate their learning activities.

In the new content of "Let's Play Tama Zoo," 23 movies are embedded in the same dot codes as several audio files. This functionality may enable the teachers to enhance the learning activities for the students with hearing challenges by using the original handmade contents with movies.

In Japan, a new course of study began in April 2011, and the subject of Foreign Language (English) is newly required in the fifth and sixth grades at all elementary schools. For this application, several new sound pens and side readers were released. Such packages will provide the students native pronunciations. However, these packages cost more than $150 each, making it impossible for each school to buy enough volumes for all students. Thus, more moderately priced and easy-to-handle software and hardware are required for teachers to make original handmade teaching materials for each individual student in their class.

CONCLUSION

This chapter reports various school activities conducted using original handmade teaching materials with dot codes and three new communication aids, which can *read* the printed dot codes on paper. The handmade sheets with the homeroom teacher's and volunteers' voices, in addition to pictures, words, and phrases, enabled the students with challenges to learn vocabulary, understand word meanings, and achieve meaningful relationships. By just lightly touching the printed dot codes on the sheet, even the students with severe mental or hand/finger challenges could reproduce the original voices and sounds with the new sound pens: Apollo Japan's Speakun and Gridmark's SPEAKING PEN.

As a result of the present efforts, students with severe mental challenges and autism could learn the relationships between pictures and words, pictures and their readings, and words and their readings. They also learned how to communicate with others and experience the pleasures and satisfactions of everyday life, and thus gained competence and confidence in themselves.

By performing extensive coding in an assembly source program in the Grid Onput system, more than one audio file can be linked to one dot code, thus easily producing advanced content such as a bilingual (trilingual, and so on) supplementary reader. Several multimedia files can be linked to the same dot code as audio files, thus enabling the development of multimedia content such as "Let's Play Tama Zoo." The latest Grid Onput system may enable schoolteachers to enhance school activities for students with both *speaking* and *hearing* challenges.

ACKNOWLEDGMENT

Shigeru Ikuta thanks "Grant-in-Aids for Scientific Research" (C) (#22530992) and "Challenging Exploratory Research" (#20653068). He also thanks "The Tokyu Foundation for Better Environment" (#292) and the "Institute of Human Culture Studies" (#024) at Otsuma Women's University.

The authors thank all the students and teachers at the School for the Mentally Challenged at Otsuka, Kirigaoka School for the Physically Challenged, Seibi Special Needs School, Moto-Hachioji-Higashi Elementary School, and Kashi-wagi Elementary School. The authors would like to express their sincere gratitude to Ms. Flynn Rachel Deborah for her reading and revising the manuscript. The authors would like to thank Enago (www.enago.jp) and PenPoint Editing (penpoint-editing.com) for the English language review.

REFERENCES

Ace Center. (2000). *Voice output communication aids*. Retrieved December 13, 2011, from http://atschool.eduweb.co.uk/acecent/html/resvoca.html

Anderson, C., Anderson, K., Ezoe, T., Fukushima, K., & Ikuta, S. (2008, June). *Facilitating universal design with sound card reader*. Paper presented at the meeting of the NECC 2008, San Antonio, TX.

Anderson, C., Fukushima, K., & Ikuta, S. (2009). Technology use for students with mild disabilities in the United State. *Otsuma Journal of Social Information Studies*, *18*, 113–126.

Apollo Japan. (2005). *Screen code*. Retrieved December 11, 2011, from http://www.apollo-japan.ne.jp/

Apollo Japan. (2008). *Garyu-tensei*. Retrieved December 30, 2011, from http://www.apollo-japan.ne.jp/pdt_tensei.html; http://www.apollo-japan.ne.jp/qa_grts.pdf

Axistive. (2011). *What is a voice output communication aid?* Retrieved December 13, 2011, from http://www.axistive.com/what-is-a-voice-output-communication-aid.html

Belson, S. (2003). *Technology for exceptional learners*. Boston, MA: Houghton-Mifflin.

Dell, A. G., Newton, D. A., & Petroff, J. G. (2008). *Assistive technology in the classroom: Enhancing the school experiences of students with disabilities*. Upper Saddle River, NJ: Pearson Education.

Disabled Living Foundation. (2011). *Living made easy for children*. Retrieved December 13, 2011, from http://www.livingmadeeasy.org.uk/children/communication-aids-with-voice-output-1413/

Edyburn, D. L. (2000). Assistive technology and mild disabilities. *Focus on Exceptional Children, 32*(9), 1–24.

Gateway. (2011). *Voice output communication aids* (VOCAs). Retrieved December 13, 2011, from http://www.gateway2at.org/page.php?page_ID=3&gen_ID=12&mensub_ID=4&submen_ID=4&AtDet_ID=55

Gridmark. (2004). *Grid onput*. Retrieved December 11, 2011, from http://www.gridmark.co.jp/product/speakingpen.html

Ikuta, S. (2008a). Present and future issue of information communication technology in education [in Japanese]. *Hagemi, 318*, 4–8.

Ikuta, S. (2008b). School activities with audios for the students with disabilities. In Koreeda, K. (Ed.), *Examples of school activities useful for the special needs education* (pp. 72–73). Tokyo, Japan: Gakken.

Ikuta, S. (2011). Communication with sound pens and magic papers [in Japanese]. *Jissen Shogaiji Kenkyu, 458*(8), 46–49.

Ikuta, S., & Ezoe, T. (2008). *Hello book 1*. Tokyo, Japan: Shinjuku Japanese Language Institute.

Ikuta, S., & Ezoe, T. (2009a). *Hello book 2*. Tokyo, Japan: Shinjuku Japanese Language Institute.

Ikuta, S., & Ezoe, T. (2009b). *Emi & Alex with sound reader* (Vol. 1). Tokyo, Japan: Shinjuku Language Institute.

Ikuta, S., & Ezoe, T. (2009c). *Emi & Alex with sound reader* (Vol. 2). Tokyo, Japan: Shinjuku Language Institute.

Ikuta, S., Nemoto, F., Ishitobi, R., & Ezoe, T. (2011). Long-term school activities for the students with intellectual and expressive language challenges: Communication aids using voices and sounds. *Society for Information Technology & Teacher Education International Conference* (pp. 3237-3242). Chesapeake, VA: AACE.

Inclusive Design Research Center. (2011). *Voice output communication aids*. Retrieved December 13, 2011, from http://idrc.ocad.ca/index.php/resources/technical-glossary/49-voice-output-communication-aids

Ishitobi, R., Ezoe, T., & Ikuta, S. (2010). "Tracing" is "speaking": Communicating and learning using supportive sound books [in Japanese]. *Computers & Education, 29*, 64–67.

Johnston, L., Beard, L. A., & Carpenter, L. B. (2007). *Assistive technology: Access for all students*. Upper Saddle River, NJ: Pearson Education.

Kaneko, S., Ohshima, M., Takei, K., Yamamoto, L., Ezoe, T., Ueyama, S., & Ikuta, S. (2011). School activities with voices and sounds: Handmade teaching materials and sound pens [in Japanese]. *Computers & Education, 30*, 48–51.

Kendall, W. (1978). Public Law 94-142: Implications for the classroom teacher. *Peabody Journal of Education, 55*(3), 226–230. doi:10.1080/01619567809538191

Koseko, K., & Kitashima, S. (1980). *Jizo (Stone statue) with a school bag* (Randoseru-wo Shotta Jizo-san, in Japanese). Tokyo, Japan: Shinnihon Shuppan.

Ministry of Education. Culture, Sports, Science and Technology-Japan. (2001). *The state of special needs education in 21ˢᵗ century in Japan*. Retrieved December 15, 2011, from http://www.mext.go.jp/b_menu/shingi/chousa/shotou/006/toushin/010102.htm

Nemoto, F., & Ikuta, S. (2010). "Tracing" is "speaking": A student acquiring the happiness of communication using "sound pronunciation system" *Computers & Education, 28*, 57–60.

Office of Special Education and Rehabilitation Services. (2004). *Disabilities that qualify infants, toddlers, children, and youth for services under IDEA 2004.* Retrieved December 12, 2011 from http://www.ldonline.org/article/12399

Office of Special Education and Rehabilitative Services. (1997). *IDEA '97: The law.* Retrieved December 12, 2011, from http://www2.ed.gov/offices/OSERS/Policy/IDEA/the_law.html

Ohshima, M., Shimada, F., Yamamoto, L., Nemoto, F., Ezoe, T., Suzuki, J., & Ikuta, S. (2007). Use of "sound pronunciation system" in elementary schools *Computers & Education, 23*, 76–79.

Ohshima, M., Sugibayashi, H., Shimada, F., Yamamoto, L., Nemoto, F., Ishitobi, R., & Ikuta, S. (2008). A useful audio device for curricular and extracurricular activities. *19th Annual Conference of the Information Technology and Teacher Education (SITE), Assessment & E-Folios* (pp. 5140-5145). Chesapeake, VA: AACE.

Okawara, H., Uchikawa, T., Shiraishi, T., Kaneko, S., Sugibayashi, H., & Hara, Y. (2008). Use of "sound pronunciation system" for students with physically handicapped [in Japanese]. *Computers & Education, 24*, 40–43.

OKIdata. (2009). *GridLayouter & grid content studio.* Retrieved December 23, 2011, from http://www.okidata.co.jp/solution/gridmark/

Olympus Inc. (1999). *Scan talk.* Retrieved December 11, 2011, from http://www.olympus.co.jp/jp/news/1999b/nr990823r300j.cfm

Sussex Community. (2011). *Voice output communication aid* (VOCA). Retrieved December 13, 2011, from http://www.sussexcommunity.nhs.uk/index.cfm?request=c2007983

Vanderheiden, G. (1984). High and light technology approaches in the development of communication systems for the severe physically handicapped persons. *Exceptional Education Quarterly, 4*(4), 40–56.

ADDITIONAL READING

Bauer, A. M., & Ulrich, M. E. (2002). "I've got a Palm in my pocket": Using handheld computers in an inclusive classroom. *Teaching Exceptional Children, 35*(2), 18–23.

Beck, J. (2002). Emerging literacy through assistive technology. *Teaching Exceptional Children, 35*(2), 44–48.

Best, S., Heller, K., & Bigge, J. (2005). *Teaching individuals with physical or multiple disabilities* (5th ed.). Upper Saddle River, NJ: Merill/Prentice Hall.

Beukelman, D., & Mlrenda, P. (2005). *Augmentative & alternative communication: Supporting children & adults with complex communication needs.* Baltimore, MD: Paul H. Brookes Pub. Co.

Bigge, J., Best, S. J., & Heller, K. W. (2001). *Teaching individuals with physical, health or multiple disabilities.* Upper Saddle River, NJ: Merrill/Prentice Hall.

Block, M. (2000). *A teacher's guide to including students with disabilities in general physical education.* Baltimore, MD: Paul H. Brookes Pub. Co.

Bugaj, C. R., & Norton-Darr, S. (2010). *The practical (and fun) guide to assistive technology in public schools.* Washington, DC: International Society for Technology in Education.

Cook, A. M., & Hussey, M. (2002). *Assistive technologies: Principles and practice* (2nd ed.). St. Louis, MO: Mosby.

DeCosta, D. C., & Glennen, S. L. (1997). *Handbook of augmentation and alternative communication*. San Diego, CA: Singular Publishing Group.

Dell, A. G., Newton, D. A., & Petroff, J. G. (2011). *Assistive technology in the classroom: Enhancing the school experiences of students with disabilities* (2nd ed.). Upper Saddle River, NJ: Pearson Education.

Edyburn, D. L. (2002). *What every teacher should know about assistive technology*. Boston, MA: Allyn & Bacon.

Farrenkopf, C., & McGregor, D. (2003). Physical education and health. In M. C. Holbrook & A. J. Koenig (Eds.), *Foundations of education: Vol. 2. Instructional strategies for teaching children and youths with visual impairments* (pp. 437-463). New York, NY: American Foundation for the Blind.

Friend, M., & Bursuck, W. D. (2002). *Including students with special needs: A practical guide for classroom teachers* (3rd ed.). Boston, MA: Allyn & Bacon.

Gray, T., & Silver-Pacuilla, H. (2011). *Breakthrough teaching and learning*. Baltimore, MD: Springer. doi:10.1007/978-1-4419-7768-7

Hersh, M., & Johnson, M. A. (2008). *Assistive technology for visually impaired and blind people*. Baltimore, MD: Springer. doi:10.1007/978-1-84628-867-8

Hersh, M. A., & Johnson, M. A. (2003). *Assistive technology for the hearing-impaired, deaf and deafblind*. New York, NY: Springer. doi:10.1007/b97528

Heward, W. L. (2003). *Exceptional children: An introduction to special education* (7th ed.). Upper Saddle River, NJ: Merrill/Prentice Hall.

Hulit, L. M., & Howard, M. R. (2002). *Born to talk: An introduction to speech and language development* (3rd ed.). Boston, MA: Allyn & Bacon.

Jaehnert, K. (2005). *Selecting an augmentative and alternative communication (AAC) device for your child*. Retrieved December 16, 2011, from http://affnet.ucp.org/ucp_channeldoc.cfm/1/14/86/86-86/3916

Kapperman, G., & Sticken, J. (2003). A case for increased training in the Nemeth Code of Braille mathematics for teachers of students who are visually impaired. *Journal of Visual Impairment, 97*(2), 110–113.

Lasardo, A., & Notari-Syverson, A. (2001). *Alternative approaches to assessing young children*. Baltimore, MD: Paul H. Brookes Pub. Co.

Lindfors, J. W. (1987). *Children's language and learning* (2nd ed.). Boston, MA: Allyn & Bacon.

Mittal, V. O., Mitchell, I. M., & Van der Loos, H. F. M. (2010). *Design and use of assistive technology*. New York, NY: Springer.

Oishi, M. M. K., Yanco, H. A., Aronis, J., & Simpson, R. C. (1998). *Assistive technology and artificial intelligence*. New York, NY: Springer.

Raymond, E. B. (2004). *Learners with mild disabilities* (2nd ed.). Boston, MA: Allyn & Bacon.

Robitaille, S. (2010). *The illustrated guide to assistive technology and devices: Tools and gadgets for living independently*. New York, NY: Demos Medical Pub.

Sadao, K. C., & Robinson, N. B. (2010). *Assistive technology for young children: Creating inclusive learning environments*. Baltimore, MD: Paul H. Brooks Pub. Co.

Schmidt, M., Weinstein, T., Niemic, R., & Walberg, H. (1986). Computer assisted instruction with exceptional children. *The Journal of Special Education, 19*(4), 493–501. doi:10.1177/002246698501900411

Sullivan, M., & Lewis, M. (2000). Assistive technology for the very young: Creating responsive environments. *Infants and Young Children, 12*(4), 34–52. doi:10.1097/00001163-200012040-00009

Theng, L. B. (2011). *Assistive and augmentative communication for the disabled: Intelligent technologies for communication, learning and teaching.* New York, NY: Information Science Reference. doi:10.4018/978-1-60960-541-4

Vaughn, S., Bos, C. S., & Schumm, J. S. (2000). *Teaching exceptional, diverse, and at-risk students in the classroom* (2nd ed.). Boston, MA: Allyn & Bacon.

Wendt, O., Quist, R. W., & Lloyd, L. L. (2011). *Assistive technology: Principles and applications for communication disorders and special education.* Bingley, UK: Emerald Group Pub. Ltd.

KEY TERMS AND DEFINITIONS

Assistive Technology Tool: Should have an individual and widespread useful function in supporting each student with disabilities. A tool being quite helpful to a certain student might not be useful to others. To investigate most suitable tool for each student might be one of the most important tasks for the schoolteachers especially at special needs schools.

Audio Device: As Sound Reader presented in this chapter that can decode the ST dot codes printed on the paper and reproduce the original audios is one of the valuable communication tools.

Communication Aids: Such as voice output communication aids (VOCAs) and the present sound pens are one of the key components for all the students to facilitate communication with classmates, homeroom teachers, families, and others.

Dot Code: Is a group of two-dimensional placed dots that can be printed on the sheet with the ordinary color printer. In some systems, audios are encoded and directly printed out as dot codes on the paper, but in recent developed systems only the linkage between the dot code and the corresponding audio or the multimedia file is embedded.

Handmade Teaching Materials: That should be prepared by homeroom teachers are the key components in supporting the individual needs and desires for each student with various challenges. Suitable easy-to-handle software is inevitable to make *original* handmade teaching materials.

Scanner Pen: For multimedia presentation, that can interpret the linkage between the dot codes printed on the paper and the real multimedia file stored in a secondary memory in a computer and reproduce the original multimedia on a PC screen or tablet, is one of the useful teaching aids.

School Activity: Performed especially at special needs school might be highly facilitated by using *original* and *individual* handmade teaching materials and aids suitable for each student with disabilities.

Sound Pens, SPEAKING PEN and Speak-un: Presented in this chapter, that can interpret the linkage between the dot codes printed on the paper and the real audio files stored in a sound pen and reproduce the original audios, are one of the useful communication tools for all the students.

Chapter 12
"Evaluator":
A Grading Tool for Spanish Learners

Paz Ferrero
Universidad Autónoma de Madrid, Spain & Ciudad Universitaria de Cantoblanco, Spain

Rachel Whittaker
Universidad Autónoma de Madrid, Spain & Ciudad Universitaria de Cantoblanco, Spain

Javier Alda
University Complutense of Madrid, Spain

ABSTRACT

Computational linguistics can offer tools for automatic grading of written texts. "Evaluator" is such a tool. It uses FreeLing as a morpho-syntactic analyzer, providing words, lemmas, and part of speech tags for each word in a text. Multi-words can also be identified and their grammar identified. "Evaluator" also manages leveled glossaries, like the one developed by the Instituto Cervantes, as well as other electronically available dictionaries. All these glossaries enable the tool to identify most words in texts, grading them into the six levels scale of the Common European Framework of Reference for Languages. To assign a lexical level to the text under analysis, a statistical distribution of leveled qualified lemmas is used. Other ways to assign a lexical level to a text by using corpora of a preset level are also suggested. The syntactic analysis is based on a collection of grammar structures leveled by following the descriptors given by the Instituto Cervantes. These grammar structures are identified within the text using quantitative indices which level a text by comparing it with a given corpus. Finally, semantic identification is done using semantic fields as defined by the Instituto Cervantes. Latent Semantic Analysis is also used to group texts dealing with the same topic together. All these methods have been tested and applied to real texts written in Spanish by native speakers and learners.

INTRODUCTION

This contribution is based on the PhD dissertation titled *Definition and analysis of quantitative linguistic parameters for automatic assessment tools applicable to Spanish as a Foreign Language*

DOI: 10.4018/978-1-4666-2530-3.ch012

(Ferrero 2011), in which the three authors of this chapter were involved. It describes and applies some automatic methods to quantitatively evaluate reference levels of texts written in Spanish by learners of Spanish as second foreign language to obtain the "Diploma de Español como Lengua Extranjera" (DELE), according to the six

Copyright © 2013, IGI Global. Copying or distributing in print or electronic forms without written permission of IGI Global is prohibited.

main levels described in the Common European Framework of Reference (CEFR): A1-A2, B1-B2, C1-C2. Official human evaluators had previously and independently scored those texts we analyzed automatically. The reference level is given with a confidence parameter that measures the reliability of the level given. In this section, we present an overview of the process, before explaining the sources we have used and describing in detail the modules which make up "Evaluator." We have, then, designed a prototype whose morpho-syntactic analyzer, FreeLing (Padró, 2006; Padró, 2009), is the tool used as the first step to process the lemmas of the Spanish texts. After this, those lemmas are automatically assessed lexically, syntactically, and semantically.

The evaluation of lexical competence is based on the classification of lexis into the levels given by the Plan Curricular del Instituto Cervantes (PCIC), our golden standard for the study. For those words not included in the PCIC list, other criteria have been developed based on the presence of those words in a combination of selected glossaries. Moreover, multiword units are also evaluated to refine the determination of the lexical level of the text. After this, the whole text is assessed with a quantitative level and given a numerical grade by applying a method derived from Zipf's law (Zipf, 1932).

The syntactic level is given by identifying categorized syntactic structures in the text being evaluated. A wide collection of syntactic structures has been created and leveled based on the PCIC, with the level being assigned depending on the complexity of the structure. The identification of these leveled structures is compared against a reference corpus with a predetermined level.

At the semantic level, we identify the content of a text following the semantic fields given by the PCIC. Then, after using customized corpora, it is possible to correlate the semantic fields of the text being tested quantitatively with the corpora. Besides this, Latent Semantic Analysis (LSA) groups texts in semantic clusters that can be identified and used for the evaluation of semantic content.

The methods developed have been tested on texts written by learners of Spanish. The results obtained using the automatic graders correlate well with the scores given by the human graders. This system is conceived to help learners of Spanish to self-assess their texts, giving them a level. "Evaluator" is able to distinguish texts among several different text contents, and to check grammatical complexity and lexical level of those texts following descriptors from the Plan Curricular of Instituto Cervantes (PCIC).

The PCIC is based on the Common European Framework of Reference (CEFR). The CEFR document recognizes that "establishing cut-off points between levels is always a subjective procedure" (Cervantes, 2006, p. 32) when situating a student text at a specific level. However, using linguistic descriptors and an automatic tool to do the grading, assessment should respect a standard, and be objective and systematically reliable. Our aim with this tool was to achieve this reliability in the assessment of learners' written texts. Figure 1 shows the general design of the tool we have been describing.

We conceive "Evaluator" as a compact tool (see Figure 1). At present, in its experimental stage, we input a text and the tool outputs a leveled text according to its vocabulary, grammar, and content independently. In this contribution we describe the basic mechanism of "Evaluator" as a prototype. However, our aim is to create an automatic tool to evaluate texts written by learners of Spanish as a second language which can be used by the learners themselves to assess their progress.

STATE OF THE ART

From the beginning of this research in 2006 until its completion in 2011, we have been tracking the development and research in automatic evaluation

Figure 1. General diagram of the "Evaluator" tool

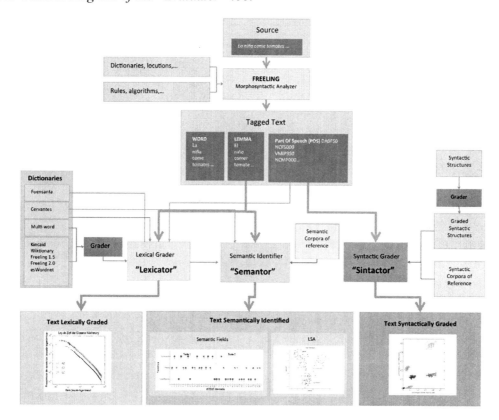

by a number of authors and institutions. During this time, researchers have developed tools and innovative products for, or in, institutions, companies and universities. Such investigation requires interdisciplinary knowledge and skills, covering linguistics, computer science, psychology, mathematics, statistics, evaluation and teaching of languages. Here we refer to our main sources in this very wide field.

Many institutions, researchers and teachers are interested in describing and developing specific evaluation criteria which are both meaningful and valid, reliable and accurate in describing levels of learning. We can consider that research on automatic information evaluation in general, and on texts in particular, began with Ellis Page in 1966 with his Project Essay Grade (PEG) (Page, 1966; Page, 1994; Page, Poggio & Keith, 1997). Since then, a number of new tools have been developed.

Several U.S. educational institutions, such as Educational Testing Service, propose tests which offer fast results in exams like the new TOEFL, in which most data are processed with automatic assessment systems (Cumming et al., 2006).

Another step in adapting education systems to technology has been taken by the National Assessment of Educational Progress (Gorman, 2010). These new methods have been shown to improve student achievement (Grimes, 2010). Moreover, at an official level, some educational assessment is already automatic. For example, the Educational Testing Service has evaluated tests (Burstein, Chodorow & Leacock, 2004) and recommends tools such as "MetaMetrics ®" ("Metrametrics," 2012) or "Lexile" ("Lexile. The Lexile Framework for Reading," 2012). These are useful both during the writing process, since they help to evaluate a written text, and also for reading, because they can be used to diagnose and measure difficulties for reading a text. Lexile also provides parameters that measure text complexity.

In the case of Spanish, however, there are few knowledge systems designed to assess texts into levels using CEFR. One that does this is DI-ALANG Test Server, a closed evaluation system used by the language department of the National University for Distance Education (Universidad Nacional de Educación a Distancia, UNED). DIALANG is described as a resource that "provides tests of different language skills, carefully designed and validated, along with a wide range of feedback and expert advice on how to improve students knowledge" (UNED, 2011). However, in 2005, studies on the use of DIALANG emphasized the need to validate it with other systems and to make it possible for learners to use it to produce their own tests (Alderson, 2005).

In the field of evaluation of Spanish as a foreign language, in 2006 the Instituto Cervantes published the *Plan Curricular Plan del Instituto Cervantes* (PCIC), a publication which has become an authorized reference for research on Spanish written texts. The PCIC describes the CEFR reference levels for Spanish. The PCIC is based on directions given by the Threshold Level Series (1978, 1990), on recommendations from the *Common European Framework of Reference for Languages: Learning, Teaching, Assessment* (CEFR, 2001), and on descriptions in the *Guide for the Production of Reference Level Descriptions for National and Regional Languages* (Council of Europe, 2005). Their criteria for materials selection and setting levels have been based mainly on knowledge and experience of experts and professionals in teaching Spanish as a second language (Bordón, 2004; Sánchez & Santos, 2004; Bordón, 2006). However, the PCIC does not use "inventories with statistical frequency, or linguistic data produced in [...] assessment situations" (Cervantes, 2006, p. 26), as the *Guide* recommended, in relation to the production of descriptions of reference levels for national and regional languages.

With regard to commercial products, there are some Spanish companies working to provide tools and related services for word processing and information retrieval, like, for example, "Daedalus." Other companies working with the Spanish language are the Ecuadorian "Signum" or the Spanish "Molino de Ideas." "Signum" offers language services like text processing, modules with dictionaries, thesaurus or spell-checkers to corporate systems or individual users.

In the area of university research, Coh-Metrix, a tool for text analysis, is an interesting development. For it, the University of Memphis team has developed 60 parameters and other modules to measure reading complexity, cohesion, and coherence, either for reading comprehension (Graesser, McNamara & Lowerse, 2010) or for studying the writing process (Crossley, McNamara, Weston & McLain, 2010).

Among Spanish universities working on Natural Language Processing, there are number of groups working on multivariate statistical methods (LSA, LSC, PCA). In this area, the tools developed by the Speech Technology Group of the Universidad Politécnica de Madrid are able to identify groups of words, or clusters, whose semantics is applied to voice-activated devices (Lucas, Fernández, Ferreiros, López & San Segundo, 2010). The Group of Advanced Interactive Tools at the Universidad Autónoma de Madrid has contributed several studies on the generation of conceptual models obtained from free-response tests evaluated automatically (Pérez, 2007). There are also a number of studies coming from the collaboration between the Universitat Pompeu Fabra, the Universitat de Barcelona and the Laboratoire Informatique d'Avignon, aimed at designing Dis-Seg, a discourse segmenter (da Cunha, San Juan, Torres-Moreno, Lloberes & Castellón, 2010a). This syntactic and discursive segmenter uses the FreeLing morpho-syntactic analyzer, and is based on Spanish lexical and syntactic rules, and especially on discourse markers, conjunctions, verb forms and punctuation (da Cunha & Torres-

Moreno, 2010c). This tool, DisSEg, is the only one in the area of parsing using the discursive framework of Rhetorical Structure Theory (RST) (Mann & Thompson, 1988). This tool can also be very useful for analyzing the syntactic complexity of segments within a clause or sentence (da Cunha, San Juan, Torres-Moreno, Lloberes & Castellón 2010b). Furthermore, by segmenting the text into sentences marked by conjunctions and discourse markers, this tool can identify and compare syntactic-discursive relations both within a text and in relation to other texts. This application would be very useful for evaluating the logical structure of a text, and its relation to its context, aspects which DELE experts in the Instituto Cervantes at present assess manually.

It is clear, then, that this chapter on Natural Language Processing covers a number of different fields, including Applied Linguistics, Computational Linguistics, Computational Semantics, and Computational Evaluation. Here, as we said, we have mentioned the main sources used in the study.

"EVALUATOR": MODULES AND STRUCTURE

In this section we summarize the modules, programs and functions that make up "Evaluator." There are four main modules in "Evaluator": "Analizator," "Lexicator," "Sintactor," and "Semantor." The first module, "Analizator," processes data and prepares them for the analysis of three linguistic levels carried out by the other three. The first, "Analizator," includes a number of features which provide important information for evaluating the text. Although this module does not appear in Figure 1, for lack of space, it would be located between the results of FreeLing and the other three modules. These modules use dictionaries and reference corpora to compute the results of "Evaluator."

Figure 1 presents an outline of the process and information flow. It shows the process from the original input (text) to the output (the grade for that text) at different levels, and the implementation of different methods. The modules are written and executed in Matlab. In these modules and functions, we have implemented algorithms and processing routines for lexical, syntactic, and semantic levels. As shown in the figure, the first step in the processing of a text is carried out by FreeLing, which parses it and does the morpho-syntactic analysis. It tags each word with its lemma and its Part of Speech (PoS). These elements, lemma and PoS tags, are key items used by "Evaluator" and its modules to evaluate a text.

Analizator

"Analizator" is a module that works on the file processed by FreeLing. It submits its information to various functions or routines that calculate and process different aspects of the text. It produces a file containing results that will be used by the other modules.

A first evaluation by "Analizator" identifies lemmas and their repetition, using a routine able to detect word repetitions, lemmas, and PoS. By using some features of FreeLing analysis, sentence and paragraph endings can be recognized, after which "Analizator" calculates their frequencies of occurrence in a text. This function can do this evaluation of the frequency of occurrence of any item (punctuation marks, markers, words, lemmas, etc.) within the text units. The results are used extensively throughout the subsequent analysis.

Another important function of "Analizator" is devoted to sorting words into the CEFR six levels scale. It is a key function for the process leading to giving a text its lexical level. This function processes all our available dictionaries: Cervantes, Kincaid, Wiktionary, FreeLing 1.5, FreeLing 2.1, esWordnet, and the multiword glossary (described below). It generates three variables for each of the items of discourse. When a lemma is identified, the leveling is done first by the level given by the Instituto Cervantes dictionary, which is taken as an authorized reference. If the lemma is not in this dictionary, then it is passed to a process of evaluation using our combined dictionaries criterion. In fact, most multiwords are leveled using the Instituto Cervantes glossary criteria, since it has a wide coverage. If a multiword is not listed in that index, we use another file containing leveled multiwords which we prepared to complete the one distributed with FreeLing. Rules to level multiwords contained in this file have been extracted from the Instituto Cervantes' Curriculum (PCIC). After a first round using this strategy, the system leaves some words unleveled. This occurs, for example, with words ending in "-mente." After chopping this ending and recovering its lemma, a new evaluating round takes place, in order to have as many leveled lemmas and words as possible.

To prepare the syntactic analysis, "Analizator" includes a function that recognizes grammatical structures. To do this, we compute the grammatical structures already identified and qualified by levels (from A1 to C2) which we have collected and leveled following the Instituto Cervantes descriptors. This identification process includes the definition of wildcards that enable us to process inflectional categories. The function assigns a syntactic level to each PoS depending on the level of the structure it belongs to. The results of this function are important for syntactic classification of the analyzed text. This is completed in "Sintactor."

For the semantic analysis, firstly, "Analizator" classifies lemmas into the semantic fields defined by PCIC. To do this, we again use the Instituto Cervantes glossary. The system uses several methods of counting, including repetitions and weights for the semantic allocation, depending on the surrounding words. These variations can be applied depending on the type of analysis to be carried out in the "Semantor" module. In this function, we have applied a stop list to remove certain lemmas, based on grammatical category. That is, the stop list filters some conjunctions, prepositions, determiners, and auxiliary verbs.

These grammatical functions have been identified using PoS tags. Once this identification is done, data are grouped to form histograms of occurrence of the lemmas identified in semantic fields and thematic areas. These results will be used for the semantic identification of the text by "Semantor."

The last function in "Analizator" at the semantic level calculates parameters of interest in Latent Semantic Analysis (LSA). This analysis is performed within each text. The units of analysis can be split to a sentence level. The function uses the method of Principal Component Analysis (PCA) adapted to various options that can be controlled easily. These options control the use of global and local averages weights and frequencies. For example, Landauer proposes the use of the logarithm of frequency (Landauer, Foltz & Laham, 1998), by which those words appearing only once in the text are removed. Global weight can be included, using criteria related to entropy or different statistical distributions. It also normalizes a word found in a number of texts to refine its weight or importance. The result of this function is a set of variables that identifies the semantic content of a text. These results will be processed and used by "Semantor."

Summarizing, the module "Analizator" creates a data file containing the results for each of the texts. These results are used by the other three modules to present the overall analysis and to level the text lexically and syntactically, and also for its semantic identification. We now look at each of the three modules and how they use the input from "Analizator."

"Lexicator"

This module is specifically devoted to lexical analysis and leveling of a text. It includes several routines to count the number of letters and vowels in each word. With this function, it is possible to know the statistical distribution of the number of letters, the appearance of vowels, the existence of written accent, and the presence of multiwords.

However, the main purpose of "Lexicator" is to give a lexical level to the text. To do this, it is able to apply a number of different strategies. One of them is based on the analysis of the percentage of words belonging to a set of controlled dictionaries. Other grading criteria are based on Zipf's law (Ha, Sicilia-García, Ming & Smith, 2002), and on assigning the lemmas to the CEFR six levels scale (A1, A2, B1, B2, C1, C2). This means that lemmas are sorted according to their frequency. From here, some statistical parameters are given to provide an overall value of the lexical level of the text. This value is typically given with a tendency, and with its reliability level. All these data, when evaluated for a collection of texts, produce figures and comparative data and represent levels and scores clearly in graphs.

"Sintactor"

As explained above, the program "Sintactor" uses the results obtained from "Analizator," especially those results associated with the level of each PoS within a text, and with the identification of grammatical structures in the text. It first identifies the syntactic structures, and then calculates quantitative parameters related to the syntactic level of the text.

"Sintactor" is made up of a set of modules that process syntactic structures in different steps. In a first phase, a collection of syntactic structures is processed and graded using descriptors given by the PCIC. These structures are located in a file containing 2586 different structures, with their respective levels. This set of structures was generated for this research and may undergo future revisions. The file is configured using different combinations of PoS. A specific level is also attached to each structure for grading purposes, according to the PCIC´s criteria of syntactic complexity at different stages of learning.

After structure identification, another routine identifies the level for each PoS. This routine takes into account the fact that a given PoS may appear in different grammatical structures with different levels. The highest level of the structures where it appears is taken as the level of the PoS.

In addition, "Sintactor" can use corpora to compare the syntactic structures identified in the text under analysis. In our case, we use a corpus made up of 36 Christmas speeches given by King Juan Carlos I, from 1975 to 2010. This corpus plays an important role, since we take it as an authorized reference, graded at a B2 level in grammar, according to our leveled structures.

By considering the PoS identification both in the corpus and in the text under analysis, we are able to calculate the deviation of the grammar of the text with respect to the grammar of the corpus. This comparison makes possible an overall evaluation of the text at a syntactic level. The results are again represented graphically.

"Semantor"

This module takes as input the results from "Analizator." It uses the semantic fields defined by the Instituto Cervantes in the PCIC together with some thematic areas given by one of the glossaries we use, the Fuensanta glossary (López, 1999). The 28 semantic fields of the PCIC are presented using the concepts of General Notions (GN) and Specific Notions (SN). "Semantor" creates a vector of 28 components, one for each semantic field defined by the Cervantes. The vector for each text is compared with those corresponding to other texts to find semantic consistency in the subject matter. We have also defined, at a more general level, four areas: Mathematics, Language, Science, and Social Sciences, using a two-dimensional plot to locate any text in any of the Fuensanta López thematic areas.

Finally, "Semantor" can perform a principal component analysis (PCA) of a collection of texts. This analysis allows us to group texts into clusters, or clouds, in terms of their semantic content. To this end, we either use a reference corpus with a specified reference level, or more reference corpora for semantic reference. These reference corpora allow us to define regions in the diagram of the eigenvectors obtained from the principal component analysis. The module is designed to apply Latent Semantic Analysis (LSA) with great flexibility and efficiency.

At this stage of the prototype of evaluation system, and due to the high computational cost, we have not included the results obtained by processing the text using esWordnet glossary. However, we believe that, after a more effective implementation of the identification algorithms, the use of esWordnet might produce valuable results for semantic analysis.

"EVALUATOR": LEXICAL, SYNTACTIC, AND SEMANTIC LEVELS

Lexical Grading

As we said, our proposal for grading vocabulary in texts written by Spanish learners is based primarily on the index of general notions and specific notions of PCIC. The difficulty of our research is how to actually grade the lexical level of a given text.

First of all, we take a text written in Spanish and presented in a flat format as an ASCII file (untagged and unmarked). After processing it using FreeLing, the file is treated by "Analizator" and "Lexicator" modules. As any given lemma can be graded at different levels depending on the semantic field, and also on the PoS value, we grade them with the average level of all the occurrences in the PCIC for that lemma. As a result, we obtain a text whose lemmas are classi-fied into levels (see right plot in figure 2). Since any text has words at all levels, two key questions immediately arise from this basic classification: what is the level of the text? What intervenes to produce a grade B1, B2, C1 or C2 for a text? In our research, we tried to answer these two questions by investigating innovative ways of processing the lexical information.

To do this it is important to control and clas-sify the largest number of words in the text pos-sible. This task is accomplished by using different types of glossaries (see left plot of figure 2). In addition, using multiple dictionaries may provide some other criteria for evaluation: vocabulary richness of the text, repetitions, specificity of words, or the identification of a word as a gen-eral or specific notion.

Figure 2. Lemmas identified from the 36 Christmas message of the King Juan Carlos I by using the avail-able glossaries. The left plot shows the percentage of lemmas identified by each glossary. After applying the methods for grading those lemmas, the histogram on the right is obtained. Standard deviations are represented as a red rectangle on the left plot, and as a blue rectangle in the right plot.

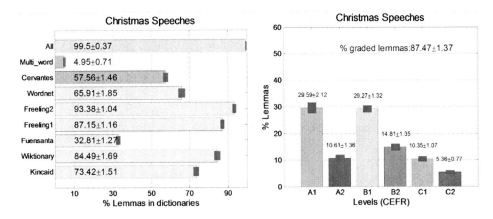

The electronic glossaries available are:

- Kincaid (Kc): It contains 2022 grammatically disambiguated lemmas and is the result of translating the original English version into Spanish. Kincaid developed this dictionary to be used in writing easy technical manuals for the US Navy. This glossary is useful to produce Controlled or Simplified English texts (Thomas, Jaffe, Kincaid & Stees. 1992).
- Wiktionary (Wk): It contains 5207 lemmas appearing in more than 27 million words written from 6527 TV series captions. In it, words are sorted in terms of their frequency of appearance ("Wiktionary," 2008).
- Fuensanta López (Fu): It contains 5273 lemmas related to nouns and verbs used in academic texts for high school. This glossary also classifies their lemmas into semantic areas. These areas do not coincide with the semantic fields defined in the PCIC of the Instituto Cervantes (López, 1999).
- FreeLing 1.5 (F1): It contains 7156 lemmas compiled by Padró and accompanies the distribution of FreeLing (Padró, 2006).
- FreeLing 2.1 (F2): It contains 76214 disambiguated lemmas. It has been developed and updated periodically to improve analysis by FreeLing (Padró, 2009).
- esWordnet (Wn): Its Spanish version has 93425 lemmas and multiwords, excluding adverbs. It facilitates the task of relating words semantically (Atserias, Climent, Farreres, Rigau, & Rodríguez, 1997; Padró, Reese, Agirre & Soroa, 2010).
- Cervantes: It is the glossary of the Plan Curricular del Instituto Cervantes with 8662 lemmas leveled according to the PCIC rules and the Common European Framework of Reference levels (Cervantes, 2006).

- Multiword: This glossary originated from the multiword glossary distributed with FreeLing system (Padró, 2006; Padró, 2009). We have extended the number of multiwords from 1480 to 5868 entries. These multiwords have been leveled automatically using the descriptors given by the PCIC.

When working with these glossaries we have made a number of assumptions. On the one hand, we assume that a dictionary corresponds to a higher level the larger the number of entries. This means that we postulate that the Kincaid's dictionary corresponds to level B1-B2, while the Wiktionary glossary corresponds better to B2 level; the glossary of FreeLing 1.5 would fall between levels B2-C1, and FreeLing 2.0 and esWordnet glossaries could be C1-C2 level. Besides this, we apply the criterion that when some words appear in one glossary but not in another, this is a level indicator. This criterion helps us to have more lemmas leveled by the method of combining dictionaries. The hypothesis given at the beginning of the paragraph, connecting the level of the dictionary with the number of entries, would be accurate enough if these dictionaries were nested, as happens with the glossaries produced for learners at different levels. However, in our research, we did not have this kind of nested dictionaries available in electronic form.

Using the available dictionaries, we postulate a different strategy that links the presence of a lemma in a combination of glossaries with the level of the lemma. In this way, we obtain a combination of leveled glossaries as follows:

Kc+Wk+F1+F2+WN: B1-B2
Wk+F1+F2+Wn: B2
F1+F2+Wn: C1
F2+Wn: C1
F2: C2
Wn: C2

In these combinations we have not used the Fuensanta glossary because it is restricted to nouns and verbs. The proposed combinations have been tested and positively correlated using the Instituto Cervantes glossary as a golden standard for reference. Only when a given lemma does not appear in the Cervantes glossary so we apply the method based on the combination of dictionaries. By using this method, we have managed to identify and grade many more words. When only using the Cervantes glossary, the percentage of graded lemmas was around 40% - 45%, but at present we can grade as many as 70%-80% of the lemmas in a text. Besides, the multiword glossary accounts for an additional 5% - 10% of lemmas. Obviously, having a larger number of lemmas leveled, means a more reliable grading of a complete text.

At this point, the most important problem in automatic evaluation is to score the global lexical level of any text. After identifying the lexical level of each word, we use three different approaches in order to identify the overall level of a text. We now describe these approaches:

• K-2000 Method for frequency ranges.

We name this method K-2000 because the Kincaid dictionary has 2000 lemmas. Our approach is based on a diagnosis method used by the Oxford 3000™ Profiler (2008), or Oxford 3000™ Text Checker (2011), a tool that evaluates a text based on the Oxford 3000 lemmas dictionary. Our method is similar, but uses the Kincaid translated glossary which has 2022 lemmas. The Oxford 3000 method diagnoses the level of a text according to the percentage of words in the text being analyzed that are found in the Oxford dictionary. The Oxford 3000 method proposes that a text with 95%-100% of its vocabulary in the Oxford dictionary can be considered to be low-intermediate, or B1; one with between 90%-95% as high-intermediate level, or B2; and those texts with 75%-90% of their words in the Oxford dictionary would be graded as advanced,

or C1-C2. This, of course, responds to the fact that each level contains more infrequent vocabulary.

In our case, our reference dictionary has fewer words (2022) than the Oxford dictionary (3000). According to Paul Nation, a list of 2000 words is a good number to cover basic vocabulary, and a larger list will begin to include academic, and even specific vocabulary (Nation & Kyongho, 1995, p. 35 and ff.). The simple transposition of the ranges given by the Oxford 3000 method to the Kincaid glossary would produce the following levels:

95%-100%: Level A1-A2
90%-95%: Level B1
80%-90%: Level B2
75%-80%: Level C1
<75%: Level C2.

• Method based on Zipf's law.

When sorting lemmas of a text by their frequency of appearance, the order obtained follows an intrinsic law that applies to every language. This law is written as:

$$\log_{10} P_r = \log_{10} C - \alpha \log_{10} r,$$

where P_r is the frequency of occurrence of a word, r is the rank of that word, and $\log_{10}$ means the logarithm function. C and α are constants. This relation is also applicable when considering lemmas belonging to any of the six CEFR levels. Thus, by combining the results obtained from the ordering of the whole set of lemmas of a text, and the six orderings obtained for each level, it is possible to define some parameters which describe how the lemmas of the same level are located along the Zipf's law curve. In Figure 3, the colored dots distinguish the six CEFR levels. The words appearing first (i.e. having a higher frequency of occurrence) belong to levels A1 and A2, while those appearing at the end of the

Figure 3. Representation of Zipf's law for the set of lemmas contained in the Wiktionary glossary. Colored dots represent lemmas classified into the CEFR six level scale. Black dots are ungraded words moved out of the curve to make the figure clearer.

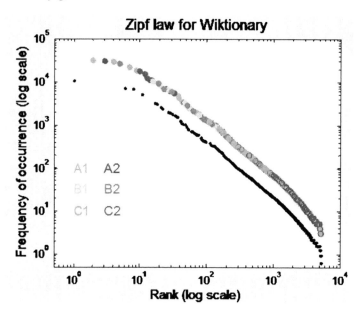

graph are less frequent and correspond to higher levels (C1 and C2).

This method produces an overall parameter that we name "level," along with a tendency and reliability parameter. Level is calculated in steps corresponding to CEFR six levels. Tendency shows how a text moves towards a lower or higher level with respect to one described previously. Finally, as the distribution of the words within Zipf's law gives a relation derived from the equation, there is a parameter that measures the deviation of the actual distribution with respect to the expected one. This parameter measures the reliability for the level assigned by this method. We have found that this reliability improves the longer the text.

• Method of level based on intervals and text length.

This method calculates the percentage range for the lexis at the six levels expected. The percentage also depends on text length. To obtain ranges of

percentages, we have used a corpus containing 36 Christmas discourses of King Juan Carlos I as a reference corpus, as explained above. We postulate that these discourses belong to the B2 level, tending towards C1. The writer, then, has used standard, everyday vocabulary in order for the speeches to be understood by most Spanish native viewers, since they are written to be addressed to the average Spanish audience at Christmas Eve.

To produce the intervals, we apply the following method. First of all, we merged all the discourses into a single file. Then, we chopped this file into blocks with a preset number of words. What actually happens is that some blocks are a little longer, because we end each block when its last clause finishes with a period. In this way, we can process each block in order to obtain the lemmas distribution into the CEFR six levels scale. The mean and standard deviation of the percentage of lemmas at each level are worked out on blocks with the same number of words. These values are used to define the ranges characterizing the level of the discourse for a given length of

Table 1. Ranges of percentages for the corpus of the King's speeches

Length (# words)	A1	A2	B1	B2	C1	C2
200	10.2 - 16.1	6.4 - 10.7	28.3 – 35.4	19.2 - 26.8	12.2 - 18.7	5.3 - 10.4
300	9.4 - 14.3	6.3 - 10.0	28.3 - 34.7	21.0 - 27.1	13.2 - 19.0	6.0 - 10.5
500	8.4 - 11.9	6.3 - 8.7	28.2 - 33.2	23.0 - 27.1	13.2 - 19.0	6.0 - 10.5
1000	7.4 - 9.7	6.0 - 7.6	28.1 - 31.3	24.9 - 28.0	16.4 - 20.0	8.3 - 11.1
1500	6.7 - 8.6	5.7 - 7.0	26.7 - 30.5	25.0 - 29.4	17.6 - 20.7	9.5 - 11.5

the text. Table 1 shows the range of percentages for each level and each length. These results are shown graphically in Figure 4. Table 1 shows that the longer the text, the narrower the range, indicating that reliability improves as the length of the text increases.

The procedure applied to this corpus could be applied to corpora graded at different levels. The results of this analysis would be a collection of ranges in percentages. When a text is under analysis, the system should locate the distribution of the lemmas of the text into the CEFR scale of six levels, and its distribution would fit into the different ranges obtained for each level. Thus, the best fitting case is selected as the level of the text.

Since the method already takes into account text length, this approach to grading would be easier and more reliable than other methods which have problems when dealing with short texts.

Syntactic Grading

Syntactic analysis and grading begins with the creation of a collection of syntactic structures that we have organized according to CEFR reference levels. The classification was done following descriptors and examples given by the PCIC. We have built these structures from simple ones, increasing their complexity and, therefore, their level. We have a great variety of phrases, insert-

Figure 4. Percentages at the CEFR six levels as a function of block length in the corpus of the King's speeches. This plot corresponds to a B2 level.

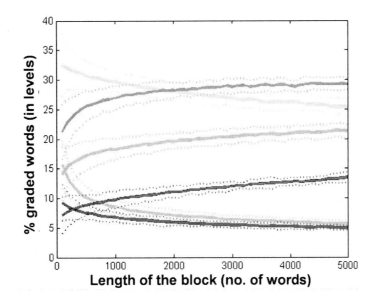

Table 2. Distribution of structures in the six CEFR levels

Level	# (total 2586)	%
A1	54	2.09
A2	178	6.88
B1	812	31.40
B2	1004	38.82
C1	497	19.22
C2	41	1.59

ing more categories like adjectives, participles, adverbs, and pronouns to produce more complex structures (Miller 1962, Chomsky 1989). This produced a total of 2586 structures, distributed as shown in Table 2.

Another useful approach to define syntactic level and structures was inspired by the criteria proposed by Kellog Hunt, with his concept of T-unit or "minimum terminal unit" (Hunt, 1977, 101). These indices are useful to analyze the syntactic maturity of school children writing in English as their mother tongue, and have also been found revealing for Spanish (Torres, 1993; Véliz 1988; Véliz, 1999). In a similar way, Derivational Theory of Complexity (DTC) proposes parameters that measure syntactic complexity from the number of transformations that can occur in a clause or in a basic unit. It was found that syntactic complexity in a native language increased with age of the learner, that is, with learning experience (Miller & McKean, 1964).

There are three indices proposed by Hunt and Véliz to measure syntactic maturity of a text: the length of the minimum terminal unit, the length of main clauses, and the index of subordinate clauses. These are also calculable and measurable indices and, therefore, indicators to quantify syntactic level (Olloqui & López, 1991). The minimum terminal unit proposed by Hunt consists of a main clause and all subordinate dependent clauses. Coordinated and juxtaposed clauses are considered independent, and so each is a different

minimum terminal unit (Rodríguez, 1999; Martín et al., 2005).

In our study, we start by applying primary and secondary indices as proposed by Hunt (Hunt, 1965) and applied by Véliz (Véliz, 2004); then, we use our leveled syntactic structures; and, finally, we apply a maximum level criterion based on counting PoS. All these allow us to define quantitative variables associated with the grammatical structures appearing in a given text.

Similarly, we may compute some indices relating to the number of grammatical categories inside a terminal unit. According to Hunt, the greater or lesser use of categories such as adjectives, gerunds, etc. also indicates a more mature a text. Interestingly, text scores with different levels of maturity were shown to be similar across different languages (Hunt, 1977, p. 101).

From "Evaluator," numerical results in the form of clausal indices are obtained by calculating the average number of, for example, adjective clauses, by identifying the relative markers, or of nominal clauses by using the completive markers, or circumstantial clauses by counting the adverbial and prepositional markers. In fact, it is very easy to compute indices related with grammar categories by recovering the PoS related to the required elements. Although calculation of these indices produces a great array of numerical data about the grammar of a text, it is not yet clear how to relate these values with the overall level of the text under analysis.

On the one hand, we can assume that high quality texts will contain more complex syntax or syntagmatic structures. This complexity can be quantified by the previously defined indices (Torres, 1993, p. 15). Some authors propose that the degree of syntactic complexity identifies the stage or level the learner has reached (Checa & Lozano, 2002; Wolfe-Quintero, Inagaki & Kim, 1998). Consequently, syntactic maturity depends on the linguistic mental representation that a learner has first in his/her mother language and, then, in a new language. On the other hand, it is obvious that syntactic complexity can make a text hard to understand, and so inefficient (Véliz, 1999).

To give an idea of the type of results for syntactic complexity, we present data in Tables 3, 4 and 5, for several parameters. Among them, indices # 8 and 9, inspired by Hunt, give measures of variety and complexity (Martín, Hidalgo & Whittaker, 2001; Bloor & Bloor, 2004). First, Table 3 compares two texts: King Juan Carlos I's 1992 Christmas message and a short text written by a young native speaker of Spanish (pen-pal letter 1_16).

Processing the same indices, we show in Tables 4 and 5 the results obtained for the set of 36 Christmas speeches of the King Juan Carlos I (Table 4), and also for a collection of 44 texts (Table 5) on the same topic (pen-pal letters), written by two groups (G1 and G2) of native Spanish writers.

From the indexes presented in Tables 3, 4, and 5, the most significant ones are the number of content words (#4), the percentage of different words (#5), and the average number of determiners in the noun phrases (#9). The King´s speech is expected to be more syntactically mature than the pen-pal letter, as is the case. This is expressed in the higher value of index #9, showing that the sentences are more complex in the case of King´s speech. On the other hand, we notice that, as the pen-pal letter is a shorter text, it has a larger percentage of different words.

A comparison between the two sets of texts in Tables 4 and 5 shows some interesting features. For example, indices #4 and #6 in all the pen-pal texts are higher than those in the King's speeches. By contrast, index #8, which represents the number

Table 3. Comparative analysis of calculated indices, including indices 8 and 9, for two texts

#	Concept	King's 1992 Speech	Pen Pal Letter 1_16
1	N° tokens	1629	150
2	N° sentences	58	8
3	N° words / sentence	24.91	16.37
4	N° of content words (%)	796 (48.86%)	86 (57.33%)
5	N° of function words (%)	580 (35.60%)	34 (22.67%)
6	% different words percentage	38.62%	59.54%
7	N° of locutions (%)	81 (4.97%)	8 (5.33%)
8	N° of noun phrases (%)	170 (10.44%)	14 (9.33%)
9	Average determiners in noun phrases	1.55	1.00

Table 4. Mean values and standard deviations of calculated indices for the King's speeches

#	Concept	36 King Speeches
1	N° tokens	1406 ± 343
2	N° sentences	49 ± 14
3	N° words / sentence	21.34 ± 5.02
4	N° of content words (%)	714 ± 171 (50.88% ± 1.53%)
5	N° of function words (%)	496 ± 125 (35.60% ± 2.39%)
6	% different words percentage	35.29% ± 1.46%
7	N° of locutions (%)	64 ± 19 (4.50% ± 0.65%)
8	N° of noun phrases (%)	154 ± 35 (11.08% ± 0.81%)
9	Average determiners in noun phrases	1.63 ± 0.08

Table 5. Mean values and standard deviations of calculated indices for texts by native Spanish writers

#	Concept	23 Pen Pal Letters (G1)	21 Pen Pal Letters (G2)
1	N° tokens	155 ± 31	164 ± 41
2	N° sentences	9 ± 3	9 ± 3
3	N° words / sentence	17.81 ± 4.88	18.85 ± 5.72
4	N° of content words (%)	87 ± 18 (55.80% ± 3.38%)	91 ± 23 (55.65% ±3.97%)
5	N° of function words (%)	41 ± 11 (26.15% ± 3.56%)	43 ± 12 (26.08 ± 3.30%)
6	% different words percentage	62.06% ± 5.54%	60.77% ± 4.92%
7	N° of locutions (%)	9 ± 3 (5.67% ± 2.03%)	8 ± 3 (4.71% ± 1.13%)
8	N° of noun phrases (%)	15 ± 5 (9.22% ± 2.05%)	14 ± 3 (8.78% ± 1.68%)
9	Average determiners in noun phrases	1.39 ± 0.20	1.33 ± 0.28

of noun phrases, and #9, which shows the average number of determiners in noun phrases, are greater for the King's speeches than for the pen-pal letters. The results for indices #4 and #6 confirm that a greater length of a text does not imply the use of a greater number of different content words. The tables show that, in texts with a higher level, that is, the King's speeches, the sentences are longer (index #3) and there are more determiners (index #9). These results show that the number of noun phrases (index #8) and the average number of determiners in noun phrases (index #9) are directly related to the stage of maturity of a text. We can, then, use this type of analysis to evaluate the level of a text. However, there is not a simple relationship between this type of index and the final evaluation of the level of a non-native writer's text, as shown by Barrio (2004).

Parametric Grading of the Syntactic Level

Another interesting way to grade the syntactic level of a text is to analyze the histogram distribution of the structures and the PoS in terms of their level (within the CEFR six levels) carefully. The two distributions - the one for the structures and the one for the PoS- can be arranged to form one for each level. Doing this, it is possible to establish the level of the text by comparing the six pair parameters of the text we are analyzing, with respect to the same parameters of the corpus processed with a preset syntactic level. Figure 5 shows the location of the six pairs for each text in the King's Christmas message corpus. The horizontal axis corresponds to the PoS and the vertical axis to the grammatical structures. As a result, the two distributions -grammatical structures and PoS- allow us to calculate the syntactic level of any text when compared with a reference corpus which has been previously leveled.

Semantic Identification

The module devoted to semantic analysis of a text included in "Evaluator" relies on a number of strategies. In this section we will describe the use of the semantic fields given by the PCIC and the application of Latent Semantic Analysis method.

Semantic Fields

The "Index of general and specific notions" of the PCIC is our basic framework to organize and identify the vocabulary of a text semantically, and even to disambiguate it to some extent. When recognizing the lemmas of a text, "Analizator" also collects information about the semantic fields corresponding to each lemma. A given lemma may belong to several different semantic fields, producing an

Figure 5. Two-dimensional plot of the six pairs of parameters describing the distribution of the PoS (horizontal axis) and the identified grammatical structures (vertical axis) for the 36 Christmas messages in the corpus of the King Juan Carlos's speeches

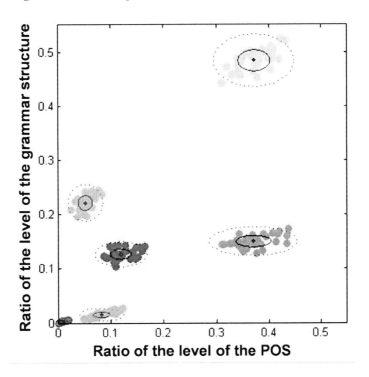

ambiguity that we need to solve. Another possibility is that some lemmas can be repeated throughout the text, indicating some emphasis, specificity or, perhaps, the writer's poor vocabulary. Semantic disambiguation can distinguish semantic fields for most lemmas in a sentence. At the same time, there are some words, or lemmas, containing semantic information which is not useful at this stage of the analysis. These are prepositions, determiners, and auxiliary verbs. Because of this, a weighting factor is calculated to enhance the semantic field in which more lemmas appear. Using this weighting strategy, it is possible to refine semantic identification. As our only authorized source for semantic identification is the PCIC, we must restrict this analysis to those lemmas identified by the Cervantes glossary. It would be interesting to expand this identification by using esWordnet to relate lemmas not appearing in the Cervantes glossary but connected through esWordnet with other lemmas that do belong to it.

The PCIC defines 7 general notions, and 20 specific notions. Thus, "Semantor" defines a multidimensional vector with 27 components for a given text. Each component has a value proportional to the appearance of lemmas belonging to the corresponding semantic field. This value has been evaluated by considering the presence of repeated lemmas, and by using the weighting factor described. Therefore, to compare two texts we may operate with those vectors, characterizing their semantic fields. This can be extended to a collection of texts by defining a correlation matrix. The method works better when a corpus of text, with similar length and dealing with the same topic, works as a reference.

In order to test this, we produced a corpus of 114 texts written by native Spanish speakers, and used them to characterize a collection of 40 texts written by 20 students of Spanish as a second language. Each student writes two texts (text #1 and text #2) along the Intermediate DELE test. The PCIC notions let us identify the semantic content of each text automatically. The results are summarized in Figure 6. The corpus contained texts on three different topics: a complaint letter ("Reclamación"), a pen-pal letter ("Penpal"), and a composition describing a place which is special for the writer ("Lugar Especial"). Each text is semantically analyzed and the blue dots identify the topic that best fits with the text. The larger they are, the greater the reliability in the identification. The cross under the dots indicates correct identification. The dots without crosses correspond to text dealing with a subject that is different from the three under analysis.

Latent Semantic Analysis

One of the methods used by "Evaluator" to identify the semantic content of a text is based on techniques of multivariate statistics, that is, frequency of appearance methods and array-based indexing (Kochandy, 2006). Latent Semantic Analysis, based on the analysis of the frequency of appearance of words, studies the semantic content of a text compared to other texts or, better still, using a corpus with a preset semantic content. The main target of this method is to extract the semantics of a text by analyzing the statistical correlation of the frequency of word occurrence with respect to the frequency of occurrence in other texts, or in a corpus. The comparison may also be intra-textual, comparing the semantic content among sentences,

paragraphs, or units of arbitrary length within a text. The method is based on the assumption that, if several related texts have the same semantic content, they use a similar set of words and their frequencies of occurrence are alike.

Basically, LSA is strongly connected to the method of Principal Component Analysis (PCA), being PCA better suited for classification purposes. PCA and LSA methods have been used successfully in the study of texts (Landauer & Dumais 1997; Biber, 1998). They are also applied in experimental sciences (López-Alonso, Alda & Bernabéu, 2002a; López-Alonso & Alda 2002b; López-Alonso, Rico-García & Alda 2004a; López Alonso & Alda 2004b; Ferrero & Alda, 2007), biomedical sciences (Kintsch, 2002; Heinzle & Haynes, 2009), social sciences (Dunteman, 1989), text assessment in psychology (Olmos, León, Escudero, & Jorge-Botana, 2009), and also in the humanities (Sigley, 1997; Venegas, 2006; Venegas, 2009). This diversity in its application is possible because PCA and LSA are basic statistical techniques in the field of multivariate analysis.

Principal Component Analysis works in the following way. To begin to apply the method, we obtain the frequencies of the lemmas with semantic importance in the text. We also have to include a stop list to filter out those lemmas with no semantic information. The frequencies of appearance are organized in a matrix of numbers. In this matrix, the rows give the frequency of occurrence of lemmas in the text. The columns contain the frequencies of occurrence of a particular lemma

Figure 6. Identification of semantic content in native Spanish letters using the PCIC semantic fields

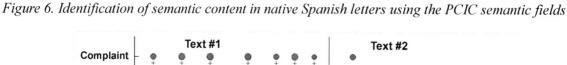
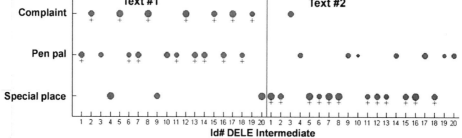

in all the analyzed texts. In the case of our study, we have many more lemmas than analyzed texts, so the array has more columns than rows. At this point, we find various possibilities to pre-process the frequency values, using various mathematical transformations. Landauer proposed taking the logarithm of the frequencies (Landauer, Dennis & Kintsch, 2007), which can be interesting when considering a large corpus where the value frequencies are high. In that case, the use of the logarithmic function reduces the range of values. Other changes can be used to normalize the frequencies of a lemma in a whole text or to weight the frequency values of the lemmas to solve the problem of texts of different length (Ziempekis & Gallopoulos, 2006).

After the pre-processing, PCA acts on the frequency matrix. The method identifies the relationships between texts through the analysis of the frequency of appearance of lemmas. One of the most common metrics for this procedure comes from the analysis of the variance-covariance matrix. Each element in this matrix compares two texts correlating the frequencies of the lemmas appearing in both texts. The variance and covariance values are organized in a $N \times N$ matrix. If the texts had absolutely nothing to do with each other, their mutual covariance would be zero, and only the elements on the diagonal would have values other than zero. However, this is not what happens in text analysis. Therefore the variance-covariance matrix has always the non-zero off-diagonal terms, indicating that the texts are connected.

From a semantic point of view, it is interesting to obtain a few uncorrelated texts containing the semantic content of all the original texts. This is precisely what it is achieved by the application of the PCA and the LSA. In our nomenclature we denominate these texts as "synthetic texts," and some other authors call them "pseudo-texts" (Jorge-Botana, León, Olmos & Escudero, 2010).

From a mathematical point of view, PCA diagonalizes the original variance-covariance matrix. We must remember that this diagonaliza-

tion process will create a new matrix with zeros off the diagonal. This means that "synthetic texts" have no relation between them. Another important result obtained from the PCA is the eigenvalues and eigenvectors set produced after diagonalizing. The PCA transformation can be seen as a rotation from a system of coordinates where the variance-covariance matrix is not diagonal to a new coordinate system where this matrix is diagonal. The change of this system of coordinates can be described by a rotation matrix. This rotation matrix is a $N \times N$ matrix. The elements of this matrix can be interpreted as the coordinates of some eigenvectors that describe the rotation. Actually, the component #i of the eigenvector #j means the importance of the principal component #j, that is, the "synthetic text" #j, in the original text #i. So, each "synthetic text" has an associated eigenvalue explaining the importance of the given "synthetic text" in the original text set. In addition, due to the mathematical procedure, eigenvalue #1 is the most important. The rest of eigenvalues are consecutively ordered in terms of their importance. Using a well-established grouping strategy, it is possible to identify those "synthetic texts" that are independent of the others. This procedure minimizes the dimensionality of the problem.

In Figure 7 we show how the texts under analysis are located in those regions where the other texts are grouped into clusters depending on the topic of the text. This graph shows how LSA may identify correctly the semantic content of the text.

CONCLUSION

In this contribution we have presented a method for the automatic assessment of texts written by learners of Spanish as a foreign language, which works at three linguistic levels: lexical, syntactic, and semantic. The tool, "Evaluator," uses the results obtained from a morpho-syntactic analyzer

Figure 7. Graphical representation of the 114 native Spanish texts using the components of the eigenvectors #2 and #3. The colored dots correspond to the 114 texts from the corpus. They have been located in separate regions of this diagram according to semantic content. The numbered stars correspond to the 40 texts written by learners of Spanish as L2. The figure shows how the 40 texts are located around the clouds of the corpus, depending on their semantic content.

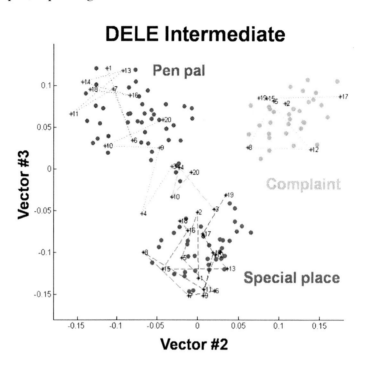

(FreeLing). "Evaluator" is made up of a number of modules that compute different parameters in a text. These parameters are automatically retrieved by specific modules and devoted to the lexical ("Lexicator"), syntactic ("Sintactor"), and semantic ("Semantor") levels. The ultimate goal is to provide a system able to grade a written text according to the six levels of the Common European Framework of Reference for Spanish learners.

"Evaluator" requires leveled glossaries or a leveling strategy based on the combination of several glossaries. It also uses a list to identify locution and phrasal structures in order to increase the number of lemmas correctly processed and leveled. This is important because correct identification and grading of individual lemmas will provide a more reliable assessment of the text's level. We have proposed three different methods which can be used to calculate a value for the lexical level of any text. The module "Lexicator" performs this task.

For syntactic analysis, "Evaluator" requires a collection of grammatical structures. Descriptors published in the Plan Curricular del Instituto Cervantes have been used to grade the different grammatical structures. These structures are identified and tracked throughout a Spanish text to obtain a set of indices. After this, the module "Sintactor" produces a level value for structures in a text, depending on the different indices defined, and also on the distribution of grammatical structures as PoS into the six CERF levels.

"Semantor" works to identify the semantic content of a text. It is able to group those texts dealing with the same, or similar, topics by computing semantic fields defined by the PCIC and, also, by applying LSA supported by a well constructed reference corpus. Both methods are reliable enough to discern if a given text is related to an expected subject or a specific thematic area.

The aim behind the construction of "Evaluator" was to provide a tool which learners of Spanish as a foreign language could use to track their development as writers in this language, inputting their texts and receiving automatic feedback in the form of a recognizable level. This would be useful not only on a personal level, but could help students to take decisions like whether to sit for an expensive written examination, for example. It is hoped that teachers and examiners too, in the future, will be able to use the tool, at least as a first stage in evaluating written texts, since it would give them an objective measure of the level of lexis and grammar. We hope, too, that more researchers will continue developing modules, and refining those which exist at present.

FUTURE RESEARCH DIRECTIONS

Advances in computational linguistics and natural language processing have opened up new ways to produce tools to apply automatic evaluation to second language writing. However, most advances have been made in English as a second/foreign language. Tools and systems for automatic evaluation of Spanish language are still under research. In our contribution, we have seen a number of problems that arose when working at the different levels of language. Here, we suggest some possible directions that should be taken in order to reach the goal.

At the lexical level, we have seen how the availability of leveled dictionaries is key to successful grading. Although the PCIC can be considered as the golden standard for leveling words and lemmas of a text, the number of lemmas is limited. Clearly, there is a need for more electronic dictionaries available to improve reliability in the leveling of texts. The best types of dictionaries would be those nested and targeted to

different levels of learning skills. Different layers of nested dictionaries would help to classify a word at the six levels of the CEFR. At the same time, glossaries to identify locutions and phrasal structures, usually working as collocations in a text are required. Another area of improvement for the method based on the range of percentages in the histogram of levels would be the production of leveled corpora. The method labeled K-2000 is really a very basic tool to distinguish between low levels of learning. The method based on the analysis of Zipf's law may require some tuning in the definition of the statistical parameters governing it. Besides this, the semantic ambiguity shown by some words should be solved by connecting the semantic module with the lexical one.

At the syntactic level, the collection of structures we have defined and leveled can be expanded to include both specific and general types of structures. These structures can be identified in the text by using the part of speech tag and a searching algorithm. This searching algorithm could be refined to identify discontinuous structures, those broken in the text when other elements are embedded in them. Grammatical agreement could be followed by processing the variations of the PoS referring to gender, person, or number. Besides this, the knowledge extracted from the analysis by "Evaluator" might serve as feedback to improve the accuracy of FreeLing. The definition of grammatical indices could be also adapted to identify different types of discourse, registers, and styles.

The work on semantic identification uses the semantic fields created by the PCIC. By using them, we can classify any text using a multidimensional vector with as many components as semantic fields. The process of finding the semantic field can be weighted by considering the semantic field of other words in a sentence. Here, the implementation of a fast algorithm to map esWordnet onto the text being analyzed would affect the semantic analysis of a text positively. And, finally, while the application of principal component analysis through LSA has allowed us to cluster texts into clouds, we believe it is still possible understand the semantics of any text much more deeply using this method. For example, it is possible to identify those lemmas whose distributions among texts are not comparable to the distribution of other lemmas. Such "anomalous" lemmas would be of interest to identify their specificity and their use as advanced level words within a collection of texts of a similar level.

REFERENCES

Alda, J., & Ferrero, P. (2007). *Análisis computacional de textos aplicados a una muestra de publicaciones en óptica. Algunas cuestiones de ciencia. Libro Homenaje al profesor Manuel Quintanilla* (pp. 655–667). Prensas Universitarias de Zaragoza.

Alderson, J. C. (2005). *Diagnosing foreign language proficiency: The interface between learning and assessment*. London, UK: Continuum International Publishing Group.

Atserias, J., Climent, S., Farreres, J., Rigau, G., & Rodríguez, H. (1997). Combining multiple methods for the automatic construction of multilingual WordNets. In *Proceedings of International Conference on Recent Advances in Natural Language Processing* (RANLP'97). Retrieved from http://nlp.lsi.upc.edu/papers-grup/papers/atserias97.pdf

Barrio, M. (2004). *Experimental study of textual development in Spanish students of English as a foreign language in Segundo de Bachillerato: Features of written register in compositions of argumentative genre.* Unpublished doctoral thesis, Departamento de Filología Inglesa, Universidad Autónoma de Madrid.

Biber, D., Conrad, S., & Reppen, R. (1998). *Corpus linguistics: Investigating language structure and use*. Cambridge University Press. doi:10.1017/CBO9780511804489

Bloor, T., & Bloor, M. (2004). *The functional analysis of English*. Oxford University Press.

Bordón Martínez, T. (2004). *La evaluación de la expresión oral y de la comprensión auditiva. Vademécum para la formación de profesores. Enseñar español como segunda lengua(L2)/lenguas extranjeras (LE)* (pp. 983–1001). Madrid, Spain: Sociedad General Española de Librería.

Bordón Martínez, T. (2006). *La evaluación de la lengua en el marco de E/L2: Bases y procedimientos*. Madrid, Spain: Cuadernos de didáctica del español/LE, Arco Libros-Muralla.

Burstein, J., Chodorow, M., & Leacock, C. (2004). Automated essay evaluation: The Criterion online writing service. *AI Magazine, 25*(3), 27-36. Retrieved June 11, 2011, from http://www.aaai.org/ojs/index.php/aimagazine/article/view/1774/1672

Cervantes, I. (2006). *Plan curricular del Instituto Cervantes. Niveles de referencia para el español. A1, A2, B1, B2, C1, C2*. Madrid, Spain: Biblioteca Nueva.

Checa García, I., & Lozano, C. (2002). *Los índices de madurez sintáctica de Hunt a la luz de las distintas corrientes generativistas. XVII Encuentro de la Asociación de Jóvenes Lingüistas (AJL)*. Alicante.

Chomsky, N. (1989). *El conocimiento del lenguaje: Su naturaleza, origen y uso*. Madrid, Spain: Alianza Editorial.

Council of Europe. (2005). *Reference level descriptions for national and regional languages (RDL): Draft guide for the production of RDL (Version 2)*. Strasbourg, France: Language Policy Division.

Crossley, S. A., McNamara, D. S., Weston, J., & McLain Sullivan, S. T. (2010). *The development of writing proficiency as a function of grade level: A linguistic analysis.* University of Memphis. Retrieved June 11, 2011, from http://wpal.memphis. edu/main/pdf/The_development_of_writing_Proficiency_tech_report.pdf

Cumming, A., Kantor, R., Baba, K., Eouanzoui, K., Erdosy, U., & James, M. (2006). Analysis of discourse features and verification of scoring levels for independent and integrated prototype written tasks for the new TOEFL. *Monograph Series,* April 2006. Educational Testing Services (ETS). Retrieved June 11, 2011, from http://www. ets.org/Media/Research/pdf/RR-05-13.pdf

da Cunha, I., San Juan, E., Torres-Moreno, J.-M., Lloberes, M., & Castellón, I. (2010b). Di-Seg: Un segmentador discursivo automático para el español. *Procesamiento del Lenguaje Natural, 45,* 1451-52. Retrieved June 11, 2011, from http://www.sepln.org/ojs/ojs2.2/index.php/pln/article/view/776

da Cunha, I., SanJuan, E., Torres-Moreno, J.-M., Lloberes, M., & Castellón, I. (2010a). Discourse segmentation for Spanish based on shallow parsing. *Lecture Notes in Computer Science, 6347,* 13-23. Retrieved June 11, 2011, from http://springerlink.com/content/r402013247484361/

da Cunha, I., & Torres-Moreno, J. M. (2010c). Automatic discourse segmentation: Review and perspectives. *International Workshop on African Human Languages Technologies* (pp. 17-20). Djibouti Institute of Science and Information Technologies, Djibouti. Retrieved June 11, 2011, from http://lia.univ-avignon.fr/fileadmin/documents/Users/Intranet/fich_art/paper_iria.pdf

DIALANG. (2009). *Test server.* Retrieved June 11, 2011, from http://www.lancs.ac.uk/research-enterprise/dialang/about

Dunteman, G. H. (1989). *Principal component analysis. Quantitative Applications in the Social Sciences, 69.* Sage Publications, Inc.

Ferrero, A., Alda, J., Campos, J., López-Alonso, J. M., & Pons, A. (2007). Principal component analysis of the photo-response non uniformity of a matrix detecto. *Applied Optics, 46,* 9–17. doi:10.1364/AO.46.000009

Ferrero, P. (2011). *Definición y análisis de parámetros lingüísticos cuantitativos para herramientas automáticas de evaluación aplicables al español como lengua extranjera.* Unpublished doctoral dissertation, Facultad de Filosofía y Letras de la Universidad Autónoma de Madrid, Madrid.

Gorman, S., & National Center for Education Statistics. (2010). *National assessment of educational progress writing computer-based assessment* (3 pp.). Brochure published by National Center for Education Statistics (NCES). Retrieved June 11, 2011, from http://nces.ed.gov/nationsreportcard/pdf/writing/2010470.pdf

Graesser, A. C., McNamara, D. S., & Louwerse, M. M. (2010). Methods of automated text analysis. In M. L. Kamil, P. D. Pearson, E. B. Moje, & P. Afflerbach (Eds.), *Handbook of reading research,* Vol. 4. Mahwah, NJ: Erlbaum. Retrieved June 11, 2011, from http://sites.google.com/site/graesserart/files/Methods-of-automated-text-analysis.pdf?attredirects=0

Grimes, D., & Warschauer, M. (2010). Utility in a fallible tool: A multi-site case study of automated writing evaluation. *Journal of Technology, Learning, and Assessment, 8*(6). Retrieved June 11, 2011, from http://escholarship.bc.edu/ojs/index.php/jtla/article/download/1625/1469

Ha, L. Q., Sicilia-García, E. I., Ming, J., & Smith, F. J. (2002). Extension of Zipf's law to words and phrases. In *Proceedings of the 19th International Conference on Computational Linguistics,* Vol. 1 (pp.1-6). Taipei, Taiwan.

Heinzle, J., & Haynes, J.-D. (2009). Multivariate functional connectivity between fine-grained cortical activation patterns. In *Eighteenth Annual Computational Neuroscience Meeting, 10*(1), 76. Berlin.

Hunt, K. W. (1965). *Grammatical structures written at three grade levels. Research Report.* National Council of Teachers of English.

Hunt, K. W. (1977). Early blooming and late blooming syntactic structures. In C. R. Cooper & L. Odell (Eds.), *Evaluating writing: Describing, measuring, judging* (pp. 99-104). National Council of Teachers of English (NCTE).

Jorge-Botana, G., León, J. A., Olmos, R., & Escudero, I. (2010). Latent semantic analysis parameters for essay evaluation using small-scale corpora. *Journal of Quantitative Linguistics, 17*(1), 1–29. doi:10.1080/09296170903395890

Kintsch, W. (2002). The potential of latent semantic analysis for machine grading of clinical case summaries. *Journal of Biomedical Informatics, 35*(1), 3–7. doi:10.1016/S1532-0464(02)00004-7

Konchady, M. (2006). *Text mining application programming.* Boston, MA: Charles River Media.

Landauer, T. K. S., Dennis, S., & Kintsch, W. (Eds.). (2007). *Handbook of latent semantic analysis.* Institute of Cognitive Science, University of Colorado.

Landauer, T. K., & Dumais, S. T. (1997). A solution to Plato's problem: The latent semantic analysis theory of the acquisition, induction, and representation of knowledge. *Psychological Review, 104*(2), 211–240. doi:10.1037/0033-295X.104.2.211

Landauer, T. K., Foltz, P. W., & Laham, D. (1998). Introduction to latent semantic analysis. *Discourse Processes, 25*, 259-284. Retrieved June 11, 2011, from http://www.knowledge-technologies. com/papers/IntroLSA1998.pdf

Lexile. (2012). *The Lexile framework for reading.* Retrieved March 25, 2012, from http://www.lexile.com/

López-Alonso, J. M., & Alda, J. (2002a). Bad pixel identification by means of the principal component analysis. *Optical Engineering (Redondo Beach, Calif.), 41*, 2152–2157. doi:10.1117/1.1497397

López-Alonso, J. M., & Alda, J. (2004a). Operational parametrization of the 1/f noise of a sequence of frames by means of the principal components analysis in focal plane arrays. *Optical Engineering (Redondo Beach, Calif.), 42*, 257–265.

López-Alonso, J. M., Alda, J., & Bernabéu, E. (2002b). Principal component characterization of noise for infrared images. *Applied Optics, 41*, 320–331. doi:10.1364/AO.41.000320

López-Alonso, J. M., Rico-García, J. M., & Alda, J. (2004b). Photonic crystal characterization by FDTD and principal component analysis. *Optics Express, 12*, 2176–2186. doi:10.1364/OPEX.12.002176

López Martínez, F. (1999). *El vocabulario básico de orientación didáctica.* Facultad de Letras de la Universidad de Murcia, España. Retrieved June 11, 2011 from http://digitum.um.es/xmlui/handle/10201/196

Lucas Cuesta, J. M., Fernández Martínez, F., Ferreiros López, J., López Ludeña, V., & San Segundo Hernández, R. (2010). Clustering of syntactic and discursive information for the dynamic adaptation of language models. *Procesamiento de Lenguaje Natural, 45*, 175-182. Retrieved June 11, 2011, from http://www.sepln.org/ojs/ojs-2.2/index.php/pln/article/view/790

Mann, C. W., & Thompson, A. S. (1988). Rhetorical structure theory: Toward a functional theory of text organization. *Text 8*(3), 243-281. Retrieved June 11, 2011, from http://discurso-uaq.weebly.com/uploads/2/7/7/5/2775690/mann02.pdf

Martín Uriz, A., & Whittaker, R. (Eds.). (2005). *La composición como comunicación: Una experiencia en las aulas de lengua inglesa en bachillerato.* Ediciones de la Universidad Autónoma de Madrid.

Martín Uriz, A. M., Hidalgo, L., & Whittaker, R. (2001). *Desarrollo y complejidad de la frase nominal en composiciones de estudiantes.* Paper presented at the XIX Congreso de la Asociación Española de Lingüística Aplicada.

McNamara, D. S., Louwerse, M. M., Cai, Z., & Graesser, A. (2006). *Coh-Metrix 2.0.* Retrieved June 11, 2011 from http://cohmetrix.memphis.edu/CohMetrixDemo/demo.htm

Metametrics. (2102). *Lexile framework for writing.* Retrieved March 25, 2012, from http://www.metametricsinc.com/lexile-framework-writing/

Miller, G. (1962). Some psychological studies of grammar. *The American Psychologist, 17*(11), 748–762. doi:10.1037/h0044708

Miller, G. A., & McKean, K. O. (1964). A chronometric study of some relations between sentences. *The Quarterly Journal of Experimental Psychology, 16*, 297–308. doi:10.1080/17470216408416385

Nation, P., & Kyongho, H. (1995). Where would general service vocabulary stop and special purposes vocabulary begin? *System, 23*(1), 35-41. Retrieved June 11, 2011, from www.victoria.ac.nz/lals/staff/publications/paul-nation/1995-Hwang-Special-purposes.pdf

Olloqui de Montenegro, L., & López Morales, H. (Eds.). (1991). *La investigación de la madurez sintáctica y la enseñanza de la lengua maternal. La enseñanza de español como lengua maternal* (pp. 113–132). Universidad de Puerto Rico.

Olmos, R., León, J., Escudero, I., & Jorge-Botana, G. (2009). Análisis del tamaño y especificidad de los corpus en la evaluación de resúmenes mediante el LSA. Un análisis comparativo entre LSA y jueces expertos. *Revista Signos, 42*(69), 71-81. Retrieved June 11, 2011, from http://www.scielo.cl/scielo.php?script=sci_arttext&pid=S0718-09342009000100004&lng=en&nrm=iso&ignore=.html

Oxford University Press. (2008). *Oxford 3000™ profiler.* Retrieved April 2, 2012, from http://www.oup.com/oald-bin/oxfordProfiler.pl

Oxford University Press. (2011). *Oxford 3000™ text checker.* Retrieved April 2, 2012, from http://oaadonline.oxfordlearnersdictionaries.com/oxford3000/oxford_3000_profiler.html

Padró, L. (2006). *FreeLing user manual 1.5.* Retrieved June 11, 2011, from http://www.smo.uhi.ac.uk/~oduibhin/oideasra/interfaces/userman15.pdf

Padró, L. (2009). *FreeLing user manual 2.1.* Retrieved June 11, 2011, from http://xavi.ivars.me/arxius/manuals/freeling/freeling-userman.pdf

Padró, L., Reese, S., Agirre, E., & Soroa, A. (2010). Semantic services in FreeLing 2.1: WordNet and UKB. *Principles, Construction, and Application of Multilingual Wordnets: Proceedings of the 5th Global Wordnet Conference*, Narosa. Retrieved June 11, 2011, from http://www.lsi.upc.edu/~nlp/papers/padro10a.pdf.

Page, E. B. (1966). Grading essays by computer: Progress report. In *Notes from the 1966 Invitational Conference on Testing Problems* (pp. 87-100).

Page, E. B. (1994). Computer grading of student prose, using modern concepts and software. *Journal of Experimental Education, 62*(2), 127–142. doi:10.1080/00220973.1994.9943835

Page, E. B., Poggio, J. P., & Keith, T. Z. (1997). Computer analysis of student essays: Finding trait differences in the student profile. *Annual Meeting of the American Educational Research Association: Vol. 8.* Retrieved June 11, 2011, from http://www.eric.ed.gov/ERICWebPortal/content-delivery/servlet/ERICServlet?accno=ED411316

Pérez Marín, D. R. (2007). *Adaptive computer assisted assessment of free-text students answers: An approach to automatically generate students conceptual models.* Doctoral dissertation, Escuela Politécnica Superior, Universidad Autónoma de Madrid. Madrid.

Rodríguez Fonseca, L. (1999). *Qué nos dicen y qué no nos dicen los índices de madurez sintáctica? Estudios de lingüística hispánica: homenaje a María Vaquero* (pp. 523–535). Universidad de Puerto Rico.

Sánchez Lobato, J., & Santos Gargallo, I. (2004). *Vademécum para la formación de profesores. Enseñar español como segunda lengua (L2)/ lengua extranjera (LE).* Madrid: Sociedad General Española de Librería.

sci_arttext&pid=S007117131999003400013&lng=es&nrm=iso

Sigley, R. (1997). Text categories and where you can stick them: A crude formality index. *International Journal of Corpus Linguistics, 2*(2), 199–237. doi:10.1075/ijcl.2.2.04sig

Thomas, M., Jaffe, G. J., Kincaid, P. J., & Stees, Y. (1992). *Learning to use simplified English: A preliminary study* (pp. 69–73). Technical Communication.

Torres González, A. N. (1993). *Madurez sintáctica en estudiantes no universitarios de la zona metropolitana de Tenerife.* Doctoral dissertation, Universidad de La Laguna. Tenerife.

UNED. (2011). *Level test.* Retrieved June 11, 2011, from http://portal.uned.es/portal/page?_pageid=93, 1336773 & _dad = portal & _schema = PORTAL

Véliz, M. (1988). Evaluación de la madurez sintáctica en el discurso escrito. [RLA]. *Revista de Lingüística Teórica y Aplicada, 26,* 105–140.

Véliz, M. (1999). Complejidad sintáctica y modo del discurso. *Estudios Filológicos, 34,* 181-192. Retrieved June 11, 2011, from http://www.scielo.cl/scielo.php?script=

Véliz, M. (2004). Procesamiento de estructuras sintácticas complejas en adultos mayores y adultos jóvenes. *Estudios Filológicos, 39,* 65-81. Retrieved June 11, 2011, from http://www.scielo.cl/scielo.php?pid=S0071-17132004003900004&script=sci_arttext

Venegas, R. (2006). La similitud léxico-semántica en artículos de investigación científica en español: Una aproximación desde el análisis semántico latente. *Revista Signos, 39*(60), 75-106. Retrieved June 11, 2011 from http://www.scielo.cl/scielo.php?script=sci_arttext&pid=S0718-09342006000100004&lng=es&nrm=iso

Venegas, R. (2009). Toward a method for assessing summaries in Spanish using LSA. In *Proceedings of the Twenty-Second International FLAIRS Conference* (pp. 310-311).

Wiktionary. (2008). *User: Matthias Buchmeier.* Retrieved March 25, 2012, from http://en.wiktionary.org/wiki/User:Matthias_Buchmeier#Spanish_frequency_list

Wolfe-Quintero, K., Inagaki, S., & Kim, H.-Y. (1998). *Second language development in writing: Measure of frequency, accuracy and complexity. Second Language Teaching and Curriculum Center.* University of Hawaii.

Ziempekis, D., & Gallopoulos, E. (2006). TMG: A Matlab toolbox for generating term-document matrices. In J. Kogan, C. Nicholas, & M. Teboulle (Eds.), *Grouping multidimensional data: Recent advances in clustering* (pp.187-210). Text Collections, Springer.

Zipf, G. (1932). *Selected studies of the principle of relative frequency in language.* Cambridge, MA: Harvard University Press.

ADDITIONAL READING

Attali, Y., Bridgeman, B., & Trapani, C. (2010). Performance of a generic approach in automated essay scoring. *Journal of Technology, Learning, and Assessment, 10*(3). Retrieved April 14, 2011 from http://escholarship.bc.edu/jtla/vol10/3/

Attali, Y., & Burstein, J. (2006). Automated essay scoring with e-rater® V.2. *Journal of Technology, Learning, and Assessment, 4*(3). Retrieved April, 14, 2012, from http://escholarship.bc.edu/jtla/vol4/3/

Enbar, N. (1999). *This is e-rater. It'll be scoring your essay today.* Retrieved January 15, 2010, from http://www.businessweek.com/bwdaily/dnflash/jan1999/nf90121d.htm

Graesser, A. C., McNamara, D. S., Louwerse, M. M., & Cai, Z. 2004. Coh-Metrix: Analysis of text on cohesion and language. *Behavior Research Methods, Instruments, and Computers, 36*, 193-202. Retrieved March 25, 2012, from http://cohmetrix.memphis.edu/CohMetrixWeb2/HelpFile2.htm

Mislevy, R. J., Behrens, J. T., Bennett, R. E., Demark, S. F., Frezzo, D. C., & Levy, R. … Winters, F. I., 2010. On the roles of external knowledge representations in assessment design. *Journal of Technology, Learning, and Assessment, 8*(2). Retrieved March 25, 2012, from http://www.jtla.org

O'Donnell, M. (2012). UAM corpus. Retrieved March 25, 2012, from http://www.wagsoft.com/CorpusTool/index.html

Wright, B. D., & Stenner, A. J. (1999). One Fish, two fish: Rasch Measures reading best. *Popular Measurement, 1*, 34–38.

KEY TERMS AND DEFINITIONS

Assessment/Evaluation: both terms mean to score a test analyzed by several indices or criteria.

CEFR Six Levels Scale: A1, A2 for lower and higher beginner stage, B1, B2 for lower and higher intermediate level, and C1, C2 for advanced and proficiency levels, respectively.

Index/Indices: Refer to parameters or notions to be computerized.

LSA/PCA: Refer to *Latent Semantic Analysis* and *Principal Components Analysis* respectively. Their methods are based on multivariate statistics.

PCIC: Plan Curricular del Instituto Cervantes.

PoS (Part of the Speech): A tag to identify grammatical categories such as noun, verb, adjective, adverb, etc.

Section 5
Devices and Simulators

Chapter 13

New Communication Technologies for Inclusive Education in and outside the Classroom

Ana Iglesias
Universidad Carlos III de Madrid, Spain

Juan Francisco López
Spanish Centre of Captioning and Audio Description, Spain

Belén Ruiz-Mezcua
Universidad Carlos III de Madrid, Spain

Diego Carrero Figueroa
Spanish Centre of Captioning and Audio Description, Spain

ABSTRACT

This chapter explores new communication technologies and methods for avoiding accessibility and communication barriers in the educational environment. It is focused on providing real-time captions so students with hearing disabilities and foreign students, among others, could participate in an inclusive way in and outside the classroom. The inclusive proposals are based on the APEINTA educational project, which aims for accessible education for all. The research work proposes the use of mobile devices for teacher and students in order to provide more flexibility using the APEINTA real-time captioning service. This allows using this service from anywhere and at anytime, not only in the classroom.

INTRODUCTION

Historically, students with functional diversity (students with special needs, students with disabilities, etc.) and foreign students have found accessibility and communication barriers while trying to access the educational system. For instance, most of the hearing impaired students do not regularly assist to the classroom because they usually face communication difficulties with the teacher or other classmates. Foreign students can also find those communication barriers when they do not have enough level in listening and understanding the language spoken in the classroom.

This chapter presents new ways of communication for inclusive education inside and outside

DOI: 10.4018/978-1-4666-2530-3.ch013

Copyright © 2013, IGI Global. Copying or distributing in print or electronic forms without written permission of IGI Global is prohibited.

the classroom. The research work is based on the inclusive proposals of the APEINTA project (Iglesias et al, 2009) which main aim is to provide accessibility in education, whether it is in or out of the classroom.

APEINTA is the result of collaboration among the Department of Computer Science and the Department of Electronic Technology, Universidad Carlos III, and the Spanish Centre of Captioning and Audiodescription (CESyA)[1]. This project was initially supported by the Ministry of Science and Innovation (2007 I+D projects - EA2008-0312) within the program of Studies and Analyses - Actions to Improve the Quality of Higher Education and the Activity of University Professors. Currently, the research presented in this chapter is being partially supported by France Telecom España S.A. and the MA2VICMR (S2009/TIC-1542), GEMMA (TSI-020302-2010-141) and SAGAS (TSI-020100-2010-184) research projects.

The APEINTA project is focused in two main inclusive proposals: the first one deals with eliminating the communication barriers that hearing impaired students or foreign students usually find in the classroom, providing automatic real-time captioning and other mechanisms to ease the communication with the teacher and others students; the second one also deals in providing an accessible Web learning platform with accessible digital resources, so every student can access them, with independence of the place where he is.

The work presented in this chapter is focused in the first proposal, studying new communication technologies for making easier the communication inside and outside the classroom among the course's participants (teachers and students), stimulating the inclusive and collaborative education.

Real-time captioning has been demonstrated as a very useful tool in educational environments for all students. Students with hearing impairments can literally read the teacher discourse and they can participate in an inclusive way during the class thanks to real-time captioning. Foreign students who do not completely understand the teacher

discourse are able to see the correct spelling in the captions, providing additional support to these students. But captioning can be useful for all the students, not only for students with disabilities or foreign students. For instance, real-time captioning can compensate noisy backgrounds, as it usually occurs in a classroom. Captioning is also useful in places where sound is not allowed, for instance, when the student is watching a pre-recorded or on-line video from the Web learning platform when travelling in public transport and he is not wearing earphones.

At this point, it is important to remark that APEINTA project has been awarded with the prize of the Spanish Confederation of Families of Deaf people (FIAPAS) in its 2009 call for applied research work related to hearing impairment in the area of education, where the first architecture of APEINTA was presented. It has also won the delegates award of the 2011 edition of the Web Accessibility Challenge in 8th International Cross-disciplinary Conference on Web Accessibility (W4A'11[2]), sponsored by Microsoft, where the new communication mechanism in APEINTA and its new architecture described in this chapter were presented.

BACKGROUND

During last decades, educators, pedagogues, psychologists, scientists, researchers and, in general, people from very different disciplines related to education have tried to achieve anti-discriminatory education environments according to the current laws related with inclusive education. These laws try to ensure an inclusive education system at all levels as a right of persons with functional diversity, rejecting segregation and discrimination.

There exist international and national laws which regulate the inclusive education. For instance, internationally, the normative of the United Nations remarks that students have to be educated in the least restrictive environment, according to the *UN Convention of the Rights of the Child* (UN, 1989), the *UNESCO Salamanca Statement* (UNESCO, 1994) and the *UN Convention on the Rights of Persons with Disabilities* (UN, 2006).

Traditionally, sign language interpreters have been the most common resource applied in order to improve the deaf students' inclusion. However, nowadays not every student with hearing disability uses sign language, thus signing does not provide deaf students full access to the classroom information (Marschark et al, 2005). Moreover, the high costs associated to this method it is not a cheap method of accessibility in the classroom.

Nowadays, some researchers around the world are working in lectures transcription based on Automatic Speech Recognition (ASR) in order to ease the access to the information in the classroom to students with hearing disabilities. Some previous works have demonstrated the benefits of speech technologies for students with disabilities (Newell & Gregor, 2000; Bain et al., 2005; Wald, 2004). The most relevant and oldest work using speech technologies in education is the Liberated Learning Consortium (LLC) (Leitch and MacMillan, 2001), in collaboration with IBM[3]. They developed ViaScribe software based on the ASR ViaVoice (Bain et al., 2005). Another interesting project is the Spoken Lecture Processing Project which was initially designed for video indexing (Glass et al., 2004).

Most of the current works in transcribing use ViaVoice system, although we can find in the literature other initiatives as VUST (Kheir and Way, 2007) from the Villanova University, which uses the Microsoft Speech Recognition Engine (MSRE). On the other hand, other initiatives developed their own ASR system instead of using commercial ones. That is the case of iCAMPUS (MIT, 2003) developed in the M.I.T. or the CHIL Project (Lamel et al, 2006).

Most of the research works in ASR for educational environments are developed for English language, but currently research works in other languages are emerging in education, as the LEC-TRA Project (Trancoso et al., 2008) in Portuguese, which demonstrated the utility of speech technologies on recorded media, like videos or audio files; The eScribe project (Bumbalek et al., 2010) in Czech or the APEINTA project in Spanish (Iglesias et al., 2009) among others, which presents some of its last research works in this chapter.

APEINTA Project is the first initiative in real-time transcription and captioning of spoken Spanish lectures. Moreover, it also provides students with different methods to see transcriptions within individual devices (Personal Digital Agendas –PDA-, laptops, etc.) or in a projection screen for all the audience. Furthermore, APEINTA can be considered as one of the few projects that pay attention to speech problems of the students. Text To Speech (TTS) tools are used in the classroom, so foreign language students or students with speaking difficulties are able to participate in the class with their comments or questions thanks to this service. Moreover, an accessible e-learning platform with accessible pedagogical resources is provided in this inclusive educational project.

This chapter is focused in the study of new communication technologies for avoiding accessibility barriers in educational environments and it is based on the APEINTA real-time captioning service. The works presented in this chapter are centered on analyzing the utility of the use personal devices for interacting with this APEINTA service, from the teacher side and from the student side.

The use of mobile phones by the teacher is proposed to speak through and connect to the APEINTA real-time captioning service in order to be transcribed and received by the students. Previous researchers in voice recognition have developed different applications in mobile phones relying on embedded ASR (Vargas and Kiss, 2008), as software for dialing, phone book search, command-and-control, etc., but most of them were based on recognizing isolated speech, this is, single words included in a database of the domain, or discontinuous speech, full sentences separated by silences. This kind of ASR based on isolated or discontinuous speech are easier to develop and lighter than the ASRs based on continuous speech, composed by naturally spoken sentences (Karat et al., 2007). Even though this difficulties, continuous voice recognition systems are been used in commercial projects, as the Hammilton Cap Tel phones (Endres, 2009). This new commercial service allows users with hearing loss to listen to and read captions through the use of a specially designed CapTel phone. Captions appear on the CapTel phone display screen in nearly real time, but not in real-time because of the high complexity of the voice recognition algorithms that implies a variable delay as a side effect. Moreover, this service is only in English language and requires a special device to use it.

That is why in this chapter we propose to send the voice signal from the mobile phone to a separated server where an ASR for continuous speech recognition is installed, instead of embedding the ASR in the mobile phone itself. eScribe project (Bumbalek, 2010) proposed something similar for the Czech language. They proposed a first approach to use human transcribers and later combining ASRs with human editors for error fixing, because ASR systems for Czech languages are not very advanced yet to provide enough accuracy levels for the service. In this chapter, the study is done with Spanish language in order to provide ubiquitous real-time captioning technically based on IP streaming and displaying the transcription online, available on a web page, so the captions can be accessed from any student device with 3G or Wi-Fi connections.

It has been also studied the usefulness of tablets for the students to receive the captions and transcriptions on them. Among the recent devices that have been made available in the market, tablets are creating a great impact and almost every month a new device is announced that goes beyond previous ones in mobility and performance. It is reasonable to foresee that in the next future most people will own and use tablets in their daily life. They would carry them

permanently and even elder people would also be familiar with those devices. That is why we chose this personal device for this work.

In the last years, tablet-PCs and pen-based technology have had a great impact on education environments (Berque et al., 2010). In many cases, this new technology devices have been used to overcome the obstacles that traditional instructional methods show for effective learning and teaching in engineering and computer science courses, as "text-based or static mediums to convey equation- and graphics-heavy concepts, a disconnect between theoretical lecture presentations and applied laboratory or homework exercises, and a difficulty in promoting collaborative activities that more accurately reflect an engineering approach to problem solving" (Huettel et al., 2007). This kind of devices offer the possibility to integrate technologies and this is the reason why the Spanish Centre of Subtitling and Audiodescription (CESyA)[4] has been involved in different research projects to develop applications and interaction models over them, applied to mitigate hearing or visual impairments in different environments (theatres, museums, education, etc.) (DeCastro et al., 2011). One of these projects is the APEINTA project presented here.

SYSTEM ARCHITECTURE

The objective of APEINTA is to provide an inclusive education for all students, regardless of any kind of disability they may have. It is a technological bet for inclusive education. This project proposes the use of new technologies in the fields of computing and electronic technology to overcome the barriers in the access to education and learning that unfortunately they still exist in the classroom.

The APEINTA project was initially centered on two different inclusive proposals: one focused in providing an inclusive environment within the classroom and the other addressing inclusive

Figure 1. Initial architecture of APEINTA

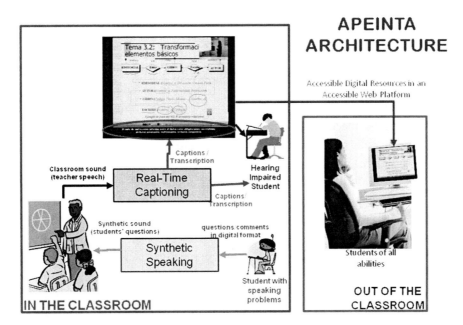

education outside the classroom (Iglesias et al, 2009). Figure 1 shows the first architecture of APEINTA project, where these proposals were well differentiated. Now, both proposals are explained in detail:

1. **In the classroom:** In this inclusive proposal two mechanisms are used to overcome the communication barriers that still exist today in the classroom. One is the application of automatic speech recognition mechanisms (ASR: Automatic Speech Recognition) to provide real-time transcriptions, useful for all those students who have temporary or permanent hearing impairment. This service is called *real-time captioning service* (or transcription service) and it deals with eliminating the difficulties that hearing impaired students or foreign students, for instance, usually find in the classroom. The other is the use of speech synthesis mechanisms (TTS: Text To Speech) to provide support for oral communication between teacher and students. This service is called

synthetic speaking service and it is useful for eliminating the communication barriers that foreign students or students with speaking problems, for instance, find in the classroom. It allows these students to participate in an inclusive mode in the classroom with their questions or comments through this service, avoiding embarrassment or disabilities problems among others.

2. **Outside the classroom.** This proposal provides an accessible education platform in the Web where students can access accessible digital resources at any time with independence of the place or device where they are accessing the information.

This first architecture of APEINTA presented some limitations for teacher and students that we wanted to tackle in this research work. This work is mainly centered in the real-time captioning service, but the results obtained in this work can be easily applied in the future to other services, as the synthetic speaking service.

The main limitation of the captioning service was that the first prototype of APEINTA was intended only to overcome the communication barriers inside the classroom, but is this service useful for all the communication sceneries between the teacher and the students? For instance, what happens if a student with hearing disabilities has a question and he wants to go to the teacher's office for a tutorship? The teacher and the student could find communication problems and the real-time captioning could be also useful in this scenario. It is not the only one and many other use cases can rise during the interactions between teacher and student.

Therefore, we are currently studying new communication methods between the teacher and the captioning service of APEINTA, so the teacher would not need to be physically connected with the APEINTA server, allowing him to use it anywhere.

Moreover, we are studying new communication methods for the students, analyzing if their own personal devices (smart phones, mobile phones, tablets, etc.) can be used for receiving the captions, so they do not need to carry specific and sometime heavy equipments (personal computers, laptop, etc.) to anywhere they could need the captions. They only requirement is the installation of a specific light software in their devices or simply connect to the captioning service through Internet.

Next sections detail these research works carried out during the lasts years in the framework of the APEINTA project.

NEW COMMUNICATION METHODS FOR THE TEACHER

When we talk about providing accessibility in the classrooms as a really crucial and special environment due to its strictly direct relation to people's individual and social development, we are focusing in the way people interact and share information to detect potential barriers which could difficult that information flow.

New communication methods are analyzed in this chapter in order to provide an alternative channel differing from the classical audio one. This chapter is centered in how to offer to the students other ways to receive the information without the need of hearing the teacher's voice.

In the communication process, we can detect two relevant sides to be taken into account: the transmitter and the receiver. In this chapter, in order to limit the problem to explain it more easily, we will focus in magisterial classes, were the teacher assumes the role of information sender and the students assume the role of information receivers. Therefore, these two sides are the ones that will interact with any intermediate system inserted between them to provide an alternative channel.

In previous phases of the real-time captioning service of APEINTA, the teacher had to be physically placed in the classroom because this service was created just to be used into the classroom. This was required because the Automatic Speech Recognition (ASR) software used in this service of APEINTA requires a microphone connected to the computer where it was installed to receive the audio stream from the teacher's voice. Figure 2 shows the initial architecture of this service. This restriction implies several problems that increase the deployment costs and requires some effort from the teacher to use it, because this architecture reduces de range of use of the system to the microphone's one. Therefore, each system deployment required a computer in the classroom, maybe even a network connection if the class is intended to be accessible outside the classroom, and if we think about it, this avoids many possibilities of remote administration in fail cases, requiring a person to go to the classroom to solve any problem. Those are not desirable situations with associated costs that are potentially removable if we move the real-time captioning server outside the classroom.

Therefore, one of our main aims in this research work is to decouple the microphone and the speech recognition audio input. In order to do it, we have studied how to replace the usual microphone

Figure 2. Previous architecture of the APEINTA real-time transcription system

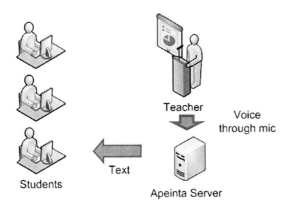

audio input, directly plugged in the computer, with a device with audio streaming capability through the network. Obviously, this solution will imply that the system will need an Internet connection with enough bandwidth to receive an audio stream but this new configuration does not reduce the number of sceneries where the system can work. This is, if the room where the system is going to be placed does not have an Internet connection or if it has any problem to receive remote live audio through the network, it still could work with the classical architecture of the service (with a high quality microphone plugged in the computer).

At this point, it is decided to use IP stream voice with the APEINTA captioning service, where the speech recognition system is working. Now it is time to decide what sort of device is better to be used by the teacher for that approach. Some years ago, there could be only a few options for it, but nowadays we have many devices to do the job (tablets, smart phones, etc.), all of them ensuring that our prototype could fulfill the requirements needed for APEINTA (good voice signal, etc.).

The use of smart phones was the choice to develop our application because this sort of devices is widely used and nowadays most of the people have one of them in their pockets as a personal device. Thus, teachers would not need other spe-

cific hardware for interacting with the service. iOS, Android, Windows Phone, Blackberry OS, etc. are just some of the most obvious options in terms of mobile operative systems to develop the application. At this point, to implement the first prototype of this new channel of communication we established our criteria to choose one of them: it is better if to paid licenses are not required for development; the system should have good market coverage and expectations for the next years; it should have an streaming API or, at least, capabilities to do so; and finally, it should use a well known programming language and IDE to reduce the development time. With that premises, we finally developed an application over Android, this is, in Java language, based in open source projects were its only interface was the one that allows the user to configure the connection with the APEINTA service, shown in Figure 3.

Therefore, the new architecture of the captioning service of APEINTA is detailed in Figure 4, where a mobile phone can be used for the communication teacher-APEINTA_captioning_ser-

Figure 3. Mobile application interface for configuring the APEINTA service connection

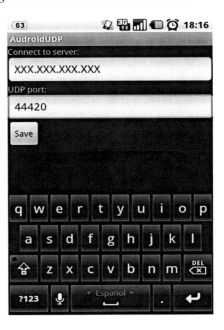

Figure 4. New architecture of the APEINTA real-time transcription system

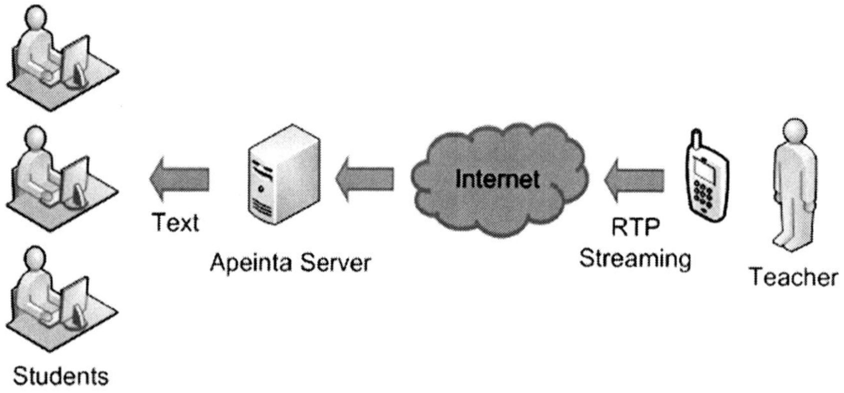

vice by using the Realtime Transport Protocol (RTP) for transmitting streaming data.

With this new application, the teacher could stream his voice from his mobile phone to the system but there is still something to do to make the whole system work. The APEINTA server's interface must be adapted to receive that audio stream and redirect that input to the Automatic Speech Recognition software of the captioning service. At this point, the decisions taken for the implementation of this first prototype were completely dependent on the way the ASR software is configured in APEINTA to receive the audio.

In our case, we used Dragon NaturallySpeaking as our ASR engine in APEINTA due to the characteristics of its API to develop applications with it. However, one of its main disadvantages for the APEINTA system is that it can only run one recognition engine per CPU so we cannot apply multitasking in our system to use one server to process many audio streams. Actually, this problem is common for most of commercial ASRs. This is why we are currently working on looking for new solutions to this problem: studying different ASRs, even studying the possibility of developing our own multi-task ASR.

Moreover, another difficulty found related to the use of Dragon Naturally Speaking client was that this ASR software is configured to receive the audio through directly plugged-in microphones, not through the network. This implies that it is necessary to find a workaround to redirect the input to the software. In order to overcome this problem, in our first implementation, we chose a mixed hardware/software solution to receive the stream by using a player to receive the stream coming from the network and decode the audio to play it through an audio card. That card, then, would be connected to the system as if it were the microphone, making the audio input available to be chosen by Dragon Naturally Speaking.

Finally, we obtained a system where the teacher is able to send his voice over an RTP streaming in any mobile network through Pulse-Code Modulation (PCM) or Adaptive Multi-Rate (AMR) audio encoding methods. So it is important to remark that it could be also used with low bandwidth Internet connections to the transcription server. That is to say, it allows using the captioning service through a connected screen or through an HTTP connection.

With the architecture exposed, it must be explained that some terms had to be taken into account to make the system work because, it is a great advantage to replace the microphone by a mobile phone and give the system a huge flexibility to be accessed but streaming audio from a mobile phone can imply coverage and bandwidth problems while being used. Knowing that, several low bandwidth audio encoders with several configurations were used during the implementation process to find which one offered a satisfactory bandwidth – quality ratio to be included in the application. The low bandwidth requirement is an obvious need in order to reduce the number of audio glitches in some environments but it has always to be in mind that it is mandatory to have enough audio quality in the receiver, this is, after decoding, as the audio stream has to be injected into the speech recognition system.

USE OF NEW PERSONAL DEVICES FOR THE STUDENTS

Once the problem of communicating the teacher with the system providing an alternate way to the classical microphone plugged into the computer, it is time to pay attention to the communication between the students and the captioning service of APEINTA because there are several different ways to provide the information contained in the server as a result from the speech recognition process usually applying caption formatting to improve their readability.

If we attend to the way the people is able to see the captions, this is, to the place where the captions are being showed, we can distinguish between open captioning and closed captioning.

Open captioning is the term applied to the way of showing the text to be read by several people simultaneously, for example, projected on a big screen during an event. This is often an easy and cheap solution to provide captioning in events because it only needs one device to show the captions for the whole crowd of users but, by the other hand, it can cause distraction or it can hide graphic information for all those ones who just don't need it. Thus, for all those environments or events where open captioning can be confusing, distracting, or simply, undesired, closed captioning must be raised as the alternate choice.

Closed captioning is the other option we have while showing captions in an event, or more specifically for this case, in a class. This sort of captioning works as an individual resource for each person, showed in a personal device as a computer, laptop, mobile phone, tablet, etc. or definitely, in any screen intended to be used by only one user at each time. By using these personal devices, students in difficulties as hearing disabilities or foreign language problems can access to the transcript generated in real-time while the teacher speaks. This configuration implies higher costs because it requires a device for each caption viewer and a system with caption sending and receiving capabilities but it solves the some open captioning disadvantages and does not require any amendment in the classroom or using any additional equipment. The key idea of open and closed captioning is that there is no solution fitting every event, environment or set of users. There will be some events more thought to include open captioning but we could find some others were closed captioning will be the best option. With this in mind, it was chosen to include both options in APEINTA so it could cover any situation 'ad-hoc'.

For the sake of solving the lack of accessibility at education, this research work was developed in order to study the use of tablets, this new personal device in this scenario. Previously smartphones, captioning glasses, laptops, and personal computers were studied as students' devices for receiving captions in the APEINTA project (Jiménez et al., 2010).

In order to implement a first prototype of this approximation, the iPad tablet was selected for it. The iPad device was chosen because it provides a 9.7" LED-Backlit screen with 1024x768 pixels resolution. This feature allows designing a user interface with larger fonts and buttons than the ones designed for conventional smartphones interfaces. Besides, it also offers an orientation sensor which enables screen adjustment for the application interface according to the device orientation.

The application was developed giving more priority its usability, looking for a simple and intuitive use, following the graphic and compositional guidelines for the iOS operating system. A special emphasis was taken on the accessibility of its interface in order to ensure the compatibility with the iOS native accessibility functions (i.e. screen reader). The application was also designed to take advantage of the iPad capabilities. This developed application also adapts its interface to both vertical and horizontal orientations of the device to respectively display the transcription like a continuous text blocks queue or like successive captions. The images in Figure 5 and 6 show both operating modes respectively.

In captioning mode, the application displays the classic couple of text lines which makes easier the tracking of the teacher's current speech easier. By the other hand, in transcription mode, the application shows a global view of the speech. By this way, every new text block is placed at the end of the page and the user can access not only to the current speech but to the previous context too.

As additional feature, the application provides the capability of managing the class notes

Figure 5. iPad application for receiving the real-time transcription: Transcription mode

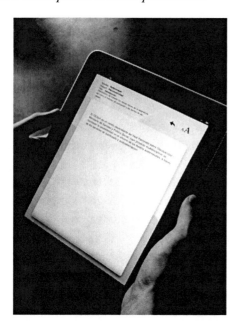

by saving all the text received from the classes, making them accessible once the class is finished. Hence, a new educational resource is provided complementarily to the usual class notes, so the student can focus in the information provided and not only in transcribing what is being said during the session.

FUTURE RESEARCH DIRECTIONS

Although this research work is focused on the APEINTA real-time captioning service, new communication technologies and methods can be analyzed for the other services of APEINTA like, for instance,, designing these services to be based on the cloud computing paradigm.

Dealing with the teacher and students' devices, a comparison of which are the preferred devices for being used with the APEINTA services is recommended.

The iPad application introduced in this chapter is prepared only for receiving captions, but it can be easily extended to include the text-to-speech functionality of APEINTA and better interaction and usability capabilities. That is, students could send textual messages to the teacher via the iPad and they would be later reproduced with computer voice in the teacher's device. This new function-

Figure 6. iPad application for receiving the real-time transcription: Captioning mode

ality would allow taking part of the class in an inclusive way to students that could not assist physically. For instance, this functionality is very useful for students that are in the hospital.

Dealing with the APEINTA real-time captioning service, the use of the Dragon Naturally Speaking ASR software in this service implies a big disadvantage that we want to solve. This ASR, as it occurs with most of the ASR software for continuous speaking recognition, only allows one recognition server per CPU. It is a single task application. This lack in the ASR software limits tremendously the functionality of the real-time captioning service. For instance, it is prepared for transcribe only the speech of one person. This is not a problem for magisterial classes, were the teacher is almost the only speaker, but when the aim is to transcribe everything in the classroom (questions, comments and participation from all the students, not only from the teacher), it becomes a big problem. That is why we are working on analyzing other ASRs for continuous speaking or even in developing our own ASR software.

Moreover, we are studying the inclusion of other accessible proposals in the APEINTA project.

CONCLUSION

This chapter proposes new communications methods for inclusive education in and outside the classroom, which are mostly based on the captioning service of the APEINTA project, which main functionality is to convert the teacher's speech to captions. This APEINTA service is focused on removing the accessibility and communication barriers that students with hearing disabilities or foreign students, for instance, usually find in the classrooms.

The APEINTA real-time captioning service was initially created to be used inside the classroom, but in this chapter its functionality is extended thanks to the proposal of alternative communication methods for both teacher and students in order to provide ubiquitous real-time captioning from anywhere and at anytime.

On the one hand, we propose the use mobile devices by the teacher while using the APEINTA captioning service. Previously in APEINTA, the teacher needed to be physically near the system server because he needed a plugged-in microphone to use this service. Currently, thanks to the use of mobile devices studied in this chapter, the teacher can use its own mobile phone by installing a light application to connect with the APEINTA captioning service, just requiring an internet connection.

On the other hand, the usefulness of tablet-PCs as personal devices for the students to receive the captions is studied. The portability, screen size and performance characteristics of this new device and the great impact and acceptation that it has had among the students during the lasts months make it a good option as student device for receiving captions.

REFERENCES

Bain, K., Basson, S., & Wald, M. (2005). Speech recognition in university classrooms: Liberated learning project. In *Proceedings of 5th Annual International ACM Conference on Assistive Technologies* (pp. 192-196)

Berque, D. A., & Konkle, L. M. (2010). *The impact of tablet PCs and pen-based technology on education: New horizons*. Purdue University Press, 2010. ISBN: 9781557535313

Bumbalek, Z., Zelenka, J., & Kencl, L. (2010). E-Scribe: Ubiquitous real-time speech transcription for the hearing-impaired. In *Proceedings of the 12th International Conference on Computers Helping People with Special Needs, ICCHP'10,* (pp. 160-168).

De Castro, M., Ruiz, B., Sanchez-Pena, J. M., Crespo, A. G., & Iglesias, A. (2011). *Tablets helping elderly and disabled people.* Ambient Assisted Living Forum 2011 (AAL 2011).

Endres, F. (2009). Americans with Disabilities Act paved the way for CapTel and Web CapTel. *The Hearing Journal, 62*(3), 48–50.

Glass, J., Hazen, T., Hetherington, L., & Wang, C. (2004). Analysis and processing of lecture audio data: Preliminary investigations. *Proceedings of Human Language Technology NAACL, Speech Indexing Workshop* (pp. 9-12).

Huettel, L. G., Forbes, J., Franzoni, L., Malkin, R., Nadeau, J., Nightingale, K., & Ybarra, G. A. (2007). *Transcending the traditional: Using tablet PCs to enhance engineering and computer science instruction. Frontiers in Education Conference - Global Engineering: Knowledge Without Borders. Opportunities Without Passports.*

Iglesias, A., Moreno, L., Revuelta, P., & Jiménez, J. (2009). APEINTA: A Spanish educational project aiming for inclusive education in and out of the classroom. In *Proceedings of the 14th Annual SIGSE Conference on Innovation & Technology in Computer Science Education (ITICSE'09), 41*(3), 393-393.

Jiménez, J., Revuelta, P., Iglesias, A., & Moreno, L. (2010). Evaluating the use of ASR and TTS technologies in the classroom: The APEINTA project. *ED-MEDIA 2010-World Conference on Educational Multimedia, Hypermedia & Telecommunications, AACE* (pp. 3976-3980).

Karat, C. M., Vergo, J., & Nahamoo, D. (2007). Conversational interface technologies. In Jacko, J. A. (Ed.), *The human-computer interaction handbook: Fundamentals, evolving technologies, and emerging applications (human factors and ergonomics)*. Lawrence Erlbaum Associates Inc. doi:10.1201/9781410615862.ch19

Kheir, R., & Way, T. (2007). Inclusion of deaf students in computer science classes using real-time speech transcription. In *Proceedings of ACM SIGCSE Conference on Innovation and Technology in Computer Science Education* (ITiCSE'07), (pp. 261–265).

Lamel, L., Bilinski, E., Adda, G., Gauvain, J., & Schwenk, H. (2006). The LIMSI RT06s lecture transcription system. *Proceedings of the 5ᵗʰ International Workshop Machine Learning for Multimodal Interaction*, (pp. 457-468).

Leitch, D., & MacMillan, T. (2001). *Liberated learning project year II report: Improving access for persons with disabilities in higher education using speech recognition technology.* Nova Scotia, Canada: Saint Mary's University.

Marschark, M., Sapere, P., Convertino, C., & Seewagen, R. (2005). Access to postsecondary education through sign language interpreting. *Journal of Deaf Studies and Deaf Education, 10*, 38–50. doi:10.1093/deafed/eni002

MIT. (2003). *ICAMPUS projects.* Spoken Lecture Processing. Retrieved from http://icampus.mit.edu/projects/SpokenLecture.shtml

Newell, A. F., & Gregor, P. (2000). *User sensitive inclusive design— In search of a new paradigm.* CUU '00. Retrieved from http://doi.acm.org/10.1145/355460.355470

Trancoso, I., Martins, R., Moniz, H., Mata, A. I., & Viana, M. C. (2008). The LECTRA Corpus – Classroom lecture transcriptions in European Portuguese. *Proceedings of the Sixth International Language Resources and Evaluation* (LREC'08).

UNESCO. (1994). *The Salamanca statement and framework for action on special needs.* World Conference on Special Needs Education: Access and Quality, Salamanca, Spain. Retrieved from http://www.unesco.org/education/pdf/SALAMA_E.PDF

United Nations. (1989). *Convention on the rights of the child*. Retrieved from http://www.unesco.org/education/pdf/CHILD_E.PDF (retrieved on January, 2012).

United Nations. (2006). *Convention on the rights of persons with disabilities*. Retrieved from http://www.un.org/disabilities/documents/convention/convoptprot-e.pdf

Varga, I., & Kiss, I. (2008). Speech recognition in mobile phones. In Tan, Z.-H., & Lindberg, B. (Eds.), *Automatic speech recognition on mobile devices and over communication networks* (pp. 301–325). Retrieved from. doi:10.1007/978-1-84800-143-5_14

Wald, M. (2004). Using automatic speech recognition to enhance education for all students: Turning a vision into reality. *34th ASEE/IEEE Frontiers in Education Conference*, (pp. 22-25).

Karat, C. M., Vergo, J., & Nahamoo, D. (2007). Conversational interface technologies. In Jacko, J. A. (Ed.), *The human-computer interaction handbook: Fundamentals, evolving technologies, and emerging applications (human factors and ergonomics)*. Lawrence Erlbaum Associates Inc. doi:10.1201/9781410615862.ch19

Kheir, R., & Way, T. (2007). Inclusion of deaf students in computer science classes using real-time speech transcription. In *Proceedings of ACM SIGCSE Conference on Innovation and Technology in Computer Science Education* (ITiCSE'07), (pp. 261–265).

Varga, I., & Kiss, I. (2008). Speech recognition in mobile phones. In Tan, Z.-H., & Lindberg, B. (Eds.), *Automatic speech recognition on mobile devices and over communication networks* (pp. 301–325). Retrieved from. doi:10.1007/978-1-84800-143-5_14

ADDITIONAL READING

Berque, D. A., & Konkle, L. M. (2010). *The impact of tablet PCs and Pen-based technology on education: New horizons*. Purdue University Press.

Bumbalek, Z., Zelenka, J., & Kencl, L. (2010). E-Scribe: Ubiquitous real-time speech transcription for the hearing-impaired. In *Proceedings of the 12th International Conference on Computers Helping People with Special Needs, ICCHP'10*, (pp. 160-168).

Iglesias, A., Moreno, L., Revuelta, P., & Jiménez, J. (2009). APEINTA: A Spanish educational project aiming for inclusive education In and Out of the classroom. In *Proceedings of the 14th Annual SIGSE Conference on Innovation & Technology in Computer Science Education (ITICSE'09)*, *41*(3), 393-393.

KEY TERMS AND DEFINITIONS

Automatic Speech Recognition (ASR): Software that automatically converts spoken words (an audio speech) into readable text.

Inclusive Education: Education in equal conditions for all the students, nevertheless of their functionalities, capabilities or special needs.

Mobile Phone: It is a personal device which allows making and receiving phone calls over a radio link.

Personal Device: It is a device which belongs to an individual or family. In this chapter, we refer to electronic personal devices which allow students to receive the real-time captioning (mobile phone, laptops, tablets, smart phones, etc.) or which allow the teacher to connect with the APEINTA captioning service.

Real-Time Captioning: Is a captioning method in which captions are simultaneously prepared and transmitted at the time of the speech.

RTP Connection: It is a connection which uses the Real-time Transport Protocol (RTP). This protocol provides data delivery in real-time and it can be implemented over both TCP and UDP protocols.

Tablet: It is an electronic personal device. It is a kind of new mobile computer of reduced size and weight.

ENDNOTES

[1]   Spanish Centre of Captioning and Audiodescription (CESyA): www.cesya.es

[2]   2011 W4A Conference. 8th International Cross-Disciplinary Conference on Web Accessibility: http://www.w4a.info/2011/index.shtml

[3]   IBM enterprise (http://www.ibm.com/us/en/)

[4]   CESyA: Spanish Centre of Subtitling and Audiodescription. http://www.cesya.es

Chapter 14
Educational Applications of Clickers in University Teaching

Francisco J. Liébana-Cabanillas
University of Granada, Spain

Myriam Martínez-Fiestas
University of Granada, Spain

Francisco Rejón-Guardia
University of Granada, Spain

ABSTRACT

The purpose of this chapter is to contextualize the situation of the use of remote response devices or clickers in education and identify the benefits that tools such as Q-Click software can bring to university teaching and to different groups of students. To fulfil this objective, the authors conducted research in classes with students who rated 149 different aspects related to the use of such software, including its use in class, benefits, and implications for follow-up assessment of the subject, attention, and class quality. This information was then compared to other groups of students studying the same subject who did not use clickers in class. The findings confirm the original proposal verifying the usefulness of these tools in university teaching for the important consequences for students and teachers.

INTRODUCTION

The real interest of young people in Information Technology and Communication (ICT) is a phenomenon that has been widely studied in scientific literature because of its implications and social consequences. It is common knowledge that today's youth have the highest rates of use of computers, Internet access, email, and mobile phones, among other technologies (*National In-*

stitute of Statistics, INE, 2011). A college education should therefore use these tools to improve processes and outcomes of student learning (Wan et al., 2007) to meet the targets set in the European Higher Education Area (EHEA).

The analysis of the implementation of ICT in teaching began several decades ago as its advantages, which reinforced the educational level of students, were recognized. Ferro et al. (2009) summarizes the main advantages of using ICT in university teaching. ICTs:

DOI: 10.4018/978-1-4666-2530-3.ch014

Copyright © 2013, IGI Global. Copying or distributing in print or electronic forms without written permission of IGI Global is prohibited.

1. Break space-time barriers in teaching and learning activities.
2. Create open and flexible learning processes.
3. Improve communication between the various players in the teaching and learning process.
4. Personalize education.
5. Provide quick access to information.
6. Facilitate interaction with information.
7. Raise the interest level and motivation of students.
8. Improve educational effectiveness.
9. Allow the teacher more time for other tasks.
10. Support follow-up learning.

To date there have been many innovations that have been implemented in teaching: (i) multimedia tools (Alférez et al., 2010), (ii) whiteboards (Murillo, 2010), (iii) web sites (Gates, 2011), (iv) wikis (Ortiz de Urbina and Mora, 2011), (v) forums (Benitez et al., 2011), (vi) Mobile Learning (Liaw et al., 2009), (vii) second life (Checa, 2010) and even (viii) microblogging networks (Liébana-Cabanillas et al., 2011).

The use of remote response devices, electronic voting systems, systems and audience response clickers, began in the sixties (Chafer, 2009), although it was not until the nineties when their use began to flourish. Although these devices were originally used for management meetings, opinion surveys, and conventions, etc. (Ruiz-Jimenez et al., 2010), such tools are widely used in some American universities (Harvard, Massachusetts-Amherst, Colorado, etc.). Recently, these devices are also being used in Spanish universities (Navarra, Barcelona, Granada, Seville, Madrid, etc.) since remote response devices reinforce the quality of education, and improve student performance and the productivity of teachers.

These are devices that allow students to obtain information found in the classroom in an agile, fast and simple via a transmitter (clicker) and receiver system connected by infrared or Bluetooth, to communicate and record responses that students make.

The information obtained in the interaction is processed immediately, allowing instant feedback between teacher and student, which demonstrates class understanding and knowledge on a regular basis, as well as potential problems that students may have with the subject.

This chapter is structured in three main sections. It begins by analyzing the current state of electronic voting systems or clickers as a technology that complements professor lectures in the classroom. After this general introduction, the operation and implications of these tools in university teaching is described. Finally, the benefits to students and teachers that are gained from integrating these technologies in education systems are analyzed. Specifically, the case of Q-Click software implemented in different courses of the Faculty of Economics and Business, University of Granada, is discussed.

PRESENT STATUS OF ELECTRONIC VOTING SYSTEMS

Today, the challenges and commitments proposed by the European Higher Education Area (EHEA) are in the process of transforming our educational system based on "teaching" into one based on "learning." This improvement process should be interactive and collaborative and is based on three basic principles (University Coordination Council, MEC, 2005): 1) greater involvement and student autonomy, 2) use of active methodologies, case studies, teamwork, mentoring seminars, and multimedia technologies and 3) a review of the role of teachers as creative agents in learning environments that encourage students.

These principles raise the need for new ICT applications in the field of university education. An audience response system is a useful tool to help comply with these proposed principles.

Electronic voting systems or clickers are small transmitters that transmit coded responses to questions posed by the teacher, allowing students to quickly answer questions (Kenwright, 2009) without the rest of the class seeing the response. Therefore, a class may never see the individual answers their classmates provide, but they may see answers in aggregate form, verifying the overall results.

This tool was initially used in classrooms as continuous evaluation systems were implemented. Continuous evaluation is designed to improve student involvement and understanding of a subject, versus traditional evaluation systems (González-Rosende et al., 2008) that don't have the same impact on the development of student skills.

This procedure has been used in different fields ranging from teaching biomedical subjects (Berry, 2009) to mathematics (Marrero, 2011) and sociology (Shaffer y Collura 2009a), demonstrating clickers' importance and effectiveness in the field of university education.

OPERATIONS AND IMPLICATIONS OF REMOTE RESPONSE SYSTEMS

It is very easy for students to operate these tools, though it is somewhat more complex for teachers, who must do some work prior to launching the system. The different stages in the commissioning and operation of such tools are outlined below:

Stage 1: Teacher Preparation

In order to operate the system, teachers must do the following tasks to ensure proper, effective use by the part of the students.

1. Installation of certified software.
2. Assign student groups based on subject enrolment.
3. Assign each student a personalized remote control and identification number to track answers in the database.
4. Write the questions that the students will answer using the application.

5. Design a lesson plan for the academic term in question.
6. Develop a student manual that explains the operation and objectives of the online response system.
7. Conduct a practice session.

Currently, there are different many different kinds of "clicker" software available, including Educlick, Enjoy, Qwizdom and Q-Click, among others. All systems have essentially the same components: survey software and applications and hardware, composed mainly of response devices (clickers or remote controls), the answer receiver and a session storage system.

In our case, we used Q-Click software purchased by the Faculty of Economics and Business, University of Granada in the academic year 2011/2012.

After the activation of the users / students, the tool is ready for operation. From the Home menu, the professor has access to and control of all sessions and the responses and questions from each one.

Once the teacher has accessed the application they assign students to groups either manually or by importing data according to the format specified by the software. This application allows teachers to organize as many groups or courses as they teach, entering personal information for each student for future access and to use the information.

Given the high cost of clickers, some universities require students to pay a security deposit for their unit at the beginning of each year to prevent misuse, and cover damage or loss. Other universities provide teachers with different packs of remote controls that must be personally distributed to students when necessary. From our point of view, the first option is the ideal, as it would ensure that all students have a clicker to use for all subjects, reducing costs and achieving greater diffusion of this tool. However, in our experience the second option is better because it ensures that a student will have the clicker when it is necessary (and it

Figure 1. Screen shot of Q-Click home menu. Teacher accessible and screen shot of class information uploaded into the Q-Click software (© 2012, Q Click; Used with permission)

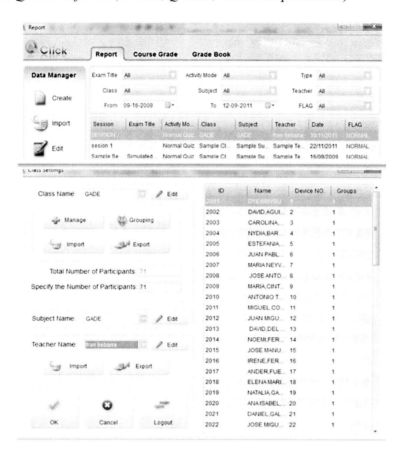

has not been forgotten at home, or lost, for example). A drawback to the second option is that it requires extra work for the teacher since they are then responsible for storage and transport of the clickers. When we used the clickers, we designated two students per group to be responsible for the delivery and collection of each clicker at the beginning and end of each class.

Stage 2: Students See and Respond to Questions

Once the teacher has uploaded the questions that will be evaluated, the pupils will see them displayed one at a time to answer in the amount of time pre-set by the teacher. Figure 4 demonstrates a screen shot of a multiple-choice question. The

student numbers are displayed at the top of the screen, and as students answer the question, the user number changes colour, so the teacher can assess the number of responses for each question in the established time frame.

The program allows students to change incorrect answers as many times as necessary during the within the allotted time frame for each question.

Stage 3: Time Frames and Answering the Questions

It is important to note that there are two ways to ask questions using this system. The first way is to require students to read and answer the question in a specific time frame. Alternatively, students may be given time to read the question "off the clock," and then have a specific amount of time in which to enter their answer. If the teacher opts to use the second method, the question must be shown for a longer period of time than in option number 1. In our opinion, given the objectives of these tools, the first option is better because the student is aware of the available time, and they usually respond more quickly than when presented with the second option when they tend to enter delayed responses.

The software automatically and continuously identifies the questions that the students answer as the teacher moves forward through the material.

One of the most popular clicker features is a review of students' response results at the end of each thematic block of material. This feature shows the number of questions students have answered correctly. Aside from the multiple choice answer features, there are also other ways for students to review material, like games for the students, contests to see who answers first, or games in which incorrect answers are eliminated leaving only one winner, and so on. The aim of all of these applications is to stimulate and generate interest from students about the course material.

Stage 4: Verification of Results and Comments on the Results

After students answer the questions, the teacher can see the results of the student responses. This

Figure 2. Students entering responses using clickers (© 2012, Q Click; Used with permission)

information can be displayed to show answers from the whole group, or results can be sorted to show only answers from one student or for questions related only to a particular topic. Using the results information a teacher can determine which theoretical issues have not been clear enough and add new content to the course if necessary. Teachers can also sort results to assess student knowledge, and determine possible questions for the final evaluation. In addition, the teacher can display this information to the students right after the response time for a question has ended, creating very dynamic class sessions.

Figure 3 shows the percentage of correct, incorrect and unanswered questions and details the histogram of each of the questions presented to students.

Stage 5: Saving Student Information and Response for Continuous Evaluation

To complete the process, all of information from each student is saved to create reports that quantify the learning of each user. Many different types of reports are available through the application including longitudinal analysis by groups or student, by teacher, by degree, or by type of question.

This information can be exported to other software to integrate with the mark of the final evaluation, in order to streamline marking for teachers.

Benefits of Integrating Electronic Audience Response System in University Teaching

Scientific literature has proposed numerous benefits and some drawbacks to the implementation and use of electronic response systems in university teaching. As we understand that the ultimate goal of these tools is learning, we propose grouping benefits for students on two levels: formal learning, through academic achievement and academic assessment; and informal learning

Figure 3. Percentage of correct, incorrect and unanswered questions and details the histogram of each of the questions presented to students (© 2012, Q Click; Used with permission)

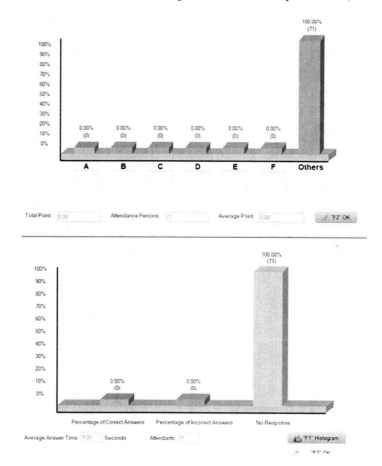

through participation, student motivation and satisfaction from the use of clickers. A brief literature summary of each type of benefit follows:

With respect to formal learning, clickers:

1. Improve the final results of the students who decide to use this technology (Liu et al., 2003, Kennedy and Cutts, 2005, Poirier and Feldman, 2007; Morling et al., 2008, Berry, 2009).

2. Improve learning by students (Kennedy and Cutts, 2005; Beatty et al., 2006; Poirie and Feldman, 2007; Morling et al., 2008; Yourstone et al., 2008; Chafer, 2009).

3. Promote student assessment (Wit, 2003; Roschelle et al., 2004; DeLosh Carpenter, 2005) and monitoring (Berry, 2009).

4. Encourage attendance and involvement of students as they prepare for classes in advance (Chafer, 2009).

5. Reduce classroom teaching time enabling teachers to spend more time on other educational activities to enrich student education (Anderson et al., 2011)

6. Produce rapid feedback for teachers on both content and quality of instruction (Draper & Brown, 2002, Barrett et al., 2005; Chafer, 2009, Collinge, 2009; Weerts et al, 2009).

7. Improve student responsiveness (Dallaire, 2011).
8. Reduce truancy levels (Ruiz et al., 2010).

With respect to informal learning, clickers:

1. Improve student participation in class (Stowell and Nelson, 2007; Martyn, 2007; Shaffer and Collura, 2009) and commitment (Bruff, 2009).
2. Generate a positive and active environment in the classroom, leading to a better formal learning process (Caldwell, 2007, Morales 2011).
3. Reduce some public rejection depending upon the level of anonymity among students in answering the questions (Davis, 2003, Nicol and Boyle, 2003, Fies and Marshall, 2006).
4. Enliven classes (Beekes, 2006, Shaffer and Collura, 2009) reducing boredom (Stowell and Nelson, 2007).
5. Promote individual monitoring of each student (Draper et al., 2002).
6. Improve student satisfaction (Chafer, 2009).
7. Increase student motivation (Caldwell, 2007; Simpson and Oliver, 2006; d'Inverno et al., 2003; Bruff, 2009).
8. Encourage group discussion (Weerts et al, 2009) and help facilitate large groups (Greer and Heaney, 2004).
9. Increase student participation (Berry, 2009, Collinge 2009).

Despite their many advantages, some drawbacks of using of clickers have been identified, including the following:

- System limitations allowing only multiple choice questions and exercises with concrete results.
- Lack of teacher skill and knowledge to manage and use the tool efficiently.

- Discomfort on the part of students who prefer traditional systems of education and evaluation.
- Rejection from students who are not interested in continuous evaluation by the teacher.

However, these possible disadvantages are easily mitigated through teacher initiative, planning and experience with the tool. It must be noted that initially, the implementation of clickers requires special involvement by faculty due to the additional workload in preparation and follow-up when clickers are used.

An Interactive Response System in University Teaching: A Practical Application with Q-Click

The main objective of this research is to confirm the advantages of teaching university students using clickers in class, and propose the following questionnaire based on the conclusions of Ruiz et al. (2010):

To analyze the importance of interactive response systems and specifically, Q-Click Software, a questionnaire containing the content above was given to each student in the following courses during the academic year 2011/2012:

- Introduction to Marketing, Business Administration Degree program (total enrollment 32 students).
- Introduction to Marketing, Business Administration and Law dual degree program (total enrolment 51 students).
- Business Management-1, Business Administration and Law dual degree program (total enrolment of 66 students).

These three subjects were chosen for this research since they are very similar despite being part of different degree programs. These subjects also have the same teacher reducing potential errors

Table 1. A sample of the questionnaire regarding clickers given to business students at the University of Granada

I believe the use of interactive response systems improves my level of class participation
I believe the use of interactive response systems improves my level of attention in class
I believe the use of interactive response systems improves assimilation of the class subject matter
I believe the use of interactive response systems improves my learning in the subject
I believe that the use of interactive learning systems will improve my mark in this class
I believe the use of interactive response systems improves the teaching quality of this class
In summary, I believe interactive response systems are useful

due to teaching differences or course contents. In addition, none of the students who responded to the questionnaire had any similar experiences in any stage of their previous education.

The questionnaire consists of six statements with one question for each attribute, answered using a Likert rating scale from 1 (strongly disagree) to 7 (strongly agree) and a final question about the usefulness of the tool. The statements are outlined in Table 1.

SPSS software, version 15.0, was used for the statistical analysis of the data. Specifically, a descriptive analysis of the sample for the variables measured and bivariate analysis by parametric tests were done. The results from each question are outlined below.

Assessment of Class Participation

The very nature of the clicker software and voluntary nature of the response allows the teacher to know the rate of student participation and Q-Click software use with absolute certainty. Data analysis reveals that the average score on the scale of 1-7 was 6.01 points, with the maximum (mode = 7) being repeated with the most frequency as shown in Table 2. These results are corroborated by many authors including Chafer (2009), Berry (2009) and Ruiz et al. (2010).

In addition, the frequency distribution of figure 4, confirms the high valuation that students gave the proposed tool.

Finally, the hypothesis was contrasted using the Student *t*-test for independent samples as shown in Table 3. The results reveal no significant differences by gender in the assessment of class participation using clickers (p = 0.607).

During the course we found that students who used this tool had improved attention in class. This, coupled with continuous assessment during the semester, and the valuation of the responses from the interactive response system proved that there was an improvement in attention during class. The average score of this attribute on the 7-point scale was 5.84. The most repeated score was also the top possible score (mode = 7), as shown in Table 4, again aligning our results with those of Berry (2009) and Ruiz et al., (2010).

In addition, the frequency distribution shown in Figure 4, confirms the high valuation that students gave clickers.

Like the assessment for class participation, there were no significant differences in the valu-

Table 2. Descriptive analysis of the rate of class participation reported by students

N	VALID	149
	MISSING	0
Mean		6.01
Median		6.00
Mode		7
Standard Deviation.		1.112
Range		6

Table 3. Student t-test for independent samples of the valuation of class participation by reported by students

Independent Samples Test		Levene's Test for Equality of Variances		t-test for equality of means						
		F	Sig.	T	df	Sig. (2-tailed)	Mean Difference	Std Error Difference	95% Confidence Interval of the Difference	
		Lower	Upper	Lower	Upper	Lower	Upper	Lower	Upper	Lower
Improved Class Participation	Equal variances assumed	0.791	0.375	-0.515	147	0.607	-0.098	0.191	-0.475	0.279
	Equal variances not assumed			-0.511	104.975	0.610	-0.098	0.192	-0.479	0.283

Table 4. Descriptive analysis of the valuation of attention in class reported by students

N	Valid	149
	Missing	0
Mean		5.84
Median		6.00
Mode		7
Standard Deviation		1.361
Range		6

ation of attention in class by gender when using clickers (p = 0.235) once the hypothesis was contrasted with the Student *t*-test for independent samples as shown in Table 5.

Assessment of Content Assimilation

As previously mentioned, none of the students had ever used clickers before, so we believe they are a good way to assess in-class content assimilation. The average score that students gave this question in the classroom assessment on the 7-point scale was 5.57. The most frequently repeated score was one of the highest possible scores (mode = 6) as shown in Table 6, endorsing the results by Chafer (2009) and Ruiz et al., (2010).

In addition, the frequency distribution shown in Figure 4, confirms the high valuation that the students gave clickers.

Table 5. Student t-test for independent samples of the valuation of attention in class reported by students

Test for independent samples		Levene's Test for Equality of Variances		t-test for equality of means						
		F	Sig.	t	df	Sig. (2-tailed)	Mean Difference	Std Error Difference	95% Confidence Interval of the Difference	
		Lower	Upper	Lower	Upper	Lower	Upper	Lower	Upper	Lower
Improved Attention	Equal variances assumed	0.169	0.682	-1.192	147	0.235	-0.277	0.233	-0.737	0.182
	Equal variances not assumed			-1.198	108.961	0.234	-0.277	0.231	-0.736	0.181

Table 6. Descriptive analysis of the valuation of content assimilation reported by students

N	Valid	149
	Missing	0
Mean		5.57
Median		6.00
Mode		6
Standard Deviation		1.332
Range		6

In this issue, significant differences by gender were revealed once the hypothesis was contrasted with the Student *t*-test for independent samples as shown in Table 7 (p = 0.019) and 8. For this survey question, the women's valuation (5.76) was higher than the men's (5.23).

Assessment of Learning

Learning is undoubtedly one of the key benefits sought by the implementation of electronic response systems (Morling et al., 2008; Yourstone et al., 2008; Chafer, 2009, Ruiz et al., 2010). In our case the assessment of learning with clickers corroborates the hypothesis and results in the use of Q-Click. The average assessment made by students about classroom learning using clickers in the proposed 7-point scale was 5.52. The highest repeated score was one of the top possible scores (mode=6) as shown in Table 9.

In addition, the frequency distribution shown in Figure 4, confirms the high valuation that the students gave clickers.

Like the questions on class learning, there were significant differences by gender once the hypothesis was contrasted with the Student *t*-test for independent samples as shown in Table 10 (p = 0.033) and 11; once again the women's assessment (5.69) was higher than the men's (5.21).

Assessment of Future Marks

Due to the answers to the previous questions, it is not surprising that students felt that the use of clickers would help them improve their final

Table 7. Student t-test for independent samples of the valuation of content assimilation reported by students

Test for independent samples		Levene's Test for Equality of Variances		t-test for equality of means							
		F	Sig.	t	Df	Sig. (2-tailed)	Mean Difference	Std Error Difference	95% Confidence Interval of the Difference		
		Inferior	Superior	Inferior	Superior	Inferior	Superior	Inferior	Upper	Lower	
Improved Content Assimilation	Equal variances assumed	1.647	0.201	-2.380	147	0.019	-0.534	0.224	-0.977	-0.091	
	Equal variances not assumed			-2.279	94.652	0.025	-0.534	0.234	-0.999	-0.069	

Table 8. Statistical analysis of group content assimilation reported by students

Group statistics	Gender	N	Mean	Standard Deviation	Standard Error Mean
Improved Content Assimilation	Male	53	5.23	1.436	0.197
	Female	96	5.76	1.238	0.126

Table 9. Descriptive analysis of the valuation of class learning reported by students

N	Valid	149
	Missing	0
Mean		5.52
Median		6.00
Mode		6
Standard Deviation		1.318
Range		6

mark in the course. For this question, the average response on the scale was 5.16 points, with three modal values and scores 4.5 and 6, (as shown in the distribution frequencies in Figure 4).

There are several modes. The lowest of the values is shown.

In addition, the frequency distribution shown in Figure 4 confirms the high valuation that students gave clickers.

Finally, the hypothesis was contrasted with the Student *t*-test for independent samples. The results in Table 13, show no significant differences by gender in the assessment of future marks as a result of as as using clickers (class participation using the proposed tool (p = 0.958).

Assessment of Teacher Quality

Based on the results of the previous questions, it seems logical that students would positively appraise clickers as far as teacher quality is concerned. The average score for this question was 5.52 points, with the most repeated score being one of the top (mode = 6) as shown in Table 14.

IMPROVED TEACHING QUALITY

Finally, the hypothesis was contrasted with the Student *t*-test for independent samples as shown in Table 15, and it reveals the absence of signifi-

Table 10. Student t-test for independent samples for the valuation of learning reported by students

Test for independent samples		Levene's Test for Equality of Variances		*t*-test for equality of means						
		F	Sig.	t	df	Sig. (2-tailed)	Mean Difference	Std Error Difference	95% Confidence Interval of the Difference	
		Inferior	Superior	Inferior	Superior	Inferior	Superior	Inferior	Upper	Lower
Improved Learning	Equal variances were assumed	0.666	0.416	-2.153	147	0.033	-0.480	0.223	-0.920	-0.040
	Equal variances were not assumed			-2.068	95.370	0.041	-0.480	0.232	-0.941	-0.019

Table 11. Group statistical analysis on improved learning reported by students

	Gender	N	Mean	Standard Deviation	Standard Error Mean
Improved Learning	Male	53	5.21	1.419	0.195
	Female	96	5.69	1.234	0.126

Table 12. Descriptive analysis of the valuation of future marks reported by students

N	Valid	149
	Missing	0
Mean		5.16
Median		5.00
Mode		4(a)
Standard Deviation		1.494
Range		6

cant differences by gender in the assessment of teaching quality resulting from the use of clickers (class participation using clickers (p = 0.266).

Assessment of Clicker Utility

To complete the assessment of the student survey, we asked for a general assessment of the utility of audience response systems. Students gave an averagen score of 6.13 with the highest repeated score being the highest possible (mode = 7) as shown in Table 16.

Finally, the hypothesis contrasted with the Student *t*-test for independent samples shown in Table 17, reveals the absence of significant differences by gender in the assessment of the utility of clickers (participation in class the proposed tool (p = 0.108).

As demonstrated above, in the opinion of the students surveyed the use of electronic response systems:

- Improves the level of student participation in class.
- Improves the level of student attention in class.
- Improves the assimilation of course content by students.
- Improves the level of learning of the subject by the students.
- Improves the expectation of future student marks.
- Improves the quality of teaching of the subject
- Confirms the usefulness of the interactive response system used.

There are no significant differences by gender, for most attributes, except in the assessments related to the questions on the assimilation of content and level of learning where women are valued clickers more positively than men on both issues.

In conclusion, the data obtained have been considered highly satisfactory and confirm the authors' intention to use this tool in coming academic years.

Table 13. Student t-test for independent samples of the assessment of future grades reported by the students

Test for independent samples		Levene's Test for Equality of Variances		t-test for equality of means							
		F	Sig.	t	Df	Sig. (2-tailed)	Mean Difference	Std Error Difference	95% Confidence Interval of the Difference		
		Lower	Upper	Lower	Upper	Lower	Upper	Lower	Upper	Lower	
Improves My Grade	Equal variances assumed	,610	,436	,053	147	,958	,014	,256	-,493	,520	
	Equal variances not assumed			,052	104,573	,958	,014	,259	-,500	,527	

Table 14. Descriptive analysis of the assessment of teaching quality reported by students

N	Valid	**149**
	Missing	**0**
Mean		5,52
Median		6,00
Mode		6
Standard Deviation.		1,287
Range		6

FUTURE RESEARCH DIRECTIONS

The incorporation of technology in university classrooms in the form of remote response devices or electronic voting systems has led to improved active learning by students, promoting better understanding and greater retention of class content (Mareno et al., 2010).

The introduction of these tools in the classroom has created active learning environments (Bruff, 2009) in which students interact with the subject

Figure 4. Frecuency distribution (© 2012, Q Click; Used with permission)

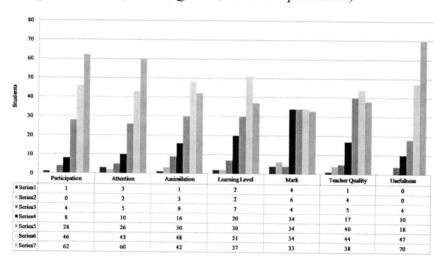

Table 15. Student t-test for independent samples of the assessment of teacher quality reported by students

Independent Samples Test		Levene's Test for Equality of Variances		t-test for equality of means							
		F	Sig.	t	df	Sig. (2-tailed)	Mean Difference	Std Error Difference	95% Confidence Interval of the Difference		
		Lower	Upper	Lower	Upper	Lower	Upper	Lower	Upper	Lower	
Improved Teaching Quality	Equal variances assumed	0.024	0.877	-1.116	147	0.266	-0.246	0.220	-0.681	0.189	
	Equal variances not assumed			-1.116	107.210	0.267	-0.246	0.220	-0.682	0.191	

Table 16. Descriptive analysis of the assessment of clicker utility reported by students

N	Valid	149
	Missing	0
Mean		6.13
Median		6.00
Mode		7
Standard deviation		1.045
Range		4

through special software managed by remote controls or Clickers. This interaction has improved formal and informal learning as shown by the data analysis from the student surveys.

Specifically, research supports the use of this tool and demonstrates that it has led to improved participation, increased student attention in class, improved content assimilation, facilitated learning, improved the expectation of higher marks, and improved students' perceptions of teaching quality. In short, this positive response validates clicker use in Marketing subjects.

Despite the advantages outlined above and the results described in the research, we feel that future researchers should:

- Contrast the long-term effect of the use of electronic voting systems to the immedi-

ate effects confirmed through this research. Long-term sustainability of the following aspects should be considered class participation, attention in class, content assimilation, learning level, and teaching quality rating and, especially the effect on the mark in the subject.

- Analyse the impact that Clickers may have on the type of teaching and methodology use in class.

- Expand the sample of students who participated in the initiative.

- Evaluate students using clickers and compare students' results to marks attained in classes that did not use clickers.

- Compare the marks of classes using clickers to the previous marks attained in the same course prior to the introduction of clickers.

- Conduct qualitative analysis to understand the social aspects of using these tools.

- Develop a behaviour model of students using such tools in order to determine how to generate formal and informal learning.

- Expand on why men and women value the system differently when evaluating the formal knowledge acquired with the use of the tool.

Table 17. Student t-test for independent samples of the assessment of clicker utility reported by students

Independent Samples Test		Levene's Test for Equality of Variances		t-test for equality of means							
		F	Sig.	t	df	Sig. (2-tailed)	Mean Difference	Std Error Difference	95% Confidence Interval of the Difference		
		Lower	Upper	Lower	Upper	Lower	Upper	Lower	Upper	Lower
Utility	Equal variances assumed	0.781	0.378	-1.617	146	0.108	-0.288	0.178	-0.640	0.064
	Equal variances not assumed			-1.553	95.512	0.124	-0.288	0.186	-0.657	0.080

CONCLUSION

The use of interactive controls, clickers or remote response devices has proven to be useful to encourage interactivity in the classroom and to provide rapid feedback to improve the learning process and achieve the aforementioned objectives.

Of all the dimensions analyzed the overall utility of clickers is the most valued with a mean score of 6.13 on the Likert scale. The least valued dimension was future marks using clickers which had a mean score of 5.16. Since all dimensions were ranked a score above 5 in all programs where the research was conducted, we believe that the use of clickers is clearly justified.

These results support those obtained in other studies about the benefits that the use of clickers provide for formal and informal university learning. Specifically, this research reiterates how the use of this tool has led to a breakdown of space-time barriers in teaching and learning activities, created a more open and flexible training process, improved communication between different actors in the teaching and learning process, increased student interaction in class, increased interest and motivation of students and improved educational effectiveness.

However, we found significant differences by gender in the case of assimilation of contents and level of learning, where women valued these two issues more than men.

All teachers, at some point in their career have had the need to connect with students in a non-traditional way by exploiting the potential that students manifest. We feel fortunate that we were able to use remote response systems to engage students' interest in technology and harness such potential. With clickers, we were able to forge stronger human and academic connections with our students. For us, the use of remote response systems has been so successful that for the 2011/2012 academic year, we are integrating this tool in 100% of the subjects taught despite the level of reorganization necessary for a successful integration.

REFERENCES

Alférez, M. J., Samos, J., Ochoa, J., & Quiles, J. L. (2010). Desarrollo de un juego como herramienta multimedia de aprendizaje y evaluación. *Ars Pharm*, 2(51), 132–136.

Anderson, L., Healy, A. F., Kole, J. A., & Bourne, L. E. (2011). Conserving time in the classroom: The clicker technique. *Quarterly Journal of Experimental Psychology*, 8(64), 1457–1462. doi: 10.1080/17470218.2011.593264

Barrett, S. M., Bornsen, S. E., Erickson, S. L., Markey, V., & Spiering, K. (2005). The personal response system as a teaching aid. *Communication Teacher*, 3(19), 89–92. doi:10.1080/14704620500201806

Beatty, I. D., Gerace, W. J., Leonar, W. J., & Dufresne, R. J. (2006). Designing effective questions for classroom response system teaching. *American Journal of Physics*, 74(1), 31–39. doi:10.1119/1.2121753

Beekes, W. (2006). The "millionaire" method for encouraging participation. *Active Learning in Higher Education*, 1(7), 25–36. doi:10.1177/1469787406061143

Benítez, Mª. D., Cruces, E. Mª Pastor & Sarrión, Mª. D. (2011). *Revista de Formación e Innovación Educativa Universitaria, 1*(4), 1-12.

Berry, J. (2009). Technology support in nursing education: Clickers in the classroom. *Nursing Education Perspectives*, 5(30), 295–298.

Bruff, D. (2009). *Teaching with classroom response systems: Creating active learning environments*. San Francisco, CA: Jossey-Bass.

Caldwell, J. E. (2007). Clickers in the large classroom: Current research and best-practice tips. *CBE Life Sciences Education*, 6(1), 9–20. doi:10.1187/cbe.06-12-0205

Carpenter, S. K., & DeLosh, E. L. (2005). Application of the testing and spacing effects to name learning. *Applied Cognitive Psychology*, *19*, 619–636. doi:10.1002/acp.1101

Chafer, E. (2009). *Una introducción a los sistemas de respuesta interactiva. Electrónica y Comunicaciones: Monográfico TICs en las aulas. Elementos Didácticos para la enseñanza* (pp. 56–57). Editorial Cypsela.

Checa, F. (2010). El uso de mataversos en el mundo educativo: gestionando conocimiento en Second Life. *Revista de Docencia Universitaria*, *2*(8), 147–159.

Collinge, J. (2009). In a regular series on how to use technology in training, Justin Collinge sings the praises of voting technology. *Technology Tools*. Retrieved November 11, 2009, from http://www.trainingjournal.com/tj/2340.html# Consejo de Coordinación Universitaria. (2005). *Ministerio de Educación y Ciencia.*

D'Inverno, R., Davis, H., & White, S. (2003). Using a personal response system for promoting student interaction. *Teaching Mathematics and Its Applications*, *22*(4), 163–169. doi:10.1093/teamat/22.4.163

Dallaire, D. H. (2011). Effective use of personal response "clicker" systems in psychology courses. *Teaching of Psychology*, *38*(3), 199–204. doi:10.1177/0098628311411898

Davis, S. M. (2003). Observations in classrooms using a network of handheld devices. *Journal of Computer Assisted Learning*, *19*, 298–307. doi:10.1046/j.0266-4909.2003.00031.x

Draper, S. W., & Brown, M. I. (2004). Increasing interactivity in lectures using an electronic voting system. *Journal of Computer Assisted Learning*, *20*, 81–94. doi:10.1111/j.1365-2729.2004.00074.x

Ferro, C., Martínez, A.I., Otero, Mª C. (2009). Ventajas del uso de las TICs en el proceso de enseñanza – aprendizaje desde la óptica de los docentes universitarios españoles. *Revista electrónica de Tecnología Educativa, 29*, 1-100.

Fies, C., & Marshall, J. (2006). Classroom response systems: A review of the literature. *Journal of Science Education and Technology*, *15*, 101–109. doi:10.1007/s10956-006-0360-1

González-Rosende, M. E., Vega, S., Girbés, M. S., Ortega, J., Segura, E., & Hernández, J. M. (2008). *La evaluación continua en el espacio Europeo de Educación Superior*. VI Jornadas de Redes de Investigación en Docencia Universitaria. Retrieved November 9, 2009, from http://www.eduonline.ua.es/jornadas2008/

Greer, L., & Heaney, P. J. (2004). Real-time analysis of student comprehension: An assessment of electronic student response technology in an introductory earth science course. *Journal of Geoscience Education*, *52*(4), 345–351.

Instituto Nacional de Estadística. INE. (2010). *Encuesta sobre equipamiento y uso de Tecnologías de Información y Comunicación en los hogares* (TIC-H). Madrid, Spain: Ed INE.

Kennedy, G., & Cutts, Q. (2005). The association between students' use of an electronic voting system and their learning outcomes. *Journal of Computer Assisted Learning*, *21*, 260–268. doi:10.1111/j.1365-2729.2005.00133.x

Kenwright, K. (2009). Clickers in the classroom. *TechTrends: Linking Research and Practice to Improve Learning*, *53*(1), 74–77.

Liaw, S. S., Hatala, M., & Huang, H. (2009). Investigating acceptance toward mobile learning to assist individual knowledge management: Based on activity theory approach. *Computers & Education*, *54*, 446–454. doi:10.1016/j.compedu.2009.08.029

Liébana-Cabanillas, F. J., Rejón-Guardia, F., Guillén-Perales, A., & Martínez-Fiestas, M. (2011). *El uso de las redes sociales de microblogging: una experiencia empírica en el curso 2011-2012*. II Jornadas sobre Innovación Docente y Adaptación al EEES en las titulaciones técnicas. Septiember, 26 and 27, Granada.

Liu, T. C., Liang, J. K., Wang, H. Y., & Chan, T. W. (2003). *The features and potential of interactive response system*. Paper presented at the 2003 International Conference on Computers in Education, Hong Kong.

Mareno, N., Bremner, M., & Emerson, C. (2010). The use of audience response systems in nursing education: best practice guidelines. *International Journal of Nursing Education Scholarship, 7*, 1–17. doi:10.2202/1548-923X.2049

Marrero, I. (2011). Los clickers en el aula de matemáticas. *Revista de Didáctica de las Matemáticas, 76*, 157–166.

Martyn, M. (2007). Clickers in the classroom: An active learning approach. *EDUCAUSE Quarterly, 2*, 71–74.

Morales, L. (2011). Can the use of clickers or continuous assessment motivate critical thinking? A case study based on corporate finance students. *Higher Learning Research Communications, 1*(1), 33–42.

Morling, B., McAuliffe, M., Cohen, L., & DiLorenzo, T. M. (2008). Efficacy of "clickers" in large, introductory psychology classes. *Teaching of Psychology, 35*, 45–50. doi:10.1080/00986280701818516

Murillo, J. L. (2010). Programas escuela 2.0 y pizarra digital: Un paradigma de mercantilización del sistema educativo a través de las TICs. *Revista Electrónica Interuniversitaria de Formación del Profesorado, 13*(2), 65–78.

Nicol, D. J., & Boyle, J. T. (2003). Peer instruction versus class-wide discussion in large classes: A comparison of two interaction methods in the wired classroom. *Studies in Higher Education, 28*, 457–573. doi:10.1080/0307507032000122297

Ortiz-de-Urbina, M., & Mora, E. M. (2011). Empleo de herramientas didácticas y TICs en la resolución de casos prácticos en administración y dirección de empresas. *Revista Electrónica de ADA, 5*(2), 168–175.

Poirier, C. R., & Feldman, R. S. (2007). Promoting active learning using individual response technology in large introductory psychology classes. *Teaching of Psychology, 34*(3), 194–196. doi:10.1080/00986280701498665

Rejas, J. (2011). Propuesta de diseño de un portal virtual en educación. *EDUTEC, Revista Electrónica de Tecnología Educativa*. Retrieved Setember 23, 2010, from http://edutec.rediris.es/revelec2/revelec33/

Roschelle, J., Penuel, W. R., & Abrahamson, L. (2004). *Classroom response and communication systems: Research review and theory*. Paper presented at Annual Meeting of the American Educational Research Association. San Diego, CA, 2004.

Ruiz-Jiménez, A., Ceballos-Hernández, C., González-Guzmán, N., Ortega Fraile, F.J., Ríos Fornos, M., & Delgado Lissen, J. (2010, Febrero). Enseñanza interactiva en la docencia universitaria. *XX Jornadas Hispano Lusas de Gestión Científica*, Setúbal, Portugal, (pp. 4–5).

Shaffer, D. M., & Collura, M. (2009). Technology and teaching: Evaluating the effectiveness of a personal response system in the classroom. *Teaching of Psychology, 36*, 273–277. doi:10.1080/00986280903175749

Simpson, V., & Oliver, M. (2006). *Using electronic voting systems in lectures*. Retrieved February 12, 2010, from http://www.ucl.ac.uk/learningtechnology/assessment/ElectronicVotingSystems.pdf

Stowell, J. R., & Nelson, J. M. (2007). Benefits of electronic audience response systems on student participation, learning and emotion. *Teaching of Psychology, 34*, 253–258. doi:10.1080/00986280701700391

Wan, Z., Fang, Y., & Neufeld, D. J. (2007). The role of information technology in technology-mediated learning: a review of the past for the future. *Journal of Information Systems Education, 18*(2), 183–192.

Weerts, S. E., Miller, D., & Altice, A. (2009). Clicker technology promotes interactivity in an undergraduate nutrition course. *Journal of Nutrition Education and Behavior, 3*(41), 227–228. doi:10.1016/j.jneb.2008.08.006

Wit, E. (2003). Who wants to be... The use of a personal response system in statistics teaching. *MSOR Connections, 2*(3), 14–20.

Yourstone, S. A., Kraye, H. S., & Albaum, G. (2008). Classroom questioning with immediate electronic response: Do clickers improve learning? *Decision Sciences Journal of Innovative Education, 6*, 75–88. doi:10.1111/j.1540-4609.2007.00166.x

ADDITIONAL READING

Addison, S., Wright, A., & Milner, R. (2009). Using clickers to improve student engagement and performance in an introductory biochemistry class. *Biochemistry and Molecular Biology Education, 37*(2), 84–91. doi:10.1002/bmb.20264

Anderson, L., Healy, A. F., Kole, J. A., & Bourne, L. E. (2011). Conserving time in the classroom: The clicker technique. *Quarterly Journal of Experimental Psychology, 8*(64), 1457–1462. doi:10.1080/17470218.2011.593264

Arenas Marquez, F. J., Molleda Jimena, G., Chávez Miranda, M. E., Domingo Carrillo, M. A., & Castañeda Barrena, R. (2004). Evaluación del autoaprendizaje con herramientas basadas en las tecnologías de la información y las comunicaciones (TIC). *Revista de Enseñanza Universitaria, 23*, 7–22.

Arnaiz, P. (2011). *Experiencias de innovación educativa en la Universidad de Murcia (2009)*. Murcia, Spain: Editum Aprender.

Berry, J. (2009). Technology support in nursing education: Clickers in the classroom. *Nursing Education Perspectives, 5*(30), 295–298.

Bode, M., Drane, D., Kolikant, Y. B. D., & Schuller, M. (2009). A clicker approach to teaching calculus. *Notices of the AMS, 56*, 253-256. Retrieved January 12, 2011, from http://www.ams.org/notices/200902/rtx090200253p.pdf.

Bruff, D. (2011). Teaching with classroom response systems. Retrieved January 12, 2011, from http://derekbruff.com/teachingwithcrs

Caldwell, J. E. (2007). Clickers in the large classroom: Current research and best-practice tips. *CBE-Life Sciences Education, 6*(1), 9-20. Retrieved January 12, 2011, from http://www.lifescied.org/cgi/content/abstract/6/1/9

Chafer, E. (2009). Una introducción a los sistemas de respuesta interactiva. Electrónica y comunicaciones. *Elementos Didácticos para la Enseñanza, 242*, 56–57.

Duncan, D. (2005). *Clickers in the classroom*. Upper Saddle, NJ: Addison-Wesley.

Fies, C., & Marshall, J. (2006). Classroom response systems: A review of the literature. *Journal of Science Education and Technology, 1*(15), 101–109. doi:10.1007/s10956-006-0360-1

Gachago, D., Morris, A., & Simon, E. (2011). Engagement levels in a graphic design clicker class: Students' perceptions around attention, participation and peer learning. *Journal of Information Technology Education, 10*, 253–269.

García-Peñalvo, F. J. (2008). *Advances in e-learning: Experiences and methodologies.* Hershey, PA: Information Science Reference. doi:10.4018/978-1-59904-756-0

Kang, H., Lundeberg, M., Wolter, B., Del Mas, R., & Herreid, C. F. (2011). Gender differences in student performance in large lecture classrooms using personal response systems ('clickers') with narrative case studies. *Learning, Media and Technology, 37*(1).

Kay, R. H., & LeSage, A. (2009). Examining the benefits and challenges of using audience response systems: A review of the literature. *Computers & Education, 53*(3), 819–882. doi:10.1016/j.compedu.2009.05.001

Kern, A.L., Moore, T.J., & Akillioglu, F. C. (2007). *Cooperative learning: Developing an observation instrument for student interactions.* Frontiers in Education (FiE).

Kyei-Blankson, L. (2009). Enhancing student learning in a graduate research and statistics course with clickers. *EDUCAUSE Quarterly, 32*(4).

Levesque, A. A. (2011). Using clickers to facilitate development of problem-solving skills. *Life Sciences Education, 10*, 406–417. doi:10.1187/cbe.11-03-0024

Patterson, B., Kilpatrick, J., & Woebkenberg, E. (2010). Evidence for teaching practice: The impact of clickers in a large classroom environment. *Nurse Education Today, 30*(7), 603–607. doi:10.1016/j.nedt.2009.12.008

Ribbens, E. (2007). Why I like clicker personal response systems. *Journal of College Science Teaching, 37*(2), 60–62.

Robert, A., Bartsch, A., & Murphy, W. (2011). Examining the effects of an electronic classroom response system on student engagement and performance. *Journal of Educational Computing Research, 1*(44), 25–33.

Ruiz-Jimenez, A. Ceballos-Hernández, García-Gragera, C. J., Delgado- Lissen, J., & Gonzalez-Guzman, N. (2010). Sistemas de respuesta interactiva en la enseñanza universitaria: Algunos resultados. Edición Digital @ Tres, S.L.L. (Ed), *Nuevas formas de docencia en el área económico-empresarial,* (pp. 195-207).

Ruiz-Jimenez, A., Chávez-Miranda, M. E., & Maria Romero-Romero, G. (2009). *Utilización de mandos a distancia interactivos para la evaluación del alumno.* Innovación en Metodología Docente en el Área Económico-Empresarial. Sevilla: Edición Digital @ Tres, S.L.L. 2009.

Ruiz-Jimenez, A., Ruiz-Orcaray, V.E., García-Gragera, J.A., Arias-Martín, C., & Vazquez- Bermudez, I. (2009). Un experimento de utilización de mandos de respuesta interactivo en la asignatura dirección y gestión de la producción II. *Innovación en Metodología Docente en el Área Económico-Empresarial.* Sevilla, Spain: Edición Digital @ Tres, S.L.L.

Salinas, J. (2004). Evaluación de entornos virtuales de enseñanza-aprendizaje. In Salinas, J., Aguaded, J. L., & Cabero, J. (Eds.), *Tecnologías para la educación. Diseño, producción y evaluación de medios para la formación.* Madrid, Spain: Alianza.

Shaffer, D. M., & Collura, M. J. (2009b). Evaluating the effectiveness of a personal response system in the classroom. *Teaching of Psychology, 36*, 273–277. doi:10.1080/00986280903175749

Siau, K., Sheng, H., & Nah, F. F.-H. (2006). Use of a classroom response system to enhance classroom interactivity. *IEEE Transactions on Education, 3*(49), 398–403. doi:10.1109/TE.2006.879802

Walker, R., & Barwell, G. (2009). Click or clique? Using educational technology to address students' anxieties about peer evaluation. *International Journal for the Scholarship of Teaching and Learning, 3*(1), 1–20.

Yourstone, S. A., Kraye, H. S., & Albaum, G. (2008). Classroom questioning with immediate electronic response: Do clickers improve learning? *Decision Sciences Journal of Innovative Education, 6*, 75–88. doi:10.1111/j.1540-4609.2007.00166.x

KEY TERMS AND DEFINITIONS

Autonomous Learning: The process in which people take initiative, with or without the help of others, to diagnose learning needs, create learning objectives, identify necessary learning resources, choose and apply adequate learning strategies and evaluate learning results.

Interactive Response System: Information technology (software and hardware) that quantifies audience answers and opinions and produces instant feedback.

Interactive Teaching-Learning Systems: Complements traditional teaching methods whose objective is to increase student participation, provide incentives for learning and facilitate student teamwork.

Learning Process: The stages of knowledge acquisition.

New Technology in Education: A set of tools for the "Information Society" which assist individual learning. This new education was created due to ICTs and fulfils the objectives of the European Higher Education Area.

New Teaching Methodologies: Competencies related to teaching which represent "best practices" in the classroom and students' professional development (including, but not limited to the use of technology, methodology, tutoring, and continuous evaluation).

Self-Directed Learning: Learning through individual searches for information and experiments. This differs from self-learning since the latter refers to a reflexive act in which one learns automatically. Conscious learning through specific actions should be called autonomous or self-directed learning.

Chapter 15
The Simulator as a University Business School Support Tool:
Implementation of Simbrand

Francisco J. Liébana-Cabanillas
University of Granada, Spain

Myriam Martínez-Fiestas
University of Granada, Spain

María Isabel Viedma-del-Jesús
University of Granada, Spain

ABSTRACT

The purpose of this chapter is to discuss the use of business management simulators in university teaching, specifically the use of marketing simulators, identifying the main advantages and disadvantages for students. The marketing simulator Simbrand was used and evaluated by 104 students in a general marketing class at the University of Granada. Their responses to a survey about the implications that simulator use has on student attention, motivation, the ability to follow course material and the quality of the classes that use this tool are outlined below. The findings provide solid theoretical evidence of the usefulness and advantages of these tools in university teaching for both students and faculty.

INTRODUCTION

Fallows and Steven (2000), define competence as "the skills necessary for employment and for life as responsible citizens and are important for all students regardless of discipline they are studying." (p. 8) The acquisition of these general and specific skills helps students improve their personal and social life while training them to become good professionals (Villa & Poblete, 2008).

Competency-Based Learning (or Activity Based Learning-ABL) is a movement that defines these necessary competencies and encourages student autonomy and learning how to learn. ABL is committed to the development of multiple competencies, including key general skills such as problem solving, time management, verbal and written communication skills, interpersonal skills,

DOI: 10.4018/978-1-4666-2530-3.ch015

Copyright © 2013, IGI Global. Copying or distributing in print or electronic forms without written permission of IGI Global is prohibited.

such as teamwork, entrepreneurial competencies and achievement orientation. ABL also encourages the development of specific professional competencies.

It goes without saying that university education must provide conceptual training through the acquisition of knowledge and content. However, a *good* university education should also provide ABL and thus, encourage the development of practical and applied skills, personal values and attitudes, applicable to different work and social situations. (Smith & Van Doren, 2004).

The increasing recognition of the benefits of ABL has led to a change in the professor's role in university education. As students have become the driving force of learning, the teacher's role now focuses on organization, monitoring and student evaluation, which require the use of strategies and teaching methodologies that encourage student self-help. Therefore, new teaching tools, based especially on the use of new Information and Communication Technologies, ICT, are changing the view of the teaching-learning processes (Ferro, Martínez & Otero, 2009), encouraging students' independent learning, collaborative work, and the development of specific personal and social skills that will undoubtedly be crucial in the formation of future professionals (Echazarreta et al., 2009).

In this context, simulation games in university classrooms are powerful teaching tools that encourage the development of these skills. These simulations replicate business situations in competitive environments and different management scenarios. Participants interact with the software and achieve results based on their decisions. Simulation games differ from other active learning techniques as they address certain aspects of management that would otherwise be difficult to imitate in the classroom. These tools allow students to see the consequences of their decisions first hand and react in a virtual environment much as they would in a real world business situation. Thavikulwat (2009) explains that, "a simulation is a 'reality' in an artificial environment, a

case study with the participants inside" (p. 242) and Akilli (2007) refers to simulation games as "experiential exercises in 'learning how to learn' that provide something more than plain thinking. It's beyond thinking." (p. 3)

In addition to simulations, there are other applications of the use of ICTs in university classrooms. For example, the use of avatars in the management learning games (Thomas, 2006) or, more specifically in the implementation of "second life," (Messinger et al., 2009) a 3D interface that allows communication and interaction between virtual people in real time via the Internet.

It is clear that through these types of innovative educational initiatives, students receive practical training, which is in high demand by companies today. Students gain knowledge and experience in overcoming problems in complex and multi-dimensional environments (Clarke, 2009). Such simulations are useful not only in business, but in other fields as well and similar initiatives have also been carried out in healthcare (Pringle & Nippak, 2010; Rogers, 2011), engineering (Deshpande & Huang, 2011), and physics (Schumann et al., 2001).

In this context, this chapter examines the utility of ICTs perceived by students, specifically the use of a marketing simulator. Concretely, theoretical content and the acquisition of personal and social skills are evaluated.

A CONCEPTUAL REVIEW OF BUSINESS SIMULATORS FROM THEIR ORIGINS TO THE PRESENT

The use of simulators began more than five decades ago at the University of Washington in 1957 (Faria, 2006). Since then, the practice has become widespread in many business schools and universities (Faria & Wellington, 2004; Moratis, Hoff & Reul, 2006; Varela, 2009). Cadotte (1995) advocates simulator use proposing that business schools place too much emphasis on theory and not enough on practice.

Now, especially, the use of such tools is becoming more important in the current university environment as these instruments provide an opportunity to address the challenges posed by the European Higher Education Area (EHEA).

Furthermore, the EHEA prioritizes teamwork as a key skill due to its relevance and high value as a professional competence. Teamwork has become increasingly important in all organizations (Nielsen, Sundstrom & Halfhill, 2005), and university classrooms are no exception. As an active and participatory teaching method, simulator use promotes teamwork, helps develop analytical and reflective skills, and enhanced problem solving skills, which are all considered vital in today's job market.

The rapid growth of simulators (Graham & Gray, 1969; Horn & Cleaves, 1980; Schriesheim & Schriesheim, 1974; Zuckerman & Horn, 1973) since their inception and through the 70s and 80s has made them an innovative and attractive alternative to traditional teaching methods.

Simulators attempt to reproduce real business using the same variables that are in the business world, offering students the opportunity to develop skills that previously could only be developed through marketplace labour.

Many studies have confirmed the effectiveness of simulators in learning environments. McKenney conducted one of the earliest studies in 1962, researching the efficacy of using simulators as compared to single case studies. He concluded that students who used a simulator had higher scores than other students who learned through traditional case studies (McKenney, 1962). Subsequent studies have reached the same conclusion, demonstrating the educational value of simulators through better learning results in comparison with the use of case studies alone (Meier, Newell, & Pazer, 1969; Raia, 1966; Wolfe, 1975; Wolfe & Guth, 1975). Simulators also promote changes in development and changes in attitudes (Dekkers & Donatti, 1981).

These powerful teaching tools improve student motivation due to their game-like nature. In general, students like simulation games and tend to value them more positively than reading or case studies (Burns, Gentry & Wolfe, 1990; Faria, 2001; Gosen & Washbush, 2004). In addition to aiding theoretical reflection of the subject, they also facilitate understanding of abstract concepts (Rieber, 1996).

However, it is necessary to be cautious interpreting these results and distinguish between objective learning results and perceptions of student learning. In a 2009 study, Anderson and Lawton highlighted the importance of proper evaluation to assess learning outcomes associated with participation in a simulation. In order to determine the learning results in terms of vocabulary knowledge, understanding of basic principles, and the ability to apply these principles, other methods not based on student perceptions should be used to measure results. Still, student perception is a very useful way to understand attitudes regarding the use of simulators and learning results (Anderson & Lawton, 2009).

Simulator technology is particularly useful in subjects such as Economics (Galán et al., 2007; Izquierdo et al., 2007; Santos et al., 2008) and marketing. In these simulations students have some market information, and have to analyze the data available to make decisions related to certain marketing variables (Tonks, 2002).

Therefore, regardless of subject matter, there is no doubt about the usefulness of these technologies in university teaching. However, in order for this type of initiative to be successful, universities need certain financial, technical and personnel resources. Santos et al. (2010) suggest that educational organizations, specifically, universities should take the follow steps to aid the successful implementation of these types of experiences:

- Offer up-to-date technology to promote and improve teamwork.

- Provide continuous support for innovative pedagogical tools.
- Accept the costs for innovative teaching tools, appreciating the long process of design and
development to make them.
- Train teachers in the use of new tools.
- Disseminate the successes of these experiences for recognition in the academic field.

SIMBRAND AS A BUSINESS MANAGEMENT SIMULATION EXPERIENCE

In recent years, scientific literature has classified four types of business simulations (Clarke, 2009):

1. *Micro-simulations*, representing simulations of business activities in specific industries such as hotel management, the airline industry, financial services, or telecommunications (Romme, 2002).
2. *Macro-simulations*, providing circumstances to practice highly complex decision-making involving variables at different levels (marketing, production, financing, etc.) in the resolution of problems [for example, the impact of interest rates on business in a particular industry (Dumblekar, 2004).
3. *Interpersonal skills simulations*, referring to simulations that focus on specific training needs of students such as problem solving (Gibson, Clark & Prensky, 2007).
4. *Business acumen simulations*, referring to simulations focused on the development of skills in strategy formulation, resource allocation, new product development, competency assessment, and product portfolio modifications, among others (Bolt, 2005).

This chapter describes a simulation experience that most closely resembles the latter category, although as Bolt (2005) notes the first three types of simulation are different subsets of the fourth. The software referred to here includes each of the approaches above but as part of business acumen simulations.

This simulation project was developed as part of a Teaching Innovation Project awarded by the Junta de Andalucía (2010:142) in the 2010/2011 academic year. The objective of this project was to implement an innovative teaching approach using virtual environments in practical classes of a general marketing course at the Faculty of Economics and Business, at the University of Granada. Simbrand software, a Cesim simulator company was used to carry out this project. To use the software, students work in small groups, forming "mini-companies", and apply general theoretical marketing concepts, including product features, pricing, investment in advertising, sales forecasting, distribution channels and customer service to a simulated, but realistic mobile technology market and make joint decisions regarding these matters. Other authors have used the Simbrand simulator for similar purposes and had satisfactory results (Wei &, Yifang, 2010).

The Simbrand simulator:

- Simulates real business in a slightly simplified manner in order to maximize educational effectiveness.
- Creates a unique business environment with respect to product characteristics, market size, distribution channels, etc.
- Generates a realistic learning environment, as corroborated by other companies who have used it and confirmed its effectiveness.

The simulation interface was provided by the company Cesim through its website (http://gc4.cesim.com). Students were organized in teams of 4 or 5 people and accessed the site with a password to participate in the simulation from any computer with Internet connection at any time of day.

In this simulation, each team was a mobile technology company, and each student had a management role in their company. The managers then had to make several marketing decisions about product features, pricing, advertising investments, sales forecasting, distribution channels, customer service and research and development.

The Simbrand simulation was broken down into the following phases:

- During the first phase, the teacher introduced the simulation, explained its objectives, and the "rules of the game." Then the students learned to use the software, created teams of 4 or 5 people, and were given their access codes.
- The simulation was carried out over the course of 8 weeks. There were 7 rounds plus an introductory practice period. At the end of each round, the teams made their decisions and could immediately see the results. Using this information, each team again made decisions they deemed appropriate for the next round. In the closing session for each round, teachers outlined the results achieved and clarified doubts
- Throughout the process, each team could observe the progress of the "other companies," creating some "real world" market competition.
- Additionally, the number of teacher-student conferences was increased to clarify decision-making questions that arose after each round. There was a large increase in the number of questions as compared to other subjects in the same area and as compared to the same subject taught in previous years using traditional techniques.
- In the final phase of the simulations, students orally reported on their company's situation, including a discussion of the objectives and the decisions made for each round and an analysis of the results. In the final session the teacher held a forum

and posed questions to the groups during which time students could comment on their experiences.

The technology integration capabilities of the software enhance the decision making process:

- All members of each team have a password with which they make proposals and decisions in each round, so that at the end of a round, all members of the team have contributed to the strategy and made decisions that the group will assume as their own.
- Each team has an online intra-group forum to facilitate communication among team members.
- Additionally, the software can host inter-group forums to answer questions or discuss issues, similar to external consulting in the real world.

The simulation is organized in the following manner:

1. Each team manages a business in two markets with different characteristics: European and Asian markets. Initially, the level of demand in Asia is lower than in the European market, but its growth is expected to be extremely high.
2. Both the European and Asian markets can be divided into four segments:
   a. Two corporate segments: Companies and Big Companies
   b. Two client segments: Families and Upper Class Families.
   c. Both client groups can be divided into upper class and middle class clients.
3. Preferences differ between segments in:
   a. Sensitivity to prices.
   b. Sensitivity to advertising.
   c. Preferences for product features and design.

d.   Distribution channels to purchase products.

4.   All companies can choose between 0 and 6 products that can differ in physical attributes (batteries, aesthetics, compactness, features) or intangible attributes (customer service), divided into two markets, Europe and Asia.

5.   The distribution channels for all companies in each of the markets are malls, electronics stores and specialty shops.

6.   At the end of each round, the teams have economic and financial information, including results, balance sheets, and market situations, broken down by market, product, and sales.

7.   Additionally, all teams have access to market research to help define their strategy and keep abreast of the competition.

After this information is shared and the teams are formed, students work together in their companies sharing ideas until the "boss" of each company makes the final decision about all of the ideas proposed by the team and puts them into action. Final reports and a defence of the decisions made are prepared by each team and presented at the end of the last round of decisions.

ADVANTAGES OF USING BUSINESS SIMULATIONS IN UNIVERSITY TEACHING

Many authors have shown the advantages of using business simulation games in teaching, highlighting different aspects, including the positive emotions experienced by students during

Figure 1. Product attributes and product distribution in each market (© 2012, Cesim; Used with permission)

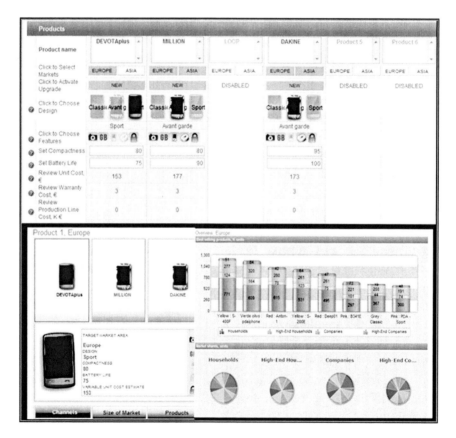

Figure 2. Segment breakdown and results (© 2012, Cesim; Used with permission)

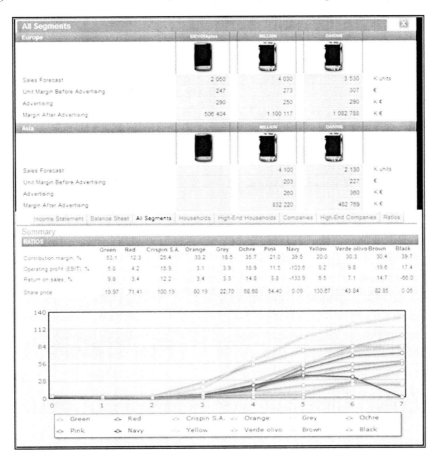

simulation experiences (Bredemeier & Greenblat, 1981; Szafran & Mandolini, 1980), improved capacity for teamwork, and conflict resolution (Teach & Govani, 1988), and improved practical application of theoretical concepts (González & Cernuzzi, 2009).

Anderson & Lawton (2009), focus on the main advantages of simulation games in review of various classical studies. The authors note that simulation games are powerful teaching tools for students that produce significant changes in three areas: learning, attitudes and behaviour.

Learning

- Teach students the terminology, concepts and principles of general business or a specific discipline.

- Help students understand the relationships between various business functions (marketing, finance, production).

- Demonstrate the difficulty of implementing business concepts that seem relatively simple (require students to apply concepts to discover the reality of business plans).

- Improve knowledge retention (it has long been accepted that participation in an activity produces greater retention of concepts and relationships than passive or traditional education).

- To enable students to transfer learning to the business world. The simulators require participants to act as managers and provide valuable business experience that can be demonstrated to future employers.

Attitudes

- Improve students´ attitudes and habits toward discipline.
- Provide a common experience for class discussion (this may be especially interesting for students with little or no business experience).
- Involve students in an active learning process.

Behaviour

- Teach students how to apply business concepts and principles to make effective decisions.
- Enable students to implement course concepts (the application of ideas as opposed to simple discussion allows students to test ideas, experiences and assess their implications. It also forces students to respond to contingencies resulting from their behaviour and decisions).
- Improve students´ ability to interact with their peers by learning and practicing interpersonal skills that assisting achieving the goals of the game.
- Provide students practice making business decisions.
- Improve business decision skills of students.

In addition to these advantages, Santos et al. (2010) notes that the virtual nature of simulators provides other advantages including:

- The flexibility to tailor learning to individual needs.
- The ability to adapt to the pace of work imposed by the teacher or workgroup.
- Personalized attention.

- The active role of the student, not only receiving information but taking a part of their training.

These authors also highlight implications of virtual simulations for teachers and universities:

Implications for Teachers

- Simulations provide flexibility for teachers and adapt to their personal needs.
- Simulations provide tools for individual follow-up and student evaluation.
- Teachers should receive training in the use of ICTs and specifically in the use of simulators before implementing them.
- Teaching material needs to be adapted to different learning environments.
- If teachers do not have access to or use tools that allow individual follow-up and students evaluation, they will have increased workloads.

Implications for Universities

- Simulator use raises the standard for innovation in education and Information and Communication Technology use.
- Virtual simulations increase accessibility for students with limited time or geographic restrictions.
- Simulators develop competencies in virtual environments.
- Qualified professors and quality teaching material is necessary for successful implementation.
- Simulators facilitate multiculturalism and multi-disciplinary work groups.
- Simulator use facilitates collaboration between different educational institutions.

Despite their many advantages, business simulators also can cause problems such as student anxiety and frustration (Doyle & Brown, 2000), and when the group size is large, motivation can be affected due to lack of control of the information handled. This dissatisfaction can result in less participation (Walters & Coalter, 1997). Therefore, some literature recommends that teams be made up of no more than three members (Wolfe & Chacko, 1983).

EVALUATING THE EDUCATIONAL EXPERIENCE

The main objective of this research was to verify the principles proposed by Anderson & Lawton (2009), about learning, attitude and behaviour among students who have experimented with the tool Simbrand.

To this end, a survey of 104 students was conducted to collect information about learning, attitude and behaviour perceptions after using Simbrand. Students from the Marketing Strategies class in the Business Studies degree program at the Faculty of Economics and Business at the University of Granada responded to the survey during the second quarter of the 2010/2011 academic year.

The final mark in the class attained by the students was based on the results of their final reports from the simulation experience, which demonstrated students' application of the theoretical concepts acquired.

The SPSS software, version 15.0, was used for statistical analysis of the data. Specifically, a descriptive analysis of the sample was conducted for the variables measured and bivariate analysis was done with parametric tests and bivariate correlations.

Learning assessment was based on student marks in the subject as the main objective indicator of the level of knowledge. The results of the analysis show a fairly high average score (7.93),

Table 1. Description of the student frequency samples

Gender	Number	%
Men	44	41.30%
Women	60	57.70%
Total	103	100.00%
Age	**Number**	**%**
19	15	14.42%
20	23	22.12%
21	19	17.31%
22	14	13.46%
23	15	14.42%
24	6	5.77%
25	6	5.77%
26	3	2.88%
27	2	1.92%
29	1	0.96%
Total	104	100.00%

which suggests that the simulation helps students acquire the right level of during the academic year. The descriptive analysis is shown in Table 2.

As Table 3 (Descriptive analysis by gender, and Student *t*-test for independent samples) show, there were no significant differences by gender on student test scores (p = 0.094).

For the *attitude assessment*, students were asked to evaluate other practical activities in the coursework (case commentary, exhibitions and other activities) as well as the simulation itself, on a 10-point grade scale.

The results, shown in Table 4, reveal that the average rating that students gave to Simbrand is

Table 2. Descriptive analysis of software learning reported by students

	Average*	**Standard deviation**
Mark from practice	7.93	1.449

*This number is 120 as it includes the total student sample present for an ordinary exam.

Table 3. Descriptive analysis of learning assessment by gender as reported by students and Student t-test for independent samples

	Gender	N*	Mean	Standard Deviation	Standard Error Mean
Mark From Practice	Male	55	7.69	1.656	0.223
	Female	65	8.13	1.224	0.152

*This number is 120 as it includes the total student sample present for an ordinary exam.

	Levine's Test for Equality of Variances		t-test for equality means						
Student T-Test	F	Sig.	t	Df	Sig. (2-tailed)	Mean Difference	Std Error Difference	95% Confidence Interval of the Difference	
	Lower	Upper	Lower	Upper	Lower	Upper	Lower	Upper	Lower
Equal variances were assumed	3.306	0.072	-1.687	118	0.094	-0.444	0.263	-0.966	0.077
Equal variances were not assumed			-1.646	97.854	0.103	-0.444	0.270	-0.980	0.091

Table 4. Descriptive analysis of the attitude towards the software reported by students

	Mean	Standard Deviation	Variance
Simbrand	7.05	1.776	3.153
Case Studies	6.91	1.719	2.954
N valid (according to the class roster)			

higher than the rest of practical activities in the coursework, which could indicate a more favourable attitude toward this type of simulator, compared to other practical assignments in the subject.

However, the descriptive analysis and hypothesis testing with the Student *t*-test for independent samples don't reveal any significant differences by gender in either case, although the attitude towards Simbrand found almost significant differences (p = 0.058).

Finally, for the *behaviour assessment* (application and implementation of the acquired concepts), two questions about the theoretical and practical knowledge were asked using a 10-point Likert scale:

1. Participation in the game provides the opportunity to demonstrate theoretical knowledge of the subject.
2. Participation in the game provides the opportunity to demonstrate practical knowledge of the subject.

The results show that students perceived the software as a generator of both theoretical and practical behaviour (with averages above 5 in all items), In this case, students reported a higher score for the practical part (7.05) than the theoretical (5.62). The descriptive analysis is shown in Table 6.

Table 7 show that students reported software usefulness to be significantly higher in practice than theory. Also, notice how the scores given by male students are higher than those given by female students in both cases (7.44 versus 6.77 for practical knowledge and 6.37 versus 5.07 for theoretical knowledge). However, when the hypothesis was tested with Student *t*-test for independent samples, significant differences were found between gender and the level of knowledge (p =

Table 5. Descriptive analysis of the attitude towards the software by gender and student t-test for independent samples

	Gender	N	Mean	Standard Deviation	Standard Error Mean
Simbrand	Male	43	7.44	1.351	0.206
	Female	60	6.77	2.003	0.259
Case Studies	Male	43	7.14	1.283	0.196
	Female	60	6.75	1.980	0.256

Student T-Test		Levine's Test for Equality of Variances		*t*-test for equality of means						95% Confidence Interval of the Difference	
		F	Sig.	t	df	Sig (2-tailed)	Mean Difference	Std Error Difference		Upper	Lower
Simbrand	Equal variances were assumed	3.982	0.049	1.919	101	0.058	0.675	0.352		-0.023	1.373
	Equal variances were not assumed			2.042	100.681	0.044	0.675	0.331		0.019	1.331
Case Studies	Equal variances were assumed	4.617	0.034	1.130	101	0.261	0.390	0.345		-0.294	1.073
	Equal variances were not assumed			1.210	100.118	0.229	0.390	0.322		-0.249	1.028

Table 6. Descriptive analysis of the theoretical and practical knowledge reported by students

	Mean	Standard Deviation	Variance
Theoretical Knowledge	5.62	2.627	6.899
Simbrand	7.05	1.776	3.153
N valid (according to class roster)			

0.013) and near significant differences were found in the case of practical knowledge (p = 0.058).

After reviewing the methodological approaches carried out on learning, attitude and behaviour proposed by Anderson & Lawton (2009) regarding the use of the simulator Simbrand, we can conclude that indeed they are important variables in the implementation and use of this tool among the sample.

FUTURE RESEARCH DIRECTIONS

As demonstrated in this chapter, new technologies in higher education, such as simulators applied to marketing management classes have many benefits. These include: promoting student learning, improving monitoring of the classes, facilitating informal learning, promoting better knowledge assimilation and creating a favourable attitude toward the subject. These results agree with those reported by several authors especially as related

Table 7. Descriptive analysis of the assessment of theoretical and practical knowledge by gender and student t-test for independent samples

	Gender	N	Mean	Standard Deviation	Standard Error Mean
Theoretical Knowledge	Male	43	6.37	2.637	0.402
	Female	60	5.07	2.524	0.326
Simbrand	Male	43	7.44	1.351	0.206
	Female	60	6.77	2.003	0.259

		Levine's Test for Equality of Variances		*t*-test for equality of means					95% Confidence Interval of the Difference	
Student T-Test		**F**	**Sig.**	**t**	**df**	**Sig (2-tailed)**	**Mean Difference**	**Std Error Difference**	**Upper**	**Lower**
Theoretical Knowledge	**Equal variances were assumed**	**0.246**	**0.621**	**2.541**	**101**	**0.013**	**1.305**	**0.514**	**0.286**	**2.325**
	Equal variances were not assumed			2.522	88.184	0.013	1.305	0.518	0.277	2.334
Simbrand	**Equal variances were assumed**	**3.982**	**0.049**	**1.919**	**101**	**0.058**	**0.675**	**0.352**	**-0.023**	**1.373**
	Equal variances were not assumed			2.042	100.681	0.044	0.675	0.331	0.019	1.331

to simulator utility in subjects such as Economics (Galán et al., 2007; Izquierdo et al., 2007, Santos et al., 2008).

Consequently, simulators are powerful teaching tools, since their use (like many new Information and Communication Technologies, or ICTs) favours autonomous learning, collaborative work and social and personal skill development, which will be necessary in students' future professional lives (Echazarreta et al., 2009).

Teachers must be aware of the importance of integrating new technologies (ICTs) in the field of education, since we live and work in a global society where technology is the core of any business and personal activity. Teachers need to lead

by example, updating teaching methodologies and transmitting knowledge in a dynamic way. From our point of view, teachers need to provide experiential education, bringing the business world reality into the university reality

Integrating technology in higher education marketing is not only in teaching a class session with a power point projector or providing educational material to students through a web platform, but needs to be a true integration of content and skills learned in the classroom to the business world. Simulators create such an opportunity, offering students the chance to apply their management skills to real market situations of limited impact.

Therefore, teachers have to strive to bring reality to education through learning, knowledge, attitudes and technology integration.

Though the use of simulators is already proven in scientific literature, we believe future researchers should:

- Contrast the sustained effect of the use of simulators, conducting a longitudinal study to assess the benefits that have been highlighted in this study and their influence on academic qualifications.
- Compare the effect of different simulators on students to observe the long-term effects of simulations.
- Assess the effect of teachers throughout the learning process, identifying factors that determine their attitudes towards this type of tool.
- Expand the student sample that participates in a similar initiative.

Finally, we would like to remind to the university business teaching community of the need to develop participatory and social initiatives for students to successfully meet the objectives set by the European Higher Education Area.

CONCLUSION

The main objective of this study was to provide an innovative way to carry out practical learning in a general marketing course. The Simbrand business simulation software gave students an opportunity to make decisions related to marketing in a simulated environment. The results, analyzed in terms of learning, knowledge and attitudes reveal that the use of ICTs in marketing subjects and specifically the use of simulation games such as Simbrand, can promote student learning, improve class monitoring and encourage informal learning. Also, the results indicate that students evaluate these tools favourably and they are considered

useful for promoting teamwork and social skills development. However, some data reported by students needs to be studied further, since men tend to overestimate the value of these tools, reporting greater learning and thus, satisfaction, than reported by women and faculty at the end of the academic year.

In short, although simulation games have been implemented since the early 50's, from our point of view it is an educational technique that has yet to be fully discovered and exploited. Based on our experience, and results, we believe that this is a very effective tool to achieve greater student involvement in the course, improving attention in class, the level of knowledge and academic results. Simulations, with their game-like formats, are powerful teaching tools that improve student motivation. In general, students like simulation games and tend to value them more positively than traditional reading or case studies (Burns, Gentry & Wolfe, 1990, Faria, 2001; Gosen & Washbush, 2004), making these tools a good way to meet the demands and challenges set by the European Higher Education Area.

REFERENCES

Akilli, G. K. (2007). Games and simulations: A new approach in education? In D. Gibson, C. Aldrich, & M. Prensky (Eds.), *Games and simulations in online learning* (pp.1-20). Hershey, PA: Idea Group Inc (IGI).

Anderson, P. H., & Lawton, L. (2009). Business simulations and cognitive learning: Developments, desires, and future directions. *Simulation & Gaming, 40*(2), 193–216. doi:10.1177/1046878108321624

Bolt, J. F. (Ed.). (2005). *The future of executive development*. Executive Development Associates. Retrieved from www.highbeam.com/doc/1P3-898719701.html

Bredemeier, M. E., & Greenblat, C. S. (1981). The educational effectiveness of simulation games: A synthesis of findings. *Simulation & Games, 12*(3), 307–332. doi:10.1177/104687818101200304

Burns, A. C., Gentry, J. W., & Wolfe, J. (1990). A cornucopia of considerations in evaluating the effectiveness of experiential pedagogies. In Gentry, J. W. (Ed.), *Guide to business gaming and experiential learning* (pp. 253–278). East Brunswick, NJ: Nichols/GP Publishing.

Cadotte, E. R. (1995). *Business simulation: The next step in management training*. Santa Monica, CA: Selections.

Clarke, E. (2009). Learning outcomes from business simulation exercises: Challenges for the implementation of learning technologies. *Education + Training, 51*(5/6), 448-459.

Dekkers, J., & Donatti, S. (1981). The integration of research studies on the use of simulation as an instructional strategy. *The Journal of Educational Research, 74*(6).

Deshpande, A. A., & Huang, S. H. (2011). Simulation games in engineering education: A state-of-the-art review. *Computer Applications in Engineering Education, 19*(3), 399–410. doi:10.1002/cae.20323

Doyle, D., & Brown, F. W. (2000). Using a business simulation to teach applied skills – The benefits and the challenges of using student teams in multiple countries. *Journal of European Industrial Training, 24*(6), 330–336. doi:10.1108/03090590010373316

Dumblekar, V. (2004). *Management simulations: Test of effectiveness*. Retrieved from http://www.unice.fr/sg/resources/articles/dumblekar_2004_management.htm

Echazarreta, C., Prados, F., Poch, J., & Soler, J. (2009). La competencia "El trabajo colaborativo": Una oportunidad para incorporar las TIC en la didáctica universitaria. Descripción de la experiencia con la plataforma ACME (UdG). *Uocpapers, Revista sobre la Sociedad del Conocimiento, 8*.

Fallows, S., & Steven, C. (2000). The skills agenda. In Fallows, S., & Steven, C. (Eds.), *Integrating key skills in higher education: Employability, transferable skills and learning for life* (pp. 8–9). London, UK: Kogan.

Faria, A. J. (2001). The changing nature of business simulation/gaming research. *Simulation & Gaming, 32*, 97–110. doi:10.1177/104687810103200108

Faria, A. J. (2006). History, current usage, and learning from marketing simulation games: a detailed literature review. *Proceedings of the Marketing Management Association* (pp. 138-139). Nashville, TN.

Faria, A. J., & Wellington, W. J. (2004). A survey of simulation game users, former-users, and never-users. *Simulation & Gaming, 35*(2), 178–207. doi:10.1177/1046878104263543

Ferro Soto, C., Martínez Senra, A.I., & Otero Neira, M.C. (2009). Ventajas del uso de las TICs en el proceso de enseñanza-aprendizaje desde la óptica de los docentes universitarios españoles. *Revista Electrónica de Tecnología Educativa, 29*.

Galan, J. M., Izquierdo, L. R., Izquierdo, S. S., López, A., Pascual, J. A., & Posada, M. … Villafanez, F. A. (2007). LABEXNET: Un laboratorio de economía experimental en Internet. *RELIEVE Revista Electrónica de Investigación y Evaluación Educativa, 13*(1). Retrieved from http://www.uv.es/RELIEVE/v13n1/RELIEVEv13n1_5.htm

Gibson, D., Clark, A., & Prensky, M. (2007). *Games and simulations in online learning*. Hershey, PA: Idea Group Inc. (IGI).

González, E., & Cernuzzi, L. (2009). Apoyando el aprendizaje de habilidades empresariales mediante la utilización de un simulador. In Sánchez, J. (Ed.), *Nuevas ideas en informática educativa* (pp. 8–19). Santiago de Chile.

Gosen, J. J., & Washbush, J. (2004). A review of scholarship on assessing experiential learning effectiveness. *Simulation & Gaming, 35*, 270–293. doi:10.1177/1046878104263544

Graham, R. G., & Gray, C. F. (1969). *Business games handbook*. New York, NY: American Management Association.

Horn, R. E., & Cleaves, A. (1980). *The guide to simulations/games for education and training*. Beverly Hills, CA: Sage Publications. doi:10.1177/1046878195264008

Izquierdo, L. R., Galán, J. M., Santos, J. I., Izquierdo, S. S., & Del Olmo, R. (2007). Mathematica como herramienta docente en Economía. In J. A. González Manteca, & R. Carrasco Gallego (Eds.), *Proceedings of the International Conference on Industrial Engineering and Industrial Management: XI Congreso de Ingeniería de Organización* (pp. 1019-1028). Madrid.

McKenney, J. (1962). An evaluation of a business game in an MBA currículo. *The Journal of Business, 35*(3). doi:10.1086/294511

Meier, R. C., Newell, W. T., & Pazer, H. L. (1969). *Simulation in business and economics*. New Jersey: Prentice Hall.

Messinger, P. R., Stroulia, E., Lyons, K., Bone, M., Niu, R., Smirnov, K., & Perelgut, S. (2009). Virtual worlds – past, present, and future: New directions in social computing. *Decision Support Systems, 47*, 204–228. doi:10.1016/j.dss.2009.02.014

Moratis, L., Hoff, J., & Reul, B. (2006). A dual challenge facing management education: simulation-based learning and learning about CSR. *Journal of Management Development, 25*(3/4), 213. doi:10.1108/02621710610648150

Nielsen, T. M., Sundstrom, E., & Halfhill, T. (2005). Group dynamics and effectiveness: Five years of applied research. In Wheelan, S. A. (Ed.), *Handbook of group research and practice* (pp. 285–311). Thousand Oaks, CA: Sage. doi:10.4135/9781412990165.d21

Pringle, J. D., & Nippak, P. I. (2010). Winston simulations as an instruction tool to teach healthcare change management: The influence of repeat simulation testing, gender and additional instructions on performance scores. *The Journal of Health Administration Education, 27*(1), 27–43.

Raia, A. (1966). A study of the educational value of management games. *The Journal of Business, 39*(3), 339–352. doi:10.1086/294863

Rieber, L. P. (1996). Animation as feedback in a computer-based simulation: Representation matters. *Educational Technology Research and Development, 44*(1), 5–22. doi:10.1007/BF02300323

Rogers, L. (2011). Developing simulations in multi-user virtual environments to enhance healthcare education. *British Journal of Educational Technology, 42*(4), 608–615. doi:10.1111/j.1467-8535.2010.01057.x

Romme, A. G. L. (2002). *Microworlds for management education and learning.* University Faculty of Economics & Business Administration, UNICE. Retrieved from www.unice.fr/sg/resources/articles/romme_2002_microworlds-management-ed-learning.pdf

Santos, B., Bueno, Y., de Pablo, I., & Borrajo, F. (2010). Innovación en docencia virtual: Los simuladores de gestión empresarial. *Relada, 4*(2), 150–158.

Santos, J. I., Galán, J. M., Izquierdo, L. R., & Olmo, R. (2008). Laboratorio de teoría de juegos en internet. In Saiz Bárcena, L., Millán, I., & Santos Martín, J. I. (Eds.), *Insights on current organization engineering* (pp. 141–142). Burgos, Spain: Universidad de Burgos.

Schriesheim, C. A., & Schriesheim, J. (1974). *Divergence of practitioner opinion and empirical evidence: The case of business simulation games.* Paper presented at the 34th Annual Meeting of the Academy of Management, Seattle.

Schumann, P. L., Anderson, P. H., Scott, T. W., & Lawton, L. (2001). A framework for evaluating simulations as educational tools. *Developments in Business Simulation & Experiential Learning, 28,* 215- 220. Retrieved from http://ABSEL.org

Smith, L. W., & Van Doren, D. C. (2004). The reality-based learning method: a simple method for keeping teaching activities relevant and effective. *Journal of Marketing Education, 26*(1), 66–74. doi:10.1177/0273475303262353

Szafran, R. F., & Mandolini, A. F. (1980). Student evaluation of a simulation game. *Teaching Sociology, 8,* 21–37. doi:10.2307/1317045

Teach, R., & Govani, G. (1988). Simulation game performance: An examination of the effect of time pressure, method of team formation, and formal planning. *Developments in Business Simulation & Experiential Learning, 21,* 83–85.

Thavikulwat, P. (2009). The architecture of computerised business gaming simulations. *Simulation & Gaming, 35*(2), 242–269. doi:10.1177/1046878104263545

Thomas, S. (2006). Pervasive learning games: Explorations of hybrid educational gamescapes. *Simulation & Gaming, 37,* 41–55. doi:10.1177/1046878105282274

Tonks, D. (2002). Using marketing simulations for teaching and learning: Reflections on an evolution 1. *Active Learning in Higher Education, 3*(2), 177–194. doi:10.1177/1469787402003002006

Varela, O. E. (2009). El rol de las escuelas de negocios en el desarrollo de destrezas gerenciales: Análisis conceptual. *Academia. Revista Latinoamericana de Administración, 42,* 73–89.

Villa, A., & Poblete, M. (2008). *Aprendizaje basado en competencias. Una propuesta para la evaluación de las competencias genéricas.* Bilbao, Spain: Ediciones Mensajero.

Walters, B. A., & Coalter, T. M. (1997). Simulation games in business policy courses: is there value for students? *Journal of Education for Business, 72*(3), 170–174. doi:10.1080/08832323.1997.10116849

Wei, L., & Yifang, L. (2010). The application of marketing simulative teaching platform in the marketing professional teaching. *Value Engineering, 34.*

Wolfe, J. (1975). Effective performance behaviors in a simulated policy and decision-making environment. *Management Science, 21*(8). doi:10.1287/mnsc.21.8.872

Wolfe, J., & Chacko, T. I. (1983). Team-size effects on business game performance and decision making behaviours. *Decision Sciences, 14*(1), 121–133. doi:10.1111/j.1540-5915.1983.tb00173.x

Wolfe, J., & Guth, G. (1975). The case approach versus gaming in the teaching of business policy: An experimental evaluation. *The Journal of Business, 48*(3). doi:10.1086/295761

Zuckerman, D., & Horn, R. (1973). *The guide to simulations/games for education and training.* Lexington, MA: Information Resources.

ADDITIONAL READING

Arquero, J. L., & Jimenez, S. M. (1999). Influencia del estudio de casos en la mejora del aprendizaje, adquisición de capacidades no técnicas y motivación en análisis contable. *Revista de Enseñanza Universitaria, Extraordinario*, 225-241.

Arteaga, R., & Duarte, A. (2010). Motivational factors that influence the acceptance of Moodle using TAM. *Computers in Human Behavior, 26*(6), 1632–1640. doi:10.1016/j.chb.2010.06.011

Ben-Zvi, T. (2010). The efficacy of business simulation games in creating decision support systems: An experimental investigation. *Decision Support Systems, 49*, 61–69. doi:10.1016/j.dss.2010.01.002

Brennan, R., & Ahmad, S. j. (2005). Using case studies in management education: The student perspective. *International Journal of Management Education, 4*(3), 21–30. doi:10.3794/ijme.43.124

Burguillo, J. C. (2010). Using game theory and competition-based learning to stimulate student motivation and performance. *Computers & Education, 55*(2), 566–575. doi:10.1016/j.compedu.2010.02.018

Dominguez, J. (1992). The need for a new generation of business games for management education. *Simulation/Games for Learning, 22*(1), 40-47.

Ebner, M., & Holzinger, A. (2007). Successful implementation of user-centered game based learning in higher education: An example from civil engineering. *Computers & Education, 49*(3), 873–890. doi:10.1016/j.compedu.2005.11.026

Faria, A. J., & Wellington, W. J. (2004). A survey of simulation game users, former-users, and never-users. *Simulation & Gaming, 35*, 178–207. doi:10.1177/1046878104263543

Fripp, J. (1993). *Learning through simulations: A guide to the design and use of simulations in business and education*. London, UK: McGraw-Hill.

Greenblat, C. S., & Duke, R. D. (1975). *Gaming-simulation*. New York, NY: John Wiley.

Horn, R. E., & Cleaves, A. (1980). *The guide to simulations/games for education and training*. Beverly Hills, CA: Sage Publications. doi:10.1177/1046878195264008

Kolb, D. A., Rubin, I. M., & McIntyre, J. M. (1984). *Organisational psychology: An experiential approach*. Englewood Cliffs, NJ: Prentice-Hall.

Kumar, R., & Lightner, R. (2007). Games as an interactive classroom technique: Perceptions of corporate trainers, college instructors and students. *International Journal of Teaching and Learning in Higher Education, 19*(1), 53–63.

Lee, A. (2010). Simulation games: Shifting from conceptual learning to experiential learning. *Blended Learning in Practice, July* 36–49.

Lin, Y. L., & Tu, Y. Z. (2012). The values of college students in business simulation game: A means-end chain approach. *Computers & Education, 58*(4), 1160–1170. doi:10.1016/j.compedu.2011.12.005

Marting, E. (1957). *Top management decision simulation: The AMA approach*. American Management Association.

Mussons, J., & Comajuncosa, J. (2005, September). *Nuevas técnicas de formación e investigación empresarial mediante el desarrollo de un simulador de negocios complejo en entorno real*. Paper presented at the Meeting IX Congreso de Ingeniería de Organización, Gijón.

Nemerow, L. G. (1996). Do classroom games improve motivation and learning? *Teaching and Change, 3*(4), 356–366.

Randel, J. M., Morris, B. A., Wetzel, C. D., & Whitehill, B. V. (1992). The effectiveness of games for educational purposes: A review of the research. *Simulation & Gaming, 23*(3), 261–276. doi:10.1177/1046878192233001

Schwab, J. (1973). The practical 3: Translation into curriculum. *The School Review, 81*(4), 501–522. doi:10.1086/443100

Segon, M., & Booth, C. (2009). Enhancing management competence through business simulations. *Journal of Business & Policy Research, 4*(2), 111–123.

Sharif, A. M., & Ranchhod, A. (2009, July). *Using the markstrat business simulation to develop strategic management behaviours.* Paper presented at the European and Mediterranean Conference on Information Systems 2009 (EMCIS2009).

Tan, K. H. (2007). Comparing games and case methods in enhancing student learning. *International Journal of Innovation and Learning, 4*(3), 224–236. doi:10.1504/IJIL.2007.012379

Tao, Y. H., Chen, C. J., & Sun, S. Y. (2009). What influences college students to continue using business simulation games? The Taiwan experience. *Computers & Education, 53*, 929–939. doi:10.1016/j.compedu.2009.05.009

Tao, Y. H., & Yeh, R. C. (2009). Personal response system: A model-based case study in Taiwan. *Proceedings of the 14th Annual Meeting of Asia Pacific Region of Decision Sciences Institute.* Shanghai.

Virvou, M., Katsionis, G., & Manos, K. (2005). Combining software games with education: Evaluation of its educational effectiveness. *Journal of Educational Technology & Society, 8*(2), 54–65.

Vos, L., & Brennan, R. (2010). Marketing simulation games: Student and lecturer perspectives. *Marketing Intelligence & Planning, 28*(7), 882–897. doi:10.1108/02634501011086472

Whiteley, T. R., & Faria, A. J. (1989). A study of the relationship between student final exam performance and simulation game participation. *Developments in Business Simulation & Experiential Exercises, 16*, 78–82.

Wierenga, B. (2011). Managerial decision making in marketing: The next research frontier. *International Journal of Research in Marketing, 28*(2), 89–101. doi:10.1016/j.ijresmar.2011.03.001

Xiaowu, Z., Yan, Y., & Xuanzhong, S. (2010). Dynamic case teaching and learning: Business education in web-based simulation environment. *5th International Conference on Computer Science and Education (ICCSE)* (pp. 667-670). doi:10.1109/ICCSE.2010.5593523

Zantow, K., Knowlton, D. S., & Sharp, D. C. (2005). More than fun and games: reconsidering the virtues of strategic management simulations. *Academy of Management Learning & Education, 4*(4), 451–458. doi:10.5465/AMLE.2005.19086786

KEY TERMS AND DEFINITIONS

Active Learning: A method that makes the student the protagonist in their academic development. Students take an active, conscious role in their own formations.

Activity Based Learning: A learning model that encourages the development of general and specific competencies to facilitate personal and professional development.

Educational Technology Integration: Integration of traditional teaching tools (lectures and practical work) with modern technological developments that increase student learning and provide experiences relevant to their professional future (simulation games, wikis, websites, multimedia tutorials, etc.).

Practical Learning: The autonomous application of theoretical learning to hands-on situations in order to develop skills for personal or professional life outside a classroom setting.

Simulation Game: Innovative technological tools that offer students the opportunity to apply knowledge acquired in a subject to different virtual business situations.

Student Educational Reality: A student's situation based on his or her relationship with coursework through learning, knowledge, attitude and technology integration.

Virtual Learning Environment: Educational software designed for students to use to acquire knowledge and develop skills through flexible, autonomous learning experiences.

Compilation of References

3 DLES. (2011). Retrieved from http://3dles.com/

Ábalos, N., Espejo, G., López-Cózar, R., Callejas, Z., & Griol, D. (2010). A multimodal dialog system for an ambient intelligent application in home environments. *Lecture Notes in Computer Science, 6231*, 491–498. doi:10.1007/978-3-642-15760-8_62

Abascal, J., & Moriyón, R. (2002). Tendencias en interacción persona computador. *Revista Iberoamericana de Inteligencia Artificia, 16*, 9–24.

Ace Center. (2000). *Voice output communication aids.* Retrieved December 13, 2011, from http://atschool. eduweb.co.uk/acecent/html/resvoca.html

AENOR. (2004). *UNE 139802:2003 Aplicaciones informáticas para personas con discapacidad. Requisitos de accesibilidad al ordenador. Software.* In *Software. Requisitos de calidad y ergonomía.* Asociación Española de Normalización y Certificación, AENOR.

Agrega. (2012). *Agrega: Repository of digital educational objects.* Retrieved November 2012 from http://agrega. hezkuntza.net

Aguilar, L. A. (1991). El informe Warnock. *Cuadernos de Pedagogía, 197,* 62–64.

Ai, H., Litman, D., Forbes-Riley, K., Rotaru, M., Tetreault, J., & Purandare, A. (2006). Using systems and user performance features to improve emotion detection in spoken tutoring dialogs. *Proceedings of Interspeech '06-ICSLP,* (pp. 797–800).

Aimeur, E., Dufort, H., Leibu, D., & Frasson, C. (1997). Some Justifications for the Learning by Disturbing Strategy. *Proceedings of International Conference on Artificial Intelligence in Education,* (pp. 119-126).

Akilli, G. K. (2007). Games and simulations: A new approach in education? In D. Gibson, C. Aldrich, & M. Prensky (Eds.), *Games and simulations in online learning* (pp.1-20). Hershey, PA: Idea Group Inc (IGI).

Alart, N., Barlam, R., Girona, M., & Lasala, M. J. (2010). Espurn@, metodología i cooperació per al canvi. *Perspectiva escolar,* Vol. 344, (pp. 32-42). Barcelona.

Alda, J., & Ferrero, P. (2007). *Análisis computacional de textos aplicados a una muestra de publicaciones en óptica. Algunas cuestiones de ciencia. Libro Homenaje al profesor Manuel Quintanilla* (pp. 655–667). Prensas Universitarias de Zaragoza.

Alderson, J. C. (2005). *Diagnosing foreign language proficiency: The interface between learning and assessment.* London, UK: Continuum International Publishing Group.

Aleven, V., McLaren, B., Roll, I., & Koedinger, K. (2004). Toward tutoring help seeking: Applying cognitive modeling to meta-cognitive skills. In J. C. Lester, R. M. Vicario, & F. Paraguaçu (Eds.), *Proceedings of Seventh International Conference on Intelligent Tutoring Systems, ITS 2004* (pp. 227-239). Berlin, Germany: Springer Verlag.

Aleven, V., Ogan, A., Popescu, O., Torrey, C., & Koedinger, K. (2004). Evaluating the effectiveness of a tutorial dialog system for self-explanation. *Proceedings of International Conference on Intelligent Tutoring Systems,* (pp. 443-454).

Aleven, V., Roll, I., McLaren, B. M., Ryu, E. J., & Koedinger, K. R. (2005). An architecture to combine meta-cognitive and cognitive tutoring: Pilot testing the help tutor. *Proceedings of 12th International Conference on Artificial Intelligence in Education* (pp. 17–24). Amsterdam, The Netherlands: IOS.

Aleven, V., McLaren, B. M., Roll, I., & Koedinger, K. R. (2006). Toward meta-cognitive tutoring: A model of help seeking with a cognitive tutor. *International Journal of Artificial Intelligence in Education, 16,* 101–128.

Aleven, V., Stahl, E., Schworm, S., Fischer, F., & Wallace, R. M. (2003). Help seeking and help design in interactive learning environments. *Review of Educational Research, 73*(2), 277–320. doi:10.3102/00346543073003277

Alférez, M. J., Samos, J., Ochoa, J., & Quiles, J. L. (2010). Desarrollo de un juego como herramienta multimedia de aprendizaje y evaluación. *Ars Pharm, 2*(51), 132–136.

Allegro, Free software. (1998). *A game programming library.* Retrieved on January 14, 2012, from http://www.liballeg.org

Allwood, J., Traum, D., & Jokinen, K. (2000). Cooperation, dialogue and ethics. *International Journal of Human-Computer Studies, Special Issue on Collaboration. Cooperation and Conflict in Dialogue Systems, 53*(6), 871–914.

Alvarez, M. (2006). *Second Life and school: The use of virtual worlds in high school education. Undergraduate term paper for the course "Game for Web.".* San Antonio, TX, USA: Trinity University.

Andeani, G., Fabbrizio, D. D., Gilbert, M., Gillick, D., Hakkani-Tur, D., & Lemon, O. (2006). Let's DISCOH: Collecting an annotated open corpus with dialogue acts and reward signals for natural language helpdesks. *Proceedings of IEEE Workshop on Spoken Language Technology (SLT'06),* (pp. 218–221).

Anderson, C., Anderson, K., Ezoe, T., Fukushima, K., & Ikuta, S. (2008, June). *Facilitating universal design with sound card reader.* Paper presented at the meeting of the NECC 2008, San Antonio, TX.

Anderson, C., Fukushima, K., & Ikuta, S. (2009). Technology use for students with mild disabilities in the United State. *Otsuma Journal of Social Information Studies, 18,* 113–126.

Anderson, J. R., Corbett, A. T., Koedinger, K. R., & Pelletier, R. (1995). Cognitive tutors: Lessons learned. *Journal of the Learning Sciences, 4*(2), 167–207. doi:10.1207/s15327809jls0402_2

Anderson, L., Healy, A. F., Kole, J. A., & Bourne, L. E. (2011). Conserving time in the classroom: The clicker technique. *Quarterly Journal of Experimental Psychology, 8*(64), 1457–1462. doi:10.1080/17470218.2011.593264

Anderson, P. H., & Lawton, L. (2009). Business simulations and cognitive learning: Developments, desires, and future directions. *Simulation & Gaming, 40*(2), 193–216. doi:10.1177/1046878108321624

André, E., & Pelachaud, C. (2010). Interacting with embodied conversational agents. In Jokinen, K., & Cheng, F. (Eds.), *New trends in speech-based interactive systems.* Springer Publishers.

Andre, E., Rehm, M. L., Minker, W., & Bifihler, D. (2004). *Endowing spoken language dialogue systems with emotional intelligence* (pp. 178–187). Irsee, Germany: Tutorial and Research Workshop Affective Dialogue Systems. doi:10.1007/978-3-540-24842-2_17

Angehrn, A. (2001). C-VIBE: A virtual interactive business environment addressing change management learning. *Proceedings of IEEE International Conference on Advanced Learning Technologies (ICALT'01),* (pp. 174-177).

Angehrn, A., Nabeth, T., Razmerita, L., & Roda, C. (2001). K-InCA: Using artificial agents for helping people to learn new behaviours. *Proceedings of IEEE International Conference on Advanced Learning Technologies (ICALT'01),* (pp. 225-226).

Angeli, A. D., & Brahnam, S. (2008). I hate you! Disinhibition with virtual partners. *Interacting with Computers, 20*(3), 302–310. doi:10.1016/j.intcom.2008.02.004

Anttonen, J., & Surakka, V. (2005). Emotions and heart rate while sitting on a chair. *Proceedings of CHI 2005* (pp. 491-499). ACM Press.

Apollo Japan. (2005). *Screen code.* Retrieved December 11, 2011, from http://www.apollo-japan.ne.jp/

Apollo Japan. (2008). *Garyu-tensei.* Retrieved December 30, 2011, from http://www.apollo-japan.ne.jp/pdt_tensei.html; http://www.apollo-japan.ne.jp/qa_grts.pdf

Arbib, M. (2003). The evolving mirror system: A neural basis for language readiness. In Christiansen, M., & Kirby, S. (Eds.), *Language evolution* (pp. 182–200). Oxford, UK: Oxford University Press. doi:10.1093/acprof:oso/9780199244843.003.0010

Argyle, M., & Cook, M. (1976). *Gaze and mutual gaze.* Cambridge, UK Cambridge: University Press.

Arias, J. L. G. (2011). *Diseño y desarrollo de una herramienta informática para apoyo en educación especial con soporte de pizarra digital interactiva.* Master Thesis, Escuela Superior de Ingeniería Informática. Universidad de Vigo.

Arias, C., & Estape, M. (2005). *Disfonía infantil.* Barcelona, Spain: Ars Medical.

Aronso, A. (1993). *Clinical voice disorders* (3rd ed.). New York, NY: Thieme.

Arroyo, I., & Woolf, B. P. (2005). Inferring learning and attitudes from a Bayesian network of log file data. In C. K. Looi, G. Mc Calla, B. Bredeweg, & J. Breuker (Eds.), *Proceedings of the 12th International Conference on Artificial Intelligence in Education, Frontiers in Artificial Intelligence and Applications* (Vol. 125, pp. 33-40). Amsterdam, The Netherlands: IOS Press.

Arroyo, I., Cooper, D. G., Burleson, W., Woolf, B. P., Muldner, C., & Christopherson, R. (2009). *Emotion sensors go to school.* Paper presented at the 14th International Conference on Artificial Intelligence in Education (AIED 2009): Building Learning Systems that Care: From Knowledge Representation to Affective Modelling.

Atienza, R., & Zelinsky, A. (2002). Active gaze tracking for human-robot interaction. *Proceedings of 4th IEEE International Conference on Multimodal Interfaces* (pp. 261-266).

Atkinson, R. (2002). Optimizing learning from examples using animated pedagogical agents. *Journal of Educational Psychology, 94*(2), 416–427. doi:10.1037/0022-0663.94.2.416

Atserias, J., Climent, S., Farreres, J., Rigau, G., & Rodríguez, H. (1997). Combining multiple methods for the automatic construction of multilingual WordNets. In *Proceedings of International Conference on Recent Advances in Natural Language Processing* (RANLP'97). Retrieved from http://nlp.lsi.upc.edu/papers-grup/papers/atserias97.pdf

Atwell, E., Howarth, P., & Souter, C. (2003). The ISLE corpus: Italian and German spoken learners' English. *ICAME JOURNAL - Computers in English Linguistics, 27,* 5-18.

Augusto, J. (2009). Ambient intelligence: Opportunities and consequences of its use in smart classrooms. *Italics, 8*(2), 53–63.

Axistive. (2011). *What is a voice output communication aid?* Retrieved December 13, 2011, from http://www.axistive.com/what-is-a-voice-output-communication-aid.html

Babu, S., Suma, E., Barnes, T., & Hodges, L. F. (2007). *Can immersive virtual humans teach social conversational protocols?* IEEE Virtual Reality Conference March 10–14, NC.

Bailey, F., & Moar, M. (2002). *The vertex project: Exploring the creative use of shared 3D virtual worlds in the primary (K-12) classroom.* SIGGRAPH'02.

Bailly, G., Raidt, S., & Elisei, F. (2010). Gaze, dialog systems and face-to-face communication. *Speech Communication, 52*(6), 598–612. doi:10.1016/j.specom.2010.02.015

Bain, K., Basson, S., & Wald, M. (2005). Speech recognition in university classrooms: Liberated learning project. In *Proceedings of 5th Annual International ACM Conference on Assistive Technologies* (pp. 192-196)

Bannan-Ritland, B. (2003). The role of design in research: The integrative learning design framework. *Educational Researcher, 32*(1), 21–24. doi:10.3102/0013189X032001021

Barkand, J., & Kush, J. (2009). GEARS a 3D virtual learning environment and virtual social and educational world used in online secondary schools. *Electronic Journal of e-Learning, 7*(3), 215-224.

Barlam, R., Lasala, M. J., Marín, J., Masalles, J., & Pinya, C. (2010). Espurnik, proposta educativa en tres dimensions. *AULA de Innovación Educativa, 205*(19), 77-78. Retrieved April 13, 2012, from http://aula.grao.com/revistas/aula/205-lenguas-integradas-y-competencias-basicas/espurnik-propuesta-educativa-en-tres-dimensiones

Barlam, R., Marín, J., & Oliveres, C. (2011). Enseñar en la sociedad del conocimiento. Reflexiones desde el pupitre. *Cuadernos de Educación, 63.*

Barlow, J. P., Birkets, S., Kelly, K., & Slouka, M. (1995). What are we doing online? *Harper's, 291*(1), 35–46.

Baron-Cohen, S., Golan, O., & Ashwin, E. (2009). Can emotion recognition be taught to children with autism spectrum conditions? *Philosophical Transactions of the Royal Society B. Biological Sciences, 364,* 3567–3574. doi:10.1098/rstb.2009.0191

Barrett, S. M., Bornsen, S. E., Erickson, S. L., Markey, V., & Spiering, K. (2005). The personal response system as a teaching aid. *Communication Teacher, 3*(19), 89–92. doi:10.1080/14704620500201806

Barrio, M. (2004). *Experimental study of textual development in Spanish students of English as a foreign language in Segundo de Bachillerato: Features of written register in compositions of argumentative genre.* Unpublished doctoral thesis, Departamento de Filología Inglesa, Universidad Autónoma de Madrid.

Barry, S. (1994). Speech viewer 2. *Child Language Teaching and Therapy, 10,* 206–213. doi:10.1177/026565909401000207

Bartle, R. A. (2004). *Designing virtual worlds.* New Riders Pub.

Bashar, A., Parr, G., McClean, S., Scotney, B., & Nauck, D. (2010, 7-9 July 2010). *Learning-based call admission control framework for QoS management in heterogeneous networks.* Paper presented at the Proc. of Networked Digital Technologies (NDT 2010), Part II, Prague, Czech Republic.

Basogain, X., Olabe, M., Espinosa, K., & dos Reis, A. (2009). *Supporting the education with 3D environments and MUVEs.* X Congreso Internacional de Interacción Persona – Computador, INTERACCION'2009.

Baylor, A. L., & Kim, Y. (2005). Simulating instructional roles through pedagogical agents. *International Journal of Artificial Intelligence in Education, 15*(2), 95–115.

Beatty, I. D., Gerace, W. J., Leonar, W. J., & Dufresne, R. J. (2006). Designing effective questions for classroom response system teaching. *American Journal of Physics, 74*(1), 31–39. doi:10.1119/1.2121753

Beekes, W. (2006). The "millionaire" method for encouraging participation. *Active Learning in Higher Education, 1*(7), 25–36. doi:10.1177/1469787406061143

Bell, M. W. (2008). Toward a definition of virtual worlds. *Journal of Virtual Worlds Research, 1*(1), 1–5.

Belson, S. (2003). *Technology for exceptional learners.* Boston, MA: Houghton-Mifflin.

Benítez, Mª. D., Cruces, E. Mª Pastor & Sarrión, Mª. D. (2011). *Revista de Formación e Innovación Educativa Universitaria, 1*(4), 1-12.

Berque, D. A., & Konkle, L. M. (2010). *The impact of tablet PCs and pen-based technology on education: New horizons.* Purdue University Press, 2010. ISBN: 9781557535313

Berry, J. (2009). Technology support in nursing education: Clickers in the classroom. *Nursing Education Perspectives, 5*(30), 295–298.

Bersano, L. (2007). *Aprendiendo, desarrollo y evaluación de una herramienta informática para niños y niñas con necesidades educativas especiales.* Master's thesis, Politécnico di Torino.

Beun, R.-J., de Vos, E., & Witteman, C. (2003). Embodied dialog systems: Effects on memory performance and anthropomorphisation. *Proceedings of International Conference on Intelligent Virtual Agents,* (pp. 315-319).

Biber, D., Conrad, S., & Reppen, R. (1998). *Corpus linguistics: Investigating language structure and use.* Cambridge University Press. doi:10.1017/CBO9780511804489

Bickmore, T. (2003). *Relational agents: Effecting change through human-computer relationships.* PhD Thesis, Media Arts & Sciences, Massachusetts Institute of Technology.

Bickmore, T. W., & Picard, R. W. (2005). Establishing and maintaining long-term human-computer relationships. *ACM Transactions on Computer-Human Interaction, 12*(2), 293–327. doi:10.1145/1067860.1067867

Black, M., Tepperman, J., Kazemzadeh, A., Lee, S., & Narayanan, S. (2008). *Pronunciation verification of English letter-sounds in preliterate children.* Paper presented at the 10th International Conference on Spoken Language Processing (ICSLP - Interspeech), Brisbane, Australia.

Blázquez, J. P. (2008). *Aprendiendo: desarrollo y evaluación de una herramienta informática para niños y niñas con necesidades educativas especiales.* Master's thesis, Universidad Politécnica de Madrid.

Bloom, B. S. (1956). *The taxonomy of educational objectives: Classification of educational goals. Handbook 1: The cognitive domain.* New York, NY: McKay Press.

Bloor, T., & Bloor, M. (2004). *The functional analysis of English.* Oxford University Press.

Blumenfeld, P. C., Soloway, E., Marx, R. W., Krajcik, J. S., Guzdial, M., & Palincsar, A. (1991). Motivating project-based learning: Sustaining the doing, supporting the learning. *Educational Psychologist*, *26*(3), 369–398. doi:10.1207/s15326985ep2603&4_8

Blurton, C. (1999) New Directions of ICT-Use in Education, *World Communication and Information Report*, Retrieved December 11, 2011 from http://www.unesco.org/education/educprog/lwf/dl/edict.pdf.

Bohus, D., & Rudnicky, A. (2005). LARRI: A language-based maintenance and repair assistant. *Spoken Multimodal Human-Computer Dialogue in Mobile Environments*, *28*, 203–218. doi:10.1007/1-4020-3075-4_12

Bolich, B. J. (2001). Peer tutoring and social behaviors: A review. *International Journal of Special Education*, *16*(2).

Bolt, J. F. (Ed.). (2005). *The future of executive development.* Executive Development Associates. Retrieved from www.highbeam.com/doc/1P3-898719701.html

BOPV. (2009). *ORDEN de 17 de noviembre de 2009, de la Consejera de Educación, Universidades e Investigación, por la que se convocan ayudas para la elaboración de Objetos Digitales Educativos (ODEs) en la Comunidad Autónoma Vasca.* Boletín Oficial del País Vasco nº 253, lunes 7-dic-2009.

BOPV. (2010). *ORDEN de 15 de junio de 2010, de la Consejera de Educación, Universidades e Investigación, por la que se convocan ayudas para la elaboración de Objetos Digitales Educativos (ODEs) en la Comunidad Autónoma Vasca.* Boletín Oficial del País Vasco nº 128, martes 6-jul-2010.

Bordón Martínez, T. (2006). *La evaluación de la lengua en el marco de E/L2: Bases y procedimientos.* Madrid, Spain: Cuadernos de didáctica del español/LE, Arco Libros-Muralla.

Bordón Martínez, T. (2004). *La evaluación de la expresión oral y de la comprensión auditiva. Vademécum para la formación de profesores. Enseñar español como segunda lengua(L2)/lenguas extranjeras (LE)* (pp. 983–1001). Madrid, Spain: Sociedad General Española de Librería.

Bos, J., Klein, E., Lemon, O., & Oka, T. (1999). The verbmobil prototype system - A software engineering perspective. *Journal of Natural Language Engineering*, *5*(1), 95–112. doi:10.1017/S1351324999002132

Branco, P., Firth, P., Encarnao, L. M., & Bonato, P. (2005). Faces of emotion in human-computer interaction. *Proceedings of CHI 2005* (1236-1239). New York, NY: ACM.

Brave, S., & Nass, C. (2008). Emotion in human-computer interaction. In Sears, A., & Jacko, J. A. (Eds.), *The human computer interaction handbook: Fundamentals, evolving technologies and emerging applications* (2nd ed.). New York, NY: Lawrence Earlbaum Associates, Taylor & Francis Group.

Bredemeier, M. E., & Greenblat, C. S. (1981). The educational effectiveness of simulation games: A synthesis of findings. *Simulation & Games*, *12*(3), 307–332. doi:10.1177/104687818101200304

Brennan, W. K. (1984). *Curriculum for special needs (children with special needs series).* Philadelphia, PA: Open University Press.

Brito, L., Nava, O., & Mejía, J. A. (2007). *Desarrollo de objetos reutilizables aplicados en el aprendizaje virtual.* In *Proceedings of IV Simposio Pluridisciplinar sobre Diseño, Evaluación y Desarrollo de Contenidos Educativos Reutilizables, SPDECE 07*, September 2007, Bilbao.

Bruff, D. (2009). *Teaching with classroom response systems: Creating active learning environments.* San Francisco, CA: Jossey-Bass.

Bruffee, K. A. (1999). *Collaborative learning: Higher education, interdependence, and the authority of knowledge.* Johns Hopkins University Press. doi:10.2307/358879

Bueno de la Fuente, G. (2006). *Organización, gestión de la información e interoperabilidad: Metadatos.* Curso de Tecnologías Aplicadas al Desarrollo de Contenidos Educativos Multimedia Interactivos CNICE. Retrieved November 2012 from http://www.tecnotic.com

Bumbalek, Z., Zelenka, J., & Kencl, L. (2010). E-Scribe: Ubiquitous real-time speech transcription for the hearing-impaired. In *Proceedings of the 12th International Conference on Computers Helping People with Special Needs, ICCHP'10*, (pp. 160-168).

Burleson, W., & Picard, R. W. (2007). Evidence for gender specific approaches to the development of emotionally intelligent learning companions. *IEEE Intelligent Systems, 22*(4), 62–69. doi:10.1109/MIS.2007.69

Burns, A. C., Gentry, J. W., & Wolfe, J. (1990). A cornucopia of considerations in evaluating the effectiveness of experiential pedagogies. In Gentry, J. W. (Ed.), *Guide to business gaming and experiential learning* (pp. 253–278). East Brunswick, NJ: Nichols/GP Publishing.

Burstein, J., Chodorow, M., & Leacock, C. (2004). Automated essay evaluation: The Criterion online writing service. *AI Magazine, 25*(3), 27-36. Retrieved June 11, 2011, from http://www.aaai.org/ojs/index.php/aimagazine/article/view/1774/1672

Cadotte, E. R. (1995). *Business simulation: The next step in management training*. Santa Monica, CA: Selections.

Caldwell, J. E. (2007). Clickers in the large classroom: Current research and best-practice tips. *CBE Life Sciences Education, 6*(1), 9–20. doi:10.1187/cbe.06-12-0205

Callejas, Z., & López-Cózar, R. (2008). Influence of contextual information in emotion annotation for spoken dialogue systems. *Speech Communication, 50*(5), 416–433. doi:10.1016/j.specom.2008.01.001

Campbell, N. (2007). On the use of nonverbal speech sounds in human communication. In Campbell, N. (Ed.), *Verbal and Nonverbal Communication Behaviors* (*Vol. 4775*, pp. 117–128). LNAI. doi:10.1007/978-3-540-76442-7_11

Carpenter, A., & Windsor, H. (2006, 24 January 2010). A head of the game? - Games in education. *Serious Games Source*. Retrieved from http://seriousgamessource.com/features/feature_061306_ahead_of_the_game.php

Carpenter, S. K., & DeLosh, E. L. (2005). Application of the testing and spacing effects to name learning. *Applied Cognitive Psychology, 19*, 619–636. doi:10.1002/acp.1101

Casacuberta, F., García, R., Llisterri, J., Nadeu, C., Pardo, J. M., & Rubio, A. (1991). Development of Spanish corpora for speech research (Albayzin). In *Proceedings of the Workshop International Cooperation Standardization Speech Databases Speech I/O Assessment Methods*, (pp. 26-28). Chiavari, Italy.

Casacuberta, F., & Vidal, E. (1987). *Reconocimiento automático del habla*. Barcelona, Spain: Marcombo-Boixareo Editores.

Cassell, J. (2000). Embodied conversational interface agents. *Communications of the ACM, 43*(4), 70–78. doi:10.1145/332051.332075

Cassell, J., Sullivan, J., Prevost, S., & Churchill, E. F. (2001). *Embodied dialog systems*. The MIT Press.

Catizone, R., Setzer, A., & Wilks, Y. (2003). Multimodal dialog management in the COMIC Project. *Proceedings of EACL'03 Workshop on Dialog Systems*: *Interaction, Adaptation, and Styles of Management*, (pp. 25–34).

Cavazza, M., de la Camara, R. S., & Turunen, M. (2010). How was your day? A companion ECA. *Proceedings of AAMAS'10 Conference*, (pp. 1629-1630).

Cerva, P., & Nouza, J. (2007). Design and development of voice controlled aids for motor-handicapped persons. In *Proceedings of the 11th International Conference on Spoken Language Processing (Interspeech'07-Eurospeech)*, Antwerp, Belgium, (pp. 2521-2524).

Cervantes, I. (2006). *Plan curricular del Instituto Cervantes. Niveles de referencia para el español. A1, A2, B1, B2, C1, C2*. Madrid, Spain: Biblioteca Nueva.

Chafer, E. (2009). *Una introducción a los sistemas de respuesta interactiva. Electrónica y Comunicaciones: Monográfico TICs en las aulas. Elementos Didácticos para la enseñanza* (pp. 56–57). Editorial Cypsela.

Chan, T.-W., & Baskin, A. B. (1988). Studying with the prince: The computer as a learning companion. *Proceedings of International Conference on Intelligent Tutoring Systems*, (pp. 194-200).

Checa García, I., & Lozano, C. (2002). *Los índices de madurez sintáctica de Hunt a la luz de las distintas corrientes generativistas. XVII Encuentro de la Asociación de Jóvenes Lingüistas (AJL)*. Alicante.

Checa, F. (2010). El uso de mataversos en el mundo educativo: gestionando conocimiento en Second Life. *Revista de Docencia Universitaria, 2*(8), 147–159.

Chomsky, N. (1989). *El conocimiento del lenguaje: Su naturaleza, origen y uso.* Madrid, Spain: Alianza Editorial.

Chou, C.-Y., Chan, T.-W., & Lin, C.-J. (2003). Redefining the learning companion: The past, present and future of educational agents. *Computers & Education, 40*, 255–269. doi:10.1016/S0360-1315(02)00130-6

Chu, S.-W., O'Neill, I., Hanna, P., & McTear, M. (2005). An approach to multistrategy dialog management. *Proceedings of Interspeech '05-Eurospeech*, Lisbon, Portugal, (pp. 865–868).

Clarke, E. (2009). Learning outcomes from business simulation exercises: Challenges for the implementation of learning technologies. *Education + Training, 51*(5/6), 448-459.

Clark, H., & Wilkes-Gibbs, D. (1986). Referring as a collaborative process. *Cognition, 22*, 1–39. doi:10.1016/0010-0277(86)90010-7

CNICE. (2006). Accesibilidad, TIC y educación. *Serie Informes, 17*. Retrieved December 20, 2012, from http://ares.cnice.mec.es/informes/17

Cole, R., Mariani, J., Uszkoreit, H., Varile, G. B., Zaenen, A., Zampolli, A., & Zue, V. (Eds.). (1997). *Survey of the state of the art in human language technology.* Cambridge University Press.

Collinge, J. (2009). In a regular series on how to use technology in training, Justin Collinge sings the praises of voting technology. *Technology Tools*. Retrieved November 11, 2009, from http://www.trainingjournal.com/tj/2340.html# Consejo de Coordinación Universitaria. (2005). *Ministerio de Educación y Ciencia.*

Conati, C. (2002). Probabilistic assessment of user's emotions in educational games. *Applied Artificial Intelligence, 16*, 555–575. doi:10.1080/08839510290030390

Conati, C., & Maclaren, H. (2009). Empirically building and evaluating a probabilistic model of user affect. *User Modeling and User-Adapted Interaction, 19*(3), 267–303. doi:10.1007/s11257-009-9062-8

Corradini, A., Mehta, M., Bernsen, N. O., & Charfuelán, M. (2005). Animating an interactive conversational character for an educational game system. *Proceedings of the International Conference on Intelligent User Interfaces*, (pp. 183–190).

Cortarelo, V. L. (2007). *Desarrollo de herramientas de apoyo docente basadas en agentes animados para educación especial.* Master's thesis, Universidad Politécnica de Madrid.

Cosi, P., Delmonte, R., Biscette, S., Cole, R. A., Pellom, B., & van Vuren, S. (2004). Italian literacy tutor: Tools and technologies for individuals with cognitive disabilities. In *Proceedings of the ESCA ETRW NLP Speech Technology Advanced Language Learning Systems Symposium*, Venice, Italy, (pp. 207–214).

Council of Europe. (2005). *Reference level descriptions for national and regional languages (RDL): Draft guide for the production of RDL (Version 2).* Strasbourg, France: Language Policy Division.

Crossley, S. A., McNamara, D. S., Weston, J., & McLain Sullivan, S. T. (2010). *The development of writing proficiency as a function of grade level: A linguistic analysis.* University of Memphis. Retrieved June 11, 2011, from http://wpal.memphis.edu/main/pdf/The_development_of_writing_Proficiency_tech_report.pdf

Cruse, D. A. (1986). *Lexical semantics.* Cambridge University Press.

Cuadrillero Menéndez, J. A., Serna Nocedal, A., & Corrochano, J. H. (2007). Estudio sobre la granularidad de objetos de aprendizaje almacenados en repositorios de libre acceso. In *Proceedings of IV Simposio Pluridisciplinar sobre Diseño, Evaluación y Desarrollo de Contenidos Educativos Reutilizables*, SPDECE 07, September 2007, Bilbao.

Cuayáhuitl, H., Renals, S., Lemon, O., & Shimodaira, H. (2006). Reinforcement learning of dialog strategies with hierarchical abstract machines. *Proceedings of IEEE/ACL SLT '06 Workshop*, (pp. 182–186).

Cucchiarini, C., Lembrechts, D., & Strik, H. (2008, April). *HLT and communicative disabilities: The need for cooperation between government, industry and academia.* Paper presented at LangTech 2008, Rome, Italy.

Cumming, A., Kantor, R., Baba, K., Eouanzoui, K., Erdosy, U., & James, M. (2006). Analysis of discourse features and verification of scoring levels for independent and integrated prototype written tasks for the new TOEFL. *Monograph Series,* April 2006. Educational Testing Services (ETS). Retrieved June 11, 2011, from http://www.ets.org/Media/Research/pdf/RR-05-13.pdf

D'Mello, S. K., Craig, S. D., Gholson, B., Frankin, S., Picard, R., & Graesser, A. C. (2005). Integrating affect sensors in an intelligent tutoring system. *Proceedings of Workshop on Affective Interactions: The Computer in the Affective Loop at IUI,* (pp. 7-13).

da Cunha, I., & Torres-Moreno, J. M. (2010c). Automatic discourse segmentation: Review and perspectives. *International Workshop on African Human Languages Technologies* (pp. 17-20). Djibouti Institute of Science and Information Technologies, Djibouti. Retrieved June 11, 2011, from http://lia.univ-avignon.fr/fileadmin/documents/Users/Intranet/fich_art/paper_iria.pdf

da Cunha, I., San Juan, E., Torres-Moreno, J.-M., Lloberes, M., & Castellón, I. (2010b). Di-Seg: Un segmentador discursivo automático para el español. *Procesamiento del Lenguaje Natural, 45,* 1451-52. Retrieved June 11, 2011, from http://www.sepln.org/ojs/ojs2.2/index.php/pln/article/view/776

da Cunha, I., San Juan, E., Torres-Moreno, J.-M., Lloberes, M., & Castellón, I. (2010a). Discourse segmentation for Spanish based on shallow parsing. *Lecture Notes in Computer Science, 6347,* 13-23. Retrieved June 11, 2011, from http://springerlink.com/content/r402013247484361/

Dallaire, D. H. (2011). Effective use of personal response "clicker" systems in psychology courses. *Teaching of Psychology, 38*(3), 199–204. doi:10.1177/0098628311411898

Davis, S. M. (2003). Observations in classrooms using a network of handheld devices. *Journal of Computer Assisted Learning, 19,* 298–307. doi:10.1046/j.0266-4909.2003.00031.x

De Carolis, B., Pelachaud, C., Poggi, I., & Steedman, M. (2003). APML, a markup language for believable behavior generation. In Prendinger, H., & Ishizuka, M. (Eds.), *Life-like characters: Tools, affective functions and applications.* Berlin, Germany: Springer.

De Castro, M., Ruiz, B., Sanchez-Pena, J. M., Crespo, A. G., & Iglesias, A. (2011). *Tablets helping elderly and disabled people.* Ambient Assisted Living Forum 2011 (AAL 2011).

de Rosis, F., Cavalluzzi, A., Mazzotta, I., & Novielli, N. (2005). Can embodied dialog systems induce empathy in users? *Proceedings of AISB '05 Virtual Social Characters Symposium,* (pp. 1-8).

De Vicente, A., & Pain, H. (2002). *Informing the detection of the student's motivational state: An empirical study.* Paper presented at the 6th International Conference on Intelligent Tutoring Systems (ITS 2002).

Decker, D., & Piepmeier, J. A. (2008). Gaze tracking interface for robotic control. *40th Southeastern Symposium on System Theory* (pp. 274-278).

Dehn, D. M., & van Mulken, S. (2000). The impact of animated interface agents: A review of empirical research. *International Journal of Human-Computer Studies, 52*(1), 1–22. doi:10.1006/ijhc.1999.0325

Dekkers, J., & Donatti, S. (1981). The integration of research studies on the use of simulation as an instructional strategy. *The Journal of Educational Research, 74*(6).

Del Soldato, T., & Du Boulay, B. (1995). Implementation of motivational tactics in tutoring systems. *Journal of Artificial Intelligence in Education, 6*(4), 337–378.

Dell, A. G., Newton, D. A., & Petroff, J. G. (2008). *Assistive technology in the classroom: Enhancing the school experiences of students with disabilities.* Upper Saddle River, NJ: Pearson Education.

Deshpande, A. A., & Huang, S. H. (2011). Simulation games in engineering education: A state-of-the-art review. *Computer Applications in Engineering Education, 19*(3), 399–410. doi:10.1002/cae.20323

Deutschmann, M., Outakoski, H., Panichi, L., & Schneider, C. (2010). Virtual learning, real heritage benefits and challenges of virtual worlds for the learning of indigenous minority languages. *Conference Proceedings International Conference ICT for Language Learning,* 3rd Conference ed.

Dev/World Bank. (2007). *ICT-in-education toolkit for decision makers, planners & practitioners,* version 2.0. Retrieved 1 December, 2011, from www.ictinedtoolkit.org

DIALANG. (2009). *Test server*. Retrieved June 11, 2011, from http://www.lancs.ac.uk/researchenterprise/dialang/about

Dillenbourg, P., Schneider, D., Synteta, P., et al. (2002). Virtual learning environments. In A. Dimitracopoulou (Ed.), *Proceedings of the 3rd Hellenic Conference "Information & Communication Technologies in Education"* (pp. 3-18). Kastaniotis Editions, Greece.

Dillenbourg, P., & Self, J. (1992). *People power: A human-computer collaborative learning system in intelligent tutoring systems* (pp. 651–660). Berlin, Germany: Springer-Verlag.

Dimberg, U. (1990). Facial electromyography and emotional reactions. *Psychophysiology*, *19*, 643–647. doi:10.1111/j.1469-8986.1982.tb02516.x

D'Inverno, R., Davis, H., & White, S. (2003). Using a personal response system for promoting student interaction. *Teaching Mathematics and Its Applications*, *22*(4), 163–169. doi:10.1093/teamat/22.4.163

Dis/e-lms. (2011). *What are e-learning pros and cons?* Retrieved 1 December, 2011, from http://e-lms.org/product-overview/elearning-faq/127-elearning-advantages-and-disadvantages

Disabled Living Foundation. (2011). *Living made easy for children*. Retrieved December 13, 2011, from http://www.livingmadeeasy.org.uk/children/communication-aids-with-voice-output-1413/

Dix, A., Finlay, J., Abowd, G., & Beale, R. (2004). *Human-computer interaction*. Prentice Hall.

D'Mello, S., Jackson, T., Craig, S., Morgan, B., Chipman, P., White, H., et al. (2008). *AutoTutor detects and responds to learners affective and cognitive states*. Paper presented at the International Conference of Intelligent Tutoring Systems, Workshop on Emotional and Cognitive Issues.

Donegan, M., Morris, J. D., Corno, F., Signorile, I., Chio, A., & Pasian, V. (2009). Understanding users and their needs. *Universal Access in the Information Society*, *8*(4), 259–275. doi:10.1007/s10209-009-0148-1

Douglas, C. E., Campbell, N., Cowie, R., & Roach, P. (2003). Emotional speech: Towards a new generation of databases. *Speech Communication*, *40*, 33–60. doi:10.1016/S0167-6393(02)00070-5

Doyle, D., & Brown, F. W. (2000). Using a business simulation to teach applied skills – The benefits and the challenges of using student teams in multiple countries. *Journal of European Industrial Training*, *24*(6), 330–336. doi:10.1108/03090590010373316

Dr. Speech. Tiger DRS INC. (1999). *Tool for a comprehensive speech/voice assessment*. Retrieved January 14, 2012, from http://www.drspeech.com

Draper, S. W., & Brown, M. I. (2004). Increasing interactivity in lectures using an electronic voting system. *Journal of Computer Assisted Learning*, *20*, 81–94. doi:10.1111/j.1365-2729.2004.00074.x

Driscoll, M. (2000). *Psychology of learning for instruction*. Boston, MA: Allyn & Bacon.

Du Boulay, B., & Luckin, R. (2001). Modelling human teaching tactics and strategies for tutoring systems. *International Journal of Artificial Intelligence in Education*, *12*, 235–256.

Duchowski, A. (2007). *Eye tracking methodology: Theory and practice*. Springer.

Duffy, T., & Cunningham, D. (1996). Constructivism: Implications for the design and delivery of instruction. In Jonassen, D. H. (Ed.), *Handbook of research for educational telecommunications and technology* (pp. 170–198). New York, NY: MacMillan.

Dumblekar, V. (2004). *Management simulations: Test of effectiveness*. Retrieved from http://www.unice.fr/sg/resources/articles/dumblekar_2004_management.htm

Dunteman, G. H. (1989). *Principal component analysis. Quantitative Applications in the Social Sciences, 69*. Sage Publications, Inc.

Echazarreta, C., Prados, F., Poch, J., & Soler, J. (2009). La competencia "El trabajo colaborativo": Una oportunidad para incorporar las TIC en la didáctica universitaria. Descripción de la experiencia con la plataforma ACME (UdG). *Uocpapers, Revista sobre la Sociedad del Conocimiento, 8*.

Edlund, J., Gustafson, J., Heldner, M., & Hjalmarsson, A. (2008). Towards human-like spoken dialog systems. *Speech Communication*, *50*(8-9), 630–645. doi:10.1016/j.specom.2008.04.002

Edyburn, D. L. (2000). Assistive technology and mild disabilities. *Focus on Exceptional Children, 32*(9), 1–24.

Ekman, P. (1999). Basic emotions. In Dalgleish, T., & Power, T. (Eds.), *The handbook of cognition and emotion* (pp. 45–60). Sussex, UK: John Wiley & Sons.

Ekman, P., & Friesen, W. V. (1978). *Facial action coding system (FACS): A technique for the measurement of facial action*. Palo Alto, CA: Consulting Psychologists Press.

El Kaliouby, R., & Robinson, P. (2005). Generalization of a vision-based computational model of mind-reading. *First International Conference on Affective Computing and Intelligent Interaction*. Beijing, China.

Elhadad, M., & Robin, J. (1996). An overview of SURGE: A reusable comprehensive syntactic realization component. *Proceedings of the Eighth International Natural Language Generation Workshop*, (pp. 1–4).

Emeneau, M. B. (1956). India as a linguistic area. *Linguistics* (pp. 32:3-16).

Emeneau, M. B. (1980). *Language and linguistic area. Essays by Murray B. Emeneau (Selected and introduced by Anwar S. Dil)*. Stanford, CA: Stanford University Press.

Endres, F. (2009). Americans with Disabilities Act paved the way for CapTel and Web CapTel. *The Hearing Journal, 62*(3), 48–50.

Engwall, O. (2008). *Can audio-visual instructions help learners improve their articulation?-an ultrasound study of short term changes* (pp. 2631–2634). INTERSPEECH.

Er, N. F., & Dag, H. (2009). *Comparison of cost-free computational tools for teaching physics*. Paper presented at the Fifth International Conference on Soft Computing, Computing with Words and Perceptions on Systems Analysis, Decision and Control (ICSCCW 2009).

Eskenazi, M. (2009). An overview of spoken language technology for education. *Speech Communication, 51*(10), 832–844. doi:10.1016/j.specom.2009.04.005

Espurna. (2010). Retrieved from http://www.youtube.com/watch?v=Fe1k8gwKGM8&feature=related

Espurna. (2011). Retrieved from http://www.espurna.cat/

Espurna-Ning. (2011). Retrieved from http://espurna.ning.com/

Espurnik. (2011). Retrieved from http://www.youtube.com/watch?v=x4fy3_t5K0Y&feature=youtu.be&hd=1

European Disability Forum. (1999). *European manifesto on the information society and disabled people*. Brussels, Belgium: European Disability Forum.

European Institute for Design and Disability. (2004). *The EIDD Stockholm declaration*. Stockholm, Sweden: Author.

Fallows, S., & Steven, C. (2000). The skills agenda. In Fallows, S., & Steven, C. (Eds.), *Integrating key skills in higher education: Employability, transferable skills and learning for life* (pp. 8–9). London, UK: Kogan.

Faria, A. J. (2006). History, current usage, and learning from marketing simulation games: a detailed literature review. *Proceedings of the Marketing Management Association* (pp. 138-139). Nashville, TN.

Faria, A. J. (2001). The changing nature of business simulation/gaming research. *Simulation & Gaming, 32*, 97–110. doi:10.1177/104687810103200108

Faria, A. J., & Wellington, W. J. (2004). A survey of simulation game users, former-users, and never-users. *Simulation & Gaming, 35*(2), 178–207. doi:10.1177/1046878104263543

Fasel, B., & Luettin, J. (2003). Automatic facial expression analysis: A survey. *Pattern Recognition, 36*, 259–275. doi:10.1016/S0031-3203(02)00052-3

Felder, R. M., & Silverman, L. K. (1988). Learning and teaching styles in engineering education. *English Education, 78*(7), 674–681.

Felder, R. M., & Soloman, B. A. (1993). *Learning styles and strategies* (Vol. 2).

Feldman, R. S., & Rim, B. (1991). *Fundamentals of nonverbal behavior*. Cambridge University Press.

Feliz, T., & Santoveña, S. M. (2009). *El proyecto Added Value of Teaching in a Virtual World (AVATAR) (Valor añadido de la enseñanza en un mundo virtual)*. Programa Comenius, Lifelong Learning Programme.

Feng, D., Shaw, E., Kim, J., & Hovy, E. (2006). An intelligent discussion-bot for answering student queries in threaded discussions. *Proceedings of International Conference on Intelligent User Interfaces*, (pp. 171-177).

Fernaeus, Y., Hakansson, M., Jacobsson, M., & Ljungblad, S. (2010). How do you play with a robotic toy animal? A long-term study of pleo. In *Proceedings of the 9th International Conference on Interaction Design and Children* (pp. 39-48). ACM.

Ferrero, P. (2011). *Definición y análisis de parámetros lingüísticos cuantitativos para herramientas automáticas de evaluación aplicables al español como lengua extranjera.* Unpublished doctoral dissertation, Facultad de Filosofía y Letras de la Universidad Autónoma de Madrid, Madrid.

Ferrero, A., Alda, J., Campos, J., López-Alonso, J. M., & Pons, A. (2007). Principal component analysis of the photo-response non uniformity of a matrix detecto. *Applied Optics, 46*, 9–17. doi:10.1364/AO.46.000009

Ferrier, L., Shane, H., Ballard, H., Carpenter, T., & Benoit, A. (1995). Dysarthric speakers' intelligibility and speech characteristics in relation to computer speech recognition. *Augmentative and Alternative Communication, 11*(3), 165–175. doi:10.1080/07434619512331277289

Ferro Soto, C., Martínez Senra, A.I., & Otero Neira, M.C. (2009). Ventajas del uso de las TICs en el proceso de enseñanza-aprendizaje desde la óptica de los docentes universitarios españoles. *Revista Electrónica de Tecnología Educativa, 29.*

Ferro, C., Martínez, A.I., Otero, Mª C. (2009). Ventajas del uso de las TICs en el proceso de enseñanza – aprendizaje desde la óptica de los docentes universitarios españoles. *Revista electrónica de Tecnología Educativa, 29*, 1-100.

Fies, C., & Marshall, J. (2006). Classroom response systems: A review of the literature. *Journal of Science Education and Technology, 15*, 101–109. doi:10.1007/s10956-006-0360-1

Forbus, K. D., Whalley, P. B., Evrett, J. O., Ureel, L., Brokowski, M., Baher, J., & Kuehne, S. E. (1999). CyclePad: An articulate virtual laboratory for engineering thermodynamics. *Artificial Intelligence, 114*(1-2), 297–347. doi:10.1016/S0004-3702(99)00080-6

Fryer, L., & Carpenter, R. (2006). Bots as language learning tools. Language learning and technology. *Language Learning & Technology, 10*(3), 8–14.

Fryer, L., & Carpenter, R. (2006). Emerging technologies: Bots as language learning tools. *Language Learning & Technology, 10*(3), 8–14.

Galan, J. M., Izquierdo, L. R., Izquierdo, S. S., López, A., Pascual, J. A., & Posada, M. ... Villafanez, F. A. (2007). LABEXNET: Un laboratorio de economía experimental en Internet. *RELIEVE Revista Electrónica de Investigación y Evaluación Educativa, 13*(1). Retrieved from http://www.uv.es/RELIEVE/v13n1/RELIEVEv13n1_5.htm

García-Gómez, R., López-Barquilla, R., Puertas-Tera, J.-I., Parera-Bermúdez, J., Haton, M.-C., & Haton, J.-P. ... Hohmann, S. (1999). *Speech training for deaf and hearing impaired people: ISAEUS Consortium.* Paper presented at the 6th European Conference on Speech Communication and Technology (Eurospeech-Interspeech), Budapest, Hungary.

Garzotto, F., & Bordogna, M. (2010). Paper-based multimedia interaction as learning tool for disabled children. In *Proceedings of the 9th International Conference on Interaction Design and Children* (pp. 79-88). ACM.

Gateway. (2011). *Voice output communication aids* (VOCAs). Retrieved December 13, 2011, from http://www.gateway2at.org/page.php?page_ID=3&gen_ID=12&mensub_ID=4&submen_ID=4&AtDet_ID=55

Gibson, D., Clark, A., & Prensky, M. (2007). *Games and simulations in online learning.* Hershey, PA: Idea Group Inc. (IGI).

Girard, J., Paquette, G., Miara, A., & Lundgren, K. (1999). Intelligent assistance for web-based telelearning. In Lajoie, S., & Vivet, M. (Eds.), *AI in education – Open learning environments.* IOS Press.

Gizatdinova, Y., & Surakka, V. (2010). Automatic edge-based localization of facial features from images with complex facial expressions. *Pattern Recognition Letters, 31*(15), 2436–2446. doi:10.1016/j.patrec.2010.07.020

Glass, J., Hazen, T., Hetherington, L., & Wang, C. (2004). Analysis and processing of lecture audio data: Preliminary investigations. *Proceedings of Human Language Technology NAACL, Speech Indexing Workshop* (pp. 9-12).

Glass, J., Flammia, G., Goodine, D., Phillips, M., Polifroni, J., & Sakai, S. (1995). Multilingual spoken-language understanding in the MIT Voyager system. *Speech Communication*, *17*, 1–18. doi:10.1016/0167-6393(95)00008-C

Goleman, D. (1998). *Working with emotional intelligence*. New York, NY: Bantam Books.

González, M. (2005). Cómo desarrollar contenidos para la formación online basados en objetos de aprendizaje. *Revista de Educación a Distancia, 3*. Retrieved December 20, 2012, from http://www.um.es/ead/red/M3/

González, E., & Cernuzzi, L. (2009). Apoyando el aprendizaje de habilidades empresariales mediante la utilización de un simulador. In Sánchez, J. (Ed.), *Nuevas ideas en informática educativa* (pp. 8–19). Santiago de Chile.

González-Rosende, M. E., Vega, S., Girbés, M. S., Ortega, J., Segura, E., & Hernández, J. M. (2008). *La evaluación continua en el espacio Europeo de Educación Superior*. VI Jornadas de Redes de Investigación en Docencia Universitaria. Retrieved November 9, 2009, from http://www.eduonline.ua.es/jornadas2008/

Gorman, S., & National Center for Education Statistics. (2010). *National assessment of educational progress writing computer-based assessment* (3 pp.). Brochure published by National Center for Education Statistics (NCES). Retrieved June 11, 2011, from http://nces.ed.gov/nationsreportcard/pdf/writing/2010470.pdf

Gosen, J. J., & Washbush, J. (2004). A review of scholarship on assessing experiential learning effectiveness. *Simulation & Gaming*, *35*, 270–293. doi:10.1177/1046878104263544

Graesser, A. C., McNamara, D. S., & Louwerse, M. M. (2010). Methods of automated text analysis. In M. L. Kamil, P. D. Pearson, E. B. Moje, & P. Afflerbach (Eds.), *Handbook of reading research*, Vol. 4. Mahwah, NJ: Erlbaum. Retrieved June 11, 2011, from http://sites.google.com/site/graesserart/files/Methods-of-automated-text-analysis.pdf?attredirects=0

Graesser, A. C., Chipman, P., Haynes, B. C., & Olney, A. (2005). AutoTutor: An intelligent tutoring system with mixed-initiative dialogue. *IEEE Transactions on Education*, *48*(4), 612–618. doi:10.1109/TE.2005.856149

Graesser, A. C., Person, N. K., & Harter, D. (2001). Teaching tactics and dialog in AutoTutor. *International Journal of Artificial Intelligence in Education*, *12*, 23–39.

Graesser, A. C., Wiemer-Hastings, K., Wiemer-Hastings, P., & Kreuz, R.TRG. (1999). AutoTutor: A simulation of a human tutor. *Journal of Cognitive Systems Research*, *1*, 35–51. doi:10.1016/S1389-0417(99)00005-4

Graham, R. G., & Gray, C. F. (1969). *Business games handbook*. New York, NY: American Management Association.

Gratch, J., Wang, N., Okhmatovskaia, A., Lamothe, F., Morales, M., van der Werf, R. J., & Morency, L. (2007). Can virtual humans be more engaging than real ones? In J. A. Jacko (Ed.), *Proceedings of the 12th International Conference on Human-Computer Interaction (HCI'07): Intelligent Multimodal Interaction Environments* (pp. 286-297).

Gratch, J., Rickel, J., Andre, J., Badler, N., Cassell, J., & Petajan, E. (2002). Creating interactive virtual humans: Some assembly required. *IEEE Intelligent Systems*, *17*(4), 54–63. doi:10.1109/MIS.2002.1024753

Gratch, J., Wang, N., Gerten, J., Fast, E., & Duffy, R. (2007). *Creating rapport with virtual agents. Intelligent Virtual Agents* (pp. 125–138). Springer.

Gratch, J., Wang, N., Okhmatovskaia, A., Lamothe, F., Morales, M., van der Werf, R., & Morency, L. P. (2007). *Can virtual humans be more engaging than real ones? HCI Intelligent Multimodal Interaction Environments* (pp. 286–297). Springer. doi:10.1007/978-3-540-73110-8_30

Greer, L., & Heaney, P. J. (2004). Real-time analysis of student comprehension: An assessment of electronic student response technology in an introductory earth science course. *Journal of Geoscience Education*, *52*(4), 345–351.

Gridmark. (2004). *Grid onput*. Retrieved December 11, 2011, from http://www.gridmark.co.jp/product/speakingpen.html

Grigoriadou, M., Tsaganou, G., & Cavoura, T. (2003). Dialog-based reflective system for historical text comprehension. *Proceedings of Workshop on Learner Modelling for Reflection at Artificial Intelligence in Education*.

Grimes, D., & Warschauer, M. (2010). Utility in a fallible tool: A multi-site case study of automated writing evaluation. *Journal of Technology, Learning, and Assessment, 8*(6). Retrieved June 11, 2011, from http://escholarship.bc.edu/ojs/index.php/jtla/article/download/1625/1469

Griol, D., Gracia-Herrero, J., & Molina, J. M. (2011). The EducAgent platform: Intelligent conversational agents for e-learning applications. In Novais, P., Preuveneers, D., & Corchado, J. M. (Eds.), *Ambient intelligence – Software and applications. Advances in Intelligent and Soft Computing Series* (*Vol. 92*, pp. 117–124). Springer.

Griol, D., Hurtado, L. F., Segarra, E., & Sanchis, E. (2008). A statistical approach to spoken dialog systems design and evaluation. *Speech Communication, 50*(8-9), 666–682. doi:10.1016/j.specom.2008.04.001

Griol, D., Molina, J. M., Callejas, Z., & López-Cózar, R. (2012). (in press). Desarrollo de actividades de evaluación para un sistema on-line de aprendizaje de idiomas. *Revista Relada, 6*.

Griol, D., Molina, J. M., & Corrales, V. (2011). Lecture Notes in Computer Science: *Vol. 7023. The VoiceApp System: Speech technologies to access the Semantic Web* (pp. 393–402). CAEPIA. doi:10.1007/978-3-642-25274-7_40

Gros, B. (2000). *El ordenador invisible: Hacia la apropiación del ordenador en la enseñanza*. Barcelona, Spain: Gedisa.

Guha, M., Druin, A., & Fails, J. (2010). Investigating the impact of design processes on children. In *Proceedings of the 9th International Conference on Interaction Design and Children* (pp. 198-201). ACM.

Gustafson, J., Elmberg, P., Carlson, R., & Jönsson, A. (1998). An educational dialogue system with a user controllable dialogue manager. *Proceedings of ICSLP, 98*, 33–37.

Gutiérrez, R. (2003). *Patología de la comunicación humana: Una taxonomía integradora*. Conferencia de clausura del XVI Congreso Nacional de Fepal, (pp. 467-486). Sevilla, Spain: Universidad de Sevilla.

Ha, L. Q., Sicilia-García, E. I., Ming, J., & Smith, F. J. (2002). Extension of Zipf's law to words and phrases. In *Proceedings of the 19th International Conference on Computational Linguistics*, Vol. 1 (pp.1-6). Taipei, Taiwan.

Hall, J. K. (1999). A prosaics of interaction. The development of interactional competence in another language. In Hinkel, E. (Ed.), *Culture in second language teaching and learning. Cambridge applied linguistics series* (pp. 137–151). Cambridge, UK: Cambridge University Press.

Han, J., & Kamber, M. (2006). *Data mining: Concepts and techniques* (2nd ed.). San Francisco, CA: Elsevier.

Hansen, D. W., & Majaranta, P. (2012). Basics of camera-based gaze tracking. In Majaranta, P. (Eds.), *Gaze interaction and applications of eye tracking: Advances in assistive technologies* (pp. 21–26). Hershey, PA: IGI Global.

Harel, I., & Papert, S. (1990). *Instructionalist products vs. constructionist tools: The role of technology-based multimedia in children's learning*. Cambridge, MA: MIT Media Laboratory.

Harnard, S. (1990). The symbol grounding problem. *Physica D. Nonlinear Phenomena, 42*, 335–346. doi:10.1016/0167-2789(90)90087-6

Hatzis, A. (1999). *Optical logo-therapy: Computer-based audio-visual feedback using interactive visual displays for speech training*. Unpublished doctoral dissertation, University of Sheffield, U.K.

Hatzis, A., Green, P., Carmichael, J., Cunningham, S., Palmer, R., Parker, M., & O'Neill, P. (2003). *An integrated toolkit deploying speech technology for computer based speech training with application to dysarthric speakers*. Paper presented at the 8th European Conference on Speech Communication and Technology (Eurospeech-Interspeech), Geneva, Switzerland.

Hatzis, A., Green, P.-D., & Howard, S.-J. (1997). *Optical logo-therapy (OLT): A computer-based real time visual feedback application for speech training*. Paper presented at the 5th European Conference on Speech Communication and Technology (Eurospeech-Interspeech), Rhodes, Greece.

Hawley, M., Enderby, P., Green, P., Brownsell, S., Hatzis, A., & Parker, M. … Carmichael, J. (2003). STARDUST: Speech training and recognition for dysarthric users of assistive technology. In *Proceedings of the 7th Conference of the Association for the Advancement of Assistive Technology in Europe* (AAATE). Dublin, Ireland.

Hawley, M., Enderby, P., Green, P., Cunningham, S., & Palmer, R. (2006). Development of a voice-input voice-output communication aid (VIVOCA) for people with severe dysarthria. *Computer Science, 4061*, 882–885.

Haykin, S. (1999). Self-organizing maps. In *Neural networks - A comprehensive foundation* (2nd ed.). Prentice-Hall.

Hazlett, R. (2003). Measurement of user frustration: A biologic approach. *Extended Abstracts CHI 2003* (pp. 734-735). New York, NY: ACM.

Heffernan, N. T. (2003). Web-based evaluations showing both cognitive and motivational benefits of the Ms. Lindquist tutor. In Hoppe, U., Verdejo, F., & Kay, J. (Eds.), *Artificial intelligence in education* (pp. 115–122). Amsterdam, The Netherlands: IOS Press.

Heinzle, J., & Haynes, J.-D. (2009). Multivariate functional connectivity between fine-grained cortical activation patterns. In *Eighteenth Annual Computational Neuroscience Meeting, 10*(1), 76. Berlin.

Heldner, M., Edlund, J., & Hirschberg, J. (2010). Pitch similarity in the vicinity of backchannels. *Proceedings of Interspeech, 2010*, 3054–3057.

Hemmert, F., Hamann, S., Lowe, M., Zeipelt, J., & Joost, G. (2010). Co-designing with children: A comparison of embodied and disembodied sketching techniques in the design of child age communication devices. In *Proceedings of the 9th International Conference on Interaction Design and Children* (pp. 202-205).ACM.

Hernández, J., Pennesi, M., Sobrino, D., & Vázquez, A. (2011). Experiencias educativas en las aulas del siglo XXI. *Fundación Telefónica,* Madrid 2011 (pp. 404-409). Retrieved April 13,2012 from http://es.scribd.com/doc/58800585/Experiencias-educativas-en-las-aulas-del-siglo-XXI

Hernández-Trapote, A., López-Mencía, B., Bersano, L., & Hernández-Gómez, L. (2007). *Aprendiendo: Uso de la tecnología de agentes conversacionales personificados en el ámbito de la educación especial.* Paper presented at the Simposio Nacional de Tecnologías de la Información y las Comunicaciones en la Educación. Congreso Español de Informática. Zaragoza, Spain.

Herschensohn, J. (2007). *Language development and age.* New York, NY: Cambridge University Press. doi:10.1017/CBO9780511486487

Hew, K. F., & Brush, T. (2007). Integrating technology into K-12 teaching and learning: Current knowledge gaps and recommendations for future research. *Educational Technology Research and Development, 55*(3), 223–252. doi:10.1007/s11423-006-9022-5

Hew, K. F., & Cheung, W. S. (2010). Use of three-dimensional (3-D) immersive virtual worlds in K-12 and higher education settings: A review of the research. *British Journal of Educational Technology, 41*, 33–55. doi:10.1111/j.1467-8535.2008.00900.x

Hietanen, J. K., Leppänen, J. M., Peltola, M. J., Linna-aho, K., & Ruuhiala, H. J. (2008). Seeing direct and averted gaze activates the approach–avoidance motivational brain systems. *Neuropsychologia, 46*(9), 2423–2430. doi:10.1016/j.neuropsychologia.2008.02.029

Hiltz, R. (1990). Evaluating the virtual classroom. In Harasim, L. (Ed.), *Online education: Perspectives on a new environments* (pp. 133–184). New York, NY: Praeger Publishers.

Hiltz, S. R., & Wellman, B. (1997). Asynchronous learning networks as a virtual classroom. *Communications of the ACM, 40*(9), 44–49. doi:10.1145/260750.260764

Hmelo-Silver, C. E. (2004). Problem-based learning: What and how do students learn? *Educational Psychology Review, 16*(3), 235–266. doi:10.1023/B:EDPR.0000034022.16470.f3

Honeyman, M., & Miller, G. (1993). *Agriculture distance education: A valid alternative for higher education? Proceedings of the 20th Annual National Agricultural Education Research Meeting* (pp. 67–73).

Hornof, A. (2009). Designing with children with severe motor impairments. In *Proceedings of the 27th International Conference on Human Factors in Computing Systems* (pp. 2177-2180). ACM.

Horn, R. E., & Cleaves, A. (1980). *The guide to simulations/games for education and training.* Beverly Hills, CA: Sage Publications. doi:10.1177/1046878195264008

Hubal, R. C., Frank, G. A., & Guinn, C. I. (2000). AVATALK virtual humans for training with computer generated forces. *Proceedings of 9th Conference on Computer Generated Forces and Behavioral Representation*, Orlando, (pp. 617–623).

Huettel, L. G., Forbes, J., Franzoni, L., Malkin, R., Nadeau, J., Nightingale, K., & Ybarra, G. A. (2007). *Transcending the traditional: Using tablet PCs to enhance engineering and computer science instruction. Frontiers in Education Conference - Global Engineering: Knowledge Without Borders*. Opportunities Without Passports.

Hugin Expert A/S. (2011, 19 August 2011). Hugin Lite - Evaluation. *Hugin expert: The leading support tool.* Retrieved from http://www.hugin.com/productsservices/demo/hugin-lite

Hugin Lite. (2012, 18 January 2012). Hugin help pages. *Hugin Lite*. Retrieved from http://download.hugin.com/webdocs/manuals/7.4/Htmlhelp/descr_NPC_algorithm_pane.html

Hunt, K. W. (1977). Early blooming and late blooming syntactic structures. In C. R. Cooper & L. Odell (Eds.), *Evaluating writing: Describing, measuring, judging* (pp. 99-104). National Council of Teachers of English (NCTE).

Hunt, K. W. (1965). *Grammatical structures written at three grade levels. Research Report*. National Council of Teachers of English.

Hyönä, J., Tommola, J., & Alaja, A.-M. (1995). Pupil dilation as a measure of processing load in simultaneous interpretation and other language tasks. *The Quarterly Journal of Experimental Psychology, 48A*, 598–612.

Hyrskykari, A., Majaranta, P., & Räihä, K.-J. (2005). From gaze control to attentive interfaces. *Proceedings of HCII 2005*, Las Vegas, NV.

Hyrskykari, A., Majaranta, P., Aaltonen, A., & Räihä, K.-J. (2000). Design issues of iDict: A gaze-assisted translation aid. *Proceedings of Eye Tracking Research and Applications, Symposium* (ETRA 2000) (pp. 9-14). New York, NY: ACM.

Iglesias, A., Moreno, L., Revuelta, P., & Jiménez, J. (2009). APEINTA: A Spanish educational project aiming for inclusive education in and out of the classroom. In *Proceedings of the 14th Annual SIGSE Conference on Innovation & Technology in Computer Science Education (ITICSE'09), 41*(3), 393-393.

Ikuta, S., Nemoto, F., Ishitobi, R., & Ezoe, T. (2011). Long-term school activities for the students with intellectual and expressive language challenges: Communication aids using voices and sounds. *Society for Information Technology & Teacher Education International Conference* (pp. 3237-3242). Chesapeake, VA: AACE.

Ikuta, S. (2008a). Present and future issue of information communication technology in education [in Japanese]. *Hagemi, 318*, 4–8.

Ikuta, S. (2008b). School activities with audios for the students with disabilities. In Koreeda, K. (Ed.), *Examples of school activities useful for the special needs education* (pp. 72–73). Tokyo, Japan: Gakken.

Ikuta, S. (2011). Communication with sound pens and magic papers [in Japanese]. *Jissen Shogaiji Kenkyu, 458*(8), 46–49.

Ikuta, S., & Ezoe, T. (2008). *Hello book 1*. Tokyo, Japan: Shinjuku Japanese Language Institute.

Ikuta, S., & Ezoe, T. (2009a). *Hello book 2*. Tokyo, Japan: Shinjuku Japanese Language Institute.

Ikuta, S., & Ezoe, T. (2009b). *Emi & Alex with sound reader* (Vol. 1). Tokyo, Japan: Shinjuku Language Institute.

Ikuta, S., & Ezoe, T. (2009c). *Emi & Alex with sound reader* (Vol. 2). Tokyo, Japan: Shinjuku Language Institute.

Inclusive Design Research Center. (2011). *Voice output communication aids*. Retrieved December 13, 2011, from http://idrc.ocad.ca/index.php/resources/technical-glossary/49-voice-output-communication-aids

Inman, C., Wright, V. H., & Hartman, J. A. (2010). Use of Second Life in K-12 and higher education: A review of research. *Journal of Interactive Online Learning, 9*(1).

Instituto Nacional de Estadística. INE. (2010). *Encuesta sobre equipamiento y uso de Tecnologías de Información y Comunicación en los hogares* (TIC-H). Madrid, Spain: Ed INE.

Instru/cypr. (2011). *Process of education*. Retrieved 1 December, 2011, from http://cyprain.blogspot.com/2010/02/process-of-education.html

Ishitobi, R., Ezoe, T., & Ikuta, S. (2010). "Tracing" is "speaking": Communicating and learning using supportive sound books [in Japanese]. *Computers & Education, 29*, 64–67.

ISO/IEC. (1999). *ISO/IEC 13407: Human-centred design processes for interactive systems*.

Isokoski, P., Joos, M., Martin, B., & Spakov, O. (2009). Gaze controlled games. *Universal Access in the Information Society, 8*(4), 323–337. doi:10.1007/s10209-009-0146-3

Izquierdo, L. R., Galán, J. M., Santos, J. I., Izquierdo, S. S., & Del Olmo, R. (2007). Mathematica como herramienta docente en Economía. In J. A. González Manteca, & R. Carrasco Gallego (Eds.), *Proceedings of the International Conference on Industrial Engineering and Industrial Management: XI Congreso de Ingeniería de Organización* (pp. 1019-1028). Madrid.

Jackendoff, R. (2007). *Language, consciousness and culture*. Cambridge, MA: MIT Press.

Jan, D., Roque, A., Leuski, A., Morie, J., & Traum, D. (2009). *A virtual tour guide for virtual worlds. Intelligent Virtual Agents* (pp. 372–378). Springer.

Jaques, P. A., Vicari, R. M., Pesty, S., & Martin, J.-C. (2011). *Evaluating a cognitive-based affective student model*. Paper presented at the 4th International Conference of Affective Computing and Intelligent Interaction (ACII 2011) Part I.

Jauregi, M. K., Canto, S., de Graaff, R., & Koenraad, T. (2010). Social interaction through video-webcommunication and virtual worlds: An added value for education. In *Short paper in CD Proceedings Online Education, Berlin*, (pp. 1-6). Berlin, Germany: ICWE.

Jensen, F. V., & Nielsen, T. D. (2007). *Bayesian networks and decision graphs* (2nd ed.). Berlin, Germany: Springer. doi:10.1007/978-0-387-68282-2

Jerónimo, J. A. (2011). *Promover el aprendizaje en los mundos virtuales con una docencia innovadora*. Universidad Nacional Autónoma de México, Virtual Educa México 2011.

Jia, J. (2002). *The study of the application of a keywords-based chatbot system on the teaching of foreign languages*. University of Augsburg.

Jiménez, J., Revuelta, P., Iglesias, A., & Moreno, L. (2010). Evaluating the use of ASR and TTS technologies in the classroom: The APEINTA project. *ED-MEDIA 2010-World Conference on Educational Multimedia, Hypermedia & Telecommunications, AACE* (pp. 3976-3980).

Johnsen, K., Dickerson, R., Raij, A., Lok, B., Jackson, J., & Shin, M. … Lind, D. S. (2005). Experiences in using immersive virtual characters to educate medical communication skills. *Proceedings VR 2005* (pp. 179-186). IEEE.

Johns, J., Mahadevan, S., & Woolf, B. (2006). *Estimating student proficiency using an item response theory model. Intelligent Tutoring Systems* (pp. 473–480). Springer.

Johnson, W. L., LaBore, L., & Chiu, Y. C. (2004). A pedagogical agent for psychosocial intervention on a handheld computer. *Proceedings of AAAI Fall Symposium on Dialogue Systems for Health Communication*, (pp. 22-24).

Johnson, W. L., Wang, N., & Wu, S. (2007). Experience with serious games for learning foreign languages and cultures. *Proceedings of the SimTecT Conference*.

Johnson, D. W., Johnson, R. T., & Smith, K. A. (1991). *Active learning*. Interaction Book Co.

Johnson, W., Rickel, J., & Lester, J. (2000). Animated pedagogical agents: Face-to-face interaction in interactive learning environments. *Journal of Artificial Intelligence in Education, 11*, 47–78.

Johnston, L., Beard, L. A., & Carpenter, L. B. (2007). *Assistive technology: Access for all students*. Upper Saddle River, NJ: Pearson Education.

Jokinen, K., & Pärkson, S. (2011). Synchrony and copying in conversational interactions. *Proceedings of the 3rd Nordic Symposium on Multimodal Communication* (pp. 18-24). NEALT Proceedings Series 15.

Jokinen, K., Harada, K., Nishida, M., & Yamamoto, S. (2010a). Turn alignment using eye-gaze and speech in spoken interaction. *Proceedings of Interspeech 2010*, Makuhari Messe, Japan.

Jokinen, K., Nishida, M., & Yamamoto, S. (2010b). On eye-gaze and turn-taking. *Proceedings of the Workshop on Eye Gaze in Intelligent Human Machine Interaction* (EGIHMI '10) (pp. 118-123). New York, NY: ACM.

Jokinen, K., Nishida, M., & Yamamoto, S. (2010c). Collecting and annotating conversational eye-gaze data. *Proceedings of Multimodal Corpora: Advances in Capturing, Coding and Analyzing Multimodality* (MMC 2010), LREC-2010. Valetta, Malta.

Jokinen, K. (2009). *Constructive dialogue management – Speech interaction and rational agents.* John Wiley & Sons.

Jokinen, K., Kanto, K., & Rissanen, J. (2004). Adaptative user modelling in AthosMail. *Lecture Notes in Computer Science, 3196*, 149–158. doi:10.1007/978-3-540-30111-0_12

Jonassen, D. H. (2000). Transforming learning with technology: Beyond modernism and postmodernism or whoever controls the technology creates the reality. *Educational Technology, 40*(2), 21–25.

Jorge-Botana, G., León, J. A., Olmos, R., & Escudero, I. (2010). Latent semantic analysis parameters for essay evaluation using small-scale corpora. *Journal of Quantitative Linguistics, 17*(1), 1–29. doi:10.1080/09296170903395890

Kain, A. B., Hosom, J. P., Niu, X., Van Santen, J. P. H., Fried-Oken, M., & Staehely, J. (2007). Improving the intelligibility of dysarthric speech. *Speech Communication, 49*(9), 743–759. doi:10.1016/j.specom.2007.05.001

Kaneko, S., Ohshima, M., Takei, K., Yamamoto, L., Ezoe, T., Ueyama, S., & Ikuta, S. (2011). School activities with voices and sounds: Handmade teaching materials and sound pens [in Japanese]. *Computers & Education, 30*, 48–51.

Karat, C. M., Vergo, J., & Nahamoo, D. (2007). Conversational interface technologies. In Jacko, J. A. (Ed.), *The human-computer interaction handbook: Fundamentals, evolving technologies, and emerging applications (human factors and ergonomics)*. Lawrence Erlbaum Associates Inc.doi:10.1201/9781410615862.ch19

Karna, E., Nuutinen, J., Pihlainen-Bednarik, K., & Vellonen, V. (2010). Designing technologies with children with special needs: Children in the centre (CIC) framework. In *Proceedings of the 9th International Conference on Interaction Design and Children* (pp. 218-221). ACM.

Keller, J. M. (1983). Motivational design of instruction. In Reigeluth, C. M. (Ed.), *Instructional-design theories and models: An overview of their current status* (Vol. 1, pp. 386–434). Hillsdale, NJ: Lawrence Erlbaum Associates.

Kelly, D., & Tangney, B. (2002). *Incorporating learning characteristics into an intelligent tutor.* Paper presented at the 6th International Conference Intelligent Tutoring Systems (ITS 2002).

Keltner, D., & Lerner, J. S. (2010). Emotion. In Fiske, S. T., Gilbert, D. T., Lindzey, G., & Jongsma, A. E. (Eds.), *Handbook of social psychology* (5th ed., Vol. 1, pp. 317–352). Hoboken, NJ: Wiley.

Kendall, W. (1978). Public Law 94-142: Implications for the classroom teacher. *Peabody Journal of Education, 55*(3), 226–230. doi:10.1080/01619567809538191

Kendon, A. (1967). Some functions of gaze direction in social interaction. *Acta Psychologica, 26*, 22–63. doi:10.1016/0001-6918(67)90005-4

Kendon, A. (2005). *Gesture: Visible action as utterance.* Cambridge University Press.

Kennedy, G., & Cutts, Q. (2005). The association between students' use of an electronic voting system and their learning outcomes. *Journal of Computer Assisted Learning, 21*, 260–268. doi:10.1111/j.1365-2729.2005.00133.x

Kenneth, D. (1966). *Voice therapy for children with laryngeal dysfunction.* Paper presented at the Annual Convention of the American Speech and Hearing Association. Washington, USA

Kenny, P., Parsons, T., & Rizzo, A. (2009). *Human computer interaction in virtual standardized patient systems. Human-Computer Interaction: Interacting in Various Application Domains* (pp. 514–523). Springer. doi:10.1007/978-3-642-02583-9_56

Kenwright, K. (2009). Clickers in the classroom. *TechTrends: Linking Research and Practice to Improve Learning, 53*(1), 74–77.

Kerly, A., Ellis, R., & Bull, S. (2008). Children's interactions with inspectable and negotiated learner models. *Proceedings of International Conference on Intelligent Tutoring Systems*, (pp. 132-141).

Kerly, A., Ellis, R., & Bull, S. (2008). CALM system: A dialog system for learner modelling. *Knowledge-Based Systems, 21*(3), 238–246. doi:10.1016/j.knosys.2007.11.015

Kerly, A., Ellis, R., & Bull, S. (2008). Dialog systems in e-learning. *Proceedings of, AI-08*, 169–182.

Ketelhut, D. J. (2007). The impact of student self-efficacy on scientific inquiry skills: An exploratory investigation in River City, a multi-user virtual environment. *Journal of Science Education and Technology, 16*(1), 99–111. doi:10.1007/s10956-006-9038-y

Kheir, R., & Way, T. (2007). Inclusion of deaf students in computer science classes using real-time speech transcription. In *Proceedings of ACM SIGCSE Conference on Innovation and Technology in Computer Science Education* (ITiCSE'07), (pp. 261–265).

Khiat, A., Matsumoto, Y., & Ogasawara, T. (2004b). Task specific eye movements understanding for a gaze-sensitive dictionary. *Proceedings of the 9th International Conference on Intelligent User Interface* (IUI 04) (pp. 265-267). New York, NY: ACM.

Kim, Y. (2007). Desirable characteristics of learning companions. *International Journal of Artificial Intelligence in Education, 17*(4), 371–388.

Kinnear, P. R., & Gray, C. D. (2010). *PASW statistics 17 made simple*. East Sussex, UK: Psychology Press.

Kintsch, W. (2002). The potential of latent semantic analysis for machine grading of clinical case summaries. *Journal of Biomedical Informatics, 35*(1), 3–7. doi:10.1016/S1532-0464(02)00004-7

Kiung, N. G., Liew, Y. T., Saripan, M. I., Abas, A. F., & Noordin, N. K. (2008). Flexi e-learning system: Disabled friendly education system. *European Journal of Soil Science, 7*(2).

Klein, J. T. (2005). Integrative learning and interdisciplinary studies. *Peer Review, 7*(4), 8–10.

Kluge, S., & Riley, L. (2008). Teaching in virtual worlds: Opportunities and challenges. *Issues in Informing Science and Information Technology, 5*.

Koller, D. (1999). Probabilistic relational models. In S. Džeroski & P. Flach (Eds.), *Proceedings of the 9th International Workshop of Inductive Logic Programming (ILP-99)* (Vol. 1634, pp. 3-13). Pittsburgh, PA: Springer.

Konchady, M. (2006). *Text mining application programming*. Boston, MA: Charles River Media.

Kornilov, A.-U. (2004). *The biofeedback program for speech rehabilitation of oncological patients after full larynx removal surgical treatment*. Paper presented at the 9th International Conference Speech and Computer (SPECOM), St. Petersburg, Russia.

Koseko, K., & Kitashima, S. (1980). *Jizo (Stone statue) with a school bag* (Randoseru-wo Shotta Jizo-san, in Japanese). Tokyo, Japan: Shinnihon Shuppan.

Kumar, R., & Rose, C. P. (2011). Architecture for building dialog systems that support collaborative learning. *IEEE Transactions in Learning Technology, 4*(1), 21–34. doi:10.1109/TLT.2010.41

Lamel, L., Bilinski, E., Adda, G., Gauvain, J., & Schwenk, H. (2006). The LIMSI RT06s lecture transcription system. *Proceedings of the 5th International Workshop Machine Learning for Multimodal Interaction*, (pp. 457-468).

Landauer, T. K. S., Dennis, S., & Kintsch, W. (Eds.). (2007). *Handbook of latent semantic analysis*. Institute of Cognitive Science, University of Colorado.

Landauer, T. K., Foltz, P. W., & Laham, D. (1998). Introduction to latent semantic analysis. *Discourse Processes, 25*, 259-284. Retrieved June 11, 2011, from http://www.knowledge-technologies.com/papers/IntroLSA1998.pdf

Landauer, T. K., & Dumais, S. T. (1997). A solution to Plato's problem: The latent semantic analysis theory of the acquisition, induction, and representation of knowledge. *Psychological Review, 104*(2), 211–240. doi:10.1037/0033-295X.104.2.211

Land, M. F., & Furneaux, S. (1997). The knowledge base of the oculomotor system. *Philosophical Transactions of the Royal Society of London. Series B, Biological Sciences, 352*(1358), 1231–1239. doi:10.1098/rstb.1997.0105

Langacker, R. W. (1999). *Grammar and conceptualization*. New York, NY: Mouton de Gruyter. doi:10.1515/9783110800524

Lantolf, J. P. (2009). Second language learning as a mediated process. *Language Teaching*, *33*(2), 79–96. doi:10.1017/S0261444800015329

LaPlante, M. P., Hendershot, G. E., & Moss, A. J. (1992). Assistive technology devices and home accessibility features: Prevalence, payment, need, and trends. *Advance Data from Vital and Health Statistics*, *217*, 2–13.

Lasala, M. J. (2011). *Proyectos educativos en aula d'acollida basados en mundos virtuales 3D: Fem una platja (hagamos una playa)*. En: Experiencias educativas en las aulas del siglo XXI. Innovación con TIC.

Lasala, M. J. (2011b). *Espurnik'11*. Retrieved from http://www.slideshare.net/aulaacollidacunit/ficha-prctica-espurnik11

Lasala, M. J. (2011c). *Experiencias didacticas mundos virtuales y redes sociales en la enseanza secundaria obligatoria*. Retrieved from http://www.slideshare.net/aulaacollidacunit/experiencias-didcticas-mundos-virtuales-y-redes-sociales-en-la-enseanza-secundaria-obligatoria

Latham, A., Crockett, K. A., McLean, D., & Edmonds, B. A. (2012). Conversational intelligent tutoring system to automatically predict learning styles. *Computers & Education*, *59*(1), 95–109. doi:10.1016/j.compedu.2011.11.001

Lave, J., & Wenger, E. (1991). *Situated learning: Legitimate peripheral participation*. Cambridge, UK: University of Cambridge Press. doi:10.1017/CBO9780511815355

Lazzaro, N. (25 October, 2011). Why we play games: Four keys to more emotion without story. *XEO Design*. Retrieved from http://www.xeodesign.com/xeodesign_whyweplaygames.pdf

Lee, C., Soong, F. K., & Paliwal, K. K. (1996). *Automatic speech and speaker recognition: Advanced topics*. Boston, MA: Kluwer Academic Publishers. doi:10.1007/978-1-4613-1367-0

Leitch, D., & MacMillan, T. (2001). *Liberated learning project year II report: Improving access for persons with disabilities in higher education using speech recognition technology*. Nova Scotia, Canada: Saint Mary's University.

Lemon, O., Georgila, K., & Henderson, J. (2006). Evaluating Effectiveness and portability of reinforcement learned dialog strategies with real users: The TALK TownInfo evaluation. *Proceedings of IEEE-ACL SLT'06*, Palm Beach, Aruba, (pp. 178–181).

Lester, J. C., Converse, S. A., Kahler, S. E., Barlow, S. T., Stone, B. A., & Bhogal, R. S. (1997). The persona effect: Affective impact of animated pedagogical agents. In *Proceedings of the SIGCHI Conference on Human Factors in Computing Systems*, (pp. 359-366).

Lester, J. C., Stone, B. A., & Stelling, G. D. (1999). Lifelike pedagogical agents for mixed-initiative problem solving in constructivist learning environments. *User Modeling and User-Adapted Interaction*, *9*, 1–44. doi:10.1023/A:1008374607830

Lexile. (2012). *The Lexile framework for reading*. Retrieved March 25, 2012, from http://www.lexile.com/

Lezak, M. (1983). *Neuropsychological assessment*. New York, NY: Oxford University Press.

Liaw, S. S., Hatala, M., & Huang, H. (2009). Investigating acceptance toward mobile learning to assist individual knowledge management: Based on activity theory approach. *Computers & Education*, *54*, 446–454. doi:10.1016/j.compedu.2009.08.029

Liébana-Cabanillas, F. J., Rejón-Guardia, F., Guillén-Perales, A., & Martínez-Fiestas, M. (2011). *El uso de las redes sociales de microblogging: una experiencia empírica en el curso 2011-2012*. II Jornadas sobre Innovación Docente y Adaptación al EEES en las titulaciones técnicas. Septiember, 26 and 27, Granada.

Ligori, M. B., & Van Veen, K. (2006). Constructing a successful cross-national virtual learning environment in primary and secondary education. *AACE Journal*, *14*(2), 103–128.

Ligorio, M. B. (2001, March). *Euroland: A virtual community*. Paper presented at the Conference Computer Supported Collaborative Learning. Maastricht, Amsterdam.

Ligorio, M. B., & Trimpe, J. D. (2000). *Euroland: Active knowledge building through different formats of mediated communication*. Unpublished, Katholieke University of Nijmegen, Netherlands.

Ligorio, M. B., Talamo, A., & Simons, R. S. (2000, March). *Euroland: A virtual world fostering collaborative learning at a distance*. Paper presented at the First Research Workshop of EDEN Research and Innovation in Open and Distance Learning, Prague.

Litman, D. J., & Silliman, S. (2004). ITSPOKE: An intelligent tutoring spoken dialog system. *Proceedings of Human Language Technology Conference: North American Chapter of the Association for Computational Linguistics*, (pp. 5-8).

Liu, T. C., Liang, J. K., Wang, H. Y., & Chan, T. W. (2003). *The features and potential of interactive response system.* Paper presented at the 2003 International Conference on Computers in Education, Hong Kong.

Liu, Y., & Chee, Y. S. (2004). Designing interaction models in a multiparty 3D learning environment. *Proceedings of 12th International Conference on Computers in Education (ICCE 2004)*, (pp. 293–302).

LMS/blog. (2011). *What LMS is best for pupils, teachers and program developers? Advantages vs disadvantages.* Retrieved 1 December, 2011, from http://njw789.blogspot.com/

LMS/Simply. (2011). *Advantages of using a learning management system.* Retrieved 5 December, 2011, from http://www.simplydigi.com/blog/2011/05/24/advantages-of-using-a-learning-management-system

LMS/time. (2011). *The LMS- Learning systems made easy!* Retrieved 5 December, 2011, from http://www.timelesslearntech.com/blog/5-advantages-of-using-the-learning-management-system-lms/

LMS-Adv/Micro. (2011). *Five advantages of using a learning management system.* Retrieved 5 December, 2011, from http://www.microburstlearning.com/knowledgecenter.php

Locke, J. L. (1997). A theory of neurolinguistic development. *Brain and Language, 58*, 265–326. doi:10.1006/brln.1997.1791

López Martínez, F. (1999). *El vocabulario básico de orientación didáctica.* Facultad de Letras de la Universidad de Murcia, España. Retrieved June 11, 2011 from http://digitum.um.es/xmlui/handle/10201/196

Lopez, M. C. I. (2009). *El desarrollo de las habilidades de alfabetización emergente en el contexto de la lectura de cuentos.* PhD Thesis, Departamento de Didáctica y Organización Escolar. Universidad de Murcia.

López-Alonso, J. M., & Alda, J. (2002a). Bad pixel identification by means of the principal component analysis. *Optical Engineering (Redondo Beach, Calif.), 41*, 2152–2157. doi:10.1117/1.1497397

López-Alonso, J. M., & Alda, J. (2004a). Operational parametrization of the 1/f noise of a sequence of frames by means of the principal components analysis in focal plane arrays. *Optical Engineering (Redondo Beach, Calif.), 42*, 257–265.

López-Alonso, J. M., Alda, J., & Bernabéu, E. (2002b). Principal component characterization of noise for infrared images. *Applied Optics, 41*, 320–331. doi:10.1364/AO.41.000320

López-Alonso, J. M., Rico-García, J. M., & Alda, J. (2004b). Photonic crystal characterization by FDTD and principal component analysis. *Optics Express, 12*, 2176–2186. doi:10.1364/OPEX.12.002176

López-Cózar, R., & Araki, M. (2005). *Spoken, multilingual and multimodal dialog systems: Development and assessment.* John Wiley and Sons.

López-Cózar, R., Callejas, Z., & Griol, D. (2010). Using knowledge of misunderstandings to increase the robustness of spoken dialogue systems. *Knowledge-Based Systems, 23*(5), 471–485. doi:10.1016/j.knosys.2010.03.004

López-Mencía, B. (2011). *Agentes conversacionales personificados en sistemas interactivos: Diseño y evaluación.* PhD Thesis, Universidad Politécnica de Madrid.

Lopez-Mencia, B., Pardo, D., Hernandez-Trapote, A., Hernandez, L., & Relaño, J. (2010). A collaborative approach to the design and evaluation of an interactive learning tool for children with special educational needs. In *Proceedings of the 9th International Conference on Interaction Design and Children* (pp. 226-229). ACM.

Lopez-Mencia, B., Pardo, D., Roa-Seiler, N., Hernandez-Trapote, A., Hernandez, L., & Rodriguez, M. (2010). *Look at me: An emotion learning reinforcement tool for children with severe motor disability.* Paper presented at Multimodal Corpora: Advances in Capturing, Coding and Analyzing Multimodality -LREC 2010.

Lucas Cuesta, J. M., Fernández Martínez, F., Ferreiros López, J., López Ludeña, V., & San Segundo Hernández, R. (2010). Clustering of syntactic and discursive information for the dynamic adaptation of language models. *Procesamiento de Lenguaje Natural, 45,* 175-182. Retrieved June 11, 2011, from http://www.sepln.org/ojs/ojs-2.2/index.php/pln/article/view/790

Maguire, M., Elton, E., Osman, Z., & Nicolle, C. (2006). Design of a virtual learning environment: For students with special needs. *An Interdisciplinary Journal on Humans in ICT Environments, 2*(1), 119–153.

Maier, A., Haderlein, T., Eysholdt, U., Rosanowski, F., Batliner, A., Schuster, M., & Nöth, E. (2009). PEAKS- A system for the automatic evaluation of voice and speech disorders. *Speech Communication, 51,* 425–437. doi:10.1016/j.specom.2009.01.004

Mairesse, F., Gasic, M., Jurcícek, F., Keizer, S., Thomson, B., Yu, K., & Young, S. (2009). Spoken language understanding from unaligned data using discriminative classification models. *Proceedings of ICASSP, 09,* 4749–4752.

Majaranta, P., Bates, R., & Donegan, M. (2009). Eye-tracking. In Stephanidis, C. (Ed.), *The universal access handbook* (pp. 587–606). Lawrence Erlbaum Associates, Inc. doi:10.1201/9781420064995-c36

Majaranta, P., & Räihä, K.-J. (2007). Text entry by gaze: Utilizing eye-tracking. In MacKenzie, I. S., & Tanaka-Ishii, K. (Eds.), *Text entry systems: Mobility, accessibility, universality* (pp. 175–187). Morgan Kaufmann.

Malone, T. W. (1981). Toward a theory of intrinsically motivating instruction. *Cognitive Science, 6*(4), 333–369. doi:10.1207/s15516709cog0504_2

Mancini, M., Castellano, G., Bevacqua, E., & Peters, C. (2007). Lecture Notes in Computer Science: *Vol. 4418. Copying behaviour of expressive motion* (pp. 180–191). Berlin, Germany: Springer.

Mann, C. W., & Thompson, A. S. (1988). Rhetorical structure theory: Toward a functional theory of text organization. *Text 8*(3), 243-281. Retrieved June 11, 2011, from http://discurso-uaq.weebly.com/uploads/2/7/7/5/2775690/mann02.pdf

Manzoni, J. F., & Angehrn, A. (1997). Understanding organizational dynamics of IT-enabled change: A multimedia simulation approach. *Journal of Management Information Systems, 14*(3), 109–140.

Mareno, N., Bremner, M., & Emerson, C. (2010). The use of audience response systems in nursing education: best practice guidelines. *International Journal of Nursing Education Scholarship, 7,* 1–17. doi:10.2202/1548-923X.2049

Marín, D. P. (2010). *Uso de agentes conversacionales pedagógicos en sistemas de aprendizaje híbrido (b-learning).* Paper presented at IV Seminario de Investigación en Tecnologías de la Información Aplicadas a la Educación, Madrid, Spain.

Marrero, I. (2011). Los clickers en el aula de matemáticas. *Revista de Didáctica de las Matemáticas, 76,* 157–166.

Marschark, M., Sapere, P., Convertino, C., & Seewagen, R. (2005). Access to postsecondary education through sign language interpreting. *Journal of Deaf Studies and Deaf Education, 10,* 38–50. doi:10.1093/deafed/eni002

Marsella, S. C., Johnson, W. L., & LaBore, C. M. (2003). Interactive pedagogical drama for health interventions. In Hoppe, I. U. (Eds.), *Artificial intelligence in education: Shaping the future of learning through intelligent technologies* (pp. 341–348). Amsterdam, The Netherlands: IOS Press.

Martín Uriz, A. M., Hidalgo, L., & Whittaker, R. (2001). *Desarrollo y complejidad de la frase nominal en composiciones de estudiantes.* Paper presented at the XIX Congreso de la Asociación Española de Lingüística Aplicada.

Martín Uriz, A., & Whittaker, R. (Eds.). (2005). *La composición como comunicación: Una experiencia en las aulas de lengua inglesa en bachillerato.* Ediciones de la Universidad Autónoma de Madrid.

Martinez - Otero Perez. V. (2003). *Teoría y práctica de la educación.* Madrid, Spain: CCS.

Martínez González, R. A., Miláns del Bosch, M., Pérez Herrero, H., & Sampedro Nuño, A. (2007). Psychopedagogical components and processes in e-learning. Lessons from an unsuccessful on-line course. *Computers in Human Behavior, 23*(1). Retrieved December 20, 2012, from http://www.sciencedirect.com/

Martínez-Celdrán, E. (1989). *Fonología general y Española: Fonología funcional*. Barcelona, Spain: Teide.

Martyn, M. (2007). Clickers in the classroom: An active learning approach. *EDUCAUSE Quarterly, 2*, 71–74.

Massaro, D. (2006). Embodied agents in language learning for children with language challenges. In K. Miesenberger, J. Klaus, W. Zagler, & A. Karshmer (Eds.), *Proceedings of the 10th International Conference on Computers Helping People with Special Needs, ICCHP 2006* (pp. 809-816). University of Linz, Austria. Berlin, Germany: Springer.

Massaro, D., Cohen, M., Beskow, J., & Cole, R. (2000). Developing and evaluating conversational agents. In Cassell, J., Sullivan, J., Prevost, S., & Churchill, E. (Eds.), *Embodied conversational agents* (pp. 287–318). Cambridge, MA: MIT Press.

Mattasoni, M., Omologo, M., Santarelli, A., & Svaizer, P. (2002). On the joint use of noise reduction and MLLR adaptation for in-car hands-free speech recognition. *Proceedings of International Conference on Acoustics, Speech, and Signal Processing (ICASSP '02)*, (pp. 289–292).

Mayer, R. E., & Moreno, R. (1998). A cognitive theory of multimedia learning: Implications for design principles. *Electronic Proceedings of the CHI '98*.

Mayo, M., & Mitrovic, A. (2001). Optimizing ITS behaviour with Bayesian networks and decision theory. *International Journal of Artificial Intelligence in Education, 12*(2), 124–153.

Mazzone, E., Iivari, N., Tikkanen, R., Read, J., & Beale, R. (2010). Considering context, content, management, and engagement in design activities with children. In *Proceedings of the 9th International Conference on Interaction Design and Children* (pp. 108-117). ACM.

McKenney, J. (1962). An evaluation of a business game in an MBA currículo. *The Journal of Business, 35*(3). doi:10.1086/294511

McNamara, D. S., Louwerse, M. M., Cai, Z., & Graesser, A. (2006). *Coh-Metrix 2.0*. Retrieved June 11, 2011 from http://cohmetrix.memphis.edu/CohMetrixDemo/demo.htm

McQuiggan, S. W., Mott, B. W., & Lester, J. C. (2008). Modeling self-efficacy in intelligent tutoring systems: An inductive approach. *User Modeling and User-Adapted Interaction, 18*(1 - 2), 81-123.

McTear, M. F. (2004). *Spoken dialog technology*. Springer. doi:10.1007/978-0-85729-414-2

Meier, R. C., Newell, W. T., & Pazer, H. L. (1969). *Simulation in business and economics*. New Jersey: Prentice Hall.

Menezes, P., Lerasle, F., Dias, J., & Germa, T. (2007). Towards an interactive humanoid companion with visual tracking modalities. *International Journal of Advanced Robotic Systems, •••*, 48–78.

Messinger, P. R., Stroulia, E., Lyons, K., Bone, M., Niu, R., Smirnov, K., & Perelgut, S. (2009). Virtual worlds – past, present, and future: New directions in social computing. *Decision Support Systems, 47*, 204–228. doi:10.1016/j.dss.2009.02.014

Metametrics. (2102). *Lexile framework for writing*. Retrieved March 25, 2012, from http://www.metametricsinc.com/lexile-framework-writing/

Meza, I., Riedel, S., & Lemon, O. (2008). Accurate statistical spoken language understanding from limited development resources. *Proceedings of ICASSP, 08*, 5021–5024.

Millar, S. (2010). Using eye gaze in school. In Wilson, A., & Gow, R. (Eds.), *The eyes have it! The use of eye gaze to support communication* (pp. 28–34). Edinburgh, UK: CALL Scotland, The University of Edinburgh.

Miller, G. (1962). Some psychological studies of grammar. *The American Psychologist, 17*(11), 748–762. doi:10.1037/h0044708

Miller, G. A., & McKean, K. O. (1964). A chronometric study of some relations between sentences. *The Quarterly Journal of Experimental Psychology, 16*, 297–308. doi:10.1080/17470216408416385

Miller, G., & Johnson, L. P. (1976). *Language and perception*. Cambridge, UK: Cambridge University Press.

Ministry of Education. Culture, Sports, Science and Technology-Japan. (2001). *The state of special needs education in 21st century in Japan*. Retrieved December 15, 2011, from http://www.mext.go.jp/b_menu/shingi/chousa/shotou/006/toushin/010102.htm

Minker, W. (1998). Stochastic versus rule-based speech understanding for information retrieval. *Speech Communication, 25*(4), 223–247. doi:10.1016/S0167-6393(98)00038-7

Miretti, M. (2003). *La lengua oral en la educación inicial.* Rosario, Argentina: Homo Sapiens.

MIT. (2003). *ICAMPUS projects.* Spoken Lecture Processing. Retrieved from http://icampus.mit.edu/projects/SpokenLecture.shtml

Mohamad, Y., Velasco, C., & Tebarth, H. (2005). Development and evaluation of emotional interface agents in training of learning disabled children. In *Proceedings of the First Workshop on Emotion in HCI.*

Molka-Danielsen, J., & Deutschman, M. (2009). *Learning and teaching in the virtual world of Second Life.* Trondheim, Norway: Tapir Academic Press.

Moncloa. (2009). *Council of Ministers 2009-07-31.* La Moncloa. Retrieved November 2012 from http://www.lamoncloa.gob.es

Montoro, G., Haya, P. A., Alamán, X., López-Cózar, R., & Callejas, Z. (2006). A proposal for an XML definition of a dynamic spoken interface for ambient intelligence. *Proceedings of International Conference on Intelligent Computing (ICIC'06),* (pp. 711–716).

Montoya, Z. (2009). *El desarrollo del lenguaje. Carta de la Salud, 155.* Santiago de Cali, Colombia: Fundación Valle del Lili.

Morales, L. (2011). Can the use of clickers or continuous assessment motivate critical thinking? A case study based on corporate finance students. *Higher Learning Research Communications, 1*(1), 33–42.

Moratis, L., Hoff, J., & Reul, B. (2006). A dual challenge facing management education: simulation-based learning and learning about CSR. *Journal of Management Development, 25*(3/4), 213. doi:10.1108/02621710610648150

Moreno, R., Mayer, R., Spires, H., & Lester, J. (2001). The case for social agency in computer-based teaching: Do students learn more deeply when they interact with animated pedagogical agents? *Cognition and Instruction, 19*(2), 177–213. doi:10.1207/S1532690XCI1902_02

Morling, B., McAuliffe, M., Cohen, L., & DiLorenzo, T. M. (2008). Efficacy of "clickers" in large, introductory psychology classes. *Teaching of Psychology, 35,* 45–50. doi:10.1080/00986280701818516

Mostow, J. (2012). Why and how our automated reading tutor listens. *Proceedings of International Symposium on Automatic Detection of Errors in Pronunciation Training (ISADEPT),* (pp. 43-52).

Mühlpfordt, M., & Wessner, M. (2005). Explicit Referencing in chat supports collaborative learning. *Proceedings of 6th International Conference on Computer-Supported Collaborative Learning* (CSCL'05), (pp. 662-671).

Muñoz, A. M. (2007). *La parálisis cerebral. Technical report, Observatorio de la Discapacidad Institutos de Mayores y Servicios Sociales.* IMSERSO.

Muñoz, K., McKevitt, P., Lunney, T., Noguez, J., & Neri, L. (2011). An emotional student model for game-play adaptation. *Entertainment Computing, 2*(2), 133–141. doi:10.1016/j.entcom.2010.12.006

Murillo, J. L. (2010). Programas escuela 2.0 y pizarra digital: Un paradigma de mercantilización del sistema educativo a través de las TICs. *Revista Electrónica Interuniversitaria de Formación del Profesorado, 13*(2), 65–78.

Nakano, Y., & Nishida, T. (2007). Attentional behaviours as nonverbal communicative signals in situated interactions with conversational agents. In Nishida, T. (Ed.), *Engineering approaches to conversational informatics* (pp. 85–102). John Wiley & Sons, Ltd.doi:10.1002/9780470512470.ch5

Nation, P., & Kyongho, H. (1995). Where would general service vocabulary stop and special purposes vocabulary begin? *System, 23*(1), 35-41. Retrieved June 11, 2011, from www.victoria.ac.nz/lals/staff/publications/paul-nation/1995-Hwang-Special-purposes.pdf

National Dissemination Center for Children with Disabilities. (2011). *Speech and language impairments.* Washington, DC: Author.

Nemoto, F., & Ikuta, S. (2010). "Tracing" is "speaking": A student acquiring the happiness of communication using "sound pronunciation system" *Computers & Education, 28,* 57–60.

Nesbit, J., Belfer, K., & Vargo, J. (2003). A convergent participation model for evaluation of learning objects. *Canadian Journal of Learning and Technology, 28*(3).

Newell, A. F., & Gregor, P. (2000). *User sensitive inclusive design—In search of a new paradigm.* CUU '00. Retrieved from http://doi.acm.org/10.1145/355460.355470

Newport, E. L., Bavelier, D., & Neville, H. J. (2001). Critical thinking about critical periods: Perspectives on a critical period for language acquisition. In Dupoux, E. (Ed.), *Language, brain, and cognitive development.* Cambridge, MA: MIT Press.

Ngiam, J., Khosla, A., Kim, M., Nam, J., Lee, H., & Ng, A. Y. (2011) *Multimodal deep learning.* NIPS Workshop on Deep Learning and Unsupervised Feature Learning. 2010.

Nicol, D. J., & Boyle, J. T. (2003). Peer instruction versus class-wide discussion in large classes: A comparison of two interaction methods in the wired classroom. *Studies in Higher Education, 28,* 457–573. doi:10.1080/030750 7032000122297

Nielsen, J. (1993). *Usability engineering.* Cambridge.

Nielsen, T. M., Sundstrom, E., & Halfhill, T. (2005). Group dynamics and effectiveness: Five years of applied research. In Wheelan, S. A. (Ed.), *Handbook of group research and practice* (pp. 285–311). Thousand Oaks, CA: Sage. doi:10.4135/9781412990165.d21

Norman, D. A., Ortony, A., & Russell, D. M. (2003). Affect and machine design: Lessons for the development of autonomous machines. *IBM Systems Journal, 42*(1), 38–44. doi:10.1147/sj.421.0038

Oester, A.-M., House, D., Protopapas, A., & Hatzis, A. (2002). Presentation of a new EU project for speech therapy: OLP (Ortho-Logo-Paedia). In *Proceedings of the XV Swedish Phonetics Conference,* Stockholm, Sweden, (pp. 45–48).

Office of Special Education and Rehabilitation Services. (2004). *Disabilities that qualify infants, toddlers, children, and youth for services under IDEA 2004.* Retrieved December 12, 2011 from http://www.ldonline. org/article/12399

Office of Special Education and Rehabilitative Services. (1997). *IDEA '97: The law.* Retrieved December 12, 2011, from http://www2.ed.gov/offices/OSERS/Policy/IDEA/the_law.html

Oh, A., & Rudnicky, A. (2000). Stochastic language generation for spoken dialog systems. *Proceedings of ANLP/NAACL Workshop on Conversational Systems,* (pp. 27–32).

Ohshima, M., Sugibayashi, H., Shimada, F., Yamamoto, L., Nemoto, F., Ishitobi, R., & Ikuta, S. (2008). A useful audio device for curricular and extracurricular activities. *19th Annual Conference of the Information Technology and Teacher Education (SITE), Assessment & E-Folios* (pp. 5140-5145). Chesapeake, VA: AACE.

Ohshima, M., Shimada, F., Yamamoto, L., Nemoto, F., Ezoe, T., Suzuki, J., & Ikuta, S. (2007). Use of "sound pronunciation system" in elementary schools *Computers & Education, 23,* 76–79.

Okawara, H., Uchikawa, T., Shiraishi, T., Kaneko, S., Sugibayashi, H., & Hara, Y. (2008). Use of "sound pronunciation system" for students with physically handicapped [in Japanese]. *Computers & Education, 24,* 40–43.

OKIdata. (2009). *GridLayouter & grid content studio.* Retrieved December 23, 2011, from http://www.okidata.co.jp/solution/gridmark/

Oliver, R. (2002) *The role of ICT in higher education for the 21st century: ICT as a change agent for education.* Retrieved 14 November, 2011, from http://www. edna. edu.au

Oliver, R. (2000). Creating meaningful contexts for learning in web-based settings. In *Proceedings of Open Learning* (pp. 53–62). Brisbane, Australia: Learning Network, Queensland.

Olloqui de Montenegro, L., & López Morales, H. (Eds.). (1991). *La investigación de la madurez sintáctica y la enseñanza de la lengua maternal. La enseñanza de es-pañol como lengua maternal* (pp. 113–132). Universidad de Puerto Rico.

Olmos, R., León, J., Escudero, I., & Jorge-Botana, G. (2009). Análisis del tamaño y especificidad de los corpus en la evaluación de resúmenes mediante el LSA. Un análisis comparativo entre LSA y jueces expertos. *Revista Signos, 42*(69), 71-81. Retrieved June 11, 2011, from http://www.scielo.cl/scielo.php?script=sci_arttext&pid= S0718-09342009000100004&lng=en&nrm=iso&ignore=.html

Olympus Inc. (1999). *Scan talk*. Retrieved December 11, 2011, from http://www.olympus.co.jp/jp/news/1999b/nr990823r300j.cfm

Ortiz-de-Urbina, M., & Mora, E. M. (2011). Empleo de herramientas didácticas y TICs en la resolución de casos prácticos en administración y dirección de empresas. *Revista Electrónica de ADA, 5*(2), 168–175.

Ortony, A., Clore, G. L., & Collins, A. (1990). *The cognitive structure of emotions*. New York, NY: University Press.

Öster, A.-M. (1996). *Clinical applications of computer-based speech training for children with hearing impairment*. Paper presented at the 4th International Conference on Spoken Language Processing (ICSLP-Interspeech), Philadelphia (PA), USA.

Oxford University Press. (2008). *Oxford 3000™ profiler*. Retrieved April 2, 2012, from http://www.oup.com/oald-bin/oxfordProfiler.pl

Oxford University Press. (2011). *Oxford 3000™ text checker*. Retrieved April 2, 2012, from http://oaadonline.oxfordlearnersdictionaries.com/oxford3000/oxford_3000_profiler.html

Oxford, R. (1989). *The role of styles and strategies in second language learning. ERIC Digest- ED317087*. Washington, DC: ERIC Clearinghouse on Languages and Linguistics.

Oxford, R., Ehrman, M., & Lavine, R. (1991). *Style wars: Teacher-student style conflicts in the language classroom, Challenges in the 1990s for college foreign language programs* (pp. 1–25). Heinle & Heinle Pub.

Padró, L. (2006). *FreeLing user manual 1.5*. Retrieved June 11, 2011, from http://www.smo.uhi.ac.uk/~oduibhin/oideasra/interfaces/userman15.pdf

Padró, L. (2009). *FreeLing user manual 2.1*. Retrieved June 11, 2011, from http://xavi.ivars.me/arxius/manuals/freeling/freeling-userman.pdf

Padró, L., Reese, S., Agirre, E., & Soroa, A. (2010). Semantic services in FreeLing 2.1: WordNet and UKB. *Principles, Construction, and Application of Multilingual Wordnets: Proceedings of the 5th Global Wordnet Conference*, Narosa. Retrieved June 11, 2011, from http://www.lsi.upc.edu/~nlp/papers/padro10a.pdf.

Page, E. B. (1966). Grading essays by computer: Progress report. In *Notes from the 1966 Invitational Conference on Testing Problems* (pp. 87-100).

Page, E. B., Poggio, J. P., & Keith, T. Z. (1997). Computer analysis of student essays: Finding trait differences in the student profile. *Annual Meeting of the American Educational Research Association: Vol. 8*. Retrieved June 11, 2011, from http://www.eric.ed.gov/ERICWebPortal/contentdelivery/servlet/ERICServlet?accno=ED411316

Page, E. B. (1994). Computer grading of student prose, using modern concepts and software. *Journal of Experimental Education, 62*(2), 127–142. doi:10.1080/00220973.1994.9943835

Paireekreng, W., Rapeepisarn, K., & Wong, K. W. (2009). Time-based personalised mobile game downloading. In Pan, Z., Cheok, D. A., & Müller, W. (Eds.), *Transactions on Edutainment II, LNCS 5660 (Vol. 2*, pp. 59–69). Berlin, Germany: Springer-Verlag. doi:10.1007/978-3-642-03270-7_5

Pala, K., & Ganagashetty, S. V. (in press). Experience of speech perception mediates lexical learning. In *Proceedings of International Conference on Speech and Prosodic Interfaces*.

Pala, K., Singh, A. K., & Gangashetty, S. V. (2011). Games for academic vocabulary learning through a virtual environment. In *Proceedings of International Conference on Asian Language Processing (IALP)*, (pp. 295-298). IEEE

Pantic, M., & Rothkrantz, L. J. (2000). Automatic analysis of facial expressions: The state of the art. [PAMI]. *IEEE Transactions on Pattern Analysis and Machine Intelligence, 22*, 1424–1445. doi:10.1109/34.895976

Paquette, G. (2002). *Designing virtual learning centers*. Retrieved December 22, 2011, from http://hal.archives-ouvertes.fr/docs/00/19/06/67/PDF/Paquette-Gilbert-Chap16-2001.pdf

Paquette, G., Bergeron, G., & Bourdeau, J. (1993). The virtual classroom revisited. *TeleTeaching '93 Proceedings*, Trondheim, Norway.

Paradis, M. (2004). *A neurolinguistic theory of bilingualism*. Amsterdam, The Netherlands: John Benjamins.

Partala, T., & Surakka, V. (2002). Pupil size variation as an indication of affective processing. *International Journal of Human-Computer Studies, 59*, 185–198. doi:10.1016/S1071-5819(03)00017-X

Partala, T., & Surakka, V. (2004). The effects of affective interventions in human–computer interaction. *Interacting with Computers, 16*, 295–309. doi:10.1016/j.intcom.2003.12.001

Partala, T., Surakka, V., & Lahti, J. (2004). Affective effects of agent proximity in conversational systems. *Proceedings of NordiCHI, 2004*, 353–356. New York, NY: ACM. doi:10.1145/1028014.1028070

Pekrun, R. (2006). The control-value theory of achievement emotions: Assumptions, corollaries, and implications for educational research and practice. *Educational Psychology Review, 18*(4), 315–341. doi:10.1007/s10648-006-9029-9

Pekrun, R., Frenzel, A. C., Goetz, T., & Perry, R. P. (2007). The control value theory of achievement emotions. An integrative approach to emotions in education. In Schutz, P. A., & Pekrun, R. (Eds.), *Emotion in education* (pp. 13–36). London, UK: Elsevier. doi:10.1016/B978-012372545-5/50003-4

Pekrun, R., Goetz, T., & Perry, R. P. (2005). *Achievement emotions questionnaire (AEQ). User's manual*. University of Munich.

Pelgrum, W. J., & Anderson, R. E. (1999). *ICT and the emerging paradigm for life long learning: A worldwide educational assessment of infrastructure, goals and practices*. International Association for the Evaluation of Educational Achievement.

Peña, J. (1988). *Manual de logopedia*. Barcelona, Spain: Masson.

Per/minu. (2011). *Perceived advantages and disadvantages*. Retrieved 1 December, 2011, from http://minutebio.com/blog/2009/03/24/perceived-advantages-and-disadvantages/

Perelló, J. (1990). *Trastornos del habla*. Barcelona, Spain: Masson.

Perelló, J., Miquel, J. A. S., & Llorach, A. (1973). *Alteraciones de la voz*. Barcelona, Spain: Científico-Médica.

Perelló, J., & Tortosa, F. (1989). *Fundamentos audiofoniátricos*. Barcelona, Spain: Científico-Médica.

Pérez Marín, D. R. (2007). *Adaptive computer assisted assessment of free-text students answers: An approach to automatically generate students conceptual models*. Doctoral dissertation, Escuela Politécnica Superior, Universidad Autónoma de Madrid. Madrid.

Pérez-Marín, D., & Pascual-Nieto, I. (2011). *Conversational agents and natural language interaction: Techniques and effective practices*. Hershey, PA: IGI Global. doi:10.4018/978-1-60960-617-6

Picard, R. (1999). Affective computing for HCI. In H.-J. Bullinger & J. Ziegler (Eds.), *Proceedings of HCI International (the 8th International Conference on Human-Computer Interaction) on Human-Computer Interaction: Ergonomics and User Interfaces*, Vol. I. (pp. 829-833). Hillsdale, NJ: L. Erlbaum Associates Inc.

Picard, R. W. (1995). *Affective computing*. Unpublished Technical report. Massachusetts Institute of Technology (MIT).

Picard, R. W. (2009). Future affective technology for autism and emotion communication. *Philosophical Transactions of the Royal Society B. Biological Sciences, 364*, 3575–3584. doi:10.1098/rstb.2009.0143

Picard, R. W., Papert, S., Bender, W., Blumberg, B., Breazeal, C., & Cavallo, D. (2004). Affective learning –A manifesto. *BT Technology Journal, 22*(4), 253–269. doi:10.1023/B:BTTJ.0000047603.37042.33

Pickering, M., & Garrod, S. (2004). Towards a mechanistic psychology of dialogue. *The Behavioral and Brain Sciences, 27*, 169–226. doi:10.1017/S0140525X04000056

Pinker, S. (2007). *The stuff of thought*. New York, NY: Viking.

Pittermann, J., Pittermann, A., & Minker, W. (2010). *Handling emotions in human-computer dialogues*. Springer. doi:10.1007/978-90-481-3129-7

Poikela, E., & Nummenmaa, A. R. (2006). *Understanding problem-based learning*. University of Tampere.

Poirier, C. R., & Feldman, R. S. (2007). Promoting active learning using individual response technology in large introductory psychology classes. *Teaching of Psychology, 34*(3), 194–196. doi:10.1080/00986280701498665

Polsani, P. R. (2003). Use and abuse of reusable learning objects. *Journal of Digital Information, 3*(4).

Pon-Barry, H., Schultz, K., Bratt, E. O., Clark, B., & Peters, S. (2006). Responding to student uncertainty in spoken tutorial dialog systems. *International Journal of Artificial Intelligence in Education, 16*, 171–194.

Pond, W. K. (2003). *Lifelong learning–The changing face of higher education. eLearning Summit, 2003*. California: La Quinta Resort.

Porayska-Pomsta, K., Mavrikis, M., & Pain, H. (2008). Diagnosing and acting on student affect: The tutor's perspective. *User Modeling and User-Adapted Interaction, 18*, 125–173. doi:10.1007/s11257-007-9041-x

Portela, J. R. L. (2010). *Diseño y usabilidad de interfaces hombre-máquina con agentes animados para apoyo a la enseñanza en educación especial*. Master's thesis, Universidad Politécnica de Madrid.

Prendinger, H., Ma, C., Yingzi, J., Nakasone, A., & Ishizuka, M. (2005). Understanding the effect of life-like interface agents through users' eye movements. *Proceedings of the 7th International Conference on Multimodal Interfaces* (ICMI '05) (pp. 108-115). New York, NY: ACM.

Pressman, R. (2009). *Software engineering: A practitioner's approach*. McGraw Hill.

Priego, L., & López, F. (2006). *Metodología para el uso de estándares internacionales en la creación de objetos de aprendizaje*. Retrieved from http://www.cs.buap.mx/~cuartocongreso/webs/apdf/A14.pdf

Pringle, J. D., & Nippak, P. I. (2010). Winston simulations as an instruction tool to teach healthcare change management: The influence of repeat simulation testing, gender and additional instructions on performance scores. *The Journal of Health Administration Education, 27*(1), 27–43.

Puyuelo, M. (1997). *Casos clínicos en logopedia*. Barcelona, Spain: Masson.

Puyuelo, M. (2003). *Manual de desarrollo y alteraciones del lenguaje: aspectos evolutivos y patología en el niño y adulto*. Barcelona, Spain: Masson.

Puyuelo, M., Rondal, A., & Wiig, E. (2000). *Evaluación del lenguaje*. Barcelona, Spain: MASSON.

Qianping, W., Wei, T., & Bo, S. (2007). *Research and design of edutainment*. Paper presented at the First IEEE International Symposium on Information Technologies and Applications in Education (ISITAE '07).

Qvarfordt, P., Beymer, D., & Zhai, S. (2005). RealTourist – A study of augmenting human-human and human-computer dialogue with eye-gaze overlay. *INTERACT 2005, LNCS 3585/2005*, (pp. 767-780).

Rabiner, L. R., & Juang, B. H. (1993). *Fundamentals of speech recognition*. Prentice-Hall.

Rabiner, L. R., Juang, B. H., & Lee, C. H. (1996). An overview of automatic speech recognition. In Lee, C. H., Soong, F. K., & Paliwal, K. K. (Eds.), *Automatic speech and speaker recognition: Advanced topics* (pp. 1–30). Kluwer Academic Publishers. doi:10.1007/978-1-4613-1367-0_1

Rabiner, L., & Schafer, R. (1978). *Digital processing of speech signals*. Upper Saddle River, NJ: Prentice-Hall.

Raia, A. (1966). A study of the educational value of management games. *The Journal of Business, 39*(3), 339–352. doi:10.1086/294863

Rajae-Joordens, R. J. E. (2008). Measuring experiences in gaming and TV applications: Investigating the added value of a multi-view auto-stereoscopic 3D display. In Westerink, J. H. D. M., Ouwerkerk, M., & Overbeek, T. J. M. (Eds.), *Probing experience: From assessment of user emotions and behaviour to development of products* (*Vol. 8*, pp. 77–90). Netherlands: Springer.

Randel, J. M., Morris, B. A., Wetzel, C. D., & Whitehill, B. V. (1992). The effectiveness of games for educational purposes: A review of recent research. *Simulation & Gaming, 23*(3), 261–276. doi:10.1177/1046878192233001

Rantanen, V., Niemenlehto, P.-H., Verho, J., & Lekkala, J. (2010). Capacitive facial movement detection for human-computer interaction to click by frowning and lifting eyebrows. *Medical & Biological Engineering & Computing, 48*(1), 39–47. doi:10.1007/s11517-009-0565-6

Rapeepisarn, K., Wong, K. W., Fung, C. C., & Depickere, A. (2006, 4-6 December). *Similarities and differences between "learn through play" and "edutainment".* Paper presented at the 3rd Austrasalian Conference on Interactive Entertainment (IE 2006), Perth, Australia.

Rasmussen, M. H., Mostow, J., Tan, Z. H., Lindberg, B., & Li, Y. (2011, August). *Evaluating tracking accuracy of an automatic reading tutor.* Paper presented at the 2011 Workshop on Speech and Language Technologies in Education (SLaTE), Venice, Italy.

Rasseneur, D., Delozanne, E., Jacoboni, P., & Grugeon, B. (2002). Learning with virtual agents: Competition and cooperation in AMICO. *Intelligent Tutoring Systems: 6th International Conference* (pp. 129-142).

Regil, L. (2003). *Interactividad y construcción de la mirada.* Barcelona, Spain: Infonomía.

Rehm, M., Nakano, Y., Andre, E., & Nishida, T. (2009). From observation to simulation: Generating culture-specific behavior for interactive systems. *AI & Society, 24*(3), 267–280. doi:10.1007/s00146-009-0216-3

Reiser, R. (2001a). A history of instructional design and technology: Part I: A history of instructional media. *Educational Technology Research and Development, 49*(1), 53–64. doi:10.1007/BF02504506

Reiser, R. (2001b). A history of instructional design and technology: Part II: A history of instructional design. *Educational Technology Research and Development, 49*(2), 57–67. doi:10.1007/BF02504928

Reiter, E. (1995). NLG vs. templates. *Proceedings of the Fifth European Workshop in Natural Language Generation,* (pp. 95–105).

Rejas, J. (2011). Propuesta de diseño de un portal virtual en educación. *EDUTEC, Revista Electrónica de Tecnología Educativa.* Retrieved Setember 23, 2010, from http://edutec.rediris.es/revelec2/revelec33/

Resta, P., & Laferrière, T. (2007). Technology in support of collaborative learning. *Educational Psychology Review, 19*(1), 65–83. doi:10.1007/s10648-007-9042-7

Revuelta, F. I. (2011). Competencia digital: Desarrollo de aprendizajes con mundos virtuales en la escuela 2.0. *Edutec-e. Revista Electrónica de Tecnología Educativa, 37.*

Rheingold, H. (1993). *The virtual community: Homesteading on the electronic frontier.* Reading, MA: Addison-Wesley.

Rickel, J., & Johnson, W. L. (1999). Animated agents for procedural training in virtual reality: Perception, cognition, and motor control. *Applied Artificial Intelligence, 13,* 343–382. doi:10.1080/088395199117315

Rico, M., Camacho, D., Alaman, X., & Pulido, E. (2009). A high school educational platform based on virtual worlds. *2nd Workshop on Methods and Cases in Computing Education (MCCE 2009),* Barcelona, Spain, (pp. 46-51).

Rico, M., Martínez-Muñoz, G., Alamán, X., Camacho, D., & Pulido, E. (2010). A programming experience of high school students in a virtual world platform. *International Journal of Engineering Education, 2010.*

Rieber, L. P. (1996). Animation as feedback in a computer-based simulation: Representation matters. *Educational Technology Research and Development, 44*(1), 5–22. doi:10.1007/BF02300323

Roda, C., Angehrn, A., & Nabeth, T. (2001). Dialog systems for advanced learning: Applications and research. *Proceedings of BotShow '01 Conference,* (pp. 1-7).

Roda, C., Angehrn, A., & Nabeth, T. (2001). Matching competencies to enhance organizational knowledge sharing: An intelligent agents approach. *Proceedings of 7th International Netties Conference,* (pp. 931-937).

Rodger, S. H., Bashford, M., Dyck, L., Hayes, J., Liang, L., Nelson, D., & Qin, H. (2010). Enhancing K-12 education with Alice programming adventures. *Proceedings of ITiCSE, 2010,* 234–238.

Rodríguez Fonseca, L. (1999). *Qué nos dicen y qué no nos dicen los índices de madurez sintáctica? Estudios de lingüística hispánica: homenaje a María Vaquero* (pp. 523–535). Universidad de Puerto Rico.

Rodríguez, W. R., & Lleida, E. (2009, September). *Formant estimation in children's speech and its application for a Spanish speech therapy tool.* Paper presented at the 2009 Workshop on Speech and Language Technologies in Education (SLaTE), Wroxall Abbey Estates, United Kingdom.

Rodríguez, W. R., Saz, O., & Lleida, E. (2010, September). *ARTICULA - A tool for Spanish vowel training in real time*. Paper presented at the 2010 Workshop on Second Language Studies Acquisition, Learning, Education and Technology, Tokio, Japan.

Rodríguez, W. R., Saz, O., Lleida, E., Vaquero, C., & Escartín, A. (2008, October). *COMUNICA - Tools for speech and language therapy*. Paper presented at the First Workshop on Children, Computer and Interaction (WOCCI), Chania, Grece.

Rodríguez, W. R. (2011). *Tecnologías del habla en la educación de la voz infantil alterada*. Zaragoza, Spain: Editorial Académica Española.

Rodríguez, W. R., Saz, O., & Lleida, E. (2012). A prelingual tool for education of altered voices. *Speech Communication, 54*(5), 583–600. doi:10.1016/j.specom.2011.05.006

Rogers, L. (2011). Developing simulations in multi-user virtual environments to enhance healthcare education. *British Journal of Educational Technology, 42*(4), 608–615. doi:10.1111/j.1467-8535.2010.01057.x

Rollings, A., & Adams, E. (2003). *On game design*. Old Tappan, NJ: Pearson.

Romme, A. G. L. (2002). *Microworlds for management education and learning*. University Faculty of Economics & Business Administration, UNICE. Retrieved from www.unice.fr/sg/resources/articles/romme_2002_microworlds-management-ed-learning.pdf

Roschelle, J., Penuel, W. R., & Abrahamson, L. (2004). *Classroom response and communication systems: Research review and theory*. Paper presented at Annual Meeting of the American Educational Research Association. San Diego, CA, 2004.

Rosé, C. P., Moore, J. D., VanLehn, K., & Allbritton, D. (2001). A comparative evaluation of Socratic versus didactic tutoring. *Proceedings of Cognitive Sciences Society*.

Ruiz, C. (1994). El proyecto MUSA. *Apanda, 2*, 14–19.

Ruiz-Jiménez, A., Ceballos-Hernández, C., González-Guzmán, N., Ortega Fraile, F.J., Ríos Fornos, M., & Delgado Lissen, J. (2010, Febrero). Enseñanza interactiva en la docencia universitaria. *XX Jornadas Hispano Lusas de Gestión Científica*, Setúbal, Portugal, (pp. 4–5).

Saari, T., Turpeinen, M., Kuikkaniemi, K., Kosunen, I., & Ravaja, N. (2009). Emotionally adapted games – An example of a first person shooter. In Jacko, J. A. (Ed.), *Human-Computer Interaction, Part IV, HCII 2009, LNCS 5613* (pp. 406–415). Berlin, Germany: Springer-Verlag. doi:10.1007/978-3-642-02583-9_45

Sabourin, J., Mott, B. W., & Lester, J. C. (2011). *Modelling learner affect with theoretical grounded dynamic Bayesian networks*. Paper presented at the 4th International Conference of Affective Computing and Intelligent Interaction (ACII 2011) Part I.

Sánchez Benavente, R., & García Cuenca, A. (2003). *Diseño de contenidos accesibles para personas con discapacidad intelectual*. Paper presented at I Jornadas Científico-Técnicas IAE / AFANIAS: La accesibilidad a Internet de personas con discapacidad intellectual, Madrid, Spain.

Sánchez Gómez, M. (2007). *Buenas prácticas en la creación de Serious Games (Objetos de aprendizaje Reutilizables)*. In *Proceedings of IV Simposio Pluridisciplinar sobre Diseño, Evaluación y Desarrollo de Contenidos Educativos Reutilizables*, SPDECE 07, September 2007, Bilbao.

Sánchez Lobato, J., & Santos Gargallo, I. (2004). *Vademécum para la formación de profesores. Enseñar español como segunda lengua (L2)/ lengua extranjera (LE)*. Madrid: Sociedad General Española de Librería.

Sánchez, J., & Romance, A. R. (2000). Multimedia. In Rios, J. M., & Cebrián de la Serna, M. (Eds.), *Nuevas tecnologías de la información y de la comunicación aplicadas a la educación*. Málaga, Spain: Aljibe.

Sanders, E., & Stappers, P. (2008). Co-creation and the new landscapes of design. *CoDesign, 4*(1), 5–18. doi:10.1080/15710880701875068

San-Segundo, R., Pardo, J., Ferreiros, J., Sama, V., Barra-Chicote, R., & Lucas, J. (2010). Spoken Spanish generation from sign language. *Interacting with Computers, 22*(2), 123–139. doi:10.1016/j.intcom.2009.11.011

Santos, B., Bueno, Y., de Pablo, I., & Borrajo, F. (2010). Innovación en docencia virtual: Los simuladores de gestión empresarial. *Relada, 4*(2), 150–158.

Santos, J. I., Galán, J. M., Izquierdo, L. R., & Olmo, R. (2008). Laboratorio de teoría de juegos en internet. In Saiz Bárcena, L., Millán, I., & Santos Martín, J. I. (Eds.), *Insights on current organization engineering* (pp. 141–142). Burgos, Spain: Universidad de Burgos.

Sarrafzadeh, A., Alexander, S., Dadgostar, F., Fan, C., & Bigdeli, A. (2008). How do you know that I don't understand? A look at the future of intelligent tutoring systems. *Computers in Human Behavior, 24*(4), 1342–1363. doi:10.1016/j.chb.2007.07.008

Sarramona López, J. (2000). *Teoría de la educación: Reflexión y normativa pedagógica*. Barcelona, Spain: Ariel.

Saz, O., Yin, E., Lleida, E., Rose, R., Vaquero, C., & Rodríguez, W. R. (2009). Tools and technologies for computer-aided speech and language therapy. *Speech Communication, 51*(10), 948–967. doi:10.1016/j.specom.2009.04.006

Schank, R. (2002). *Designing world-class e-learning: How IBM, GE, Harvard Business School, and Columbia University are succeeding at e-learning*. McGraw-Hill Professional.

Schriesheim, C. A., & Schriesheim, J. (1974). *Divergence of practitioner opinion and empirical evidence: The case of business simulation games*. Paper presented at the 34th Annual Meeting of the Academy of Management, Seattle.

Schumann, P. L., Anderson, P. H., Scott, T. W., & Lawton, L. (2001). A framework for evaluating simulations as educational tools. *Developments in Business Simulation & Experiential Learning, 28*, 215- 220. Retrieved from http://ABSEL.org

Schutz, P. A., & Pekrun, R. (Eds.). (2007). *Emotion in education*. San Diego, CA: Elsevier.

Serra, M., Vallejo, J., Goday, P. S., & Cabrero, F. J. (1982). Trastornos de la fluidez del habla: Disfemia y taquifemia. *Rev. Logop. Fonoaud, 2*(2), 69–78.

Shaffer, D. M., & Collura, M. (2009). Technology and teaching: Evaluating the effectiveness of a personal response system in the classroom. *Teaching of Psychology, 36*, 273–277. doi:10.1080/00986280903175749

Shank, P. (2005). *The value of multimedia in learning*. Adobe Motion Design Center.

Shaw, E., Johnson, W. L., & Ganeshan, R. (1999). Pedagogical agents on the Web. *Proceedings of International Conference on Autonomous Agents,* (pp. 283-290). ACM Press.

Sheehy, K. (2010). Virtual environments: Issues and opportunities for researching inclusive educational practices. In Peachey, A., Gillen, J., Livingstone, D., & Smith-Robbins, S. (Eds.), *Researching learning in virtual worlds*. Human-Computer Interaction Series. doi:10.1007/978-1-84996-047-2_1

Sheehy, K., & Ferguson, R. (2008). Educational inclusion, new technologies. In Scott, T. B., & Livingston, J. L. (Eds.), *Leading edge educational technology*. New York, NY: Nova Science.

Shurville, S., & Browne, T. (2007). Introduction: ICT-driven change in higher education: Learning from e-learning. *Journal of Organisation Transformation & Social Change, 3*(3), 245–250. doi:10.1386/jots.3.3.245_2

Sibert, J. L., Gokturk, M., & Lavine, R. A. (2000). The reading assistant: Eye gaze triggered auditory prompting for reading remediation. *Proceedings of the Symposium on User Interface Software and Technology (UIST '00)* (pp. 101-107). New York, NY: ACM.

Sicilia, M, A., & García, E. (2003). On the concepts of usability and reusability of learning objects. *International Review of Research in Open and Distance Learning, 4*(2).

Sigley, R. (1997). Text categories and where you can stick them: A crude formality index. *International Journal of Corpus Linguistics, 2*(2), 199–237. doi:10.1075/ijcl.2.2.04sig

Simpson, V., & Oliver, M. (2006). *Using electronic voting systems in lectures*. Retrieved February 12, 2010, from http://www.ucl.ac.uk/learningtechnology/assessment/ElectronicVotingSystems.pdf

Smith, L. W., & Van Doren, D. C. (2004). The reality-based learning method: a simple method for keeping teaching activities relevant and effective. *Journal of Marketing Education, 26*(1), 66–74. doi:10.1177/0273475303262353

Sobrino, A. (2000). Evaluación del software educativo. In Reparaz, C., Sobrino, S., & Mir, J. I. (Eds.), *Integración curricular de las nuevas tecnologías*. Barcelona, Spain: Ariel.

Sommerville, I. (2004). *Software engineering* (7th ed.). Addison-Wesley.

Speech Viewer, I. B. M., III. (2005), *Software for speech therapy*. This product has been discontinued. Retrieved January 14, 2012, from http://www.synapseadaptive.com/edmark/prod/sv3/

Staudte, M., & Crocker, M. W. (2009). Visual attention in spoken human-robot interaction. *Proceedings of the 4th ACM/ IEEE International Conference on Human Robot Interaction (HRI '09)* (pp. 77-84). New York, NY: ACM.

Stemmer, B., & Whitaker, H. A. (2008). *Handbook of the neuroscience of language*. San Diego, CA: Academic Press.

Stowell, J. R., & Nelson, J. M. (2007). Benefits of electronic audience response systems on student participation, learning and emotion. *Teaching of Psychology, 34*, 253–258. doi:10.1080/00986280701700391

Sucar, L. E., & Noguez, J. (2008). Student modeling. In Pourret, O., Naïm, P., & Marcot, B. (Eds.), *Bayesian networks: A practical guide to applications* (pp. 173–185). West Sussex, UK: J. Wiley & Sons.

Surakka, V., Illi, M., & Isokoski, P. (2004). Gazing and frowning as a new human-computer interaction technique. *ACM Transactions on Applied Perception, 1*(1), 40–56. doi:10.1145/1008722.1008726

Surakka, V., Sams, M., & Hietanen, J. K. (1999). Modulation of neutral face evaluation by laterally presented emotional expressions. *Perceptual and Motor Skills, 88*, 595–606. doi:10.2466/pms.1999.88.2.595

Surakka, V., & Vanhala, T. (2011). Emotions in human-computer interaction. In Kappas, A., & Krämer, N. (Eds.), *Face-to-face communication over the Internet: Emotions in a Web of culture, language, and technology* (pp. 213–236). Cambridge University Press. doi:10.1017/CBO9780511977589.011

Susi, T., Johannesson, M., & Backlund, P. (2007). *Serious games: An overview*. Technical report, University of Skovde (HS-IKI-TR-07-001).

Sussex Community. (2011). *Voice output communication aid* (VOCA). Retrieved December 13, 2011, from http://www.sussexcommunity.nhs.uk/index.cfm?request=c2007983

Swartout, W., Traum, D., Artstein, R., Noren, D., Debevec, P., & Bronnenkant, K. … Piepol, D. (2010). Ada and Grace: Toward realistic and engaging virtual museum guides. *Intelligent Virtual Agents* (pp. 286-300). Springer.

Swerts, M., & Krahmer, E. (2005). Audiovisual prosody and feeling of knowing. *Journal of Memory and Language, 53*, 81–94. doi:10.1016/j.jml.2005.02.003

Sykes, J. (2006). Affective gaming: Advancing the argument for game-based learning. In Pivec, M. (Ed.), *Affective and emotional aspects of human-computer interaction* (pp. 3–7). Amsterdam, The Netherlands: IOS Press.

Szafran, R. F., & Mandolini, A. F. (1980). Student evaluation of a simulation game. *Teaching Sociology, 8*, 21–37. doi:10.2307/1317045

Takagi, H. (1998). Development of an eye-movement enhanced translation support system. *Proceedings of the Third Asian Pacific Computer and Human Interaction* (pp. 114-119). IEEE Computer Society.

Talmy, L. (2000). *Toward a cognitive semantics*. Cambridge, MA: MIT Press.

Tao, J., & Tan, T. (2005, 22-24 October 2005). *Affective computing: A review*. Paper presented at the Affective Computing and Intelligent Interaction (ACII 2005), Beijing, China.

Tartaro, A., & Cassell, J. (2008). Playing with virtual peers: Bootstrapping contingent discourse in children with autism. *Proceedings of the 8th International Conference for the Learning Sciences-Volume 2* (pp. 382-389).

Taylor, K., & Moore, S. (2006). Adding question answering to an e-tutor for programming languages. *Proceedings of 26th SGAI International Conference on Innovative Techniques and Applications of Artificial Intelligence*, (pp. 193-206). Cambridge, UK: Springer.

Teach, R., & Govani, G. (1988). Simulation game performance: An examination of the effect of time pressure, method of team formation, and formal planning. *Developments in Business Simulation & Experiential Learning, 21*, 83–85.

Tepperman, J., Silva, J., Kazemzadeh, A., You, H., Lee, S., Alwan, A., & Narayanan, S. (2006). *Pronunciation verification of children's speech for automatic literacy assessment.* Paper presented at the 9th International Conference on Spoken Language Processing (ICSLP - Interspeech), Pittsburgh (PA), USA.

Thavikulwat, P. (2009). The architecture of computerised business gaming simulations. *Simulation & Gaming, 35*(2), 242–269. doi:10.1177/1046878104263545

The New Media Consortium & the EDUCAUSE Learning Initiative. (2007). *The 2007 horizon report* (pp. 18).

Thomas, M., Jaffe, G. J., Kincaid, P. J., & Stees, Y. (1992). *Learning to use simplified English: A preliminary study* (pp. 69–73). Technical Communication.

Thomas, S. (2006). Pervasive learning games: Explorations of hybrid educational gamescapes. *Simulation & Gaming, 37*, 41–55. doi:10.1177/1046878105282274

Tinio, V. L., & UNDP, Asia-Pacific Development Information Programme and e-ASEAN Task Force. (2003). *ICT in education.* e-ASEAN Task Force.

Tonks, D. (2002). Using marketing simulations for teaching and learning: Reflections on an evolution 1. *Active Learning in Higher Education, 3*(2), 177–194. doi:10.1177/1469787402003002006

Torey, Z. (2009). *The crucible of consciousness.* Cambridge, MA: MIT Press.

Torrance, E. P., & Myers, R. E. (1970). *Creative learning and teaching.* HarperCollins Publishers.

Torres González, A. N. (1993). *Madurez sintáctica en estudiantes no universitarios de la zona metropolitana de Tenerife.* Doctoral dissertation, Universidad de La Laguna. Tenerife.

Trancoso, I., Martins, R., Moniz, H., Mata, A. I., & Viana, M. C. (2008). The LECTRA Corpus – Classroom lecture transcriptions in European Portuguese. *Proceedings of the Sixth International Language Resources and Evaluation* (LREC'08).

Traum, D., Roque, A., Leuski, A., Georgiou, P., Gerten, J., & Martinovski, B. … Vaswani, A. (2007). Hassan: A virtual human for tactical questioning. *Proceedings of the 8th SIGdial Workshop on Discourse and Dialogue* (pp. 71-74).

Ullman, M. T. (2001a). A neurocognitive perspective on language: The declarative/procedural model. *Nature Reviews. Neuroscience, 2*(1), 717–726. doi:10.1038/35094573

Ullman, M. T. (2001b). The declarative/procedural model of lexicon and grammar. *Journal of Psycholinguistic Research, 30*(1). doi:10.1023/A:1005204207369

Ultsch, A. (2007). Emergence in self-organizing feature maps. In *Proceedings Workshop on Self-Organizing Maps* (WSOM '07), Bielefeld, Germany.

UNED. (2011). *Level test.* Retrieved June 11, 2011, from http://portal.uned.es/portal/page?_pageid=93, 1336773 & _dad = portal & _schema = PORTAL

UNESCO. (1994). *The Salamanca statement and framework for action on special needs.* World Conference on Special Needs Education: Access and Quality, Salamanca, Spain. Retrieved from http://www.unesco.org/education/pdf/SALAMA_E.PDF

United Nations. (1989). *Convention on the rights of the child.* Retrieved from http://www.unesco.org/education/pdf/CHILD_E.PDF (retrieved on January, 2012).

United Nations. (2006). *Convention on the rights of persons with disabilities.* Retrieved from http://www.un.org/disabilities/documents/convention/convoptprot-e.pdf

Unity Technologies. (2011, 19 August 2011). *Unity 3.* Retrieved from http://unity3d.com/unity/

US Department of Labor. (1999). *Futurework—Trends and challenges for work in the 21st century.* Quoted in EnGauge, "21st Century Skills," North Central Regional Educational Laboratory. Retrieved 31 May, 2002, from http://www.ncrel.org/engauge/skills/21skills.htm

Usability.gov. (2011). *Usability.gov is the primary government source for information on usability and user-centered design.* HHS Web Communications and New Media Division, U.S. Department of Health and Human Services. Retrieved December, 2012, from http://www.usability.gov/about/index.html

Valle, R. E. (2011). TIC y accesibilidad: Programa Red XXI Educacyl Digital. *Educación Especial y Mundo Digital, 2*, 202–215. Almería, Spain: Universidad de Almería.

Van Eck, R. (2006). Digital game-based learning: It's not just the digital natives who are restless. *EDUCAUSE Review*, *41*(2), 16–30. Retrieved from http://www.educause.edu/EDUCAUSE+Review/EDUCAUSEReviewMagazineVolume41/DigitalGameBasedLearningItsNot/158041

Vanderheiden, G. (1984). High and light technology approaches in the development of communication systems for the severe physically handicapped persons. *Exceptional Education Quarterly*, *4*(4), 40–56.

Vanhala, T., & Surakka, V. (2008). Computer-assisted regulation of emotional and social processes. In Or, J. (Ed.), *Affective computing: Focus on emotion expression, synthesis, and recognition* (pp. 405–420). Vienna, Austria: I-Tech Education and Publishing. doi:10.5772/6168

Vanhala, T., Surakka, V., Courgeon, M., Martin, J.-C., & Jacquemin, C. (in press). Voluntary facial activations regulate physiological arousal and subjective experiences during virtual social stimulation. [in press]. *ACM Transactions on Applied Perception*.

Vaquero, C., Saz, O., Lleida, E., Marcos, J., & Canalís, C. (2006). VOCALIZA: An application for computer-aided speech therapy in Spanish language. *Proceedings of IV Jornadas en Tecnología del Habla*, (pp. 321–326).

Varela, O. E. (2009). El rol de las escuelas de negocios en el desarrollo de destrezas gerenciales: Análisis conceptual. *Academia. Revista Latinoamericana de Administración*, *42*, 73–89.

Varga, I., & Kiss, I. (2008). Speech recognition in mobile phones. In Tan, Z.-H., & Lindberg, B. (Eds.), *Automatic speech recognition on mobile devices and over communication networks* (pp. 301–325). Retrieved from. doi:10.1007/978-1-84800-143-5_14

Vázquez Reyes, C. M., & Fernández Rota, M. E. (2002). *El proyecto de la Agencia Europea sobre la aplicación de las Tecnologías de la Comunicación e Información a la educación del alumnado con necesidades educativas especiales*. Tecnoneet.

Véliz, M. (1999). Complejidad sintáctica y modo del discurso. *Estudios Filológicos, 34*, 181-192. Retrieved June 11, 2011, from http://www.scielo.cl/scielo.php?script=

Véliz, M. (2004). Procesamiento de estructuras sintácticas complejas en adultos mayores y adultos jóvenes. *Estudios Filológicos, 39*, 65-81. Retrieved June 11, 2011, from http://www.scielo.cl/scielo.php?pid=S0071-17132004003900004&script=sci_arttext

Véliz, M. (1988). Evaluación de la madurez sintáctica en el discurso escrito. [RLA]. *Revista de Lingüística Teórica y Aplicada*, *26*, 105–140.

Venegas, R. (2006). La similitud léxico-semántica en artículos de investigación científica en español: Una aproximación desde el análisis semántico latente. *Revista Signos, 39*(60), 75-106. Retrieved June 11, 2011 from http://www.scielo.cl/scielo.php?script=sci_arttext&pid=S0718-09342006000100004&lng=es&nrm=iso

Venegas, R. (2009). Toward a method for assessing summaries in Spanish using LSA. In *Proceedings of the Twenty-Second International FLAIRS Conference* (pp. 310-311).

Vicsi, K., Roach, P., Oester, A., Kacic, Z., Barczikay, P., & Sinka, I. (1999, August). *SPECO: A multimedia multilingual teaching and training system for speech handicapped children*. Paper presented at the 6th European Conference on Speech Communication, Budapest, Hungary.

Vila, J. M. (2008). Alteraciones del habla. *Pediatría Integral, 11. XXII Congress of the Society of Pediatric Outpatient and Primary Care*, (pp. 56-59).

Villa, A., & Poblete, M. (2008). *Aprendizaje basado en competencias. Una propuesta para la evaluación de las competencias genéricas*. Bilbao, Spain: Ediciones Mensajero.

Voice Games Model 5167B. Key Elemetrics. (2010). *Tool for voice therapy*. Retrieved January 14, 2012, from http://www.kayelemetrics.com/index.php?option=com_product&view=product&Itemid=3&controller=product&cid%5B%5D=53&task=pro_details

VoxGames. (2009). *Software for speech and voice therapy*. CTS Informatica, Brasil. Retrieved January 14, 2012, from http://www.ctsinformatica.com.br/#voxGames.html{paginaProduto!7&1

Vygotsky, L. S. (1978). *Mind in society*. Harvard University Press.

W3C. (2012). *Web accessibility initiative.* Retrieved December, 2012, from http://www.w3.org/WAI/

Wahlster, W. (Ed.). (2006). *SmartKom: Foundations of multimodal dialog systems.* Springer. doi:10.1007/3-540-36678-4

Wald, M. (2004). Using automatic speech recognition to enhance education for all students: Turning a vision into reality. *34th ASEE/IEEE Frontiers in Education Conference,* (pp. 22-25).

Walsh, S. (2011). *Exploring classroom discourse. Language in Action Routledge Introductions to Applied Linguistics.* Routledge.

Walters, B. A., & Coalter, T. M. (1997). Simulation games in business policy courses: is there value for students? *Journal of Education for Business, 72*(3), 170–174. doi:10.1080/08832323.1997.10116849

Wang, H., Chignell, M., & Ishizuka, M. (2006). Empathic tutoring software agents using real-time eye tracking. *Proceedings of the 2006 Symposium on Eye Tracking Research & Applications* (ETRA '06) (pp. 73-78). New York, NY: ACM.

Wang, N., & Johnson, L. W. (2008). The politeness effect in an intelligent foreign language tutoring system. *Proceedings of 9th International Conference Intelligent Tutoring Systems,* (pp. 70-280).

Wang, Y., Wang, W., & Huang, C. (2007). Enhanced semantic question answering system for e-learning environment. *Proceedings of AINAW'07 Conference,* (pp. 1023-1028).

Wan, Z., Fang, Y., & Neufeld, D. J. (2007). The role of information technology in technology-mediated learning: a review of the past for the future. *Journal of Information Systems Education, 18*(2), 183–192.

Warnock, M. (1979). Children with special needs: The Warnock Report. *British Medical Journal, 1,* 667–668. doi:10.1136/bmj.1.6164.667

Watt, D., & Fabricius, A. (2002). Evaluation of a technique for improving the mapping of multiple speakers' vowel space in the f1–f2 plane. *Leeds Working Papers in Linguistics and Phonetics, 9,* 159–173.

WCAG 2.0 (2008) *Web content accessibility guidelines 2.0.* Retrieved December 20, 2012, from http://www.w3.org/TR/WCAG20/

Weerts, S. E., Miller, D., & Altice, A. (2009). Clicker technology promotes interactivity in an undergraduate nutrition course. *Journal of Nutrition Education and Behavior, 3*(41), 227–228. doi:10.1016/j.jneb.2008.08.006

Wei, L., & Yifang, L. (2010). The application of marketing simulative teaching platform in the marketing professional teaching. *Value Engineering, 34.*

Wellman, B., Salaff, J., Dimitrova, L. G., Garton, L., Gulia, M., & Haythornthwaite, C. (1996). Computer networks as social networks: Collaborative work, telework, and virtual community. *Annual Review of Sociology, 22,* 213–238. doi:10.1146/annurev.soc.22.1.213

Weng, F., Varges, S., Raghunathan, B., Ratiu, F., Pon-Barry, H., & Lathrop, B. ... Shriberg, L. (2006). CHAT: A conversational helper for automotive tasks. *Proceedings of the 9th International Conference on Spoken Language Processing (Interspeech-ICSLP),* (pp. 1061–1064).

Westerinck, J. H. D. M., Ouwerkerk, M., Overbeek, T. J. M., Pasveer, W. F., & De Ruyter, B. (2008). *Probing experience: From assessment of user emotions and behaviour to development of products.* Dordrecht, The Netherlands: Springer.

Wik, P., & Hjalmarsson, A. (2009). Embodied conversational agents in computer assisted language learning. *Speech Communication, 51*(10), 1024–1037. doi:10.1016/j.specom.2009.05.006

Wiktionary. (2008). *User: Matthias Buchmeier.* Retrieved March 25, 2012, from http://en.wiktionary.org/wiki/User:Matthias_Buchmeier#Spanish_frequency_list

Wilcock, G., & Jokinen, K. (2011). Emergent verbal behaviour in human-robot interaction. In L.-C. Delgado, et al. (Eds.), *Proceedings of the Third International Conference on Spoken Dialogue Systems: Ambient Intelligence (IWSDS),* (pp. 375–380). Granada, Spain, September 2011.

Wiley, D. A. (2000). Connecting learning objects to instructional design theory: A definition, a metaphor, and a taxonomy. *Learning Technology, 2830*(435), 1–35.

Williams, J., & Young, S. (2007). Partially observable Markov decision processes for spoken dialog systems. *Computer Speech & Language*, *21*(2), 393–422. doi:10.1016/j.csl.2006.06.008

WiloStar3D. (2011). Retrieved from http://www.wilostar3d.com/

Wit, E. (2003). Who wants to be... The use of a personal response system in statistics teaching. *MSOR Connections*, *2*(3), 14–20.

Witkowski, M., Arafa, Y., & deBruijn, O. (2001). Evaluating user reaction to character agent mediated displays using eye-tracking equipment. *Proceedings of the Symposium on Information Agents for Electronic Commerce* (AISB'01) (pp. 79-87).

Wolfe, J. (1975). Effective performance behaviors in a simulated policy and decision-making environment. *Management Science*, *21*(8). doi:10.1287/mnsc.21.8.872

Wolfe, J., & Chacko, T. I. (1983). Team-size effects on business game performance and decision making behaviours. *Decision Sciences*, *14*(1), 121–133. doi:10.1111/j.1540-5915.1983.tb00173.x

Wolfe, J., & Guth, G. (1975). The case approach versus gaming in the teaching of business policy: An experimental evaluation. *The Journal of Business*, *48*(3). doi:10.1086/295761

Wolfe-Quintero, K., Inagaki, S., & Kim, H.-Y. (1998). *Second language development in writing: Measure of frequency, accuracy and complexity. Second Language Teaching and Curriculum Center*. University of Hawaii.

Woolf, B. P. (2009). *Building intelligent interactive tutors: Student-centered strategies for revolutionizing e-learning*. Burlington, MA: Elsevier, Inc.

Woolf, B., Burleson, W., Arroyo, I., Dragon, T., Cooper, D., & Picard, R. (2009). Affect-aware tutors: recognising and responding to student affect. *International Journal of Learning Technology*, *4*(3/4), 129–164. doi:10.1504/IJLT.2009.028804

World Health Organization. (2011). *World report on disability*. Geneva, Switzerland: World Health Organization.

Yamazaki, H., Kitamura, K., Harada, K., & Yamamoto, S. (2008). *Creation of learner corpus and its application to speech recognition*. International Conference on Language Resources and Evaluation, LREC2008, Marrakech, Morocco.

Yates, K. A. (2007). *Towards a taxonomy of cognitive task analysis methods: A search for cognition and task analysis interactions*. Unpublished Doctoral Dissertation, University of Southern California, Los Angeles.

Yonezawa, T., Yamazoe, H., Utsumi, A., & Abe, S. (2007). Gaze-communicative behavior of stuffed-toy robot with joint attention and eye contact based on ambient gaze-tracking. *Proceedings of the 9th International Conference on Multimodal Interfaces* (ICMI '07) (pp. 140-145). New York, NY: ACM.

Young, S., Evermann, G., Gales, M., Hain, H., Kershaw, D., & Liu, X. (2006). *The HTK book*. Cambridge, UK: Cambridge University.

Yourstone, S. A., Kraye, H. S., & Albaum, G. (2008). Classroom questioning with immediate electronic response: Do clickers improve learning? *Decision Sciences Journal of Innovative Education*, *6*, 75–88. doi:10.1111/j.1540-4609.2007.00166.x

Ziempekis, D., & Gallopoulos, E. (2006). TMG: A Matlab toolbox for generating term-document matrices. In J. Kogan, C. Nicholas, & M. Teboulle (Eds.), *Grouping multidimensional data: Recent advances in clustering* (pp.187-210). Text Collections, Springer.

Zipf, G. (1932). *Selected studies of the principle of relative frequency in language*. Cambridge, MA: Harvard University Press.

Zuckerman, D., & Horn, R. (1973). *The guide to simulations/games for education and training*. Lexington, MA: Information Resources.

Zue, V. W., & Glass, J. R. (2000). Conversational interfaces: Advances and challenges. *Proceedings of the IEEE*, *88*, 1166–1180. doi:10.1109/5.880078

About the Contributors

David Griol Barres obtained his Ph.D. degree in Computer Science from the Technical University of València (Spain) in 2007. He has also a B.S. in Telecommunication Science from this University. He is currently Professor at the Department of Computer Science in the Carlos III University of Madrid (Spain). He has participated in several European and Spanish projects related to natural language processing and dialogue systems. His research activities are mostly related to the development of statistical methodologies for the design of spoken dialogue systems. His research interests include dialogue management/optimization/simulation, corpus-based methodologies, user modeling, adaptation and evaluation of spoken dialogue systems and machine learning approaches. Before starting his Ph.D. study, he worked as a network engineer in Motorola. He is a member of ISCA (International Speech Communication Association), IEEE (Institute of Electrical and Electronics Engineers), and AEPIA (Spanish Association of Artificial Intelligence).

Zoraida Callejas Carrión is Assistant Professor in the Department of Languages and Computer Systems at the Technical School of Computer Science and Telecommunications of the University of Granada (Spain). She completed a PhD in Computer Science at University of Granada in 2008 and has been a visiting researcher in University of Ulster (Belfast, UK), Technical University of Liberec (Liberec, Czech Republic) University of Trento (Trento, Italy), and Technical University of Berlin (Berlin, Germany). Her research activities have been mostly related to speech technologies and in particular to the investigation of dialogue systems. Her results have been published in several international journals and conferences. She has participated in numerous research projects, and is a member of several research associations focused on speech processing and human-computer interaction.

Ramón López-Cózar Delgado is Professor at the Faculty of Computer Science and Telecommunications of the University of Granada (Spain). His main research interests in the last 15 years include spoken and multimodal dialogue systems, focusing on speech processing and dialogue management. He has coordinated several research projects, has published a number of journal and conference papers, and has been invited speaker at several scientific events addressing these topics. In 2005 he published the book "Spoken, Multilingual and Multimodal Dialogue Systems: Development and Assessment" (Wiley). Recently he has co-edited the book "Human-Centric Interfaces for Ambient Intelligence" (Elsevier Academic Press, 2010), in which he has coordinated the section concerning speech processing and dialogue management. He is a member of ISCA (International Speech Communication Association), FoLLI (Association for Logic, Language and Information), AIPO (Spanish Society on Human-Computer Interaction) and SEPLN (Spanish Society on Natural Language Processing).

* * *

Xavier Alamán holds a PhD in Computer Science (UCM-1993), a MSc. Artificial Intelligence (UCLA-1990), a MSc. Computer Science (UPM-1987), and a MSc. Physics (UCM-1985). He has served as the Dean of the School of Engineering, Universidad Autónoma de Madrid, from 2000 to 2004. He got the tenure in the same university in 1998. Previously he was an IBM researcher for 7 years. His research interests include Ambient Intelligence and Virtual Worlds. He has been main researcher in several R&D projects in these areas and has contributed with more than 50 publications.

Javier Alda is Professor of Optics at the University Complutense of Madrid. He has written more than 100 research papers in several areas of optics, ranging from laser beam propagation to industrial application of optical systems. During the last 5 years he has become increasingly interested in the algorithms and procedures of computational linguistics. In this topic he has contributed with some implementations of automatic scoring strategies to assess the level of the writing of learners of Spanish as a second language.

Andoni Eguíluz is Professor at Engineering Faculty at the University of Deusto (Bilbao, Spain) since 1991, Graduate in Computer Science Engineering, best year's record (UD), 1991, Fellow of the Advanced Study Program of the Massachusetts Institute of Technology (MIT, USA), 1996, and Cofounder and manager of gizer.net (2004-2011), a spin-off company for development of social technology projects and technology for accessibility. He has been director and researcher on a number of software projects regarding accessibility, multimedia, web, graphical 3D interaction, graphical interfaces, compiling environments, compiler generators, et cetera. Actually working on projects related to technology & audiovisual contents oriented to education, multimedia, audiovisual & web accessibility, technology & innovation.

Emi Endo, Bachelor of Health and Physical Education, Schoolteacher, School for the Mentally Challenged at Otsuka, University of Tsukuba, 1-5-5 Kasuga, Bunkyo-ku, Tokyo 112-0003 Japan, graduated in School of Health and Physical Education at University of Tsukuba. She was a short-distance track athlete. She started as a helper in a welfare institution for three years and then worked as a part-time schoolteacher at the Krigaoka School for the Physically Challenged and Special Needs Education School for the Visually Impaired, both affiliated with the University of Tsukuba. She is now a 1st and 2nd joint class homeroom teacher at School for the Mentally Challenge at Otsuka, University of Tsukuba, and has been conducting many school activities using original handmade teaching materials with dot codes.

Takahide Ezoe, Principal, Shinjuku Japanese Language Institute, 2-9-7 Takadanobaba, Shinjuku-ku, Tokyo 169-0075 Japan, started to teach Japanese for foreign students in 1975. In the 1970s, most Japanese universities did not have students from overseas, and therefore, there was no established Japanese language teaching method. He thus began to develop his own teaching method (Ezoe method), now one of the most well known in Japan. While developing the method, Mr. Ezoe made great efforts to visualize the structure of Japanese language in order to make learning easy for everyone. This "Ezoe grammar structure" is now adopted by a number of educational institutions in Japan, including schools for the deaf. Mr. Ezoe also developed a device called Sound Reader, which is available for various textbooks and grammar cards. He always supports Dr. Ikuta's advanced study on creative school activities with original handmade teaching materials with dot codes.

Paz Ferrero graduated in Latin and Greek in 1986 from University Complutense of Madrid. In 2002 she graduated in English from University Autónoma of Madrid. She obtained her PhD degree in 2011 at University Autónoma of Madrid working on the development of automatic tools for the assessment of text written in Spanish. Currently she teaches at the Alcobendas Vocational School and she is involved in a research project dealing with the application of Latent Semantic Analysis for unsupervised text scoring.

Diego Carrero Figueroa, Graduate in Audiovisual Systems Engineering from the University Carlos III of Madrid, holds a Master in Multimedia and Communications from the University Carlos III of Madrid. He worked for two years in the Computer Science Department at the same University. Currently develops its activities as researcher at the Spanish Centre for Subtitling and Audio Description (CESyA). His interests are biometrics, pattern recognition, and speech processing. He has also published several articles in the field of biometrics.

Suryakanth V. Gangashetty is working as an Assistant Professor at IIIT Hyderabad from 2006. He completed his BE (Computer Science and Engineering) from Govt. (BDT) College of Engineering Davangere in 1991, M.Tech (Systems Analysis and Computer Applications) from Karnataka Regional Engineering College Surathkal in 1998 and Ph.D (Neural Network Models for Recognition of Consonant-Vowel Units of Speech in Multiple Languages) from Indian Institute of Technology Madras in 2005. Before joining to IIIT Hyderabad, he worked as a Senior Project Officer at Speech and Vision Laboratory, IIT Madras. He did his post-doctoral studies (PDF) at Carnegie Mellon University (CMU) Pittsburgh (PA, USA) during April 2007 to July 2008. He also worked as a visiting research scholar at OGI Portland (USA) for three months during the summer of 2001. He is author of about 80 papers published in national as well as international conferences and journals. He co-authored two book chapters in edited volumes published by Springer and World Scientific publishing company. He is a life member of the CSI, IE, IUPRAI, ASI, IETE, ORSI, and ISTE. He has reviewed papers for reputed conferences and journals. His research interests include speech processing, neural networks, multimedia signal processing, pattern recognition, soft computing, machine learning, image processing, natural language processing, artificial intelligence, and fuzzy logic. His Ph.D. research work at IIT Madras was nominated for the IBM outstanding PhD student award of the year 2005 as judged by IBM IRL New Delhi, in the all India level competition.

Mª Luz Guenaga, PhD in Computer Science (2007), Dr. Europeus mention, University of Deusto, wrote a thesis titled "Integral Accessibility of digital resource centres for people with visual disability." During her predoctoral stay at the Braillenet Laboratory, Paris VI University, she carried out research on accessibility and visual impairment. She has coordinated several R&D projects nationwide and contributed to the dissemination of her activity as a lecturer at the Univ. of Deusto, organizing several international conferences like the workshop "ICT and accessibility" or "the 5th Symposium on Image/Video Communications over Fixed and Mobile Networks" supported by the IEEE. She was selected to be part of the Young Researcher Consortium at the International Conference on Computers Helping People with Special Needs 2006.

Luis Alfonso Hernández Gómez, Engineer in Telecommunications in 1982, PhD in Telecommunications Engineering in 1988, Tenured Professor at U.P.M since 1994, is member of the Signal Processing Applications Group (GAPS) in the Signals, Systems and Communications Department (SSR) of

Universidad Politécnica de Madrid (UPM). His research interests are mainly centred in the design and evaluation of human-technology interactive systems where has directed various doctoral theses and has written numerous articles. Dr. Hernández Gómez has coordinated an important number of research and technology transfer projects with both public and private sectors. He has also been Scientific Consultant at different Spanish companies, Evaluator at the Spanish National Agency for Scientific Evaluation and Member of the scientific committee of EUSIPCO, INTERSPEECH, and LREC (ELRA).

Shigeru Ikuta, Sc.D., Professor, Otsuma Women's University, School of Social Information Studies, 2-7-1 Karakida, Tama, Tokyo 206-8540 Japan, is an education technologist, teacher educator in science, and special educator with a focus on student learning and development on the basis of communication aids. He completed his graduate work and earned a doctorate in science at Tohoku University in Sendai, Japan. He was working as a Professor of Computation Chemistry at Tokyo Metropolitan University for twenty-nine years and is honored to be an Emeritus Professor. He moved to University of Tsukuba and has started collaborative works with schoolteachers at the special needs schools, affiliated with the University. He has been conducting many school activities in cooperation with the schoolteachers using original handmade teaching materials with dot codes in supporting the students with various challenges both at the special needs and ordinary schools.

Ana Iglesias is Ph.D. in Computer Sciences and currently is a member of the faculty of the Computer Science Department of Carlos III University of Madrid (Spain), since February 2006. Since 2000, she is working at the Advanced Databases Group in the Computer Science Department at Carlos III University of Madrid and she is also a member of the Spanish Centre of Caption and Audiodescription (CESyA) since 2005. She has been working and managing several national research projects on education, accessibility, advanced database technologies, and others. Her research interests include accessibility, education, database design and advanced database technologies, among others, and she is co-author of several publications in international journal and congresses related to these research lines.

Kristiina Jokinen is Adjunct Professor and Project Manager at University of Helsinki and leads the 3I (Intelligent Interactive Informatics) research group. She is Adjunct Professor of Interaction Technology at University of Tampere, and Visiting Professor at University of Tartu, Estonia. Her research focuses on spoken dialogue systems, human-human and human-machine interaction, and multimodal communication, and she has played a leading role in many collaborative research projects. Her publications include e.g. the book "Constructive Dialogue Modelling - Speech Interaction and Rational Agents" (John Wiley) and textbook "Spoken Dialogue Systems" with M. McTear (Springer). She is Secretary-Treasurer of SIGDial.

Satomi Kaiami, Bachelor of Music, Schoolteacher, School for the Mentally Challenged at Otsuka, University of Tsukuba, 1-5-5 Kasuga, Bunkyo-ku, Tokyo 112-0003 Japan, completed the Undergraduate Programs of Music Education at Tokyo College of Music. She started as a schoolteacher at Matsudo Special Needs School, Chiba Prefecture. She is now working at School for the Mentally Challenged at Otsuka, University of Tsukuba, under the teacher exchange program between the University of Tsukuba and Chiba Prefecture. She is a first-year homeroom teacher at junior high school division and has been developing many handmade teaching materials in cooperation with her colleague, Fumio Nemoto. She wants the students with disabilities to acquire the ability of expressing himself/herself and gain competence and confidence.

María José Lasala graduated in History from the Universidad Autónoma de Barcelona (1990). She has worked as educator in special education centers and currently has a tenured position as teacher at the "Ernest Lluch High School," Cunit, Spain. She is in charge of the "Aula de Acogida" (Welcome course) since 2008. She has used many new technologies in this course, such as blogs, social networks, QR codes, collaborative writing tools, and virtual worlds. She has given several courses and seminars on these topics to other secondary education teachers. She is the co-ordinator of the Espurnik initiative, a project involving virtual worlds in secondary education.

Francisco J. Liébana-Cabanillas is an Assistant Professor in the Marketing and Market Research Department at the University of Granada (Spain) and holds a Ph.D. Business Sciences in this university. He has a degree in Business and Administration Science and a Master in Marketing and Consumer behavior, from the University of Granada. His main area of research and interest the field is the effectiveness of the mobile and online banking, the results of which are reflected in various papers, which have been presented at the EMAC, INBAM, AEMARK, JORNADAS HISPANOLUSAS, EDULEARN, ICERI, et cetera. His recent works have appeared in *Expert Systems with Applications, The Service Industries Journal, Advances in Intelligent and Soft-Computing series of Springer,* et cetera. He is currently working on different research projects in Internet social networks, Internet ad effectiveness, and new technologies acceptance.

Eduardo Lleida was born in Spain in 1961. He received the M.Sc. degree in Telecommunication Engineering and the Ph.D. degree by the Universitat Politecnica de Catalunya (UPC), Spain, in 1985 and 1990, respectively. From 1986 to 1988, he was involved in his Doctoral work at the Department of Signal Theory and Communications at the Universitat Politecnica de Catalunya From 1989 to 1990 he worked as Assistant Professor, and from 1991 to 1993, he worked as Associate Professor in the Department of Signal Theory and Communications at the Universitat Politecnica de Catalunya. From February 1995 to January 1996, he was with AT&T Bell Laboratories, Murray Hill, NJ as a consultant in Speech Recognition. Currently, he is a full Professor of Signal Theory and Communications in the Department of Electronic Engineering and Communications at the University of Zaragoza, where he is heading a research team in speech recognition and signal processing.

Tom Lunney, BSc (Hons), MSc, P.G.C.E, PhD, MIEEE, MBCS, received his degrees in Mathematics and Computer Science from Queen's University Belfast, and is now a Senior Lecturer in Computer Science at the University of Ulster. His research areas include concurrent and distributed systems, artificial intelligence, networks, and multi-modal computing. He has presented papers at a range of international conferences and participated in the organizing committees for many highly-respected international conferences and workshops. He has taught at a number of other institutions including Queens University, Belfast and The University of Pau, France. He is currently Course Director for postgraduate Masters programmes in the University of Ulster.

Myriam Martínez-Fiestas is an Assistant Professor in the Marketing and Market Research Department at the University of Granada (Spain) and hold a Ph.D. Business Sciences in this university. She has a degree in Business and Administration Science, a degree in Law, a Master in Marketing and Consumer behavior, from the University of Granada, and a Executive Master in Law and Business, from *Garrigues* Studies Centre, in collaboration with Harvard Law School. Her main area of research and interest is green consumer behavior and effectiveness of the green advertising, the results of which are reflected in various papers, which have been presented in different conferences, including AEMARK, INTED, UNIVEST, ICERI, JORNADAS HISPANOLUSAS, Interdisciplinary Workshops, and EDULEARN. She is currently working on different research projects in emotion ads effectiveness and green consumer behavior.

Juan Mateu is a Technical Engineer in Computer Management from the Polytechnic University of Valencia where he later obtained a Master's degree in Software Engineering, Formal Methods and Information Systems. Currently, he combines his professional activity as a teacher of Computer Science in secondary education and training cycles with research in the application of virtual worlds in the teaching-learning process. He recently started his PhD research at the Autonomous University of Madrid under the supervision of Xavier Alaman, focusing in the implementation of an architecture for educational applications using virtual worlds and tangible interfaces.

Päivi Majaranta is a Senior Researcher at the University of Tampere, Finland, where she also received her PhD in Interactive Technology in 2009. Majaranta has been involved in several research projects related to eye tracking, including her work as the scientific coordinator of the European Network of Excellence on Communication by Gaze Interaction (COGAIN, 2004-2009). Majaranta is especially interested in the application of eye tracking in gaze-aware natural interfaces.

Fumio Nemoto, Bachelor of Literature, Schoolteacher, School for the Mentally Challenged at Otsuka, University of Tsukuba, 1-5-5 Kasuga, Bunkyo-ku, Tokyo 112-0003 Japan, graduated in Department of Education, Faculty of Literature, at Toyo University. He started as a part-time schoolteacher at Seibi Special Needs School, Suginami-ku, Tokyo, and moved to School for the Mentally Challenged at Otsuka, University of Tsukuba. He is the chief of senior high school division. He has developed many handmade teaching aids and tools to support individual needs and desires of each student. He has been conducting many school activities using communication aids and original handmade teaching materials with dot codes. He wants every student with disabilities to express his/her thoughts and feelings to others. He has been collaborating with Professor Shigeru Ikuta, Otsuma Women's University for more than seven years.

Paul McKevitt is Chair in Digital MultiMedia at the Magee Campus of the University of Ulster. Previously, he was Visiting Professor of Intelligent MultiMedia Computing in the Institute of Electronic Systems, Aalborg University, Denmark, Lecturer and British EPSRC (Engineering and Physical Sciences Research Council) Advanced Fellow in the Department of Computer Science, University of Sheffield, England and Research Scientist and Research Fellow in The Department of Computer Science, New Mexico State University, New Mexico, USA. He has published numerous research papers in international conferences, research books and journals and has been awarded 3 UK/international patents. He obtained his Ph.D. (Exeter, 1991), M.Sc. (New Mexico, 1988), and B.Sc. (Hons.) (Dublin, 1985) degrees in Computer Science and M.Ed. degree in Education (Sheffield, 1999).

Beatriz López Mencía, MEng in Telecommunications from Universidad Politécnica de Madrid (UPM) in 2005, has just obtained a PhD in Telecommunications Engineering in the Signals, Systems and Communications Department (SSR) from the same university. Her research career is focused in the field of human computer interaction. Following a design and evaluation approach, her research analyses a full scope of aspects relevant to the inclusion of embodied conversational agents in two application areas: task-oriented spoken language dialogue systems (SLDSs) and educational applications for children with special educational needs. She has several publications and she has participated in research forums and roundtables. From an industrial point of view, she held a 3-month academic stay in Deutsche Telekom Laboratories, where she worked in the Quality and Usability Lab. Currently she is involved in several research projects and she works as User Experience consultant at different Spanish Companies.

Iratxe Mentxaka has a degree in Pedagogy with a specialization in Management and Innovation of Learning Centers and new technologies applied to education by the University of Deusto (Bilbao, Spain) since 2005. She is a researcher at DeustoTech Learning at the Deusto Foundation working on instructional design, educational object evaluation and innovation in the classroom. She has experience as educational consultant, as master on-line tutoring and as responsible for the management, programming, and evaluation of socio-cultural activities in civic centers. She has also participated in seminars about cyber-bullying and Web 2.0. Actually she collaborates in several research projects about technology enhanced learning.

Jose Manuel Molina is Full Professor at the Carlos III University of Madrid (Spain) and director of the Department of Computer Science. Previously he has been director of the Ph.D. Program in Computer science and Technology of this University. He obtained Ph.D. and B.S. degrees in Telecommunication Science from the Technical University of Madrid. He is currently the Director of the research group of Applied Artificial Intelligence (www.giaa.inf.uc3m.es). His research areas are focused on the application of artificial intelligence in multi-agent systems, fuzzy logic, evolutionary computation, artificial vision, multi-sensor systems, signal processing, context-aware systems, and user-centered applications to access information and services. He is author of more than 40 contributions in international journals with impact factor, more than 150 papers in international conferences, and 16 books.

Karla Muñoz is full time Ph.D. student at the University of Ulster (UU), Magee campus. She has a M.Sc. in Computing and Intelligent Systems from the University of Ulster and a B.Sc. in Electronic Systems Engineering from Tecnológico de Monterrey, Mexico City. In 2008, she was granted a Vice Chancellor's Research Scholarship (VCRS) by the UU to sponsor her Ph.D. studies and was awarded with the 8over8 prize, which is allocated to the top performing student on the M.Sc. Computing with Specialism course at the UU. She was sponsored during her M.Sc. studies at UU by the high level scholarship for Latin America (AL-AN) of the European Union (EU) Program. She has presented papers in workshops and international conferences. Karla's research interests include HCI, e-learning, problem-based learning, user-modeling, virtual and game-based learning environments, intelligent tutoring systems, data mining, and AI techniques for reasoning and making decisions under uncertainty.

Luis Neri is full-time Professor of the Physics and Mathematics Department at the Design, Engineering and Architecture School of Tecnológico de Monterrey, Mexico City Campus (ITESM-CCM). He holds a Ph.D. in Physics from Mexico National University and has over 30 years of experience as Professor. He holds a certificate in Problem-Based Learning and Collaborative Learning techniques from ITESM and also delivers seminars, which assist the qualification of teachers in active learning methods. He is author and co-author of several Physics books and Blackboard courses approved by ITESM. He has published several scientific papers and research chapters in education, astrophysics and alternate energy sources, and has participated in several national and international conferences in these areas. Dr. Neri is member of the "e-Learning research group" at ITESM-CCM, which is comprised of academics interested in designing electronic and technological systems that encourage learning processes in the subjects of physics, mathematics, and computation.

Ismael Pascual Nieto received the Ph.D. degree in Computer Science and Engineering from the Universidad Autonoma de Madrid in 2009. He has published more than 20 papers in international journals and conferences. He has co-edited the book "Conversational Agents and Natural Language Interaction: Techniques and Effective Practices," and organized the 1st APLEC-2010 Workshop.

Julieta Noguez is Associate Professor and Researcher at the Department of Computer Science, Tecnológico de Monterrey, Mexico City Campus (ITESM-CCM). Julieta Noguez has a M.Sc. and a Ph.D. in Computer Science from ITESM. She has more than 70 publications in journals and proceedings of international conferences, and has supervised eight M.Sc. and two Ph.D. theses. She is member of the Mexican AI Society and IEEE. At ITESM-CCM, she was granted with the Best Professor Award in 2000 and the Best Professor at Graduate Level Award in 2009. She is also member of the National Research System (level 1) from the Science and Technology Mexican Council and leader of "e-Learning research group" at ITESM-CCM since April 2005. Her main research interests include intelligent and affective tutoring systems, virtual laboratories, collaborative learning, probabilistic reasoning, project oriented learning, active learning, edutainment and e-learning.

Kiran Pala has done Bachelor's in Computer Science and Information Technology from Jawaharlal Nehru Technological University-Hyderabad and doing graduate research in Cognitive Science at International Institute of Information Technology Hyderabad (IIIT H), India. I am affiliated to Language Technologies Research Center (Anusaaraka Lab), one of the research centers that focuses on issues related to Language Technologies Natural Language Processing and Machine Translation. I also did some work in the Speech Perception focusing on the Auditory Perceptual Variations, Changes in Language Faculty and existence of Cognitive Structures, and also interactive assistance for adult learners. Before joined to IIIT H, he has served for more than 3 years as Software Developer and Language Engineer in information technology industry especially in development tools for learning. He is an author of about 20 papers presented and published in national as well as international conferences and journals. He has co-authored two book chapters in edited volumes. He has reviewed papers for reputed conferences and journals. Broadly, his research interests include human-learning and cognition, psycholinguistics, natural language processing and machine learning, and cognitive neuroscience.

Juan Francisco López Panea works at the Spanish Center for Subtitling and Audio Description (CESyA) as a Technician-Researcher, focused in the use of new devices to provide accessible content. He is researching in the field of the Automatic Speech Recognition applied for live subtitling in broadcast television and educational environments. As telecommunications engineer, he worked for three years at Telefónica I+D in projects related to ubiquitous access for multimedia content, especially in home networks and new mobile platforms. In this field, he developed software for low resources devices and integrated web technologies and VoIP solutions to provide better distribution channels for personal contents and communication. Now, his current work and interests are related to the use of automatic speech recognition to provide automatic live subtitling in the way to reach accessible education and leisure for the deaf people.

David Díaz Pardo has an MEng in Telecommunications Engineering from Universidad Politécnica de Madrid (2002). He is currently doing a PhD and holds a research position in the same university, under the supervision of Luis Hernández, in the Signal Processing Applications Group (GAPS). His research interests include, firstly, human-technology interaction, with the primary focus of developing new analytical perspectives for the evaluation of the users' experience, especially in the context of applying multimodal interaction technology in novel areas of application (smart, personalised services involving spoken dialogue at home, in public spaces or in mobile scenarios). A second, related, area of interest is the study of rhythm in human speech, with a view to improve the naturalness of conversation with machines and develop strategies to improve robustness when communication breakdown occurs.

Diana Perez-Marin received the Ph.D. degree in Computer Science and Engineering from the Universidad Autonoma de Madrid in 2007. She is currently a Lecturer and Researcher at the Universidad Rey Juan Carlos. She has published more than 40 papers in journals such as *Computers and Education* and *Journal of Educational Technology and Society*. She has edited the book "Conversational Agents and Natural Language Interaction: Techniques and Effective Practices" (Information Science Reference, 2011), and she has co-authored the book "Las TIC en la Educación" (Anaya, 2011). She has also organized two international workshops on the Adaptation and Personalization in E-B/Learning using Pedagogic Conversational Agents, APLEC-2010 and APLEC-2011 integrated into PALE 2011 together with the international conferences UMAP-2010 and UMAP-2011.

Ana Pérez-Pérez is a M. S. and PhD student in Computer Science at University of Granada, Spain. She has also a B. S. in Computer Science from this university. Her research interests and activities have been related to speech technologies and include dialogue systems, multimodal systems, and ambient intelligence, among others. She is currently participating in several research projects related to these areas. She is a member of SEPLN (Spanish Society on Natural Language Processing).

Francisco Rejón-Guardia is an Assistant Professor in the Marketing and Market Research Department at the University of Granada (Spain) and holds a Ph.D. Business Sciences in this university. He is currently working on different research projects relating to effectiveness of advertising on the Internet Social Networks, the results of which are reflected in various papers to conference proceeding, and chapters in different books (AEMARK, Interdisciplinary Workshops, EDULEARN, Handbook of Research on Business Social Networking: Organizational, Managerial, and Technological Dimensions). His main research interest is Internet advertising effectiveness and new technologies acceptance.

Susana Romero is a Professor and the person in charge of laboratories in the Department of Industrial Technologies at Engineering Faculty at the University of Deusto (Bilbao, Spain) since 1997. She participates, organizes, and/or evaluates numerous projects, conferences, contests, training courses, and resources for the teaching of the electronics and the microcontrollers. Between them the use of the Microbotic stands out as educational tool. Her publications in books and magazines have turned on the electronics from an educational point of view. She collaborates with DeustoTech Learning research unit of the Deusto Foundation in educational projects. At the moment she is working on projects of adaptation to the European Higher Education Area at the University of Deusto, and she is member of Guides of Learning's evaluation committee at the same university.

William R. Rodriguez was born in Colombia in 1976. He received a B.Sc. in Biomedical Engineering by the University of Science and Development in 2002 in Bogotá, ME and Ph.D. degree in Biomedical Engineering by the University of Zaragoza in 2008 and 2010, respectively. His research interests are new technologies for elderly and applications of speech technologies such as voice therapy tools and computer-aided applications for handicapped children. He has published several journal and conference papers related to speech technologies for disabilities applications. He is the PreLingua's creator and his current work involves the improvement of this tool and how to estimate reliable acoustical parameters from vocalic sounds in altered voices.

Belén Ruiz-Mezcua is Ph.D. in Sciences Physics for Telecommunications School of Polytechnic University of Madrid. She has been Adjunt Vicechancellor of Research in Carlos III University from 2007 until 2011 and she is a member of the faculty in Computer Science department of Carlos III University of Madrid (Spain). She is the head of Spanish Centre of Caption and Audiodescription (CESyA) since 2005. Her researches are focussed in speech and speaker recognition, accessibility on web and accessibility is products, services and applications and technologies applied to disable people. She works and manages several international projects, and she is co-author of several publications in international journal and congresses.

Araceli Sanchis de Miguel is Professor at the Carlos III University of Madrid (Spain) and is currently the director of the CAOS group (www.caos.inf.uc3m.es) at this university. She obtained Ph.D. degree in Computer Science from the Technical University of Madrid. She is author of more than 20 articles in JCR journals and has participated in over 80 international conferences. He has also worked on research projects, leading some of them at the Carlos III University of Madrid.

Oscar Saz Torralba was born in Spain in 1980. He received a B.Sc. in Telecommunications Engineering by the University of Zaragoza in 2004 and a Ph.D. by the University of Zaragoza in 2009. He is currently a Fulbright scholar at the Language Technologies Institute of the School of Computer Science at Carnegie Mellon University in Pittsburgh, USA. His research interests are new applications of speech technologies such as oral interfaces for handicapped individuals and computer-assisted language learning; areas where he has published several journal and conference papers. His current work involves the study of applying conversational environments into computer assisted pronunciation training of second language learners of English.

Alvaro Hernández Trapote receives his Ph.D. in Computer Science from the Universidad Politécnica of Madrid. Among his main research interests are the study of the user factors in interactive systems. In his thesis research those related with biometrics applications were analyzed as privacy, invasiveness, or perception of security. He is also interested in ECAs capabilities for dialogue management and empathy behaviour, also applied for encouraging the learning experience of students with special needs. In 2008, he held a visiting research in KTH (Stockholm, Sweeden) during three months working in the TMH department. He has also worked in different national and European projects jointly with Spanish companies and is member of scientific committee of LREC.

María Isabel Viedma-del-Jesus is PhD in Psychology from the University of Granada and Assistant Professor at the Department of Marketing and Market Research at the University of Granada. Dr. Viedma-del-Jesus has participated in many congresses and scientific meetings in both national (Spanish) and international contexts in the areas of psychology (such as annual meetings organized by the Society for Psychophysiological Research and Spanish Congress of Psychophysiology) and marketing and market research (such as Congreso Anual de Marketing-AEMARK-). Dr. Viedma-del-Jesus has published papers in influential journals such as *Scientometrics, Psychophysiology, Psychopharmacology, Tobacco Control, Psicothema, Motivation & Emotion, Behavioral Psychology and Quality & Quantity*, among others. Her main research topics are: scientific study of emotion, psychophysiology, social marketing and consumer behavior, bibliometric analysis, and new technologies applied to teaching.

Rachel Whittaker is a Senior Lecturer in the English Department at the Madrid Universidad Autónoma, where she teaches discourse analysis and academic reading and writing at undergraduate level, and academic writing and Content and Language Integrated Learning (CLIL) in Master's programmes. She has published widely on writing at secondary level in CLIL and EFL contexts using data from corpora of foreign language writing (The UAM Corpus of Written Interlanguage, The UAM-CLIL Corpus). Working in the framework of Systemic Functional Linguistics, she is interested in linguistic evidence for text quality in writing, and applications to literacy education.

Index

CPSIA information can be obtained at www.ICGtesting.com
Printed in the USA
BVOW050545020713

324521BV00007BB/111/P

9 781466 625303